Conte

D0193503

The Michelin Red Guide Switzerland makes it so easy to choose where to spend the night and to find that special restaurant.

Following the explanatory pages – in several languages – to crack the symbols, signs and abbreviations, the selection of hotels includes comprehensive up-to-date information on their amenities (swimming pools, tennis courts, saunas, gardens) as well as their dates of annual closure, their telephone and fax numbers and which credit cards are accepted.

The Red Guide also recommends and classifies a selection of restaurants from those serving a carefully prepared dish of the day to the starred establishment with a reputation for exceptional cuisine.

All selected hotels and restaurants are located on the town plans. Local maps and a mine of useful information are invaluable to the traveller.

Every year the Michelin Red Guide Switzerland revises its selection of establishments and it makes the ideal companion publication to the Michelin Green Guide Switzerland.

VOCABULARY

Terms used in the hotel industry are underlined

German	English	German	English
Bahnhof	Railway station	Kursaal	Casino
Brücke	Bridge	Markt	Market
Bündnerstube	Traditional sitting-room from the Grisons	Meublé	Hotel (no restaurant)
Burg	Feudal castle	Münster	Important church (cathedral)
Café	Tea room (in German-Switzerland)	Ober...	High, upper
Carnotzet	In hotels of the Vaud and the Valais, a room used for the consumption of cheese-dishes and local wines	Pass	Mountain pass
		Pension	Pension, boarding house
		Rathaus	Town Hall
Denkmal	Monument or memorial	Restaurant	Place where lunch and dinner may be had. In some German-Swiss towns, many "Restaurants" serve only drinks, as in cafés, unless there is a notice saying "Speise-Restaurant"
Fähre	Ferry		
Fall	Waterfall, cascade		
Garni	Hotel (no restaurant)		
Garten	Garden		
Gasse	Street, alley	Schloss	Castle, château
Gasthaus	Inn (with restaurant if indicated)	Schlucht	Gorge
		Schwimmbad	Swimming pool
Gletscher	Glacier	See	Lake
Grotto	Grotto (in Ticino, a bar serving local wines)	Spielplatz	Sports ground
		Strandbad	Bathing beach
Hafen	Port, harbour	Strasse	Street
Haupt...	As a prefix: main, chief, head	Tal	Valley
		Talsperre	Dam
Kirche	Church	Tobel	Ravine
Kleintaxi	Small taxi	Tor	Gate (of a town)
Kloster	Monastery, convent, abbey	Unter...	Under, lower
		Verboten	Forbidden, prohibited
Kurhaus	Spa. Usually a large isolated establishment with simple furnishings. There are also thermal and mountain "Kurhäuser", used more as places to stay than as overnight stops	Wald	Forest, wood
		Wirtschaft	Very modest inn, used mostly by local people; "pub"
		Zytgloggeturm	Clock-tower
		Zeughaus	Arsenal

BRIEF VOCABULARY FOR SKIERS

German	French	English
Skischule	École de ski	Ski school
Skilehrer	Moniteur de ski	Ski instructor
Abfahrt	Départ, piste	Ski run
Schi, Ski (Bergski, Talski)	Ski (amont, aval)	Top ski, bottom ski
Kanten	Carres	Ski edges
Bindung	Fixation	Ski bindings
Skistock	Bâton	Ski stick
Skiwachs	Fart	Ski wax
Schussfahrt	Descente directe	Straight run
Querfahrt	Traversée	Traversing
Schneepflug, Stemmen	Position de chasse-neige	Stem position
Abrutschen	Dérapage	Side slipping
Kurvenschwung, Bogen	Virage	Curve, swing, turn
Wedeln	"Godille"	Wedling
Spezialslalom	Slalom spécial	Special slalom
Riesenslalom	Slalom géant	Giant slalom
Abfahrtslauf	Descente libre	Clear run
Kombination	Combiné	All-round test
Langstreckenlauf	Course de fond	Long distance race
Sprungschanze	Tremplin de saut	Ski jumping
Skilift	Téléski, remonte-pente	Ski lift
Sessellift	Télésiège	Chairlift
Kabinenbahn	Télécabine	Cable-car
Schwebebahn	Téléphérique	Cable-car
Drahtseilbahn	Funiculaire	Funicular
Lawine	Avalanche	Avalanche
Schutzhütte	Refuge	Refuge
Skiwerstatt	Atelier de réparation de skis	Ski repair shop
Rodelbahn	Piste de luge	Sledge run
Eisbahn	Patinoire	Skating rink

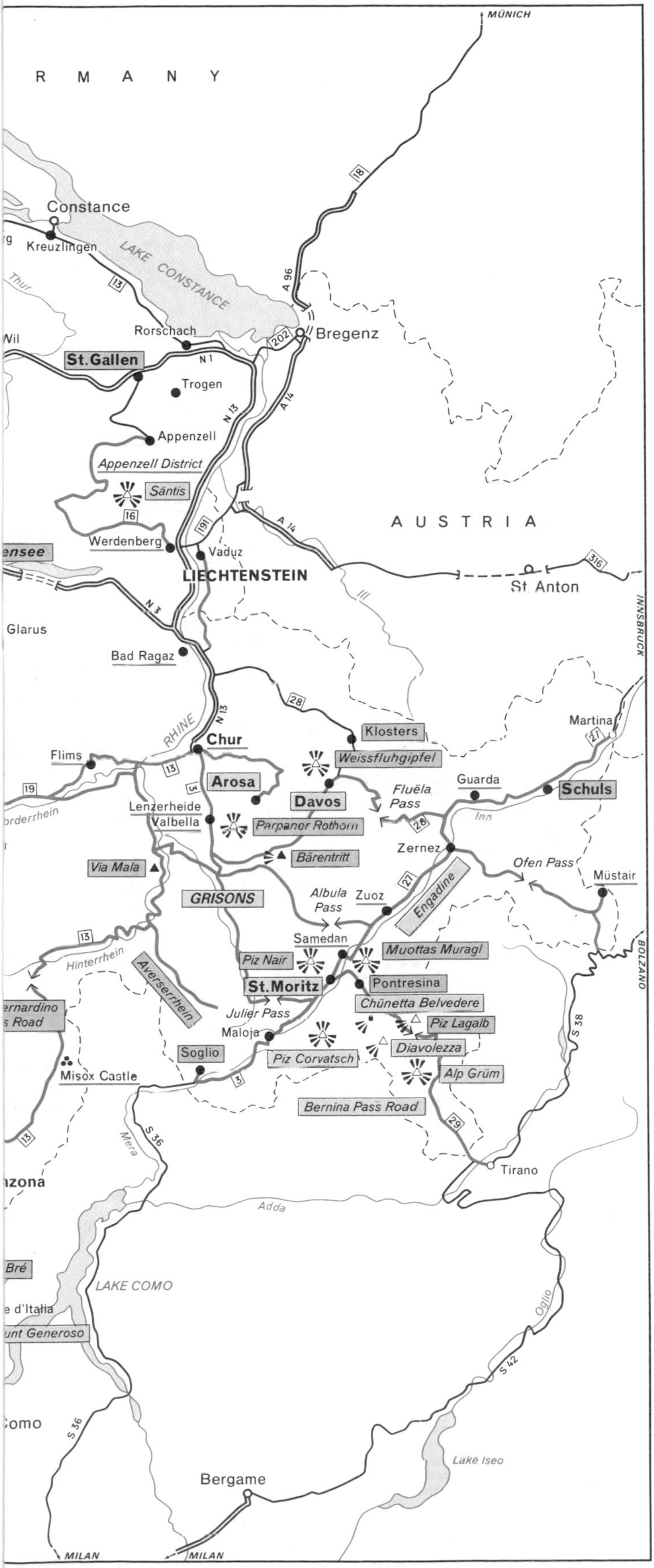

GERMANY

MÜNICH

Constance
Kreuzlingen
LAKE CONSTANCE
Thur
13
rg
Wil
Rorschach
St. Gallen
N 1
Trogen
Appenzell
Appenzell District
Säntis
16
N 13
Werdenberg
Vaduz
LIECHTENSTEIN
ensee
N 3
Glarus
Bad Ragaz

Bregenz
A 96
202
A 14
AUSTRIA
191
A 14
III
St Anton
316
INNSBRUCK

28
Klosters
Martina
27
Weissfluhgipfel
RHINE
N 13
Chur
Arosa
Flims
19
13
Davos
Fluéla Pass
Guarda
Schuls
orderrhein
Lenzerheide
Valbella
Parpaner Rothorn
28
Inn
Via Mala
Bärentritt
Zernez
Ofen Pass
Müstair
GRISONS
Albula Pass
Zuoz
27
Engadine
BOLZANO
Samedan
13
Hinterrhein
Piz Nair
Muottas Muragl
Averserrhein
St. Moritz
Pontresina
ernardino
s Road
Julier Pass
Maloja
Chünetta Belvedere
Piz Lagalb
S 38
Soglio
Piz Corvatsch
Diavolezza
Misox Castle
Alp Grüm
3
Bernina Pass Road
29
13
Mera
S 36
Tirano
nzona
Adda
Bré
LAKE COMO
e d'Italia
unt Generoso
Ortio
S 42
Como
S 36
Bergame
Lake Iseo
MILAN
MILAN

GERMANY

LAKE CONSTANCE

Wil

N1

St.Gallen ★★

Altstätten

Appenzell District ★

Werdenberg ★

Vaduz

LIECHTENSTEIN

Walensee ★★

AUSTRIA

Näfels

N3

Glarus

Maienfeld

★ Bad Ragaz

RHINE

Chur ★

19

Vorderrhein

Davos ★★★

Schuls ★★

Inn

Engadine ★★★

San Bernardino
Pass Road ★★

Hinterrhein

★★★St.Moritz

Bernina Pass Road ★★★

2

13

Bellinzona

Adda

LAKE COMO

Oglio

Lake Iseo

SWITZERLAND : A HOLIDAY PLAYGROUND

As soon as he sets foot on Swiss soil, the foreigner yields himself to a country profoundly devoted to the promotion of its heritage and to the development of tourism.

As specialists in the hotel business, jealous of a well-earned reputation, the Swiss know how to create for him, at any place and in any season, an atmosphere to suit his taste: picturesque or luxurious surroundings, comfort, spotless cleanliness and a warm welcome. The foreigner is also offered a wide variety of amusements: he can choose between the most colourful folk festivals and the most popular

Shop sign

sporting or cultural events. The Confederation is provided with a close network of railways and roads. As the true crossroads of Europe and an important international air centre, it extends a warm welcome to the peaceful invasion of tourists and sportsmen.

WHEN SHOULD YOU VISIT SWITZERLAND?

The "sporting" seasons – The month of June, during which the ice-cap is in good condition for mountaineering, will also be preferred by the tourist who cannot imagine the Alpine pastures without their new carpet of flowers.

High summer is not always a guarantee of steady, fine weather in the mountains unless you try your luck in the Engadine, the Valais or the Ticino. None the less, this remains the most lively season. While work in the fields is in full swing, the motorist will find all the great Alpine routes open and the sightseer will be delighted by the spectacle of rushing torrents and waterfalls (in the plain, this is the time to see the Aare and the Rhine in full flood), and the climber can tackle clean, dry rock. *For more details on mountaineering and skiing, see p 23.*

When the first snow falls, all tourist activity turns to winter sports. To welcome the rush of town dwellers eager to forget the mists of the plains and to disport themselves on sunny slopes, every resort draws on all the resources of its constantly perfected hotel and sporting accommodation.

The "restful" seasons – In spring and summer the shores of the Swiss lakes offer ideal conditions for a restful stay. On the southern slopes of the Alps, Lake Lugano and Lake Maggiore are traditionally sought-after in early spring and the warming effect of the *Föhn (qv)* transforms Lakes Lucerne and Thun into little Rivieras early in April. The Lake Geneva area (the Vaud Riviera) is at its most charming in the season of the grape harvest (early October).

Until the end of November, a fine Indian summer may be very favourable to an art-lover's tour in Switzerland. The cities of the Mittelland, with their old stones warmed by the autumn light, then appear in the full majesty of their setting.

ARTS AND CRAFTS

The map below indicates a selection of Swiss specialities suitable for travel souvenirs *(for gastronomic specialities see p 33).*
The craft centres of Zürich and Stein am Rhein hold exhibitions on different themes with a view to the promotion of Swiss popular arts and crafts.

PLACES TO STAY

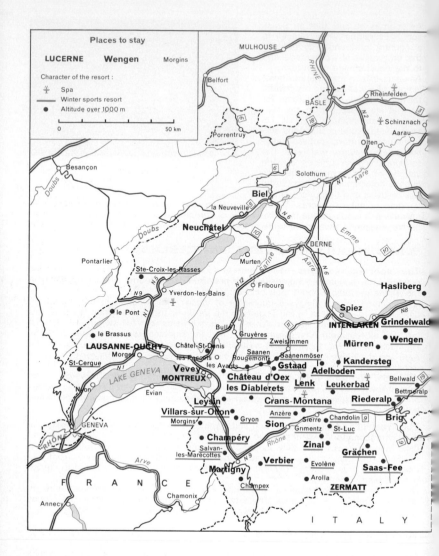

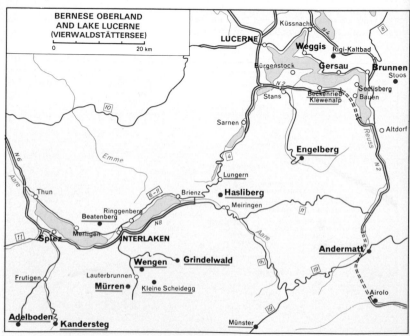

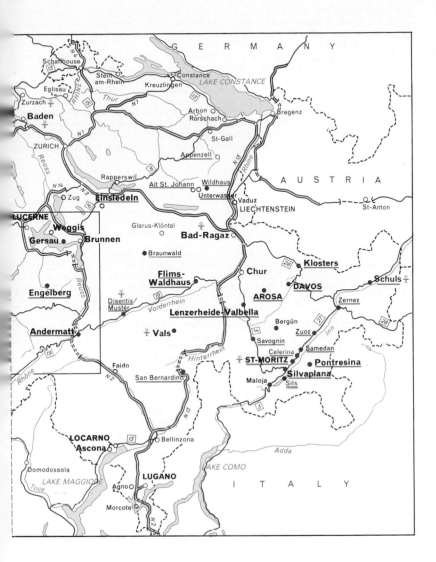

FACILITIES

The mention facilities under the individual headings in the body of the guide indicates that a resort is located on these maps.
For the winter sports resorts consult the table at the end of the Practical Information.

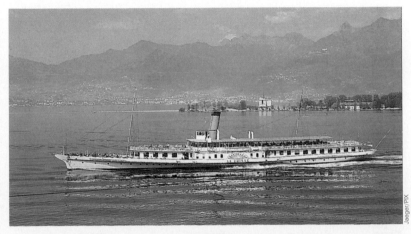

Lake Geneva

THE SWISS CONFEDERATION

The Swiss Confederation is endowed with a highly original physiognomy. Although the country is small, it boasts a wide variety of ethnic groups, languages and religions; yet, despite the different types of landscape, there exists a strong sense of geographical identity.

Every year crowds of tourists travel to Switzerland to discover or rediscover its charming, peaceful atmosphere: imposing mountain ranges crowned by famous peaks, smiling valleys, treacherous gorges, huge snowfields, impetuous springs and gushing torrents, fertile plains, flower-decked villages dotted among the mountains, prosperous cities spreading along the peaceful shores of the lakes.

Art lovers too will be seduced by Switzerland's architecture and cultural heritage: the looming silhouette of a fortified castle, the noble lines of a baroque monastery and the audacity of modern feats of engineering will appeal to their artistic sensitivity. They will be delighted to stop and admire a pretty fountain, or visit a tiny hamlet where the chalets shine like brand new toys.

A FEW FIGURES

The territory of the Swiss Confederation has an area of 41 300km² - 15 942sq miles or about a quarter of that of England and Wales. It could be contained in a circle with a radius of 115km - 70 miles (the distance from London to Portsmouth). If the whole of Switzerland were levelled to its average altitude, it would lie 1 350m - 4 428ft above sea level.

According to the figures released by the National Bureau of Statistics (1990 census), the present population of Switzerland is estimated at 6 873 700 inhabitants, including over 1.2 million foreigners. This means there are 166 people to each square kilometre, a ratio comparable to that of the Paris region. One-fifth of the population is concentrated within the five largest towns: Zürich, Basle, Geneva, Berne and Lausanne.

A selection of Swiss mountains over 4 000m - 13 123ft

Mount Rosa (Valais)	4 634m - 15 203ft
Dom (Mischabel; Valais)	4 545m - 14 941ft
Weisshorn (Valais)	4 505m - 14 780ft
Matterhorn (Valais)	4 478m - 14 692ft
Dent Blanche (Valais)	4 357m - 14 295ft
Grand Combin (Valais)	4 314m - 14 153ft
Finsteraarhorn (Valais)	4 274m - 14 022ft
Aletschhorn (Valais)	4 195m - 13 763ft
Breithorn (Valais)	4 165m - 13 665ft
Jungfrau (Berne-Valais)	4 158m - 13 642ft
Mönch (Berne-Valais)	4 099m - 13 448ft
Schreckhorn (Berne)	4 078m - 13 379ft
Piz Bernina (Grisons)	4 049m - 13 284ft
Lauteraarhorn (Berne)	4 042m - 13 261ft

Switzerland's largest lakes

Lake Geneva	580km² - 224sq miles
Lake Constance (Bodensee)	540km² - 208sq miles
Lake Neuchâtel	217km² - 84sq miles
Lake Lucerne	114km² - 44sq miles
Lake Lugano	48km² - 19sq miles
Thun Lake	48km² - 19sq miles

A SELECTION OF PICTURESQUE VILLAGES

Village	Canton	Village	Canton
Gandria	Ticino	Morcote	Ticino
Giornico	Ticino	St-Ursanne	Jura
Gruyères	Fribourg	Soglio	Grisons
Guarda	Grisons	Stein am Rhein	Schaffhausen
Kippel	Valais	Zuoz	Grisons

Introduction

The Matterhorn

L. Degonda / O.N.S.T.

DESCRIPTION OF THE COUNTRY

Switzerland consists of a lowland area (the Mittelland or Middle Country) between the mountain barriers of the Alps and the Jura, which both arose in the Tertiary Era.

SWISS ALPS

The Alps cover 3/5 of Helvetian territory, making Switzerland the second most Alpine country in Europe after Austria, where the proportion reaches 2/3. Setting aside that part of the Grisons which lies to the east of the Hinterrhein Valley – a high valley like the Engadine, which, with its extra-continental climate, is more typical of central Europe – the Swiss Alps, like the French, belong to the western Alpine group, that is, to the steepest and most contorted chain, and are, therefore, most affected by erosion. The culminating point of this world of lakes and glaciers is Mount Rosa (altitude at the Dufour Peak, 4634m – 15203ft), although the St. Gotthard Massif (Pizzo Rotondo – 3192m – 10473ft), which may be called the water-tower of Europe, represents the keystone of the whole structure in spite of its monotonous outlines. The lack of symmetry of its transverse section has been, no doubt, the most striking feature of the mountain chain, since the sinking of the Po Plain closed its eventful geological history. A motorist crossing a pass like the St. Gotthard is made aware of the sharp contrast between the relatively gentle slopes of the north face and the sudden descent which occurs on the south.

In the longitudinal direction, the remarkable depression which slashes through the mountains from Martigny to Chur and is drained in opposite directions by the Rhône and the Vorderrhein, forms a great strategic and tourist highway.

The glaciers – The Swiss Alps at present comprise about 2000km² – 772sq miles of glaciers. The most typical are the valley glaciers and the Aletsch Glacier is the most extensive in Europe (169km² – 65sq miles).

Moving downstream, a **névé** *(Firn* in German), or snowfield in which snow accumulates and is compacted into ice, is succeeded by a slowly-moving **tongue of ice** *(Gletscher* in German or glacier), traversed by a close network of crevasses.

Breaks or "steps" in the downward slope, which in the case of a torrent would form cascades or rapids, are marked by confused and unstable masses of ice **(seracs)** which, on the Rhône Glacier, have all the appearance of a petrified cataract.

The **moraines** are accumulations of rocky debris brought down by the glacier. They often soil the whiteness of its tongue of ice and sometimes mask it completely as at the Steingletscher *(qv)*. Once they have come to a halt they form characteristic embankments along their edges known as lateral moraines *(illustration overleaf)*.

The heritage of the Quaternary glaciers – Only about 100 centuries ago the predecessors of the present glaciers, which were abundantly fed, completely filled the depression between the Jura and the Alps. Within the mountain system these solid rivers reached gigantic proportions. The Rhône Glacier, in what is now the Valais, was at least 1 500m – 5 000ft thick.

Everywhere these giants left their mark. It is largely to them that motorists owe the unexpected features that may brighten their journey through a high mountain valley. Alternate shrinkings and spreadings, faults breaking the longitudinal skyline, the rocky bars or **bolts** obstructing certain valley floors and sometimes blocking them completely, are to be found everywhere, together with tributary **hanging valleys** described as **scoops** because of their U-shaped cross-sections, which show a very marked break in level as they join the main valley *(see sketch overleaf)*.

When the ice disappeared, the new flow of river waters immediately began to soften these contrasts. **Connecting gorges** then made deeper cuts, through the bolts, as in the Aare Gorges, or connecting the bed of a hanging valley with that of the main valley as in the Trient Gorges.

But the Alpine torrents were not only destructive: they also built up obstacles in the form of **cones of rubble**, of which the largest example in Switzerland is the cone of Illgraben as seen from Leuk.

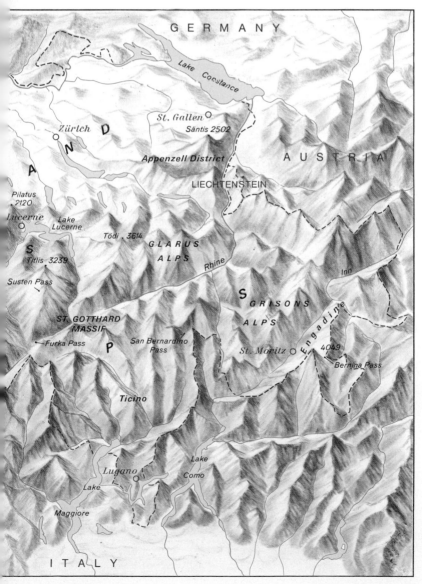

ALPINE RELIEF

For the benefit of tourists unfamiliar with particular forms of mountain relief — whether due to torrents or glaciers — some general points about their features and the geographical terms relating to them are given below.

FLUVIAL RELIEF	GLACIAL RELIEF

Upper Valley: Erosion

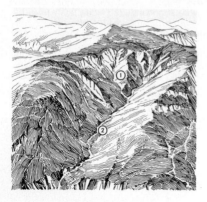

Torrent formed basin
1) Half funnel shaped and deeply ravined drainage basin
2) Outflow channel

Former glacial basin
1) Flattened trough
2) Steep sides

Middle Valley: Transference

Torrent formed valley
1) V-shaped valley
2) Very steep sided valley

Former glacial valley
1) U-shaped valley with wide base, often embanked
2) Shoulder

Lower Valley: Deposition

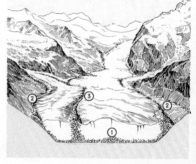

Cone of rubble

When the slope is too gentle to allow the torrent to wash down debris this piles up into a cone of rubble

Moraines
1) Ground moraine
2) Lateral moraine
3) Medial moraine

ALPINE VEGETATION

Vegetation is closely bound to climatic and soil conditions. In the mountainous areas vegetation is also influenced by the height and degree of exposure to the prevailing winds and sun, thus the slopes facing south.

The south-facing slope, free from forests, favours settlement and cultivation while the sparsely populated north-facing slope, with its shade and humidity, favours the growth of great dense forests. This contrast is particularly marked when the valley runs from west to east.

Above the agricultural land, which extends to about 1 500m – 4 921ft, is the zone dominated by coniferous forest. At 2 200m – 7 218ft the dense forest ceases and makes way for the mountain pasture *(alp)* where sturdy, short-stemmed species, bilberry and Alpine flowers grow. At 3 000m – 9 842ft the mineral zone takes over with moss and lichen clinging to the rock faces of an otherwise desolate landscape.

Forests – Below are the essential characteristics of the most familiar types of conifers so well represented in the Alps.

Norway Spruce – In French: *Epicéa;* in German: *Fichte;* in Italian: *Abete rosso.* Essentially a mountain species to be found on northward-facing slopes.

It has a slim, pointed crest and a generally "hairy" appearance, with branches curled like a spaniel's tail. The bark is reddish and becomes very wrinkled as it grows old. Prickly needles. The cones hang down and when ripe fall in one piece to the ground.

Spruce or Fir – In French: *Sapin;* in German: *Tanne;* in Italian: *Abete bianco.* The tree has a broad head, flat on the top, like a stork's nest, in the older specimens. The bark is various shades of grey. The cones stand up like candles and, when ripe, disintegrate on the branch, dropping their scales. The needles are soft and grow in rows like the teeth of a comb. They have a double white line on their inside surface.

Larch – In French: *Mélèze;* in German: *Lärche;* in Italian: *Larice.* This is the only conifer in the Swiss Alps which sheds its needles in winter.

The tree is found on sunny slopes in the high mountains, especially in the Valais and the Grisons. Conoo are very small. Tho light shade of the thin, pale green needles does not prevent grass from growing, and this makes the shelter of larch-woods pleasant for tourists.

Larch

Arolla Pine – In French: *Pin arolle;* in German: *Arve;* in Italian: *Pino cembro.* A characteristic feature of the many species of pine is the arrangement of their needles in tufts of two to five, held together by a scaly sheath. Their cones have hard, tough scales.

The Arolla Pine can be recognized by the shape of its branches, which are deeply curved like those of a candelabrum. The tree is often damaged by the wind.

Flora – The term "Alpine plants" is reserved for those which grow above the upper limits of the forests. The early flowering of these species, which are usually small and lusty, is caused by the brevity of the growing season (June-August). The disproportionate size of the bloom, when compared with the plant as a whole, and its bright colouring are directly connected with the high ultra-violet content of the light at high altitude.

Among the multitude of floral species found in the high Alpine area, a majority have come from different habitats: plains or lower slopes (Dandelion or cornflower) capable of adapting to a rugged climate; Mediterranean (Carnation, Narcissus); Arctic (Buttercup, Alpine poppy) and Siberian (Edelweiss).

Some of the indigenous species (Colombine, Mountain Valerian) have survived from the Quaternary glacial period.

The best time to admire Alpine flora is from May to July, but August still provides flowers in the high mountain pastures and ridges.

Protection of Alpine flora – The picking of certain Alpine flowers which are particularly threatened, like the Cyclamen, Alpine Aster, Primrose and Edelweiss is strictly controlled on Swiss territory.

| Alpine Columbine | Purple Gentian | Martagon Lily | Fire Lily. |

ALPINE CLIMATE

Compared with conditions prevalent in the neighbouring plains, the Alpine climate appears infinitely variable according to difference of altitude, mountain formation and exposure.

The breezes – During the warm season the variations of temperature caused every day as different levels in a mountain valley grow warmer or cooler, produce local winds called *brises,* similar to sea and land breezes elsewhere.

Towards midday the warm, expanding air in the valleys moves up the natural corridors to the heights, where it causes the formation of clouds around the mountaintops. This temporary increase in clouds in the afternoon is a sign of steady, fine weather, but walkers will do well, because of it, to make for the belvederes very early. About 5pm the valley breeze dies away and the air suddenly turns colder. Soon the mountain breeze, which is usually stronger, will sweep the valley in the opposite direction.

The Föhn – This wind, which usually occurs in the settled cold season, causes a complete upset in the Alpine weather. The Föhn, as it is called in German, is most keenly felt on the north side of the Alps in the upper Aare and Reuss Valleys.

The phenomenon is caused by the movement of a deep barometric depression along the northern slope of the Alps. The air drawn in by this depression first sheds its load of moisture on the Italian side of the mountain chain, where thunderstorms and heavy rain occur at this time. It then pours violently over the crest-line, growing warmer and more compressed as it loses height, and turns into a dry, hot wind, while the atmosphere clears. In the mountains, when this happens, everyone is on the alert. Torrents are suddenly in spate, avalanches thunder and the water of the great lakes is lashed into fury. The risk of disastrous forest fires is also increased. Some communities then apply a code of strict rules, which may be seen posted in cafés in the upper Reuss Valley; it goes so far as to forbid smoking absolutely. In human beings the *Föhn* causes such marked discomfort that a laboratory at Basle has put a special "anti-*Föhn*" preparation on the market.

But the *Föhn* also has beneficial effects: it melts the snow, so that animals can be put out to grass early on Alpine pastures. It also enables certain Mediterranean vegetation (maize, vines, chestnut trees) to flourish far beyond their normal geographical limits in favourably situated valleys. In short, the occurrence of the *Föhn* is an event of first-class importance in the daily life of the mountainous districts of Switzerland.

SWISS JURA

The Jura, which culminate at the Crêt de la Neige (alt 1 723m – 5 653ft) in France, appear on Swiss territory as a sheaf of strongly-folded, calcareous mountain-chains curving for 200km – 125 miles between the Dôle (alt 1 677m – 5 502ft) and the Lägern (alt 859m – 2 819ft – above Baden). In France the Jura drop towards the plain of the Saône in a gigantic staircase of plateaux; in Switzerland the last ridges of the massif form above the Mittelland *(see below)* a continuous rampart, rising at a bound to more than 1 000m – 3 000ft to face the wonderful spread of the Bernese Alps and the Mont Blanc Massif.

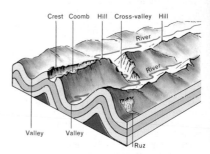

Diagrammatic section of a Jurassic fold

The parallel **valleys** are separated by the hills.
The slashes made by erosion on the flanks of the hills form the **ruz** (a term derived from the name Val de Ruz).
The **cross-valley** cuts across the hill, connecting two valleys.
The **coomb** runs longitudinally along the top of a hill; its escarped edges are called **crests**.

The green countryside of the Jura mountain system reveals a regularly folded structure derived from the movements of the earth's crust, which built up the Alpine chain in the Tertiary Era.

However beside this "fixed swell" of valleys and hills there is still room on this side of the frontier for high, almost level plateaux like that of the Franches Montagnes *(qv)*. The effects of erosion have developed in this solid block a whole system of cuttings and enclosed valleys *(see diagram)* and have laid bare, for the greater benefit of the tourist, rock escarpments which might not have been expected.

MITTELLAND OR MIDDLE COUNTRY

From Lake Geneva to Lake Constance, between the Alps and the Jura, stretches a gently sloping *glacis* on the surface of which lies the mass of debris torn from the Alps. The hydrographical network of the Aare River shows that all the drainage here feeds the Rhine through a furrow running along the foot of the last ridge of the Jura. Before the Quaternary ice age the Rhône itself flowed through this depression, in which a string of lakes (those of Biel and Neuchâtel) and marshy areas now lie.

In fact, the Mittelland is a region of hills deeply divided by clefts – ravines and winding, steep-walled valleys. The vital centres of Swiss agriculture are to be found in the Mittelland and the largest cities of the Confederation are concentrated there.

To get the best of a panorama go up to the viewpoints and summits early in the morning.

HISTORICAL NOTES

Early Helvetia – The present territory of the Confederation was colonized by the Romans in the 1C BC and later invaded by the Barbarians – Burgundians and Alamans – whose ethnic characteristics and differing temperaments are to be found today among the Romansh and Germanic Swiss. In the Middle Ages it was included in the great body of the Holy Roman Empire. The gradual decline of this Empire enabled certain feudal dynasties, like the families of Zähringen, Savoy, Kyburg and Habsburg, to emerge as real territorial powers at the beginning of the 13C. Meanwhile, as in Germany, certain cities (Zürich, Berne), which had enjoyed the favour of the distant Emperor, already had the status of free towns, while the small isolated communities in the mountains were almost autonomous.

Founding pact – In the Alpine valleys near Lake Lucerne, the "Waldstätten" (Forest States) of Uri, Schwyz and Unterwalden, showed great discontent when the Habsburgs appointed the government by bailiffs. On 1 August 1291, representatives of the three communities signed a pact of mutual assistance "to last, if God will, forever". This pact is the beginning of the Helvetic Confederation. *For the legendary version see p 144.*

Struggle against the Habsburgs – The 14C saw a continual struggle by the "original cantons" against the Austrian Habsburgs. Pitted against the heavy cavalry formed from the flower of High German nobility, the Confederate infantry triumphed at Morgarten (1315), Laupen (1339), Sempach (1386) and Näfels (1388). Meanwhile, several towns or *Länder* (peasant communities) joined the earlier nucleus. Lucerne did so in 1332, Zürich in 1351, Glarus and Zug in 1352 and Berne in 1353. This group is known in Swiss history as the VIII Cantons.

Territorial expansion – Inspired by their feats of arms, the cantons felt a taste for adventure and a wish to extend their political influence farther afield. Swiss military prestige was brilliantly vindicated by the victories of Grandson *(qv)* and Murten *(qv)* over the Duke of Burgundy, Charles the Bold, in 1476. In the Italian theatre of operations the belligerents vied with one another for the services of Swiss contingents, and the Confederates did not fail to exact payment in rich territorial concessions. But the over-ambitious anti-French policy of Cardinal Schiner *(qv)* led his countrymen into the losing camp at Marignano. A perpetual alliance was then signed with François I. Henceforth, Switzerland withdrew from the scene of international politics, though it continued to furnish the courts of Europe with selected troops. The last bonds of dependence on the Empire; however, had, been broken. At the beginning of the 16C the confederal jigsaw puzzle acquired Fribourg, Soluthurn, Basle, Schaffhausen and Appenzell.

The territories of the "allied countries" (Valais and the Grisons Leagues) and those of the "bailiwicks" (Thurgau, Ticino), which were held in subjection by one or several cantons, fitted into the gaps of the XIII Cantons *(see Bellinzona).*

From the Reformation to the invasion – The Reformation preached by Zwingli *(qv)* and Calvin found fruitful soil for expansion in Switzerland, thanks to the critical works of humanists like Erasmus. It was spread throughout Romansh Switzerland by Bernese arms and struck deeply into the still imperfectly welded organization of the XIII Cantons. The Confederates, anxious to avoid disastrous schisms in their ranks, took care to refrain from the murderous religious strife in neighbouring states (Wars of Religion and the Thirty Years War). This gave substance to the Swiss tradition of neutrality, which was fortified by the formal recognition of Swiss sovereignty by the signatories of the Treaty of Westphalia (1648).

Under the French Revolution, the Directory imposed the status of a unified and centralized Republic (the "Helvetian Republic") on the Swiss people, to whose temperament it was quite unsuited. Switzerland then became a battlefield for the French against their allied enemies (Austrians, Prussians and Russians). More serious still, internal disorder and factions were rife in the country. After allowing time for the situation to get worse, Napoleon imposed his Act of Mediation – 1803.

The federative nature of the Helvetian State was recognized, but a triple equality "of the cantons between themselves, of the town dwellers between themselves and of the people of the country and the towns" was proclaimed. Six new cantons – Aargau, St Gallen, Graubünden (the Grisons), the Republic of Ticino, Thurgau and Vaud – were added to the political majority. Yet French hegemony meant, for Switzerland, annexations (the Jura and the Valais) and conscription which was bitterly resented, to say nothing of the disastrous economic effects of the continental blockade.

From the Pact of 1815 to the Constitution of 1848 – After the fall of the Napoleonic Empire the accession of three new territories – the Valais, the Republics of Geneva and Neuchâtel – brought the number of cantons to 22. At the Congress of Vienna the great European powers proclaimed the perpetual neutrality of Switzerland. But internal difficulties threatened the foundations of the state; among them were the deep religious divisions which led in 1846 to the conclusion of a separatist League of Roman Catholic cantons known as the **Sonderbund**. The Diet, which represented all the other cantons, met at Berne, proclaimed the dissolution of the Sonderbund and intervened by force of arms. A considerable display of force enabled General Dufour, the commander of the Confederate Army, to end hostilities very quickly and open the way to a general reconciliation. The Constitution of 1848, which was established after these events and revised in 1874 and more recently in 1978 *(see Democracy in Action p 25)*.

Contemporary Switzerland – In a world frequently disturbed by war, Switzerland has not ceased to maintain its neutrality; but to do this it has had to keep vigilant watch over its frontiers during great international conflicts. Switzerland has used its neutrality to develop humanitarian functions which do it honour.

The International Red Cross was founded thanks to the efforts of Henri Dunant in 1863. Since the beginning of this century Geneva has been chosen as the seat of many international organizations.

LANGUAGE AND RELIGION

One of the successes standing to the credit of the Swiss Confederate regime is the coexistence of several distinct language and confessional groups in a single community. It is true that since the 19C the industrialization of the country, by causing large movements of population, especially between the towns, has made religious intolerance unthinkable.

Races and languages – *For linguistic majority in each canton see the chapter on the Swiss Cantons.*

At the fall of the Roman Empire in the 5C the present territory of French-speaking Switzerland was occupied by the Burgundians, who were forced to flee from Gaul, and who fairly quickly adapted themselves to Roman civilization and adopted the Christian religion, or more exactly the Arian heresy.

However, just before, the Alamans, other barbarians from the north, had already invaded the plateau but were driven back by the Burgundians to the Sarine (*Saane* in German) River. Being regarded as a frontier, the Sarine became the very symbol of the plurality of languages in Switzerland.

One of the most interesting single points on the line of demarcation between French and German is the town of Biel, a bilingual city *par excellence*.

The German-speaking Swiss are 64% of the Helvetian people. **Schwyzerdütsch,** which is a German-Swiss dialect of the Swabian group, has many local variations. It is used in daily conversation, while classical German is reserved for official business and correspondence.

On the other hand, the French-speaking group (18%) have seen their dialect fall more and more into disuse. Italian (11%) is spoken almost entirely throughout the Ticino and in part of the Grisons (Graubünden).

As for Romansh, which is not a dialect, but a language of Latin origin, it is used only by 7% of the Swiss in the Grisons Canton *(qv)*, especially in the Engadine and Grisons Oberland.

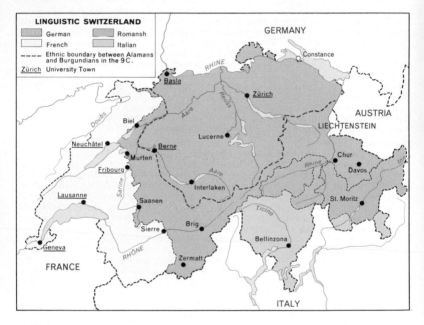

German, French and Italian are regarded as the official languages of the Confederation and are used as such by the authorities and the federal civil service. At least two of these three are taught compulsorily in schools.

Romansh was recognized as a fourth national language in 1938. The Romansh League has done all it can to preserve and even spread its use in schools and in the press.

The religious question – *For religious majority in each canton see pp 26-27.*

Until the middle of the 19C the religious question was acute, and it long seemed an obstacle to unity in the Confederation. This was proved by the Sonderbund war *(qv)*. But since 1848 complete tolerance is the rule.

Today the Protestants represent 44.3% of the population of Helvetian origin and the Roman Catholics 47.6%. Most of French Switzerland is Protestant except the cantons of Fribourg and the Valais. Central Switzerland is Roman Catholic and the north and east are Protestant.

The Swiss Protestant temperament, in its fundamentally democratic and patriotic aspects, owes much more to the forceful personality of a man like Zwingli *(qv)* than to the strict doctrine of one like Calvin *(qv)*, whose influence was felt chiefly in Geneva. The rather loose organization of the Protestant churches reflects the federalist structure of the country and allows subsidized State churches to exist alongside free churches supported by the donations of the faithful.

The Roman Catholics are attached to six dioceses: Basle (See of Solothurn), Lausanne-Geneva-Fribourg (See of Fribourg), Sion, Chur, St Gallen and Lugano. The regular clergy are distributed among a small number of large abbeys like those of St-Maurice, Einsiedeln and Engelberg.

Finally, many dissident Catholic or Protestant churches and philosophical sects have found fruitful soil in Switzerland.

FAMOUS SWISS

From legendary heroes to famous artists... religious reformers to scholars... a country as small as Switzerland does not lack famous citizens. Mentioned below are a few that are known internationally.

14C: William **Tell** *(qv);* Arnold von **Winkelried** *(qv).*

15C: St Nicholas of **Flüe** *(qv).*

15 and 16C: Cardinal Matthew **Schiner** *(qv);* Ulrich **Zwingli** *(qv);* Joachim von Watt known as **Vadian** *(qv);* Theophrastus Bombastus von Hohenheim, known as **Paracelsus,** natural scientist and alchemist; François de **Bonivard** *(qv).*

16 and 17C: Domenico **Fontana,** architect and his student Carlo **Maderno.**

17C: Kaspar Jodok von **Stockalper** *(qv).*

17 and 18C: Jakob and Johann **Bernoulli,** mathematicians.

18C: Daniel **Bernoulli,** mathematician; Jean Etienne **Liotard,** painter; Leonhard **Euler,** mathematician; Jean-Jacques **Rousseau** *(qv);* Salomon **Gessner,** poet and painter; Horace Bénédict de **Saussure,** physicist.

18 and 19C: Jacques **Necker,** financier and statesman; Johann Caspar **Lavater,** philosopher; Johann David **Wyss,** writer; Johann Heirich **Pestalozzi** *(qv);* General Frederic de **Laharpe** *(qv);* Guillaume Henri **Dufour,** Swiss army general; Léopold **Robert,** painter; Albert Bitzius known as Jeremias **Gotthelf,** writer; Rodolphe **Toepffer,** known for his drawings.

19C: Louis **Agassiz,** geologist; Nikolaus **Riggenbach,** engineer (built rack-railways *see Rigi* p 172); Jacob **Burckhardt,** philosopher; Gottfried **Keller,** poet; Henri Frédéric **Amiel,** writer; Conrad Ferdinand **Meyer,** author, poet.

19 and 20C: Arnold **Böcklin,** painter; Henri **Dunant,** founder of the Red Cross; César **Ritz,** businessman and hotelier; Carl **Spitteler,** poet; Ferdinand **Hodler** *(qv),* painter; Ferdinand de **Saussure,** linguist; Felix **Vallotton,** painter; Carl Gustav **Jung,** psychoanalyst; Charles Ferdinand **Ramuz** *(qv),* writer; the world famous clown Adrien Wettach, better known known under the name of **Grock;** Ernest **Ansermet,** orchestra conductor; Fréderic Sauser known as Blaise **Cendrars,** writer; Edouard Jeanneret-Gris known as **Le Corbusier,** architect; Frank **Martin** and Arthur **Honegger,** musicians and the actor Michel **Simon.**

20C: Alberto **Giacometti,** painter and sculptor; Mario **Botta,** architect; Hans **Erni** *(qv),* painter; Jean **Tinguely,** sculptor; Max **Frisch,** writer; Friedrich **Dürrenmatt,** writer.

In addition to the above names, one must include Swiss "expatriates" who chose to adopt a different nationality – for instance, the French writers Madame **de Staël,** Benjamin **Constant** – and, conversely, those foreigners who decided to settle in Swiss territory – the painters Conrad **Witz, Holbein** the Younger, Paul **Klee,** the artist Daniel **Spoerri,** the author Hermann **Hesse,** the film director Charlie **Chaplin,** the writer Georges **Simenon,** the cigar importer Zino **Davidoff,** etc.

CONQUEST OF THE HEIGHTS

The many dramatic or glorious episodes of the struggle between man and the mountains have never ceased to arouse public interest. The victories of the 19C over the supposedly most inaccessible peaks gradually destroyed the superstitious dread with they were regarded by popular imagination *(see Pilatus),* but mountaineering still has many critics as well as a growing number of devotees.

Switzerland, with its many "over 4000m – 13123ft" peaks *(p 14)* is a happy hunting-ground for the climber. We are told that as long ago as the 14C six monks from Lucerne undertook to climb the Pilatus, not without suffering, after this exploit, the reproaches of their Father Superior. One of the first climbs recorded to the credit of Switzerland was that of the Titlis, which was accomplished in 1744 by four peasants from Engelberg. In 1792 Spescha, a monk from Disentis, conquered the Oberalpstock. The year 1811 was marked by an outstanding expedition: the **Meyer brothers,** rich merchants of Aarau, reached the Valais, via the Grimsel and, starting from the Lötschental, climbed the **Jungfrau** (4158m – 13642ft).

At the same time, Frenchmen and Austrians were attacking their highest peaks. In 1786 the guide **Jacques Balmat,** of Chamonix, reached the summit of the **Mont Blanc;** he repeated his expedition in 1787 with the Swiss physicist, De Saussure *(see Michelin Green Guide, Alpes du Nord – in French only).* The Austrians, for their part, made the first ascent of the Grossglockner (3797m – 12457ft) in 1800.

In 1813 the Breithorn (4165m – 13665ft) was conquered in its turn; then the Tödi in 1824 and the Piz Bernina (4049m – 13284ft) in 1850. Until then the Swiss had more or less monopolized these exploits. From 1840 onwards the British recorded some famous first ascents in the Alpine chronicle: the **Stockhorn** in 1842 and the **Wasenhorn** in 1844, by. **J. D. Forbes;** the **Pic Dufour** (4634m – 15204ft) in 1855 by the three **Smyth** brothers; the **Eiger** in 1858 by **Barrington;** and above all, in 1865, the **Matterhorn** (Cervin – 4478m – 14692ft) by **Edward Whymper** *(qv).* These successes, with those of the French and Italians, make the 19C the great period of mountaineering.

The conquest of the slopes – Introduced into the country at the end of the 19C, **downhill skiing** has become very popular due to the country's incredible network of ski lifts and cable-cars and its superb mountain climate.

The Swiss snowfields have attracted British skiers who revolutionized competitive skiing by codifying the downhill race and slalom *(for more details see Michelin Green Guide to Austria);* and in the resorts of Mürren and Zermatt they have established a British "atmosphere"!

The courses at the Swiss official school of skiing reflect the general tendencies of Swiss teaching. The constant aim is to improve the average rather than to produce brilliant individuals. **Cross-country skiing** has attracted a great number of skiers due to the numerous signposted trails offered and guides present. In the spring the Valais High Road, the crossing of the glaciers in the Bernese Alps, and the run down the Diavolezza (Bernina Massif) attract many ski enthusiasts.

ECONOMY

Improved communications and the increase of population have led the Swiss economy to specialized dairy farming and large-scale industry.

The growing needs of the industrial population have led the country to make up with imports for the shortage of agricultural products, which represent only half of its total consumption. Only Britain imports more foodstuffs per head of its people.

Dairy farming – In this mountainous country, agriculture is restricted by the severe climate and the high proportion of non-productive land (25.6%) represented by lakes, glaciers and barren rocky slopes.

In the more hospitable areas, fodder, pasture and dairy farming have outstripped arable farming, which is hindered by the damp climate and rough ground.

Two breeds of cattle are the best known: the brown beasts known as the Schwyz breed, and the red and white Simmentals, which are the more numerous.

Efforts have been concentrated on milk production, and a complete industry has sprung from this speciality: the production of butter, cheese, preserved milk, milk chocolate (Lindt, Nestlé, Suchard, Tobler) and malted milk, exports of which have built up an excellent reputation abroad.

Forestry – The forests cover just over 1 million hectares – 247 million acres (that is to say 1/4 of the country's area) of which 70% are conifers with a majority of spruce trees. The forests have not only an invaluable ecological role but they supply the country with one of the few raw materials which can meet the country's needs.

Industry – As a continental state, isolated by high mountain barriers and poor in mineral resources, the Confederation seemed unlikely to have an industrial future; but it has made up for natural shortcomings by the ingenuity and enterprise of its inhabitants. To overcome mountain barriers, they bored long tunnels, built steeply graded, winding railways and perfected the rack-railway, able to climb to over 3 000 m – 10 000ft *(see Gornergrat)*. A network of roads, constantly improved, completes this equipment.

Situated at the crossroads of the great trade routes, Switzerland has become the centre of Europe.

The Confederation has turned to manufactures which require skilled labour but only a minimum of raw materials (watches, electrical machinery, embroidery and silks), the high quality of its products securing it a prominent place in the international market. Industrial operations are directed by highly qualified technicians, assisted by teams of research workers. With a generous supply of capital and skilled, conscientious employees, success appears clearly in the mechanical, electrical, chemical and textile trades.

Machinery – The metals are made into machine-tools, especially for the watch and clock and textile industries, diesel engines (Baden, Zürich), locomotives (Winterthur), agricultural and printing machinery, and spare parts for aircraft, which are exported all over the world. Precision equipment (optical instruments, calculating machines, scientific and medical equipment) and the growing output from the electrical industry satisfy all demands.

Motor vehicles – Switzerland has no national motor industry except for heavy lorries and coaches (MOWAG, NAW – grouping together Saurer, Berna and FBW).

Watch and clock industry – The watch and clock trade is third in importance to the chemical industry and machine-tool industry so far as exports are concerned.

Textiles – Silk-work and embroidery have been practised for several centuries in the east and centre of the country (Basle ribbons, Zürich silks, St Gallen and Appenzell embroidery and Glarus cotton goods).

The output of synthetic fabrics (Lucerne) has tended to take the place of the silk industry.

Chemical products – The requirements of the textile industry for dyestuffs have created an active chemical industry of which Basle is the centre. Pharmaceutical products, dyes and synthetic perfumes are among the chief exports.

Energy – In a country lacking in coal and oil, water power has become the chief source of energy. The systematic development of the hydro-electric resources requires large-scale projects *(see the Grande Dixence Dam)*. However, it is estimated that the usable resources of the country will be fully employed before the year 2000. In September 1990 the Swiss population voted a moratorium stalling the construction of nuclear power stations for the ten years to come. As a result, the country will have to intensify and diversify its hydro-electric resources in order to meet the ever-increasing demands in energy.

Tourism – As a source of foreign currency, tourism is an important industry in the Confederation. However, owing to economic crises and weather conditions, its contribution varies from year to year.

Banking – The economic prosperity of Switzerland, its political and monetary stability and the thrift of its people have encouraged the accumulation of capital in the banks. The abundance of foreign investment in the country is profitable, in the first place, to national industry and trade. Moreover, this capital enables the Confederation to finance undertakings it has had to establish outside its territory in order to circumvent foreign protectionist measures (textile and food industries) and, by investing money in foreign business and stocks, partly to restore its trade balance, which is compromised by the excess of imports over exports.

Another proof of the foresight of the people, is the way **insurance** has played a prominent part in the Swiss economy. Its private insurance and reinsurance companies have branches all over the world.

A brief record of Swiss successes – The following were discovered or perfected by the Swiss: vitamins, DDT, the first rack-railway in Europe, the first practical gas turbine, the incorporation of milk in chocolate and flour, the modern formula for life insurance, the self-winding watch, the recording chronometer, plastic wrappings, etc.

DEMOCRACY IN ACTION

The Constitution of 1848, revised in 1874 and in 1978, set up a modern federative state in place of the former Confederation of Cantons on which each canton had applied an individualist policy, having its own coinage, postal services and customs.

The Communities – Liberty of the individual, liberty of faith and conscience, liberty of the press and of association are recognized by the Constitution, which gives every Swiss citizen aged over twenty the right to vote and to be elected. Women, at last, obtained the vote in federal elections in 1971 but they do not always have a say in cantonal and community affairs. However, the whole regime rests upon the principle of the sovereignty of citizens living in 3000 free communities and forming the very basis of the national will.

In all matters the community is competent to decide in the first instance and the canton intervenes only on appeal. A revealing detail may be found in the fact that in order for a foreigner to acquire Swiss nationality he must first be admitted to the "corps of citizens" of a given community.

A Landsgemeinde at Glarus

Cantonal authority – Each canton has kept its political sovereignty, with its own constitution and legislative body. In each of the 23 cantons *(pp 26-27)* executive power belongs to the State Council and legislative power to the Grand Council.

The practice of direct democracy still survives in a few mountain cantons like Appenzell, Glarus and Unterwalden. Here, every spring, all active citizens meet in the open and are called upon to vote by a show of hands on all questions affecting the community. These highly ceremonious meetings are called the **Landsgemeinden** *(see the Calendar of Events).*

The federal authorities Legislative power is exercised by two assemblies, the National Council and the Council of States; executive power by a college of seven members, the Federal Council. The two assemblies, when sitting jointly, form the Federal Assembly. The National Council represents the people with one deputy being elected for more than 30000 inhabitants (200 members); each canton or half-canton is represented by at least one seat. The Council of States, which represents the cantons, has 46 members, or 2 per canton regardless of the size of the population.

This bicameral system, similar to American parliamentary institutions, protects as far as possible the interests of the small communities.

Executive power resides in the Federal Council. Its seven members are elected for a four-year term (by the Federal Assembly), and each administers a department, that is to say, a ministry. The annual election of the President – whose official title is President of the Confederation – and of the Vice-President appears to be a mere formality, the Vice-President always succeeding the President and his successor being chosen from a roster drawn up by agreement. These traditions reveal Swiss distrust of over-brilliant individuals and everything that suggests a presidential regime.

The sovereign people – Decisions by the Federal Assembly can be taken only after a favourable vote of the two chambers. But here again popular sovereignty appears. If within 90 days after a decision by the Assembly, signatures can be obtained from 50000 citizens, the entire population is then called upon to decide whether a law should finally be accepted or rejected. This is the right of referendum, which in practice has a conservative influence. The average citizen of Vaud is fond of saying: "The referendum is our right to say No when Berne has said Yes".

The Swiss people also have the right to initiate legislation. Thus, 100000 citizens may demand an amendment of the Articles of the Constitution or the adoption of new articles. Thus, the popular will finds expression at every level of political activity and exercices a permanent control over the country's institutions.

During a referendum held in early December 1992, the Swiss nation answered no to joining the EEE *(Espace Economique Européen)*, the first step towards the European Community and, subsequently, European Union.

For historical information on the country
consult the table and notes in the Introduction.

THE SWISS CANTONS

Under the shield: the name of the canton and its official abbreviation (used for car registration).
On the map: the boundaries of the cantons and their capitals.
In the alphabetical list, the name of the canton is given in English with its local name, or its alternative name. The area, population, language and religious majorities follow.
Abbreviations — F.: French, G.: German, I.: Italian, P.: Protestant, R.C.: Roman Catholic.

Appenzell — Inner-Rhoden (AI): 172km² — 66sq miles — pop 13 870 (G.-R.C.).
              Ausser-Rhoden (AR): 243km² — 94sq miles — pop 52 229 (G.-P.).
The bear, which represents the Abbey of St Gallen, adorns the shield of the canton.

Aargau — 1 404km² — 542sq miles — pop 507 508 (G.-P.).
The name means "the country of the Aare" and the river is represented by wavy lines. The three stars represent the three districts which together form the canton.

Basle (Basel, Bâle) — Basle District (BL): 482km² — 165sq miles — pop 233 488 (G.-P.).
                 Basle Town (BS): 37km² — 14sq miles — pop 198 411 (G.-P.).
The town was the seat of a prince-bishop. Its arms include a bishop's crosier (red for Basle District, black for Basle Town).

Berne (Bern) — 6 050km² — 2 659sq miles — pop 958 192 (G.-P.). *For the origin of the coat of arms see p 54.*

Fribourg — 1 670km² — 645sq miles — pop 213 571 (F.-R.C.).
The shield of Fribourg is black and white, the colours of the Dukes of Zähringen.

Geneva (Genève, Genf) — 282km² — 109sq miles — pop 379 590 (F.-P.). *For the origin of the coat of arms see p 94.*

Glarus — 684km² — 2654sq miles — pop 38 508 (G.-P.).
Its coat of arms represents St Fridolin, the patron saint of the district.

Grisons (Graubünden) — 7 106km² — 2 744sq miles — pop 173 890 (G.-P.).
The modern history of Graubünden, known as the Grisons in English and Rhaetia in ancient times, begins with the alliance of the three Leagues founded in the 14 and 15C.
The League of God's House gathered the subjects of the Bishop and Chapter of Chur under the shield charged with "an ibex passant sable" (chur and environs, Engadine).
The Grey League (shield half sable, half argent, i.e., black and white), from which the Grisons gets its name, ruled the upper Rhine Basin.
The banner of the Ten Jurisdictions League (a cross of gold and blue quartering) flew in the Prättigau, the district of Davos and Arosa.

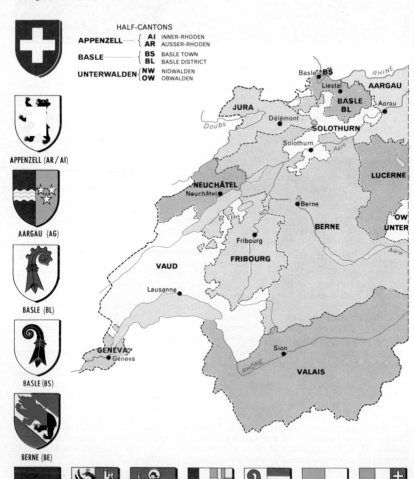

Jura − 837km² − 323sq miles − pop 66 163 (F.-.R.C.). *For the origin of the coat of arms see Delémont p 80.* The canton was formed on 24 September 1978 by popular vote ratifying a Federal decree of 9 March 1978. Its three districts, Delémont (the capital), Porrentruy and Franches Montagnes were formerly the northern part of the canton of Berne.

Lucerne (Luzern). − 1 492km² − 576sq miles − pop 326 268 (G.-R.C.).

Neuchâtel − 797km² − 308sq miles − pop 163 985 (F.-P.).
The present coat of arms dates from the proclamation in 1848 of the Republic of Neuchâtel. The white cross on a red ground commemorates its adhesion to the Confederation.

St Gallen − 2 014km² − 778sq miles − pop 427 501 (G.-R.C.).
The fascine on the shield recalls the union of the various districts which were joined in 1803, when the canton was formed.

Schaffhausen − 298km² − 115sq miles − pop 72 160 (G.-P.).
Schaffhausen means "the sheep's house" (Schaf = sheep).

Schwyz − 908km² − 350sq miles − pop 111 964 (G.-R.C.).
The shield of Schwyz used to be plain red. Later, it was charged with a white cross and became the emblem of the entire Swiss Confederation.

Solothurn − 791km² − 305sq miles − pop 231 746 (G.-R.C.).

Ticino − 2 811km² − 1 085sq miles − pop 282 181 (I.-R.C.).

Thurgau − 1 013km² − 391sq miles − pop 209 362 (G.-P.).
The two lions in the coat of arms were borrowed from the arms of the Counts of Kyburg.

Unterwalden − Nidwalden (NW): 276km² − 107sq miles − pop 33 044 (G.-R.C.).
Obwalden (OW); 491km² − 190sq miles − pop 29 025 (G.-R.C.).
The arms bear the keys of St Peter: those of Nidwalden are on a red ground ; those of Obwalden on a red and white ground.

Uri − 1 076km² − 415sq miles − pop 34 208 (G.-R.C.).

Valais (Wallis) − 5 226km² − 2 018sq miles − pop 249 817 (F.-R.C.).
The shield is red and white to commemorate the episcopal banner of Sion. It bears thirteen stars representing the thirteen *dizains* (districts) of the canton.

Vaud (Vadt) − 3 219km² − 1 243sq miles − 601 816 (F.-P.).
The green flag was adopted when the Lemanic Republic was founded in 1798. The white flag with the motto "Liberté et Patrie" was adopted when Vaud joined the Confederation in 1803.

Zug − 239km² − 92sq miles − pop 85 546 (G.-R.C.).

Zürich − 1 729km² − 667sq miles − pop 1 179 044 (G.-P.).

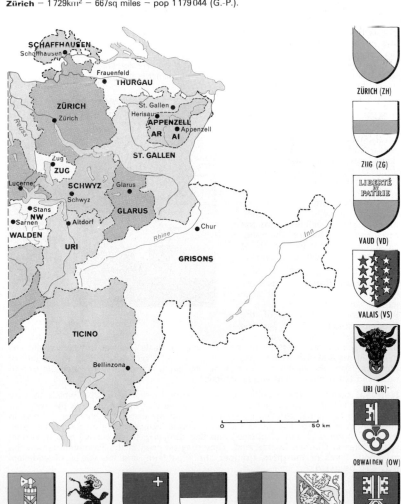

PICTURESQUE SWITZERLAND

TRADITIONS AND FOLKLORE

Swiss folklore can always point to a rich collection of local costumes. None the less, it is in the mountains that the foreigner must seek out people who wear their traditional costumes every day. The Gruyère and the Valais are favoured areas in this respect.

The *armailli* (herdsman) of Gruyère still wears the *bredzon*, a short cloth or canvas jacket with puffed sleeves – a heritage from the Empire period – embroidered with thorn-points and, on the lapels, with edelweiss. The straw toque edged with velvet is called a *capette*. Similar costumes are found in all the pastoral districts of the Bernese Oberland, although less often, but the man's jacket there is often made of velvet.

At Evolène the women's working dress includes a simple frock, with a red and white kerchief for the neck, and a straw hat with a brim edged with velvet and turned down over the ears, while the crown is encircled by crochet-work ribbons arranged in bands. On high feast days the women of Evolène put on a rustling silk apron and the *mandzon* (a sort of jacket with long sleeves); they wear a very flat, round felt hat on top of a white lace bonnet.

Traditional costumes of the Appenzell

Pastoral traditions – These are still very much alive in mountain districts like the Anniviers Valley *(qv)* where the whole life of the people is governed by the movements of cattle from the villages to the mayen *(qv)* and the high Alpine pasture *(alp)*. On all the north side of the chain, the trek to the alp gives rise to joyful and picturesque parades (late May, early June). Endless lines of beasts with beribboned and flower-decked horns move along the roads with cow-bells tolling, escorted by herdsmen burdened with the kit they need for living in the chalets (the strongest carry a huge cheese-boiler on a yoke). In the Valais (at Verbier and the Balme Pass – between Trient and Argentière) the end of the journey is marked by cow fights, after

which the "queen" of the herd may wear the giant bell reserved for her.

High summer, being a time of hard and sometimes frantic labour, hardly favours amusements. However, a midsummer festival sometimes varies the solitude of the *armaillis* by bringing a crowd of friends and relations up from the valleys.

The return from the alp, the *désalpe*, equally spectacular, causes great liveliness on the roads and in the villages. The open-air performances of *William Tell* at Interlaken begin with a procession of this kind.

Urban traditions – These are generally of a patriotic and civic nature, like the commemoration of the Escalade at Geneva or the *Knabenschiessen* at Zürich *(see the Calendar of Events)*. In quite a

Off to the mountain pastures for summer

different spirit, more like the Rhenish customs, the Basle Carnival, in which all classes mingle in masked dances and processions, brings a touch of frivolity to the city of Erasmus. From behind the mask of some grotesque figure the merrymaker is free to taunt and tease friends and acquaintances.

National sports – The activities of shooting and gymnastic clubs, which concern more than 1/3 of the male population over 19 years of age, appear to the onlooker in the form of martial parades by sportsmen and the display of sporting trophies in inns and cafés. As for the traditional rustic sports, like wrestling on the grass, stone throwing, *hornuss* (a sort of cricket) and flag throwing, these survive only at certain village fêtes in German Switzerland. They may be seen in the Emmental where the cavernous tones of the great trumpet, the Alpenhorn, and the voices of yodellers may also be heard.

Calendar of Events
The most important Swiss festivals are listed in a table, in the Practical Information section at the end of the Guide.

URBAN SCENE

Certain large Swiss villages and towns offer admirable examples of town-planning to those who can view them from well-chosen vantage points.

In any case there is hardly a city of the Mittelland which does not guard jealously, sometimes even too severely, some fragment of its medieval character. Here the old quarters are residential and have not suffered the unhappy fate of the ancient nuclei of so many other European towns often dilapidated or damaged by war.

Fountains – Fountains, always charmingly decked with flowers, add a welcoming note to the livelier squares and streets of many towns and cities. The central columns are carefully painted and gilded and often support an animal or an allegorical subject such as a warrior, a hero of legend or most likely a "banneret" (a man-at-arms carrying a banner with the crest of the town).

Justice Fountain, Berne

Arcades (in German: Lauben) – Originating beyond the Alps, this form of building became popular in the north from the 14C onwards, when it was adopted by the gentlemen of Berne. Consequently the arcaded streets in many towns of the Mittelland can be regarded today as evidence of a period of Bernese hegemony.

Outdoor painting – This has been very popular since the Renaissance, not only in districts with sunny skies and a dry climate like the Engadine (1) but also in many towns of German Switzerland, where façades are proudly decorated with vast allegorical or historical compositions inspired by Olympus as well as by the Bible.

All over the Confederation historic monuments and public buildings have shutters painted with chevrons in the colours of the canton's coat of arms.

Covered bridges – This type of building is very popular in all German Switzerland. Besides providing towns like Lucerne with pleasant walks under shelter, it fulfils a technical requirement, for the protection of a roof considerably reduces the cost of maintenance of a structure made wholly of timber. The latest covered bridge built in Switzerland dates from 1943 (Hohe Brücke, on the road from Flüeli to Kerns – p 176). Some localities built on hillsides (Lausanne, Erlenbach, Thun) have covered public staircases, also built entirely of wood.

Oriels (in German: Erker) – These corbelled loggias, sometimes built in two storeys, are to be seen in the northeastern towns where they are elaborate works of art decorated with carving and painting. With more modest means, the Engadine peasant builds these original openings on the grey walls of his house.

Official buildings – The word comfortable well describes the impression of middle-class ease given by Swiss public buildings such as the town hall (Rathaus) of which even the smallest city is so proud. The most successful of these buildings bear valuable witness to the quality of civil architecture in the Gothic, Renaissance and classical periods. Their internal arrangements – rooms richly ornamented and furnished with stucco, woodwork, glazed cabinets and especially magnificent porcelain stoves – show a sophisticated way of life.

The old corporation headquarters (Zunfthaus) vie with this luxury. One in Zürich houses the collection of pottery of the Swiss National Museum.

Oriel window in Stein am Rhein

These buildings often display collections of the decorative arts which flourished at the time they were being built and during their heyday.

Finally, it is very revealing that important buildings like the great Gothic cathedrals which monopolize attention at the expense of their surroundings are Swiss specimens of foreign styles. The Helvetian genius comes to fruition much less in single masterpieces than in the general design of a group of buildings, a street or a simple country church.

---

(1) Do not confuse mural painting and sgraffito. On the latter, read The Engadine House p 85.

RURAL ARCHITECTURE

The Swiss peasant's house, carefully kept and adorned with flowers, shows – especially in German Switzerland – a remarkable care for comfort and propriety as well as a highly developed practical sense.

House in the Bernese Oberland
(Jungfrau District)

The roof is low-pitched, with wide eaves on all sides, and in the high valley is still covered with shingles weighted with large stones. Decoration is profuse: beams are carved with facets and the props of the roof are elaborately finished.

The Oberland mountaineer is very proud of these refinements and calls his house his *Schali* (chalet or little château). This is the type of house that has made the Swiss chalet known the world over.

House in Central Switzerland
(Lucerne District)

A highly distinctive form of building, recognizable by its steep roof and separate weatherboards sheltering the row of windows on each storey. The ground floor is high above the ground and can be reached only from the side, up an out door staircse.

House in the Appenzell
(near Trogen)

In this rainy district farm buildings must be grouped in a single block, and wooden shingles, laid like the scales of a fish, form a protective covering even on the façades. The gable of the dwelling house always faces the valley. At ground level are the windows of the cellar, where women working at fine embroidery find an even temperature. The shutters can be folded back vertically, so as to fit into a groove at the top of the window.

Bernese Country House
(Emmental)

A huge roof, reaching down to the first floor at the sides, also covers a large barn. The most prosperous peasants, imitating the townsmen, often do away with the triangular roof over the gable and build in its place a majectic timber arch (indicated by a red dotted line), which is fully panelled.

House in the Ticino
(Foroglio, Bavona Valley)

A stone building with primitive arrangements: communication between storeys is only by outdoor stairs and wooden galleries.

The walls have to be made very thick (up to 0.90 m — 3ft) owing to the irregular shape of the stones used. The roof is of stone slabs. The upper part of the gable is left open to the winds or enclosed with a rough partition of superimposed planks.

House in the Valais
(Evolène)

In the villages of the French-speaking Valais, wooden houses are often tall. the living quarters (wooden part) are joined by open sided galleries to the kitchen block (masonry), partly visible on the right.

In the foreground is a *raccard* or *mazot*, a small building which serves as a granary or store *(see text and illustration p 207).*

House in the Engadine. — *The peculiar arrangement of this dwelling is illustrated and described in detail on p 85.*

RELIGIOUS ART

As an international crossroads, Switzerland has always freely welcomed the most varying artistic influences; this is proved by its cathedrals and abbey churches. In the countryside the church towers have sharply-gabled roofs, shaped like a circumflex accent. Sometimes sharply pointed spires or shining onion-shaped domes indicate sanctuaries which are often beautifully decorated and form an essential feature of the landscape. The following descriptions do not include the churches of Italian Switzerland. These show a development of religious architecture similar to that of Lombardy.

Romanesque Art – Specimens of this are rare on the north slope of the Alps and illustrate two different architectural traditions. In German Switzerland a building like the Abbey Church of All Saints at Schaffhausen, which is simply a cold, bare hall with a flat ceiling supported by pillars, recalls the Rhenish sanctuaries which were still being built very late in the Middle Ages, on the plan of the ancient Christian basilicas. In Romansh Switzerland, the great nave of Payerne, with barrel vaulting, and the abbey church at Romainmôtier, bear witness to the Burgundian Romanesque influence.

Gothic Art – The early 13C cathedral of Lausanne is the finest specimen; it shows a very original process of assimilation of the various methods established by French craftsmen. The Renaissance style had little influence on religious architecture in Switzerland, where Gothic persisted until the middle of the 16C. The increasingly complicated design of vaulting (star vaulting in the chancels) and furniture and the appearance of precious alterpieces with

Interior of the abbey church at Payerne

Flamboyant decoration (Chur Cathedral) are characteristic of the later period. The style of the latter, known as Late Gothic, is plentifully represented all over German Switzerland and the Grisons.

Baroque Art – From the 17C onwards the Counter-Reformation, resulting from the Council of Trent, brought to the Alps a great many missionaries belonging to orders more interested in direct action than in mysticism. Franciscans, Capuchins and Jesuits sought permanently to associate a new religious art with this Catholic revival; it was to take the place of Gothic, which had become a symbol of barbarism. The researches of the great, fashionable architects from Italy and the Ticino were widely drawn upon. Stucco and frescoes covered every available surface. Gigantic rood screens, exalted the dogma of the Real Presence with their gilding and gave prominence to the Virgin and the Saints. It was then that the great Swiss Benedictine abbeys took on their present florid look.

Nevertheless alongside these grandiloquent masterpieces of **Vorarlberg** baroque a rural vigour survived in many sanctuaries of the Valais and the Grisons. This was the time when a mountain retreat like the Conches Valley (Goms Valley of the upper Rhône) had its local dynasties of altar builders, such as the Ritzes, and organ makers, such as the Carlens. From refinement to refinement, church baroque reached its highest degree in the ornate Collegiate Church of Arlesheim, before expiring gently about 1770. After this, for a century and a half, imitation of the antique reigned supreme.

Contemporary Research – In the search for a new religious architecture which, while taking advantage of the opportunities afforded by reinforced concrete, respects the notions of mystery and meditation proper to a sacred place, Central Europe and especially German Switzerland are the leading exponents. There is a real overall unity about the buildings of Karl Moser, who showed the way with his Church of St Anthony in Basle and of his pupils Fritz Metzger (St Charles in Lucerne), Hermann Baur (St Nicholas of Flüe in Berne), and Otto Dreyer (St Joseph in Lucerne). These huge churches are startling at first sight, yet the most critical visitor cannot remain blind to the poise of their towers, the masterly distribution and variation of their lighting and the richness of some pieces of furniture, including goldsmith's work. Thanks to the artists of the St Luke's Society, a Romansh group led by the painter Cingria, the churches of less radical design, built at the same time in French Switzerland, are decorated in a fresh and vigorous style.

Michelin Green Guides for North America:

California
Canada
New York
New England
Quebec
Washington

SOME FEATURES OF SWISS LIFE

Military duty – Although Switzerland is a neutral country, do not be surprised to find soldiers in uniform and armed at crossroads, military convoys along the roads, shooting practise in the fields. This unusual scene is because military service plays a prominent part in the life of the Swiss citizen. With its continual mixing of classes and ethnic groups the Army is an essential agent of "Helvetization". All men fit for service can be called up to serve in the Swiss army between the age of 20 and 50, 55 in the case of officers. Women may volunteer to serve in the SFA *(Service Féminin de l'Armée)*.

The Swiss Army is a militia without "regular" units. "Active" service begins only at general mobilization. There is no provision for performing civilian service instead of military service.

The Army has a general only in time of war or general mobilization (General Guisan, 1939-45).

Full-time service (at 20 years of age) does not usually exceed 4 months, but it is followed. Reservists aged between 20 and 32 belong to the "élite" and are obliged to undergo eight 3-week trainınarly andg sessions. From 33 to 42 years old they join the *land-wehr,* where they are expected to follow three 2-week courses. Finally, between 43 and 50, the men accede to the *landsturm,* where they only have to train for two weeks a year.

The Swiss soldier keeps all his equipment at home: uniform, rifle, ammunition, gas mask... Apart from the training periods, shooting practise with service weapons remains compulsory; a certain number of marks must be scored every year, and these are noted in the soldier's pay book.

Many Swiss carry on training for pleasure: common on Sunday mornings is the crackling of gunfire heard even in the remotest valleys.

The years when soldier-citizens are not called up for training, they nonetheless have to submit to an arms and equipment inspection carried out by their local municipality.

Swiss Navy – With its some 30 cargo ships sailing the oceans, Switzerland ranks 50th out of the 111 countries with a merchant marine and among the forerunners of landlocked nations.

Electoral duty – Although held, if at all possible, on a given Sunday, the various elections – communal, cantonal and federal – occur in the citizen's calendar with a frequency that may seem surprising to the foreigner.

It cantons like Berne and Zürich, which are very much attached to strict control of the various budgets, it is a common joke that votings are as frequent as *jass,* the Swiss game of poker. Voting may take place about the building of a bus-shelter (communal) or the diversion of a mountain torrent (cantonal) just as much as about the fixing of prices (federal). *See Democracy in Action p 25.* The larger number of elections explains the lack of interest on the part of the electorate (35-50% participation, while for cantonal votings participation can be as low as 30%).

Work and leisure – Switzerland remains one of the countries in the world where the working week is the longest: 2 000-2 300 hours a year.

Once the working day has ended, the Swiss will relax with a newspaper – they are, in fact (in spite of radio and television), said to be the most avid readers of newspapers in the world!

Newspapers can still be found piled up on a street corner – payment is left to the discretion of the individual; while in a café or restaurant, although the newspaper is free, it is attached to a wooden pole.

Dinner in German Switzerland is a rather sketchy affair; it is usually just a *café au lait* and *Rosti.* After dinner the Swiss may linger in a café or brasserie, amidst the cigar smoke, with a simple glass of wine or a mug of beer (spirits are rarely served outside the home) and even a plate of sausage and ham. The influence of women is particularly felt in the campaign against alcoholism: Alkoholfreis Restaurants exist in towns of any importance. These restaurants do not serve alcoholic beverages – not even beer!

More rarely, for home life must not be disturbed, a *fondue* is the pretext for friendly reunions which may go on far into the night.

For more details on Swiss gastronomic specialities see p 33.

Generally speaking the Swiss go to bed early. Evening programmes at the cinema begin at 8.30pm with an intermission in the middle of the main film. There is no question of night life (after midnight) except in Geneva and Lausanne.

The casinos or *Kursaals* are sought-after chiefly for their concerts, dance orchestras, variety programmes etc., as public gambling *(maximum stake: 5Frs)* is forbidden throughout Switzerland.

Swiss love of music is evident in the seasonal festivals and daily concerts given in the leading tourist resorts.

For further information see the Calendar of Events.

The introduction of chocolate to Europe
The Swiss chocolate-makers of today enjoy an enviable reputation. However it was not until the mid-19C that they started making chocolate bars. Chocolate was one of the foodstuffs that the New World contributed to the Old Word in the 17C. Initially introduced as a drink, it was popular in the 17C coffee houses of Oxford, Marseilles and Vienna. James Baker opened the first chocolate factory in New England and by 1876 the Swiss M D Peter was making milk chocolate on a commercial scale.

FOOD AND WINE

A country combining the culinary traditions of France, Germany and Italy, Switzerland is rich in gastronomical specialities which, although unsophisticated, are nonetheless wholesome and tasty, and deserve to be sampled.

Meals in restaurants – The menu usually offered in Swiss restaurants includes soup (both at midday and in the evening), an *entrée* (lake or river fish, eggs, cheese puffs, etc.) and a meat dish with vegetables; an extra charge is often made for dessert, however. *A la carte* dishes are very generous.

Fondue – The great hard cheeses, Gruyère and Emmental, which carry the fame of the Swiss dairy industry abroad, form the basis of *fondue,* a preparation which is a national institution among the French Swiss.
As might be expected, every Romansh canton, especially Vaud, Neuchâtel and Fribourg, claims to have the secret of the mixture of Gruyère, Emmental, Vacherin and the other ingredients which will make the best *fondue.* In all cases the basic recipe is as follows: boil some white wine in an earthenware cooking-pot – the *caquelon* – the bottom of which must first be rubbed with garlic. Pour in all the grated cheese and stir constantly until the mixture is quite liquid. Then add spices and kirsch, etc. Serve boiling hot on a carefully regulated brazier. The *fondue* is eaten by dipping little cubes of bread, held on a long fork, into the pot. And bad luck to the clumsy fellow who lets his bread fall into the pot! He has to buy a bottle of wine – known locally as a Fendant *(see Swiss Wines below).*
Raclette is a Valais speciality. It is prepared by toasting one side of a slice of Valais cheese (the soft cheese of Bagnes or Conches – Goms) at a fire. When the cheese melts it is scraped directly onto the plate with a knife or a wooden blade. The *raclette* is eaten with gherkins and with bread or potatoes cooked in their jackets.

Meat, pork and fish – Under the heading of butcher's meat, the most original Swiss speciality is the dried meat of the Grisons, **Bündnerfleisch.** This is raw beef smoked and dried, served in thin slices. Apart from this delicacy, the most frequent meat dishes are fillet of veal *(Schnitzel)* and pork chop. However, the people of Zürich, who have the reputation of being gourmets, have popularized dishes such as minced veal (or calf's liver) with cream *(geschnetzeltes Kalbsfleisch)* and *Leberspiessli* (calf's liver cooked on a spit, with bacon). In contrast with this rather poor selection, the pork-butchers' shops offer an extraordinary variety of *Wurst* (sausages). The German Swiss eat a lot of mild-tasting food: *Gnagi* (knuckle of pork, much enjoyed in Berne for a four o'clock snack), *Klöpfer* (saveloy) at Basle, *Schüblig* at St Gallen, *Kalbsbratwurst* (veal sausage) at Zürich, *Salsiz* (small salamis) in the Engadine. The French Swiss prefer smoked sausages having a stronger taste *(boutefas* in Payerne, *longeole* in Geneva, etc).
Drawing on these resources the monumental **Berner Platte** (Bernese Dish) brings together bacon, sausages, ham, sometimes boiled beef, pickled cabbage *(Sauerkraut)* and potatoes or green beans.
The national dish of German Switzerland is the golden **Rösti** (potatoes boiled, diced, fried and finally baked in the oven with fried onion rings and bacon bits).
The rivers and lakes produce a wide variety of fish such as trout, pike, dace, tench, carp and perch (fishing nets on the shores of Lake Geneva). All these species are seasoned according to local tradition and will delight many a gourmet.

Sweets and desserts – Fresh cream enters into the composition of many sweets and desserts such as meringues and *Schaffhauserzungen* (baked biscuits with fresh cream). The kirsch-cake of Zug and the *Leckerli* of Basle – spiced bread made with honey and almonds – have their faithful followers.
Swiss chocolate, of time-honoured reputation, is used to make delicious cakes and sweets. In hotels, one often finds small chocolate bars on one's pillow or bed side table.

SWISS WINES

There are less than 14 000ha – 34 600 acres of vineyards which makes up only 36% of the wine consumed nationally. Of the white wine of Vaud, the best known vintages are Lavaux, Dézaley, Féchy, Aigle and Yvorne.
Many varieties of white and red wine are to be found in the Valais. Fendant is white, and so is Johannisberg, which has a more delicate bouquet like the Rhine wines. Dôle, the most popular red wine in Switzerland, is a fragrant blend obtained by mixing black *pinot* and *gamay* grapes, which make up most of the Burgundy wine crop.
Although Cortaillod is a strong, heavy, red wine, most of the wines from Neuchâtel, such as Auvernier, Boudry and Colombier, are light, sparkling, white wines drawn from a noble vine, the Chasselas, which grows on chalky soil.
Ticino vines yield heady, highly alcoholic wines, such as Mezzana – both red and white – and Nostrano – red – which are pleasant with dessert.
The red, white and rosé wines (Süssdruck) from the eastern area of the country and the Alpine Valley of the Rhine by contrast, are most appreciated for their light and subtle quality.

Serving the wine: the "star" – The diversity of vines and soil allows a choice wide enough to accompany a well-furnished menu.
The white wines of the Vaud (Dorin) and the Fendant of the Valais, the Neuchâtel wines *(see above)* and that of Biel (Twanner) go with *hors-d'œuvre* and fish. A Cortaillod or good Dôle are strong enough to match roasts and venison. Johannisberg and the Malvoisie of the Valais, and some Ticino vintages, are excellent dessert wines. Kirsch from Zug, *marc* from the Valais and Williamine pleasantly finish a meal.
Some white wines are expected to "make a star". Those from Neuchâtel are bottled very early and hold carbonic gas in suspension. When uncorked and poured from a height (see how the waiters do it) they foam in the glass and form a sort of star.
Local wines are served in restaurants in decanters of 2, 3 and 5 décis *(décilitres).*

Sights

Clock Tower, Berne

M. Martin/VLOO

AARAU © Aargau

Michelin map **216** folds 16 and 17 or **427** fold 5 – Alt 383m – 1 273ft – Facilities

This is the Aargau canton capital, one of the richest in Switzerland, thanks to the textile and machine industries of the Aare and Rhine areas. It is pleasantly placed at the foot of the Jura. The best **general view** of the old town is to be had from the bridge over the Aare. It rises in terraces from the river and is dominated by the towers of the belfry, the church and the old castle.

Old Town – A delightful stroll may be taken through the old quarters. In their narrow streets the tourist will find fine houses, sometimes adorned with oriel windows and wrought iron emblems whose style recalls the long Bernese domination. There are façades covered with frescoes and roofs with stepped gables and eaves.

Parish Church (Stadtkirche) – The church is perched on the extreme edge of a spur running west. It is surmounted by an elegant late 17C belfry. The fine Fountain of Justice (1643) is in a small adjacent square, and from a point nearby, there is a pleasant view of the countryside.

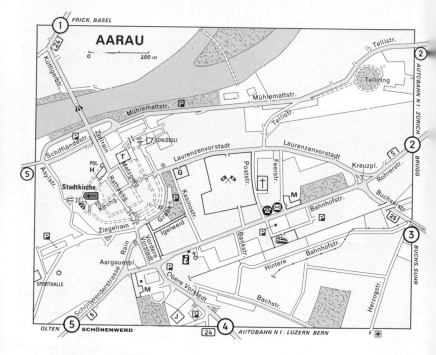

EXCURSIONS

★**Schönenwerd** – *4.5km – 3 miles southwest on ⑤, the Olten road.*
A modern quarter, owing its existence to the Bally boot and shoe factories, has grown up outside the old town of Schönenwerd, dominated by a 12C collegiate church.

★★**Boot and Shoe Museum** (Schuhmuseum) ⊘ – The museum is installed in the Felsgarten house, where the founder of the firm lived and opened his offices and first workshops. It contains valuable collections of all periods tracing the history of footwear, through the centuries, among the most varied peoples. The exhibition, unique of its kind, is completed by corporative emblems, books on travel and shoe craft and royal and imperial orders concerning the manufacture of boots and shoes.

★**Hallwil Castle** ⊘ – *18km – 11 miles southeast on ③, the Suhr road. From Teufenthal go to Hallwil, Boniswil and then take the road to Seengen.*
This lovely castle spreads over two islands in the river Aare, which flows out of the nearby lake, Hallwiler See. Built and enlarged from the 11-16C, then restored, its crenellated walls can be seen through the trees.
Enter by the drawbridge and through the court of honour to reach the second island.
A museum of popular art and traditions has been set up in the central building. On the first island, the tower of the main building is open to visitors : the first floor is occupied by the furnished apartments of a 17C lord while the second floor presents the living quarters of a 19C bourgeois.

The chapter on art and architecture in this guide gives
an outline of artistic achievement in the country
providing the context of the buildings and works of art
describrd in the Sights sectlon.

This chapter may also provide ideas for touring.
It is advisable to read it at leisure.

★★ ADELBODEN Berne   Pop 3 347

Michelin map **217** fold 16 or **427** fold 13 – Local map see BERNESE OBERLAND –
Alt 1 356m – 4 446ft – Facilities

Adelboden lies in the wide, sunny **basin**★★ at the upper end of the Engstligen Valley.
It is one of the highest of the fashionable resorts in the Bernese Oberland and one of
the best known, both in summer and in winter, for its healthy and agreeable climate.
The village clusters half-way up the slope, facing a majestic skyline of limestone
mountains. The most striking feature is the snow-covered, flat top of the Wildstrubel
(alt 3 243m – 10 640ft), completing the great mountain circle of the Engstligenalp,
from which the powerful **Engstligen Cascade**★★★ (Engstligenfälle) bursts forth,
leaping from a rocky shelf and forming a most impressive spectacle.

AIGLE Vaud   Pop 7 825

Michelin map **217** fold 14 or **427** fold 12 – Local maps see VALAIS and VAUD ALPS
– Alt 417m – 1 369ft

A wine and industrial centre as well as a military depot, Aigle is a pleasant small
town at the junction of the Rhône and Ormonts Valleys; it is surrounded by famous
vineyards, which, although walled, extend down from the heights and into the town
itself.
Stroll along the shaded Gustave-Doret Avenue (beside the torrent of the Grande
Eau) and into the town's centre by the unusual Jerusalem Alley (Ruelle de
Jérusalem), with its covered wooden galleries decked with flowers. To the east of
the village, the castle and church of St Maurice – with its Gothic stone steeple –
form a pleasant architectural group.

Castle – Like the town this 13C feudal fortress is surrounded by vineyards. It
originally belonged to the house of Savoy but was captured and rebuilt by the
Bernese in the 15C. Restored recently the stronghold retains its curtain walls
bristling with pepperpot roofed towers and turrets. It now houses period furniture
and a local museum. The covered sentry-walk is decorated with mural paintings of
fruit and flowers.

Wine Museum ⊙ – The Wine Museum (Musée de la Vigne et du Vin) is located in
several rooms of the main building and three floors of the main tower. On display
are glassware, coopers' casks, tubs and tools, labels... from the 17C to the present
day. Note the two enormous old winepresses. There is also a luminous **tapestry**
(1943) by Jean Lurçat.

ALTDORF Ⓒ Uri   Pop 8 282

Michelin map **217** fold 10 or **427** fold 15 – Local maps see Lake LUCERNE and
ST.GOTTHARD MASSIF – Alt 462m – 1 516ft –Facilities

Altdorf, the key to the St Gotthard Pass on the north side of the Alps, stands
between Lake Lucerne and the defiles of the Upper Reuss Valley. It preserves all
the dignity of a small, old-fashioned capital town. The traveller will notice the
southern influences already apparent in the city: the assortment of groceries, the
restaurant menus, the presence of Ticino characteristics in the people and traces of
the **binario** (see Andermatt below), all of which will prepare him for a greater
change of scene.

William Tell Monument (Telldenkmal) – The statue of the famous archer of Uri
stands in the main square of the town. The work dates from 1895 and is interesting
chiefly for the fact that it created Tell's physical type, since made familiar all over
the world by a postage stamp bearing his effigy (illustration p 146).
The statue is appropriately erected in this canton, which was the first to throw off
foreign tutelage (p 144).
A small **Tell Museum** ⊙ has been set up at Bürglen on the Klausen Pass road (qv).

EXCURSION

★**Bauen** – Pop 174. Facilities. 10km – 6 miles northwest.
At the foot of the mountains, this lovely village nestles in a verdant, flowered
landscape on the west bank of Lake Uri.
The **site**★, with its small church (1812 neo-baroque interior), flower-decked hotels
chalets, and its foliage (pine, palm, banana and monkey puzzle trees) resembles a
small Riviera-like resort due to its pleasant micro-climate.

★ ANDERMATT Uri   Pop 1 319

Michelin map **217** south of fold 10 or **427** fold 15 – Local maps see BERNESE
OBERLAND and ST.GOTTHARD MASSIF – Alt 1 436m – 4 711ft – Facilities

Andermatt lies at the junction of the St Gotthard, Furka and Oberalp roads in an
austere but beautiful curve of the Urseren Valley, which is the heart of the
St Gotthard Massif.
The life of the town, which is marked by a touch of southern animation, flows
along the narrow main street, some sections of which still show the typical Italian
binario (road with granite paving stones).
In winter, when snow covers the neighbouring slopes, dotted with anti-avalanche
barriers, Andermatt receives many skiers, attracted by its easy access.
The main sporting centres are the Nätschen District (towards the Oberalp Pass),
which is regularly served by local trains and chairlifts, as are the Gemsstock slopes,
equipped with a cable-car.

Michelin map 𝟤𝟣𝟩 fold 16 and 𝟤𝟣𝟫 fold 3 or 𝟦𝟤𝟩 folds 13 and 22

This place is well known to specialists in human geography for the extraordinary nomadic habits of the people, who are always on the move between the vineyards of the Rhône Valley, the chief villages (Vissoie, for instance), the mid-mountain pastures *(mayens)* and the Alps, to name their various fields of activity in ascending order of altitude.

The **Anniviers Valley** has remained to this day the domain of a few enthusiastic mountaineers attracted by the primitive charm of resorts like **Zinal.**

FROM SIERRE TO ZINAL

49km – 30 miles – about 2 1/2 hours – Itinerary ③ of the Valais local map.

Sierre *– See Sierre.*

The route leaves the Brig road at the edge of the Forest of Finges and climbs quickly above the Sierre Basin, where the large aluminium works of Chippis are located. The hotels of Montana and Crans stand in a row, very high on the north slope of the Rhône Valley.

Niouc and its chapel mark the beginning of the way through the Anniviers Valley. Below, the Navisence flows in a deep ravine. Upstream the view opens up over the snowfields of the Zinalrothorn and the Ober Gabelhorn, on either side of the twin peaks of the Besso.

Pontis Chapel (Chapelle des Pontis) – At the edge of the precipice, which the road skirts by means of a tunnel, this little sanctuary gives those perpetual wanderers, the people of Anniviers, a chance to invoke the protection of the Virgin and St Christopher.

The chalets of Pinsec stand on the opposite slope, along a very steep ridge.

Vissoie – This lovely perched village is identified by its square feudal tower and small rustic church.

When climbing the hairpin bends from Vissoie to St-Luc, the tourist's gaze is once more drawn to the astonishing site of Pinsec. Here the mountain skyline opens out with the Matterhorn Peak rising in the distance.

St-Luc – Facilities. This delightful hamlet has been converted into a winter sports resort. The viewing table at the entrance to the village offers an impressive **view★★** of the valley and the whole mountain range, dominated by Mount Marais (2 412m – 7 915 ft) on the left and by Mount Boivin (2 995m – 9 825ft) on the right.

The road along the mountainside from St-Luc to Chandolin soon enters woods. During this run you will get splendid glimpses of the Anniviers Valley below, Sierre in the Rhône Valley and rising behind the Wildhorn and Wildstrubel Massifs.

★★**Chandolin** – Facilities. Alt 1 936m – 6 348ft. Chandolin is approached by the new village, a skiing resort consisting of modern chalets and lowish blocks of flats built in accordance with local tradition.

Continue on foot.

This will bring you to the old village, dotted with picturesque wooden bungalows, one of the highest permanently inhabited places in Europe.

This little settlement clings to the slope within view of a splendid **panorama★★** of the Valais Alps (from left to right : Zinalrothorn, Besso, Ober Gabelhorn, the Zinal Peak and the Dent Blanche). From beside the cross, standing on a knoll behind the church, there is a good view.

Return to Vissoie and go south on the road to Grimentz.

The road first climbs the west face of Roc d'Orzival, which at times becomes a *corniche* overlooking the ravine. At the bottom of the ravine, between magnificent rocky sides, flows the Navisence. Snowy crests block the horizon.

★**Grimentz** – Facilities. This lovely resort facing the Corne de Sorebois, which separates the Zinal and Moiry Valleys, has preserved several *mazots (illustration p 207).*

★**Moiry Valley** – *13km – 8 miles from Grimentz.* This valley is an extension of the Anniviers Valley. The route reveals after 2km – 1 mile a lovely waterfall (on the left), Grimentz (on the right) and straight ahead the Dent Blanche (appropriately named as *dent blanche* means white tooth). At 4km – 2 1/2 miles there is a **view★** (to the left) of Grimentz and the Anniviers Valley. 1 km – 1/2 mile farther the **Moiry Dam** is visible in front of Dent Blanche; it soon seems as if the dam bars the road yet the road goes round it and after a tunnel opens out on the left. From the middle of the dam (alt 2 249m – 7 379ft) there is a **view★** onto the reservoir, Pennine Alps and their glaciers.

Continue along the road *(mediocre),* with its numerous small waterfalls. Overlooking the reservoir, at the end of the dam, there is a striking **view★** onto the Moiry and Zinal (on the left) Glaciers. The road ends at a smaller lake facing the Moiry Glacier.

Return to Grimentz and take the road to Zinal.

★★**Zinal Valley** – The road offers a superb **view★★**: in the foreground of the Zinal Valley with the town of Ayer high up on the east side, prolonged northwards by the Anniviers Valley which is blocked in the far distance by the snow-covered mass of the Wildstrubel. The valley lined with spruce then narrows and seems to shrink beside the overwhelming Weisshorn Mountain. After crossing the Navisence and passing by the Pralong hydro-electric power station, the road passes through **Zinal** (facilities), a well-known centre for mountaineering, and ends 2km – 1 mile farther on at the place called Tsoudounaz in a small corrie at the foot of the Zinal Glacier.

APPENSELL © Appenzell (Inner-Rhoden)   Pop 4 781

Michelin map **216** fold 21 or **427** fold 7 – Local map see APPENZELL DISTRICT –
Alt 789m – 2 589ft – Facilities

Appenzell lies at the foot of the green foothills of the Alpstein, in a pastoral
landscape in the heart of the "original eastern Switzerland" that its canton
represents. It is a small old-fashioned town showing a compromise, typical of
Germanic countries, between rural and city life. (It is a *flecken,* a word denoting
communities that are neither towns nor villages).

The very name of Appenzel *(Abbatis cella,* the Abbot's cell) dates from the early
settlement of the country by the monks of St Gallen.

A walk in the **main street** (Hauptgasse) offers various temptations (embroidery
shops, Appenzell cakes decorated with portraits of cowmen in yellow breeches and
scarlet waistcoats). It lies between the church, with its astonishing baroque
embellishments, and the Löwendrogerie, the curved gable of which bears a series
of paintings of medicinal plants with this mournful comment: "Many plants against
illness, none against death."

EXCURSIONS

★★**Hoher Kasten** ⊘ – Alt 1 795m – 5 890ft. *7km – 4 miles southeast on the road to
Weissbad and Brülisau. Cable-car leaves from Brülisau.*
The ride up in the cable-car offers a view below of spruce trees, mountain pastures
and shepherds' huts; to the right the wooded ravine with Sämtisersee lying at the
bottom; and straight ahead the massive limestone spur of the Hoher Kasten. From
the belvedere *(view indicator),* higher up than the restaurant but easily accessible,
is a wide **panorama★★**: west and northwest, of the town of Appenzell and the hills
of the surrounding Appenzell District; to the east, the view plunges down to the
Rheinthal and its river, winding from Lake Constance (to the north) to the
Liechtenstein Mountains (to the south), with the Austrian Alps in the background.
The Alpstein Massif and its highest peak, Säntis, are clearly visible to the
southeast.

★★**Ebenalp** ⊘ – Alt 1 640m – 5 380ft. *7km – 4 miles   about 1 1/2 hours –
following the Weissbad-Wasserauen road to its terminus, plus 8 minutes by cable-
car.*
The Ebenalp is a promontory of Alpine height, edged with cliffs jutting out over the
Appenzell country.
From Ebenalp you can return on foot *(about 1 1/2 hours)* to Wasserauen by way of
the **tunnel-grotto of Wildkirchli** (80m – 262ft long), where excavations have laid bare
traces of the oldest prehistoric settlement in Switzerland, and by the **Seealpsee★**,
whose dark waters lie at the foot of the Rossmad.

APPENZELL DISTRICT

Michelin map **216** folds 21 and 22 or **427** folds 7 and 8

The country of Appenzell and the great Alpine coomb of the Toggenburg (Upper
Thur Valley) are separated by an administrative border-line, for Appenzell has been
a separate canton since 1513, while the Toggenburg is still under the control of
St Gallen, as it was when the famous abbey was at the height of its power. None
the less, they form a single tourist area, for they are attached geographically to the
pre-Alpine chain of the Alpstein, whose jagged crests, culminating in Säntis
(alt 2 502m – 8 207ft), lie above the Rhine Valley, facing the Vorarlberg Mountains.
Motorists crossing the Austrian frontier at St Margrethen-Höchst should take
advantage of a visit to St Gallen and leave road no 7 for one of the little winding
roads leading to Trogen and Heiden,
within sight of Lake Constance.

Life in the Appenzell – The Appenzell
country is a soft, undulating landscape
of green hills dotted with farms *(p 30)* at
the foot of the Alpstein's northern
barrier. Its rich townships with their
pretty, curvilinear gabled houses still
hold meetings of the traditional Landsgemeinden *(p 25).* These assemblies of
peasants, who wear swords as a mark
of their dignity as active citizens, take
place in the Appenzell for the Inner-
Rhoden half-canton (Catholic) at Trogen and alternately at Hundwil for the
Ausser-Rhoden half-canton (Protestant).
See the Calendar of Events. Traditions
are still very much alive in the Appenzell: the women's pretty ceremonial
dress, characterised by a *coiffe* with
immense tulle wings, the consumption
of special dishes like Appenzell fat
cheese (one of the strongest Swiss
cheeses) and that of the small, dry
sausages called *Alpenklübler.* Another
old custom which has survived is that of
fine old-fashioned embroidery, which
continues to flourish as a cottage industry in Inner-Rhoden.

A coiffe

39

★⬛ SITTER VALLEY AND STOSS ROAD

From St Gallen to Altstätten

34 km – 21 miles – about 2 hours – Local map below
Certain sections of these roads carry parallel tram-lines. Be careful at unguarded level-crossings!

★★St. Gallen – *Time: 2 hours. See St. Gallen.*

The recommended route from St. Gallen affords pleasant views all along the Sitter Valley. This is at first a deep ravine, but turns into a softly undulating depression dotted with farms in the purest style of local tradition. The most typical example is a group of buildings 1km – 1 1/2 mile southeast of the Hundwil road-fork.

Stein – As you cross this village, located on a plateau (alt 823m – 2 700ft) and thus higher up than its neighbours, there are wide views of the surrounding countryside. In the chalet-restaurant is a demonstration **cheese dairy** (Schaukäserei) ⊘ where, in a picturesque atmosphere (musical automata), you can observe the production of the famous Appenzell cheese.

Appenzell – *See Appenzell.*

Gais – At the beginning of the last century this market town was still drawing many adherents of whey cures. On the main square there is a fine example of baroque architecture to be seen in the row of curved-gabled houses.

★Stoss – *1/4 hour on foot Rtn.* In 1405 this plateau was the scene of a battle which ensured the liberation of Appenzell from the Austrian yoke. To enjoy the very distant **panorama★★** of the Rheinthal and the Vorarlberg Alps, go up to the commemorative chapel and, to its right, the obelisk which is marked out from afar by a clump of trees.

Altstätten – Altstätten lies in the heart of the Rheinthal – in the Alpine section of the Rhine Valley between the Grisons and Lake Constance (Bodensee) – on a warm inner plain with orchards, vineyards and crops of maize. It has a very medieval character, especially noticeable along its picturesque Marktgasse (Market Street). This street is lined with pointed-gabled houses, built on pillared arcades for the convenience of pedestrians, who can walk under cover. The Engelplatz, with its flower-decked fountain and crooked houses, makes another pretty picture.

The highway code states that on difficult mountain roads the ascending vehicle has priority.
On "postal" roads drivers must comply with the directions of the drivers of the post bus service.

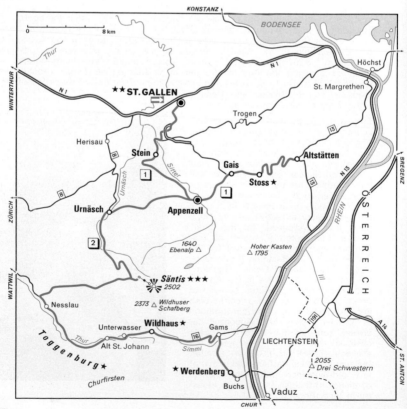

★② THE TOGGENBURG

From Appenzell to Buchs
62 km – 39 miles – about 2 1/2 hours – Local map opposite

Appenzell – *See Appenzell.*

Urnäsch – The village is known for its **folklore museum** ⊙ located in a 19C chalet with small, low-ceilinged rooms and crooked floors. On the ground floor, display cases contain sumptuous costumes and extraordinary hats; the first floor contains a collection of local costumes, paintings and painted figurines as well as a forge and carpenter's shop. The second floor exhibits an Appenzell interior; displayed on the top floor are a music room, dairy and old wooden toys.

A short distance past Appenzell, between Urnäsch and Schwägalp, the road emerges from the bottom of a dell, planted here and there with fir and ash trees, to come out at the foot of the impressive cliffs of the north face of Säntis.

★★★ Säntis – *See Säntis.*

The section from Schwägalp to Nesslau over the barely perceptible "pass" of the Kräzeren (alt 1 300m – 4 264 ft) leads along the southwest barrier of the Alpstein (Silberplatten, Lütispitz). Alpine formations with many traces of landslides succeed the parklands. The spa of Rietbad is framed in a valley dotted with green knolls. Between Nesslau and Wildhaus, uphill from two wooded clefts, the High Toggenburg Valley spreads harmoniously, dotted with dwellings whose walls are protected by weather-boarding. During the climb from Unterwasser (facilities) to Wildhaus you may admire the deeply folded escarpments of the Wildhuser-Schafberg and the surprisingly serrated crests of the Churfirsten. In conjunction with Alt St Johann (facilities), these two resorts exploit a vast snowfield.

★Wildhaus – Facilities. The pleasant resort lies on the plateau separating the Toggenburg from the Rheinthal, within sight of the Wildhuser Schafberg, the Churfirsten and the Drei Schwestern. Wildhaus is the birthplace of the great reformer **Zwingli** *(qv)*, whose home may still be seen.

From Wildhaus to Gams, the road drops towards the Rheinthal, whose appearance marks the end of the drive. From the hairpin bends immediately before Gams you will appreciate the size of this trough, dominated on its eastern side by the mountains of the Vorarlberg and of Liechtenstein. These are separated by the Feldkirch Gap, negotiated by the road and railway to the Arlberg Region of Austria.

★Werdenberg – *See Werdenberg.*

ARENENBERG CASTLE Thurgau

*Michelin map **216** fold 9 or **427** fold 7 – 1.5km – 1 mile west of Ermatingen and north of Salenstein*

The little Arenenberg Castle, surrounded by gardens and a fine park, stands on a terrace overlooking the western basin of Lake Constance, Untersee.

A Swiss Malmaison – The castle was built in the 16C and became, in 1817, the property of Queen Hortense, the daughter of Joséphine de Beauharnais and wife of the former King of Holland, Louis Bonaparte. Hortense and her son, the future Napoleon III, spent every summer at Arenenberg until her death in 1837, and the Empress Eugénie and the Prince Imperial stayed frequently there after the fall of the Second Empire. In 1906 Eugénie presented Arenenberg to the canton of Thurgau and it was transformed into a museum.

★Napoleonic Museum ⊙ – The works of art and furniture collected by the former owners have remained in the castle. Note Queen Hortense's drawing-room, furnished in the style of the period, the library, the bedrooms and the boudoirs, which contain many mementoes of the imperial family. From Queen Hortense's bedroom there is a wide **view** over Lake Constance and Reichenau Island. Near the castle a small chapel contains a fine marble statue of Queen Hortense.

★ AREUSE GORGES

*Michelin map **216** fold 12 and **217** fold 4 or **427** fold 12 – Local map see Swiss JURA*

These gorges are part of the Travers Valley *(qv)* itinerary.

Tour – *About 1 hour on foot starting from Noiraigue railway station, where there is a car park.*
Once beyond the Plan-de-l'Eau hydro-electric power station the path descends to the heavily-forested valley floor to follow the Areuse along its channelled course. The steep limestone sides of this V-shaped gorge rise to jagged crests.
Half-way down a belvedere offers a good plunging view of the narrowest part of the gorge where the torrent rushes over cascades. An old hump-backed bridge adds a romantic touch to this attractive **beauty spot★**.
Champ-du-Moulin – *A surfaced path leads through the woods to this hamlet.*
The house, standing on its own, to the left of the path, is where the famous philosopher, **Jean-Jacques Rousseau**, spent the month of September 1764 during his period of exile in Switzerland. Although dating from 1722 the Renaissance windows originally came from a house in Valangin.
Beyond, the scattered hamlet of Champ-du-Moulin, stands in a woodland setting at the southern end of the gorge.
Climb back up to Champ-du-Moulin railway station *(1/2 hour on foot)*, from where there is another good view of the southern end of the defile. It is possible to take one of the many trains back to Noiraigue.

★★★ AROSA Graubünden (Grisons) Pop 2 271

Michelin map **218** fold 5 or **427** fold 17 – Local map see GRISONS – Alt 1 742m – 5 715ft – Facilities

The elegant resort of Arosa spreads its hotels in the Upper Schanffig Basin of the Plessur Valley. It charms the visitor at once in its setting of gently sloping woodlands, reflected in small lakes.

Access – *From Chur to Arosa 31km – 19 miles – about 1 hour.* The **Arosa road★**, (or **Schanfigg Valley road★**) a high, winding, picturesque *corniche* along the Schanfigg, passes through flower-decked villages with quaint churches. During the last part of the journey the road cuts through unusual sharp limestone ridges, which are convex and wooded on the north side and concave and barren on the south side. Note, on the outskirts of Langwies, the railway viaduct stretched across the chasm.

The resort – The Chur road passes through **Aeusser-Arosa**, the chief centre of activity and location of the railway station and the lakes. The road then emerges from the forest and ends at **Inner-Arosa**, where the upper depression of the Plessur (Aroser Alp) begins. The nearby centre of **Maran** is more isolated; visitors to Arosa walk to it along delightful, gently-sloping paths through the woods (*Eichhörnliweg*: "squirrel path"). The settlement spreads over the open Alpine pastures.
The Arosa Weisshorn cable-car is the ski-lifts' backbone in winter, Arosa's real season. Skiers are offered a choice of easy, intermediate or difficult runs, some of which drop over 1 000m – 3 000ft.

★★**Weisshorn** ⊘ – Alt 2 653m – 8 704ft. *Access in 20 min by cable-car.*
The climb up to the mid-station, Law Mittel (alt 2 013m – 6 640ft) offers wide vistas of Arosa, its lakes, verdant basin and mountains. From the top *(viewing table)* there is a magnificent **panorama★★** of the Grison Alps' neighbouring heights and snowy ridges, blocked to the south by Piz Kesch, Piz Ela and Erzhorn; Arosa is visible and Chur can be seen to the northwest at the foot of Calanda Mountain.

★ ASCONA Ticino Pop 4 540

Michelin map **219** north of folds 7 and 8 or **427** fold 24 – Local map see LOCARNO: Excursions – Alt 210m – 689ft – Facilities – Town plan in the current Michelin Red Guide Switzerland

Ascona's site on Lake Maggiore's shore resembles Locarno's and its relation to the mouth of the Maggia River. Like its large neighbour, it enjoys the river delta's flat lands as sports grounds.
This colourful fishing village, which has long been a favourite with artists, has become a substantial resort (Ascona Music Festival in September).

Church of Our Lady of Misericord – The church adjoins the cloisters of the Collegio Papio. Founded in 1399 and reconstructed in the 15C – except for its chancel which is Gothic – it is known for its 15-16C cycle of polychrome **frescoes** *(some in very bad condition)*. The frescoes are in the nave (St Christopher, Holy Father, St Sebastian) and on the walls and vaulting of the chancel (Old and New Testament). Note also the beautiful **altarpiece**, above the high altar, depicting the life of the Virgin (said to be by Giovanni Antonio della Gaia – 1519).

EXCURSIONS

★★**Ronco Tour** – *17km – 11 miles – about 1 1/2 hours. See Locarno: Excursions.*

Brissago Islands ⊘ – Tourists should take the time to visit these tiny islands.

Telephone Numbers
By dialling 111 you will obtain
- addresses of chemists on duty
- addresses of the nearest hospital and/or doctor
By dialling 117 you will obtain
- police in case of an emergency
By dialling 120 you will obtain
- in winter snow report and avalanche bulletin
By dialling 140 you will obtain
- the Touring-Secours motor breakdown service (open 24 hours)
By dialling 162 you will obtain
- weather forecasts
By dialling 163 you will obtain
- information about snow-bound roads and whether you need chains etc.
The operators usually speak French, German and Italian depending on the region and English in the main cities and major resorts.

Michelin map **427** fols 4 or **216** folds 4-5 − 11km − 7 miles southeast of Basle

It is to the Roman general Munatius Plancus, a friend of Julius Caesar, that Switzerland owes the existence of the "colonia raurica" ruins, the oldest Roman settlement situated alongside the Rhine, founded in 44-43 BC. It is believed that the actual colonization of the Augst site dates back to the year 10 BC.

An Important Ancient City − By the year 200 AD the city of Augst had considerably expanded, featuring a population of 20 000, and had become a prosperous centre for both trade and craft. Owing to its privileged location on the northern border of the Roman Empire, Augst also enjoyed a thriving artistic activity, demonstrated by the many imposing public buildings.

It would appear that, towards the end of the third century (circa 260), characterised by severe political unrest, most of the city was destroyed when the Alamans delivered an assault on the defensive system known as the Limes. In order to keep their control over this strategic passage of the Rhine, the army built the powerful Kaiseraugst stronghold slightly north of Augst soon after the year 300 AD. Most of these fortifications were still standing after the fall of the Roman Empire and served to protect the local population during the early Middle Ages.

Excavation work − During the 16C, a century strongly influenced by the doctrines of the great Basle humanists, the famous jurist **Amerbach** *(see Basle)* was the first to carry out scientific research, making use of the excavation work formerly conducted by the tradesman Andreas Ryff, also a native of Basle. Subsequent excavations were conducted on an irregular basis.

In 1839, the Historical and Archaeological Society of Basle (Historische und Antiquarische Gesellschaft zu Basel) commissioned research to be carried out on the Roman city. From 1878 onwards, this antique site was to be the object of in-depth, scientifically-based investigations which have continued up to the present day.

The Antique Ruins − *Tour: 1/2 hour to one day, depending on the route. French leaflets and plans of the different tours are on sale at the museum. The ruins are signposted in French and German.* Around twenty monuments have been restored, including the **theatre**, the largest Roman ruin in Switzerland with a seating capacity

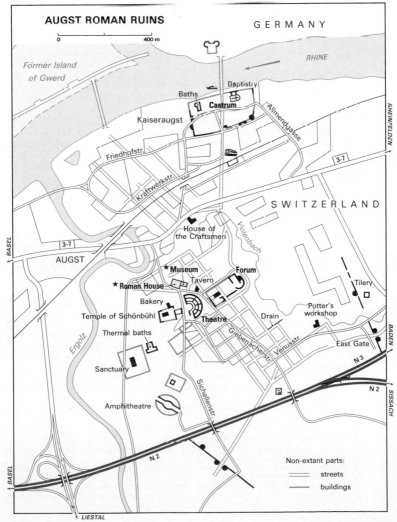

of 8 000. Today it is used as a venue for outdoor concerts and live performances. The administrative, political and religious core of the city was the **forum**, consisting of the basilica, the Temple of Jupiter and the curia (display of mosaics in the cellar). Markets and various local festivities were held at the forum.

★**Roman House** ⊘ – This building, whose premises were of a residential and commercial nature, is a faithful reconstruction of the type of house common in Augst under the Roman Empire. The main rooms – kitchen, dining-room, bedroom, bathroom, workshop and boutique – contain authentic artefacts and utensils found on the

Roman mosaic

Röme museum, Augst

site, as well as replicas. The floor of the steamroom carries a diagram (cross-section) of the hypocaust, an ingenious heating system devised by the Romans in which hot air circulated under the floor and between double walls.

★**Roman Museum (Römermuseum)** ⊘ – Adjoining the Roman House, this museum presents a selection of exhibits representative of the 700 000 objects unearthed during the excavations. The **silver hoard**★★ discovered at the foot of the Kaiseraugst fortifications in 1962 features many precious objects, including 68 items belonging to a sumptuous table set: dishes decorated with mythological scenes, tumblers, spoons, candelabra, platters, etc. This treasure also contained three silver ingots which experts were able to trace back to the year 350 AD thanks to their stamp. It is thought that the treasure might have been buried during the German invasion in 352-353 AD.

AVENCHES Vaud   Pop 2 505

Michelin map ☷ fold 5 or ☷ fold 12 – 4km – 2 miles south of Lake Murten – Alt 473m– 1 574ft

Avenches is built on the site of the former capital of the Helveti. The Roman city of Aventicum, founded by the Emperor Augustus, had some 10 000 inhabitants and flourished throughout 2C AD. It was destroyed in 259 AD. The Renaissance château which stands in the centre of the town dates from the late 16C. It was commissioned by the bishops of Lausanne, who in those days held the office of suzerain lords.

The modern town, formerly the Capitol, is much smaller than the ancient city, the size of which can be judged from the excavated ruins.

At the time of the Legions – The town was defended by a ring of fortifications about 6km – 4 miles round, with walls over 7m – 23ft high, crowned with battlements; semicircular towers abutting against the wall's inner surface were used as observation posts; one of them, the "Tornallaz", survives, but it has been badly restored. One is allowed to visit the remains of the amphitheatre, the Roman arena and a large sanctuary known as the "storkery", of which only one pilaster has survived. Recent excavations have revealed the ruins of a portico and temple podium. The amphitheatre could seat an audience of 8 000.

★**Roman Museum** ⊘ – The museum is housed in a square tower, built in the Middles Ages over the main entrance to the Roman amphitheatre. It contains objects discovered during the excavations. On the ground floor are displayed a very fine statue of a wolf suckling Romulus and Remus, several inscriptions, mural paintings and mosaics. On the first floor, visitors will appreciate the copy of a golden bust of the Emperor Marcus Aurelius (the original is in the Archaeological and Historical Museum of Lausanne), some bronze pieces, a display of coins minted at Aventicum and a statue in Carrara marble celebrating the cult of Minerva. On the second floor, utensils and pottery complete the collection.

Cailler, Suchard, Kohler, Nestlé, Lindt, Tobler...

Attractive presentations, mouth-watering contents characterise the high-quality confectionery of the Swiss chocolate-makers.
During the 19C and early 20C Swiss chocolate-makers acquired an international reputation for their delectable products.
Like a good wine, one should savour the aroma and taste. Dark, white or milk, chocolate comes in many forms - cake, mini-slabs, sweets and a variety of shapes - and is often combined with various other ingredients (nuts, raisins, ginger).

BADEN Aargau
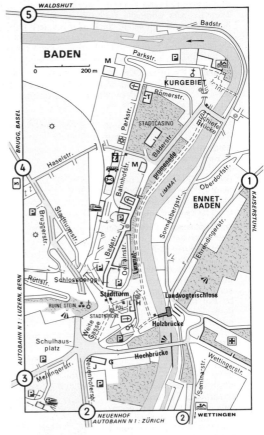

Michelin map **216** folds 6 and 7 or **427** fold 5 – Alt 385m – 1 273ft – Facilities

Baden lies at the foot of the last spurs of the Jura. It occupies a picturesque **site** ★ on the banks of the Limmat. The spa and the industrial quarters extend below the old town, standing on a spur overlooking the river, dominated by the ruins of Stein Castle (Ruine Stein). This imposing fortress served as an arsenal and a place of refuge for the Austrians during their unsuccessful campaigns against the Swiss, which ended in the victories for Swiss independence at Morgarten (1315) and Sempach (1386). In 1415 the Confederates seized and burnt it. It was rebuilt in the 17C by inhabitants of Baden with the help of the Catholic cantons, but it was destroyed again in 1712 by the people of Berne and Zürich. Baden is an industrial centre known the world over for its electro-mechanical engineering.

SIGHTS

★**Old Town** – From the modern road bridge (Hochbrücke) there is a fine **view**★ of the old town. Its houses with their stepped gables and fine brown roofs, pierced by many dormer windows, come down to the Limmat, which is crossed by an old covered wooden bridge (Holzbrücke).

The parish church (Stadtkirche) and the city tower (Stadtturm), which is adorned with a belfry and corner turrets and roofed with glazed tiles, dominate the whole.

Bailiffs' Castle (Landvogteischloss) ⊘ – The castle stands near the Holzbrücke, on the east bank of the Limmat.

A **museum** is housed in the keep of the old castle, which served as a residence for the bailiffs from 1415 to 1798.

There are collections of arms, period furniture, paintings and sculpture, pottery, bronze and coins of Roman origin, found in the district, and costumes of the Aargau Canton. From the upper floors of the museum there are pleasant views of the covered bridge and the old town.

Spa – Known in Roman times as Aquae Helvetiae, Baden became one of Switzerland's most important spas towards the end of the Middle Ages. With its nineteen hot sulphur springs, yielding about 1 million litres – 200 000 gallons of salty water a day at a temperature of 48°C (118°F), it is now a well-known spa specialising in the treatment of rheumatism and respiratory disorders.

The Limmat-Promenade along the river is a pleasant walk.

EXCURSION

★**Wettingen Abbey (Ehem. Zisterzienserkloster Wettingen)** ⊘ – 3km – 2 miles south of Baden, between the railway and the Limmat.

This former Cistercian abbey, founded in the 13C in fulfillment of a vow, by Count Heinrich von Rapperswil, now houses a school.

The Gothic **cloisters** have been glazed in and now display a collection of stained glass. On the inner walls are the serried ranks of statues portraying former abbots and monks.

Following a fire the abbey church was rebuilt in 1517. The **interior**★ is richly decorated with frescoes, paintings, stucco and marble. This elaboration is continued in the pulpits, altarpieces, lecterns and statues. Of particular note are the splendidly carved **choirstalls**★★ dating from the early 17C. Vigorously carved heads adorn the cheekpieces while the stall backs portray the founders of the abbey as well as the Fathers of the Church.

Calendar of Events
The most important Swiss festivals are listed in a table, in the Practical Information section at the end of the Guide.

★★★ **BASLE** (Basel, Bâle) [C]   Pop 178 428

Michelin map 216 fold 4 or 427 fold 4 – Local map see Swiss JURA – Alt 273m – 895ft – Plan of conurbation in the current Michelin Red Guide Switzerland

Situated on the northwest border of Switzerland, facing Alsace and the Baden region, Basle is washed by the Rhine river at the point when it becomes navigable, thus opening up opportunities for maritime trade. The second largest city in the country, Basle has become a major industrial and commercial centre on account of its strategic geographical location; today its prosperity is derived from banking, insurance, sea traffic and the primary sector. In spring, the city hosts a **Fair** which attracts over one million visitors every year. In June it also organises the International Art Exhibition (Art Internationale Kunstmesse), seen as one of the major events in the realm of modern art.

The city was originally founded as part of the Roman settlement of Augusta Raurica, created in 44 BC. In 1032 it became part of the Germanic Empire but later came under the rule of a prince-bishop, vassal of the Emperor: these events are recalled in the town's coat of arms, which bears an episcopal cross. It was only in 1501 that it joined the Helvetic Confederation.

A Major Religious Crisis – From 1431 to 1448, the Council of Basle endeavoured to reform the clergy and bring heretics back to the church. However, its existence was to be threatened by the serious disagreements dividing the Pope and his bishops, and Eugenius IV tried to form another council at Ferrara. The Council of Basle then offered the papal tiara to Amadeus VIII, Duke of Savoy, who accepted and took the title of Pope Felix V. This was the beginning of the Great Schism ended in 1449, when Amadeus renounced the papacy.

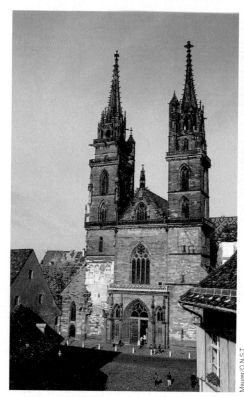

Cathedral, Basle

A Reformed City – An open city during the Reformation, Basle soon adopted the new confession (in 1529), such as it had been advocated by Johannes Hussgen, known by the name of OEcolampade. This former monk and priest preached a moderate reform, respecting the attachment the faithful showed towards Catholic practices; consequently, the city came to enjoy a reputation of tolerance, which has endured up to the present day. Because of its openness and geographical location, Basle welcomed many French Huguenots who had fled from their country following the Revocation of the Edict of Nantes. They introduced silk weaving into Basle, paving the way for industrial expansion. The town started to manufacture silk ribbons, used for decorating hats and crinolines, an activity in which it came to specialise. This was soon supplanted by the related industry of dying: the creation of the Geigy factory in 1785 signalled the beginning of the chemicals industry in Basle.

The charming old town and its quaint classical hotels are the vestiges of the 18C, seen as the "golden age" of Basle.

The Carnival – Deeply entrenched in Alaman territory, the Basle Carnival dates from the Middle Ages; strangely enough, it is the only Catholic celebration which has survived in Protestant country after the Reformation. Created to mark the beginning of Lent, the carnival interrupts the daily life of the Basle population by three days of processions and mascarades, meticulously governed by coded rituals. Today's carnival is the result of a long process which only reached its definitive form in 1946, inspired by the traditional carnival processions enacted by the guilds of the city. On the first Monday (Shrove Monday), at 4 o'clock in the morning, all the lights are switched off and the "Morgestraich", a custom going back to the 18C, heralds the start of the festivities.

The participants, sporting masks and costumes and divided into "gangs" of 20 to 200 people, line up behind a coloured Chinese lantern which can reach 3m – 10ft high. The procession then marches through the streets of the city to the strains of fifes and drums, ending up in the local restaurants at 6 o'clock, where they are served onion pie and soup made with flour. These colourful displays of masks and musical performances – highly organised or conducted individually – continue to enliven the town until the following Wednesday. Tuesday afternoon is reserved for children: do not miss the procession of little boys.

★ **OLD TOWN** *3 hours*

★★ **Cathedral (Münster) (CY)** ⊘ – The great 12C building was partly rebuilt in the 14 and 15C and restored in the 19C. It is built of red sandstone and surmounted by two Gothic towers (view). Between the towers is a porch dating from the mid-13C. The recessed arches of the main doorway are decorated with small statues of prophets and angels and garlands of foliage and flowers. Statues of the Tempter and of a Foolish Virgin stand on the right. Going round the building to the left you will reach the Romanesque portal of St Gall. It shows Christ the Judge on the tympanum, the Wise and Foolish Virgins on the lintel and the Resurrection of the Dead over the main vault.

Inside the cathedral, at the end of the north aisle, is an 11C low relief in red sandstone representing the martyrdom of St Vincent. Also in the north aisle another 11C low relief depicts apostles conversing in twos under the arches.

The partly Romanesque east end is adorned with a frieze and modillions. It faces the « Pflaz » terrace – a reminder of the former bishop's palace. There is a pretty **view**★ of the Rhine, the town, the Black Forest and the Vosges.

Going on around the cathedral you will pass through a narrow, dark passage into 15C Gothic cloisters, extended by other cloisters of the same period.

Cross the square and take on the right the Augustinergasse.

The Augustinergasse is lined with 16C houses.

★ **Ethnographic Museum (Museum für Völkerkunde) (CY M¹)** ⊘ – The museum houses an extensive **natural history** (mainly of Switzerland) and a prehistory section.

Its ethnographic section displays about 140 000 objects: masks, arms, carvings... and Oceanian and Pre-Columbian works of art.

Particularly worth noting is the Melanesian section (ground floor): a Papuan temple hut, masks, totems etc. There is an interesting Indonesian collection. Several galleries exhibit precious textiles. Displayed in another gallery are objects from Ancient Egypt. The upper floors contain geological displays and a didactic presentation of prehistory and the natural sciences.

After the museum continue straight ahead by the Rheinsprung, an alleyway lined with 15 and 16C houses, which affords a good view of the Rhine, the town, the Mittlere Rheinbrücke and its chapel covered with glazed tiles. The Rheinsprung slopes down to the Eisengasse, a busy street lined with shops, which leads to the Market Square.

Market Square (Marktplatz) (BY) – Lined with corbelled houses, it is the scene of a market held in front of the town hall near the 16C Wine Growers' Guild Hall.

Town Hall (Rathaus) (BY H) ⊘ – The building was erected between 1504-14 in the Late Gothic style and was enlarged and restored between 1898-1902. The façade is decorated with frescoes and flanked by a modern belfry adorned with pinnacles. The inner courtyard is ornamented with heavily-restored 17C frescoes and a statue of the town's founder, Munatius Plancus. The State Council Chamber is also open.

At the far end of the Marktplatz, take the Marktgasse (Market Street) on the left which leads to the Fischmarktplatz.

The Fischmarktplatz (Fish Market Square), a lively sector of Basle's business quarter, is ornamented with the Fish Market Fountain.

★ **Fish Market Fountain (Fischmarktbrunnen) (BY)** – A Gothic column is surmounted by a Madonna and two saints. The original (1390) is in the Historical Museum.

★ **Old Streets (BY)** – Take the Stadthausgasse on the left and then continue along the Schneidergasse. This leads to the Spalenberg, a steep small street lined with antique and craft shops. Turn left into the Gemsberg which leads to a square lined with 13 and 14C houses. The flower-decked Chamois Fountain adds to the charm of the square. Turn right into the Heuberg where you will see old 13 and 14C houses.

Holbein Fountain (Holbeinbrunnen) (BY) – Left of the Spalenvorstadt. The 16C fountain represents a bagpiper inspired by an engraving by Dürer, and peasants dancing, based on a drawing by Holbein.

Spalen Gate (Spalentor) (ABY) – A fine 13-14C monumental gate. Two battlemented towers frame the central part, which is crowned by a glazed-tiled, pointed roof. The summit of the west façade is adorned with Basle's coat of arms.

Go back by the Spalenvorstadt and turn left at the road junction.

Church of St Peter (Peterskirche) (BY) – This Late Gothic church was built in pink sandstone. 14 and 15C frescoes may be seen in the south aisle and in the chapel to the left of the chancel.

On the left of the east end of the church, take the Petersgasse, full of medieval charm.

The Blumenrain leads to the Mittlere Rheinbrücke giving access to the east bank of the Rhine. At the end of the bridge, go down some steps on the right.

Oberer Rheinweg (CY) – This esplanade set along the Rhine affords a pretty **view**★, especially from the bridge, the **Wettsteinbrücke**, at the east end: of the old quarters of Basle, the towers of the cathedral and of the churches, the palaces and the small artisans' cottages by the water's edge.

Cross the Wettsteinbrücke.

BASEL

Barfüsserpl.	**BY** 3	Fischmarkt	**BY** 18
Brunngässlein	**CY** 9	Gemsberg	**BY** 20
Augustinergasse ..... **CY** 2	Centralbahnstr.	**CZ** 12	Innere
	Eisengasse	**BY** 15	Margarethenstr.	**BZ** 29

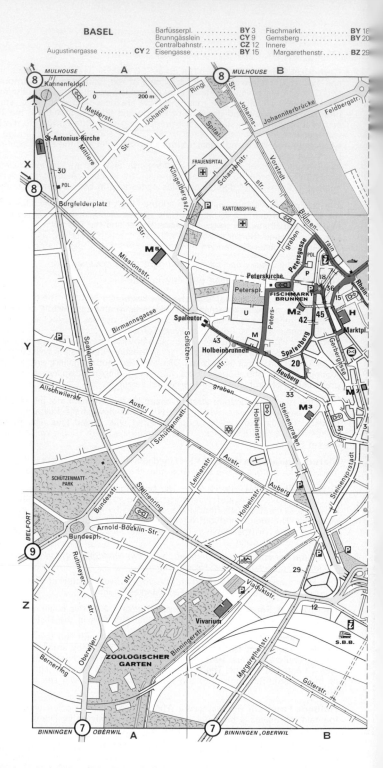

★★★ **Fine Arts Museum (Kuntsmuseum) (CY)** ⊙ – The works of art are exhibited in rotation, with the result that the visitors are not always able to see them all at the same time.

Particular emphasis is laid on 15 and 16C paintings and drawings, as well as on 19 and 20C art.

Most of the early works shown here belonged to a 16C art collector from Basle, Basilius Amerbach, whose father was a friend of both Erasmus and Holbein. Donated to the city in 1661, they served as a starting-point for the creation of the museum.

Entrance courtyard – Here stand sculptures by Rodin (The Burghers of Calais), Alexandre Calder and Edouardo Chillida.

The gallery surrounding the entrance courtyard presents works by two 19C Swiss painters, Arnold Böcklin and Ferdinand Hodler.

Ground Floor – To the right lies the Prints Gallery, in which sumptuous collections of drawings and engravings are exhibited in rotation.

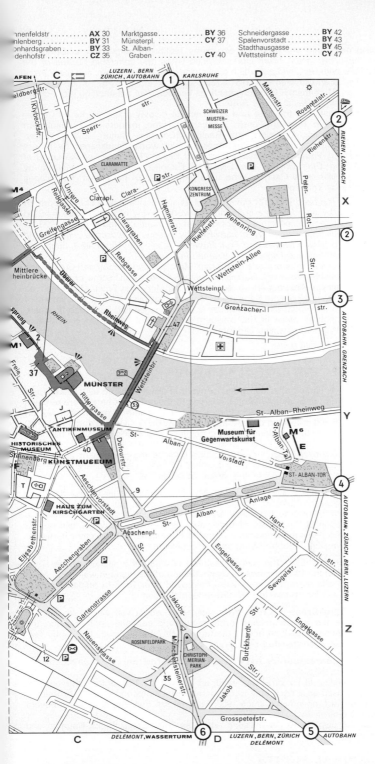

First floor – Rooms 1 to 15 are devoted to pictorial art in the Upper Rhine covering the period 1400 to 1600.

An admirable series of altarpiece panels, *The Mirror of the Holy Salvation,* by the Basle master, Konrad Witz (c1440-45), is characterized by an exact observation of masses, a charming landscape (the St Christopher panel), and careful composition and colour harmony study.

The Alsatian painter, Martin Schongauer (c1445-91), drawing from the experiences of Konrad Witz and his followers, depicts tender family scenes, notably in *Mary and Child in Their Room.*

Next is Grünewald (d 1528) and his *Christ on the Cross,* frightfully bruised and tortured with terrifying realism, and his famous contemporary from Strasbourg, Hans Baldung Grien with his *Death of a Young Girl* .

Niklaus Manuel Deutsch (c1484-1530), a Bernese, had a taste for eerie and narrative subjects, as is shown in his *Judgement of Paris* and *Pyramus and Thisbe.* Hans Holbein the Younger, one of the greatest painters of all time, marked the peak of the Renaissance. Around twenty paintings sum up the essence of his work.

His pessimistic and analytical art expresses reality in simple forms. One may admire the *Christe in the Tomb* with stiffened limbs, the admirable *Portrait of the Artist's Wife with Her Children,* which evokes inexpressible sadness, and the *Portrait of Erasmus as an Old Man* with his shrewd gaze.

Rooms 16 to 21 contain 17C Dutch paintings, including an outstanding work of the young Rembrandt, *David before Saul.*

The rooms situated in the east and north wings display major works by Caspar Wolf and Yohann Heinrich Füssli, paintings by the masters of Romanticism (Delacroix, Géricault, Daumier) and Realism (Courbet, Manet), and a superb collection of Impressionist and Post-Impressionist works: landscapes by Monet *(Snow Scenes),* Pissarro *(The Harvesters)* and Sisley *(The Banks of the Loing at Moret);* *Young Girl Lying in the Grass* by Renoir; *Montagne Ste-Victoire* by Cézanne; *Ta Matete* by Gauguin who uses large areas of flat colour; landscapes and portraits by Van Gogh.

Second Floor – The history of 20C painting and its successive stages of development are illustrated by an admirable collection of works, many of which were handed down by well-known collectors. Cubism, a movement created around 1908, is particularly well represented with canvases by Braque *(Landscape, Pitcher and Violin),* Picasso *(Bread Loaves and Fruit Bowl on Table, The Aficionado),* Juan Gris *(The Violin)* and Fernand Léger *(The Woman in Blue).*

German Expressionism is present with Franz Marc *(Tierschicksale)* and Emil Nolde *(Vorabend: Marschlandschaft),* Surrealism with Salvador Dali. Some of the rooms contain examples of Abstract art attributed to Juan Miró, Max Ernst, Mondrian, van Doesburg, Vantongerloo and Kandinsky. Visitors may also admire the works of Henri Rousseau – known as *Le Douanier* – Marc Chagall and Paul Klee. Pop Art, too, finds its rightful place in the museum with faithful adepts such as Jasper Johns, Andy Warhol and Claes Oldenburg.

Retourn to Münsterplatz.

ST. ALBAN DISTRICT (ST. ALBAN-TAL) (DY)

This district was named after the oldest convent in town, founded by the bishop of Basle in 1083. Of the former building belonging to the order of Cluny, there remains only a wing of the Romanesque cloisters, integrated into a private house and visible from the old graveyard of St-Alban's Church (Gothic chancel and tower, 19C nave, etc). It was in this residence that the painter **Arnold Böcklin** spent his childhood days.

The town's traditional paper industry, dating back to the creation of a canal by monks in the 12C, is evidenced by a number of mills; view over the canal and several mills at the beginning of the street, St-Alban-Tal.

★**Paper Museum** (Basler Papiermühle) (DY M⁶) ⊘ – In 1980, this former flour mill attached to Klingental Convent, later converted into a paper mill (1453), was turned into a museum devoted to the many aspects of the paper industry. It provides a lively presentation of the history of paper and paper-related activities, laid out on four levels. The museum workshops organise demonstrations on each particular theme: paper-making, founts, typography and binding.

Mühlegraben (DY E) – The heavily-restored vestiges of a section of the Basle remparts, built in the 14C, comprise a reconstitution of the wooden wall-walk. Most of the city's medieval fortifications were destroyed after 1860, in response to the demographic increase prompted by 19C industrialization.

St. Alban-Berg-Cross – Cross the canal, from where you can make out the foundations of the town's former fortifications, and continue on foot along the path which leads up St-Alban hill. At the top, the St Alban gateway (St. Alban-Tor) built in the 13C, is surrounded by a pretty garden.

Museum of Contemporary Art (Museum für Gegenwartskunst) ⊘ – *In an outbuilding of the Fine Arts Museum.*

A modern building lit by large bay windows adjoining a 19C factory, this unusual ensemble is used as a backdrop to temporary exhibitions on the most prominent contemporary art movements since 1960: Minimal Art, Conceptual Art, Arte Povera and Free Figurative Art.

The museum displays works by such artists as Frank Stella, Bruce Nauman and Joseph Beuys.

ADDITIONAL SIGHTS

★★★**Zoological Garden** (Zoologischer Garten) (AZ) ⊘ – This zoo of international fame was founded in 1874 and is one of the largest in Switzerland (the Berne Zoo is 13ha – 32 acres as well). It includes more than 5600 animals from each of the five continents. The zoo specializes in the reproduction and rearing of threatened species: rhinoceroses (from Asia), gorillas, spectacled bear...

Its park, with its ponds where swans, ducks and flamingoes and other exotic birds splash about, is equipped with all the necessary facilities to make your stay at the zoo pleasurable (restaurants, picnic areas, children's play areas etc). The children's zoo has young or newborn animals which the children can touch and ponies or elephants on which they may ride.

Several buildings are entirely devoted to one species, such as the Monkey Pavilion, the Aviary, the Elephant House, the Wild Animal House, etc.

The visit ends with a stop at the **vivarium,** where a wide variety of fish (sea and freshwater) are displayed, along with rare amphibian and reptile species. Before leaving, do not miss the penguins and king penguins, the zoo's star attractions.

★ **Kirschgarten Museum (Haus zum Kirschgarten) (CZ)** ⊘ – The museum is housed in an 18C mansion. On the ground floor there is a fine collection of 16-19C watches, porcelain stoves and a large collection of porcelain figurines.
On the first and second floors the visitor can admire drawing-rooms adorned with Aubusson tapestries, pictures and French furniture; boudoirs; 18 and 19C costumes; a dining room; a music room; and a kitchen with a magnificent battery of copper pans and utensils.
On the third floor there is a curious collection of old toys: dolls' houses, miniature carriages, boats and vintage cars.
The cellar contains porcelain and ceramics from Switzerland, Germany, France and China; and carved casks, one of which dates from 1723 and held 10 000 litres – 2 200 gallons.

★ **Historical Museum (Historisches Museum) (CY)** ⊘ – This was a former Franciscan church (14C). In the basement are exhibited Gallic and Roman ceramics, 5-7C barbarian jewellery from burial grounds in the Basle area, and Romanesque sculpture.
Near the stairway leading down stands a popular 17C *Lällenkönig*, with a small happy face, rolling eyes and a protruding tongue.
In the nave there are stalls from Basle's cathedral and columns from 14-17C fountains. In the aisles several 15-17C rooms have been reconstructed with period furnishings, stained glass, coins and medals; the south aisle contains Gothic tapestries, coffers and 15C craftwork; in the north aisle are mementoes of the Basle Corporations.
In the chancel may be seen an altarpiece by Yvo Strigel of Memmingen (1512), religious sculptures and stained glass (15-16C). Liturgical objects are to be found in the small north sacristies. The treasury in the basement contains the museum's original collections: the 16C Amerbach and the 17C Faesch. Basle jewellery and treasures from the Corporations may be seen. The lower tier of the gallery contains fragments of the Dance of Death by Konrad Witz (15C), tombstones and inscriptions dating back to the Council of Basle *(p 46)*.
Go down to the small south sacristy to see the treasure (12-16C) of Basle Cathedral; note the silver-and-gold reliquary bust of St Ursula, commissioned by the people of Basle to hold the relics of the saint and of her companions. In the basement may be seen *objets d'art* (not from Basle) of the 13 and 14C as well as mementoes of **Erasmus**, who died in Basle in 1536.

★ **Museum of Antiquities (Antikenmuseum Basel und Sammlung Ludwig) (CY)** ⊘ – The exhibits illustrate the various periods of Antiquity from pre-Hellenic times to the decline of the Roman era. Special emphasis is given to Greek art of the first millennium BC.
On the ground floor are assembled marble sculptures and bronze statuettes dating from the Archaic and Classical eras (600-300 BC). Note the funerary stela (480 BC), locally referred to as "the relief of the Basle doctor". The basement features works dating back to Roman and Hellenic times: clay statuettes, small bronzes, funerary stelae from Phrygia, a set piece representing Achilles and Penthesilea and several Roman tombs, including a fine marble sarcophagus decorated with the legend of Medea.
On the first floor, a superb collection of Attic vases (520-350 BC) is on display. They are attributed to an artist known as the "Berlin painter" and include a huge amphora complete with lid, bearing the twin figures of Athena and Hercules. The remaining exhibits consist of jewellery and coins (Sicily and southern Italy).
On the second floor, visitors may admire a series of Greek vases belonging to the Geometric (1100-700 BC) and Archaic (620-500 BC) eras. The earlier works are characterised by black figures set against a light clay background. They are shown together with weapons from ancient Greece and Italy, as well as Etruscan artefacts (votive-statuettes and bronze miniatures).

The Carnival Fountain (Fasnachtsbrunnen) (CY F) – The playing waters of the fountain are the centre of attraction on the esplanade in front of the municipal theatre. Nine cleverly articulated metallic structures in perpetual motion, are a good example of the wit and ingenuity of the sculptor **Jean Tinguely** (1925-1991). Tinguely studied at the local Academy of Fine Arts before leaving for Paris. With his "strange machines", made of various materials and discarded objects, he defied the artistic conventions of his time and gently poked fun at modern society.

Museum of Casts (Skulpturhalle) (AY M⁵) ⊘ – This complements the previous museum as it houses a great many casts of Greek statues, including an impressive collection of plasters used for the Parthenon sculptures.

Museum of the City and Cathedral (Stadt- und Münstermuseum) (CX M⁴) ⊘ – The museum is located in what is left of a monastery founded in the 13C and partly destroyed in 1860. Medieval sculptures from Basle Cathedral can be admired in detail: originals or copies, in red sandstone or wood, of gargoyles, recumbent figures, statues (several equestrian statues) friezes, low reliefs,...
The other rooms contain stalls and capitals, as well as models and drawings of old Basle. They also feature plaster reproductions of the "St Gall Gate" and the main entrance to the town.

Historical Museum of Pharmacy (Pharmazie-historisches Museum) (BY M²) ⊘ – The museum contains instruments and medicines used in the past as well as a reconstruction of a laboratory and a pharmacy with 18-19C wood panelling. Note also an unusual portable medicine chest of the 18C and a fine collection of jars dating from the 16 to the 19C.

Collection of Old Musical Instruments (BY M³) ⊘ – A remarkable display of 16-20C string, wind and percussion instruments may be seen. Audio equipment enables the visitor to hear the instruments playing.

Museum of Contemporary Art (Museum für Gegenwartskunst) (DY) ⊘ – A modern building, with large picture windows overlooking the River Rhine, provides a pleasant setting for temporary exhibitions devoted to the main artistic currents of the 70s and 80s. It has displayed works by many outstanding figures, namely Joseph Beuys, Frank Stella and Bruce Nauman.

Museum of Architecture (Architekturmuseum) (BY M⁷) ⊘ – The temporary exhibitions cover the work of an architect or a contemporary movement.

Church of St Anthony (St Antoniuskirche) (AX) – This church was built from 1925-31 according to the plans of the architect Moser. The barrel-vaulted nave is roofed with coffered vaulting while the side aisles have coffered ceilings as well. Multicoloured windows illuminate the great main body of the church.

THE PORT (HAFEN) *via Untere Rebgasse* (CX)

Since the Middle Ages, the town has played a part in trade between the North Sea and the Mediterranean, Swabia and Burgundy.

River navigation ceased following the building of the great Alpine roads and railway lines and it was not until 1907 that traffic resumed as far as Antwerp and Rotterdam. Since then, the port of Basle, which is the terminus for navigation on the Rhine, has enabled Switzerland to take part in maritime traffic. Its main docks extend downstream as far as the Petit-Huningue, where an obelisk and a viewing table mark the junction of the French, German and Swiss frontiers.

The proximity of the border is an obstacle to extension of the port which could only be envisaged on French and German territory as in the case of the Blotzheim aerodrome which is run jointly with Mulhouse.

The port of Basle Town and Basle District (Bâle-Ville and Bâle-Campagne) are equipped to handle the largest motor vessels and barges. Coal, hydrocarbons, grain, metallurgical products and industrial raw materials make up most of this traffic, which is mainly concerned with imports.

General view ⊘ – From the silo terrace of the Swiss Navigation Company there is a wide **panorama★** of the town and port installations. Beyond them lies the plain of Alsace with the Vosges, the Black Forest and the Jura forming a backcloth.

★"From Basle to the High Seas" Exhibition (Unser Weg zum Meer) ⊘ – This exhibition records various aspects of Swiss navigation on the Rhine and illustrates the vital part played by this waterway in the foreign trade of the Confederation.

Tour by boat ⊘ – In summer, excursions on the Rhine and the Kembs Canal, comprising a general tour of the port, are organised. *For details of embarkation points see the town plan* (BY).

EXCURSIONS

★★Augst Roman Ruins – *See Augst Roman Ruins.*

★Liestal – *16km – 10 miles southeast.*
This charming locality extending over the wooded slopes of the Ergolz Valley is the chief town of the Basle District. Stroll down its main street (Rathausstrasse) lined with painted 19C houses, leading from the city's medieval gate to its red sandstone Town Hall, decorated with Renaissance frescoes which were restored in 1900. On the heights of Schleifenberg, the Aussichtsturm belvedere affords a lovely view of the Rhine and the landscape stretching until the Alps. The surrounding forests offer many possibilities of pleasant walks for ramblers.
During the summer season, a little **steam train** for tourists (Waldenburger Dampfzug) links Liestal to Waldenburger, located 14km – 9 miles to the south.

★Rheinfelden – *17km – 10.5 miles east by* ③. *Believed to be the oldest city in Aarau, Rheinfelden is the last stopping place for* **cruises along the Rhine**. Many of its ancient monuments are still standing: medieval tower and ramparts, Gothic church with Baroque additions, etc. It is also a pleasant spa town dotted with fine parks.
The **Feldschlösschen Brewery** ⊘, a red and yellow brick building, is one of the oldest in the country; it was founded in 1876.

★Chapel of St Chrischona – *8km – 5 miles – about 1/4 hour. Leave Basle by* ② *to Riehen. At the post office at Riehen turn right towards Bettingen.*
The road runs through the residential suburds of Basle and Bettingen before climbing to St Chrischona Chapel. From a terrace nearby there is a **panorama★** extending from Säntis in the east to the Jura mountain ranges in the west. Basle can be seen nestling in the Rhine plain.

★Bruderholz Water Tower (Wasserturn) ⊘ – *3.5km – 2 miles. Leave Basle by* ⑥ *and bear right in Jacobsbergsstrasse to go to Bruderholz.*
A water tower stands on the great esplanade of the Battery, so-called in memory of the redoubts built by the Confederates in 1815 during the last compaign of the Allies against Napoleon I. A stairway (164 steps) leads to the top of the tower, which commands a lovely **panorama★** of Basle, the Jura and the Black Forest.

Muttenz – *5km – 3 miles southeast.*
In the town centre stands the **"Pfaarrfkirche"**, a strange fortified church surrounded by crenellated circular walls; originally of Romanesque inspiration, it was subsequently remodelled in the 15 and 16C. The small single nave, with its carved wooden ceiling, presents some superb fragments (restored) of early Renaissance religious frescoes.

Use the Index to find more information about a subject mentioned in the guide
- towns, places of interest, isolated sites, historical events or natural features.

★ BEATENBERG Berne   Pop 1 373

Michelin map **217** fold 7 or **427** fold 13 – Local maps see BERNESE OBERLAND and INTERLAKEN : Excursions – Alt 1 150m – 3 773ft – Facilities

Access from Interlaken 10km – 6.5 miles to the other end of the village; access also by funicular from the Thun road (qv).

The winding but excellent road *(connecting to the Scheidgasse Street in Unterseen)*, climbing amidst fir trees, offers good glimpses of Interlaken, the Jungfrau and Thun Lake.

Beatenberg, a terraced resort, extending along more than 7km – 4.5 miles, consists mainly of hotels and holiday chalets nestled in the trees. It overlooks Thun Lake and, further to the right, the Niesen, while on the left one may admire the sweeping ranges of the Jungfrau and the Mönch for an all-encompassing view, go up to the Niederhorn.

★★ Niederhorn ⊘ – Alt 1 950m – 6 397ft. *Access by chairlift.*

From the summit *(viewing tables)* of this mountain covered with Alpine pastures is a spectacular **panorama★★**; south beyond Thun Lake onto the glaciers of the Jungfrau Massif; southwest onto the Niesen and far in the distance Mont Blanc, barely visible; west onto the summit of the Stockhorn; northwest as far as the Neuchâtel and Murten Lakes; north onto the mountains preceding the Emmental; and east beyond Lake Brienz, onto the cliffs of the Brienzer Rothorn.

BELLINZONA Ⓒ Ticino   Pop 16 849

Michelin map **218** south of fold 12 or **427** folds 24 and 25 – Local map see GRISONS – Alt 223m – 732ft – Facilities

Bellinzona is an unavoidable point of passage for traffic using the St Gotthard, Lukmanier or San Bernardino routes. It lies on the Italian side of the Alps and for a thousand years has been a stronghold guarding the Ticino Valley. In 1803 it became the administrative centre of the canton, which took the name of the river.

★ Castles – The fortifications of Bellinzona, built between the 13 and the 15C, rested on three castles connected by walls, a great part of which can still be seen. These castles still bear the names of Uri, Schwyz and Unterwalden in spite of the bitter memories left in the country by the administration of bailiffs, appointed by the Forest Cantons, who ruled the country.

Castle of Uri (Castello Grande) – This, certainly the oldest of the three castles, is built on a rocky height at the end of a defile which it thus commanded. Its two squat, square towers could be seen from afar while the height on which it stood deflected the St Gotthard road towards the mountainside. Considerable remains of its walls, with their Italian machicolations can be seen from different vantage points in the town.

★ Schwyz Castle (Castello di Montebello) – *Access: by a ramp which starts from the railway station road (Viale Stazione).* This great citadel, built on a lozenge-shaped plan, was completely restored in 1903, and is now typical of forts built in the Lombard military architectural style. It houses an archaeological and historical museum.

Unterwalden Castle (Castello di Sasso Corbaro) – The road up to Schwyz goes on as far as the third castle.

The Unterwalden Castle is the upper stronghold of the Bellinzona fortifications. It stands among chestnut groves and should be noted chiefly as a **belvedere★**. From the terrace of the outer court, the view of the Lower Ticino Valley as far as Lake Maggiore is pleasant.

There is a museum of costumes and traditions of the Ticino region in the castle.

Michelin map 217 fold 6 or 427 fold 13 – Local map see EMMENTAL – Alt 548 m –
1 797ft – Plan of the conurbation in the current Michelin Red Guide Switzerland.

The seat of the Swiss federal authorities, Berne also houses the headquarters of
several international organisations. It lies inside a steep-sided loop of the Aare and
faces the Alps. In 1405 the town was consumed by a terrible fire. It was
subsequently rebuilt with yellowish-green sandstone and, thanks to its general
plan, remains a model of adaptation to a site. Berne has been a university town
since 1834; it is also an important centre for industry and scientific research.
The Rose Garden (Rosengarten, **CY**) offers a nice overall **view**★ of the old town,
nestling in one of the loops of the Aare river.

HISTORICAL NOTES

Foundation of Berne – A 15C chronicle describes the foundation of the town by
Duke Berchtold V of Zähringen in 1191 as follows: wishing to create a city, the Duke
asked for the advice of his huntsmen and his chief master of hounds. One of them
answered: "Master, there is a good site in the river bend where your Castle of
Nydegg stands". The Duke visited the spot, which was then thickly wooded, and
ordered that a moat be dug on the present site of the Kreuzgasse (a street running
up to the cathedral). However, it was thought better to draw the line of the moat
farther west, where the clock tower stands today. As game was very abundant the
Duke agreed with his advisers to give the new town the name of the first animal
caught at the hunt. It so happened that this was a bear (Bär). The Duke, therefore,
named the town Bärn (Bern) and gave it a bear as its coat of arms.

The great days of Berne's history – From the 14 to the 16C, Berne followed a
clever policy of expansion and played a pre-eminent part in the Confederation.
Many annexations, such as those of Burgdorf and Thun after the struggle with the
Kyburgs, secured its hegemony on both banks of the Aare.
In the 15C the conquest of Aargau enabled it to extend to the Lower Reuss, and its
resolute attitude in the Burgundian wars placed it in the front rank of Swiss
cantons. In the 16C, by annexing the Gruyère and Vaud districts, Berne dominated
all the country between the Lower Reuss and Lake Geneva.

Berne in the Confederation – When the Constitution of 1848 was drafted after
the defeat of the Sonderbund *(qv)*, Berne was chosen by common consent as the
seat for the federal authority. The choice was amply justified by the leading
political part the city had played for several centuries and its privileged position in
the centre of the Confederation and at the dividing line between the Latin and
Germanic cultures. Though the city became the seat of the Federal Chambers, the
civil service and the federal postal and railway services, this did not make it the
capital of the Confederation or the administrative centre of the country as are
London or Washington. The federal system prevented any one town from enjoying
a political pre-eminence.

Ferdinand Hodler – One of the most important Swiss painters of the 20C, Hodler,
was born in Berne in 1853 (d 1918 in Geneva). Orphaned at the age of 12, Hodler
became apprentice to Ferdinand Sommer (a painter of Swiss landscapes for
tourists) in Thun; he spent some time in Langenthal (Berne), as well. At 19 he went
to Geneva to copy the romantic landscapes painted by Calame. With the help of
his professor Barthélemy Menn (1815-93), a student of Ingres and friend of Corot,
Hodler broke with conventional painting. Among his many canvases painted at that
time are portraits, some of which point to his later large, monumental masterpieces. A trip to Spain (1878-79) enabled Hodler to admire the technique of
Velázquez and Titian, as well as Raphael's compositions. As a result his style
evolved, his technique was perfected and his palette brightened. During this period
Hodler painted a number of landscapes: the Alps and Thun Lake *(qv)* were his
preferred subjects.
Although the major artistic currents (Realism, Symbolism, Art Nouveau) of the time
can be found in his works, Hodler as of 1885, branched off to adopt Parallelism.
This style can be found in both his allegorical works *(Night, 1889-90; Day,
1899-1900; p 57)*, as well as his historical canvases *(The Retreat of Marignan;
p 226)*, which earned Hodler first prize in 1897 in a competition organised by the
Swiss National Museum in Zürich and the vigorous *William Tell (illustration p 146)*.
Hodler no longer copied nature; his landscapes were simplified became plainer.
The lake's reflection accentuates the symmetry, and his inclination to paint in
monochrome – blue was his preferred colour – and confirms the unity of his
compositions.
At the end of his life, Hodler was painting landscapes, which reflected almost
lunar-like landscapes where only lines and volumes were produced and no trace of
life or death.

★★ OLD BERNE *2 1/2 hours*

The old part of town, now a pedestrian-zone, is still delightfully evocative of the
Middle Ages. The ancient towers, the pretty **fountains** decorated with flowers and
statues, and the narrow streets festooned with flags offer a most pleasant
perspective. The streets are flanked by long arcades which form a huge shopping
mall. The old town centre is served by trams and trolley buses sporting both
federal and regional emblems. In summer visitors may hire barouches for a
charming drive round town.

*6km – 3 1/2 miles of arcades and some streets are reserved for pedestrians only.
From Easter to the end of October the principal monuments are floodlit until
midnight.*

    Start from the Bahnhofplatz.

Church of the Holy Spirit (Heiliggeist-Kirche) **(AZ)** – This baroque church was built between 1726-29.
Take the Spitalgasse, a bustling street lined with arcades which boasts many shops. There is a piper's fountain in the centre.

Bärenplatz (BZ) – In former days, this square was occupied by a large bear pit. Today it is a vast esplanade, a lively meeting place surrounded by pavement cafés.

Prison Tower (Käfigturm) **(BZ A)** – This gate marked the western boundary of the town from 1250-1350. It was restored in the 18C.

★**Marktgasse (BZ)** – The Marktgasse is smart and lively and is the main street of the old town. With its luxury shops and its many florists' windows it is the centre of intense activity: fine 17 and 18C houses present a series of arcades, giving great unity to the whole.
You will notice the fountain named for Anna Seiler (Seilerbrunnen), who in 1354 provided the town with its first hospital. Further on, the Marksman's Fountain (Schützenbrunnen) depicts a standard-bearer with, between his knees, a small bear wearing armour and firing a gun.
On the Kornhausplatz, you will see the Ogre Fountain (Kindlifresserbrunnen). It represents an ogre devouring a small boy and holding other children in reserve under his left arm.

★**Clock Tower** (Zytgloggeturm) **(BZ)** ⊘ – This was the town's west gate from 1191 to 1250. Its famous chimes start pealing at four minutes to the hour. With its 16C Jack (on the Kramgasse side) and its many painted figures, especially the delightful little bear cubs filing past to the sound of the Fool's small bells, this picture postcard scene is the most popular souvenir of Berne. The tour inside the clock enables you to admire the clock's inner workings.

Kramgasse

★**Kramgasse (BZ)** – The Kramgasse, a more crowded prolongation of the Marktgasse, has kept its original character. In the first street to the right after the clock tower you will see old houses with oriel windows and corner turrets. Along the Kramgasse notice the Zähringen Fountain with its bear wearing armour and holding the Zähringen coat of arms in his paw, and the Samson Fountain, surmounted by a statue of the giant forcing open the jaws of a lion.
At no 49 stands **Albert Einstein's** ⊘ house. It was there that the great scientist wrote his theory of relativity in 1905. Sixteen years later he was awarded the Nobel Prize for Physics on account of his outstanding research work on protons. Visitors may learn about his stay in Berne – which lasted from 1902 to 1909 – by consulting a collection of miscellaneous documents and by visiting his study and his bedroom. The latter contained a writing desk where Einstein could work standing up.

At the end of the Kramgasse, turn left into the Kreuzgasse leading to the Rathausplatz.

The Rathausplatz is ornamented with a fountain, with a banneret (Vennerbrunnen) by Hans Gieng (1542).

Town Hall (CY H) – This is the seat of the Berne Municipal Council (the legislative assembly of the city of Berne) and of the Grand Council (the legislative assembly of the canton). It was erected between 1406-17 and has been much restored, but remains, with its double staircase and covered porch, one of the most typical buildings in the city of Berne.

Return to the Kreuzgasse which leads to the Gerechtigkeitsgasse.

There the Justice Fountain (1543) can be seen *(photograph p 29)*.

On the left of the Nydeggasse, which is a continuation of the Gerechtigkeitsgasse, is the Church of the Nydegg (Nydeggkirche) built in the 14C on the foundations of a fortress which was destroyed in 1270.

Nydegg Bridge (Nydeggbrücke) **(CY)** – The bridge spans the Aare and affords attractive **views**★ of the quarters huddled in the meander of the river and the wooded slopes which overlook it.

★**Bear Pit** (Bärengraben) **(CZ)** ⊘ – Since the end of the 15C the bears of Berne have been popular favourites. They receive many visits, not only from tourists but also from the Bernese, who are particularly fond of them. A woman of Berne even bequeathed them a legacy!

Turn about. At the entrance to the Gerechtigkeitsgasse turn left into the Junkerngasse.

The Junkerngasse is lined with old houses; at no 47 stands the **Erlacher Hof**, a fine 18C dwelling in the classical style.
Approaching the cathedral from the east, one has a pleasant general view of the tall tower, the nave and flying buttresses, and the pinnacles surmounting the buttresses. Go around the building to the left until you come to a fine terrace planted with trees and flowers. From the terrace there is a bird's-eye **view**★ of the

Aare locks and to the right, the Kirchenfeldbrücke Bridge, which spans the river Aare over a distance of 40m-135ft.
Go up to the Münsterplatz (the cathedral square), where you will see the Moses Fountain.

★**Cathedral of St Vincent** (Münster) (BCZ) ⊘ – The most recent of the great Gothic churches in Switzerland, generally called a cathedral, is in reality a collegiate church. The first stone was laid in 1421, building went on until 1573, and the tower, over 100m – 328ft high, the highest in Switzerland, was finished only in 1893. The **tympanum**★★ of the main portal, by the Master Erhard Küng, is remarkable. It illustrates the Last Judgment with a multitude of figures (234), some still painted. The Damned and the Elect are very realistically treated. There are statues of prophets on the recessed arches, Wise and Foolish Virgins in the embrasures (left and right respectively) and *grisaille* frescoes dating from the beginning of the 16C on either side of the portal.

Enter the church by the right-hand door in this façade. Tourists who do not mind a climb can take a spiral staircase of 270 steps on the left. This leads to the platform ⊘ of the tower from where there is a **panorama**★★ with, in the foreground, the various quarters of the town, with their fine reddish-brown tiled roofs, many turrets and belfries, the bridges over the Aare

and, in the background, the majestically spreading chain of the Bernese Alps. The nave is a vast structure with network vaulting and painted bosses adorned with coats of arms.

The chancel has great 15C stained-glass windows by Hans Acker, depicting the Passion and the Crucifixion in the centre; other windows depict the Victory of the 10 000 Knights, and the Magi are on the left. The stalls are in the Renaissance style.

On leaving the cathedral, cross the Münsterplatz and take on the left the Münstergasse (several narrow covered passages leading to the Kramgasse) to Casino Square. Just before reaching the bridge (Kirchenfeldbrücke) take the Bundesterrasse on the right.

The Bundesterrasse is a promenade overlooking the Aare Valley.

Federal Palace (Bundeshaus) (BZ) ⊘ – The Federal Assemblies are housed in this heavy, domed building, the design of which was inspired by the Florentine Renaissance. The commentary during the guided tour through the various debating chambers (Council of the States, National Council) will enlighten the visitor on the workings of Swiss democracy *(p 25)*.

From the terrace which is to the south of the Federal Palace there is a pleasant view of the Aare, the town and in the background, the Bernese Alps.

ADDITIONAL SIGHTS

★★**Fine Arts Museum** (Kunstmuseum) (BY) ⊘ – This museum contains a very fine collection of 13C-20C paintings. It also possesses a remarkable collection of works by Paul Klee (1879-1940), who lived in Berne for many years.

On the ground floor, a room is devoted to the Italian Primitive artists of the 13C to 15C, including Fra Angelico *(Madonna and Child)* and Duccio, whose *Maestá* reflects the Byzantine style characteristic of the Sienese school.

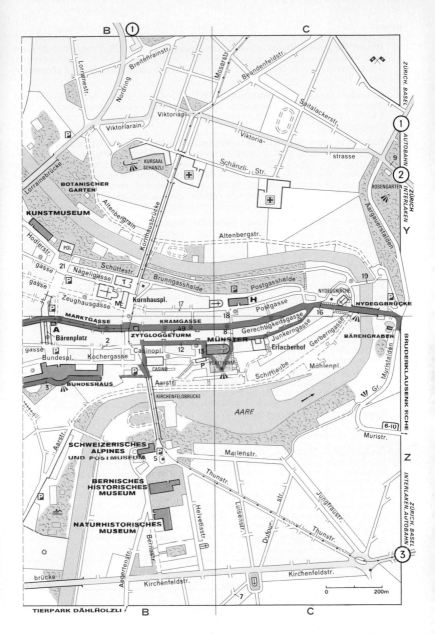

The Swiss Primitives of the 15C and 16C – especially those of the Master of the Carnation from Berne and the Master of Berne – show detailed execution but also a certain stiffness and naivety.

The 16C school, which favours the portrayal of religious scenes, is represented by the Bernese painter Niklaus Manuel Deutsch (c1484-1530), whose style and composition were already akin to the art of the Renaissance *(St Luke Painting the Virgin, The Martyrdom of the 10 000 Knights of Mount Ararat)*, and by two excellent portraits of Luther and his wife from the workshop of the German painter Cranach. On the ground floor are exhibited works of Swiss and European painters of the 19C and 20C. The work of Albert Anker (1831-1910) revolves around simple themes: scenes of everyday life and portraits of people and children *(Old Woman Warming Herself, Young Girl Knitting)*.

The French School is represented by Delacroix, by the major Impressionists including Monet, as well as Cézanne, Renoir, Pissarro, Manet, Sisley, Bonnard, who belonged to the Nabis group and Utrillo, who painted scenes of Montmartre. A special exhibition is devoted to the native-born artist Ferdinand Hodler. Along with the great allegorical frescoes that reflect his concern for death *(Day, Night, Disillusioned Souls)*, visitors may admire his deeply nostalgic landscapes *(Thun Lake and the Stockhorn)*, as well as his portraits *(Young Girl with a Poppy)* and self-portraits (*The Madman* pictures him with wild, menacing features). On the first floor there are also paintings by the Expressionist artists Rouault, Soutine and Modigliani, as well as works by Picasso, one of the leaders of the Cubist School. One of the galleries is reserved for paintings from the first half of the 20C, including works by Cuno-Amiet, who used a palette of bright, warm colours. There is also a large collection by the Cubist painters Braque, Picasso, Juan Gris and Fernand Léger.

Found in five rooms in the basement is a rich **Paul Klee collection.** The museum owns over 2 000 drawings as well as oils, gouaches and watercolours which trace the artist's development *(the works done on paper are exhibited in rotation)*. The striving for colour effects gives rise to square paintings *(Pictorial Architecture in Red, Yellow and Blue)*, to Divisionist works from the years 1930-32 *(Ad Parnassum)* and to paintings with figures and signs against a coloured background *(Flowers in Stone,* 1940).

Botanical Garden (Botanischer Garten) **(BY)**   This vast garden, tastefully arranged, descends to the banks of the Aare in terraces. Fountains and pools here and there add to the pleasure of the visit. The greenhouses contain a collection of tropical plants.

★★**Natural History Museum** (Naturhistorisches Museum) **(BZ)** ⊘ – The great Wattenwyl Hall on the ground floor is quite remarkable. The African animals it contains are shown in their natural surroundings. On the ground floor dioramas display fauna from Asia. The first floor contains a fine collection of vertebrates from the local fauna, and of Arctic mammals. The biological nature of the whale is also outlined. The second floor is devoted to birds, reptiles, gemmology, petrogeology and insects. The third floor is reserved for collections relating to mineralogy and palaeontology.

★★**Bernese Historical Museum** (Bernisches Historiches Museum) **(BZ)** ⊘ – This Neo-Gothic building contains various historical, prehistorical, archaeological and ethnographical collections.

From the lower mezzanine, where you can visit the Pourtalès Room and its 18C furniture, proceed to the upper mezzanine, which houses the Oriental collection belonging to Henri Moser Charlottenfels. A miniature model of the city is displayed on the first floor, together with several collections, including the booty captured from the Burgundians at Grandson and Murten in 1476. It includes standards, embroideries and tapestries which belonged to Charles the Bold, Duke of Burgundy. Among the tapestries is one with the coat of arms of Philip the Good woven in a Flemish workshop in 1466.

Other tapestries from Flemish looms, and especially from Tournai, attract attention by their fine design and rich colours. Examples are *The Judgment of Trajan and Herkenbald,* woven in the 15C and inspired by paintings by Roger van der Weyden; *The Magi* (1460), *The Life of St Vincent* (belonging to the cathedral), and others illustrating several episodes in the life of Julius Caesar.

On the second floor is the giant scale (1 752), which was at the Berne arsenal; it weighed cannons of 2 tons! A number of rooms illustrate the daily lives of the Bernese during the 19 and 20C.

A bronze group with fountains by Romagnoli stands in the Helvetiaplatz, commemorating the 1865 founding of the International Telegraphic Union in Paris.

★★**Swiss Alpine Museum** (Schweizerisches Alpines Museum) **(BZ)** ⊘ – A short documentary film called "Gondwana and the Alps", illustrating the formation of the Swiss Alps and their geological composition, can serve as an introduction to the discovery of this wonderful mountain range, its conquest by man and its scientific exploration. A miniature relief map, showing the different types of mountains, reproduces several famous valleys and summits (Matterhorn, Piz Bernina, Dents du Midi). The art of mountaineering as well as the development of life-saving equipment, climbing gear and the instruments and techniques used in high mountain areas testify to man's relentless efforts to tame this savage monster and make it accessible to

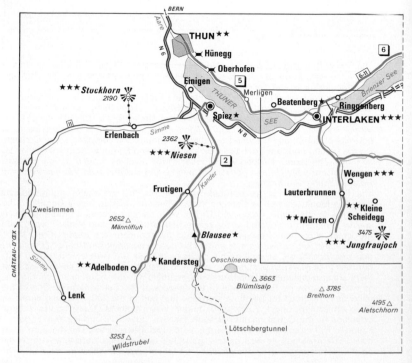

travellers. The Alps also fascinated many painters, as is demonstrated by the works of Ferdinand Hodler, *The Climb* and *The Fall*. Other rooms are devoted to meteorology, housing conditions, everyday life, traditional costumes and lore, regional flora and fauna, and a cartographic representation of the Alps.

★ **Swiss Postal Museum** (Schweizerisches PTT-Museum) (**BZ**) ⊘ – The Postal Museum shows the development of the Swiss postal service from ancient times to the present day. The first floor explains the history of modern telecommunications. A large stamp collection in the basement will attract the attention of collectors.

★ **Dählhölzli Zoo** (Tierpark) ⊘ – *Entrance in the Jubilämsstrasse* (**CZ**). This fine 13ha – 32 acre park has about 1 000 animals kept in large enclosures.

Vivarium – The aviary contains hundreds of tropical birds with brilliant plumage. There are also rare specimens of local fauna, many reptiles and fish.

★ **Church of St Nicholas** (Bruder Klausenkirche) – *Leave by the Muristrasse* (**CZ**). This is dedicated to St Nicholas of Flüe, familiarly known in Switzerland as "Bruder Klaus" (Brother Nicholas – *qv*). It is built on a broad esplanade and has a detached bell tower. With its simple lines it is one of the most representative specimens of modern architecture in Switzerland.

EXCURSIONS

★★ **Gurten** ⊘ – *Alt 858 m – 2 815 ft – 2.5km – 1 1/2 miles about 1/2 hour including 10 minutes by funicular. Leave Berne by the Monbijoustrasse* (**AZ**), *the Belp-Thun road, and at the entrance to Wabern turn right towards the lower funicular station.*
The Gurten, a magnificent belvedere with a **panorama**★★ of Berne and the Bernese Oberland, is a pleasant place in which to stroll; it also has facilities for children.

Enge Peninsula – *4 km – 2 1/2 miles north, located in the first bend of the Aare. Leave Berne by* ⑦ *on the road to Biel. After the Tiefenau railway station bear left and at a crossroads bear right onto the Reichenbachstrasse as far as a modern Protestant church (Matthäuskirche).*
A board indicates the location of the archaeological remains of Enge: the ramparts of the ancient Helvetian town and Roman vestiges (1C). Among the latter are the ruins of a small oval amphitheatre, the smallest in Switzerland; and a couple of hundred yards farther on in the forest are the public baths.

★★★ BERNESE OBERLAND

Michelin map **217** folds 6 to 10 and 16 to 20 or **427** folds 13 to 15

This massif set in the heart of Switzerland, marked to the north by the crescent-shaped Lakes of Thun and Brienz, to the east by the Grisons, to the south by the Upper Valais and to the west by the Vaud and Fribourg Alps, abounds in sights – natural and man-made   of international renown: natural – the Jungfrau and Eiger, the Rhône Glacier, the Trümmelbach Falls, Thun Lake... man-made – the resorts of Interlaken and Grindelwald and the Jungfraujoch, the highest rack railway in Europe.

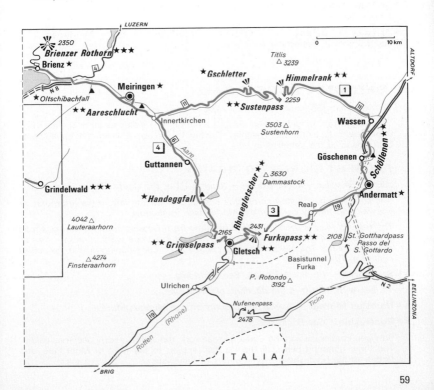

Taking advantage of the great number of natural curiosities and "playgrounds" suited for Alpine sports in the relatively small area between the Aare and the Rhône, Swiss tourist genius has made the Bernese Oberland the most remarkable natural holiday resort in Europe.

For a century a dazzling view of the Jungfrau from the Höheweg promenade at Interlaken has been a lasting memory for visitors to this wonderfully equipped area. The region is also known as an international centre of mountaineering.

Conquest of the Eigerwand – One of the most dramatic episodes after the conquest of the Matterhorn was that of the north face of the Eiger *(qv)*. In 1858 the summit (3970 m – 13025ft) had been reached by the Englishman, Barrington. The south and southwest spurs had been conquered in 1874 and 1876. From 1935 onwards many attempts were made to climb the north face: that year, two Germans were killed; the next year, three roped teams of Germans and Austrians met their death.

The story of these tragic failures raised such a storm of protest that the cantonal authorities in Berne forbade any further attempt. The ban was lifted in 1937, however, the year marked by the failure of the Austrian, Rebitsch and the German, Wiggerl Vörg. In 1938 Vörg and his companion, Anderl Heckmair, made secret preparations for an attempt in which they were determined to succeed. Though two Austrians, Kasparek and Harrer, started before them, they overtook them on the second day and decided to join forces with the rival team. Their slow and difficult progress, threatened at every step by the danger of storms and avalanches, was anxiously watched from the valley. Forewarned by the press and the radio, the whole world hung on the details of their progress. When at last, after long days of struggle, they surmounted the final crest, blinded by fatigue and storm, they were not immediately aware of their victory!

Their difficult descent by the west face, in the midst of a blizzard, sealed the success of their expedition.

TOUR

Recommended itineraries. – Organised according to time (longest to shortest) needed.

★★★**Jungfrau Region** – Tour by car, cable-cars and train from Interlaken – allow 2 days. *See Interlaken : Excursions.*

★★★**Round tour of the Three Passes (Grimsel, Furka, Susten)** – Starting from Interlaken – allow at least 1 day. This includes the itineraries ④, ③ and ① *(see below).*

★★★① **Susten Pass Road** – From Andermatt to Meiringen – about 2 1/2 hours. *See Susten Pass Road.*

★② **Kander Valley** – From Spiez to Kandersteg – about 2 1/2 hours. *See Kander Valley.*

★★★③ **Furka Pass Road** – From Gletsch to Andermatt – about 2 1/4 hours. *See Furka Pass Road.*

★④ **Grimsel Pass Road** – From Meiringen to Gletsch – about 1 1/2 hours. *See Grimsel Pass Road.*

★★⑤ **Thun Lake** – From Thun to Interlaken – about 1 hour. *See Thun.*

★⑥ **Lake Brienz** – From Interlaken to Meiringen – about 3/4 hour. *See Brienz.*

Blue Thistle

D'après photo Champroux/ JACANA

★★★ BERNINA PASS ROAD

Michelin map 218 folds 15 and 16 or 427 folds 17 and 26.

This magnificent mountain road climbs up the Bernina Valley as far as the pass and then descends along the Poschiavo Valley to Tirano; it links the Engadine in Switzerland to the Valtellina in Italy.

FROM ST MORITZ TO TIRANO

56km – 34 miles – about 2 hours – Itinerary ⑦ of the Doubs Basins local map

It is advisable not to start across the Engadine slope too late in the afternoon, or you will find the icy corrie of the Morteratsch in shadow.

The Bernina Pass is usually blocked by snow from October to May. The pass road is not cleared at night. The railway – the highest in Europe without racks – runs all the year round. The Swiss customs control is at Campocologno and the Italian control at Piattamala.

★★★**St. Moritz** – *Time: 1 1/2 hours. See St. Moritz.*

Leave St. Moritz in the direction of Pontresina.

★★**Muottas Muragl** – *Access and description see Muottas Muragl.*

★★**Pontresina** – *See Pontresina.*

Between Pontresina and the Chünetta road fork, the valley quickly becomes wilder. The three glittering peaks of the Piz Palü appear to the right of Munt Pers, and farther to the right, the snowy summits of Bellavista.

Morteratsch Glacier

★★★ **Chünetta Belvedere** — Alt 2 083m − 6 832ft. *From the Bernina road 2km − 1 mile Rtn − plus 1 hour on foot Rtn.* After branching off on the road to the Morteratsch Glacier, leave your car before the wooden bridge leading to Morteratsch station, Cross this bridge and the railway track and after passing a bed of stones brought by the torrent, take a path going uphill to the right, under the larches. After 20 minutes, at the second fork, when the view opens out, turn to the right to climb to the belvedere.

From there you will see the grand picture formed by the **Morteratsch Corrie**, overlooked from left to right by the Piz Palü, Bellavista, the cloven summit of the Piz Bernina (highest point: 4 049m − 13 284ft), the Piz Morteratsch with its heavy snow-cap and the Piz Boval. The lower end of the glacier dies away in the foreground; it is framed by terminal moraines and divided longitudinally by a central moraine. The **view**★★ is splendid directly after two hairpin bends followed by a level-crossing.

To the right of Bellavista the glorious twin peaks of the Bernina Massif − Piz Bernina and Piz Morteratsch − appear. From the latter descends the Morteratsch Glacier − a truly breathtaking sight. After this the road emerges into the Upper Bernina Depression.

★★★ **Diavolezza** ⊘ − Alt 2 973m − 9 754ft. *About 1 hour Rtn from the Bernina road, including 9 minutes by cable-car.*

For generations of mountaineers and skiers the Diavolezza refuge (now a restaurant) has been the starting-point of one of the most famous glacier runs in Europe. Thanks to the cable-car, tourists can now reach this high mountain pass and admire its spectacular glacier landscape.

At Curtinatsch via the upper opening of the Arlas Valley, the three peaks of the Piz Palü reappear to the right.

★★ **Piz Lagalb** ⊘ − *Access by cable-car in 8 minutes; leave from Curtinatsch.* Through a rocky terrain *(on foot − 1/4 hour Rtn)* one reaches the snowy peak of Piz Lagalb (alt 2 959m − 9 708ft) from where there is a **panorama**★★ which reveals about forty of the main peaks in the Grisons: to the southwest, the Diavolezza Range and its northern glaciers; to the south the lovely green lake, Lago Bianco, and other lakes (natural); to the right of the Diavolezza, the small Lej de la Diavolezza sparkles at the bottom of a crater-like pit.

Farther on, where the road begins to skirt the first lakes of the Bernina, the Piz Cambrena, in its turn, stands out clearly.

★★ **Bernina Pass** − Alt 2 328m − 7 638ft. After leaving the valley, followed throughout its length by the railway and in which the Lago Bianco lies, the road climbs to the Bernina Pass from where there are clear **views**★★★ of the Piz Cambrena and its glacier.

★★★ **Alp Grüm** ⊘ − Alt 2 091m − 6 860ft. *From the "Ospizio Bernina" station (accessible by car along a downhill road starting from the Bernina Pass), about 1 hour Rtn, including 10 minutes by rail.* A well-known belvedere overlooks the Palü Glacier and the Poschiavo Valley.

From the Bernina Pass to the Rösa Plateau the road dips into the **Agone Valley**, framed between the warmly coloured slopes of the Piz Campasc and the Cima di Cardan. It then follows a winding course, taking advantage of every natural feature to maintain a practicable gradient. For a long time, looking back, the Cambrena group offers glimpses of its glaciers. Forest vegetation is once more reduced to a few clumps of stunted larch. You will make your entry to La Rösa facing the majestic, rocky Teo cirque.

From La Rösa to Poschiavo the wooded slopes, clothed with spruce, grow darker. 1km − 2/3 mile after two hairpin bends, in a section where the road winds above a green valley, a widely sweeping stretch of corniche reveals, lying below, the villages of San Carlo and Poschivo, overshadowed by the icy shoulder of the Pizzo Scalino.

Poschiavo − The main street of the town, running between tall, uniform buildings with regularly spaced windows quite unlike those of the Engadine, introduces the traveller from the Bernina to transalpine surroundings. The early 16C Church of San Vittore on the main square shows in its architecture the peculiar position of the Grisons as a transit area not only for men and goods but also for artistic influences. Although the general appearance of the building, with its low-pitched roof and especially its slim campanile with five storeys of arches, is Lombard in style, the network of star vaulting, most remarkable in the chancel, derives from a typically Germanic style belonging to the last Flamboyant Gothic period. Lake Poschiavo (a hydro-electric reservoir) is the best feature of the Poschiavo-Miralago section. Very high on the steep and wooded eastern slope stands the steeple of San Romerio.

Miralago − From this hamlet, whose name − "look at the lake" − refers to the **view★**, a glance upstream will give you your last glimpse of a mountain skyline.

From Miralago to **Tirano** the downward slope is steep again. Vineyards and tobacco fields become more frequent. At Brusio notice the railway loop. The pilgrims' church of the Madonna di Tirano, in the Renaissance style, marks the arrival on Italian soil.

★ BEX SALT MINE Vaud

Michelin map **217** fold 14 or **427** fold 12

This 300-year-old **mine** ⊙ is still fully operational and produces 150 tons of salt daily. It consists of 40km − 25 miles of galleries, shafts, passageways and steps, originally hollowed out by means of chisels and sledgehammers. The salt is obtained through traditional means of extraction. A stream of fresh water is injected into the salt rock, flooding its every crevice, until the brine shows a salt content of 30%. This technique is known as leaching. The water is then evaporated through boiling, leaving a salt deposit at the bottom of the container. Part of the mine has been made into a museum which can be visited on foot and in a small-size train. To illustrate the history of the mine, a diaporama and a permanent exhibition have been set up in a former brine reservoir, first excavated in 1826. The exhibits include the various tools and pieces of machinery which have served the mining industry over the past centuries.

★ BIEL (BIENNE) Berne   Pop 51 893

Michelin map **216** fold 14 or **427** folds 12 and 13 − Local map see Swiss JURA − Alt 438m − 1 437ft − Facilities

Lying at the foot of the last spurs of the Jura and on the shore of the lake that bears its name, Biel is a good excursion centre and its bathing beach, not far from Nidau, is much appreciated. It marks the linguistic dividing-line between French and German *(map p 22)*: 1/3 of the inhabitants speak French. The modern lower town contrasts with the old quarters of the upper town.

Life at Biel − Biel is an extremely busy town. The population has grown over tenfold within a century, thanks to the watch and clock industry, which still employs about 6 000 persons. The first "Omega" watch factory was set up at Biel in 1879.

Supplementary industries have been established to mitigate possible economic crises (precision machine-tool works, wire-mills and graphic-art workshops).

The problem of bilingualism is interesting at Biel: both German and French are official languages on an equal footing. It is not unusual to come across two Bielese people conversing without difficulty, each in his own language.

The Ring

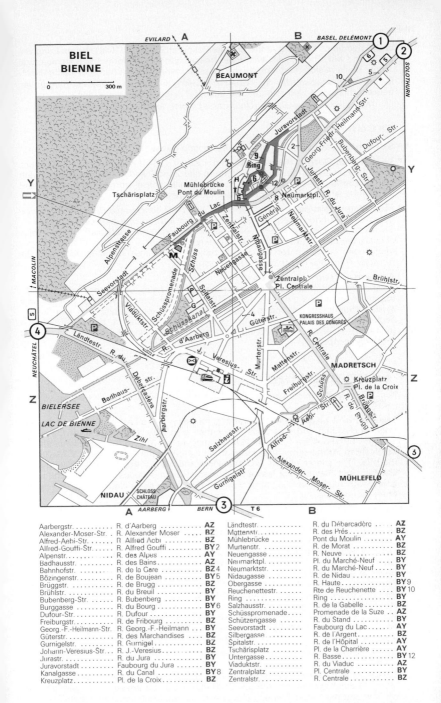

BIEL
BIENNE

0   300 m

SIGHTS

★**Schwab Museum** (**AY M**) ⊘ – Here are housed collections formed from discoveries made by Colonel Schwab (1803-69), a pioneer in the research of the prehistoric period in Romansh Switzerland. It contains the best-known examples of the lake-dwellers' era. To finds made in Lakes Biel, Neuchâtel and Murten are added those from the Gallo-Roman settlement at Petinesca and La Tène (discovered by Schwab in 1857).

From the museum go along the Faubourg du Lac (Seevorstadt) then take the Rue du Bourg (Burggasse) on the left.

★**Old Town** (**BY**) – This is very picturesque. The tourist will find many fountains and façades decorated with numerous and remarkable wrought iron signs, often brightly painted.

Rue du Bourg (Burggasse) – On this street are the town hall, notable for its stepped gable and façade adorned by windows with red sandstone mullions, and a Fountain of Justice (1744).

Ring – This charming square was the centre of old Biel, when the town was governed by the prince-bishops of Basle, from the 11C to the Revolution. Justice was done here; the accused appeared before the members of the Council seated in a semi-circle, and it was from this arrangement that the Ring drew its name.

63

In the middle of the Ring is the curious Banneret Fountain (1546), symbolizing the militia and war. The houses, with their arcades and turrets, form a fine architectural group, while beside them stands the massive tower of the Church of St Benedict.

Rue Haute (Obergasse) **(BY 9)** – Lined with Bernese-arcaded *(p 29)* and Burgundian houses, this street also features the beautiful Angel's Fountain (1564).

Then take the Rue Basse (Untergasse) which leads to the lake district.

EXCURSIONS

★★ **St Peter's Island (St Petersinsel)** – *Description below.*

★ **Taubenloch Gorges** (Taubenlochschlucht) – *2.5km – 1 1/2 miles – about 1 1/2 hours.* Leave Biel by ② and the road to Solothurn and Zürich, and at Bözingen take a path just before the Suze Bridge, near a wire-mill. These gorges, often wild and mysterious, are served by an excellent tourist path.

★ **Magglingen (Macolin)** – *8km – 5 miles – about 1/2 hour. Leave Biel by ①200m after going under a bridge between two bends, turn left into the by-road to Evilard.* Go on to Magglingen, where you will find an extensive **panorama**★ of the Swiss plateau, the lakes at the foot of the Jura and the Alps. Magglingen is known for its Federal School of Gymnastics. *It is accessible by funicular from Biel (west on the town plan).*

Aarberg – *11km – 7 miles south.* A canal links this small yet prosperous town to Biel Lake. The upper town, joined to the lower town by a covered bridge (16C) over the Aare, is worth a visit. Its **main square**★ (Stadtplatz), oblong in shape and paved, is embellished with two flower-decked fountains and lined with classical façades and a small 15C church (restored). *A picturesque second-hand sale is held annually the last Friday and Saturday in April.*

★ LAKE BIEL (BIELER SEE)

Michelin map **216** folds 13 and 14 or **427** folds 12 and 13 – Local map see Swiss JURA

Lake Biel is of glacial origin. It stretches for 15km – 9 miles at the foot of the last ridge of the Jura and was once larger than it is now, for the level of the water dropped by about 2m – 7ft in 1878 to uncover a score of lake-dwellings on the south shore. At the same time some of the waters of the Aare were deflected from the lake. "The shores of Lake Biel are wilder and more romantic than those of Lake Geneva... but they are not less smiling", wrote Jean-Jacques Rousseau. The north shore, with villages nestling amidst vineyards – such as La Neuveville *(qv)* – is the more picturesque.

★★ **St. Peter's Island (St. Petersinsel)** ⊘ – *By boat from Biel or la Neuveville. Allow half a day for the whole excursion.* St. Peter's Island, at the extreme southwest end of the lake, really became a peninsula when the lake's water level was lowered, but it has kept its traditional name of island. In the autumn of 1765 it was visited by Jean-Jacques Rousseau, who recalls his idyllic stay there in *The Confessions of J. J. Rousseau* and in *Reveries of the Solitary Walker.* The tourist can easily walk round the north side of the island and enjoy pretty glimpses of the lake, especially towards the village of Ligerz (Gléresse). After seeing the small landing-stage used by Rousseau, you will come upon the house in which he lived. St. Peter's Island and its neighbour, the small **Rabbits Island** (joined to the shore by a strip of marshy land since the waters of the lake were lowered), are nature reserves providing a delightful haven of peace for migratory birds, hare and deer.

★ **North Shore** – In this French-speaking section of the lake are some charming old towns.

Cressier – Set back from the lake, this old wine-growers village has preserved some of its old buildings: on the Rue des St-Martin there is a house (1576) with an oriel window and the Vallier Château (1610) with its pointed turrets lies nearby.

Le Landeron – Nearer to the lake, this small village is hemmed in by vegetable gardens and orchards. The charm of this village lies in its unique long shaded square adorned with two fountains with bannerets. It is defended at each end by a fortified gate (1659 north side, 1596 south side) and lined with old houses. The town hall (15C) is built onto the Martyrs Chapel. At no 36 note the house dating from 1550.

La Neuveville – *See La Neuveville.*

BREMGARTEN Aargau   Pop 5 280

Michelin map **216** folds 17 and 18 or **427** fold 5 – Alt 386m – 1 266ft

Bremgarten is built at the base of a bend of the Reuss, which encircles its walls. In the time of the Habsburgs it was a fortress and a bridgehead. Although less imposing, its site may be compared with those of Berne and Fribourg.

From the Lucerne road, or from the Casinoplatz, there is a fine **general view** of the old town, whose roofs rise in terraces from the river. This can be crossed on a 16C covered bridge, in the middle of which stand two little chapels.

Former gateways or fortified towers – the Obertor (Upper Gate) and the Hexenturm (Witches' Tower) – and attractive houses with oriel windows and overhanging roofs form an interesting picture.

★ **BRIENZ** Berne

Pop 2 849

Michelin map **217** fold 8 or **427** fold 14 – Local map see BERNESE OBERLAND – Alt 570m – 1 871ft – Facilities

Brienz lies along the shore of its lake, facing the Giessbach Falls, whose muffled roar can be clearly heard in the town. It is one of the best preserved old-fashioned summer resorts in the Bernese Oberland.

The town is a great wood-carving centre and has a technical school to maintain the tradition as well as a school for stringed instruments. Most of the carvings of bears in all sizes and positions sold as souvenirs come from the local workshops.

★★★ **Brienzer Rothorn** ⊙ – Alt 2 350m – 7 710ft. *About 3 hours Rtn (2 hours and 20 minutes by rack-railway).*
Panoramic view of the Bernese Alps, Lake Brienz (Brienzersee) and Hasli.

★★ **Giessbach Falls (Giessbachfälle)** – Impressive group of cascades.
- **Starting from Brienz** ⊙ – Main platform of Brienz-Bahnhof. *About 2 hours Rtn, including 3/4 hour by boat and funicular.*
- **Starting from Interlaken** ⊙ – Separate Interlaken – Brienzersee or Bönigen embarkation stages. *About 3 hours Rtn, including 2 hours by boat and funicular.*

★ **Ballenberg Open-Air Museum** ⊙ – *2.5km – 1 1/2 miles plus 1/4 hour on foot Rtn. It is recommended that you obtain a map of the museum at the entrance. Leave Brienz east on the Hofstetten road which branches left off the main street. Car park south of the village.*

This open-air museum, located beside the Wyssensee, was opened in 1978. About thirty buildings have been moved to this wooded and hilly site.

These homes and traditional farms, of the past or present, are grouped according to their provenance, and as a result, their similar building methods. They are often seen with their dependencies and furnished interiors – including utensils, tools and farm machinery.

Those worth special notice are the half-timbered Bernese chalet (no 311) from Rapperswil, the chalet (no 331) from Ostermundigen with its *trompe-l'œil* windows underneath the gable and the 17C Adelboden (no 1 011) chalet covered with Gothic inscriptions. The Chaux-de-Fonds (Jura) multi-purpose dwelling (no 111) stands out because of its great white façade with small windows; the Oberentfelden (Aargau) chalet (no 221) dating back to 1609 is covered by a large thatched roof. The canton of Geneva is represented by the large farmhouse (no 551) from Lancy, which was originally a small farm building containing the wine press. Of smaller size but as picturesque is the half-timbered wine grower's chalet (no 611) from the Zürich area, which was built in 1780. Strolling through the site you will go back into time as you watch the craftsman, baker or cheesemaker at work...

★ **LAKE BRIENZ**

Shorter, narrower, perhaps less picturesque but nonetheless wilder than Thun Lake, Lake Brienz is linked to its "twin" by the Aare River.

★ **North Shore** – *From Interlaken to Meiringen – 30km – 19 miles – about 3/4 hour – local map see Bernese Oberland.* From Interlaken *(qv)* to Ringgenberg the road runs through woods, climbing to the last slopes of the Harder.

Ringgenberg – Facilities. The church *(to reach it turn into the road to the landing-stage)* stands on a charming site on the edge of a steep ridge on which the village is built. From the lake shore, there are attractive views of the lake and the mountains immediately overlooking Interlaken. The building was erected in the 17C on the ruins of a castle (Burg) whose keep was used again in the building of the belfry. Between Ringgenberg and Brienz, especially on the Oberreid-Brienz section, the view opens out over **Lake Brienz**, enclosed by the Brienzer Rothorn Chain and the foothills of the Faulhorn. The best place for a halt is 600m – about 1/3 mile northeast of Oberreid, where you return to the lake shore. From this point you will begin to see, upstream, the Sustenhörner Range which reaches its highest point of 3 503m – 11 490ft in the dome-shaped Sustenhorn.

★ **Brienz** – *See above.*

★★★ **Brienzer Rothorn** – *The excursion from Brienz which includes a ride on a rack-railway takes about 3 hours Rtn. See above.*

Among the cascades which cast their spray down the nearby cliffs, the **Oltschibach Waterfall**★ is the most noteworthy.

★ **Meiringen** – *See Meiringen.*

BRIG (BRIGUE) Valais

Pop 10 602

Michelin map **217** fold 18 or **427** fold 14 – Local map see VALAIS – Alt 681m – 2 234ft – Facilities – Town plan in the current Michelin Red Guide Switzerland

Brig is located at the confluence of the rivers Rhône and Saltine. This charming town is a lively halting-place at the junction of the Simplon road *(qv)* and the road to the Rhône Glacier and the Furka. The railway station is important, as it stands on the frontier at the north end of the Simplon Tunnel, which is the longest rail tunnel in the world (19.8km – 12 miles).

The king of the Simplon – Brig owes its great attraction to the ideas and ambitions of **Kaspar Jodok von Stockalper** (1609-91) from a Valais family, who were traditionally the guardians of the Simplon Defile. Through his enterprise Stockalper amassed great riches from the trade route over the Alps during the Salt Monopoly. He was courted by emperors and kings but his wealth and success soon made him enemies and he had to flee to Italy, leaving his proud fortress unfinished. He was however to return to Brig to die a respected but ruined man.

65

Stockalper's Castle (Stockalperschloss) ⊙ – This was once the largest private residence in Switzerland. It can be recognized from afar by its three towers with bulbous domes, standing where the road to the Simplon begins.

The first building, as you come from the centre of Brig, is the Stockalper family dwelling (early 16C), flanked by a fine watch-tower. The enormous main building (built over the original warehouse by the "Great Stockalper") has eight storeys, including cellars, and is connected with the smaller house by a picturesque gallery with two tiers of arcades.

Enter the main courtyard by the gateway in the wing at right angles. This **courtyard★** is surrounded by open galleries in two or three storeys and is still very fine. The three towers set around it, with their plain stonework, make a contrast with this elegant building, directly inspired by the Tuscan Renaissance.

BRUGG Aargau   Pop 9 482

Michelin map 🟦 fold 6 or 🟥 fold 5

Founded by the Habsburgs in the early 12C, the "city of the bridges", which stands at the confluence of the Aare and the Reuss, has preserved many of its old buildings. An important industrial town, Brugg plays a central role in the country's road and railway network.

The Old City – Among the monuments still standing are the Archive Tower, the Storks' Tower (Storchenturm) and the imposing 12 and 16C **Black Tower** (Schwarzer Turm) which overlooks the bridge spanning the Aar. This vantage point affords a good view of its wooded banks and old houses. Note the 16C former Town Hall and the late Gothic Protestant church with its 18C interior decoration.

On the pretty Hofstatt Square you will find the former arsenal (17C) and the old storeroom, dating from the 18C.

Vindonissa Museum ⊙ – Housed in the museum are the finds from the Roman site of Vindonissa (see below): jewellery, arms, coins, statues, pottery, glasswork, as well as articles made of wood and leather. The 4C skeleton of a Roman woman in a sarcophagus and the model of the Vindonissa military camp are worth noting. Outside is a lapidary museum (steles, votive inscriptions).

Königsfelden Abbey – See Königsfelden Abbey.

Vindonissa's Roman Amphitheatre – At Windisch 1km – 1/2 mile via the Zürich road then on the right of Königsfelden Church take the Hauserstrasse.

This is the most important find of the Vindonissa site – a military camp which was, in the 1C, the Roman headquarters for all Switzerland and located on the present-day site of Windisch. The oval amphitheatre (112m × 98m – 367ft × 321ft) with its double wall of ashlarstone (average height 2m – 6 1/2ft) held 10 000 spectators.

★★ BRUNNEN Schwyz   Pop 6 232

Michelin map 🟦 fold 1 or 🟥 fold 15 – Local map see Lake LUCERNE – Alt 439m – 1 440ft – Facilities

Brunnen is one of the major resorts of Lake Lucerne; Hans Christian Andersen, the author of fairy tales, came here frequently on holiday.

Until the opening of the Axenstrasse (qv), Brunnen was a key port for traffic between the Schwyz and Uri cantons and a transit point of first-class importance on the St Gotthard route. It is busy today because tourists on the great transalpine route (road no 2, via Arth) and those on the coast route via Vitznau come together here.

Brunnen deserves at least a stop for its **site★★** at the head of the wild Lake Uri (Urnesee), in the heart of picturesque and historical Switzerland.

It was here in Brunnen, after the victory at Morgarten, that on 9 December 1315, the three cantons of Uri, Schwyz and Unterwalden renewed their pact of mutual assistance (for more information see Historical Notes).

★★ **Quays** – From the shady quay which prolongs the new Axenquai Promenade eastwards below the Axenstrasse, the stroller gets a complete **view★★** of Lake Uri, lying like a fiord between wild mountain spurs.

The dominant feature is the Uri-Rotstock, which rears bare twin peaks above a small glacier.

In the foreground, on the opposite shore, the tender green of the historic field of **Rütli** (Grütli for the French Swiss) shows up against the wooded slopes of the Seelisburg spur.

At the extreme point of this promontory may be seen the natural obelisk erected by the "early Cantons" to the memory of Schiller, the poet of Tell, calling it the **Schillerstein.**

A short trip in a motor-boat will give a closer view; see under Lake Lucerne.

Gourmets...

*The chapter on Food and Drink in the Introduction to this guide describes Switzerland's gastronomic specialities and best national wines. The annual **Michelin Red Guide Switzerland** offers an up-to-date selection of good restaurants.*

BULLE Fribourg   Pop 9 062

Michelin map ⚿ southwest of fold 5 or ⚿ fold 12 – Alt 769m – 2 523ft – Facilities

Bulle is in the centre of the "green Gruyère", one of the most attractive districts in Switzerland with its peaceful scenery and quaint folklore. The market town deals in timber, cattle (the black-and-white Fribourg breed) and cheese.

★★ **Museum of the Gruyère Region** ⊙ – Founded by the local writer Victor Tissot, the museum is installed in the basement of a modern building at the foot of the castle. This museum of local art is divided into two sections and is superbly arranged.

The larger first section contains 25 elevated displays exhibited thematically and several reconstructed peasant interiors: the most unusual is a room (1673) decorated with painted scenes of the life of the Prophet Elijah, as well as the cheese room, which is part of a chalet for the herders up in the mountain pastures. Admire the large variety of fine **old furniture**: tables, beds, chests, cribs... all painted, carved or decorated. The 18C Gruyère regional **costumes** are also worth noting as well as the paper crèches of the same period. Also on display are 18-19C medallions on paper from the Vosges and Bavaria, Renaissance and baroque religious statues, church plate (gold monstrance dated 1752) cowbells and horns from the Alps and a diorama of the local fauna.

The second section contains engravings and paintings of the 16-17C Italian school. Also represented are the French school, with works by Corot and Courbet (a lovely portrait of a young Bulle girl) and the Swiss school (Vallotton, Alexis Grimou). Note the several pieces of furniture, old and modern, especially the painted cupboard by Netton Bosson. Present-day traditions of the Gruyère region are illustrated by an audio-visual presentation.

Castle – An imposing building flanked by four round towers, built in 13C, in the style of Burgundy and Savoy like the castles of Rolle *(qv)* and Yverdon-les-Bains *(qv)*, by Bishop Boniface of Lausanne. Two coupled shields bearing the two cauldrons of Fribourg are painted on the walls.

BURGDORF (BERTHOUD) Berne   Pop 15 373

Michelin map ⚿ fold 15 or ⚿ fold 13 – Local map see EMMENTAL – Alt 533m – 1 749 ft

Burgdorf, at the entrance to the Emmental (the Valley of the Emme, famous for its pastures and its cheese industry – *p 84*), is a busy little town in the canton of Berne. The modern town, with its large textile works, is overlooked by the old town, crowned by its castle.

Castle – This massive brick building was erected by the Dukes of Zähringen at the end of the 12C and passed to the Bernese in 1384.

Museum ⊙ – The museum occupies three floors in the tower. The Knights' Hall, with fine old furniture, Emmental costumes, porcelain, a collection of musical instruments and mementos of **J.H Pestalozzi** *(qv)*, who worked here from 1799 to 1804, may also be seen. From the top floor there is an attractive **view** of Burgdorf and the Bernese Alps.

Church – This was built at the end of the 15C and has been much restored. There is star-vaulting in the chancel. A fine 16C rood-screen serves as an organ-loft.

EXCURSIONS

★ **Lueg Belvedere** – Alt 887m – 2 910ft. *8.5km – 5 1/2 miles – about 1/2 hour. Leave Burgdorf by the road to Wynigen.*

On leaving the town you will cross two ferro-concrete bridges over the Emme. After 1.5 km – 1 mile take a narrow, winding road to the right which passes through Gutisberg; after leaving a by-road to Wynigen on your left, park the car. You reach the top of the bluff along a very steep path among fir trees. A monument to the Bernese cavalry (1914-18) has been erected on the open space; from here the semicircular **panorama**★ includes, in the foreground, a landscape of fields and fir trees, and the Jura and the Bernese Alps on the horizon.

Sumiswald – *16km – 10 miles to the east. Leave Burgdorf by road no 23 to the south and bear left at Ramsei.*

This pretty Bernese village has fine wooden houses characteristic of the region: a large façade carries one or two tiers of windows close together; the overhanging roof is immense; the gable is often painted and decorated with designs in bright colours. The **Kramerhaus** and the **Zum Kreuz Inn** (at the Sign of the Cross) are quite remarkable.

★ CELERINA Graubünden (Grisons)   Pop 975

Michelin map ⚿ fold 15 or ⚿ fold 17 – 3 1/2 miles northeast of St Moritz – Local map see GRISONS – Facilities

Celerina (Schlarigna in Romansh) lies at the foot of the larch-clad ridge that separates the Samedan Basin from the upper levels of the High Engadine lakes. It is rather like an annexe of St Moritz, especially in the field of sports equipment. In the Cresta quarter, where the great hotels of the resort are found, the famous bobsleigh and "skeleton" runs end. Nearer the banks of the Inn, old Celerina shows an attractive group of typical **Engadine houses** *(illustration see Engadine)*.

The excursions from St Moritz can also be done from Celerina.

St John's (San Gian) – Standing alone on a bluff to the east of Celerina, the uncrowned tower of the Romanesque church is a familiar landmark in the Inn Valley. The painted ceiling and remains of frescoes date from *c* 1478.

★★★ CHASSERAL Berne

Michelin map 216 fold 13 or 427 folds 3 and 12 – 12km – 7 miles southeast of St Imier – Local map see Swiss JURA

Chasseral (alt 1 607m – 5 272ft) is the highest point of the northern Jura and commands a justly famous panorama of the Swiss alps. Hardy motorists can cross the Swiss Jura by the route shown below.
A chairlift from Nods enables one to reach the summit quickly.

FROM ST-IMIER TO LA NEUVEVILLE

33km – 21 miles – about 1 1/2 hours – Itinerary 7 on the Swiss Jura local map

☉ *The road is narrow and is generally blocked by snow between December and mid-May (April on the south side).*

St-Imier – This bustling watch- and clock-making centre is located on the south face of Mount Soleil.
St-Imier's past is recalled by the Tower of St Martin (or Queen Bertha), the bell tower, all that remains of an 11C church (destroyed in 1828) and its 12C collegiate **church** ☉ (now a Reformed church). The church's interior presents a narthex with archaic capitals (heads on the right), an apse with oven vaulting and a chancel with ogive vaulting and mural paintings (Evangelists, Christ in Majesty in an almond-shaped glory).

> *Leave St-Imier by the Neuchâtel road. 1km – 1/2 mile beyond Les Pontins, turn left into the Chasseral road.*

This road, after following the line of a typically Jurassic fold *(see diagram in the Introduction)*, comes out on the upper ridge.

> *On reaching this upper ridge, turn left towards the Hôtel du Chasseral where you will leave the car.*

★★★ **Panorama** – The Hôtel du Chasseral, situated just below the route's highest point, marks the end of the public thoroughfare. The nearby viewing table permits the visitor to take his bearings on the main peaks of the Bernese and Valais Alps and the Mont Blanc Massif. This wonderful back-cloth extends for some 250km – 156 miles.
The motorist with a little time to spare may walk to the Chasseral beacon *(1 hour Rtn by a wide, gently sloping path)* near a Swiss postal service's telecommunications relay station.
From the beacon you get a **circular view★★★** of the horizon, extending from the Swiss Alps to the northern Jura, the Vosges and the Black Forest.

> *Return to the car and make for the fork, where you turn left towards Nods, Lignières and La Neuveville.*

Before reaching La Neuveville there are good views of the Biel and Neuchâtel Lakes to be seen from the road's hairpin bends.

La Neuveville – *See La Neuveville.*

★ CHÂTEAU-D'OEX Vaud   Pop 3 110

Michelin map 217 fold 15 or 427 fold 12 – Local map see VAUD ALPS – Alt 1 000m – 3 281ft – Facilities

Château-d'Oex (pronounced Château Day) is the capital of the Enhaut District, a section of the Sarine Valley between the Tine Defile and the Bernese border. It is a little pre-Alpine mountain centre which has long lived apart, spreading its chalets and hotels at the foot of the last wooded slopes of the Gummfluh and the Vanils. This is a typical Vaud Alps family resort, highly popular on account of the many water sports facilities it offers.

Musée du Vieux Pays d'Enhaut, Château-d'Oex

Paper cutting by SAUGY "Trek to the Alpine pastures"

For more information on the principal festivals which occur in Switzerland throughout the year see the Calendar of Events.

★ **Enhaut Traditional Museum (Musée du Vieux Pays d'Enhaut)** ⊘ – Located in a three-storey building, the museum illustrates the rich historical past (12-19C) of the region. Archives, arms, craftsmen's tools and carved and painted furniture are exhibited, as well as reconstructed interiors and bedrooms (third floor) of mountain people's and weavers' homes. Stained-glass windows, 19C paper cuttings (second floor) and black bobbin pillow lace (third floor) are also worth noting. Reconstructed in two separate pavilions are a chalet which housed herders up in the mountain pastures; note the cheese room where the gigantic copper cauldron (800 litres – 176 gallons) rightly holds the place of honour; and the carpenter's work room.

Also part of the museum but located at the end of the town is the **Etambeau chalet** (18C), which houses artefacts of regional architecture. The barn presents an exhibition on alpine transport.

Swiss clock and watchmaking

Visit all or one of the following museums to admire the craftsmanship and development of this industry
La Chaux-de-Fonds: International Museum of Horology
Le Locle: Museum of Horlogy
Geneva: Horology and Enamels Museum.

LA CHAUX-DE-FONDS Neuchâtel   Pop 36 894

Michelin map **216** fold 12 or **427** fold 12 – Local map see Swiss JURA – Alt 992m – 3 254ft – Town Plan and plan of the conurbation in the current Michelin Red Guide Switzerland

La Chaux-de-Fonds is the biggest watch- and clock making centre in Switzerland as well as being one of the largest agricultural centres.

It is the capital of the Neuchâtel Mountains, and lies in an upper valley of the Jura. The town was almost entirely destroyed by fire in 1794 and afterwards rebuilt to a geometric plan.

The cradle of the clock-making industry since the early 18C, this city also plays an important part in the production of microtechnology, electronics and mechanics, as well as the tertiary sector.

La Chaux-de-Fonds has another claim to fame in that it prints postage stamps for the Confederation as well as many foreign countries.

Local celebrities – La Chaux-de-Fonds is the native town of the automaton maker Pierre Jaquet-Droz (1721-1790), the painter Léopold Robert (1794-1835), the automobile designer Louis Chevrolet (1870-1941) and the writer Frédéric Sauser, better known as **Blaise Cendrars** (1887-1961), who with Guillaume Apollinaire heralded the age of Surrealism. His life, like his literary work, was governed by his overriding passion for travel, both across land and in his mind.

Le Corbusier – The 6 October 1887 saw the birth of Charles Edouard Jeanneret. After studying painting and architecture at the local art school, he embarked upon a European tour which enabled him to meet many eminent architects. In 1918 he gained recognition as a painter when he published the Purist manifesto with Amédée Ozenfant. "After Cubism" advocated formal simplicity, economy of means and mathematical precision without however denying a role to poetry and the emotions. The same principles were to guide his work as an architect. In 1920 he changed his name and became known as Le Corbusier. The same year, together with Ozenfant and the poet Paul Dermé, he founded the literary magazine *L'Art Nouveau,* which remained in circulation until 1925. Le Corbusier was an inventive man who believed in structuring man's habitat along vertical lines. He invented the "living machine", which illustrated his views on the relationship between society and technology. His accomplishments in the field of community housing are revolutionary by their conception: he establishes an artful balance between the different elements, combining a variety of building materials and using light to enhance the cement blocks and exploit their full potential. His work is by no means limited to Europe and many examples of his creative genius can be seen in the URSS, Brazil, Japan and India. Strongly criticised or highly praised, Le Corbusier remains one of the undisputed masters of 20C architecture and his impact on modern urbanism has been considerable.

A "Le Corbusier route", illustrating his achievements in the area, can be obtained from the tourist information centre.

THE CRADLE OF THE CLOCK-MAKING INDUSTRY

From Geneva to the Jura – It was in the 16C that this craft, which had already existed for over a century, was given a new impetus.

The reformer Calvin, who held sway in Geneva, where he lived, compelled the goldsmiths to turn their attention to the making of watches, forbidding them to make "crosses, chalices and other instruments used for popery and idolatry".

A little later the development of this budding industry was spurred by the arrival in Geneva, about 1587, of French Huguenots driven from their country. Clock-making soon spread from Geneva to the Neuchâtel Jura.

Daniel Jean-Richard and the horse-dealer – In 1679 a horse-dealer coming home to the Neuchâtel mountains brought back from London a watch which was admired by everyone until, one day, it stopped. The people of Sagne, a village near

LA CHAUX-DE-FONDS

(map of La Chaux-de-Fonds showing streets, Musée International d'Horlogerie, Musée des Beaux-Arts, Musée d'Histoire Naturelle, Place Neuve, Square de l'Ouest, etc.)

BELFORT

BIEL BÄLE

BESANÇON

LE LOCLE

NEUCHÂTEL, LA SAGNE

La Chaux-de-Fonds, advised the horse-dealer to have his watch examined by a young man called Daniel Jean-Richard, who was said to be highly skilled. The apprentice managed to repair the watch, studied its mechanism and decided to make watches himself. This he did, using tools of his own design and settling at Le Locle, where he trained many workers. The watch industry subsequently spread throughout the Jura.

A world famous industry – Most of the watch-making industry today is concentrated in French-speaking Switzerland, and especially in the Jura.
The greater number of entreprises are located in La Chaux-de-Fonds, Le Locle, Biel, Neuchâtel, Solothurn and Granges. They employ about 32 000 black-coated and manual workers. The workshops have highly developed technical equipment which enables them to produce a large quantity of high-quality watches. But the search for perfection has always been very important to the Swiss watchmakers. At present the precision-tolerance for their working parts is of the order of 1/400th of a millimetre – 1/10 000th of an inch. In certain workshops the daily production of 1 000 workers could be carried away in a jacket pocket. Precision has improved – thanks to the introduction of computers.
In 1992 the 145 million watches and movements produced corresponded to 58% in value of world production.

Collection Musée International d'horlogerie

This sector, together with those of chemical products and machinery, is one of the country's largest export industries. Thus watch- and clock-making plays a major role in the economy of the Confederation, and in spite of competition from Japan and Southeast Asia, it remains an essential factor in the stability of Switzerland's balance of trade.

★★ INTERNATIONAL MUSEUM OF HOROLOGY ⊘ 1 hour

Founded in 1902, this fascinating museum has been housed since 1974 in underground rooms with the entrance on the north side of the park.
The museum illustrates the ways of measuring time chronologically from Antiquity to the present with more than 3 000 items from the world over. The theme is Man and Time.
The museum also has a centre for the restoration of antique clocks and watches and an interdisciplinary study centre about Time.
Via a footbridge crossing over striking clock mechanisms you reach the main gallery: ancient instruments for measuring time, Renaissance, 17 (exquisite enamel watches) and 18C instruments are shown. Marine chronometers, watches from the region of Neuchâtel and other countries, as well as unusual astronomical instruments, musical clocks and amusing 19C automata are also displayed.

Before leaving this gallery look to the left into the glassed-in workshop where craftsmen restore antique watches and clocks.

Continue on to the centre of scientific clocks and watches (astronomical, atomic and quartz-crystal clocks).

Go on up to the belfry from where there is a pleasant view of the museum's park; proceed into an elevated gallery which introduces modern clock-making techniques. Outside is the imposing **carillon**, a 15-ton tubular steel structure made by the sculptor Onelio Vignando and raised in 1980. Every quarter hour it chimes (the tune varies according to the season) and at night it also offers a captivating light show.

Collection Musée International d'horlogerie

ADDITIONAL SIGHTS

★ **Fine Arts Museum** ⊘ – Recently redesigned and enlarged with a new, well-lit modern annexe designed for hosting temporary displays, this museum presents a number of standing exhibitions which provide an interesting insight into the work of Swiss painters, many of which were born in La Chaux-de-Fonds. On the ground floor – note the impressive entrance hall with its mosaic tiling and sweeping staircase ornamented with carved balusters – several rooms are devoted to artists such as Charles l'Eplattenier (landscapes: *Springtime, The Doubs River*), Lucien Schwob *(Rue du Pont, Self-Portrait)*, François Barraud (portraits: *Marie and Louise, Self-Portrait).* On the first floor one room pays tribute to Léopold Robert (1794-1835), a native of La Chaux-de-Fonds. A Romantic painter who studied under Girodet and David, Robert paid frequent visits to Italy, a country from which he often drew inspiration: *Bandit with Gun, Wounded Bandit, Dancing on Capri Island.* The large canvases of Edouard Kaiser (1855-1931) illustrate a variety of professions with startling realism: *The Barons (gold casters), Engraver's Workshop, Box Maker's Workshop.* Other major figures like Hodler *(Marignan Warrior)*, Vallotton *(Sunset)* and Le Corbusier *(Woman with Bathrobe)* complete this panorama of Swiss painting.

The museum also prides itself on possessing the sumptuous **René and Madeleine Junod Collection**, featuring works from the turn of the century, or painted prior to 1950: *Les Colettes* by Renoir, *L'Estaque* by Derain, *Young Girls in a Garden* by Matisse, *View of Cagnes* by Soutine. An exhibition devoted to modern art, consisting of tapestries, sculptures and paintings executed after 1950, illustrates different contemporary schools in Europe: Manessier *(The Passion of Our Lord Jesus Christ)*, Afro *(Childhood Memories)*, Winter *(Red Spots)*, Jacobsen *(Mobile Sculpture)*, etc.

Museum of Natural History ⊘ – *On the 2nd floor (lift) of the main post office.* This collection of stuffed animals is certainly worth a visit. Various Swiss and exotic species (of African origin, particularly Angola) of mammals, birds and reptiles are exhibited. A series of dioramas present specimens in their natural setting. A room devoted to marine fauna displays several hundred types of seashells.

History and Medal Museum ⊘ – This local history museum is housed in a former mansion used for the meetings of the town council. 17 to 19C Neuchâtel interiors are on show on the first floor: bedrooms with sculpted ceilings, kitchens complete with cooking utensils, etc. The medal room presents collections of local and foreign coins, along with medals bearing the effigy of famous personalities from Switzerland (Calvin, General Dufour, Le Corbusier) and abroad (Abraham Lincoln, Louis XVI, Queen Victoria).

Zoological Garden (Bois du Petit Château) ⊘ – *Enter by rue du docteur Coullery.* Take a stroll around this pleasantly shaded park, where the different species (namely deer, stags, wolves, palmipeds) are separated by enclosures.

Peasant Museum ⊘ – *In the southwest suburb of Éplatures "Grise", 5 Rue Chevrolet.*
The museum is located in an old Jura farmhouse (1612). Although restored, the farmhouse has preserved some Gothic elements (mullioned windows on the ground floor) of the original building (1507). It is an imposing shingled structure with its wide course, triangular gable and discreet carved decoration. The interior has a pine framework with a large central fireplace. The life of the 17C well-to-do farmer is relived. There is a clockmaker's workshop, a cheese-room and a still, as well as furniture, utensils, tools, and porcelain stoves. Local lacemakers can be seen at work on the first Sunday of every month.
The life of peasants is illustrated by temporary exhibitions held every year.

EXCURSIONS

Le Locle – *8km – 5 miles to the southwest. See Le Locle.*

La Sagne – *10km – 6 miles south and after 4km – 2 1/2 miles by a road on the right which runs along the railway line.*
Fine 16-18C Jurassian farms are dotted along the road. Daniel Jean-Richard was born in this village in the 17C.
The church is favoured by its site on the flank of the ridge. Built in the 15 and 16C, it was restored partially in 1891 and then more thoroughly in 1952 and 1983. The nave has ogive vaulting.
The modern windows are glazed in plain glass, in pale shades of green, yellow, grey and violet.

★★VUE DES ALPES ROAD

From La Chaux-de-Fonds to Neuchâtel

22km – 14 miles – about 3/4 hour – Itinerary ⑧ *on the Swiss Jura local map*

Motorists coming from France will do well to approach La Chaux-de-Fonds through Morteau and Le Locle. The choice of this route will enable them to admire, as they cross the frontier, the Doubs Falls (qv).

On leaving La Chaux-de-Fonds, when going up to the Vue des Alpes, there will be attractive glimpses of the Les Ponts Valley (on the north side of the pass), the flat pale green floor of which cuts into the wooded slopes around it.

★**Vue des Alpes** – Alt 1 283m – 4 209ft. The viewing table will enable the visitor to fit names to the peaks in this tremendous **panorama**★: Finsteraarhorn, Jungfrau, Weisshorn, Dent Blanche, Mont Blanc, etc. The best light is that of a fine late afternoon.

★★**Tête de Ran** – Alt 1 422m – 4 655ft. *From the Vue des Alpes, 2.5km – 2 miles to the Tête de Ran Hotel, plus 1/2 hour on foot Rtn to reach the summit, climbing straight up the steep ridge overlooking this hotel on the right.* Lovers of panoramic views may prefer this belvedere *(steep stony path)* to that of the Vue des Alpes: the Tête de Ran is better placed for a wide view of the Jura ridges in the foreground (Val de Ruz, Chasseral and Chaumont Chains), even though fir trees hide the view to the northwest; most of Lake Neuchâtel can be seen.

On the way down through the fir trees of the southern slope, there are interesting views of the **Ruz Valley** depression. This immense "ship's hold" has not failed to strike geographers with the regularity of its features: *ruz* has, therefore, become a scientific term to describe the first stages of erosion on the side of a mountain *(diagram in the Introduction).*

Valangin – This picturesque little town nestles at the foot of an attractive 12 and 15C castle protected by an imposing curtain wall with towers (levelled). The 16C Gothic collegiate church (inside, interesting tombs and funerary plaques), the town gate with a clock tower and 16 and 17C houses make a nice, old-fashioned picture.

Between Valangin and Neuchâtel the road follows the wooded Seyon Gorges.

★★**Neuchâtel** – *Time: 2 1/2 hours. See Neuchâtel.*

★★ CHILLON CASTLE Vaud

Michelin map **217** fold 14 between Territet and Villeneuve or **427** fold 12 – Local maps see Lake GENEVA and MONTREUX

Chillon Castle is built on a rocky islet, its towers reflected in the waters of Lake Geneva. The picturesque **site**★★ lies at the centre of the lake, within sight of Montreux, the French shore and the Alps – the Dents du Midi are clearly visible. The first fortress was built in the 9C to guard the road from Avenches to Italy, which crossed the Great St Bernard after skirting Lake Geneva.

The castle became the property of the Bishops of Sion, who extended it, and then of the Counts of Savoy from 1150. It took on the appearance we know today in the middle of the 13C.

"The Prisoner of Chillon" – The castle and its dungeons have been used as a state prison more than once, but **François de Bonivard** remains the most famous prisoner.

Chillon Castle

Bonivard tried to introduce the Reformation when prior of St Victor at Geneva. His theses displeased the Duke of Savoy, who had designs on the town and was an ardent champion of Catholicism. Bonivard was arrested and cast into the castle dungeons which ever since have borne his name. He lived chained to one of the pillars – the pillar is shown to visitors, and it is said that the prisoner's footprints can be traced in the rock – for four years until he was freed by the Bernese in 1536. When he visited Chillon in 1816 on a pilgrimage to Clarens, which was the setting of Rousseau's *Nouvelle Héloïse,* **Byron** commemorated the captivity of De Bonivard in a poem, *The Prisoner of Chillon,* which helped to make the castle the most popular monument in Switzerland.

TOUR ⏱ *about 1 hour*

The moat is crossed on an 18C bridge which replaced the drawbridge. The dungeons, which were used as magazines for the Bernese fleet in the 17 and 18C, have fine ogive vaults and are hewn from the rock. Byron cut his name on the third pillar in De Bonivard's cell in 1816.

The Great Hall of the bailiffs, which bears the coat of arms of Savoy, is enhanced by a magnificent ceiling and an imposing 15C fireplace. Other interesting ornamental features are the oak columns, the fine set of furniture and the large collection of pewter. The former Banqueting Hall or "Aula Nova", decorated with timber roofing in the shape of an inverted ship's hull, houses the museum; the collections comprise pewter, armour, furniture and weapons (a musket inlaid with bone and mother-of-pearl). The "Camera Paramenti" served as a guest room when the Dukes of Savoy ruled over the town. The vast Knights' Hall, also called the Coat of Arms Room, has walls hung with the heraldic insignia belonging to the Berne bailiffs of Vevey; note the wooden throne and the dresser containing pewter pots. It leads to the Duke's Bedroom or "Camera Domini". After walking through the court of honour, you may visit a series of rooms: the chapel (painted murals), the Justice Hall or Large Room of the Count, formerly used for parties and formal receptions (note the black marble columns), the Clerks' Hall and the Lapidary Museum, displaying stones found in the moat and maquettes showing the successive stages of construction of the castle. The top of the keep (difficult access by a narrow staircase) commands lovely **views**★★ of Montreux, Lake Geneva and the Alps. The visit ends with a section of the wall-walk and two fortified towers, converted into a prison during the 17C.

For historical information on the country
consult the table and notes in the Introduction.

CHUR (COIRE) Ⓒ Graubünden (Grisons)   Pop 32 868

Michelin map **218** fold 4 or **427** fold 16 – Local map see GRISONS – Alt 585m - 1 919ft – Facilities

Chur lies in the Rhine Valley at the meeting-point of Latin and German influences and has been since the 16C the historical, administrative and religious capital of the Grisons. It is built a short distance from the Rhine on a mound of rocky debris formed by a tributary of the Plessur.

★**General View** – To the east of Chur, the first hairpin bend on the road to Arosa (Arosastrasse) makes a good observation point from which to see the town as a whole with its many belfries, and its background of steep rocky ridges, covered with eternal snow – the Calanda.

SIGHTS

Old Town – The old town (reached by climbing a stairway and passing under an old gate – Hoftor) is grouped around St Martin's which stands below the cathedral and the bishop's palace – Chur remains a cathedral city. Strolling through the town, the tourist will find narrow streets of fine houses, sometimes flanked by towers, pretty squares with fountains adorned with flowers and the arms of the Grisons canton, and finally the 15C town hall (Rathaus), all of which make for an unusual and picturesque scene.

★ **Cathedral of Our Lady** (Kathedrale) – The cathedral was built in a mixed Romanesque and Gothic style in the 12 and 13C. The exterior was remodelled after a fire in 1811. The tower is crowned with a domed belfry. The porch is adorned with painted recessed arches.

The building has an irregular plan and the axis of the nave is out of line with that of the chancel. The nave, which is roofed with ribbed vaulting, is very dark, lit as it is only by the clerestory windows on the south side.

The chancel is considerably raised and contains a very fine 15C **triptych**★ in carved and gilded wood at the high altar; it is dedicated to Our Lady and is the largest Gothic triptych in Switzerland.

Four statues depicting the Apostles and dating back to the 13C are arranged on either side of the altar.

Treasury ⊙ – It includes reliquaries of the Carolingian period and the Middle Ages and reliquary-busts of great value.

The **Bishop's Palace** (Hof) is an elegant 18C edifice.

Rhaetic Museum (Rätisches Museum) ⊙ – This museum is housed in the late 17C Buol mansion. It contains interesting displays of folklore relating to the canton, a prehistory collection and historical specimens.

Fine Arts Museum (Kunstmuseum) ⊙ – Most of the works displayed are by 18 to 20C artists and sculptors from the Grisons by birth or adoption: Barthelemy Menn, Angelica Kauffmann, Giovanni Segantini – and contemporaries, including Giovanni, Augusto and Alberto Giacometti and E.-L. Kirchner.

★ **LENZERHEIDE ROAD — SCHYN GORGES**
Round tour starting from Chur

73 km – 45 miles – about 3 hours – Itinerary ⑤ *on the Grisons local map*

After leaving Chur from the south, the uphill road, which becomes very steep, soon gives a general view of the town and the little Calenda Chain in the background. Higher up, on emerging from the first wooded section, the slope becomes gentler and you can look down on the opening of the **Schanfigg** (Plessur Valley, flowing down from Arosa – *p 42*) and the buildings of the spa at Passugg, which has given its name to one of the most popular Swiss table waters, renowned for its highly beneficial properties.

Then, as you ascend the Rabiusa Valley, you will see the ruins of Strassberg Tower standing out below the village of Malix.

The small resorts of **Churwalden** – preceded by a lonely church on the edge of the forest – and **Parpan**, mark the end of this route, which leads through open country to the Lenzerheide shelf forming the watershed and language boundary between German and Romansh.

★ **Lenzerheide-Valbella** – Facilities. The two resorts of Lenzerheide and Valbella are located in Lenzerheide Valley. The resorts' modern buildings are set in a hollow (at an altitude of 1500m - 4900ft; the hollow forms the top of the first ridge crossed by the road from Chur) enhanced by two lakes. Its popularity is due to the charming **parklike country**★, which the motorist will appreciate between Valbella and Lenzerheide-centre.

In winter the even slopes encourage downhill skiing, especially on the Piz Scalottas and the Stätzerhorn – both equipped with a long chain of chairlifts reaching up to 2861m - 9382ft at the Parpaner Rothorn.

★★ **Parpaner Rothorn** ⊙ – *Access by cable-car in 1/4 hour from Lenzerheide-Valbella.* The climb above the fir trees as far as Scharmoin (alt 1900m - 6234ft) gives way to barren slopes before reaching the rocky peak of Parpaner Rothorn (alt 2861m - 9382ft).

The superb **view**★★, which to the west reveals the Valbella hollow, its resort and clear lake, is blocked to the east by the snowy summits of the Weisshorn, Tschirpen and Aroser Rothorn.

For a wider, more open view, walk *(1/4 hour Rtn)* to a nearby mountain top such as the Ostgipfel (alt 2899m - 9511ft).

From Lenzerheide to Lenz, approaching the Chapel of San-Cassian, the view opens out towards the depression of the Oberhalbstein, its entrance narrowed between the wooded foothills of the Piz Mitgel and the more pasture-like slopes of the Piz Curvèr. The first Romansh houses, giving a foretaste of the Engadine style *(qv)* will be seen at **Lenz**.

Brienz – The church is worth visiting for the sake of its **altarpiece**★ (1519) with Flamboyant decorations, representing the Virgin surrounded by saints. Notice St Luzius, the evangelist of Rhaetia, who is depicted with the insignia of royalty.

From Lenz to Tiefencastel the road descends into the Albula Valley, which until the very end seems uninhabited; higher up, however, the perched villages of Mon and Stierva are a welcoming site on the ledges overlooked by the Piz Curvèr.

The fine mountain group of the Piz Mitgel stands out clearly. After two hairpin bends, the white church of Tiefencastel, a favourite subject for amateur photographers, appears.

Farther on, more or less in line with the road, the belfry of **Mistail** marks one of the oldest churches in the Grisons (Carolingian period).

Tiefencastel – *See St. Moritz: Julier and Albula Pass Roads.*

From Tiefencastel to the Solis Bridges, the Albula Valley narrows and the Piz Mitgel mountain group can be seen. The Albula then plunges into the Schyn Gorges.

★**Solis Bridges** – An impressive group of structures. From the road bridge you can appreciate the boldness of the railway viaduct, whose central span of 42m, rises 89m - 137ft and 292ft - above the bed of the Albula River.

Schyn Gorges – The vegetation clinging to the rocky walls of this formidable fissure makes it difficult to realize its depth. The most impressive section is the crossing of the lateral Mutten Ravine *(Tobel)*.

Thusis – *See San Bernardino Pass Road.*

The road from Thusis to Chur is described under San Bernardino Pass Road.

COLOMBIER Neuchâtel   Pop 4636

Michelin map ▨▨ fold 12 or ▨▨▨ fold 12 – 7km - 4 miles west of Neuchâtel

This village, not far from Lake Neuchâtel and known for its white wines, is dominated by the imposing mass of its castle, built in the 15C in Late Gothic style and enlarged during the next two centuries.
In 1762 the philosopher Jean-Jacques Rousseau stayed at the castle, which remained the property of the Counts of Neuchâtel for many years. The building is today a barracks and military museum.

Museum ⊙ – On the first two floors the vast common rooms, reserved for officers only, have timber ceilings and monumental chimneypieces; patriotic frescoes animate the walls of the Knights Hall on the first floor (mobilization of Swiss army in 1914) and on the second floor in the room directly above (important historical events of medieval Switzerland).
Also displayed are hundreds of arms (14-20C) – either cutting and thrusting weapons or firearms; as well as armour, flags and regimental memorabilia (portraits, uniforms...). A large gallery on the third floor exhibits cannon. At the end of the tour the guide will show you a small room on the second floor containing textiles, made in the area in the 18 and 19C, painted with an Indian pattern.

Cailler, Suchard, Kohler, Nestlé, Lindt, Tobler...

Attractive presentations, mouth-watering contents characterise the high-quality confectionery of the Swiss chocolate-makers.
During the 19C and early 20C Swiss chocolate-makers acquired an international reputation for their delectable products.
Like a good wine, one should savour the aroma and taste. Dark, white or milk, chocolate comes in many forms - cake, mini-slabs, sweets and a variety of shapes - and is often combined with various other ingredients (nuts, raisins, ginger).

★★ CONCHES VALLEY

Michelin map ▨▨ folds 18 and 19 or ▨▨▨ fold 14

The road, as it climbs up the Upper Rhône Valley, enters mountainous terrain; it serves the numerous resorts and ski lifts hanging on the side of the Aletschhorn Massif. Conches Valley (or **Goms** in German) begins at Fiesch.

FROM BRIG TO GLETSCH

54km – 32 miles – about 2 hours – Itinerary ④ *on the Valais local map*
The road which follows the Furka-Oberalp railway at a distance may be blocked by heavy snow between Brig and Oberwald for short periods.

The Upper Rhône Valley comprises four levels which cause the river to drop by 1 000m – 3 000ft.

Brig – *Time: 3/4 hour. See Brig.*

From Brig to the Grengiols fork, the road runs close to the foaming Rhône at the bottom of a narrow, winding cleft. It passes by the large, isolated baroque Hohen Flühen Chapel and serves the lower stations of the Riederalp-Greicheralp cable-car (starting from Mörel) and that of **Bettmeralp** (facilities; starting from Betten station). These lines serve a high Alpine plateau (alt 2 000m – 6 500ft), wonderfully situated within view of the Valais Alps and close to the Aletsch Glacier, the most extensive in the Alps (169km² – 65sq miles with its tributaries).

★**Riederalp,** ★★**Moosfluh** ⊙ – *Access to Riederalp by cable-car from Mörel; access to Moosfluh by chairlift from Riederalp.* Located in a **site**★ overlooking the Rhône Valley, on a shelf on the valley's north side, **Riederalp's**★ (facilities) chalets and hotels are terraced beginning at 1 930m – 6 332ft and face the mountain range separating Switzerland from Italy. Above its westernmost point is the Villa Cassel, the centre of the Aletschwald nature reserve.
From the cable-car's arrival station, walk (a few minutes) to the chairlift's departure station to go to Moosfluh.
The ride up the chairlift passes by the mid-station of Blausee, located between two small lakes, before arriving at the upper station of **Moosfluh**★★ (alt 2 335m – 7 661ft). The latter is set amidst a jumble of green rocks and dominates the spectacular curving form of the **Aletsch Glacier**★★★, lying immediately to the north at the foot of the slopes and tributary glaciers of the Aletschhorn Massif, as well as the Rhône Valley to the south.

The valley's second level or 'step' stretches from Lax to Fiesch and is marked by the appearance – confirming a gain in height – of Arolla pines *(qv)* and small barns on piles *(raccards – illustration p 207)*. This section marks the start of the upper Rhône Valley, known as the Conches Valleys (Goms).

Below, in a gorge section, the Rhône is joined by the tributary River Binna. Further up the valley, when Fiesch comes into view, it is possible to look up the valley Fieschertal, on the left, and see in the far distance the snowy peak of the Finsteraar-Rothorn.

★★★ **Eggishorn** ⊘ – Alt 2 927m – 9 603ft. *Access by cable-car from Fiesch.*
The first stage takes you up over a spruce forest and a scree of greenish-coloured, jagged rocks. From the upper station (alt 2 869m – 9 423ft) there is a superb **panorama★★★** of the Aletsch Glacier below in the immediate foreground, of the Fiesch Glacier and a nearby cascade further round to the right and of all the other neighbouring mountain peaks.
For an even wider view, climb to the top of one of the three mounds of scree which are quite close to the station. The Eggishorn summit is marked by a cross *(difficult clamber)*.
After the next change in level beyond Fiesch, the view extends back downstream to the snow-covered slopes of the Weisshorn (alt 4 505m – 14 780ft).
After a few hairpin bends notice the village of **Mühlebach,** the birthplace of Cardinal Schiner *(p 209)*, on the opposite slope.

★ **Bellwald** – Facilities. *Access by a winding road 8km – 5 miles or by cable-car from Fürgangen.*
A small summer and winter resort, Bellwald (alt 1 600m – 5 249ft), with its old larch wood chalets and hotels set on a curved terrace, is orientated southwest. It presents a wide aerial **view★** of Conches Valley – from Fiesch to Brig – across the way of Eggishorn (identified by its cross), above and to the right of the Wannenhorn Massif ⊘ and its glaciers and left onto the Alps of the Italian frontier.
The **Richinen and Steibenkreuz chairlift** offers a pleasant excursion above the grass-land with a close-up view of the Wannenhorn Glaciers; to the south, the majestic Matterhorn can be glimpsed in the distance. The valley opens out again beautifully.
The third level is the longest in the Conches Valley. The Alpine coomb now offers a bare, open landscape which the total lack of enclosures, single trees or scattered chalets makes very striking. The villages with their blackish wooden houses adorned with geraniums are grouped around slim white church towers.
Upstream, to the right of the Galenstock Summit, you will espy the Furka Gap although the pass itself is out of sight.

Reckingen – The baroque church of Reckingen is the most agreeably pro-portioned in the Conches Valley. It was built in the 18C to the plans of the parish priest, Jean-Georges Ritz, one of a family of artisans who made sculptured altars for many churches in the district. The name of this family has become world-famous since one of its members, César Ritz (born at Niederwald 1850, died 1918), achieved eminence as a hotel-keeper.
The Seilers, who made Zermatt prosperous and built the two hotels near the Rhône Glacier (at Gletsch and at the Belvédère) were also natives of the Conches Valley.

Münster – Facilities. This large village stands at the foot of the cone of debris covered with fan-shaped patches of tillage. The church with its conical-shaped spire is worth visiting for its Flamboyant **altarpiece★** dedicated to the Virgin, the work of an artist of Lucerne (1509).

Beyond Ulrichen the valley becomes wilder; the houses of Obergesteln, rebuilt in stone after a fire in the last century, have a stark appearance at first.
The Muttenhörner still seems to block the valley completely.
Above Oberwald, the last village in the Conches Valley, looking down on the village's little church with its stone avalanche screen, the road, now quite mountainous, slips into a defile which gets ever more bare as the Rhône leaps from fall to fall, and emerges on the fourth level into the Gletsch Basin, in sight of the Rhône Glacier, the source of the great river.

★★ **Gletsch** – Alt 1 759m - 5 771ft. At the junction of roads from the Furka Pass, the Grimsel Pass and the Conches Valley (Upper Valais) lies Gletsch, on the floor of a desolate basin once covered by the tongue of the Rhône Glacier. Higher up, on the road to the Furka Pass (qv), the setting of the bend in which the Belvedere Hotel stands, draws many sightseers. This well-known halt offers not only the attraction of the **Rhône Glacier★★** in which has been cut an **ice grotto★** ⊘ the walls of which reflect a bluish light, but also an immense **panorama★★** of the Bernese and Valais Alps.

Michelin map ⅗7 eastern edge of fold 11 (on the shore of Lake Geneva) or ⅘7 fold
11 – Local map see Lake GENEVA – Alt 380m – 1 246ft

This little town is crossed from end to end by a main street lined with arcaded
houses built, after the invasion by Bernese troops, in the 16C *(see Urban Scene,
p 29)*.

Château ⊙ – The château was rebuilt in a sober style in the 18C, and is
surrounded by a fine park. It belonged to Jacques Necker, a Geneva banker and a
Minister of Louis XVI. His daughter, Germaine de Staël, known as "Corinne" after
the heroine of one of her novels, lived in the château after she was considered
"undesirable" by the "ogre" Bonaparte.
There she presided over a sort of literary principality which was nicknamed "the
States General of Europe" and of which Benjamin Constant, Mme Récamier,
Schlegel and Sismondi were the principal members.
The **interior★** is elegantly furnished in the Louis XVI and Directoire styles. Worth
seeing are the library (formerly the reception room), Mme de Staël's bedroom,
Mme Récamier's room with its Chinese wallpaper, and on the first floor, drawing-
rooms adorned with Aubusson tapestries, two very expressive busts of Buffon by
Houdon and Pajou, interesting portraits by Duplessis, Gérard, Carmontelle, Girodet
and others.

Gradients in percentages

*On the continent gradients are usually represented as percentages. The following
figures will give the motorist some idea of slopes ahead*

10% 1:10   20% 1:5
14% 1:7   25% 1:4
18% 1:5.5   30% 1:3.3.

★★ CRANS-MONTANA Valais

Michelin map ⅗7 fold 16 or ⅘7 fold 13 – Local map see VALAIS – Alt 1 500m –
4 921ft – Town plan in the current Michelin Red Guide Switzerland – Facilities

MONTANA

The municipality of Montana lies on a level stretch of parkland dotted with small
lakes, facing the impressive backdrop of the Valais Alps in the far distance. To the
west it is extended by the recent resort of Crans-sur-Sierre, with which it forms the
Crans-Montana tourist complex. Seen from Montana, the Valais Alps give the
impression of rising from the near background whereas in fact the Rhône Valley
lies between them and the observer.
The splendid site of this terrace facing due south at an altitude of 1 500-1 700m –
4 900-5 600ft attracts a great many visitors both in summer and winter. It was here
that **Katherine Mansfield** stayed in 1921 and wrote some of her charming stories (*The
Garden Party, The Doll's House*, etc.).
During the winter season, skiers will enjoy the sunny slopes and the highly efficient
system of skilifts.

Approach – *From Sierre – 13km – 8 miles.*
The road leading out of Sierre follows a succession of hairpin bends, climbing
through vineyards and then pastures.
On reaching Montana, the passing motorist who wishes to return to the floor of the
Rhône Valley by a different road can find his way down along the by-road from
Crans to road no 9 – an interesting route which offers fine views of the Pennine Alps.

★★**Vermala** – Alt 1 670m – 5 479ft. *1.5km – 1 mile. Leave your car below the Café-
Restaurant du Cervin and go to the belvedere laid out on the right, at the edge of
a small escarpment.*
A bird's-eye view of the Rhône Valley with a sweeping panorama of the high
summits enclosing the Anniviers Valley (especially the Weisshorn and the
Zinalrothorn and, in the far distance, the Matterhorn).

★★**Plans Mayens** – Alt 1 622m – 5 322ft. *1.5km – 1 mile. You may stop at the edge of
the road, beside the terrace of the Restaurant du Mont-Blanc.* A wide panorama of
the Valais Alps is offered, extending to the Mont-Blanc Massif in the distance.

CRANS-SUR-SIERRE

The resort of Crans was founded in 1929 in the immediate neighbourhood of
Montana, facing the Valais Alps. It stands on a plateau open to the south and has
grown rapidly. Its famous Alpine golf courses (18 and 9 holes), modern hotels and
delightful, easy walks make it a much sought-after country resort.
In winter, skiers who love sunny slopes can make downhill runs amounting,
when snow is plentiful, to a drop of nearly 2 000m – 6 560ft. The long cable-way
linking Crans with the Wildstrubel foothills is the main item in its mechanical
equipment.

★★★**Bella Lui** ⊙– Alt 2 543m – 8 340ft. *Access by cable-car. Time for trip: 1 1/2 hours
Rtn.*
A great panorama of the Valais Alps. A magnificent ascent by cable-car over the
Rhône Valley. Halt at Croix (or Cry) d'Er (alt 2 258m – 7 408ft – T.C.S. viewing
table).

Michelin map **218** fold 5 or **427** fold 17 – Local map see GRISONS – Alt 1 560m –
5 120ft – Facilities

The resort of Davos, which owed its success first to its "cure" and then to its
winter sports, is today a lively little business centre. The name "Davos" is
commonly linked with "Parsenn", a synonym for the best-known skiing grounds.

The resort. – The town extends for nearly
4km – 2 1/2 miles without any clear distinction between Davos-Dorf and Davos-Platz,
on the floor of the mountain valley in
which the Landwasser flows before
plunging into the defile of the *Zügen*.
The torrents rush into this basin
from the southeast; the Flüela-
bach, the Dischmabach and the
Sertigbach, in particular, have
made gaps which bring
much sunshine to the re-
sort between mountains
which might screen it
on that side To the
northeast, beyond
Lake Davos,
equipped for
aquatic sports,

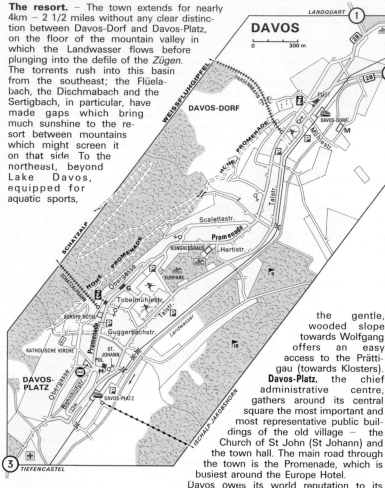

the gentle,
wooded slope
towards Wolfgang
offers an easy
access to the Prätti-
gau (towards Klosters).
Davos-Platz, the chief
administrative centre,
gathers around its central
square the most important and
most representative public buildings of the old village – the
Church of St John (St Johann) and
the town hall. The main road through
the town is the Promenade, which is
busiest around the Europe Hotel.

Davos owes its world reputation to its
skating rink which is the largest in Europe and, during the skiing season, to the
Parsenn funicular, which has opened up the most remarkable snowfields in
Switzerland to enthusiasts for winter sports. The terminus of the funicular is the
Weissfluhjoch (alt 2 693m – 8 747ft) and that of the cable-car, the Weissfluhgipfel
(alt 2 844m — 9 331ft). Both are departure points for more than thirty marked ski-
runs which are constantly patrolled by the Parsenn Service.
This whole scheme, which is completed by the cable-car running between
Parsennhütte and Weissfluhjoch and several ski-lifts, offers varied runs to
experienced skiers. Some of the ski-runs end 2 000m – 6 000ft below their starting
points (the Parsenn Derby course ends at Küblis in the Prättigau at an altitude of
813m – 2 667ft). In addition, the resort has the Strela slopes for beginners or
moderately skilled skiers. Finally, the opposite side of the valley, facing north, is
also well equipped and offers to skiers of varying skills new runs and excursions
(Pischahorn, Jakosbshorn, Rinerhorn).

SIGHTS

★★**Weissfluhgipfel** ⊙ – Alt 2 844m – 9 331ft. *About 2 1/2 hours Rtn including
35 minutes by funicular and cable-car.*
A magnificent panorama extends to the Bernese and Valais Alps.

★★**Schatzalp** ⊙ – Alt 1 863m – 6 112ft. *3/4 hour Rtn, including 5 minutes by funicular
(Schatzalpbahn) services starting simultaneously from Davos-Platz and the Schat-
zalp.* From around the Schatzalp Hotel there is a good view over the main Davos
Valley and the secondary valleys. Nearby *(10 minutes Rtn)* is a small **Alpine garden**
(alpinum). To continue the climb use the cable-cars from Schatzalp to the Strela
Pass at 2 350m – 7 710ft.

★**Hohe Promenade** – *1 hour on foot Rtn.* A perfectly planned road, level and
sometimes under trees, kept clear of snow in winter.
This walk can be reached from Davos-Dorf by the road behind the Seehof Hotel
(near the Parsenn funicular station) or from Davos-Platz by a steep path which
continues the lane to the Catholic church.

View of Davos

★★THE ZUGEN AND FLÜELA PASS ROADS
Round tour starting from Davos
135km – 84 miles – allow one day – Itinerary ① *on the Grisons local map*

Leave Davos by ③.

Frauenkirch – The small church has an avalanche fender. The nearby houses with larger wooden superstructures anticipate, for the tourist coming from the opposite direction, the German architecture of Prättigau.

★**Zügen Defile** – *You will pass alongside the defile on the way to Bärentritt (see below).* The clear, leaping waters of the Landwasser seethe impressively. The Zügen, neighbouring avalanche corridors, are often disastrous in winter.

★★**Bärentritt** – *2 hours on foot Rtn by the old road to the Zügen taking the exit east of the tunnel (on the Davos side). Park the car at Schmelzbaden.* From this point – a projecting parapet forms a belvedere – which marks the beginning of the Zügen Defile, there is an impressive downward view of the confluence 80m – 262ft below, of the Landwasser and of the torrent forming the Sägetobel Cascade on the right.

Coming out of the deep Tieftobel Ravine, you will see below you the **Wiesen Viaduct★** (210m long, central span 55m, 88m high – 60 × 180 × 288ft) one of the largest structures of the Rhaetic railways.

After Schmitten the view plunges to the left onto the Albula and the Landwasser, its affluent which we have been descending since our departure from Davos.

As far as Tiefencastel the larch woods follow a landscape of deep ravines *(Tobel);* the last of these level with Surava, serves as a backdrop for the ruins of the feudal **Belfort Castle,** a fortress perched on an escarpment.

Brienz – *See Brienz.*

Tiefencastel – *See St. Moritz: Albula Pass Road.*
From Tiefencastel to La Punt, the itinerary (Albula road) is described p 182 and from La Punt to Susch (Engadine) described p 87.

Susch – A village whose two towers (the church belfry and a tower with a bulbous steeple) stand out in front of the last wooded slopes of the Piz Arpiglias. Officially starting from Susch, the Flüela Pass road soon overlooks this village.

The first series of hairpin bends climbs quickly above the rugged Susasca Valley.

Beyond, on a 4km – 3 miles long *corniche* section, the **view★** opens out over the icy corrie enclosing the desolate coomb of the Grialetsch Valley completely covered with the greenish debris of landslides. On either side of a well-marked snowy gap you will recognize the Piz Grialetsch (on the right) and the Piz Vadret (on the left). Two hairpin bends bring the road to the entrance of the deserted Chantsura coomb, overlooked by the Schwarzhorn.

Beyond Chantsura, just after another pair of hairpin bends, a distant gap downstream calls for a halt.

The white, high-perched form of Tarasp Castle *(qv)* stands out clearly against the background of the Lower Engadine Dolomites. Nearer but less distinct the grey Steinsberg Tower guards the town of Ardez.

Flüela Pass – Alt 2383m – 7818ft. *Closed when threatened by avalanche.* Two lakes, a hospice and traces of landslides from the Schwarzhorn and the Weisshorn characterize the barren landscape of the Flüela Pass.

The descent to Davos follows a long, monotonous corridor. After the second bridge over the Flüela – notice here the first Arolla pines, outposts of the forest zone – the crests of the Weissfluh *(qv)* appear, well-known to the skiers of Davos. Beyond Tschuggen, the valley becomes more welcoming with flower-strewn fields, larch and fir woods all the way to Davos.

DELÉMONT C Jura

Michelin map **216** fold 14 or **427** fold 4 – Local map see Swiss JURA – Alt 436m
– 1 430ft

Until 1792 Delémont was the summer residence of the prince-bishops of Basle,
whose crosier appears in the arms of the town. Today it owes its importance to its
railway station and its watch and precision-instrument factories. It has been, since
1978, the capital of the new canton of Jura.

Old Town – The old or "high" town, on either side of Rue du 23-Juin, has kept its
monumental gates, 16C Renaissance fountains and noble 18C classical buildings.
The bishops' castle, the Church of St-Marcellus and the town hall are the most
representative buildings of the old town of Delémont.

Town Hall – This building with its outside staircase, baroque doorway and interior
decoration is noteworthy.

Art and History Museum of the Jura Region ⊘ – The museum contains archaeological finds
(from the prehistoric to the Merovingian era) made in the area (Roman statuettes
in bronze or terracotta), as well as ancient religious objects (parish treasure in
basement: 7C silver and enamelled crosier), mementoes of Napoleon, examples of
local crafts, furniture (first floor – 18C cupboard; 17C furnishings in prince-bishops'
portrait gallery, 18C dining room; third floor – 18C bedroom and folklore and works
by artists from the Jura).

Vorbourg Chapel – *2km – 1 mile northeast.* To arrive at the pilgrimage centre of
Our Lady of Vorbourg use the shaded road lined with a Stations of the Cross and
offering good views of Delémont. The chapel stands in a wild and wooded site
overlooking a deep valley. It contains baroque altars and walls covered with 18 and
19C ex-votos.

Every year
*the **Michelin Red Guide Switzerland***
revises the town plans:

-through routes, by-passes, new streets, one-way systems, car parks...
- the exact location of hotels, restaurants, public buildings...
Current information for easy driving in towns.

★★★ DENT DE VAULION Vaud

Michelin map **217** fold 2 or **427** fold 11 – 15km – 9 miles southwest of Vallorbe –
Local map p 116 – Alt 1 483m – 4 865ft

The Dent de Vaulion, one of the steepest summits in the Swiss Jura, provides an
immense panorama of the Alps, from the Jungfrau to the Meije and the Joux
Valley.

Climb to the Dent – *From the road from Romainmôtier to L'Abbaye, 5km – 3 miles –
about 3/4 hour.* The access road, tarred as far as the chalet on the Dent de Vaulion,
branches off from the main road on the ridge between the Vaulion and Joux
Valleys. It soon becomes very narrow *(passing only possible at certain points).*
From the chalet you can see your way to a signpost marking the summit *(viewing
table).*

★★★ **Panorama** – The great glory of this view is the Mont Blanc Massif beyond the
mists of Lake Geneva; the first ridges of the Jura towards the Joux Valley and its
lakes are also a majestic sight. Beware of the alarming precipice, a sheer drop of
over 200m – 600ft.

DISENTIS/MUSTÉR Graubünden (Grisons)

Michelin map **218** fold 2 or **427** fold 15 – Local maps see GRISONS and
ST. GOTTHARD MASSIF – Alt 1 133m – 3 717ft – Facilities

Disentis/Mustér, the centre of Romansh culture and a health resort, is the small
capital of the Upper Grisons and Oberland Valleys, colonized in the Middle Ages by
the monks of St Benedict. From its terrace it overlooks the junction of the Tavetsch
Rhine, flowing down from the Oberalp Pass to the west and the Medel Rhine from
Lukmanier Pass to the south.
In summer those who like an excursion involving little effort will find here a whole
series of short walks (with belvederes and painted chapels). In winter skiers are
offered a network of ski-lifts which take them up to the runs at an altitude of
3 000m – 9 240ft.

Abbey – This is one of the oldest Benedictine foundations in Switzerland, dating
from the 8C. The buildings, which are used by the monks as a school, are 17, 19
and 20C. The abbey, from which the town derives its Romansh name of Mustér,
forms a massive quadrilateral of buildings lying on the flank of a long, rugged
Alpine slope, the summit of which is shaded by forests.

★ **Abbey Church** (Klosterkirche) – This imposing baroque church (1695-1712) flanked by
two towers with bulbous domes, has a bright interior with well-placed tribunes.
The two tiers of windows are invisible from the nave in accordance with the
baroque rules of indirect lighting. The stucco and paintings on the vaulting were
restored in the first quarter of the 20C.

★OBERALP PASS ROAD
From Disentis/Mustér to Andermatt

31km – 19 miles – about 1 hour – Itinerary ⑤ on the St. Gotthard Massif local map

The Oberalp Pass ⊙ is usually blocked by snow from November to May; when the pass road is closed a train assures the transportation of cars between Andermatt and Sedrun.

The most notable features of the trip through the Oberalp Pass (alt 2 044m – 6 704ft), which is largely covered by a lake, are the following:

– **the upper exit from the Sedrun Basin:** after Camischolas, the road bends back to enter a wooded defile.

From the bend *(benches)* at the entrance to this defile there is a charming and curious view of the villages of the Tavetsch Valley – where the Vorderrhein rises. The villages stand on green terraces cut by sharp-edged ravines.

– **the descent from the Oberalp to Andermatt:** the view★★ soon enfilades the pastoral slopes of the Urseren Valley as far as the Furka Gap (and its hotel) and looks down on Andermatt, clustering at the foot of the debris from Urseren Forest, which has been ravaged by avalanches (notice the many protective walls built on this slope).

★**Andermatt** – *See Andermatt.*

★VORDERRHEIN VALLEY
From Disentis/Mustér to Reichenau

52km – 32 miles – about 1 3/4 hours – Itinerary ⑧ on the Grisons local map

A short distance after having left Disentis/Mustér from the northeast, upstream from the modern road bridge and railway viaduct which span the Russeinbach Ravine, stands an old covered bridge now disused. Farther on, the elegant bulbous belfry of Somvix is noteworthy.

Trun – The great building of the **Cuort Ligia Grischa** ⊙ (black and white shutters), a former residence of the Abbots of Disentis built in 1674, was in some sort the parliament and law court of the League *(see below)*. Inside, among other apartments, you may visit the Abbot's room, with 17C panelling and the Law Court decorated in the baroque style. The maple tree that may be seen at the entrance to the village, in the enclosure adjoining the 18C Chapel of St Anne (modern commemorative paintings), grew from a seedling from the maple of Trun. It was in the shade of this sacred tree – like the oak of Guernica to the Basques *(see Michelin Green Guide to Spain)* – that the pact of the Grey League was solemnly confirmed in 1424.

Ilanz – Former capital of the Grey League *(see Grisons – p 26)* – Disentis/Mustér being more the religious capital – Ilanz, founded in 1395, is the only place in the Grisons Oberland which bears the official title of "town". The most picturesque quarter which may be reached by crossing the bridge over the Rhine and following the exit route towards Vals or Vrin, still has mansions of the 17C with baroque decoration, especially the Casa Gronda (black and yellow shutters) with its corner turret, window grilles and finely-ornamented door frames.

★**Versam Road** – *From Lanz to Bonaduz 21km – 13 miles.* The road offers vistas of the Rhine Gorges as well as the Bifertenstock (Tödi Massif) Crests, to the left of the Vorab. The clearing immediately before the village of Versam is a good place to stop. It affords a **view**★ of such typical summits on the far side of the ravine as the Vorab group, with its great plateau glacier, on the left, and the Ringelspittz on the right. In the foreground is the Flimserstein Promontory, girdled with imposing cliffs. The narrow road is soon suspended on a ledge along the flank of the whitish precipices (a curious phenomenon of erosion) formed by the Rhine and its tributary, the Rabiusa, and runs through the mass of debris brought down by the Flims landslide.

Return to Lanz and the Reichenau road.

From Laax to Trin the landscape, which becomes rough and thickly wooded, reveals the original chaotic formation of the great flow of debris coming down from the Sardona Range into the Rhine Valley.

Below the road the dark waters of the small Lake Cresta will be seen. The obstruction created by the Flims landslide compels the road to cross a very steep ridge of which the summit is marked by the resort of Flims at an altitude of 1 103m – 3 618ft.

★**Flims** – *See Flims.*

The widest views on this trip are seen during the descent from Trin (pretty village high up in the mountains) to Reichenau. This is the time to look at the Reichenau Basin, where the Vorderrhein (Outer Rhine), just freed from its gorges, joins the Hinterrhein (Inner Rhine) emerging majestically from the Domleschg Basin, near Bonaduz.

Reichenau – With its three bridges forming a triangle enclosing the confluence of the Vorderrhein and the Hinterrhein, this little settlement – consisting of a castle and its outbuildings *(partly turned into an inn)* – owes its existence to a site exceptionally convenient for collecting tolls. It is still an important road junction at the fork of the main roads to the Domleschg (Thusis) and the Grisons Oberland (Disentis/Mustér).

Use the Map of Principal Sights to plan a special itinerary.

★★ DOUBS BASINS

Michelin map **216** fold 12 or **427** fold 12

The name Doubs Basins designates the area which includes the widest part of the gorges of the River Doubs, Lake Brenets (called Lake Chaillexon on the French side) and Chatelot Dam. It establishes the boundary between France and Switzerland for 43km – 26 1/2 miles and is more accessible to the motorist and offers more belvederes on the French side *(see Michelin Green Guide Jura in French only)* and yet the Swiss side offers pleasant boat trips on Lake Brenets.

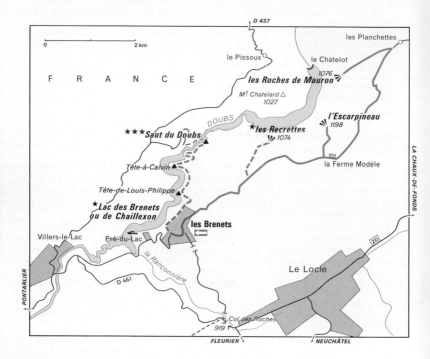

FROM LES BRENETS TO THE DOUBS FALLS

Local map above

On foot (by a forest path bordering the east bank) 2 1/4 hours Rtn or 1 hour plus return by boat.

By boat ⊙: 1 hour Rtn plus 20 minutes Rtn on foot.

Les Brenets – A small border town pleasantly terraced on the slopes which plunge into the lake of the same name.

★**Brenets Lake** – Called Lake Chaillexon on the French side, this lake was a meander of the Doubs which was transformed into a reservoir due to landslides. It is 3.5km – 2 1/2 miles long and averages a width of 200m – 656ft. At one point its sides become extremely narrow, thus forming two basins: the first (average depth 10m – 33ft) spreads over an area between gently smiling slopes; the second basin (average depth 30m – 99ft) flows between abrupt limestone cliffs – crowned with fir, Norway spruce and beech trees – the crests of which offer, now and again, profiles suggesting famous people (**Louis-Philippe, Calvin** etc...). The federal cross painted onto the rock face in 1853 and the so-called Grotto of the King of Prussia can be seen on the Swiss side.

★★★**Doubs Falls (Saut du Doubs)** – *It can be reached by the landing stage, which marks the end of the lake via a forest path.* This famous waterfall, the overfall of Brenets Lake, 27m – 89ft high, when seen from the Swiss belvedere is much less spectacular than when seen from the French side *(description in the Michelin Green Guide Jura in French only)*. The site is wooded.

SWISS VIEWPOINTS OF THE DOUBS – *Local map above*

From Les Brenets to the Mauron Rocks

11km – 7 miles – about 1 hour

Les Brenets – *See above.*

After leaving Les Brenets in the direction of Le Locle bear left at the crossroads onto the road towards Les Planchettes. The road passes through woods, climbs to the plateau, and arrives near the hamlet of Les Recrettes.

★**Les Recrettes Viewpoint** – Alt 1 074m – 3 524ft. *1/2 hour on foot Rtn.* From the belvedere there is a good **view**★ onto the loop of the Doubs made by Châtelard Mountain on the French side and the hinterland covered with fir trees and pastures.

Just before the farm *(Ferme Modèle)* bear left onto a path *(private: close the gates after you)* and continue along it for about 700m − 1/2 mile until you are right by the cliff.

Escarpineau Viewpoint − Alt 1 198m − 3 930ft. From this belvedere there is a lovely **panorama** (unfortunately blocked by pine trees in the foreground) onto the Chatelot Dam and Lake and the crests of the French Jura.

In front of the farm *(Ferme Modèle)* bear left. Before the village of Les Planchettes bear left onto a surfaced path through woodlands.

Mauron Rocks (Les Roches de Mauron) − Alt 1 076m − 3 530ft. Walk to the viewpoint, near the restaurant, from where there is a plunging view onto the Doubs, hemmed in by the Châtelard Promontory and the Chatelot Dam.

★★ EINSIEDELN Schwyz — Pop 10 869

Michelin map **216** fold 19 or **427** fold 15 − Alt 881m − 2 890ft − Facilities

The small town of Einsiedeln, which is a pleasant winter or summer resort, lies in a district of rugged hills and pinewoods intersected by torrents. It is the most famous and most frequented place of pilgrimage in all Switzerland. Its fame spreads as far as Alsace and Southern Germany.

The church and monastery buildings, forming the sumptuous ensemble we know today, were build in the 18C on the site of a monastery founded in 934 by Otto I and Duchess Reglinde of Swabia and since burnt down several times.

The town's main street runs into the east side of the huge square on which the abbey church stands. The 140m − 150yds long façade of the Benedictine abbey overlooks a great semicircular parvis, edged with arcades, in the centre of which stands a fountain to the Virgin.

It is in this impressive setting that the great festival of the Miraculous Dedications is held *(see the Calendar of Events)* and that every five years performances of *The Great Theatre of the World* by Calderón de la Barca take place.

SIGHTS

★★ **Abbey Church (Klosterkirche)** − This was built between 1719-35 in **Vorarlberg** baroque which is popular in regions around Lake Constance, and it is the most remarkable example of this style in Switzerland. Two tall towers flank the façade, which is slightly convex and very graceful.

The interior is surprisingly spacious. The length of the church, including the upper chancel, is 113m, the width of the nave 41m and the height of the Dome of the Nativity up to the lantern 37m - 370 × 131 × 118ft (Westminster Cathedral 306 × 156 × 280ft). Above all, the decoration is extraordinarily rich: the vaulting, domes and octagonal roof of the nave, the aisles and chancel are covered with frescoes and stucco.

This decoration is largely the work of the Asam brothers, who came from Bavaria. One was known as a painter, the other as an artist in stucco, but many other artists also took an active part, thus, the altars were built and painted by the Carlone brothers from Sciara (near Como) and by Milanese artists.

The chancel, which was built between 1674-80, was remodelled later and painted by Kraus, of Augsburg.

The upper chancel where the monks meet daily for divine service can be seen behind the painting of the Assumption. The wrought iron grilles of the chancel are remarkable.

Abbey church at Einsiedeln

The Holy Chapel, built at the entrance to the nave on the site of the cell occupied by St Meinrad, who was martyred in 861, contains the statue of Our Lady of Hermits, an object of special veneration for pilgrims.

In spite of the variety and exuberance of decoration the building shows great artistic unity.

Abbey Great Hall (Grosser Saal) ⊘ – This is on the second floor of the monastery buildings and is reached by going round the church to the right. Enter by the first door on the left, in the courtyard.

It was built at the beginning of the 18 C and is decorated with stucco and frescoes by Marsiglio Roncati of Lugano, and Johannes Brandenberg of Zug. At regular intervals exhibitions are held there of items from the monastery's different art collections.

★ The EMMENTAL

Michelin maps **216** folds 15 and 16 and **217** folds 6 and 7 or **427** folds 13 and 14

The Emmental, the name of which brings immediately to mind the well known "Swiss" cheese, is a large valley to the east of the canton of Berne and delimited by the Aare River and the canton of Lucorne. It is cut by the Emme River, an affluent of the Aare, which it meets up with east of Solothurn.

Originating in the Hohgant Massif, north of Lake Brienz, the Emme River crosses first a mountainous area, the slopes of which are covered with fir trees and pastures and then runs through a cheerful area of forests and fields sprinkled with chalets decked with flowers, isolated or in groups. The area's wealth comes from forestry, crop farming and cattle raising.

Emmental cheese is to German Switzerland what Gruyère cheese is to French Switzerland. It is the most widely exported of Swiss cheeses: its enormous wheels, hard interior dotted with large irregular eyes (Gruyère is more compact and has fewer and smaller eyes) and hazel-nut taste are known the world over.

TOWNS AND SIGHTS

Burgdorf; ★Lueg Belvedere – See Burgdorf.

Hasle – On the west bank of the Emme, this village is linked to the Rüegsau-schachen (east bank) by a remarkable **covered bridge** (1838). Built entirely of wood, the bridge crosses the river in one span. The Protestant church, a former chapel rebuilt in the 17C, is worth noting. Inside are small 17C stained-glass windows, heraldic bearings as well as 15C frescoes on the north wall of the nave (Last Judgment, Cruci-fixion...).

Jegenstorf – This gay and flowered town clusters its houses around a Late Gothic church, with a saddle roof, and a shingled bell tower. The interior is decorated with woodwork; the stained-glass windows are 16-18 C. The town's **"château"**, ⊘ an 18 C town house, which was added to a feudal tower, stands in a small wooded park and presents temporary exhibitions in lovely 18 C period rooms.

Kirchberg – The Protestant church (1506 restored), overlooking the village, contains, in its apse, 16 and 17 C stained-glass windows: the north side windows depict St George killing the dragon and the Bernese coat of arms; the south side shows a Virgin in Majesty and various symbolic figures. The stained glass of the central windows is modern.

★**Langnau im Emmental** – See Langnau im Emmental.

Lützelflüh – This lovely village on the Emme has a church which was built in 1494 (modernised). Inside the church are six old stained-glass windows, an organ loft (1785) and the tomb of Albert Bitzius (pseudonym of Jeremias Gotthelf) pastor and writer during the 19 C.

Marbach – *See Marbach.*

Sumiswald – *See Burgdorf: Excursions.*

Trachselwald – The 17 C Reformed church with its 18 C belltower, has in its nave a curious painted ceiling and in its apse an intriguing baroque mausoleum (1695). Outside the village, on a wooded slope, is a gracious 15 C **castle** ☉, which, although it has been restored, has kept its 12 C tower (access by a covered stairway).

Utzenstorf – *See Utzenstorf.*

Worb – A bustling, industrial centre and crossroads, this town is dominated by its two castles of the 12 and 18 C and by its Late Gothic church (carved stalls, 16 and 17 C stained-glass windows in the apse).

★★ EMOSSON DAM

Michelin map 🟥 fold 9 or 🟥 fold 21 – 24km – 15 miles southwest of Martigny

Access – *Take from Le Châtelard Giétroz the funicular which goes from the C.F.F. (Swiss railway) power station to the water tower then take the little train which stops at the base of the dam. A tiny funicular, known as "Le Minifunic", will then leave you at the Gueulaz Pass (time allowed for trip: 1 1/2 hours).* Inaugurated on the occasion of the 700th anniversary of the Swiss Confederation, this ingenious piece of technological mastery can rise to a height of 260m – 854ft in two minutes. The train trip offers lovely views of the Mont Blanc Massif.
Or access only in summer by the La Forclaz road, then the second road on the left (12 km – 7 1/2 miles) up to the dam via Finhaut (take the loop to avoid the village). On the last leg of the trip the route looks onto the Mont Blanc Massif.

Dam ☉ – The vaulted dam of Emosson rises to a height of 180m – 590ft in its site just below the Gueulaz Pass (alt 1 970m – 6 463ft). The reservoir with a capacity of 225million m³ – 7 946million ft³ and a surface area of 327ha – 808 acres is well integrated into its mountainous setting.
The building of the dam was a joint Franco-Swiss project and took eight years to complete (1967-75). The Emosson dam replaced the old Barberine dam which now lies 42m – 138ft below the surface of the water when it is at its highest level. The hydro-electric power station on the upper stage at Châtelard-Vallorcine is in French territory while the Swiss power station on the lower stage (la Bâtaz) lies on the floor of the Rhone valley. The annual production figure is approximately 850million kWh which is shared between the two national electricity companies EDF (France) and ATEL (Switzerland). From the car park terrace of the neighbouring café-restaurant, there is a magnificent **view★★** of the Mont Blanc Massif (right to left) from Aiguilles Rouges to the Mont Blanc including Maudit Mountain, Mont Blanc du Tacul, Aiguille du Midi, Aiguille du Dru, Aiguille Verte, the Aiguilles du Chardonnet and Argentière, Aiguille du Tour and Le Tour Glacier and Grands Glacier.
Go up to the Chapel of Our Lady of Snow (Notre Dame des Neiges), modern and yet traditional in appearance, the interior of which contains pretty stained-glass windows.

★★★ ENGADINE

Michelin map 🟦 folds 6, 7, 15 and 16 or 🟥 folds 17 and 18

Engadine, which has always been approached by the High Road, has a landscape quite different from that of the great, deep valleys of the Alps, where basins and gorges sometimes alternate rather monotonously. As the average altitude is about 1 500m – 4 900ft (1 800m – 5 900ft in Upper Engadine) the motorist travelling from the north through the Julier or Albula Pass will experience only a modest fall in ground level. As for the motorist coming from Italy through the Maloja Pass, he drives into the cradle of the Upper Inn without a change of level.
The Engadine Mountains, despite their 4 000m – 13 000ft (Piz Bernina – 4 049m – 13 284ft) look, in these conditions, as though they had lost their lower slopes. They are, above all, to be admired for the splendour of their glaciers.
The tourist will be attracted here even more by the continental mountain climate than by the landscape. The very varied weather, very little influenced by disturbance from the sea, is characterized by clear skies, and dry, light breezes. The rarefied air causes intense sunshine. This is most striking in winter when increased by reflection from the snow. The resort of St. Moritz has thus rightly adopted the sign of the sun.
The well-known Engadine Skimarathon assembles cross-country skiers competing over 40km – 25 miles *(for information apply to: Engadin Skimarathon, CH 7504, Pontresina).*

The Engadine house – The typical Engadine house, a massive grey structure, has plenty of room for two families under a broad gable crowning a façade sometimes interrupted by a break in its line. Floral, geometric or heraldic designs frequently cover the white walls. These may be painted for the dry climate preserves paintwork, or they may be decorated by the process known as **sgraffito.** To obtain this process the mason first applies a layer of rough, grey plaster which he then covers with a coat of limewash. Finally, by simply scraping the surface (but how skilfully) he brings out again, in grey, the designs required (rosettes, foliated scrolls, etc. in the Renaissance style).

The windows are small and irregularly placed and widen outwards. Richly wrought iron grilles, sometimes curving out at the bottom, indicate reception rooms from which charming little oriel windows *(photograph p 29)* project.

Engadine house

When not too elaborate, the *Bündnerstube (definition p 4)* of hotels and inns give a first glimpse of the local style of furnishing, which resembles that of the Tyrol. But those who wish to form a general idea of local interior furnishings should pay a visit to the Engadine Museum at St. Moritz. The most typical room is the **Sulèr**, a sort of covered court common to the barn and the living quarters, which serves as a work and meeting room. This cool, dark room, with carefully kept stone flags and a low, whitewashed vault is lit only by a wide opening in the carriage gate.

Sightseers may pause at every step in most of the villages of the Inn Valley, but they will find the most striking collection of Engadine dwellings at **Zuoz** *(qv)*. **Guarda** *(qv),* more rural but equally charming, is regarded as the "museum-village" of the Lower Engadine.

FROM ST MORITZ TO SOGLIO

33km − 20 1/2 miles − about 1 1/2 hours − Itinerary ④ *on the Grisons local map*

★★★ **St. Moritz** − *Time: 1 1/2 hours. See St. Moritz.*

As you leave St. Moritz the snowy peaks of the Piz de la Margna block the horizon.

★★★ **Piz Corvatsch** ⊙ − *Access by cable-car in 16 minutes; leave from Surlej (to the left of the Silvaplauna Lake which is reached by the causeway).*

The ride up to the mid-station of Murtel (alt 2702m − 8865ft) offers views onto the Silvaplauna and Sils Lakes, while underneath you the fir trees are little by little overcome by a rocky landscape. From the upper station (Corvatsch alt 3303 m − 10837ft) there is a magnificent **panorama**★★★ to the southwest onto the dazzling peak of Piz Corvatsch (alt 3451m − 11319ft), the neighbouring snowfields *(summer skiing),* the Bernina Range and its glaciers farther east, and to the north and west onto the valley and lakes of the Upper Engadine dominated by the northern Grisons in the background.

The road runs along the foot of the slopes of the Upper Inn Valley and skirts the **Silvaplauna and Sils Lakes**★★.

★ **Sils** − This quiet and elegant resort in the Upper Engadine includes the two townships of Sils-Baselgia and Sils-Maria at the beginning of the Inn Valley in thickly wooded countryside.

The soft lines of the landscape, both in the main valley and in the tributary Fex Valley, which is also very wide, and the lakes contribute to the restful atmosphere of the resort. Between the two lakes and in spite of the large hotels of Sils-Maria, which stand out between the trees, across the way at the foot of the slope, you will enjoy to the south at the foot of the Bernina Massif, a glimpse of the very wide glacier gap at the beginning of Fex Valley.

Sils Lake and Piz de la Margna

Friedrich Nietzsche (1844-1900) chose this village as his summer resort from 1881-88; mementoes of the philosopher can be found in his house which has been turned into a museum.

Maloja – *See Maloja.*

Maloja Pass – Alt 1 815m – 5 955ft. This pass, the lowest of the passes between Switzerland and Italy, establishes the actual boundary of Engadine and is the watershed between the Danube and Italian sides of the Grisons.

Although the pass is hardly noticeable on the Engadine side, on the other hand, on the opposite side, the Mera Torrent has carved its valley (Bregaglia Valley) much more deeply than the Inn has its valley.

Downhill from the pass the **Bregaglia Valley★★** is the continuation of the Inn Valley. A series of hairpin bends leads you to Casaccia which marks the junction with the old Septimer road from Bivio. Beyond Piz Cacciabella, which can be recognized by its small rounded snow-cap, is the typical hanging valley *(p 17)* of Albigna, intersected by a great dam.

Downhill from Löbbia, the **view★** opens towards Stampa and Vicosoprano framed on the slope facing north by magnificent firwoods interspersed by pale green clumps of larches.

The villages spread out between Vicosoprano and Promontogno – including Stampa, Giacometti's native village – show, in the evolution of their architectural style, the diminishing influence of the Engadine style (tall houses with deep sunken windows, the streets are narrow and cobbled and there are groups of little barns with rows of open gables). And even the Alpine flora is replaced by chestnut groves, vineyards and orchards.

La Porta – This bottleneck in the valley, fortified since Roman times, marks the natural frontier between Alpine and southern Bergell. The Castelmur Keep stands on a spur above the Romanesque campanile of Nossa Donna The former road, higher and still quite distinguishable, cut through the promontory more directly and passed through the old wall, substantial traces of which remain. Castelmur was the key to the Obere Strasse *(qv)* on the Italian side. Constant improvements to this road during the Middle Ages were financed largely by the lords of the domain.

★★**Soglio** – *Access by a narrow and very steep by-road* The **site★★** of this village is one of the most picturesque in the Bergell. It stands on a terrace surrounded by chestnut groves facing the rocky cirque that closes the Bondasca Valley. The smooth sides of the Pizzo Badile, which can be seen very clearly, are amongst the most amazing in the Alps Standing out clearly against the houses which cluster around the church with its Italian-style campanile, the noble façades of several Salis palaces (one now a hotel – the Hotel Palazzo Salis) evoke memories of one of the Grisons families best known abroad, many members having been in the diplomatic service.

FROM ST MORITZ TO MARTINA

78km – 48 1/2 miles – about 3 hours – Itinerary ④ *on the Grisons local map*

★★★**St. Moritz** – *Time: 1 1/2 hours. See St. Moritz.*

After the wooded slope separating St. Moritz from Celerina, the itinerary goes along the lower plateau of the Upper Engadine.

★**Celerina** – *See Celerina.*

★**Samedan** *See Samedan.*

At first the **Inn Valley** is very wide and its flat alluvial floor has to be protected against flooding by the torrent.

★**Zuoz** – *See Zuoz.*

Between Punt Ota (the traditional boundary between the Upper and Lower Engadine) and Zernez, the Valley narrows and is less built up. Near Zernez the Piz Linard appears.

Zernez – *See Zernez.*

From Zernez to Susch the road sinks into the *Clüs,* a wooded defile following the Inn. The rocky, snow-streaked faces of the Piz Linard emerge gradually.

Susch – *See Davos: Excursions.*

Beyond Susch, after a widening of the valley, commanded from its terrace by the village of Guarda, the road runs through another narrow section where it overlooks at intervals the rushing waters of the torrent from a height of about 150m – 500ft.

★**Guarda** – *Excursion from Giarsun, 2.5km – 1 1/2 miles – plus 1/2 hour sightseeing.* With its houses decorated with sgraffiti *(see The Engadine House opposite)* and family coats of arms over the doors and with its steep, narrow streets, paved with cobblestones, and its fountains, Guarda is regarded as a typical village of the Lower Engadine.

You will now see the Steinsberg Tower standing upstream, on a rocky hill against which the white village of Ardez is built.

Ardez – This village at the foot of the Steinsberg is worth a halt for its painted houses with charming flower-decked oriel windows. The theme of Original Sin has enabled the decorator of the Adam Eve House to paint a study of luxuriant foliage.

Between Ardez and Schuls the corniche road overlooks a third wooded defile, sinking finally towards its floor. From the very start it offers a first glimpse of the proud **Tarasp Castle**. The many mountain crests of the Lower Engadine Dolomites (Piz Lischana and Piz St Chalambert Mountains) follow one another in the distance as far the Swiss, Italian and Austrian frontier ridges.

★★ **Schuls** – *See Schuls.*

Downhill from Schuls, the valley narrows between the crest line marking the Italian side on the right and the slopes streaked with torrents descending from the Silvretta Massif on the left. At Martina the valley becomes a defile (to the north) below the Austrian village of Nauders. An itinerary towards the Dolomites to the south passes via the Reschenpass.

★ ENGELBERG Obwalden — Pop 2958

Michelin map **217** fold 9 or **427** folds 14 and 15 – Alt 1002m – 3287ft – Facilities

Engelberg stands on a site which, though surronded by heights, is sunny. It is the great mountain resort of central Switzerland, engaged both in tourist and religious activities. A swimming-pool, tea-rooms, tennis courts, and a skating rink are found alongside one of those great and sumptuous Benedictine abbeys which lie concealed in the high valleys of Switzerland.

The mountaineer has only to choose between the glacier formation of the Titlis and the jagged crests of the Spannörter and the Uri Rotstock, while the walker, using the ski lifts well-known during the skiing season, can easily reach such attractive sites as that of the Trübsee and even of the Titlis.

Abbey ⊙ – The monastery, which was founded in the 12C, owned the whole valley until the French invasion of 1798. Today it is a massive quadrilateral of buildings, most of which are used as a religious college.

The **church,** which also serves the parish, has the grandiose arrangement and decoration proper to buildings of the 18C baroque school. The organ is one of the largest in Switzerland.

EXCURSIONS

★★ **Titlis** ⊙ – Alt 3239m – 10627. *Viewing table.* South of Engelberg, cable-cars enable the tourist to reach the upper belvedere (alt 3020m – 9909ft) where he will enjoy a panorama extending from the Sustenhorn to the Rigi. *Allow about 3 hours for the return trip including 3/4 hour by cable-car. Excursions on foot also possible in summer.*

★ **Schwand** – *4km – 2 1/2 miles to the north – about 1 hour Schwand is approched by a steep, narrow road from where there are unencumbered views of the ring of mountains (you can turn below the chapel at Schwand). A fine Alpine beauty spot in sight of the Titlis.*

ERLENBACH Berne — Pop 1668

Michelin map **217** fold 6 or **427** fold 13 – Local map see BERNESE OBERLAND

Several **houses**★ of the most majestic Bernese type lend great distinction to the entrance to this village on the Spiez side *(information on rural architecture)*. From the central crossroads a curious covered wooden staircase leads to the terrace on which the church stands. Go round the building to reach the façade stopping in the close, which, with its tombs scattered in the grass and its bushy trees, composes, with the church itself, a romantic **picture**★.

Inside, the nave and the chancel are almost completely covered with naive paintings dating from the beginning of the 15C. Among other Biblical subjects, note the procession of Wise and Foolish Virgins (triumphal arch) and the symbols of the Four Evangelists (chancel vaulting).

★★★ **Stockhorn** ⊙ – *Access by cable-car (25 minutes).* From the top of the Stockhorn, although not very high (alt 2190m – 7185ft), there is one of the loveliest panoramas existing in the Oberland. You may even see the surefooted chamois haunting its peak. From Erlenbach to the mid-station of Chrindi (alt 1637m – 5374ft), the cable-car goes through a small, deep valley carved out by a torrent and lined with either fir trees or chalets. Between Chrindi and the upper station (alt 2139m – 7018ft) you fly over the lovely Stockenseen, a pool of emerald green water *(angling)* occupying a glacial hollow. From the upper station, walk *(1/4 hour Rtn)* to the top of the Stockhorn *(viewing table below, south side)*, surrounded by grassy and wooded slopes, for the **panorama**★★★: to the north of Thun and part of its lake, to their left the Lakes of Amsoldingen and Allmendingen; to the south onto the Stockenseen lakes and on its right and higher up of the smaller Oberstockensee Lake; Erlenbach between Walpersberg fluh and Mieschfluh Peaks; and all around like a back-cloth bristle the most renowned white summits of the French and Swiss Alps from the Jungfrau to the Mont Blanc.

Geographical terms

For specialised geographical terms referring to glaciers and glacial topography, consult the section on Alpine Relief in the Introduction.

ESTAVAYER-LE-LAC Fribourg — Pop 3808

Michelin map **217** fold 4 or **427** fold 12 — Alt 454m — 1489ft

The little town of Estavayer is built on a hill overlooking the south shore of Lake Neuchâtel. It has preserved its medieval city look (ramparts, towers, old houses...). Its pleasure boat harbour makes it a popular resort among water sports enthusiasts.

Church of St Lawrence (Église St-Laurent) — A Late Gothic building crowned with a large square tower at the transept crossing. Inside, the **chancel★** is ornamented with fine 16C stalls and a painted and gilded high altar in the baroque style and enclosed by an elaborate wrought-iron screen.

Chenaux Castle — This imposing building (13-15C) still boats its walls, quartered by round towers.

Museum ⊙ — This stately mansion (1435) built in yellow sandstone and featuring tiered bay windows was once used to store the tithes contributed by the local population. At present it houses a regional history museum: impressive collections of weapons and early engravings, reconstitution of an old kitchen and its utensils, stuffed frogs parodying human scenes (a political gathering, a game of cards), exhibition room devoted to railway transport (Swiss trains, lanterns, etc.).

★ FLIMS Graubünden (Grisons) — Pop 2258

Michelin map **218** east of fold 3 or **427** fold 16 — Local map see GRISONS — Alt 1103m — 3618ft — Facilities

The resort of Flims, is divided into two sections: **Flims-Dorf,** the traditional residential section, whose mountain houses stand on open ground at the foot of the Flimserstein Cliffs (or Crap de Flem); **Flims-Waldhaus,** where hotels are scattered in a forest of conifers on a low ridge connecting Flem Valley and the basin in which the delightful Lake Cauma lies (bathing beach — water warmed by underground hot springs).
The confused topography of the thickly wooded slopes which undulate between this point and the bottom of the Vorderrhein Gorges still recalls the chaotic appearance of this area in prehistoric times, when an enormous landslide along the axis of the present Flem Valley blocked the Rhine Valley and compelled that river to find a new course.
The terraced site of Flims, its exposure due southward and the proximity of woods well suited to walking, make it much sought-after as a family resort. In winter one can either go for wonderful walks or enjoy the ski-runs.

★★**Cassons Grat** ⊙ — *Leave from Flims, the ascent takes 1/2 hour by chairlift and cable-car.* In good weather the ride up in the chairlift at least as far as the first station (Foppa alt 1424m — 4672ft) is enchanting; you look down on green pastures, luxurious Engadine chalets adorned with flowers, and spread out in the background are the two built up areas of the resort. After Foppa the terrain becomes more desolate, however, a promising **view★** develops — it is at its best at the second station (Naraus alt 1850m — 6070ft) — onto the shelf of Flims and the snowy ridges appearing in the distance. The cable-car *(after change)* stops at Cassons (alt 2637m — 8652ft) after having hugged the magnificent Flimserstein Cliffs. Go on foot *(1/4 hour Rtn)* to the Cassons Grat (alt 2700m — 8858ft), from where the Swiss flag flies: superb **view★★** orientated south towards the Rhine Gap and the Grisons Alps and blocked to the north by ravine-like ridges.

★**Crap Masegn** ⊙ — *Leave from Murschetg (3.5km — over 2 miles southwest on the road to Oberalppass), the ride takes 25 minutes by cable-car.*
During the ascent of the Vorab, a landscape of fir trees, chalets and grazing cows unfolds before you, but from the mid-station of Crap Sogn Gion (alt 2213m — 7261ft) onwards the terrain becomes more desolate. The **view★** from the upper station of Crap Masegn (alt 2472m — 7110ft) passes from the desolation of the surrounding peaks (Fil de Rueun, Vorab and Siala) to Flims below in the Vorderrhein Valley, the Rhine's principal headstream.

A cable-car continues to Vorab (alt 2570m — 8432ft) and its glacier (summer skiing).

★★ FORCLAZ PASS ROAD

Michelin map **219** folds 1 and 2 or **427** fold 21

The convenience of a direct link between Chamonix and the great Valais road junction of Martigny makes the Forclaz Pass road one of the great international routes of the Alps.

FROM VALLORCINE TO MARTIGNY

26km — 16 miles — about 3/4 hour — tour of Emosson Dam and trek to Trient Glacier not included

The road is narrow between Vallorcine and the Swiss frontier. Customs controls at Le Châtelard.

From Vallorcine *(see Michelin Green Guide Alpes du Nord in French only)* the road runs boldly through the Tête Noire Defile.

★**Tête Noire Defile** – The most impressive section of this gorge is between the Roche Percée Tunnel and the hamlet of Tête-Noire.
Note the picturesque village of Finhaut.

★★**Emosson Dam** – *Access and description see Emosson Dam.*

To reach the pass the road then turns back into the high pastoral coomb of Trient, fissured at the foot of the Trient and Grands Glaciers, which are separated by the Aiguille du Tour.

Forclaz Pass – Alt 1527m – 5010ft. To the south the view is cut off by the detached crests of the Aiguille du Tour (visible on the extreme left, above the Grands Glacier). To the north the snow peaks of the Bernese Alps seldom emerge from the bluish mist which rises from the great Valais Depression on fine summer days. The rocky Pierre-Avoi Peak, between the Rhône and Drance Valleys, is easier to distinguish.

From Forclaz Pass, many long **pedestrian circuits** ⊘ are available in the midst of the Valais mountains to visitors keen on wild nature. One of these walks, leading to the **Trient Glacier**★ *(allow 3 hours Rtn, inaccessible in winter because of the snow)* follows an outflow channel (natural duct draining the glacier waters towards the valley) running along the mountain side and through a forest of larch, spruce and arolla pines. The path offers an open view of the Grands Glacier and Dzornevattaz Valley, as well as the Pétoudes d'en Haut and Herbagères pastures lying below Balme Pass. The ascent towards Trient Glacier is breathtaking. The "tongue" of snow – a massive powdery stretch which appears to have frozen in mid-air like a lava flow – sparkles with bluish tints as one draws nearer.
Half-way up the mountain, enjoy a well-deserved break at the "Trient refreshments stall": this former refuge, rebuilt after an avalanche in 1978, was used in the late 19C to provide accommodation for the workers in charge of the commercial exploitation of the ice.
From the pass to Martigny the view of the Martigny Basin and the gap formed by the Valais Rhône really opens out only 2.5km – 1 1/2 miles below the ridge. The rocky snag-like Pierre-Avoi is still prominent in the foreground; soon you will pick out the narrow furrow of the Drance forming a way through to the Great St Bernard. The site of Martigny and La Bâtiaz Tower become visible where the road runs between vineyards.

Martigny – *Time: 1 1/2 hours. See Martigny.*

Calendar of Events
The most important Swiss festivals are listed in a table, in the Practical Information section at the end of the Guide.

★ **FRANCHES MONTAGNES**

Michelin map **216** fold 13 or **427** fold 3

The high plateau of the Franches Montagnes (average altitude 1000m – 3281ft) between the Doubs Valley and Mount Soleil Chain is one of the most original districts in the Swiss Jura. Its low houses, pastures dotted with fir trees and natural parks where bay horses and milch cows graze, are most attractive.
Tourism flourishes in winter due to the popularity of cross-country skiing. The chief town of the district is **Saignelégier**, well-known throughout the Jura for its August horse fair *(see the Calendar of Events)*. Many fine trips can be made locally, especially to the **Jura Corniche**★ *(see below)* or in France, the **Goumois Corniche**★★.

★**Jura Corniche** – *Itinerary 9 (about 1/2 hour) of the Swiss Jura local map.* At the foot of the Rangiers Sentinel (Sentinelle des Rangiers) branch off into the St-Brais road along the crest between the Doubs Valley and the Sorne or Delémont Valley, the latter being dotted with thriving industrial villages.
To see the floor of the Doubs Valley towards St-Ursanne, halt at the belvedere 100m after passing under a high-tension cable.

★★ **FRIBOURG** Ⓒ   Pop 36355

Michelin map **217** fold 5 or **427** fold 12 – Alt 640m – 2100ft – Plan of the conurbation in the current Michelin Red Guide Switzerland

Fribourg is a remarkable **site**★★ on a rocky spur encircled by a bend of the Sarine. The deeply sunken course of the river still marks the boundary between the two great ethnic and linguistic areas of Switzerland: it is amusing to see here that places on the west bank of the river have French names, while the hamlets on the east bank are named in German. The old quarters which extend from the Sarine to the Upper Town, bristling with church towers and monasteries, still wear the aspect of a medieval city. Fribourg boasts a considerable number of sculpted **fountains** dotted on the squares and along the streets of the city. They were originally built during the Middle Ages to serve as outlets for the many springs which supplied the town with water. Later, in the 15C, they were adorned with elegantly-chiselled basins and stone columns, the work of such renowned artists as Hans Schäuffelin the Younger, Hans Geiler, Hans Gieng and Stephan Ammann.
Every three years the city of Fribourg hosts an international exhibition on photography.

HISTORICAL NOTES

From its foundations to the Reformation – In 1157 **Berchtold IV of Zähringen** founded Fribourg at a ford on the Sarine and made it a stronghold to command this important thoroughfare. When the Zähringen family became extinct, the town changed hands several times. It passed to the Kyburgs and then to the Habsburgs but finally preferred the rule of Savoy to that of Berne. Fribourg joined the Confederation in 1481 after having acquired extensive lands in the Vaud Country. Here the Reformation had no decisive influence on men's minds and the Catholic restoration inspired by Father Canisius reaffirmed the already deeply Catholic feelings of the town, which became the seat of the Bishopric of Lausanne, Geneva and Fribourg.

Bastion of Catholicism – In the 17C many religious orders were added to those already settled in Fribourg in the 13C: Franciscans, Jesuits and other communities made it the Catholic capital of Switzerland. Among its most famous and brilliant establishments were the College of St Michael, founded by the Jesuits, the Capuchin Church and Monastery, the Franciscan Monastery and the Monastery of Maigrauge, built by the Cistercians in the 13C.

The University – In 1889 the foundation of a state university blessed with a Catholic vocation gave a new impulse to the crucial role played by religious instruction in modern times. Fribourg University, one of the most prestigious seats of learning, still enjoys an excellent reputation both in Switzerland and abroad. It consists of five faculties (theology, law, social and economic sciences, languages and natural science) and fifteen independent institutes (computer technology, journalism, etc.) which welcome students from all over the world. Tuition is either bilingual or multilingual.

★★GENERAL VIEW *1/2 hour by car*

Starting from the Place de l'Hôtel de Ville, cross the Zähringen Bridge. From this great stone structure you can get a **view** down the deeply sunken course of the Sarine towards the small covered bridge, Pont de Berne, and the new Gottéron Bridge.

On leaving the bridge turn to the right on the Route de Bourguillon, passing between the Red Tower (Tour Rouge) and the Cats' Tower (Tour des Chats), relics of the old ramparts.

From the Gottéron Bridge *(leave the car on the parking area just after the bridge)*, you will see a beautiful **view**★★ of the roofs of Fribourg. About 600m 1/3 mile after the bridge turn sharply to the right and pass under the Bourguillon Gate (Porte de Bourguillon). The wooded land surrounding Loreto Chapel – a classical building inspired by the famous Italian sanctuary in the Marches region – offers several interesting **views**★ of the city and its natural site.

A steep slope will take you down to the old town.

★OLD TOWN *allow 1/2 hour on foot*

Place du Petit St-Jean – This square lies south of the quartier de l'Auge. It owes its name to St-Jean de Jérusalem, a knights' chapel built in the 13C and demolished 600 years later.

The fountain erected in memory of St Anne, the patron saint of the local tanning industry, is the work of Hans Gieng.

Berne bridge – A charming wooden bridge with oak supports spans the river Sarine over a distance of 40m - 130ft.

Start walking up the rue d'Or.

On the corner you will find the Auberge de la Cigogne (Storks' Inn), which was once a hostelry attached to the Augustinian convent. The facade features a rococo mural representing a group of storks.

Turn right into the rue des Augustins.

Augustinian Church (Église des Augustins) (D) – The interior of this building, which was commissioned by the mendicant orders, presents a large nave divided into four bays, separated by Gothic arches resting on spherical pillars. The furnishings are characteristic of the baroque period. The wooden retable surmounting the high altar – gilded and painted to resemble marble – is the work of Peter and Jacob Spring: three levels of niches flanked by columns portray religious scenes, most of which were taken from the life of the Virgin. The two retables placed at the entrance of the chancel were executed by the Ryeff workshops. The one on the right features an elegant polychrome composition, *Virgin and Child*.

On the square stands an annex to the church: a gallery with six arcades, supporting a first floor reinforced by half timbering. The monastery buildings have been converted into administrative offices.

Turn left at the end of the rue de la Lenda.

Rue de la Samaritaine – This steep, paved street will bring you back down to Place du Petit St-Jean. The Samaritans' Fountain, yet another token of Hans Gieng's talent, represents Jesus Christ and the Samaritan at Jacob's well. Level with the fountain, note the impressive Late Gothic façade, punctuated by eight picture windows embellished with Flamboyant tracery.

Go back to the car and drive to the newer part of town via Berne Bridge, the Rue des Forgerons (on the left), the Tour des Chats, the road to Stadtberg and Zähringen Bridge.

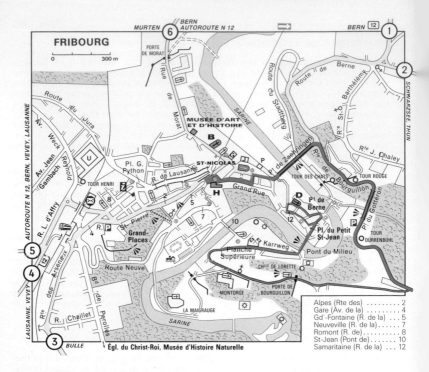

★ NEW TOWN *2 1/2 hours*

★ **Town Hall** (Hôtel de Ville) **(H)** — The town hall stands near a square famed for its lime tree, planted, it is said, on 22 June 1476 to celebrate the victory of the Confederates over **Charles the Bold** in Murten. This fine, early 16C building, complete with canopy and double staircase (17C) is dominated by a large roof of brown tiles. The belfry and its Jack-o'-the-clock figure are crowned with pinnacle turrets.

★ **Cathedral of St Nicholas** (St-Nicolas) ⊘ — The cathedral rears its fine Gothic tower above the roofs of the old town. The first stone of this building was laid in 1283. It was intended to take the place of the church dedicated to St Nicholas and built a century earlier by the founder of the town, Berchtold IV of Zähringen. Work began on the chancel, which was erected by about 1280. The far end of the church, however, was altered in the 17C by the rebuilding of an apse with three walls and five bays to replace the flat east end.

Exterior — The fine tower, 76m – 250ft high, was built in the 14C, on the octagon completed in about 1490 with a crown of pinnacles in the style of the period. The **tympanum ★ ★** of the main porch, surmounted by a rose window, is devoted to the Last Judgment: Heaven and Hell are shown on either side of the Weighing of Souls; the archivolts bear angels, prophets and patriarchs, the doorway, apostles. The sculptures in the south porch of the union of Christ and the Church, date from the first half of the 14C.

Interior — A square vestibule formed by the lower part of the tower, with side-walls adorned with fine arcades, precedes the ogive-vaulted nave. 17C pictures garnish the corner-pieces of the great arcades above and below the triforium, which is surmounted by clerestory windows (modern – 1983 – by A. Manessier).
The aisles, which also have ogive vaulting, are lit by windows designed by the Polish painter, Mehoffer (early 20C).
The 16 and 17C side chapels were provided with baroque altars in the middle of the 18C. The chancel, which is enclosed by a Gothic wrought-iron screen, is adorned with 15C **stalls ★** representing the prophets and the apostles. Above the screen a rood-beam supports a large Calvary carved in the first half of the 15C. To the right as you go in, the Chapel of the Holy Sepulchre contains a fine **Entombment** dating from 1433 and more stained glass by Manessier.
The late 15C font in the fourth bay on the south side of the chancel is made of finely carved stone. Its wooden cover is 17C. The organ, which was one of the glories of Fribourg in the 19C, was built in 1834.

★ **Art and History Museum** (Musée d'Art et d'Histoire) ⊘ — The collections displayed in the Hôtel Ratzé, an elegant Renaissance building (16C), and in a former slaughterhouse, converted in 1981, illustrate the art and history of Fribourg from its origins up to the present day. The Hôtel Ratzé houses many exhibits dating back to the Middle Ages, a period rich in artistic events. Note the Late Gothic collections of remarkable works of art executed by local artists such as Martin Gramp, Hans Fries, Hans Gieng and Hans Geiler. Fries – the town's official poet from 1501 to 1510 – exerted a strong influence over his contemporaries and several of his works are on display, including scenes from a retable. The 17C is present with works by Pierre Wuilleret and Jean François Reyff, and the 18C with paintings attributed to Gottfried Locher. In the room devoted to regional guilds and associations, a series of engravings and watercolours present the city of Fribourg and its canton. The artefacts displayed in the archaeological section can be traced back to prehistoric times, ancient Rome and the early Middle Ages.

The stone museum set up in the former slaughterhouse features a fascinating collection of fourteen 15C **statues★** taken from the Cathedral of St Nicholas, depicting the Annunciation and the Apostles. Visitors may also admire a splendid 11C Crucifixion scene from Villars-les-Moines and a group of sculptures attributed to Hans Gieng (16C), contrasting sharply with the monumental compositions of Jean Tinguely. The rest of the exhibition consists of a rare collection of objets in silver and gold (14-18C), some stunning pieces of Burgundian jewellery (7-8C) and works by Marcello (the pseudonym of the native artist the Duchess Castiglione Colonna, née Adèle d'Affry), extremely popular during the last century.
A number of 19 and 20C works, including several by Eugène Delacroix, Félix Vallotton and Ferdinand Hodler, are on show in the attic room above the former slaughter house.

Franciscan Church (Église des Cordeliers) (B) ⊙ – A Franciscan community settled in Fribourg in 1256. The monastery buildings were completed about the end of the 13C. The monastery, which then had a superb book-binding workshop and the richest library in the town, received distinguished guests passing through Fribourg; popes, cardinals, emperors and princes.
The Gothic buildings were drastically remodelled in the 18C and the nave of the church was completely rebuilt. It has a flat ceiling and is roofed with wood, but the chancel has kept its ogive vaults. The first chapel on the right contains a gilded and carved wood **triptych★** made in about 1513 for Jean de Furno, which shows Alsatian influence. The central panel depicts the Crucifixion, with Mary Magdalene at the foot of the Cross: the panel on the left shows the Adoration of the Shepherds, and that on the right, the Adoration of the Magi. The folding shutters on the left illustrate the Annunciation and those on the right, Coronation of the Virgin. The Dormition of the Virgin is painted on the predella.
Chancel – The chancel is a good example of 13C Franciscan architecture, with four keystones in the vaulting bearing the symbols of the Evangelists. It contains oak **stalls★** dating from about 1280.
On the left of the chancel is the altarpiece of St Anthony, known as *the Death of the Usurer*, painted in 1506 by the Fribourg artist Hans Fries. The picture illustrates the words of the Gospel: "Where a man's treasure is, there will his heart be also". Over the high altar stands the magnificent **altarpiece★★** by the Masters of the Carnation, painted at Solothurn and Basle in 1480 by two artists who signed their works with red and white carnations. The picture is very large (0 x 2.7m - 2b x 8 1/2ft) and was installed in the chancel during the restoration of 1936 replacing a baroque altarpiece installed in 1692. The central scene represents a Crucifixion; it is flanked by four Franciscan saints: St Bernardino of Siena, St Anthony of Padua, St Francis of Assisi and St Louis, Bishop of Toulouse. The Adoration of the Shepherds is on the left shutter, that of the magi on the right; the background suggests the Fribourg Alps. The folding shutters have an Annunciation in the centre, St Elizabeth of Hungary, patroness of the Franciscan Third Order, on the right, and St Clara of Assisi on the left.

ADDITIONAL SIGHTS

Grand-Places – In fine weather, the lawns are a popular attraction. The ornamentation of the fountain was conceived and executed by the sculptor **Jean Tinguely.**
The monument on the left commands a **view** of the rooftops of the old town, dominated by the Gothic tower of the Cathedral of St Nicholas.

Church of Christ the King (Église du Christ-Roi) – *43 Boulevard de Pérolles*. This church, completed in 1953, stands on a broad esplanade. The façade is semicircular. The interior, a successful example of building in reinforced concrete, has a curious plan with an oblong nave supported by columns. The chancel, surrounded by an ambulatory, is crowned by a dome.

Jean Tinguely the sculptor and experimental artist

*Born in Fribourg in 1925, Jean Tinguely began by studying painting at the Academy of Fine Arts in Basle. However, he soon found the courses too conventional for his liking and moved to Paris in 1953. Throughout his life, his conception of art and his passion for games and movement – reflected in his "strange machines" – marked him out as a highly eccentric character, endowed with fervent imagination. Even his very first creations, mobile volumes consisting of geometrical figures, stood out from the work of contemporary artists. In 1959 his Metamatics, accoustic machines designed for drawing and painting, could be seen as a reaction against applied abstract art. After producing compositions made of wire, sheet metal and cardboard boxes, he turned towards discarded objects (engine parts, gearwheels), which he combined with wood and material and used to make frightening machines; he subsequently staged live "happenings" at which these curious contraptions would self destruct. In 1960, when he presented his work Homage to New York in the grounds of the Museum of Modern Art of New York, the destruction of this extraordinary assemblage required the intervention of the local fire brigade. Later he adhered to the principles of Nouveau Réalisme, a term coined by the art critic Pierre Restany. Influenced by Dadaism and two of its principal exponents, Marcel Duchamp and Picabia, Tinguely went against accepted conventions by creating large, extravagant machines which, despite their arrogance, showed a strong sense of humour. In 1983, in collaboration with Niki de Saint-Phalle, he produced the Stravinsky Fountain, a gay, inventive structure which now stands in a small pond next to the Georges Pompidou Centre; it was commissioned by the City of Paris. In the years that followed Tinguely's work took on sombre overtones, resulting in scenes verging on the macabre (his exhibitions in Venice in 1987 and at the Georges Pompidou Centre in Paris in 1988). "Death has visited me, Death has caressed me. I turned her threats into a celebration, a burlesque dialogue", the artist declared towards the end of his life.
Jean Tinguely died in Berne on 30 August, 1991, having exerted a strong influence over the art of his contemporaries.*

Natural History Museum (Musée d'Histoire Naturelle) ⊙ – *In the Faculty of Science on the Route de Marly (not on plan) via the Boulevard de Pérolles.*
The museum occupies seven rooms on the first floor. The first rooms display fossils (geological and paleontological sections), a relief model of the Aletsch glacier and its region, and a splendid collection of minerals, along with a reconstitution of a "crystal cave". The other rooms, impressive by their size, are devoted to zoology. Stuffed specimens of local fauna are presented in their natural setting and a diorama shows visitors a variety of bird species, complete with recorded songs. Other displays include animals from the five continents, namely fish, reptiles, invertebrates and shellfish. The fascinating world of insects is given special attention: morphology, reproduction, evolution of the species, recorded stridulations of the grasshopper and cricket, and studies conducted under a microscope.

EXCURSIONS

★**Black Lake (Schwarzsee)** – *27km – 17 miles – about 1 hour. Leave Fribourg by ② and road N 74.*
When you reach Tafers, turn right into a picturesque road offering charming views towards the Berra on the right and towards the Guggershorn on the left.
After Plaffeien, a pretty village of varnished wooden chalets, the road climbs through the Sence Valley to end at the Schwarzee (angling) in a pretty mountain **setting★**. A pleasant resort, a summer or winter excursion centre, has grown up beside the lake.

★**Rossens Dam** – *Round tour of 55km – 34 miles. Leave Fribourg by ④, road no 12. After 13km – 8 miles take the Rossens road on the left.*
A large dam was built across the Sarine in 1948, upstream from the village of Rossens. It is of the arched type, 320m long and 83m high – 1 049 x 272ft.
The reservoir, 14km – 8 1/2 miles long, forming a magnificent pool in a pretty, steep-sided setting, is known as **Lake Gruyère**. To enjoy a good view, follow the road on the right towards Pont-la-Ville. At La Roche take road no 77 on the right and cross the lake at Corbières. At Riaz you will rejoin road no 12 to Fribourg.

Hauterive Abbey ⊙ – *7km – 4 miles southwest of Fribourg by ③. After 4.5km – 3 miles take the Marly-le-Grand exit and turn right.*
After Chesalles, a road on the left leads to the abbey which stands in a loop of the Sarine. The Cistercian abbey, founded in 1138, was secularized in 1848 but resumed the life of prayer and work in 1939. The church, built in the purest Cistercian style in 1160, has since undergone many alterations, especially in the 14 and 18C. It was furnished with stained-glass windows (14 and 15C) in the chancel (closed by a grille) with fine stalls with panels carved with human figures and crowned with openwork canopies, a 16C mural painting and in the north side aisle the recumbent figure of a knight whose feet rest on a lion. The monastery buildings were rebuilt in the 18C, with a baroque façade. Inside, the main staircase is adorned with elegant wrought-iron balustrades.
The Gothic **cloisters** were entirely remodelled in the 14C. They are roofed with painted groined vaulting with finely carved keystones.

★★★ FURKA PASS ROAD

Michelin map **217** folds 10 and 19 or **427** folds 14 and 15

The view of the Rhône Glacier and the summits of the Bernese Oberland make this high altitude itinerary unforgettable.

FROM GLETSCH TO ANDERMATT

32km – 20 miles – about 2 1/4 hours – Itinerary ③ on the Bernese Oberland local map

★★**Gletsch** – *See Conches Valley.*

Leaving Gletsch, you will be charmed by the sight of the Rhône Glacier from its upper level, which can be seen from the ledge to where it ends as a frozen cataract between rounded rocks.

★★**Rhône Glacier** (Rhonegletscher) **(Hotel Belvedere)** – *See Conches Valley.*

The road across the slopes reveals distant views of the Bernese and Valais Alps. To see the **panorama★★★** at its widest, stop near the fork of a small military road *(closed to traffic)* 1 500m – about a mile before reaching the pass and walk a little way through the fields. You will see the snow-clad peaks of the Weisshorn and the Mischabel shining in line with the gap formed by the Conches Valley (Goms — Upper Valais). Nearer, towards the Grimsel Pass, stand the barren sides of the great peaks above the 4 000m – 13 123ft line of the Bernese Oberland.

★★**Furka Pass** ⊙ – Alt 2 431m – 7 975ft. Stop at the Hotel Furkablick to admire the majestic Galenstock at close range. The Furka Pass is the highest shelf of the great longitudinal furrow that divides the Swiss Alps from Martigny to Chur. It is an essential route for tourist communications between Romansh Switzerland, the road junction of Andermatt and the Graubünden (Grisons). Since 1982 a railway tunnel through the pass has been opened linking Oberwald to Realp.
From the pass to the Hotel Galenstock the road, after a long gentle slope above the deserted valley of Garschen, skirts the foothills of the Galenstock, the most familiar peak on the run. The **panorama★★** opens out on the forbidding Urseren Valley, with the three villages of Realp, Hospental – the latter marked by an old watch-tower and a church, both well detached – and Andermatt. In line with them, in the background, you will see the zigzags of the Oberalp road. Andermatt is within easy reach.

★**Andermatt** – *See Andermatt.*

Michelin map 🔲 fold 11 or 🔲 south of fold 11 – Local map see Lake GENEVA – Alt 375m – 1 227ft – Plan of the conurbation in the current Michelin Red Guide Switzerland

Geneva is unquestionably one of the most privileged Swiss cities on account of its exceptional location. Its natural environment has been carefully protected so as to guarantee the best possible living conditions, with the result that Geneva conveys the image of a pleasant, comfortable town.

Visitors will be charmed by the opulent mansions, the harbour and its fountain, and the shimmering shores of the lake, set against a backdrop of lush vegetation and wooded mountains.

Geneva is the second seat of the United Nations after New York and it houses the headquarters of several specialised UN agencies devoted to economic, as well as social and humanitarian causes (e.g. disarmament). The town has been chosen to represent a great many international bodies such as the European Centre for Nuclear Reasearch, the World Committee of the Red Cross and the International Labour Organisation (BIT).

But Geneva, clustering around its cathedral, also remains the town of Calvin and the stronghold of the Reformation. It is an intellectual city, a nursery of naturalists and teachers and the metropolis of Romansh Switzerland with busy streets and shopping centres (Place du Molard quarter, where one of the famous Davidoff cigar shops is located on Place Longemalle). A very Helvetian atmosphere of order and discipline binds the three Genevas into one.

Geneva makes a good excursion centre. One of the more interesting **train journeys** (Lake Geneva-Mont Blanc), leaving from the Eaux-Vives quarter, allows the traveller to discover some of the most spectacular mountain scenery as well as the attractive banks of Lake Geneva.

HISTORICAL NOTES

The eagle and the key – The arms of the canton *(reproduced on p 26)* illustrate Geneva's status before the Reformation. As an Imperial town (the "half-eagle") and a bishopric (the golden key encircled by a pale),

The Jet d'eau

Geneva on the banks of the Rhône, was often defended by its rulers from the attacks of neighbouring territorial powers, especially those of the House of Savoy. The very liberal rights granted to it by its Prince-Bishop Adhémar Fabri in the 14 C marked a stage in the political and economic evolution of the city whose independent and cosmopolitan character were to be further enhanced by the religious outlook fostered by Calvin.

The town of Calvin – From 1532 onwards Reform was preached successfully at Geneva by French humanists. Shortly after Calvin settled in the town, which became "the Rome of the Protestants". Calvin behaved like a dictator, decreed laws, built new ramparts, welcomed Marot, Theodore Beza and the Scottish preacher John Knox *(see Michelin Green Guide to Scotland)* and burnt at the stake the Spanish doctor, Miguel Serveto, whose theological opinions did not please him.

However, the Dukes of Savoy could not resign themselves to the loss of their state's leading city. On 12 December 1602, Charles-Emmanuel made a surprise night attack on the ramparts of Geneva. This was the famous attempt at scaling the walls *(L'Escalade)* of which the Genevese still commemorate the failure every year *(see the Calendar of Events)*.

Geneva, capital of the mind – Intellectual life flourished in the 18 C: Jean-Jacques Rousseau, Mme d'Épinay, the banker Necker and his daughter Germaine (the future Mme de Staël), Dr Tronchin, the mountaineer and man of science, De Saussure, the painter Liotard, and Voltaire were Genevese by birth or by adoption. Diderot and D'Alembert had several volumes of their controversial 18 C French encyclopedia, *L'Encyclopédie,* printed here from 1777-79. French troops entered Geneva in 1798 and for sixteen years the town was the capital of the French "Département" of Léman. It joined the Swiss Confederation after the collapse of the Napoleonic Empire on 1 June 1814.

★★HARBOUR AND LAKE SHORES *3 hours*

One of the most famous landmarks of Geneva is the harbour and its magnificent **Jet d'Eau**, the highest fountain in the world (145m – 476ft), whose great white plume marks the city from afar. The lake itself, circled by seagulls and teaming with many boats, namely paddle steamers, is a memorable sight.

North Bank

Take a walk along the Quai du Mont-Blanc, which runs parallel to the north bank of the lake and which features stately mansions decked with flags. The route offers distant **views★★** of the surrounding mountains (Voirons, Môle, Salève, Mont Blanc on a clear day).

> *Start from the junction formed by the bridge, the street and the Quai du Mont-Blanc.*

The "prow" of the Ile Jean-Jacques Rousseau juts out downstream from the bridge. On it stands a statue of the famous writer.

The Quai du Mont-Blanc is a bustling centre of activity, frequented by both local residents and tourists, who enjoy strolling along the lake shores and visiting the cafés and souvenir shops.

Brunswick Monument (Mausolée du duc de Brunswick) **(FY B)**. – The mausoleum of Charles II of Brunswick (1804- died in Geneva in 1873), a distinguished benefactor of the town, was built in 1879 in the style of the Scaliger tombs in Verona *(Michelin Green Guide to Italy)*.

> *Proceed along Quai Wilson, the continuation of Quai du Mont-Blanc, or go to the Débarcadère des Pâquis and use the "Mouettes Genevoises", a regular shuttle service linking several points of the harbour.*

★★**Parks of Mon Repos, Perle du Lac and Villa Barton** (GX) – These three parks which are connected form the finest landscaped area in Geneva. There are elegant mansions within and in the environs of the gardens.

Farther on there is a good view of the **Little Lake** *(p 104)* towards Lausanne.

History of Science Museum (Musée d'Histoire des Sciences) **(GX)** ⊘ – In Perle du Lac stands the stately Bartholoni Villa (1825), lavishly decorated with mural paintings. This residence now houses a museum devoted to scientific equipment dating from the 18 and 19C. One of the rooms on the ground floor pays tribute to the Genevese physicist De Saussure (inventions, personal instruments and mementoes), while others display exhibits to astronomy (sundials, planetaries), navigation (sextants, compasses) and surveying (theodolites). The artefacts shown on the first floor concern the medical profession (Laennec's stethoscope, portable first-aid kits) electricity and electromagnetism, meteorology (thermometers, barometers) and physics (models of steam engines, various measuring devices, including an acoustic spoon used for calculating the speed of sound crossing water).

★**Botanical Garden** (Jardin botanique) **(FX)** ⊘ – This 17ha – 42-acre garden, conceived as a pleasant recreational spot, may also be seen as a living museum of the plant kingdom. It features a **rock garden★★**, where plants are divided into geographical groups, a deer pen and aviary, and a series of hothouses with a superb winter garden, containing many luxuriant species from equatorial and tropical countries. Notice boards direct visitors to the most interesting flowers.

South Bank

> *Start from Pont du Mont-Blanc.*

The quays running along the south of the lake are flanked by lawns planted with trees and decorated with pretty flower beds.

English Garden (GY) – A floral clock dominates that part of the garden which looks out onto the Quai Général Guisan. The terrace affords an interesting panorama of the harbour and, farther back, the Jura mountain range. For a good, close-up view of the fountain, situated at the end of the Jetée des Eaux-Vives, take a walk along the Quai Gustave-Ador. There, an impressive collection of sailing boats are moored to an artificial marina, confirming Geneva's reputation as an important yachting harbour.

★**La Grange Park (GY)** – It features the finest rose garden in Switzerland (flowering season mid-June) and, in the centre of the grounds, an elegant 18C residence.

Next to it lies the charming **Eaux-Vives Park★**.

Boat trips ⊘

A great many formulae are available to visitors, ranging from a quick trip round the harbour to a grand tour of the lake. *See also under Lake Geneva.*

The Geneva Escalade
This traditional festival commemorates the successful defense of the town against the Savoyards who attempted to scale the walls (l'escalade). The celebrations include a torchlight procession with the Genevese in period costume through the narrow streets of the town and along the banks of the Rhône. The procession makes a number of halts along the way when a herald on horseback reads out the official proclamation claiming victory over Savoy. To celebrate the anniversary the local confectioners make chocolate cauldrons, thus symbolising the heroic deeds of the "Motherland" who vanquished the enemy by pouring the boiling contents of a cauldron over their heads. A religious service in St Peter's Cathedral, fireworks and bangers complete the day's festivities.

★ THE OLD TOWN *1 1/2 hours*

Place Neuve – This large square, dominated by the bronze equestrian statue of General Dufour *(qv)*, a Swiss hero of the 19C, is surrounded by several stately buildings: the Academy of Music, designed in the 19C by Jean-François Bartholoni, the Grand Theatre (19C) and the Rath Museum.

Rath Museum (Musée Rath) (EY) ⊘ – This museum, fronted by a portico, was built in the 19C in conformity with Greek classicism. Temporary exhibitions, organised by the Art and History Museum, are held here.

Promenade des Bastions (FYZ) – This public garden, laid out in the 18C, follows the former lines of fortification of the town. On the right, beyond the huge plane tree, stand the universtity buildings and library.

★ **Reformation Monument (FY D)** – This monumental wall (over 100m – 329ft long) was built against a 16C rampart and kept deliberately plain. The great statues of the four Genevese reformers Farel, Calvin, Beza and Knox stand in the centre underneath the motto *Post Tenebras Lux*.

The monument was erected in 1917 and its other statues and low reliefs with explanatory texts recall the origins of the Reformed Church and its repercussions in Europe.

In front of it the arms of Geneva – bishop's key and imperial eagle – appear on the pavement between the bear of Berne and the Lion of Scotland.

University Library (Bibliothèque Universitaire) (FZ) ⊘ – The Ami-Lullin room is reserved for a permanent display of manuscripts, books and archives relating to the history of the Reformation and literary life in Geneva. The room named after **Jean-Jacques Rousseau** contains personal mementoes belonging to the writer (manuscripts, prints and a bust by Houdon).

> *Leave the Promenade des Bastions by the gate leading into Rue St-Léger, opposite the Place Neuve. Then turn left and take the road which passes under the bridge.*

Place du Bourg-de-Four – This picturesque square, located in the heart of the old town, was used for markets and trade fairs during the Middle Ages. Some of the old buildings, many of which were inns, have kept their original signs. The fountain in the middle of the square is decorated with flowers and surrounded by cafés, art galleries and antique shops.

> *Follow the Rue de l'Hôtel de Ville on the left and then, cross the Place de la Taconnerie on the right.*

★ **St Peter's Cathedral (Cathédrale St-Pierre) (FY)** ⊘ – This great building, erected between the 12 and 13C and partly rebuilt during the 15C, has been a Protestant church since the year 1536. It was given a surprising Neo-Grecian façade in the 18C.

The interior is plain but impressive. You may see Calvin's seat *(in the north aisle, just before the transept crossing)*, 15C stalls *(in the south aisle)* and the tomb of the Duke de Rohan, who was the head of the Reformed Church in France during the reigns of Henri IV of Navarre and Louis XIII *(first chapel on the south side of the chancel)*. The Chapel of the Maccabees opens out of the first bay in the south aisle. It is an elegant structure in the Flamboyant Gothic style, built by Cardinal de Brogny at the beginning of the 15C and heavily restored in the 19C.

North Tower ⊘ – The top of the tower commands a superb **panorama**★★ of Geneva, the lake, the Jura and the Alps.

> *Once out of the cathedral you are on the Cour St-Pierre.*

★ **Archaeological Site** ⊘ – In front of the west face of the Corpses' Chapel (southwest of the cathedral), a staircase leads down to the archaeological site. This vast complex contains artefacts spanning more than 2000 years of man's history. Several footbridges take visitors to the basement of the cathedral, where an audio-visual presentation explains how the country was converted to Christianity.

A first church and baptistery were built in the second half of the 4C. Less than fifty years later, Isaac, Bishop of Geneva, already possessed a palace, two cathedrals and a new baptistery. A reception hall decorated with polychrome mosaic flooring was added around 450. It has recently been restored. Subsequently, the three episcopal churches and the baptistery were replaced by a large cathedral (c 1000). Its walls were used as foundations for the present cathedral, whose construction was started in 1160. Half-way through the visit, a small museum displays replicas of the principal monuments and the various exhibits discovered during the excavation work.

> *Cross the Cour St-Pierre and turn right into Rue du Soleil Levant.*

On the corner of the street stands a bronze statue of the prophet Jeremiah, executed by Rodo.

> *The Rue du Soleil Levant leads into the Rue du Puits St-Pierre.*

★ **Maison Tavel (FY)** ⊘ – This house is the oldest in Geneva. After the great fire of 1334 – which destroyed more than half the town – it was rebuilt and gradually acquired its present appearance. Its elegant stone façade, broken by three rows of picture windows and flanked by a turret at one corner, features an amusing series of stone effigies representing heads of animals and human beings. A niche above one of the windows on the first floor carries the sculpted coat-of-arms of the Tavel family, a branch of the Genevese aristocracy who gave their name to the house. The rooms and cellars have been tastefully restored and the house is certainly worth a visit as it will enlighten you on the history of Geneva between the 14 and 19C. The town's ramparts, architecture, religious and political activities, and day-to-day life are vividly evoked through a series of interiors reconstituted on the second floor, and by several collections, of coins, early photographs, locks, door

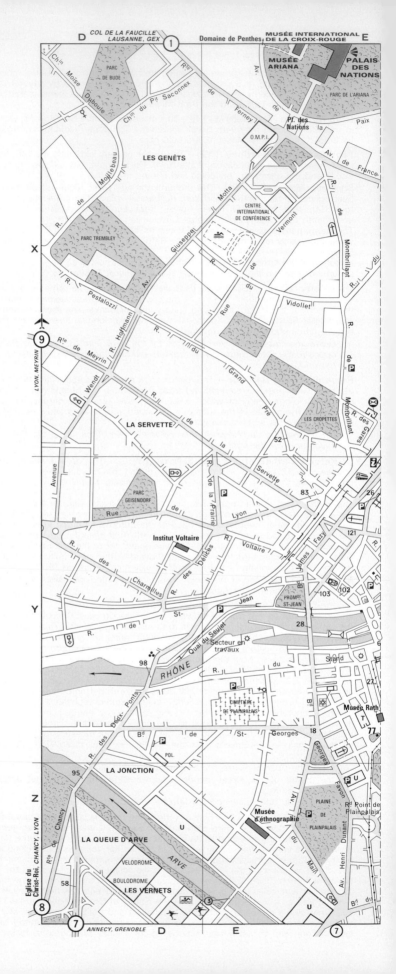

GENÈVE

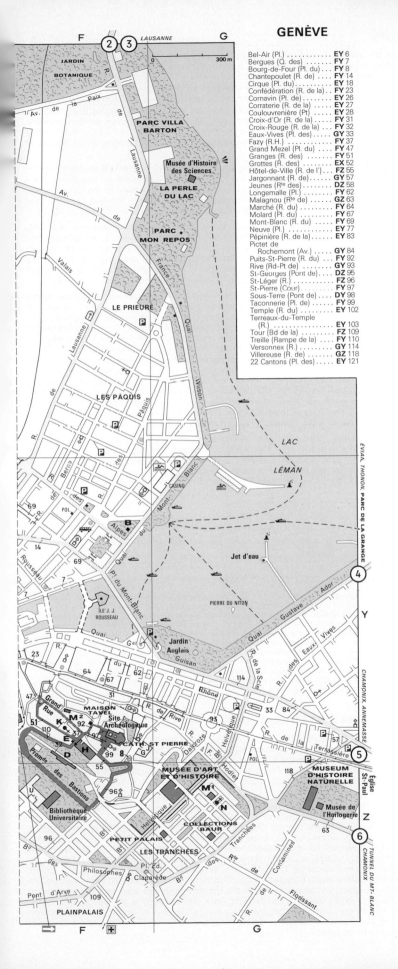

panels and roof ornaments. Admire the superb furniture, the pretty wall hangings (paper and printed calico) and the fine services made of silver and pewter (Geneva was once an important manufacturing centre). The attic displays a striking relief map attributed to the Genevese architect Auguste Magnin (1842-1903), presenting the town as it was in 1850 (copper roofs, zinc buildings and fortifications).

A few steps away from the Maison Tavel, on the opposite side of the street, the arcades of the **former arsenal** house the last remaining canon of the Helvetian Republic *(see the Historical Notes)*.

The walls carry modern mosaics executed by Cingria, illustrating three phases of the town's history.

Town Hall (FY H) – This building dates from the 16-17C and the oldest section, the Tour Baudet, was built in 1455. Go into the courtyard to see the curious cobbled ramp which made it possible to be carried on litters to the upper floors. On the ground floor you can visit the **Alabama Room** ⊘ where the first convention of the Red Cross, known as the **Geneva Convention**, was signed on 22 August 1864.

Grand'Rue (FY) – This picturesque street, one of the best preserved in the old city of Geneva, offers visitors a remarkable choice of bookstores, art galleries and antique shops. Several buildings are associated with the memory of famous people: no 40 is the house where **Jean-Jacques Rousseau** was born and the great actor Michel Simon (1895-1975) came into the world at no 27. When you reach Place du Grand-Mézel, ornamented with a flower-decked fountain, turn left.

Rue des Granges (FY) – This street is lined with large, comfortable residences built in the style of French 18C architecture. The Hôtel de Sellon at no 2 houses the **Zoubov Collection** ⊘ made up of Countess Zoubov's personal mementoes and brought back from her many trips abroad. Some items come from China (*cloisonné* enamels from Peking, painted enamels from Canton) or Russia (imperial palaces of St Petersburg). Furniture pieces signed by the greatest 18C French cabinet-makers, portraits executed by court painters such as Vigée-Lebrun, the Baron Gérard, Lampi the Elder and Lampi the Younger, as well as sumptuous carpets and tapestries decorate the different rooms of the Hôtel: the private entrance, the dining-hall, the vast lounge, the bedrooms and the boudoir of Catherine II.

At no 7 stands the house where Albert Gallatin (1761-1849) was born. This enterprising politician was to become an American statesman, who later contributed to founding the Constitution of the United States of America.

St Germanus' Church (Église St-Germain) **(FY K)** ⊘ – This 4-5C basilica was extended in the 14 and 15C. The belfry, façade and east end were renovated when the building was restored in 1959. The interior is lit by modern stained-glass windows. There are remains of a late 4C altar.

A canopied fountain surmounted by a sundial stands against the east end of the church.

Turn right into the Rue Henry-Fazy.

Pass under the Porte de la Treille (**FY E**). The Tour Baudet (1455), which houses the Executive-Council Chamber, stands on the left.

Follow on the right the Promenade de la Treille which slopes down steeply to the Place Neuve.

General Dufour, a national hero

Guillaume-Henri Dufour was born in 1787 in the German town of Constance of Swiss parents in exile. He studied in Geneva, then at the Ecole Polytechnique in Paris, before serving as an officer in Napoleon's Grand Army. He left the service in 1817 and returned to Switzerland where he founded the military academy at Thun two years later. He was responsible for reorganising the federal armed forces and was appointed chief of staff. Dufour showed his strategic skill when he commanded the federal army against the rebels of the separatist confederation of Catholic cantons in the Sonderbund War (1847).

Between 1832 and 1964 he worked on his pioneer topographical survey of Switzerland publishing a series of topographic maps at a scale of 1:100 000, known as the Dufour Map.

When he died in 1875 he was honoured with a hero's funeral. The highest point of Mount Rosa, Pointe Dufour, is named after the General.

THE INTERNATIONAL DISTRICT

Place des Nations (EX) – This huge square borders on Ariana Park and the modern buildings of international organisations and banks. Note the tall, concave structure, made of blue-tinted glass, which houses the WOIP headquarters (World Organisation of Intellectual Property). In front is a tiered waterfall flanked by bronze copies of the naiads originally conceived for the Neptune fountain in Florence.

★★**Ariana Museum (EX)** ⊘ – Founded by the Genevese patron Gustave Revilliod (1817-1890), after whose mother Ariane Revilliod-De-la Rive it was named, this museum is built in the style of an Italian palace.

The collections on the ground floor provide a riveting illustration of seven centuries of the history of ceramics in Europe, Asia and the Middle-East, running from the Middle Ages up to the present day. The exhibits include the famous Delft earthenware, porcelain from Japan and China (imported by the East India Company) and ceramics from Meissen and Sèvres (whose décors and figurines were to inspire many European manufacturers). Two educational areas explain the various techniques associated with the art of fireclay, as well as the functions of both glass and ceramics. On the first floor, several rooms are devoted to Swiss manufacturers. Contemporary trends in the production of pottery are represented in the basement with exhibits dating from the 20C, including several Art Nouveau and Art Déco pieces.

★★**Palais des Nations** (EX) ⊘ – *Entrance at 14 Avenue de la Paix, Portail de Pregny.* The palace, which stands in the Ariana Park, was built between 1929 and 1936 as the headquarters of the League of Nations. Since 1946 it has been the second centre of the United Nations, the seat of which is located in New York City *(see Michelin Green Guide to New York City)*. A new wing was added in 1973. It is one of the most active conference centres in the world.

The **Salle des Pas Perdus,** adorned with various kinds of marble donated by UN member countries, leads into the great **Assembly Room** (capacity 2000 people) where plenary meetings are held.

Pass along a gallery onto which several meeting rooms open, to reach the **Council Chamber** where the most important conferences take place. It is also called the Spanish Room in honour of Francisco de Vitoria, who founded international law. The Spanish artist José María Sert decorated this room with huge frescoes depicting the technical, social and scientific achievements of mankind.

The visit ends with a film which explains the role of the United Nations Organisation and its famous peace-keeping forces.

Park – These grounds, covering an area of 25ha - 60 acres, are planted with cedars, cypresses and many other fine species. The park features several works of art: a bronze armillary sphere bequeathed by the United States in honour of President Woodrow Wilson, an arrow-shaped monument given by the Soviet Union to celebrate the conquest of space and a bronze sculpture christened *Family,* the work of Edwina Sandys, offered to Geneva during the International Year of Childhood (1979). Seen from the park, the huge mass of the Palais des Nations, built in limestone, travertine and a variety of marble materials, offers a powerful, imposing image. The upper part of the terrace affords a nice view of Lake Geneva and the Mont Blanc mountain range.

UN Philatelic Museum ⊘ – *The museum lobby is the starting-point for visits of the Palais des Nations.* The museum presents collections of stamps and envelopes relating to the League of Nations and the United Nations, along with a wide selection of philatelic publications from all over the world. These are complemented by a new audio-visual presentation, introduced in 1989.

★**International Red Cross and Red Crescent Museum** (Musée International de la Croix-Rouge et du Croissant-Rouge) ⊘ – The museum is approached through a narrow concrete cutting carved out of a hill which lies at the foot of the building

The Genevese businessman **Henri Dunant,** who had witnessed the Battle of Solférino, when the French and the Piedmontese engaged in hostilities against the Austrians on 25 June 1859, decided to launch a movement in aid of the wounded. Four years later, he founded the Red Cross. These historical facts are shown in a panoramic diorama: at the end of the presentation the screen opens onto the figure of "Henri Dunant writing", executed by the US sculptor George Segal. A series of exhibition areas, harmoniously combining light, glass and concrete, offer a chronological description of the activities carried out by the Red Cross and the Red Crescent throughout the world (during the Russo-Turkish war between 1870 and 1875, the Muslim Turks were given permission to replace the cross by a red crescent on a white background). The Wall of Time is an inventory of the major events associated with the Red Cross between 1863 and 1988: relief to victims of wars and natural disasters, support to hostages and political prisoners, efforts to contribute to their release. An impressive archive system, featuring over 7 million cards, lists the names of those men and women who were detained in prison camps during the First World War.

Visitors can also enter a 4m^2 - 4.5yd^2 area, the replica of a real cell in which 17 prisoners spent up to 90 days. A series of films and computer terminals supply more detailed information about the action of the CICR.

The museum provides a moving insight into the history of mankind, inviting both respect and contemplation.

MUSEUMS OF THE SOUTH BANK

★★**Art and History Museum** (Musée d'Art et d'Histoire) (GZ) ⊘ – Its collections present an outline of the history of civilisation, from prehistoric times up to the mid-20C. The largest sections are those devoted to archaeology *(lower ground level)* and painting *(first floor)*. The numismatic room contains a wide range of ancient monetary weights and coins. The collections of applied art include exhibits dating from the 12-19C: sculpted furniture (15-18C), stained glass from the Middle Ages, weapons (guns, pistols with carved ivory butts) and armour made between the 12 and the 18C. Several rooms of a castle have been reconstructed, complete with relief panelling and 17C furniture.

Archaeology – Several rooms in succession are devoted to prehistory (objects of local origin), Egypt, Mesopotamia, the Near East, Greece, Rome and the Etruscans.

Painting – The celebrated altarpiece by **Konrad Witz** (1444) shows the second miraculous draught of fishes. This work is the first exact representation of landscape in European painting. Geneva and Salève can be glimpsed in the background.

Other rooms pay tribute to the Italian and Dutch schools. These are succeeded by pictures of the 17 and especially the 18C. The solemn François Duchatel with his *Dead Nun,* Rigaud and Largillière with their rather contrived, brightly-coloured paintings precede two great 18C artists in pastel. There are a number of masterpieces by Quentin de la Tour, including the *Abbé Hubert Reading,* picturesque and true to life, as well as the delicate and impish portrait of Belle de Zuylen. The second pastellist is the Genevese artist Liotard, whose long beard was well-known to all European society. His portrait of Mme d'Epinay is astonishingly fresh.

The 19C section shows some luminous landscapes by Corot, works by the Genevese artist Toepffer, as well as several pictures by Hodler, whose fierce, powerful technique is illustrated by two portraits (*The Drinkers* and *The Headmasters,* in which the central figure, a rector, bears a striking resemblance to Calvin). Tribute is paid to the Impressionist movement, with works by Pissarro (*The Harbour in Rouen)*, Monet *(Peonies)*, Cézanne *(The House in Bellevue)*, Renoir *(Summertime)* and Sisley *(The Lock at Moret-sur-Loing)*.

★ **Musical Instruments Museum** (Musée d'Instruments anciens de musique) (GZ M¹) ⊙
  – A rich collection of 16-19C musical instruments of European origin and some unusual pieces. The most striking feature of the visit is a recording performed with keyboards, as well as wind, stringed and percussion instruments.

★ **Baur Collection** (GZ) ⊙ – This museum, housed in a 19C mansion, is devoted to the art of the Far East. Several rooms are reserved for temporary exhibitions. The ground floor and first floor present collections of porcelain, stoneware, celadon and jade combining purity of form, richness of colour and delicacy of decoration. These show the evolution of ceramic art in China, from the T'ang (618-908) to the T'sing dynasty (1644-1911).
  Japanese art is displayed on the second floor. Most of the exhibits (sabres, 18C porcelain, lacquer ware, netsuke carved wooden buttons) date from the Tokugawa (1615-1868) or Meiji periods (1868-1912).

★★ **Petit Palais – Museum of Modern Art** (GZ) ⊙ – This 19C residence is seen as the "temple" of both French and European avant-garde painting from Impressionism to Surrealism (1880 to 1930), continuing into Abstract art. Founded by Oscar Ghez de Castelnuovo, a former industrialist with a passion for painting, the museum displays works of the highest quality taken from his own collection, occasionally by rotation. These shows are complemented by temporary exhibitions focusing on a particular theme, school or artist.

Ground Floor – The **Impressionist School** was born around 1830-1840 in reaction to accepted conventions ; it strived to express man's visual perception of the world in a flurry of colour and light, prompted by the minute study of nature. Impressionism and Post-Impressionism are represented by such artists as Manet *(Berthe Morisot with Veil)*, Puvis de Chavannes *(The Older Sister)*, Boudin *(Seascape)*, Caillebotte *(The Bridge of Europe)*, Fantin-Latour *(Venus Washing)*, Renoir *(Portrait of the Poetess Alice Vallière)*, Cézanne *(Along the Oise)* and Degas *(Nude Woman Washing)*.

The **Nabi Movement** (a Hebrew word meaning a prophet) resulted from the meeting of Gauguin and Sérusier at Pont-Aven in 1888 ; the latter was to become its most fervent follower *(The Cloth Merchant, The Garland of Roses)*. Other adepts included Gauguin, who produced sculptures and ceramics *(The Beautiful Angèle, Tahiti Woman)*, Emile Bernard *(Cancale Beach)*, Maurice Denis *(The Artist's Family)*, Lacombe *(The Ages of Life)*, Vuillard *(Le Grand Teddy)*, Maxime Maufra *(Place St-André-des-Arts)*, Vallotton, O'Conor, etc.
The **Louis Valtat** Room is devoted to the work of this painter, who belonged to the Fauves group: *At Maxim's, Women Bathing, Water Carriers in Arcachon*.

First Floor – The **Neo-Impressionist Movement,** also called Divisionism or Pointillism, involved painting with small dabs of colours – a technique pioneered by the Impressionists – broken up into tiny dots in order to achieve greater luminosity. Its main representatives were Signac, Cross *(Seascape with Cypresses)*, Charles Angrand *(The Seine at Dawn)*, Henri Martin *(Joie de Vivre)*, Mengarini (excellent *Nude at the Window*), Van de Velde *(The Haymaker)* and Van Rysselberghe.
At the Autumn Fair held in Paris in 1905, a group of young artists caused a sensation because of the strong, bold colours they used in their work: the **Fauvist Movement** was born. The exhibition here presents works by Van Dongen (*The Old Clown,* pathetic ; *Portrait of Kazhnweiler,* disturbing), Chabaud *(The Moulin Rouge, The Night)*, Derain *(The Picnic)*, Dufy *(Market in Marseilles)*, Othon Friesz *(Young Girls in Marseilles)*, Manguin, Marquet *(Springtime in La Frette)* and Vlaminck *(Level-Crossing on 14 July)*. The **Moïse Kisling** Room contains a retrospective of this Polish-born painter who joined the School of Paris *(Nude Portrait of Arletty)*, *(Portrait of Jean Cocteau Sitting in his Studio)*.

Second Floor (Orangerie) – Several rooms pay tribute to Nicolas Tarkhoff (1871-1930), a Russian painter belonging to the School of Paris, whose works include street scenes, maternity scenes, views of Paris and landscapes painted both at night and during the day.

First Basement – The Ernest Ansermet Room presents compositions by the "**Montmartre Group**": Utrillo *(Notre-Dame)*, Suzanne Valadon, Steinlen *(The Evening Draws In)* ; the "**Montparnasse Group**": Picasso *(Morning Serenade)*, Chagall *(The Wandering Jew)*, Foujita *(The Lion and the Lion Tamer)*, Soutine *(The Skinned Cow)* ; the **Cubists:** Lhote *(A Sunday with Alain Fournier)*, Metzinger, Marie Laurencin, Survage.
Second Basement – The Ramparts Room hosts temporary shows. Nearby, a huge vaulted niche (a vestige of Old Geneva) is used as a setting for sculptures signed by Zadkine, including a fine polychrome composition carved in wood, *Harlequin and Colombine*.

★★ **Natural History Museum** (Muséum d'Histoire Naturelle) (GZ) ⊙ – The visit is enhanced by the presentation of the various collections and of the aquariums, vivariums and terrariums.
The ground floor is reserved for local fauna, the first floor for tropical birds and mammals and the second floor for fish, amphibians, exotic reptiles and invertebrates (insects, molluscs). The third floor is devoted to the paleontology, geology and mineralogy of Switzerland and the Geneva district (do not miss the luminescent minerals).

This floor also gives a chronological account of the history of the earth, making reference to the other planets of the universe, meteorites, volcanoes, earthquakes and the continental drift. The fourth floor enlightens visitors on the geology of the country. The most interesting exhibit is a relief map of Switzerland, at a scale of 1:100 000, which clearly shows the three main geographical regions: the Swiss Jura, the Middle Country and the Alpine range.

Horology and Enamels Museum (Musée de l'Horlogerie et de l'Émaillerie) **(GZ)** ⊙ –
Housed in an elegant 19C mansion, this museum is concerned with the science of horology from its origins up to the present day. It also illustrates the Genevese art of enamels, applied to the ornamentation of watches, jewellery, portraits and snuffboxes between the 17 and 20C.
On the ground floor, the 15-18C period is represented by sundials, hourglasses, clocks (1700 wooden clocks, 1711 astronomers' clocks with automatons), and especially clocks made in Geneva (ornemental pieces shaped as shells and insects, executed between 1830 and 1870).
The first floor displays alarm clocks, as well as 19 and 20C enamelled clocks from Geneva, often equipped with musical mechanisms. In the attic has been reconstituted the workshop which belonged to the famous watch and clock repairer Louis Cottier.
The enamels room explains the different techniques of this delicate art, which flourished in Geneva soon after 1650. The collections on display demonstrate the fine draughtsmanship, bold colours, extreme precision and high degree of mastery which characterise the art of enamels.

ADDITIONAL SIGHTS

Barbier-Mueller Museum (FY M²) ⊙ – It presents in rotation sumptuous collections relative to so-called "primitive" cultures of the five continents. The impressive display of sculptures, ceramics, jewels, ornaments and material is enhanced by the judicious layout and lighting.

Russian Orthodox Church (Église orthodoxe russe) **(GZ N)** ⊙ – The golden domes of its cupolas are an attractive feature of this residential district, which dates from the late 19C. The building, in the style of old Moscow churches, reproduces the plan of a Greek cross. Inside, the walls, vaulting and pillars are ornamented with paintings inspired by Byzantine art. The nave is separated from the chancel by the iconostasis, forming five arches in Carrara marble, finely carved and adorned with icons. In the centre stands the sacred doorway, carved in cypress pine, gilded with intricate relief work.

Ethnographic Museum (Musée d'ethnographie) **(EZ)** ⊙ – The museum presents miscellaneous collections from all over the world, featuring both works of art and simple objects for everyday use. It also hosts temporary exhibitions, focusing on specific themes or ethnic groups.

Voltaire Institute and Museum (Institut et musée Voltaire) **(DY)** ⊙ – "Les Délices" – Voltaire's main place of residence between 1755 and 1765 – has become a centre for research into the life of its famous guest and the period in which he lived. In 1965 the Institute published the very first edition of the author's vast correspondence. The library contains an impressive display of contemporary documents.
The drawing room and its adjoining gallery present furniture, manuscripts, rare editions and portraits, together with a collection of 199 wax seals used by Voltaire in his correspondence and bearing the heraldic insignia of the author. Note the terracotta replica of Houdon's statue of Voltaire – whose official name was François-Marie Arouet – and the portrait attributed to Largillière, executed when the writer was 24 years old.

St Paul's Church (Église St-Paul) – *Leave by* ⑤. This church will appeal to visitors interested in contemporary religious art on account of Maurice Denis' contribution to its interior decoration after 1915: the nave is enriched with 14 stained-glass windows and the canvas adorning the apse illustrates the life of St Paul in the form of a superb triptych.

Church of Christ the King (Église du Christ-Roi) – *At Petit-Lancy by* ⑧. The bell tower of this modern, suburban church is linked to the rest of the building by a peristyle. The interior consists of a spacious **nave★** with coffered vaulting and exposed beams.
The south wall is decorated with a fresco by Beretta while the north wall is pierced with a stained-glass window conceived by Albert Chavaz. In the chancel, which ends in a flat chevet, a huge triptych is embellished with a fine tapestry by Alice Basset.

Domaine de Penthes – *In Pregny-Chambésy, 18 Chemin de l'Impératrice. Enter by Avenue de la Paix, north of the local map, then take the Route de Pregny.* This hilly park, covering an area of 12ha – 30 acres, is planted with fine beech trees.

★ **Historical Museum of the Swiss Abroad** (Musée des Suisses à l'Étranger) ⊙ – The Penthes Château, which welcomed the Duchess of Orléans and her sons (Comte de Paris, Duc de Chartres) in 1852, presently houses a museum devoted to Swiss relations with the rest of the world from the Middle Ages to the present day. The subjects covered include the army, as well as the postal and diplomatic services. Emphasis is placed on the Franco-Swiss alliances from 1444 to 1830, and on the mercenaries or famous Swiss personalities who served the European powers.

In the Le Fort Room, enhanced by delicate wainscoting, are a number of portraits worth noting and an oval embossed silver platter depicting, after a tapestry by Le Brun, the oath of alliance taken by Louis XIV and the Swiss cantons. The first floor evokes the French Revolution and its tragic result for Louis XVI's Swiss Guards, the French Occupation and the role of the Swiss regiments during the Empire, as well as the traditions followed by the Papal Guard, founded during the 16C *(p 209)*. Mementoes of Beatus von Fischer, Switzerland's first postmaster and the national postal system, are presented in a room arranged like an 18C salon decorated with lovely **woodwork★**: seven gilded and painted panels representing the Gods of Olympus, taken from the Reichenbach Château near Berne. The exhibition rooms on the second floor are devoted to Swiss celebrities who acquired a worldwide reputation: industrialists (Nestlé, Suchard and Kohler for chocolate, Bréguet for clockmaking), bankers (Necker), diplomats (Gallatin) and writers (Blaise Cendrars).

Military Museum of Geneva (Musée militaire genevois) ⊘ – The former stables of the château, presently renamed the General Dufour Pavilion, house a small museum which explains the role played by the Swiss army during the Second World War (figures in uniform, military equipment and armament, coupons, newspapers, instruction manuals, etc.).

★★★ LAKE GENEVA (LAC LÉMAN)

Michelin map **217** folds 11 to 14 or **427** folds 11 and 12

The Swiss shore of Lake Geneva spreads its great arc fringed with vineyards successively along the last slopes of the Jura, the ridges of the Swiss Plateau and the foothills of the Vaud Alps. This shore, especially in the Vevey-Montreux section, became, after J.-J.-Rousseau had stayed there, the refuge of the Romantics. The "pilgrimages", which became more and more frequent among "nature lovers", started a great tourist industry.

Tour – *As well as the following itineraries, the corniche section of the motorway connecting Vevey and Rennaz affords wonderful views of the Upper Lake.*

The lake by boat – The steamers of the Compagnie Générale de Navigation on Lake Geneva call regularly on the Swiss and French shores, offering many trips. Let us mention among others the afternoon trips called the Tour of the **Little Lake** (Petit Lac – starting from Geneva) and the more interesting Tour of the **Upper Lake** (Haut Lac – starting from Ouchy-Lausanne). A round trip of the lake takes between 11 to 12 hours.

HYDROGRAPHICAL NOTES

From the Geneva Fountain to Chillon Castle – In all the Alpine range there is no lake that can rival that of Geneva, with its depth of 310m and its area of 58 000ha – 1 000ft and 143 323 acres. The lake is crescent-shaped, 72km long and 13km across – 45 and 7 1/2 miles – at its widest point, between Morges and Amphion. The Little Lake between Geneva and Yvoire is usually considered separately from the Great Lake. The latter is the widest section, within which another Upper Lake can be seen off Vevey-Montreux.

For centuries Lake Geneva has been an exceptional study centre, especially for the "nursery" of naturalists established at Geneva since the Reformation. Since the datum line of Swiss altimetry was fixed at the Niton Rock (alt 374m – 1 227ft above the level of the Mediterranean at Marseilles), a rock emerging from the water in the port of Geneva, the level of the lake may be regarded as the general standard of altitude in Switzerland.

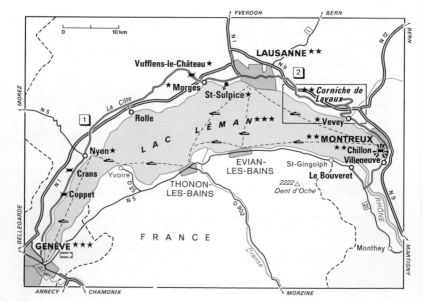

The folding of the Alps in the Tertiary Era reversed the incline of the valleys thus causing the waters to ebb and lakes to form along the edge (Lake Lucerne and Lake Geneva). The lake does not absorb the troubled waters of the Valais Rhône without a struggle: their **meeting** can be observed from the terraces or summits overlooking the towns of Vevey and Montreux. The powerful muddy flow seems to be completely engulfed; in reality, it does not mix with the lake water immediately and a layer of muddy river water remains at a depth of about 20m – 65ft until the autumn when the lake cools and mixes the river flow. The waters of the Rhône are purified and regulated in the process. However, the depth of the lake is gradually decreasing as a result of the silt deposits from the Rhône and the deepening of the river bed which causes the level of the lake to fall.

Exchange of heat between the lake waters and the atmosphere produces a very mild climate, especially in early spring and late autumn. The latter season on the Riviera of the Vaud canton is well known abroad. We also recommend a tour at the time of the grape harvest along the routes described below.

★① TOUR OF THE VINEYARDS
From Geneva to Lausanne

70km – 43 miles – about 3 hours – Local map opposite

★★★**Geneva** – *Time: 2 hours. See Geneva.*

> *Leave Geneva by ③ and by the shore road to Lausanne (which does not leave Geneva's built-up area until after Versoix).*

Coppet – *Time: 1/2 hour. See Coppet.*

Crans – *See Crans-Montana.*

★**Nyon** – *Time: 1 hour. See Nyon.*

> *Leave Nyon by ⑤, heading towards Aubonne.*

On leaving the charming port of Nyon and after Luins and the enchanting **site**★ of its little church standing alone among the vines in a clump of cypresses, you make a fast run to Bursins and then on to Mont-sur-Rolle. The view opens out. Besides the Savoy shore of the lake – with Thonon – and the summits of the Haut-Chablais, you will now see the Vaud shore from the Rolle Bay to the Naye Rocks with Lausanne between. The south-facing hills which slope down to the lake are one of the great wine-growing areas of Switzerland.

Rolle – This town lies on the north shore of Lake Geneva half-way between Geneva and Lausanne. The 13C **castle** built by a Prince of Savoy is triangular in plan, with a large tower at each corner. Out in the lake, on a small artificial island, is an obelisk erected to the memory of **General Frédéric de Laharpe** (1754-1838), a tutor of Tzar Alexander I. He introduced the latter to the new, progressive ideas. He was also a promoter of the independence of the Vaud and one of the founding fathers of the Helvetian Republic.

The run from Mont-sur-Rolle to Aubonne reveals typical villages surrounded by vineyards, like Féchy, while the **views**★★ open out towards the Little Lake as far as Geneva (fountain) and the Salève.

Immediately after leaving Aubonne, going towards Lavigny, the crossing of the Aubonne Ravine offers an attractive general view of the town.

★**Vufflens-le-Château** ⊘ – Vufflens Castle is one of the proudest buildings in all Switzerland. It stands on a plateau overlooking the ravine of the Morges, and with a fine view of the Jura, Lake Geneva and the Alps.

The castle belonged to a Savoy family and was entirely rebuilt of brick in the 15C after the Italian fashion. It was extensively restored in the 19C.

The castle consists of two quite distinct parts. The massive square keep, quartered by four towers, rises well above the rest to a lantern turret at a height of 60m – 200ft. The decorative brickwork and machicolations add an attractive note to this imposing fortress. The entrance courtyard separates the keep from the living quarters range with its four unusual slender towers each sporting a machicolated "ruffle" terminating in pointed roofs.

★**Morges** – *See Morges.*

> *Between Morges and Lausanne leave road no 1 to make a detour through St-Sulpice.*

★**St-Sulpice** – The little **St-Sulpice Church**★, a pure specimen of Romanesque art in the Vaud country and Protestant since the 16C, stands in a rustic and peaceful **setting**★ within sight of Lake Geneva and the Savoy Alps. The only traces of the former Romanesque church – which was originally a Benedictine priory – are the chancel, the transept and its crossing and tower above.

The interior is severe and simple but tempered by multicoloured decoration.

> *Return to road no 1 for the drive to Lausanne.*

The Church of St-Sulpice

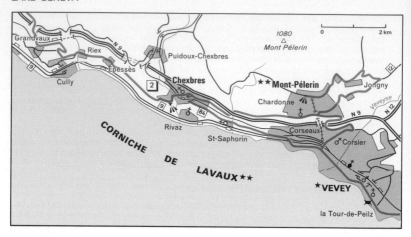

★★ 2 THE LAVAUX CORNICHE
From Lausanne to Villeneuve
39km – 24 miles – about 1 1/2 hours – Local map see above

The road described below, which crosses the motorway after the La Croix crossroads, is the same road that is sandwiched between the motorway and the coastal road (no 9) as far as the outskirts of Vevey. If traffic is too heavy take the small road from Grandvaux to the Puidoux railway station (5km – 3 miles), which then links up to the road described. It too borders and over-looks the motorway. The motorway also offers splendid views but they are often interrupted by the many tunnels.

★★ **Lausanne** – *Time: 1 hour. See Lausanne.*
Leave Lausanne by Avenue de Béthusy going towards La Rosiaz.

After this the road runs through a residential suburb and wooded ravines and emerges on a gently undulating slope planted with fruit trees within view of the Upper Lake and its Savoy shore. This is marked from left to right by the Meillerie Cliffs, the green undulations of the Gavot Plateau (behind Evian) and the Drance Delta.

Farther on, after the crossroads at La Croix, the whole of the Great Lake (Grand Lac) can be seen: the curves of the Vaud shore make a bend at the foot of the Jura, beyond the houses of Lausanne. The Yvoire Point juts out from the far shore. The once familiar sight of stately lateen-sail boats with great white sails is now a thing of the past. Two of these boats can still be seen in Ouchy and Geneva.

After a steep descent you will cross the motorway and railway.

The road then enters the Lavaux vineyard, sung by Ramuz, the writer from the Vaud. Its slopes plunge down into the Upper Lake opposite the precipitous shores of Savoy. Then come the wine-growing villages of Riex and Epesses enclosed by terraces of vines. The slope steepens and you enter the Le Dézaley District.

Where the road skirts a sharp little spur, a **belvedere**★★ with a T.C.S. viewing-table, offers a view of the Valais Rhône Valley through a gap in which the snowy Grand Combin summit appears in the distance.

A little farther on are the towns of Vevey and Montreux. They cover every bend in the shore at the foot of the characteristic Dent de Jaman and the cliffs of the Naye Rocks. During the last corniche section, between Chexbres, Chardonne and Vevey *(belvederes with benches)* look out for the Dents du Midi.

★ **Vevey** – *Time: 1 1/2 hours (for both Vevey and Mount-Pèlerin Resort). See Vevey.*

★★ **Montreux** – *See Montreux.*

★★ **Chillon Castle** – *Time: 1 hour. See Chillon Castle.*

Villeneuve – Located at the east end of the lake, this small town with vestiges recalling its ancient past, has a pleasant lake front.

The Grand'Rue, bedecked with multicoloured banners in summer, has kept its old narrow houses fronted by wooden gates. Several shops have façades decorated with quaint wrought-iron signs. Near the Place du Temple and its pretty fountain stands St Paul's Church (12C), noted for its stained-glass windows. Not far from the station, an unusual Town Hall has been set up in the former chapel of the hospital. Many world celebrities fell in love with the town and decided to make it their home. Among those whose name will forever remain associated with Villeneuve were writers like **Byron** (one hotel is named after him), Victor Hugo, Romain Rolland (he lived here from 1922 to 1938, a villa in the grounds of the Byron Hotel carries his name), and painters like Oskar Kokoscha (he died here in 1980).

When you leave Villeneuve, turn right and take the road to Noville, then cross the Rhône and turn right again towards Le Bouveret (road no 21).

Le Bouveret – This village a few miles away from the French border is the seat of the **Swiss Steam Park** (Swiss Vapeur Parc) ⊙. Along a circuit set up on the shores of the lake, near the sailing harbour, miniature trains circulate in a re-created rail-way décor in the midst of lush vegetation. Travellers may be seated on board small carriages driven by steam locomotives (Pacific 01, Waldenbourg 030, etc.) – a great favourite among children.

In summer, the **Rive-Bleue Express**, a steam engine dating back to Edwardian times, travels from Le Bouveret to Evian.

★ GIORNICO Ticino   Pop 1 048

Michelin map 218 fold 12 or 427 fold 15 – 9km – 6 miles northwest of Biasca –
Local map see ST. GOTTHARD MASSIF – Alt 378m – 1 238ft

Giornico, in a wild setting brightened by the first vineyards on the slopes of the
Upper Ticino Valley (The Leventina), is the most attractive halt on the St Gotthard
road.

The site – The stone roofs of the houses on a wooded island in the river and the
two old hump-backed bridges leading to it form a pretty picture when seen from
the bridge to the west bank of the Ticino. In the foreground the slender tower,
weathered and blackened, of the Church of Santa Maria di Castello stands among
the vines.

★St Nicholas (San Nicolao) – *On the west bank of the Ticino (the first church downstream from the bridge).*
This Romanesque church (12C) is charmingly pure and simple. Inside, the two
superimposed chancels show the very rare "confessional" arrangement dating
from the origins of the church (the crypt is half underground and supports the
upper chancel on which the relics or "sacred body" were displayed). This
arrangement enabled worshippers to place themselves literally under the protection of the patron saint of the sanctuary. The capitals in the crypt or lower chancel
and the font should be noted especially for their rustic carving (symbolic animals,
geometric designs).

GLARUS Ⓒ   Pop 5 728

Michelin map 218 north of fold 3 or 427 fold 16 – Alt 472m – 1 549ft – Facilities

Glarus lies in a deeply ravined **site**★ at the foot of the Vorder Glärnisch Cliffs. Since
its old quarters were destroyed by fire in 1861 it has had the appearance of a busy
city, built on a regular grid plan. The great Zaunplatz holds the canton's open-air
assembly (Landsgemeinde – *illustration p 25*).

A hive of industry – The row of factories, which gives a peculiar character to the
Linth Valley as the main artery of the Glarus Canton, recalls the valleys of the
Vosges.
In the 18C Pastor Andreas Heidegger introduced cotton spinning into the area. The
town enjoyed its golden age about 1860 when printing on cloth was introduced.
"Indian" fabrics from Glarus then flooded the Eastern market, as the weavers of
Glarus excelled at this technique.
Today Glarus is still the only industrial mountain canton in Switzerland. But
this municipality is also a tourist area; a resort such as **Braunwald** (facilities) keeps up
the traditions of the canton, which was a pioneer of mountaineering (the very first
shelter of the Swiss Alpine Club was built in the Tödi Massif in 1863) and skiing
(the very first Swiss Ski Championship was held at Glarus in 1905). Music Festivals
at Braunwald are extremely popular events and they also attract many music-lovers
each year.

EXCURSION

★Klöntal – *13km – 8 miles – about 3/4 hour. Leave Glarus by the road to Zürich,
then make for Riedern. In this village follow the road straight on to the Klöntal,
running up the lonely Löntsch Valley.*
At the top of a steep climb under beech trees you come into sight of Lake Klöntal
which was enlarged when the dam was built. The Glärnisch's jagged steep slopes,
rent by inaccessible ravines, plunge from a height of 2 000 m – 6 500ft into the
waters of the lake. The road climbs again to follow the lake shore and after the
second hairpin bend halt at a bench; in front of you is a superb **view**★★ of the
Klöntal.

★★★ GRANDE DIXENCE DAM

Michelin map 219 fold 3 or 427 fold 22 – Local map see VALAIS

The new Grande Dixence, the greatest feat of civil engineering the Swiss have ever
undertaken, is of the dead-weight type and 284m – 932ft tall. The first Dixence
Dam, 87m – 285ft completed in 1935, had a storage capacity of 50 million m³ –
1 765 million cu ft feeding the Chandoline power station on the floor of the Rhône
Valley opposite Sion with an average fall over 1 750m – 5 700ft. This was already
the most powerful hydro-electric installation in the world and the biggest head of
water in the world.
The Grande Dixence Dam 400m – 1/4 mile downstream from the original work –
and at an altitude of 2 365m – 7 759ft (crest of the dam) – has been built up in
stages to a height of 284m – 932ft more than two and a half times the height of
St Paul's Cathedral (to the top of the cross). About 6 million m³ – 208 million cu
ft of concrete were required – enough to build two Great Pyramids. It was
completely filled in September 1966. A further part of the project involved
drilling about 100km – 60 miles of underground tunnels to bring water from the
foot of the Matterhorn Glacier. The water was then distributed not only to the
new power station at Fionnay in the nearby Bagnes Valley, but also to the
Riddes-Nendaz and Chandoline power stations in the Rhône Valley. The hydro-
electric output of Switzerland has been increased by an annual 1 600 million kWh.

Michelin map 🔢 fold 3 or 🔢 fold 12 – Local map see Swiss JURA – Alt 440m – 1 442ft

The little town of Grandson stands near the southern end of Lake Neuchâtel. On 2 March 1476, a famous battle, in which the Confederates severely defeated the Duke of Burgundy, Charles the Bold, took place under its walls. The Duke left all his artillery and much treasure in the hands of the victors.

SIGHTS

★★**Castle** ⊘ – The first stronghold was built at the beginning of the 11 C by the lords of Grandson, but the castle, as we know it today, dates from the 13 C. After 1476 the domain of Grandson became the property of the town of Berne and Fribourg and the castle became the bailiffs' residence and was rearranged inside. The castle, with high walls, large round towers and a covered watchpath, stands on a remarkable **site★★** on the shore of the lake.
There are rooms of historic interest and collections of ancient arms. The wall-walk particularly should be seen, also the Knights' Hall (fine Renaissance stalls), a museum devoted to the Burgundian wars (dioramas) and to Charles the Bold, the great armoury, the fortresses' museum, the dungeons and the chapel as well as a museum of the Grandson District.

A car museum occupies the basement. The collection includes an 1898 Delahaye as well as the 1927 white Rolls-Royce Phantom which once belonged to Greta Garbo.

St John the Baptist – The half-Romanesque, half-Gothic church has a plain barrel-vaulted nave flanked by aisles with half-barrel vaulting. Primitive capitals surmount the monolithic columns. There is a striking contrast between the very simple nave and the chancel, which is rib-vaulted and lit by many stained-glass windows. A fine fresco depicting the Entombment is in the chapel on the south side of the chancel. The acoustic drums are also noteworthy.
Leave the church, go around to the east end and the fountain (1637); then, to the right of the church, note the former Bailiff's House, which has carved on its pediment a sun with a human face between savages wearing loincloths and brandishing clubs.

Street names are written on the town plan or indexed with a number.

Michelin map 🔢 fold 2 or 🔢 fold 21 – Local map see VALAIS – Alt 2 469m – 8 100ft

The Great St. Bernard hospice stands in a rocky gully, almost continually swept by an icy wind, on the edge of a lake which is frozen on an average of 265 days in the year and where the winter season lasts for more than eight months. The refuge exemplifies the survival of an admirable Christian tradition of help and hospitality. For nine centuries, the monks established here by St Bernard from Aosta – canons regular belonging to the Augustinian order – have taken in, comforted and rescued travellers in winter. A statue in honour of this "hero of the Alps" has been erected at the summit of the pass, on Italian soil.

Travellers caught in a snowstorm

Musée du Grand St-Bernard, Bourg-S-Pierre

Hospice. – The hospice is open throughout the year to all travellers seeking a quiet haven of peace. In the hallway stands the marble statue commissioned by Napoleon in honour of General Desaix, who was killed in the Battle of Marengo (1800).

Church – This 17C baroque church, fully incorporated into the hospice, was built on top of an early 13C sanctuary, presently serving as the crypt.
The high altar is graced by the statues of St Bernard and St Augustine. The stalls, carved in walnut, and the painted vaulting in the chancel, wildly ornate with strong, bold colours, are characteristic of the baroque period. The Holy Trinity is pictured surrounded by scenes taken from the New Testament: the Adoration of the Three Wise Men, the Annunciation and a Nativity scene. To the left, facing the chancel, stands the altar of St Bernard. On it rests a gilt walnut casket containing the remains of the illustrious saint.

Treasury – It features a fine collection of sacred objects: a polychrome 13C bust-reliquary of St Bernard, sculpted in wood and ornamented with embossed gold and precious stones, a silver pilgrim's cross gilded and studded with gems (13-14C), a Virgin and Child dating from the 15C and an illuminated 15C breviary.

Museum ⊘ – The visit starts with the **kennels**, where one can see the famous St Bernard breed, noted for its sense of loyalty, which used to accompany the monks on their errands of mercy. Nowadays the race is no longer used for rescue parties; it has been replaced by Alsatian dogs, considered to be more agile.

The **museum** recalls the long history of the pass from Antiquity to the present day: the numerous travellers it has welcomed (merchants, soldiers, pilgrims, migrants, bandits, smugglers), regional fauna and flora, the climate and everyday life at the hospice and in the pass. The archaeological artefacts include an ex-voto, a collection of coins, a handsome bronze statue of Jupiter and a finely-worked votive hand.

The history of the hospice – the statutes of the Augustinian order were committed to paper in 1438 – is illustrated by exhibitions of pictures and photographs.

★ GREAT ST. BERNARD PASS ROAD

Michelin map **219** folds 1 and 2 or **427** fold 21

The Great St Bernard Pass, connecting the Drance and Dora Baltea Valleys, carries the most historic transalpine route. Since tourist traffic began, the great tradition of hospitality has continued here since the 11C and such popular memories as that of Napoleon's crossing of the Alps in 1800 have drawn crowds attracted by the "pilgrimage". The opening of the tunnel beneath the pass has helped to separate the mass of hurried tourists crossing the frontier from the "pilgrims".

FROM MARTIGNY TO THE GREAT ST. BERNARD PASS

55km – 34 miles – about 3 1/2 hours – Itinerary 1 *on the Valais local map*

The road once beyond the fork in Bourg-St-Bernard demands careful driving because of its numerous bends. When the road is blocked by snow, tourists should travel via the tunnel. Swiss and Italian customs control are at the top of the pass in summer. Those using the tunnel will find the customs control all the year round at Gare Nord in Switzerland and Gare Sud in Italy.

Martigny – *Time: 1 1/2 hours. See Martigny.*

A short distance after Martigny, the road follows the deeply sunken Drance Valley as far Les Valettes. The smallest valleys are still planted with vines and fruit trees *(see "A first taste of Provence" under Valais)*.

Road to Mauvoisin – *75km – 46 1/6 miles from Les Valettes – about 3 1/2 hours.* Road no 21 as far as Sembrancher winds between the Drance River and the railway line.

★ **Round tour of the passes** – *Starting at Sembrancher.* When the weather is good this excursion is very pleasant.

The road continues through Vollèges (elegant bell tower), **Le Levron** (terraced mountain village), the passes of Le Lein (a rocky larch-filled hollow), Le Tronc and Les Planches (restaurant) and the tiny village of Vens *(pick up the road to Mauvoisin)*. It is a forest road at the beginning *(unsurfaced for 5km – 3 miles between Le Levron and Les Planches Pass)*, becomes a *corniche* road and then passes through woods of fir trees and larches. It affords splendid **views★** of the neighbouring valleys, the Pierre Avoi Mountain (northeast), the snowy summits of the French Alps (Mont Blanc) southwest and the Pennine Alps (Grand Combin) southeast.

★ **Verbier** – *Starting at Bagnes. See Verbier.*

From Bagnes return to the Drance Valley.

★★★ **Mauvoisin Dam** – Alt 1961m – 6433ft. The Mauvoisin Dam, which blocks a wild ravine in the Upper Bagnes Valley, is one of the highest arched-type dams in the world (237m – 778ft). This huge wall has created a reservoir of 180 million m³ – 40000 million gallons of water to feed the turbines of the Fionnay and Riddes power stations.

At Mauvoisin, make for the visitors' car park half-way between the hotel and the dam. After parking the car, take the path to the crown of the dam.

★★ **Road to Champex.** – The small **road★** from Les Valettes to Champex is difficult. There are 22 hairpin bends, mostly sharp and awkward above the Durnant which flows through 1km – 1/2 mile of the impressive gorges *(sightseeing facilities; inexperienced mountain drivers are advised to take the route via Orsières, see below)*.

★★ **Champex** – Alt 1465m – 4806ft. Facilities. Champex stands high above the Orsières Basin at the mouth of a deep wooded valley containing a delightful lake. It is an elegant resort which in summer combines the pleasures of the beach and good views. Its watery mirror reflects the majestic series of snowy summits of the Combin (Combin de Corbassière on the left, Grand Combin on the right). Those in search of views can see the range at their leisure while strolling along the Signal road connecting the hotel-belvederes of the resort.

★★ **La Breya** ⊘ – Alt 2374m – 7787ft. *1 1/2 hours Rtn, including 1/4 hour by chairlift.* A pleasant ascent by chairlift above Lake Champex; panorama of the Valais Alps.

From Champex to Orsières, the winding, surfaced road, well laid out, within sight of the Combin Massif and the Valais foothills of the Mont Blanc sloping down to the Ferret Valley, lies between broad fields of strawberries. The setting provides wonderful scenery.

Orsières – The town lies at the bottom of a hollow where the Ferret Valley, after following the whole Valais face of the Mont Blanc Massif, joins the Entremont Valley. The church has preserved its rustic belfry in the Lombard Romanesque style, although much damaged by the weather.

Among the Valais foothills of the Mont Blanc which overlook the Ferret Valley, you will see the snowy peak of the Portalet in the distance; the great pyramid of the Catogne stands out clearly; Mount Vélan rises behind the triangular Petit Vélan.

The road passes **Bourg-St-Pierre** on its right, with its rust-coloured roofs nestling at the mouth of the Valsorey Valley and its waterfall. After crossing the Valsorey and its gorges, the road overlooks Les Toules Dam of which there is a magnificent view *(a small section of the old pass road from Bourg-St-Pierre before you reach the dam is not surfaced).*

Afterwards glaciated and striated rocks and rifts filled with landslides make the landscape more and more harsh.

Bourg-St-Bernard – The installation of ski-lifts (cable-car towards the Menouve Pass), in this frontier resort at the entrance to the tunnel, have enabled a new winter sports resort, Super-St-Bernard, to be established. The last section is through the sinister Combe des Morts, swept by avalanches. To the left of the Vélan rises the fine smooth ice-cap of the Grand Combin.

Great St. Bernard Tunnel ⊙ – In view of the ever-increasing road traffic between the Rhône Valley and the Aosta Valley and to overcome the problem of snow blocking the road through the pass for over six months of the year, the Swiss and Italian governments combined to build a road tunnel, from 1959-64, which would be open all the year round and would shorten the distance from Basle to Turin to 450km – 281 miles. Some sections of the road on the Italian side are not protected. Throughout the length of the road one can admire the daring construction of this artificial highway with its viaducts cast high above the Artanavaz Gorges.

Access roads on either side of the tunnel are generally covered and have a maximum gradient of 6 % (1 in 16), they lead from below Bourg-St-Pierre on the Swiss side and above St Oyen on the Italian side.

After the Combe des Morts, it is a fast run to the Great St. Bernard Pass.

★**Great St. Bernard Pass** – *See Great St. Bernard Pass.*

★ GRIMSEL PASS ROAD

Michelin map 217 folds 9 and 19 or 427 fold 14

The road to the Grimsel, which runs along the floor of the Upper Aare Valley (Haslital), introduces the motorist to a district of rounded rocks, polished by former glaciers.

FROM MEIRINGEN TO GLETSCH

37km – 23 miles – about 1 1/2 hours – Itinerary 4 on the Bernese Oberland local map

★**Meiringen** – *See Meiringen.*

Outside Meiringen, the valley is blocked by the rocky mound of the Kirchet. Though the torrent has managed to cut through this "bolt" *(p 17)* in the well-known Aare Gorges (not visible from the road), the traveller must cross this ridge at high altitude, but this enables him to get attractive glimpses between the trees of the perfectly level basin of Innertkirchen, dominated by the great escarpments of the Burg and the pyramid of the Bänzlauistock.

★★**Aare Gorges (Aareschlucht)** – *From the road to the Grimsel, 1km – 1/2 mile – plus 1/2 hour visit. See Meiringen: Excursions.*

The valley loses its pastoral character but patches of vegetation still flourish among slabs of rock. After the bends which follow the bridge at Boden and 1 500m - about a mile downstream from Guttannen, the tourist crosses the Spreitlauibach by a gallery built in reinforced concrete. This ravine is subject to terrible avalanches which have swept the whole area clean except for part of a forest.

Guttannen – This is the only community in the Oberhasli which can be called a village. Its **Crystal Museum** ⊙ has a wide variety of minerals.

The climb continues from level to level in a **setting**★★ of rounded greenish rocks, snowfields and waterfalls. In some places the road cuts through huge blocks of extraordinarily polished, light-coloured granite.

★**Handegg Waterfall (Handeggfall)** – The Arlenbach and the Aare mingle their waters in a Y-shaped cascade which falls into a narrow gorge.

After the turquoise sheet of the reservoir-lake of Räterichsboden comes the great artificial lake of Grimsel whose muddy waters are held back by two dams anchored to the half-way Nollen Rock – the site of a hotel which took the place of the Grimsel hostel, now submerged. In line with the drowned valley, the **view**★ reaches the crests of the Finsteraarhorn (alt 4 274m – 14 022ft, highest point of the Bernese Alps) in the distance.

★★**Grimsel Pass** – Alt 2 165m – 7 103ft. A "Lake of the Dead" recalls the fighting between the Austrians and the French in 1799. From the mound behind the Hotel Grimselblick, the **view**★★ includes the desert region where the Rhône rises, the Belvedere Hotel – the only visible human habitation – near the Rhône Glacier and, from left to right, the snowy Galenstock Summit, the foot of the Rhône Glacier, the Furka Gap and its long, bare, monotonous crests stretching between the Upper Valais and the Piedmontese Toce Valley. Facing northwest you will see in the far distance the walls of the Lauteraarhorn (alt 4042m – 13 261ft).

The road then drops towards the Gletschboden, a desolate valley floor. The country loses its Arctic character and becomes more typically Alpine. The road develops hairpin bends on the Meienwand slopes and comes into sight of the terminal cataract of the Rhône Glacier, overlooked by the snowy dome of the Galenstock. You will also see Gletsch in the distance.

★★ **Gletsch** – *See Conches Valley.*

★★★ GRINDELWALD Berne   Pop 3 733

Michelin map **217** south of fold 8 or **427** fold 14 – Local map see BERNESE OBERLAND and INTERLAKEN: Excursions – Alt 1 034m – 3 392ft – Facilities

On an unforgettable site, Grindelwald, the "glacier village", is the only great mountain resort in the Jungfrau area which can be reached by car and it, therefore, attracts not only resident visitors – mountaineers or skiers according to the season – but crowds of day trippers from the district of Interlaken. The motley bustle which, on fine winter or summer days, surges exuberantly along the little town's main street, plunges the newcomer straight into the atmosphere of an Alpine capital.

★★★ **Site** – The site of Grindelwald combines a foreground full of country charm – fields planted with fruit trees or maples and dotted with pretty dwellings – with a grand rocky barrier stretching from the shoulder of the Wetterhorn to the pyramid of the Eiger.

On one hand are the high mountains, a playground for mountaineers or skilled skiers; on the other, between the Grosse and Kleine Scheidegg Ridges, with the Faulhorn between, is an immense amphitheatre-like shape of Alpine pastures and woods perfectly adapted for cross country skiing.

Access is provided by the Wengernalp railway, which serves the high altitude annexe of the Kleine Scheidegg *(qv)* which is much appreciated by skiers in early spring, and by the chain of chairlifts at First.

EXCURSIONS

★★★ **Jungfraujoch** ☉ – *See Jungfraujoch. Spend half a day on this "climb", starting by one of the two early morning trains.*

★★ **First** ☉ – *About 1 1/2 hours Rtn, including 1 hour by cable-car.* An excellent belvedere with a viewing table overlooking the Grindelwald Basin and the Wetterhorn, Schreckhorn, Fiescherhörner and Eiger Peaks.

From the terminus you are advised to go on climbing, if not to the summit of the **Faulhorn**★★★ (panorama – *5 hours on foot Rtn*), at least to the **Bachsee**★★ *(2 hours on foot Rtn).* From the shore of this little lake the Finsteraarhorn, the highest point of the Bernese Alps can be seen framed between the Schreckhorn and the Fiescherhörner.

★★ **Glacier Gorge** (Gletscherschlucht) ☉ – *2.5 km – 1 1/2 miles – on a very narrow road beginning at the end of the village, on the right, after a church, plus 1/2 hour sightseeing. This is an easy walk along well-arranged galleries.*

A rocky fissure at the bottom of which the tail of the Lower Grindelwald Glacier (Unterer Grindelwaldgletscher) appears as a narrow strip of ice.

★★★ GRISONS (GRAUBÜNDEN)

Michelin map **218** folds 1 to 7 and 11 to 17 or **427** folds 15 to 18

Three languages, two churches more or less equally represented and a political evolution towards democracy similar to that of the "original cantons" make the Grisons, which is the largest Swiss canton, a true model of the Confederation.

For the traveller this is no doubt the part of Switzerland where he can enjoy the most complete change. The Engadine, with the charm of its clear blue skies and open countryside, is the tourist lode-star of this little mountain state astride the Alps.

Geographical notes – The Grisons contain the sources of the Rhine and Inn. These two upper basins (Rhine and Inn) are separated southwest of the Silvretta by the large mountain range dotted by the Piz Linard, Piz Kesch, Piz Err and Piz Platta summits. Between these summits open the Flüela, Albula and Julier Valleys. This large Alpine area forms a vast semicircle marked out from west to east by the great Oberalp, St Gotthard, San Bernardino, Maloja, Bernina and Umbrail Passes. The Vorderrhein has its source in the Oberalp cirque and runs from Disentis/Mustér along the Grisons Oberland; the Hinterrhein comes down from the Adula Glaciers. They meet at the foot of Reichenau Castle.

The Upper Inn Valley (the river joins the Danube at Passau on the borders of Germany and Austria), because of the Engadine, is also part of ancient Rhaetia.

Historical notes – The territory of the Grisons Canton corresponds with the most mountainous parts of ancient **Rhaetia**, whose "Welsch" tribes originally peopled the area between Lake Constance and Venetia *(see Introduction: Swiss Cantons).*

The Upper Valleys of the Rhine and the Inn, protected from Germanisation, remained Romansh-speaking districts whose language, derived from Latin, was officially recognised as the fourth Swiss national language in 1938.

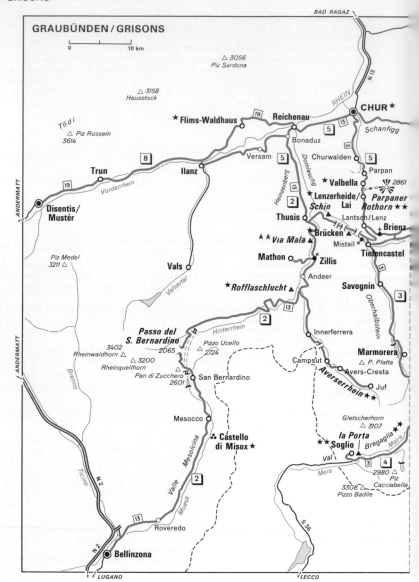

GRAUBÜNDEN / GRISONS

A transit area – Under Roman rule and throughout the Middle Ages, Rhaetia, being crossed by the High Road – the **Obere Strasse** (the Julier and especially the Septimer Pass) and the Low Road – the **Untere Strasse** (Splügen Pass) monopolised nearly all the transalpine traffic through the present territory of the Confederation. The great advantage of the High Road is that there are few passes, which are usually so frequent along transalpine roads. The only comparable cavalcade was farther west along the Great St Bernard road.

The present network of transalpine roads through the Grisons results from the implementation between 1818-23 of a programme financed jointly by Switzerland, Austria and Piedmont.

TOUR

Recommended itineraries. – Organised according to time (longest to shortest) needed for an itinerary.

★★① **The Zügen and Flüela Pass Roads** – Round tour starting from Davos – allow one day. *See Davos.*

★★② **San Bernardino Pass Road** – Road from Bellinzona to Chur – allow one day. *See San Bernardino Pass Road.*

　★③ **Julier and Albula Pass Roads** – Round tour starting from St Moritz – about 5 hours. *See St.Moritz.*

★★★④ **The Engadine** – Upper Engadine (Bregaglia Valley): road from St Moritz to Soglio – about 1 1/2 hours. Lower Engadine (Inn Valley): road from St Moritz to Martina – about 3 hours. *See Engadine.*

　★⑤ **Lenzerheide Road, Schyn Gorges** – Round tour starting from Chur – about 3 hours. *See Chur.*

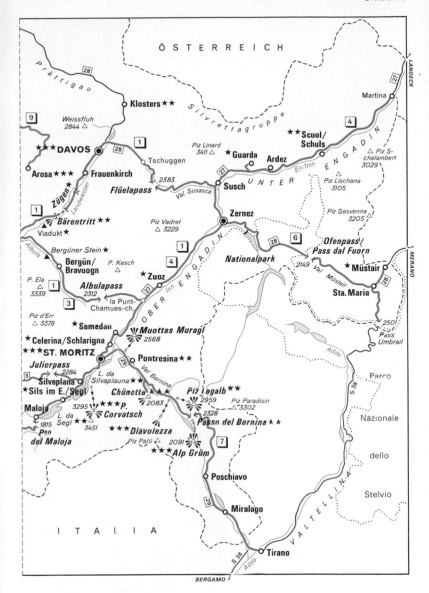

★ 6 **Ofen Pass Road** (Swiss National Park and Müstair Valley) – Road from Zernez to Umbrail Pass – about 2 1/2 hours. *See Zernez.*

★★★ 7 **Bernina Pass Road** (Bernina Valley and Poschiavo Valley) – Road from St Moritz to Tirano – about 2 hours. *See Bernina Pass Road.*

★ 8 **Vorderrhein Valley** – Road from Disentis/Mustér to Reichenau – about 1 3/4 hours. *See Disentis/Mustér.*

★ 9 **Schanfigg Road** – Road from Chur to Arosa – about 1 hour. *See Arosa.*

Telephone Numbers
By dialling 111 you will obtain
- addresses of chemists on duty
- addresses of the nearest hospital and/or doctor
By dialling 117 you will obtain
- police in case of an emergency
By dialling 120 you will obtain
- in winter snow report and avalanche bulletin
By dialling 140 you will obtain
- the Touring-Secours motor breakdown service (open 24 hours)
By dialling 162 you will obtain
- weather forecasts
By dialling 163 you will obtain
- information about snow-bound roads and whether you need chains etc.
The operators usually speak French, German and Italian depending on the region and English in the main cities and major resorts.

This little fortified town is perched on a hill in a harmonious landscape. It charms visitors to Romansh Switzerland by its friendly atmosphere, derived from the time when the whole Sarine Valley lay under the gay and kindly sway of the Counts of Gruyères (12-16 C).

SIGHTS

Arrival – *Cars should be parked (car park) outside the town.*
Visitors will immediately be charmed by the locality of Gruyères, which they approach by its main street. It is lined with old houses with twin windows and wide eaves, and slopes down to the town fountain before rising again towards the castle.
Go up to the castle on foot, noticing on the right the old grain measures hollowed out of a stone block, and then on the left, the house with delicately carved 16C window-frames of the jester Chalamala, who became famous at the court of the Counts of Gruyères.

★ **Castle** ○ – The former castle of the Counts of Gruyères now belongs to the Fribourg Canton. Most of it dates from the late 15C (façades on the courtyard of the main dwelling).
The internal arrangement of the castle recalls both the feudal period (kitchen and guardroom) and the refinements of the 18C. Their decoration, more or less tasteful, is largely the work of the Bovy family, a dynasty of artists who saved the castle from destruction in the last century and welcomed a great many foreign artists (Corot among them).
The most valuable pieces in the collections assembled here are the three mourning **copes**★ of the Order of the Golden Fleece, used by the almoners of Charles the Bold to celebrate solemn masses for the repose of the knights, who died in the campaign of 1476. These sumptuous vestments became, for the people of Fribourg, their most glorious trophy of the Battle of Murten *(p 158).* Four 16C Flanders tapestries are in a new hall.

The heraldic crane of the Counts of Gruyères can be seen in many places, over doors, in stained-glass windows and on fire-backs.

St John's – The 15C chapel stands on a pleasantly situated terrace within view of the Lower Gruyère (Bulle-Broc District), partly drowned by the reservoir of the Rossens Dam *(qv),* and of the two graceful Dent de Broc Peaks.

Follow the main street again.

In this direction it offers a view of the Moléson *(see below),* the most typical Gruyère peak.

Turn to the right in front of the fountain.

The Belluar – This picturesque defence work (the name of which is derived from the same root as *boulevard*) guarded the main entrance to the town in the days of palfreys and hackneys.

Cheese Dairy ○ – *1 km – 1/2 mile, at the entrance to Pringy.* This model cheese dairy includes a cellar and storage

The Main Street

area on the ground floor; on the first floor is the ripening area and on the second floor are galleries overlooking the demonstration area where Gruyère in wheels of 35 kilos – 77 lbs is made. Taped commentary in English.

EXCURSION

Moléson-sur-Gruyères – Facilities. *6 km – 4 miles to the southwest.*
This pretty village features an alpine **cheese dairy** ○ set up in a 17 C chalet, with a roof made up of 90 000 shingles. After an audio-visual presentation of regional specialities, visitors are shown the humble sleeping quarters of a local cowheard *(armailli).* Then they can watch a cowherd prepare Gruyère cheese according to traditional methods, baking it in an old-fashioned stove fuelled by firewood. Fresh products are kept in the milk room, while the more mature cheeses are stored in the salting house, a small square building with a shingle roof located near the farm.

A cable-car will take you up to the **Moléson Observatory** ⊘ (alt 2002m – 6500ft), which commands a panoramic view of the Gruyères area and the Swiss plateau. The observatory organises evening classes on the subject of astronomy (telescopes). During the winter season 35km – 20 miles of carefully marked-out ski runs are available to tourists.

La Locanda restaurant in Moléson-Village is the sitting for a **Wax Museum** (Historial Suisse) ⊘ which evokes famous figures in Swiss history from St Maurice to Henri Dunant.

★★ GSTAAD Berne

Michelin map **217** fold 15 or **427** fold 13 – Local map see VAUD ALPS – Alt 1080m – 3543ft – Facilities

Gstaad lies at the junction of four gently sloping valleys on the boundary between the Bernese and Vaud Alps. They are: the Upper Sarine Valley, the Lauenen Valley, the Turbach Valley and the Saanenmöser Depression. The resort is pleasing for its restful setting and the variety of its sporting and social facilities.

Thanks to the blue trains of the local railways the resort shares with **Saanenmöser** (alt 1272m – 4173ft – facilities) and even with **Zweisimmen** (facilities – equipped with a large cable-car for ascents to the Rinderberg) a magnificent skiing ground served by about sixty ski-lifts, which enable runs to be varied in accordance with individual tastes in snow or track.

★★ HÉRENS VALLEY

Michelin maps **217** fold 16 and **219** fold 3 or **427** fold 22

The Hérens Valley is one of the most accessible of the lateral valleys in the French-speaking Valais, and the tourist will find it fascinating.

The Évolène District, in a very fine setting of high mountains (Dent Blanche), gives a picture of local customs.

A living museum – Sights like that of haymaking between Évolène and Les Haudères are among the most attractive in picturesque Switzerland. The inhabitants of this high valley are unusually faithful to their traditional dress *(illustration p 28)* and wear it even while performing their daily tasks. When you see the women working in the fields in colourful groups, riding on mule-back or driving herds of cows, you are often tempted to forget the rigours of their mountain life. The men scarcely appear in these pastoral scenes. Most of them find work in local timber yards or factories.

FROM SION TO LES HAUDÈRES

29km – 18 miles – about 2 hours – Itinerary **5** *on the Valais local map.*

★★ **Sion** – *Time: 3 hours. See Sion.*

From Sion, crossing the Rhône and leaving on the right the Chandoline power station, which is fed by the Grande Dixence Dam, the road climbs in hairpin bends, affording good views of the site of Sion, which is marked by the fortified heights of Valère and Tourbillon. On arriving at Vex, the first village in the Hérens Valley, the superb rock pyramid of the Dent Blanche begins to emerge from the corrie of Ferpècle.

★★★ **Grande Dixence Dam** – *See Grande Dixence Dam. 16km – 10 miles from Vex by a narrow road – allow 2 hours.*

The road, which runs almost horizontally along a ledge, approaches the ravines overlooking the confluence of the Borgne and the Dixence. The eye will be caught by the astonishing ridge of broken country from which the Pyramids of Euseigne spring.

★ **Pyramids of Euseigne** – The road passes through a tunnel under the "crowned columns" cut out by erosion from masses of soft morainic debris and saved from destruction by their unstable, rocky crowns.

The valley shrinks and the gradient grows steeper. Arrival in the Évolène Basin is marked by the reappearance of the Dent Blanche. To the right of the Dent Blanche, in the foreground, stand the twin sharp-edged pyramids of the Dents de Veisivi.

★ **Évolène** – Facilities. This charming resort is well suited for mountaineering (Mount Collon and Dent Blanche Massifs). Its tall **wooden houses**★★, gay with bright flowers, are among the finest in the Valais *(illustration p 30)*.

Les Haudères – The chalets stand in picturesque disorder.

From here two roads lead, in one instance 12km – 8 miles to the mountaineering station of Arolla (alt 1998m – 6437ft; facilities pp 12-13) at the foot of Mount Collon, and in the other case 9km – 5 miles to Ferpècle (alt 1770m – 5807ft) at the foot of the Dent Blanche.

As the road climbs to the hamlets of La Sage, Villa and La Forclaz there are clear views of the Upper Hérens Valley.

Consult the Index to find an individual town or sight.

★ HÖLLOCH CAVE (HÖLLOCHGROTTE) Schwyz

Michelin map 🗺️ northwest of fold 2 or 🗺️ fold 15

The Hölloch Cave is known for the size of its galleries, the number of its naturally formed chambers and the beauty of its concretions. It is also the biggest cave in Europe and as a geological phenomenon enjoys a worldwide reputation.

Access – On the way out of Schwyz, take the Muotatal road *(see Schwyz for town plan)* which is narrow until you reach Hinterthal, then cross the river and turn left into a steep uphill road going to Stalden *(signpost: Stalden-Hölloch)*.
Leave the car near the "Gasthaus zur Höllgrotte" where the guide lives, and walk to the entrance to the cave.

Tour ⊙ – *Torches, hard hats and wellingtons are recommended.* The Hölloch Cave was almost unknown at the beginning of this century, but, since 1949 it has been the scene of continuous exploration. Only 1km – 1/2 mile of the galleries are open though more than 147km – 91 miles have been mapped. This underground architecture seems almost unbelievable and is fascinating: there are few stalactites or stalagmites, but by contrast there are delicate, fairylike concretions in the form of roses, chandeliers, and sea-shells which seem to moderate the grim, smooth walls of the great gulfs in the cave and the ever-increasing number of erosion holes. The "altar" and the "great pagoda" especially should be seen.

The late season (October and early November) is a good time for an artistic tour of Switzerland.
When travelling through the Mittelland (Middle Country) at this time you should get a very clear view of the Alps.

★★★ INTERLAKEN Berne   Pop 4 852

Michelin map 🗺️ folds 7 and 8 or 🗺️ fold 14 – Local maps see BERNESE OBERLAND and INTERLAKEN: Excursions – Alt 564m – 1 854ft – Town plan in the current Michelin Red Guide Switzerland – Facilities

Interlaken is the tourist centre of the Bernese Oberland.

The resort – The Latin sound of the name Interlaken recalls the clerical origin of the town; it grew up "between the lakes" from the 12C onwards, around an Augustinian monastery of which traces (cloister gallery) can still be found in the block of buildings formed by the castle and the Protestant church.
Framed between the small wooded Ranges of the Rügen and the Harder, the town is scattered today over the low plain of the Bödeli, formed by deposits from the Lombach in the north and the Lütschine in the south. These finally divided the single lake (into which the Aare used to flow between Meiringen and Thun) into two distinct sheets of water, Lakes Thun and Brienz (Thunersee and Brienzersee).

View of Interlaken

SIGHTS

★★ **Höheweg.–** This famous avenue is bordered on one side by the lawns and flower beds of the Höhematte, on the other by a row of grand hotels and behind them, the casino (Kursaal). The promenade links the urban centre of Interlaken West with the much more scattered township of Interlaken East. It offers dazzling **views★★★** of the Jungfrau summit, through the opening of the lower Lütschine Valley. The life on the avenue itself is no less attractive. It is pleasant to stroll beneath the trees, glancing at the pavilion of meteorological instruments or the well-known floral clock in the casino gardens.

A second attraction on the opposite bank of the Aare is the open-air swimming-pool and miniature golf course. These are both popular weekend activities during the summer season.

Unterseen Church – With its rustic tower crowned by a steeply-pitched roof, this building with the Mönch (on the left) and the Jungfrau (on the right) in the background makes an attractive **scene★★**.

Tourist Museum ⊘ – *At Unterseen Obere Gasse 26*. A charming renovated 17C residence with old timber beams up to 20m – 60ft long houses a small museum which retraces the development of tourism in the Jungfrau Region from the beginning of the last century up to the present day. The ground floor exhibits illustrate a century of road transport in the Oberland : the Habkern postal carriage, models of other postal vehicles and the first bicycle to have been used in Interlaken.

The milestones *(studensteine)* indicated the distance and length of time required for those on foot, to reach Berne.

On the first floor the exhibitions cover the growth of the hotel industry (accommodation in private homes, inns and hotels) and the development of the railway network (model of a locomotive from the Brünig Pass's rack railway). They also feature a number of nautical instruments and furnishings (compass, first-aid kit, siren, wheel) grouped together in the boat section. The most interesting exhibit is undoubtedly a miniature model of the *Bellevue*, the very first boat to sail on Lake Thun. The themes of the second floor are winter sports with a section on the development of skis and sledges, the growth of mountain railways such as those on the Giessbach, Wetterhorn and jungfrau and the sport of mountaineering. The top floor is reserved for temporary exhibitions.

EXCURSIONS

Nearby belvederes which can be reached by funicular or on foot

★★★ **Schynige Platte** ⊘ – Alt 2 101m – 6 891ft. *About 4 hours Rtn, including 2 hours by rack-railway starting from Wilderswil Station.*
This "climb" is especially suited to tourists who have no time to go farther into the Jungfrau Massif. From the upper station, near which are an Alpine garden, a botanical section with local flora and an hotel terrace commanding a panoramic view, it is easy to climb to the nearest summit (alt 2 067m – 6 781ft with a view towards the great Lauterbrunnen Valley and the Jungfrau) or to the Daube (alt 2 076m – 6 812ft) belvedere facing the Jungfrau, Interlaken and its lakes.

★★ **Harderkulm** ⊘ – Alt 1 323m – 4 341ft. *About 1 hour Rtn, including 1/2 hour by funicular.*
The summit affords a clear view of the two Interlaken lakes and the Jungfrau Massif.

★ **Heimwehfluh** ⊘ – Alt 670m – 2 218ft. *About 1/2 hour Rtn, including 5 minutes by funicular.*
A cool, shady hill forming a shelf overlooking Thun and Brienz Lakes. There are many shady walks, especially on the slopes of the Rügen or the Harder.

Excursions by car or by cable-car

★ **Beatenberg** – *Access and description see Beatenberg.*

★★★ **Lauterbrunnen Valley** – *18km – 11 miles – about 3 hours including 2 3/4 hours cable-car and sightseeing. Leave Interlaken to the south on the Grindelwald road.* The road runs into the wooded Lütschine Defile, losing sight of the Jungfrau for the time being.

At the road fork at Zweilütschinen, go straight ahead to Lauterbrunnen.

The valley soon widens, framed, as you go upstream, by the huge rock walls which make the Lauterbrunnen Gorge a classic example of the glacial feature: a U-shaped valley *(see illustration in the Introduction : Alpine Relief)*. Ahead, on either side of the slopes of the Schwarzmönch, appear the snowy summits of the Jungfrau (on the left) and those of the Mittaghorn-Grosshorn group (straight ahead).

Lauterbrunnen – Facilities. This village has heavy transit traffic. Motorists who wish to go to Wengen must leave their cars *(car park)*.
Here the **Staubbach Waterfall★★**, which Byron compared to the "tail of the pale horse ridden by Death in the Apocalypse", plunges 300m – 1 000ft – from the terrace at Mürren, dissolving almost entirely into fine spray.
In line with the valley you will now see, clearly detached, Breithorn Summit, to the right of the Grosshorn.

Leave your car in the Trümmelbach Falls car park.

★★★**Trümmelbach Falls** (Trümmelbachfälle) ⊘ – *3/4 hour on foot Rtn.*
A lift passing through the rock leads to the beginning of the galleries. These are very well sited over the winding fissure where the Trümmelbach leaps and boils, forcing its way through a series of great eroded pot-holes.

On returning to the lower entrance of the funicular, do not fail to walk up the path to the left (to the right when facing the mountain) and see the incredible gush of water coming from the last but one falls of the Trümmelbach Falls.
Return to your car and drive up the valley to Stechelberg, the Mürren-Schilthorn cable-car station and the place from where you can see, to the south *(1km – 1/2 mile)* the lovely, almost vertical **Sefinen Waterfall**★ (Sefinenfall).

★★**Mürren** – *Access: 10 minutes by cable-car. See Mürren.*

★★★**Schilthorn** ⊘ – *Round trip about 2 hours including 1 hour's cable-car via Stechelberg. See Mürren: Excursions.*

★★★**Grindelwald** – *20km – 12 miles to the southeast – about 3/4 hour. See Grindelwald.*
At Zweilütschinen turn left into the Schwarze Lütschine Valley. This is less steep-sided than the Lütschine Valley through which you have just come. After having climbed the ridge, formed by a former moraine, by means of a series of hairpin bends, you will begin to see the impressive mountain setting of Grindelwald *(qv)*. From left to right the following will appear in succession: the Wetterhorn group, with the great snowfield of the Grindelwald Firn the beginning, of the Upper Grindelwald Glacier (Oberer Grindelwaldgletscher), the Mettenberg, the Lower Grindelwald Glacier (Unterer Grindelwaldgletscher) and finally, at the end of the long rock face, the pyramidal shape of the Eiger.

★★★**Tour of Three Passes** (Grimsel, Furka, Susten) – *191km – 119 miles – allow a whole day (start in the early morning). Leave Interlaken to the southwest on the Meiringen road (described on p 152) then follow the roads to the Three Passes (described on pp 110, 94, 202), preferably beginning with the Grimsel Pass road.*

★**Kander Valley** – *43km – 27 miles – about 3 hours. Leave Interlaken by the road to Spiez. See Kander Valley.*
The road follows the south shores of Thun Lake and it lies opposite the wooded Nase Promontory and the Beatenberg *(qv)* terrace.
After Därlingen a *corniche* section reveals the whole of the lake and town of Thun in the distance.
At Leissigen take the road to the left towards **Aeschi**, crossing the ridge between the lake and the Kander Valley. The Aeschi **panorama**★ is a pleasantly wide view; the village marks the top of the climb. After discovering the mountain setting of Thun Lake you will see the gigantic Niesen Peak and – through the Kiental Gap – the three snowy Blümlisalp Peaks.

The rest of the excursion, from Reichenbach to Kandersteg, is described under Kander Valley.

After going up to Lake Oeschinen return to Interlaken via Spiez *(qv)*.

For other excursions from Interlaken into the Bernese Oberland, see the list of recommended itineraries under Bernese Oberland.

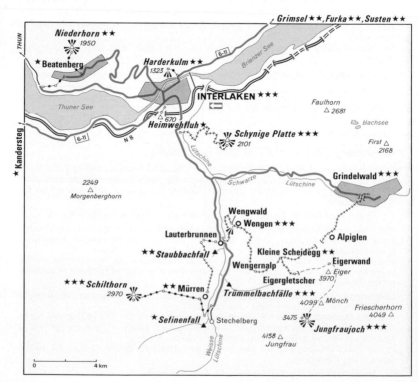

★★★Round tour by railway of the Jungfrau ⊙

Allow a whole day for the tour. Some of the slopes have gradients of 25% – 1:4. The tourist staying at Interlaken who wants to climb the Jungfraujoch should choose a day when the atmospheric conditions are the best possible in order to enjoy spectacular scenery: a veil of cloud on the summits is enough to spoil the excursion.

Wear warm clothes, and if you want to go out into the open, take sun-glasses and wear stout shoes.

Lauterbrunnen – *See Interlaken: Excursions.*

The excursion to the **Trümmelbach Falls**★★★ *(qv)* should not be missed. It takes about 1 1/2 hours from Lauterbrunnen. *Use the postal van connecting with the trains from Interlaken.*

Wengwald – Alt 1 182m – 3 878ft. Between this stopping-place and Wengen the route offers a splendid **view**★★★ of the Lauterbrunnen rift, while the **Jungfrau** emerges in the distance. This is flanked on the right by the Silberhorn, a dazzling white, conical snow-peak.

★★★Wengen – *See Wengen.*

Wengernalp – Alt 1 873 m – 6 145ft. A wild site at the foot of the rock and glacier slopes of the Jungfrau. The deep Trümmelbach Gorge in the foreground makes the height of this wall of rock still more impressive, and it is rare to pass here during the warm part of the day without seeing an avalanche.

To the left of the Jungfrau you will recognise the snowy cleft of the Jungfraujoch – the terminus of the excursion (the Sphinx observatory is visible), and then the Mönch, the glacier, Eigergletscher and the Eiger.

★★Kleine Scheidegg – Alt 2 061m – 6 762ft. Facilities. This mountain resort, isolated on the ledge connecting the Lauterbrunnen and Grindelwald Valleys, is a favourite with skiers, who find abundant snow here late in the season. In summer it is frequented by tourists seeking tranquillity. Tourists who do not go up the Jungfraujoch may admire the Grindelwald Basin and pick out the Eiger-Mönch-Jungfrau group in excellent conditions by going up to the **belvedere**★★ on the north side of the pass *(1/2 hour on foot Rtn)*.

Eigergletscher – Alt 2 320m – 7 612ft. This stop near the snout of the Eiger Glacier, much broken and stained with morainic deposits, marks the beginning of the underground section, 7km – 4 miles long, which leads to the Jungfraujoch. In spring, great numbers of skiers come here.

Eigerwand – Alt 2 865m – 9 400ft. The station is cut out of the rock. Ventilating bays giving on the north face of the Eiger afford a bird's eye view of the Grindelwald Basin and the Interlaken District. It is an impressive situation when one remembers the dramatic efforts of mountaineers to conquer this rock wall, which was climbed for the first time only in 1938.

★★★Jungfraujoch – *See Jungfraujoch.*

Alpiglen – Alt 1 616m – 5 302ft. After this resort the railway line, which hitherto has skirted the foot of the Eiger, dips towards the broad and verdant Grindelwald Basin, where the outlying fields, dotted with houses, reach out to the rock base of the Wetterhorn. Ahead is the pastoral plateau of the Grosse Scheidegg (Great Scheidegg).

★★★Grindelwald – Alt 1 057m – 3 392ft at the station. *The resort and the best excursions (to First, the Bachsee and the Glacier Gorge) are described under Grindelwald.*

Boat Trips

Many steamer and motor-boat services are run during the season on Thun Lake (Thunersee – landing stage in the Interlaken Westbahnhof) and on Lake Brienz (Brienzersee – landing-stage behind the Interlaken Ostbahnhof or at Bönigen), enabling everyone to go on trips which include stopping-places like the **Giessbach Falls**★★ (Giessbachfälle – *qv*) which is the most interesting sight on the shores of Lake Brienz or to enjoy evening cruises. Finally, lovers of aquatic sports will find sailing and water-skiing schools and boats for hire at the base at Neuhaus, on Thun Lake.

MICHELIN GREEN GUIDES

Art and architecture
Ancient monuments
Scenic routes
Landscape
Geography
History
Touring programmes
Plans of towns and buildings

A selection of guides for holidays at home and abroad

A collection of regional guides for France.

JAUN PASS ROAD

Michelin map **217** folds 5, 6 and 7 or **427** folds 12 and 13

The road to the Jaun Pass is the most mountainous in the Fribourg Alps. For the sightseer it combines lakes, rocky crests and stretches of pasture.

FROM SPIEZ TO BULLE

63km − 39 miles − about 2 1/2 hours

★**Spiez** − *See Spiez.*

Just beyond Spiez, between Wimmis and Reidenbach, the Simme Valley, to which the Port, a rocky defile cut through the Burgfluh barrier marks the lower entrance, is a corridor through verdant country showing highly developed agriculture. Many covered bridges cross the torrent. To the east the great cone-shape of the Niesen is prominent for a long time in the background.

Erlenbach − *See Erlenbach.*

From Reidenbach to the Jaun Pass, the road, making many hairpin bends in open country, offers steadily lengthening views of the valley, dotted with red roofs, in which the embanked Simme flows. The snows of the Wildhorn sparkle on the horizon due south

From the Jaun Pass (alt 1 509m − 4 951ft; winter sports) to Jaun, the road is less winding but steeper than on the Bernese side. It includes several fine high corniche sections opposite the deeply riven escarpments of the **Gastlosen**, where the people of Fribourg practise rock-climbing.

Jaun − This little town quite close to the dividing line between Romansh and German Switzerland still has a few fine old chalets and a church with a traditional shingle roof. The site is deeply shut in and is cheered by its generous cascade.

Charmey − The main attraction of this village is the surrounding countryside.

★**Javroz Bridge** − Leave the Jaun Pass for a moment to take the road to Cerniat; park the car in the car park on the right and go a few steps to the belvedere. The reinforced concrete arch with a span of 85m − 275ft crosses the deep Javroz Valley at a height of 60m − 200ft at a point where the river begins to flow into the artificial Montsalvens Lake. As far as the Montsalvens Tower, whose ruined walls recall the feudal past of the County of Gruyère, the **Jogne Valley** (Jauntal − now Romansh-speaking) remains wide and open, its lower slopes disappearing under the waters of the many-armed lake formed by the Montsalvens Dam. As in other parts of the Alps the farmers here used to use curious vehicles (half-sleighs, half-carts) well suited to local surfaces to gather in the crops. At Charmey on the 2nd Sunday in October there is a race of these vehicles.
The road becomes very hilly between Montsalvens and Bulle as it descends to the floor of the ravines, through which the Jogne and the Sarine flow, and crosses these torrents. It then affords pleasant views of the Gruyère District.

Broc − From the garden in front of the town hall, you will enjoy a lovely **view**★ of the Gruyère area with the three familiar summits of Vanil Blanc, Vudalla and Moléson as a backdrop.

Bulle − *See Bulle.*

★★**Gruyères** − *Extra distance 7km − 4 miles − allow 1 hour for sightseeing in Gruyères (qv).*

★★ JOUX VALLEY

Michelin map **217** folds 2 and 12 or **427** fold 11

The jewel of the Vaud Jura, the Joux Valley and its lake presents an agreeable stop on an otherwise hilly road which links the French boundary to Lake Geneva.

FROM VALLORBE TO NYON

57km − 36 miles − about 3 hours − Itinerary 1 *on the Swiss Jura local map*

The Marchairuz road (Le Brassus to St-George) is usually blocked by snow from November to April.

Vallorbe − *See Vellorbe.*

From Vallorbe, the road, climbing quickly up the side of the steep, wooded slope overlooking the "source" of the Orbe *(qv)*, skirts the foot of the Dent de Vaulion escarpments.

★★★**Dent de Vaulion** − *From Le Pont, 12km − 7 miles − about 1/2 hour − by the Vaulion road and then the road to the Dent, on the left, plus 1/2 hour on foot Rtn. For access and description see Dent de Vaulion.*

★★**Joux Valley** − The road then leads into the Joux Valley gently hollowed out between the minor ranges of Risoux and Tendre Mounts. After the small Lake Brenets, and the villas and hotels of **Le Pont** (facilities) scattered around it, appears Lake Joux, the largest of the Jura lakes. Its calm waters are frozen during the long harsh winter. Until a few years after the First World War this ice, cut into regular blocks, was stored at Le Pont in underground ice-houses before being sent to Paris by rail. You follow the south shore, bordered by wooded hills, wide pastures, and hospitable villages, which are both pleasant country resorts and small industrial centres employed in watch and clock-making.

The climb from Le Brassus (facilities) to the Marchairuz Pass affords pleasant views of Lake Joux and its valley, closed by the bold spur of the Dent de Vaulion.

Amburnex Coomb − *Tour from the pass road 8.5km − 5 miles. The road to the Amburnex Coomb begins a little below the Marchairuz Pass, on the slope of the Joux Valley. Close the gates behind you. Take care not to drive on the grass. Military area.* Tourists looking for a quiet halting-place will find it in this secluded coomb.

On the Nyon side, this run, which affords wonderful views of Mont Blanc, includes two different sections:

− **between the pass and St George,** the descent through the woods is interspersed with wide, flat clearings from which glimpses of Lake Geneva and the great lakeside towns (Lausanne, Thonon, Geneva) can already be had. Geneva is easy to recognize in summer, thanks to the jet of its great fountain.

− **between St George and Nyon,** the Mont Blanc is nearly always visible.

La Garenne Zoo ⊘ − This small zoo presents mostly European species (wolf, lynx, eagle, etc.).
The hairpin section between Burtigny and Begnins offers particularly open **views**★★ of the Savoy shore of Lake Geneva − note the jutting Yvoire Point − with its towns and mountains (from left to right: Den d'Oche, Voirons, Salève), and the crests of the Jura, forming a rampart above the Gex District. Nyon is close by.

★**Nyon** − *Time: 1 hour. See Nyon.*

*A map of Touring Programmes
is given at the beginning of the guide.*

*To plan a special tour
use the preceding Map of Principal Sights.*

★★★ JUNGFRAUJOCH Berne

Michelin map **217** fold 18 or **427** fold 14 − Local maps see BERNESE OBERLAND and INTERLAKEN : Excursions − Alt 3 475m − 11 401ft

This high mountain resort is the highest resort served by a rack-railway ⊘ in Europe (the last part of the trip before arriving at the resort is through a tunnel 7km − 4 miles long; for the railway tour of the Jungfrau leaving from Interlaken *see Excursions from Interlaken*). In fine weather it offers the tourist not only outstanding views but a great choice of attractions (dog sleighs, "Ice Palace"). As regards sports, the Jungfraujoch is above all a summer skiing centre. From the terrace of the Jungfraujoch Plateau and from the Sphinx's (rocky peak) belvederes a view can be had onto the great icy expanse of the Aletsch Glacier. To the north lies the Interlaken District. In the distance you will see faintly the crests of the Jura, the Vosges and the Black Forest. *Do not leave the beaten track without a guide.*

The Jungfrau

★★ JURA, SWISS

Michelin maps **216** folds 2 to 5 and 12 to 16, **217** folds 2 to 4 and 11 and 12 and **70** folds 7 to 9 and 16 and 17 or **427** folds 3, 4, 11 and 12.

The Swiss Jura, however fine its great belvederes may be, is more than a mere viewing point for the Alps and deserves more than a quick run. From the parallel valley to the cross valley *(see diagram p 20)* and from parkland to forest the motorist will find here – especially in the Bernese Jura – a whole series of sites making a harmonious transition from the Burgundian lands of the Saône Plain to the Swiss Mittelland with its German civilization.

The Swiss shield – In the past the Jura has been more often a protective *glacis* for the Confederation than a stronghold of democracy. It has remained politically divided among the surrounding towns as it was when the princes of Neuchâtel or the bishops of Basle held the keys to the main routes through it. Thus, we may speak of the Vaud Neuchâtel, Bernese, Solothurn and Basle Juras in spite of the creation of the Jura Canton in 1978.

This political division has not greatly hampered the economic progress of the Swiss Jura secured since the beginning of the 18C by the watch-and clock-making industry, born at Le Locle and La Chaux-de-Fonds *(qv)*.

Crossing the Jura – The motorist coming from France will be well advised to follow, towards the end of his run, the roads giving very open views of the Swiss Plateau (the Mittelland) with its lakes and the Alps. The itineraries along the Pichoux Gorges *(qv)*, the Vue des Alpes *(qv)* or the Joux Valley *(qv)* are especially suit-able. The Chasseral road *(qv)*, between St-Imier and Lake Biel is certainly worthy of inclusion in any list of roads crossing the Jura, on account of the wide panorama to be seen from its upper level. Many other crossings of the Jura offer sustained scenic interest over short sections, for instance the road from La Cure to Nyon via St-Cergue (no 90), an alternative to the Faucille road which is recommended, especially in winter, for its excellent surface; the road from Vallorbe to Lausanne via Cossonay (no 9), which forms a balcony over the Vaud District swithin sight of Mont Blanc; and the roads from Pontarlier to Yverdon - les - Bains via

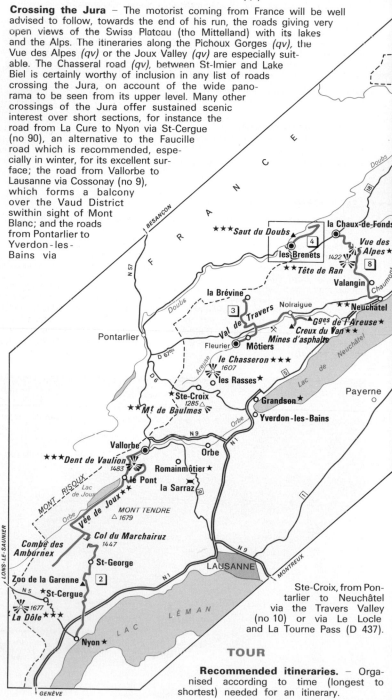

Ste-Croix, from Pontarlier to Neuchâtel via the Travers Valley (no 10) or via Le Locle and La Tourne Pass (D 437).

TOUR

Recommended itineraries. – Organised according to time (longest to shortest) needed for an itinerary.

★★⬚1 **Weissenstein Road** – Road from Porrentruy to Solothurn – about 4 1/2 hours. *See Weissenstein Road.*

★★⬚2 **Joux Valley** – Road from Vallorbe to Nyon – about 3 hours. *See Joux Valley.*

⬚3 **Travers Valley** – Road from Fleurier to Noiraigue – about 2 hours. *See Travers Valley.*

★★⬚4 **Doubs Basins** – Tour by boat, car or on foot – about 2 1/2 hours. *See Doubs Basins.*

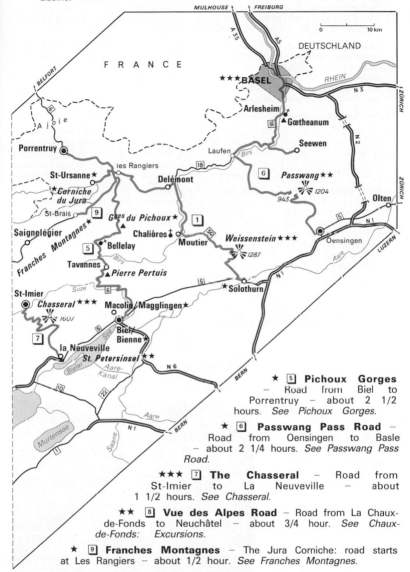

★ ⬚5 **Pichoux Gorges** – Road from Biel to Porrentruy – about 2 1/2 hours. *See Pichoux Gorges.*

★ ⬚6 **Passwang Pass Road** – Road from Oensingen to Basle – about 2 1/4 hours. *See Passwang Pass Road.*

★★★ ⬚7 **The Chasseral** – Road from St-Imier to La Neuveville – about 1 1/2 hours. *See Chasseral.*

★★ ⬚8 **Vue des Alpes Road** – Road from La Chaux-de-Fonds to Neuchâtel – about 3/4 hour. *See Chaux-de-Fonds: Excursions.*

★ ⬚9 **Franches Montagnes** – The Jura Corniche: road starts at Les Rangiers – about 1/2 hour. *See Franches Montagnes.*

★ KANDER VALLEY

Michelin map **217** folds 7 and 17 or **427** fold 13

From Thun Lake to Lake Oeschinen *(access from Kandersteg: see overleaf)* this valley is divided into two sections orientated differently: firstly the Frutigtal which goes southwest as far as Frutigen; then the Kandertal which goes south to Kandersteg.

FROM SPIEZ TO KANDERSTEG

39km – 25 miles – about 2 1/2 hours – Itinerary ⬚2 *on the Bernese Oberland local map*

This excursion ends in a cul-de-sac at Kandersteg, but the railway is fitted out to take cars through the Lötschberg Tunnel (qv) emerging in the Valais.

★**Spiez** – *See Spiez.*

Crossing the spur which separates Spiez from the Kander, the road, situated halfway up the slope, drops towards the valley floor and begins to encircle the huge Niesen Pyramid, which has almost geometrically precise lines.

★★★**Climb to the Niesen** ⊘ – Alt 2362m – 7749ft. *From Mülenen station, about 2 hours Rtn, including 1 hour by funicular.* The funicular rides above the Frutigtal and stops at the top (beacon) from where there is a magnificent **panorama**★★★ of the Bernese Oberland, Thun Lake, the Mittelland and the Jura.

Ahead, through the Kiental Gap, the three identical snowy Blümlisalp Peaks gradually appear. They are best seen from near Reichenbach.

Beyond Reichenbach, the valley, known as the Frutigtal, opens out and turns southward. Among the houses scattered on the slopes many new buildings will be seen near the road, but these conform strictly with the traditional architecture of the Bernese Oberland *(illustration p 30)*. A little before Frutigen you will see shining ahead and to the left, at the end of a new perspective along the Kander Valley, the icefields of the Balmhorn and the Altels.

Frutigen – Facilities. *1/4 hour on foot Rtn to go up to the church (following the Adelboden road for a moment and then turning up the first ramp to the right).* This large village at the confluence of the Kander and the Engstligen, a torrent flowing down from Adelboden, is the best-equipped medium altitude resort in the Lötschberg District. The church is built on a height within view of the Balmhorn and the Altels. It has a delightful **setting**★ among the lawns and trees of its close.

★★**Adelboden** – *See Adelboden.*

Crossing the Kander at the foot of the ruins of the Tellenburg – the picture formed by this tower and the railway viaduct has been widely distributed by local tourist publicity – you approach the Bühlstutz Ridge. This separates the Kandergrund shelf from the Kandersteg Basin and compels the Lötschberg railway to make a hairpin loop around the ruins of the Felsenburg, which stand out clearly on their rocky spur.

★**Blue Lake** (Blausee) ⊘ – *About 3/4 hour walk and trip by boat.*
This site comprises not only a little lake with incredibly clear, blue water, lying deep in the forest within view of the snowy Doldenhorn Summit, but also a mass of rocks among the woods, a trout-farm and a restaurant.

The road now attacks the Bühlstutz ridge in a more austere landscape of fields and woods dotted with rocks.

At last you emerge into the Kandersteg Basin with steep slopes laced with waterfalls.

★**Kandersteg** – *Description see below.*

★ **KANDERSTEG** Berne   Pop 1 077

Michelin map **217** northwest of fold 17 or **427** fold 13 – Local maps see BERNESE OBERLAND and VALAIS – Alt 1 176m – 3 858ft – Facilities

Lying at the foot of rugged escarpments, which frame the snow-peaks of the Blümlisalp to the east and dip into a green Alpine basin, Kandersteg is best known today for its position at the north end of the **Lötschberg Tunnel.** This tunnel, 14.6km – 9 miles long (Kandersteg-Goppenstein), has created, since 1913, a direct link between Berne and the Rhône Valley. The railway can convey motor-cars. *Apply for information from the Swiss National Tourist Offices or at the railway stations.*
The life of the locality is kept going in summer by the proximity of natural wonders like Lake Oeschinen and, in winter, by facilities for skiers.

EXCURSIONS

★★★**Lake Oeschinen** ⊘ – *About 1 1/2 hours Rtn, including 7 minutes by chairlift, plus a 20-minutes walk.*
The road leading to the lower chairlift station branches off the main road from Kandersteg directly after the bridge over the Oeschinen-bach, on the left. From the upper station a road leads down to the lake

Lake Oeschinen

shore *(bear to the right at a fork after a 5-minute walk)* encircled by a vast amphitheatre of cliffs, crowned by the snowy Blümlisalp Peaks. After reaching the lake, good walkers will continue to Kandersterg on foot by the direct road, avoiding the need to return to the upper chairlift station.

★★ **Klus** – *2.5km* – *2 miles* – *plus 1 hour on foot Rtn.* Follow the main road towards the floor of the valley and leave your car at the lower cable-car station at Stock. Then continue to climb, on foot, a little road which will soon cling to the rocky wall before entering a tunnel over the Klus, a wild gorge where the Kander, flowing down from the Gasterntal, rushes downwards. Go on to the bridge over the Kander after a second tunnel. Light-footed tourists will prefer to descend by the steep path, sometimes wet with spray, which leaves the road between the two tunnels.

★ **KIPPEL** Valais   Pop 370

Michelin map **217** fol 17 or **427** fold 13 – Local map see VALAIS

The remote alpine valley, **Lötschental★**, remained cut off from the outside world until the Lötschberg Railway Tunnel was built between Kandersteg in the north to Goppenstein in 1913. The River Lonza flows southwards through the valley to join the Rhône. In the past when it was extremely difficult to maintain an open road in the lower sections of the valley, due to the frequency of avalanches, the main access was by passes at an altitude of 2 500m – 8 200ft.

The people of this remote valley have remained very attached to their traditional way of life and it is well worth leaving the Valais to visit Kippel.

Access – *From the road fork at Gampel to Kippel 12km* – *7 1/2 miles* – *about 3/4 hour.*

The road climbs the steep and wild gorge of the Lower Lonza, with below, the many bridges of the Lötschberg railway. Beyond Goppenstein the road enters the great and gently spreading coomb of the upper Lötschental.

★**Kippel** – This is the most typical village in the valley, and the tourist in a hurry may want to spend all his time here. In the area around the church there are numerous blackened **wooden houses★★** with delicate friezes of dog-tooth and rosette patterns. The crowds which gather for High Mass make Sundays and feast days the best for lovers of folklore, but the Corpus Christi procession *(see the Calendar of Events)*, with its procession of "God's Grenadiers", offers the most colourful spectacle. For this occasion flags are flown and the local men bring out old-fashioned attirements with plumes, bearskin caps and buffs or belts.

Blatten – *4km* – *2 miles from Kippel.* This short excursion enables the tourist to discover the beauty of this valley which becomes ever more rugged.

★★ **KLAUSEN PASS ROAD**

Michelin map **218** folds 1 and 2 or **427** fold 15

The Klausen road connects the Reuss Valley (Uri Canton) to that of the Linth (Glarus Canton). It combines nearly all the physical and economic features of mountainous Switzerland. Within less than 50km – 31 miles the traveller passes from a high, wild primitive Alpine coomb (Urner Boden) to one of the most industrial valleys in the range (Linth Valley).

FROM ALTDORF TO LINTHAL

48km – *30 miles* – *about 2 hours*

The Klausen road is closed to vehicles with a trailer (pp 202-203).
The Klausen Pass is usually blocked by snow from November to May.

Altdorf – *See Altdorf.*

It is only a short distance from Altdorf to the next halting-place.

Bürglen – Bürglen is said to be the birthplace of William Tell and the village now has a **Tell Museum.** ⊘ The exhibits include a host of documents, chronicles, sculptures, paintings and other items relating to Switzerland's legendary hero over the past 600 years.

Between Bürglen and Unterschächen, the road, lined by a series of chapels, runs at first along the verdant cleft through which the Schächen rushes. This widens upstream and is then covered with birch, maple and fruit trees, but the south slope, quickly becoming barren, gives a foretaste of harsher sections.

From Unterschächen to the pass, two big hairpin bends facing the mouth of the Brunnital, a tributary valley ending in a cirque at the foot of the Ruchen and Windgällen precipices, lead to Urigen, the starting-point of a magnificent **corniche section★★**. From now on there is a bird's-eye view of the wild cul-de-sac of the Upper Schächental, enclosed by the gigantic Chammliberg Cliffs. The bend marked by a single rock on the side of the escarpment (600m – about 1/3 of a mile above the first tunnel on this slope on the way up) forms a **belvedere★** overlooking the Stäubi Waterfall (Stäubifall) and the hamlet of Aesch, 400m – 1 312ft below. The great snow-laden cornices of the Clariden can be seen behind the Chammliberg Cliffs.

★**Klausen Pass** – Alt 1 948m – 6 391ft. Motorists usually stop below the summit on the Schächental slope, at the Klausenpasshöhe Hotel.

From a spot near the hotel you can see, from left to right, the snowy crests of the Clariden, the Chammliberg Cliffs, the double Schärhorn Peak the rocky points of the Windgälen and finally, in line with the Schächen Gap, the Uri-Rotstock Massif on the horizon.

After passing the huts of Vorfrütt, where herdsmen shelter during the summer, you will be able to admire the north face of the Clariden and the Chlus, a corrie streaked by two cascades.

★**Urner Boden** –   The run along the bottom of this very regular cleft offers the motorist a long level stretch, unexpected at this altitude (1 300 to 1 400m – 4 250 to 4 600ft). The belfry of the chief hamlet, standing in the middle of the hollow, behind a clump of fir trees, is an attractive feature of the run down from the Klausen Pass.

There are more hairpin bends as far as **Linthal.** The Linth Valley, both agricultural, and industrial, now opens out below, abutting on the walls of the Selbsanft (Tödi Massif) upstream.

★★ KLOSTERS Graubünden (Grisons)   Pop 3 542

Michelin map 218 east of fold 5 or 427 fold 17 – Local map see GRISONS – Alt 1 194 m – 3 917ft – Facilities

In the setting, still quite rural, of the Prättigau, Klosters is a fully-equipped summer and winter resort. In summer the Silvretta Summits, jutting up on the horizon, invite mountaineers to make agreeable mountain expeditions.

In winter, the skier, using the cable-cars from Gotschnagrat and Madrisa or the railway shuttle service between Klosters and Davos, finds the famous Parsenn snowfields open to him *(qv)*.

Moreover, in March and April, spring skiing weeks are organised as excursions led by guides in the Silvretta and Vereina Massifs.

KÖNIGSFELDEN ABBEY Aargau

Michelin map 216 fold 6 or 427 fold 5 – west of Baden between Brugg and Windisch

The Franciscan Abbey of Königsfelden was founded in 1308 by Queen Elizabeth and the Habsburg family on the spot where King Albrecht I was assassinated by Duke Johann of Swabia.
The monastic buildings are now occupied by a mental hospital.

Church (Klosterkirche) ⊙ – This disused church, which stands in a pretty park, has recently been restored. It is a large Gothic building. The nave, lit by clerestory windows, has a flat wooden ceiling. The aisles are decorated with painted wooden panels representing portraits of knights and coats of arms. A memorial in the nave recalls that Königsfelden became the burial place of the Habsburgs.
The long **chancel**★ is lit by eleven windows of which the **stained glass**★, made between 1325-30, forms an interesting series. You will recognise the Childhood of Christ, the Passion, scenes from the Lives of the Saints and the Death of the Virgin. The colours, in which a silvery-yellow predominates, are iridescent; the monochrome drawing is delicately done.

KREUZLINGEN Thurgau   Pop 17 239

Michelin map 216 folds 9 and 10 or 427 fold 7 – Alt 407m – 1 335ft – Facilities

The Swiss town of Kreuzlingen is built on a former moraine of the Rhine Glacier. It forms a single town with the German city of Constance, divided only by the frontier. The town owes its name to a relic of the Holy Cross (Kreuz), which was brought back from the Holy Land in the 10C and deposited in the Basilica.

St Ulric's Basilica. – This church was built in its present form in the 17C and the interior decoration in the baroque style was done in the following century. The building was damaged by fire in 1963 and then restored in 1967.
The Olive Grove Chapel (Ölbergkapelle) contains an extraordinary group of 250 carved wooden figurines set in curious rock work and representing scenes from the Passion. These figurines are about 30cm – 1ft high and were carved at the beginning of the 18C by a Tyrolean sculptor. The work took no less than eighteen years. The chancel has a fine wrought iron parclose screen.

EXCURSION

Gottlieben – *4km – 2 miles to the west by road no 13.*
Gottlieben lies at the western end of the arm of the Rhine joining the Untersee, or lower lake, to the main basin of Lake Constance. It has a 13C castle, remodelled in the 19C. In the 15C the building was used as a prison for the deposed anti-pope John XXIII and for the Czech Reformer **Jan Hus.** Prince Louis-Napoleon Bonaparte, the future Napoleon III, lived here in 1837-38.
Near the castle is an attractive group of half-timbered houses.

Gourmets...

The chapter on Food and Drink in the Introduction to this guide
describes Switzerland's gastronomic specialities and best national wines.
The annual Michelin Red Guide Switzerland
offers an up-to-date selection of good restaurants.

★ LANGNAU IM EMMENTAL Berne   Pop 8 940

Michelin map ▨ fold 7 or ▨ fold 13 — Local map see EMMENTAL

The picturesque town of Langnau lies on the banks of the Ilfis (spanned by a covered bridge), a tributary of the Emme. Its commerce is based on forestry and Emmental cheese (main exporting centre for Emmental cheese).

Local Museum (Heimatmuseum) ⊙ — Housed in a 16C chalet, the "Chüechlihus" displays local crafts (porcelain, glasswork) and objects representing the local industries including workrooms, a room furnished in 18C painted wood, household utensils, clocks, musical instruments and old military uniforms.

Across from the museum, the 17C Reformed Church has preserved its original overly elaborate stone pulpit and a dozen small stained-glass windows with heraldic bearings.

★ **Dürsrüti Wood (Dürsrutiwald)** — *3km — 2 miles to the north (to the right of the road to Burgdorf).*
This forest of giant pine trees atop a hill, which offers pleasant views of the Langnau Valley.

★★ LAUSANNE Ⓒ Vaud   Pop 128 112

Michelin map ▨ folds 3 and 13 or ▨ fold 11 — Local maps see Lake GENEVA and Swiss JURA — Alt 455m — 1 493ft — Facilities — Plan of the conurbation in the current Michelin Red Guide Switzerland

Lausanne is a welcoming, cosmopolitan city, greatly appreciated by university students and high society people, who enjoy the lovely views it offers of the lake and the surrounding Alps.
The town is built on uneven ground. After being confined to the promontory of the present City for several centuries, Lausanne spread southward to the delightful shores of Ouchy, a former fisherman's hamlet. Its new quarters contrast sharply with the old, steep, narrow streets which lead to the cathedral.
The life of the town is concentrated between Place de la Riponne, Rue du Bourg, Place Saint-François, Rue du Grand-Chêne and Place Bel-Air. These are joined by the Grand Pont, spanning the valley where the Flon torrent once flowed.
An important centre for art and entertainment, Lausanne has acquired a worldwide reputation on account of the famous ballet troupe directed by Maurice Béjart and the classical concerts performed by the French Swiss Orchestra and the Chamber Orchestra of Lausanne. The Palais de Beaulieu and the Théâtre Municipal are frequently used to host dance performances and musical shows.
The municipality of **Vidy**, part of Lausanne, enjoys an Olympic status since it houses the International Olympic Committee (IOC) in a modern tower built with dark, smoky glass. The noble organisation was founded in 1894 by Baron Pierre de Coubertin. The Olympic Museum set up in Ouchy in June 1993 has made Lausanne the world capital of the Olympic movement.

HISTORICAL NOTES

Early Days — Recent excavations have shown that Lausanne was originally built on the site of the present "City", perched on the promontory where Neolithic skeletons have been uncovered. Southwest (at **Vidy**) part of the former Roman Lousonna has been excavated. Of particular interest is a section of Roman road, located exactly where the Geneva-Lausanne motorway now comes in.

The cathedral city — At the end of the 6C the first bishop, St Marius, came to live in the city of Lausanne; the first cathedral was built there two centuries later. In the Middle Ages, religious leadership was combined with economic and political expansion: the quarters of the Place de la Palud, the Bourg, St-Pierre, St-Laurent and St-François were added to the town.
In the 13C many religious orders settled here and the Prince-Bishop Guillaume de Champvent consecrated the new cathedral in the course of a great festival; later Pope Gregory X dedicated it in the presence of the Emperor Rudolf I of Habsburg. The city or upper town was the religious and intellectual centre; commercial activities flourished in the adjoining districts.

From the Reformation to the Bernese domination — The Reformation scored a sweeping success at Lausanne: it was preached there in 1529 by Guillaume Farel, a friend of Calvin. In 1536 the town and all the Vaud Country were occupied by the Bernese who had already been converted. All the churches of Lausanne except the cathedral and the Church of St Francis disappeared, one by one.
In 1723 the Bernese harshly suppressed an attempt by the Vaud people to recover their independence: Davel, instigator of the revolt, was beheaded at Vidy.
It was not until 1803 that the Vaud attained political autonomy, with Lausanne as its capital.

The Age of Enlightenment and its heritage — The 18C was a time of prosperity. Lausanne came under French influence, especially that of the Encyclo-paedists. Voltaire stayed here and had his play, *Zaïre,* performed. Byron and Shelley visited Lausanne in 1816 as did Wordsworth in 1790 and 1820; Dickens resided here in 1846, where he was visited by, among others, Thackeray and Tennyson and, again in 1853. T.S. Eliot stayed here in 1921-22 where he wrote *The Waste Land,* with which he gained international recognition. Literary salons flourished.
Benjamin Constant, the author of *Adolphe,* was born in Lausanne in 1767.

The university, partly installed in the 16C "Academy", brilliantly perpetuated these traditions. Very active publishers helped its fame and it has never lacked material: Sainte-Beuve delivered his speech on Port-Royal at Lausanne, and Gide adapted his *Caves du Vatican* as a play for a Students' Society. But the best known local figures were Dr Tissot, who lived in the 18C and was known as the "healer of the Sick Europe", Dr Jules Gonin – an eye surgeon specialised in operating detached retinas – and Maurice Lugeon (d 1953), an outstanding geologist and an authority on the Alps.

★★ OUCHY (AZ)

Ouchy is linked to Lausanne by its "métro", an electrically-driven funicular once known as the "rope" (cable-driven) and later as the "tyre" (mounted on wheels). Ouchy – a famous hotel resort and popular spot for Sunday strollers – has become the "lake-front" of Lausanne. It is also one of the liveliest navigation centres and sailing harbours in Lake Geneva, mainly on account of the tourist trade and the many leisure boats available for cruises.

The shaded quays, adorned with tropical plants and flowers, stretch for over one kilometre – half a mile and are prolonged eastward by the lakeside path. This charming route offers lovely **views**★★ of the harbour, Lake Geneva and the Chablais mountains.

★★ Olympic Museum (BZ) ⊘

Olympic Flag

– The embodiment of Baron Pierre de Coubertin's lofty olympic ideals, this museum enjoys a privileged location on the shores of Lake Geneva. Its setting is a charming landscape laid out as a public garden and enhanced by statues, fountains and multi-coloured pavilions. The **park**, planted with evergreen species and many other trees and shrubs (Italian cypress, juniper, magnolia) extends across terraced slopes, offering nice views of Lake Geneva, and the Savoy Alps in the far distance. All along the path which winds its way to the entrance of the museum (420m – 1 378ft, the length of an Olympic stadium), a series of statues symbolise the marriage of sport and culture.

Part of the museum has been built underground in order to preserve the natural environment. The modern ensemble inspired by a Greek temple is the work of two architects: the Mexican Pedro Ramírez Vázquez (who designed the National Anthropology Museum in Mexico City) and the Swiss Jean-Pierre Cahen, a native of Lausanne. In front of the white marble façade (the stone was shipped over from the Greek island of Thassos), two rows of four columns carry the names of the towns which hosted the Olympic Games and those of the IOC presidents. In a granite bowl ornamented with allegorical motifs illustrating the myth of Prometheus, the olympic flame burns forever.

SWISS MEDAL WINNERS AT THE LILLEHAMMER WINTER OLYMPICS - 1994

Gold medals

Gustav Weder Donat Acklin	} Two-man Bobsleigh
Andreas Schoenbaechler	Freestyle Skiing Aerials
Vreni Schneider	Alpine Skiing Ladies Slalom

Silver medals

Reto Goetschi Guido Acklin	} Two-man Bobsleigh
Vreni Schneider	Alpine Skiing Ladies Combined Downhill/Slalom
Urs Kaelin	Alpine Skiing Men's Giant Slalom
Gustav Weder Donat Acklin Kurt Meier Domenico Semerado	} Four-man Bobsleigh

Bronze medals

Hippolyt Kempf Jean-Yves Cuendet Andreas Schaad	} Nordic Combined Men's team
Vreni Schneider Alpine	Skiing Ladies Giant Slalom

Level 0 – The ground floor is largely devoted to the history of the Games, with particular emphasis on ancient Greece. Superb works of art, displayed according to their subject, evoke the origins of the Games: terracotta figures, marble and bronze sculptures, vases decorated with figures of athletes, gold laurel wreaths, *strigils* – scraping instruments used by athletes for removing the combination of oil, sand and perspiration from their body, etc. You can also see all the torches that have carried the Olympic flame since the first edition in 1936 (Berlin). Other exhibitions enlighten visitors on the life and achievements of **Baron Pierre de Coubertin** (reconstruction of his Lausanne study, furniture and personal mementoes), the various International Olympic Committees and the IOC presidents who have succeeded one another (a video film presents the world events which marked their epoch). The visit ends with an area which presents the two cities designated to stage the forthcoming summer and winter Games. Note the two fine bronze statues: *The American Athlete* by Rodin and *The Archer* by Bourdelle.

Level 1 – One side is devoted to the summer Games, the other to the winter Games. In both areas, audio-visual technology enables visitors to relive the great moments of Olympic history and share the physical effort and strong emotions experienced by top-level athletes. Opening and closing ceremonies are re-enacted on huge screens and a battery of video terminals provide answers to thousands of questions about the Games, the different events, the athletes, the records, etc.
The philatelic and numismatic department boasts a remarkable collection of stamps, coins and medals bearing the effigy of the Games.

Level 2 – Cafeteria and terrace. **View** of the park, the lake and the mountains. Sculpture by Botero, *Young Girl with Ball.*

Level-1 – Book and video library. The magnetic entrance card gives access to three films.

Elysée Museum (Musée de l'Elysée) **(BZ)** ⊘ – This large, late-18C villa with its sculpted façade is surrounded by a small park which slopes down to the lakeside and is shaded by chestnut, pine and cedar trees peopled with squirrels.
The building houses a photography museum which presents large-scale temporary exhibitions of 19 and 20C prints.

OLD TOWN *2 hours*

Place de la Palud (BY 23) – Lined by old houses and by the Renaissance façade of the Town Hall – which proudly bears the arms of the city of Lausanne – , this square is adorned with the charming Fountain of Justice (16-18C). Nearby, at no 23, an animated clock strikes the hours of the day, exhibiting a gallery of historical figures.
The curious covered staircase beyond the fountain leads through to the cathedral. In the past these steps took one to the entrance of what was known as the "Cité du Marché".

History Museum of Lausanne (Musée historique de Lausanne) **(BY M¹)** ⊘ – The rooms of the former bishop's palace have been restored to house these collections, which recall the town's history from prehistoric times up to the 20C. After leaving the first section, devoted to geology, prehistory and the Middle Ages, visitors discover a vast miniature model of the city as it was in 1638, complemented by an audio-visual presentation. The Berne period (17-18C) is liberally illustrated by documents and objects relating to politics, agriculture and everyday life. The advent of the railway and its consequences on the political scene, the expansion of tourism and business (banks, insurance companies) are among the many chapters that make up the fascinating history of the town. Several 19C window displays have been reconstructed in the last room: a general store, a grocery shop, a printing house and a photographer's studio. Note the safe which once belonged to the Kohler house (1828), characterised by original and elaborate ironwork.

★★ **Cathedral (CY)** ⊘ – This is the finest Gothic building in Switzerland. Its construction began during the episcopate of St Amadeus (1145-1159) and was completed in the mid-13C. The church was consecrated in 1275; subsequently it was entirely restored at the instigation of Viollet-le-Duc (late 19C).
The east end, the oldest part of the building, abuts two picturesque square towers and is dominated by the lantern-tower at the transept crossing. Both the latter and the bell-tower are strongly reminiscent of Anglo-Norman architecture, clearly marking the transition from Romanesque to Gothic.

The south door, known as the Painted Doorway, is adorned with a fine group of 13C sculptures originally painted and similar in execution to those of Ile-de-France. The pillars supporting the roof of the porch bear on the left, in the foreground, figures of the Prophets (Isaiah, David and Jeremiah); near the door, the Forerunners (Moses, John the Baptist, Simeon); on the right, in the foreground, three of the Evangelists (St Matthew, St Luke and St Mark); in the background, three Apostles (St Peter, St Paul and St John). The lintel is carved with two low reliefs, the Death and Assumption of the Virgin. On the tympanum the Coronation of Mary takes a unique form: Christ in Majesty takes from the hands of an angel the crown which the Virgin is ready to receive.
The Montfalcon Doorway – named after the two bishops Aymon and Sébastien de Montfalcon – was built in 1517 and completely renewed in the early 20C. It opens in the centre of the main façade, giving access to a narthex with two rounded lateral apses. Three 13C statues, two of which are sadly decapitated, represent the Virgin, Solomon and the Queen of Sheba. In a small chapel on the right, a series of mural paintings (1505) portray the life of the Virgin Mary.

The interior, plain and with a rare degree of unity, shows certain Burgundian features such as its general plan and narthex with no side chapels ; other features are influenced by the English Gothic style : the gallery runs below the clerestory windows. Note the original arrangement of stout columns, alternating with pairs of slim pillars.

In the south aisle are some very rare and unusual 13C **stalls** (removed for restoration) with exceptionally fine figures on the cheekpieces. Other stalls, in the Flamboyant style (16C) are placed in a chapel in the lower part of the north aisle.

In the south arm of the transept a 13C rose window, *Imago Mundi* (elements, seasons, months and signs of the Zodiac), is remarkably harmonious and decorative. It was already well known in the 13C, for Villard de Honnecourt drew it in his *Album,* the first collection dealing with Gothic architecture and decoration.

In the chancel is the tomb of Othon I of Grandson, who had a brilliant career at the English court and became the firm friend of Edward I. He died in 1328.

In the ambulatory note the tomb of the 13C bishop-builder Roger de Vico-Pisano.

Lausanne is one of the last towns to maintain a night-watch. From the top of the cathedral tower the night watchman cries the hour between 10pm and 2am.

Tower ⊙ – *Access to the stairway (232 steps) at the end of the south aisle.* From the top of tower there is a fine **view**★ of the town, Lake Geneva and the Alps. The parvis of the cathedral affords bird's eye views of the town and the lake.

Go round the cathedral and take on the left of the east end, the Rue Cité-Derrière, a small medieval street decorated with wrought iron signs. At right angles lies the Rue de l'Académie, where a **Pipe and Tobacco Museum** ⊙ (Musée de la pipe et objets du tabac (**CX M²**) has been set up in the basement of an antique shop. A private collector has succeeded in reuniting more than 2 500 pipes from countries all over the world, including several unusual pieces with finely-sculpted bowls.

Castle St-Maire (**CX B**) – This 15C brick and stone building was originally the residence of the bishops of Lausanne and then the Bernese bailiffs. The cantonal government sits there today. The terrace affords a sweeping **view** of the Lausanne rooftops and Lake Geneva.

> *Continue along the Rue Cité-Derrière. Then turn left into Avenue de l'Université, which leads to Place de la Riponne, situated at the foot of the promontory.*

Rumine Palace (Palais de Rumine) (**BX**) – The palace was built in the early 20C in the Italian Renaissance style, thanks to a generous legacy bequeathed by Gabriel de Rumine. It houses the library and five museums.

Fine Arts Museum (Musée des Beaux-Arts) ⊙ – *In summer this museum hosts exhibitions such as the International Tapestry Biennial (1994, 1996 ...). The rest of the year, the collections are shown in rotation. Each year temporary exhibitions are organised around a specific theme or artist.*

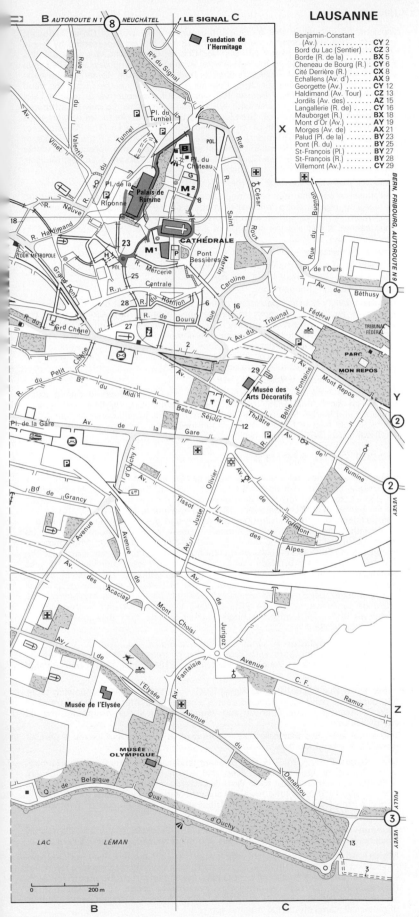

LAUSANNE

Most of the pictures in this municipal museum are the work of Swiss nationals, many of which were born in the region. The 18 and 19C are represented by F. and J. Sablet, L.-R. Ducros (water colours) and Charles Gleyre, who was visited, in his Paris studio, by the leading Impressionists. Among those who depicted their own country are German Swiss painters such as Hodler and Anker, Romansh landscape artists such as De La Rive, St-Ours, Calame, and especially natives from the Vaud area: Bosshard, Biéler and Bocion (70 pictures of the countryside around Lake Geneva, executed with great sensitivity). The more recent works may be attributed to F. Valloton, R. Auberjonois, Steinlen, Louis Soutter, etc. As far as foreign art is concerned, the French School is represented by F. Dubois *(The Massacre of St Bartholomew, The Triumvirs)*, Largillière, Rigaud *(Portrait of the Duchess of Nemours)*, Mignard and Géricault, as well as by an impressive collection of works executed by such masters as Courbet, Cézanne, Renoir, Bonnard, Degas, Matisse, Marquet, Vlaminck, Vuillard and Utrillo.

Geological Museum *– First floor, on the left.*

The museum contains rock specimens from the Jura, the Alps, Lausanne and the surrounding region, along with relief models of the Jura, the Simplon and the Matterhorn. A new exhibition area is now devoted to the Quaternary period in the Vaud canton. It displays the skeleton of a mammoth discovered near Brassus, in the Jouy Valley, in 1969.

Museum of Paleontology *– On the right, opposite the Geological Museum.*

A collection of plant and animal fossils, mostly European, are on display, alongside molluscs and skeletons of birds and mammals.

Zoological Museum *– Second floor.*

The main gallery houses specimens of flora from countries all over the world. On the left is an interesting room of comparative anatomy between Man and the animal race. On the right is a display of all the vertebrates coming from the Vaud region: birds, insects, fish, and species commonly found in forests and at high altitudes. Of particular interest is the colony of Mexican ants busy at work in their natural setting, a carefully-reconstituted tropical environment. The central gallery of the museum is devoted to mineralogy.

Archaeological and Historical Museum *– Sixth floor.*

The museum hosts temporary exhibitions of artefacts discovered during excavations on local sites. Many of the objects found near the lakes of Geneva, Lausanne and Murten feature tools and ceramic pieces from the Bronze Age, Celtic tombs, a gold bust of Marcus Aurelius and jewellery and weapons dating back to medieval times (5-7C).

ADDITIONAL SIGHTS

★ **Museum of Spontaneous Art (Collection de l'Art Brut) (AX)** ⊘ – The four floors of this unique museum – housed in the former stables of the 18C Beaulieu Château – present a selection of one thousand objects (out of some five thousand) collected by the painter Jean Dubuffet since 1945 and donated to the city.

The paintings, drawings, sculptures, modelling and embroidery on display here – made with the most unexpected materials – are all the work of people who live on the fringe of society and who have received no academic training: schizophrenics, inmates confined to prison cells or mental hospitals, spiritualist mediums, etc. The spontaneous art they produce, while reflecting their own individuality, is also reminiscent of the modern works attributed to "genuine" artists such as the Surrealist, Abstract and Naïve painters. Some of these strange objects possess strong artistic appeal: carved wood by Clément, painted fabric by Madge Gill, drawings by Guillaume Pujolle *(The Eagles)*, Woïfli, Aloïse and Scottie Wilson, sculptures by Filippo Bentivenga, huge sketches by Jaki, illustrated books by Metz, paintings by Walla...

Hermitage Foundation (CX) ⊘ – *2 Route du Signal.*
Surrounded by a fine park with rare species of trees, the former home of the Bugnions' (a family from Vaud) was built in about 1841. Since 1984 it houses large temporary exhibitions on art and history.

★★ **View from the Signal (Vue du Signal) (BX)** – Alt 643m – 2 109ft. Viewing table, telescope. This belvedere, situated near a small chapel, affords a pleasant **view** of Lake Geneva, the Savoy, Fribourg and Vaud Alps and, in the foreground, the old city of Lausanne.

Half a mile away lies **Sauvabelin Lake** and its reserve for does and ibexes, a popular place for weekend strollers.

Mon Repos Park (CY) – In this pleasant landscape garden stands the Empire-style villa where Voltaire once lived and which housed an Olympic Museum dedicated to the memory of **Baron Pierre de Coubertin**, founder of the modern Olympic Games, who lived for a long time at Lausanne and is buried there.
To the north of the park the Federal Tribunal, the supreme court of Switzerland, occupies a large building.

Museum of Decorative Arts (Musée des Arts Décoratifs) (CY) ⊘ – Temporary exhibitions of contemporary applied art and glass sculptures are held here.

Montriond Park (AY) – On this spot where in 1037 the first Truce of God was proclaimed in the district, there is a great esplanade which is reached by a ramp and a staircase. The **view**★★ extends over Ouchy, the shores of Lake Geneva to the Alps. One section of the park is taken up by a **botanical garden** ⊘, consisting of an arboretum, an alpine garden with mountain flora, flowers, succulents and a variety of medicinal, carnivorous and aquatic species.

PULLY *by ③ on the town plan*

The old village of Pully has become a residential suburb of Lausanne. From the terrace of the Church of St Germain (of Gothic origin but very much altered) a charming **view★** opens out onto the pleasure boat harbour below, the eastern part of Lake Geneva and across the way to the French side of the lake from Evian to Meillerie. In the church precincts stand a museum and the remains of a Roman villa.

Museum of Contemporary Art ⊘ – Along the shores of Lake Geneva, a number of former industrial premises have been renovated to house collections shown in rotation, each devoted to a specific theme. The exhibition halls, spacious and sparsely-decorated, covering a total area of 1 500m² – 16 150 sq ft are laid out on two levels. A specialised library, a bookstore, a shop, a cafeteria and a garden are available to visitors.

The rooms present works, including large ones, illustrating the different contemporary art trends which emerged after 1945. The American movement **Pop Art**, which reflected everyday life and the consumer society in the 1960s, is represented here by artists such as Andy Warhol, Rauschenberg and Roy Lichtenstein; **Minimal Art**, reducing shapes to the barest essentials and limiting the role of the artist, found keen adepts in Kelly, Stella and Noland; the **New Fauves** school, which gained influence in Germany in the late 1970s, privileged colour and shape; **Spatialism**, also known as Spatial Art or Spatial Movement, a trend born in Italy towards the middle of the century (Lucio Fontana), involves the use of fluorescent techniques to outline compositions suspended in space; the Italian movement **Arte Povera**, founded in the late 1960s (Merz, Zorio, Calzolari, Penone) was based on a provocative approach which illustrated reality in the simplest possible way; **New English Sculpture** was created in the early 1980s: its followers (Tony Cragg, David Mach, Bill Woodrow) drew inspiration from everyday objects (motorbike, lawnmower), to which they gave unusual shapes.

Museum ⊘ – It is located near the house where **Charles Ferdinand Ramuz** (1878-1947) lived until his death. This well-known novelist collaborated with Stravinsky, for whom he wrote *The Soldier's Tale;* he also produced such works as *Terror on the Mountain* and *Beauty on Earth.* It displays souvenirs of Ramuz (photographs, manuscripts, original works), together with paintings by R Domenjoz, M Borgeaud, V Milliquet, and by many other contemporary artists from Pully (J Lecouttre, P Besson, F Simonin, M Pellegrini, etc.). Visitors may also admire baked clay sculptures by Derain and precious objects (writing desk, model of royal barge) which belonged to the King of Siam, a resident of Pully between 1925 and 1945.

Roman Villa ⊘ – Located under the terrace of Le Prieuré Hotel (the pink paving reproduces the outline of the Roman walls).

What has been revealed of this vast and rich 2C domain is the summer residence, which is a small building with an apse made of a double semicircular wall about 3m – 10ft high and decorated on its inner wall with a polychrome **fresco** more than 20m² – 215sq ft depicting chariot races.

EXCURSIONS

Lutry – *4km – 2 1/2 miles by ③, then take road no 9.*
Pleasantly located on the shores of Lake Geneva (small sailling harbour, view of the Alps), this village and its maze of narrow streets deserve a short visit. On the main square, embellished with a fountain, stands the church with white façade and its fine Romanesque porch enhanced by arabesques. Step inside to admire the carved wooden stalls and the flower motifs painted on the vaulting.

As you leave the village, you may notice an imposing fortified castle (now a centre for social services and health care) dominating the vine-covered slopes.

Échallens ⊘ – *15km – 9 miles by ⑦, then take road no 5.*
Located in a fertile cereal-growing agricultural area, this small town boasts a fascinating **Bread and Grain Museum** ⊘ (Maison du Blé et du Pain), set up in a restored 18C farmhouse. The daily lives of peasants, millers and bakers throughout the ages are illustrated by a diorama, a collection of farming tools (seeders, ploughs, harrows), granaries and a display of different types of baking ovens and mills (manual, mechanical, grinding, and cylinder mills). At the end of the visit, rolls, loaves and croissants are prepared and baked before your eyes.

Servion Zoo ⊘ – *18km – 11 miles by ① on the road to Berne.*
This estate is home to a wide range of animal species from countries all over the world. After the Monkey Pavilion (comical black and white-ringed marmosets, so called because of the tufts of fur around their ears), visitors enter the tropical hothouse where exotic birds live in the natural state (Chinese crested mynahs, African spur-winged plovers, etc.). Alongside the Ostrich Pavilion you will find Chilean flamingoes, as well as crowned cranes and pink-backed pelicans from Africa. Next come the red deer, American buffaloes, brown bears and wolves. The last two species to be visited are the mighty Siberian tiger and the energetic wallaby. The park also features several recreational areas for picnics and outdoor games.

This guide, which is revised regularly,
incorporates tourist information provided at the time of going to press.
Changes are however inevitable owing to improved facilities and fluctuations in
the cost of living.

LENK Berne

Michelin map **217** fold 16 or **427** fold 13 – Local map see BERNESE OBERLAND –
Alt 1 068m – 3 504ft – Facilities

This charming resort is located in a vast basin surrounded by lush green cow
pastures and is crossed by the Simme (canalized) which originates only a couple of
kilometres south in the snowy Wildstrubel Range.

As a spa the town's sulpherous springs cure the patient of ailments of the joints
and the respiratory system. The town's ski lifts take the walker and skier to the
nearby slopes of Metschberg, Betelbert and Mülkerblatten (skiers only). Everyone,
however, will find something to interest them in Lenk whether it be its sports
facilities or its lovely tree-lined streets with its cheerful flower-decked chalets.

Simme Falls (Simmenfälle) – *4km – 2 1/2 miles plus 10 minutes on foot Rtn. Leave
the car in the car park to the left of the restaurant and follow the signposts
indicating "Barbarabrücke".*

Powerful and noisy, the falls tumble down the rocky face of the Wildstrubel.
Because of the fir trees you can only see the base of the falls; go back to near
the restaurant to see the top.

★ **Iffigen Falls (Iffigenfall)** – *2.5km – 1 1/2 miles plus 3/4 hour on foot Rtn.*
Leave Lenk to the south on the road to Iffigen. Park the car at the end of the
surfaced road (falls visible) and walk up the road *(rocky and steep – 15% – 1 in 6
1/2 – traffic permitted only for lorries and at fixed hours)* 2km – 1 mile. From a
bend to the left admire the falls tumbling down (80m – 262ft).

LEUK (LOÈCHE) Valais

Michelin map **217** folds 16 and 17 or **427** fold 13 – Local map see VALAIS – Alt
750m – 2 461ft

Leuk lies in terraces half-way up the slope above the Rhône Valley at the mouth of
the Dala Gorges. The little town has a severe setting very characteristic of the
southern Valais *(qv)*. This austere atmosphere is due to the barrenness of the
slopes and heavily modelled summits. From the castles' esplanade at the entrance
to the town there is an astonishing **view★** of the valley floor. The great fluvial cone
of rubble from the Illgraben, covered with mingled heath and forest vegetation
(Forest of Finges or Pfynwald) stands immediately below; it is familiar to all Swiss
school children as an example of fluvial deposition. This obstruction still forms the
natural boundary between the French-speaking Central Valais and the Upper Valais
with its German Swiss culture.

Castles – Their names recall the titles of functionaries of the Bishop of Sion, who
used to live there.

The first stronghold met with on entering the town is the **Castle of the Vidomnes** (the
vidames – secular deputies of the bishops of France under the *Ancien Régime*).
This building has become the town hall. The tall 16C structure and its stepped
gables flanked by watch-towers recall, in a much more graceful and original style,
the building at Sierre known by the same name. Farther on, the 15C **Castle of the
Majors** still has a square crenellated tower.

EXCURSION

Leukerbad (Loèche-les-Bains) – Facilities. *15km – 10 miles to the north by the direct
route – about 1/2 hour.*

This high-altitude spa, whose sulphurous, calcareous and gypsum-carrying waters
are recommended for the treatment of various disorders, was considered in the
19C to be an essential stop in the itinerary of the tourist on foot. Leukerbad marks
the end of the well-known crossing of the **Gemmi Pass** (alt 2 314m – 7 405ft), which
starts from Kandersteg in the Bernese Oberland and ends on the Valais slope in a
dizzy road cut out of the living rock.

The natural pulpit of the Gemmi (views of the Valais and Bernese Alps) offers a
grandiose spectacle to the tourist. *Cable-car to the Gemmi Pass.*

Leukerbad can also be reached through the quaint village of **Albinen**, whose
wooden houses, perched on the nearby slopes, appear to defy the laws of
gravity. The narrow, winding road offers vertiginous views of the Valais in several
places.

LIECHTENSTEIN

Michelin map **216** south of folds 21 and 22 or **427** folds 7, 8, 16 and 17

The Principality of Liechtenstein is a fragment of the former Germanic Confederation, whose territory extends from the east bank of the Rhine to the Vorarlberg
Mountains, grouping together 11 municipalities. The little state was made a
sovereign principality by the Emperor Charles VI in 1719 for the benefit of Prince
Jean Adam of Liechtenstein, and it owes the preservation of its statute largely to
the wise policy followed by Prince Johann II (the Good), the length of whose reign
(1858-1929) has only been exceeded by that of Louis XIV (1638-1715). Franz-
Joseph II ruled the country from 1939 to 1989. Since then, he has been succeeded
by his son, the heir Hans Adam. After 1919 Liechtenstein loosened its last bonds
with Austria and concluded monetary, postal, customs and diplomatic conventions
with the Swiss Confederation; today it is to all intents a part of the Swiss economic
sphere. The dividing line between the Germanic and Rhaetic civilizations is,
however, clearly marked by the southern boundary; the large villages scattered
among the orchards at the foot of some castle or around churches with pointed
spires make a contrast with the Grisons cities closely gathered among their vines.

General Information:

160km² – 61 1/2sq miles; Pop 29 386 in 1990
Official abbreviation: FL (vehicle reg)
Official language: German
Religion: Catholicism (majority)
Constitutional monarchy
The Parliament or Diet is composed of 25 members
elected for four years
The Government, elected for four years, is composed
of five members: the Head of State, his deputy and
three Federal advisors (Federal councillors).
There are no formalities on passing from Switzerland
into Liechtenstein.

VADUZ *1 1/2 hours*

Lying at the foot of the imposing **castle**, the residence of its princely family, the capital city – seat of the present government – has become a busy international tourist attraction.

Post Office. – Philatelists collect stamps issued by this small state. The post office is as great a feature of interest as the Postage Stamp Museum *(see below)*.

Liechtenstein State Art Collection (Liechtensteinische Staatliche Kunstsammlungen) ⊘ – The museum is devoted primarily to paintings and 20C graphic art. It houses a part of the famous **Prince's Art Collection★★** which contains (on the second floor) the golden carriage custom-built in Paris by Nicolas Pineau for Prince Joseph Wenzel Von Liechtenstein, Austrian ambassador to the French court in 1738.

National Museum (Liechtensteinisches Landesmuseum) ⊘ – In the restored buildings of an old inn, this museum covers the important periods of the principality's history. There is a relief model of the country, a mineralogy collection as well as collections of art from the prehistoric age, the Bronze Age, the Roman era (coins, objects), and the Alemannic period (jewellery, arms). Also exhibited are arms (medieval cutting and thrusting weapons and 16-18C fire-arms), utensils, local folk art, works of art (16C paintings, German religious sculpture) and cult objects.

Postage Stamp Museum (Briefmarken-museum) ⊘ – Located in a small gallery of the Liechtenstein Museum of Art *(see above)*, this museum highlights the principality's philatelic art.

SOUTH OF VADUZ

From Vaduz to Maienfeld

16km – 10 miles – about 3/4 hour – Local map right

> Leave Vaduz to the south on the Triesen road.

Malbun Valley (Malbun Tal) – *15km – 9 miles from Triesen.* Michelin maps **216** fold 22 and **218** fold 4 or **427** fold 16. In the heart of the country, this picturesque valley climbs to the corrie at the foot of the Sareiser Joch (alt 2 000m – 6 562ft) which is part of the Vorarlberg foothills.

St Luzisteig Defile (Engpass) – This fortified defile momentarily leaves the warm, wide Rhine Valley, only to return to it immediately.
Hemmed in between the Fläscherberg height and the steep and often snowy escarpments of the Falknis, this defile was of strategic importance so long as the road that follows it was the only road suitable for motor vehicles between Austria and the Grisons (Graubünden).
The route is still barred today by a line of fortifications, some of which were built in 1703; most of the others were built from 1831-37.
On the Grisons side of the Luziensteig. Pass the road is steep and runs through woods. For a halt you may choose the shady clearing among oak trees, 1km – 1/2 mile from Maienfeld where a Heidi Fountain (Heidibrunnen) serves as a memorial to Johanna Spyri (1827-1901), a popular Swiss writer of children's books *(Heidi).*

Maienfeld – A little Grisons town already showing a touch of southern elegance.

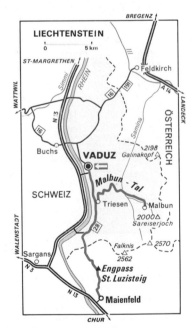

Gourmets...

*The annual **Michelin Red Guide Switzerland**
offers a selection of good restaurants.*

Michelin map ██ folds 7 and 8 or ██ fold 24 – Local map right – Alt 214m – 702ft – Facilities – Town plan in the current Michelin Red Guide Switzerland

Locarno lies in the hollow of a sunny bay which curves more sharply as the delta formed by the Maggia River juts into the waters of **Lake Maggiore**★★★ *(see Michelin Green Guide to Italy)*. It has an exceptional climate in which hydrangeas, magnolias and camellias blossom as early as March.
Visitors to this beautiful town will find pleasant walks among the gardens, along the shores of the lake and on the vine-covered slopes on which stand the villas of Orselina, and in the Cardada Hills.
The historical feature of the town is the 15C castle, **Castello Visconti**, where there is a small archaelogical museum and one of modern art.
The town became internationally famous when the Disarmament Conference of 1925 was held in its Palace of Justice (Palazzo Pretorio).

★**Madonna del Sasso** – This church is much frequented by tourists and pilgrims. It stands on the summit (355m – 1 165ft) of a wooded spur which can be reached either by car along the hairpin bends of the Via ai Monti della Trinità or in 6 minutes by funicular.
In both cases you arrive at an upper level from which a ramp interrupted by flights of stairs leads down to the basilica (excellent bird's-eye views).
The monastery was founded by Bartolomeo of Ivrea in 1487 and rebuilt in 1616. Inside the church is an altarpiece painted by Bramantino in 1522 (at the end of the south aisle) depicting the *Flight into Egypt*. From a loggia there is a fine **view**★ of Locarno and Lake Maggiore.

Ascona on Lake Maggiore

EXCURSIONS

★★**Cimetta** – The funicular going to the Madonna del Sasso is continued by a cable-car which in ten minutes climbs the **Cardada Alp** (alt 1 350m – 4 428ft) from where there is a very extensive **view**★★.
From Cardada a chairlift ⊘ goes to the top of the Cimetta (alt 1 672m – 5 482ft) where there is a fine **panorama**★★ of the Alps and Lake Maggiore.

★★**Ronco Tour** – *17km – 11 miles – about 1 1/2 hours – by a corniche road on which it is difficult to pass between Ronco and Porto Ronco. The trip is most agreeable in the late afternoon. Leave Locarno to the southwest by the Ascona road.*
A little after the great bridge over the Maggia, turn right towards Losone. In this village, after the church, turn left (road to Ascona and Verita Mountain) and right (road to Ronco) at the next crossroads. After running through a small valley containing a sawmill and a flour mill, leave the Arcegno road on your right. At the next fork bear right.
The *corniche* by-road, emerging from chestnut woods, debouches above Lake Maggiore and immediately affords a series of beautiful **bird's-eye views**★★.
Below, in succession, you will see Ascona, the two wooded **Brissago Islands** *(qv)* and finally the lakeside town of Brissago. You come into sight of Ronco.

Ronco – The village clings to the flank of a slope in a typically Mediterranean **setting**★★. The church terrace makes a good viewing point.
Taking a steep, winding road you can rejoin the coast road at Porto Ronco; turn to the left. This road has several sections cut out of the rock.

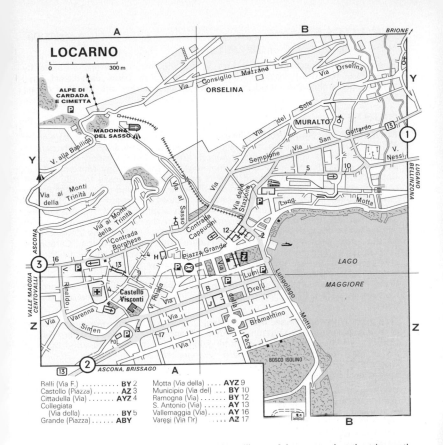

The scenery as you approach the attractive village of Ascona makes the trip worth-while.

★ **Ascona** – *See Ascona.*

The Verzasca and the Onsernone Valleys and the tributary valleys of the Maggia (Val de Campo, Val de Bosco, Val Ravona) are noted especially for the character of their Ticino villages *(illustration p 30).*

The local boat services offer pleasant trips varying from the short crossing to the pontoons on the opposite shore of the lake (Magadino) or at Ascona and Brissago, to a pleasant excursion which makes it possible in spring, summer and autumn to visit Stresa and the Borromean Islands.

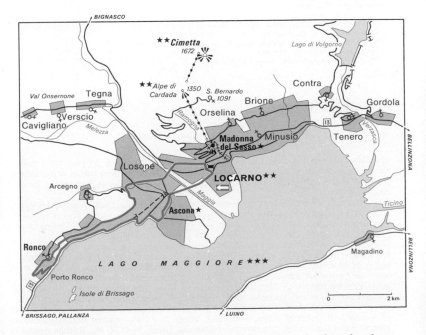

Some hotels have their own tennis courts, swimming pool, private beach, sauna or garden.
Consult the current edition of the annual **Michelin Red Guide Switzerland.**

LE LOCLE Neuchâtel

Michelin map 216 fold 12 or 427 fold 12

This small town nestling in the Jura Valley and linked to Franche-Comté by Rock Pass (Col-des-Roches) owes its prosperity to **Daniel Jean-Richard** *(qv)*, a young goldsmith who introduced the art of clockmaking into the area during the 18C.

SIGHTS

★ **Museum of Horology (Musée d'Horlogerie)** ⊘ – The **Château des Monts** is an elegant 18C mansion located on the heights of Le Locle, surrounded by a lovely park. It houses a museum containing many superb artefacts from a variety of countries and is seen as the indispensable complement to the Horology Museum of La-Chaux-de-Fonds *(qv)*. The ground floor is practically a showcase for 18C interior decoration: a large drawing-room, an antechamber, a panelled dining-hall, a library – all tastefully furnished and decorated – provide the charming setting for a splendid collection of clocks delicately worked in silver and gold. The Λ-L Perrelet room illustrates the history of clockmaking, from the very first timepiece with automatic rewinding to the tiniest digital watch. On the first floor, the Maurice-Yves Sandoz room presents clocks with miniature automatons, like the "Carabosse fairy", a gilt copper figure portraying an old woman walking with great difficulty. The second floor explains the science of horology (old instruments, clocks, watches, chronometers, precision tools, etc.).

Visitors may also see slides and a diorama on the subject, and take a look around the workshop of a local clockmaker, faithfully reconstituted in accordance with tradition.

Fine Arts Museum (Musée des Beaux-Arts) ⊘ – In addition to the rooms devoted to Swiss painting and sculpture in the 19 and 20C (Girardet, Koller, Kaiser, Mathey), the museum features an interesting display of prints executed by both Swiss and foreign artists: *Richard Wagner* by Vallotton, *The Studio* by Giacometti, *First Snowfall* by Lermite, *The Dancing Stars* by Dufy, *Portrait de Claude* by Renoir, etc.

Underground Mills (Moulins souterrains du Col-des-Roches) ⊘ – Built in the 16C to use the waters of Le Locle Valley as a new energy source, these mills expanded rapidly from the mid-17C to the late 19C: the gushing water of the river activated huge wheels, which in turn operated the various beaters, baking ovens and sawmills. In the early 20C the mills were turned into slaughterhouses and subsequently abandoned. Fortunately they were not to slip into oblivion and have now been restored to their former glory.

The exhibition in the entrance hall – explaining the different types of mills, their role and mechanism – is a good introduction to the tour.

The downstairs grotto is certainly worth a visit: it features numerous wells and galleries which the men had to dig with their bare hands, and contains several remarkable pieces of machinery (gear mechanisms, flour mills, saws, superposed wheels,...).

Swiss timepieces

Switzerland has been renowned for its high-quality timepieces ever since the master watchmaker Abraham-Louis Breguet (1747-1823) demonstrated his artistry and craft. Visit one or all of the following museums to admire the originality, artistic taste and craftsmanship of Swiss timepieces and to discover the history of this craft.

La Chaux-de-Fonds: International Museum of Horology
Le Locle: Museum of Horlogy
Geneva: Horology and Enamels Museum.

★★★ LUCERNE (LUZERN) C

Michelin map 216 fold 17 or 427 fold 14 – Local map see Lake LUCERNE – Alt 436m – 1 430ft – Facilities – Plan of the conurbation in the current Michelin Red Guide Switzerland

The fame of Lucerne as a tourist resort is kept up from year to year by a well-known music festival *(see the Calendar of Events)*. The town has a remarkable site★★★ at the northwest end of Lake Lucerne, where the Reuss River takes up its course again.

The old town, whose access by water was guarded by covered wooden bridges, abuts against a flank of the mountain on which are seven large square towers connected by walls, which are the remains of the town's fortifications. The modern quarters are on the Musegg, Gütsch and Dietschiberg Hills.

Once a simple fishermen's village, Lucerne acquired a certain fame by the foundation in the 8C of a small Benedictine monastery attached to the Alsatian abbey of Murbach. But the opening of the St Gotthard route in the 13C made the town an important staging-point between Flanders and Italy. Situated as it was near "Waldstätten" (the first Swiss Cantons – *read The Swiss national sanctuary under Lake Lucerne*), Lucerne soon established commercial contacts with both countries from which it drew great profit. It was then only a step to the conclusion of a treaty of political alliance in 1332. When the Reformation began, Lucerne assumed the leadership of Catholic resistance. There, in 1574, the Jesuits opened their first college in German Switzerland. From 1601 to 1873 Lucerne was the seat of the Apostolic Nuncio for Switzerland, Rhaetia (Graubünden, the Grisons) and Upper Germany.

★★OLD TOWN AND THE LAKE SHORE *3 hours*

Start from the Schwanenplatz (Swan Square) and make for the Kapellplatz in which stands the Chapel of St Peter.

The centre of the Kapellplatz is adorned with the Fritschi Fountain (Fritschibrunnen) which represents carnival, spring and joy. (Fritschi is a legendary character in whose honour a carnival has been held since the 15C). The Kapellgasse, a lively street lined with shops, leads to the **Kornmarkt** (Grain Market).

★Old Town Hall (Altes Rathaus) (BZ) – This fine Renaissance building, erected on the banks of the Reuss between 1602-06 and flanked by a tall, square tower, overlooks the Kornmarkt.

The Gasthaus zu Pfistern, to the right of the town hall, has a fine painted façade.

Picasso Collection (Picasso Sammlung) (BZ) ⊙ – Left of the town hall, the Am Rhyn town house (Am Rhyn-Haus), like its neighbour, is also Renaissance in style. The majority of the works (paintings, gouaches, wash drawings, engravings and a book by Picasso) exhibited date from the last 20 years of the artist's life (d 1973). This collection is a donation from the Rosengart family, Lucerne art dealers. Among the works displayed note the portrait (1956) representing Jacqueline in the artist's Cannes studio and a *Déjeuner sur l'Herbe,* a very liberal version of Manet's famous painting; Picasso is seated on the right.

Take the Kornmarktgasse on the left and then on the right, an alleyway leading to the Hirschenplatz.

Hirschenplatz (Stag Square) (AZ) – Lined with attractive, restored houses with painted façades and adorned with wrought-iron signs, this square was formerly a meeting-place. Goethe stayed at the "Goldener Adler" in 1779.

★Weinmarkt (Wine Market) (AZ) – This is a pretty square in the heart of the old town, whose old houses, covered with paintings and decorated with many signs and flags, were the seats of the various guilds.

Note no 7, the Scales' Mansion, and the Wine Market Pharmacy (Weinmarkta-potheke) built in 1530. The Gothic fountain in the centre of the square represents warriors and St Maurice, patron saint of soldiers. The original is now in the Government Palace *(see opposite).*

Follow the Kramgasse to the **Mühlenplatz** (Mills Square) **(A7)** which dates from the 16C and where markets were held.

There is a fine view of the Spreuerbrücke, the old houses on the opposite bank of the Reuss and, in the distance, of Gütsch Hill.

Spreuerbrücke (AZ) – This covered bridge, known as Mills Bridge, spans an arm of the Reuss. It was built in 1408 and restored in the 19C. The decoration of painted panels representing a Dance of Death was executed in the 17C by Kaspar Meglinger. From this bridge, in the middle of which there is a little chapel built in 1568, you will enjoy a good view of the quays of the old town and of the façade of the Jesuits' Church.

Beyond the bridge, follow the Pfistergasse for a short distance.

No 24, formerly the Arsenal, from 1567-68 to 1983, now houses the **Historical Museum** (Historisches Museum – **AZ M²**) ⊙. The collections (armour, uniforms, weights and measures, traditional dress, gold and silver plate) displayed pertain to the political and military past as well as the former economic activities of the Lucerne Canton.

Return to the quay (Reuss-Steg).

Charming houses with oriels, painted façades and flower-decked fountains make a fine sight. On the left are the towers from the old town fortifications.

The Kapellbrücke

Jesuits' Church (Jesuitenkirche) **(AZ B)**. – This large building was the first church to be built in the Jesuit style in Switzerland (1667-77). The very plain façade is framed between two tall towers surmounted by domed belfries.

The **interior★** is nobly proportioned. The vaulting in the nave is covered with frescoes and the high altar is adorned with a huge pink marble stucco altarpiece. The stucco in the nave dates from 1750 and is rococo inspired.

On the right of the church, take the Bahnhofstrasse where the Government Palace stands.

Government Palace (Regierungsgebäude) **(AZ P)** – This building with its ornate stonework in the style of the Florentine Renaissance was erected between 1557-64 for the bailiff Ritter. Since 1804 it has housed the cantonal government. In the inner court stands the original fountain of the Weinmarkt *(see previous page)* which dates from 1481.

Franciscan Church (Franziskanerkirche) **(AZ D)** – This church, built in the 13C and remodelled many times, contains fine stalls and a 17C carved wooden pulpit.

★Kapellbrücke (BZ) – This covered bridge, rebuilt after the fire of 1993, which crosses the Reuss at the point where it emerges from the lake, has become a symbol of Lucerne *(photograph on previous page)*. The bridge which was built at the beginning of the 14C and is over 200m – 656ft long, protected the town on the lake side and is flanked by an octagonal tower, roofed with tiles, called the **Wasserturm.**

It was adorned with about 100 paintings on wood in the triangles formed by the roof beams. These paintings were executed at the beginning of the 17C and restored at the beginning of the 20C. They depicted the history of Lucerne and Switzerland, and of Sts Leger and Maurice, patron saints of the town. Copies now replace the panels destroyed by fire.

Return to the Schwanenplatz.

Beyond the modern bridge (Seebrücke) which spans the Reuss, is a spacious quarter with many shops.

★Cathedral of St Leger (Hofkirche) **(BY)** – This church, dedicated to St Leger (Leodegar) the patron saint of the town – which is said to derive its name from him – was founded in 735. In 1633 all except the Gothic towers were destroyed by fire and it was rebuilt in the Renaissance style. It is a great building, reached by a monumental stairway and is surrounded by cloisters in the Italian style, containing tombs of the old families of Lucerne.

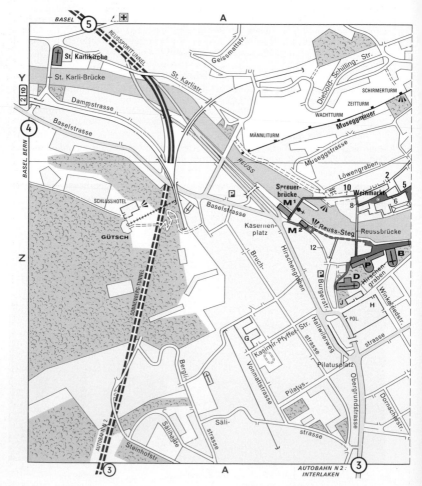

The **interior**★ is well proportioned, in the late Renaissance style. The chancel is enclosed by a wrought-iron grille and furnished with ornate stalls. Gilded and figured altarpieces adorn ten of the altars (*Piétà* – south aisle; *Death of the Virgin* – north aisle). The organ (1650) is one of the best in Switzerland.

The Shore – The quays, planted with trees and flanked by mansions, afford admirable **views**★★ (**BY**) of the town site and Lake Lucerne, and beyond of the Alpine range stretching from the Rigi to the Pilatus *(viewing tables)*. At the end of the Carlspittelerquai are pleasant green lawns and the Lido beach.

★★★ **Swiss Transport Museum** (Verkehrshaus) ⊘ – *Lidostrasse 3 (near the lake) by* ②. Opened in 1959, this museum offers to visitors of all ages an illustration of the history of transportation in Switzerland.

Swiss Railway – Two halls and one square contain a collection of around sixty railway vehicles, the largest in the country. The oldest steam locomotive dates from 1858, the most recent from 1916. This exhibition features an amazing number of electric locomotives made during the early period: the first electric tramcar (1888), the first European three-phase electric locomotive (1899), the first high-tension locomotive operating on single-phase current (1904). Other models made before 1949 include the Crocodile and the AE 8/14 (the most powerful at the time). Among the rack-railways is a 1873 model belonging to the "Vitznau-Rigi" railway (the first in Europe). Several trams and an impressive collection of reduced models complete the exhibition.

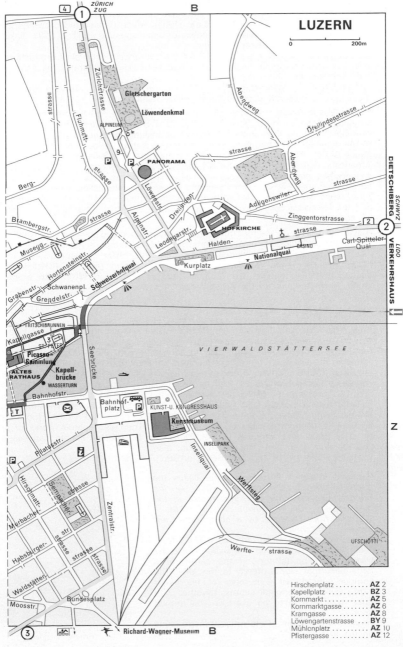

Hirschenplatz	**AZ** 2
Kapellplatz	**BZ** 3
Kornmarkt	**AZ** 5
Kornmarktgasse	**AZ** 6
Kramgasse	**AZ** 8
Löwengartenstrasse	**BY** 9
Mühlenplatz	**AZ** 10
Pfistergasse	**AZ** 12

The journey from Wassen to Göschenen is reconstituted on a large maquette of the north section of St Gotthard railway. A modern locomotive control cabin simulator reproduces the trip to St Gotthard. *Treat your children to a ride on the miniature steam train.*

Automobiles, motorcycles, cycles... – A collection of about forty automobiles occupies the ground floor: Genevese Thury-Nussberg motorcar (1877), Dufaux racing car (1905, Geneva), Zürich taxi (1908), Mercedes (Silver Arrow – 1933), Lamborghini (1968) and Ford Concept Car (1980).

The mezzanine displays sleighs, diligences and a 19C caleche. On the first floor about fifty cycles (1875 – Pennyfarthing, 1880 – Engadine four-wheeler) and motorcycles of the past and present as well as automobile motors.

Post and telecommunications – Presented in the first hall is an attractive account of the Swiss postal services through the ages. Shown are the handling of mail from the moment it drops into the box until it arrives at its destination and stamp production. There is a gallery which is especially interesting to the philatelist.

In a second hall the important historical moments of telecommunications and modern realizations in the world of the telephone, telegraph, radio and television are traced. *Some of the machines can be operated.*

Navigation, cable-cars, tourism – The ground floor exhibits the machinery of the steamboat *Pilatus* (1895). The Navigation section (first floor) presents a remarkable collection of reduced models and nautical instruments tracing the progress of navigation through the centuries. Note the shipowner's office, containing a wide range of miniature ships, marine books and seascapes donated to the museum by the shipowner Philipp Keller in 1980. The cable-car section *(second floor)* displays a cabin of the first public aerial cable-car (1908), which transported passengers to Wetterhorn and the ultra-modern cabin of the cable-car, built in 1984, linking Spielboden to Langfluh near Saas-Fee.

The tourism section shows a selection of the country's most typical products and activities and, Panorama Switzerland, a multivision show illustrates the country's most famous sites.

The paddle-wheel steamship *Rigi* (1847) – set up in a small courtyard within the museum – is presently used as a self-service restaurant.

From airships to rockets – Models of balloons and airships and the frame of a hot-air balloon can be seen beside an equipped Swissair plane. Hung above are examples of more than thirty Swiss civil or military airplanes form the bi-plane to the supersonic jet and helicopter; the larger planes are outside. On the upper floors is the astronautics section with many objects (1960s) which served the Americans during their space travels: parts of rockets, Mercury space capsule, a spacesuit, a piece of lunar rock etc. as well as accessories and models. This section includes the **Cosmorama** *(second floor)* a narrated slide show *(time: 1/2 hour)* which shows the different events in space travel on 18 large-scale screens and the **Planetarium Longines** *(ground floor)* which shows the celestial phenomena on screen.

Hans Erni Museum – On the far right of the museum, a building shelters approximately 300 canvases (plus ceramics) of Hans Erni, the contemporary painter, native of Lucerne. The collection includes works from the 1930s onwards (Symbolism, Figurative art). There is also a huge mural painting (40m – 131ft) in the auditorium which depicts the greatest thinkers and scientists of the western world, from Antiquity to the present day.

ADDITIONAL SIGHTS

Fine Arts Museum (Kunstmuseum) (BZ) ⊙ – The museum, housed in the Palace of Arts and Congresses where concerts are given during the Lucerne festival, is used for temporary exhibitions; especially in conjuction with the Music Festival.

Found in the first-floor rooms are religious carvings and 16C paintings on wood by Swiss (Martin Moser: *Story of Lazarus*) and foreign (Holbein the Younger: *Lucretia's Suicide*) artists as well as 17C (Kaspar Meglinger: *Dance of Death*) and 18C paintings (J Melchior Wyrsch, Anton Graff: portraits). The following galleries exhibit works of art (late 19 early 20C) by Swiss Realists Vallotton *(The Woman with Roses)*, Robert Zünd (landscapes), Ferdinand Hodler (portraits, landscapes, allegorical subjects) and Max Buri... They also contain works of art by Dufy *(Bois de Boulogne)*, Utrillo *(Moulin de la Galette)*, Foujita (landscape) and Vlaminck (still life). The second floor also contains works by 19 and 20C Swiss artists.

Richard Wagner Museum ⊙ – *Leave the town by the Hirschmattstrasse* **(BZ)**. *At the Bundersplatz take the Tribschenstrasse in the direction of St Niklausen. About 1km – 1/2 mile from Lucerne, by a church, turn left towards Tribschen.*

Richard Wagner's house, where he lived from 1866-72 and where he received Nietzsche stands on a promontory in the centre of a large park that slopes down to the lake. The composer produced a number of his major works here; the original scores, together with other souvenirs, may be seen on the ground floor.

There is a collection of old musical instruments on the first floor.

Richard Wagner

★**Great Panorama of Lucerne** (BY) ⊘ – In this outstanding panorama, Edouard Castres has depicted a scene from the Franco-Prussian war. In February 1871 the routed French army under General Bourbaki fled into Switzerland, where they were given asylum. Far from glorifying war Castres has portrayed all the suffering and misery.

Lion Monument (Löwendenkmal) (BY) – The dying lion is carved out of the sandstone cliff-face. It commemorates the heroism of Louis XVI's Swiss Guards.

Glacier Garden (Gletschergarten) (BY) ⊘ – This takes the tourist back to the time when the plain as far as the Jura was covered by the Reuss Glacier. Here you will see 32 giant potholes which were uncovered in 1872. These potholes, one of which is 9.5m - 29 1/2ft deep and 8m - 16ft wide, were hollowed out by water falling through crevasses in the glacier and polished by stones or mills, revolved by the water. One of them weighs six tons.

The museum contains, on the ground floor, prehistoric collections (plant and animal fossils), the reconstitution of a reindeer hunter's cave towards the end of the Ice Age, the first relief map of Central Switzerland (18C) and miniature replicas of traditional chalets.

On the first floor you can see a peasant's humble sleeping quarters and a series of documents explaining the history of the Glacier Garden. The old city of Lucerne is evoked on the second floor through a display of plans, engravings, models and 18C furniture.

Musegg Ramparts (Museggmauer) (ABY) ⊘ – The remains of the fortified city walls, include nine watch and defense towers, dating from 1350 to 1408. From the top of the Schirmer Tower (Schirmerturn-*91 steps ; destroyed by fire in 1994*) there is a **view**★ of Lucerne with the soaring spires of St Leger's Cathedral and of the lake in its mountain setting.

Church of St Charles (St Karlikirche) (AY) – This modern church was built by the architect Metzger in 1934. The porch is surmounted by great statues of the four Evangelists. Inside, the nave has a flat ceiling supported by tall columns It is decorated with frescoes and lit by yellow and purple stained-glass windows.

Museum of Natural History and Archaeology (Natur-Museum) (AZ M¹) ⊘ – Devoted mainly to the natural characteristics of central Switzerland, this museum presents on the first floor an extensive collection of Alpine minerals and fossils and a remarkable **gallery of archaeology** exhibiting objects found in the area from the Neolithic lake dwellers, the Bronze Age and Celto-Roman period. Also in this gallery, models and dioramas depict the life of the lake dweller. Found on the second floor arc zoological and botanical collections as well as aquariums, terrariums, etc.

★★**Dietschiberg** – Alt 629m – 2 064ft. At the station, take bus no 14 and get off at the Konservatorium stop. From there it is a twenty-minute walk, following signposts to Utenberg and Golfplatz. Splendid **panorama**★★ of Lake Lucerne, with Lucerne and Pilatus on the right, the Rigi on the left and the Bernese and Glarus Alps on the horizon *(viewing tables)*.

★**Gütsh** (AZ) ⊘ – Alt 523m – 1 716ft. *About 1/2 hour Rtn, including 6 minutes by funicular (station on the Baselstrasse – plan p 140).*
From the terrace of the Gütsch Castle Hotel which crowns this wooded hill on the left bank of the Reuss, the **view**★ extends over the fortified town, the lake and Alps.

BOAT TRIPS ⊘

The constantly changing views of Lake Lucerne make a trip on its waters a continual delight, even in stormy weather. Starting from Lucerne the complete tour of the lake in a comfortable boat with a restaurant takes around 6 hours. These outings introduce one to some of the most treasured historical sights: the William Tell Chapel, the Schillerstein obelisk, etc. It is also possible to combine the boat trip with a train journey through the mountains: such is the case of the "William Tell Express", which links Lucerne to the Ticino canton.

EXCURSIONS

★★★**Pilatus** – 15km – *9 miles about 3 hours, including 1 hour by rack-railway.* Michelin maps **216** fold 17 and **217** fold 9 or **427** fold 14. *Leave Lucerne by ③ and take the motorway in the direction of Interlaken. After a long tunnel, turn off the motorway to Alpnachstad. At Alpnachstad take the Pilatus rack-railway. The excursion is described under Pilatus.*

★★**Bürgenstock** – Facilities. 16km – *10 miles to the south.* Michelin maps **216** fold 17 and **217** fold 9 or **427** folds 14 and 15. *Leave Lucerne by ③. You can go up the Bürgenstock either by car from Stansstad (6km – 3 miles along a steep, narrow road) or by funicular from the landing-stage at Kehrsiten-Bürgenstock in 7 minutes. Services connect with the steamers.* The name Bürgenstock is given to a massive, wooded, rock ridge and also applies to a group of luxury hotels perched 500m – 1 500ft above the central junction (Chrüztrichter) of the lake. The favourite walk at the Bürgenstock is along the **Felsenweg**★★ *(about 1/2 hour)*, a corniche path making a panoramic circuit around the Hammetschwand spur. The summit of this (1 128m – 3 700ft) can be reached by a lift up the mountainside.

★★★**Rigi** – 24km – *15 miles – about 3 hours, including 1 hour by mountain railway. Leave Lucerne by ② road no 2.*
Leave the car at the Arth-Goldau station and take the Rigi railway to its terminus at Rigi-Kulm. The rest of the excursion is described under Rigi.

Michelin maps 📖 folds 17 and 18 and 📖 folds 9 and 10 or 📖 folds 14 and 15

Lake Lucerne is found on most maps under its German name: Vierwaldstättersee. The French name is Lac des Quatre-Cantons.

The Lake Lucerne district offers its diorama of hills and mountains, its little old-fashioned cities and its innumerable belvedere-summits to the tourist. For many visitors the stamp of a town like Lucerne typifies the charm of that central Switzerland which the road over the Brünig Pass (or Sachseln, *qv*) conveniently links with the Bernese Oberland.

HISTORICAL NOTES

The Swiss national sanctuary – Every corner in this part of Switzerland has its hero, its battlefield, its commemorative chapel or its feudal ruins. This was the cradle of Swiss democracy.

Long before the Confederation began, the **Waldstätten** (forest cantons) on the shores of the lake were already leading, like the peoples of many lonely valleys in the Alps, a life full of communal obligations. The exploitation of forests, the clearing of Alpine pastures and the distribution of the offspring of flocks and herds constantly required meetings, discussions and elections. Being accustomed to such ways, the Waldstätten adapted themselves without much difficulty to a symbolic allegiance to the Emperor when all Helvetia was part of the Germanic Holy Roman Empire. The "immediate" attachment of the District of Uri to the Empire was formally guaranteed as early as 1231, since that area deserved special treatment for its situation on the St Gotthard route.

Compagnie de Navigation du Lac des Quatre-Cantons, Lucerne

Lake Lucerne

This relative autonomy seemed threatened when the Austrian House of Habsburg, anxious to ensure the effective and profitable administration of its possessions in the region, created a corps of officials financially interested in the revenues of their estates without consulting local susceptibilities. These bailiffs quickly became unpopular. The worst affront that can be offered to a man in a state of freedom is to impose upon him, from outside, a judge who is neither a peer nor a citizen.

The position became critical when the Habsburgs, in the person of Rudolf, acceded to the Imperial throne in 1273. At the death of Rudolf, which opened the prospect of a fiercely contested election and a dangerously confused political situation, the representatives of Schwyz, Uri and Unterwalden met to conclude a permanent alliance. This mutual assistance pact did not propose disobedience to the overlords, but it categorically rejected any administrative and judicial system imposed from without and it is regarded by the Swiss as the birth certificate of the Confederation. Its original text is carefully preserved at Schwyz, and the anniversary of its signature (on 1 August 1291) is celebrated as the national festival *(see the Calendar of Events)*.

The victory of Morgarten (1315) over the troops of Leopold of Austria marked the definite liberation of the three "original" cantons.

Dawn of liberty – However surprising such a development may have seemed to the feudal society of the period, it would not have achieved its later fame but for the legendary interpretation which, from the 15C onwards, created an incomparably more colourful and dramatic version of these events. This, in turn, became one of the treasures of German literature with the **William Tell** of Schiller in 1804. This version no longer described a long struggle by alternate negotiation and armed revolt but a conspiracy long matured by the representatives of the three communities, depicted henceforth as so many victims of despotism personified by Bailiff Gessler, and solemnly sworn on the Field of Rütli, opposite Brunnen, by thirty-three spokesmen of Schwyz, Uri and Unterwalden.

After having been subjected by Gessler to the famous ordeal of the apple, the archer William Tell became the arm of justice of the conspiracy. He killed Gessler in the sunken road (Hohle Gasse) at Küssnacht *(p 12)*, opening the way to an era of liberty. Since that time the Rütli episode has been the living source of the Swiss national tradition.

"Protector of the Fatherland" – The District of Unterwalden (more exactly the half-canton of Obwalden) which is crossed by the Brünig route, is proud to number among its sons the hermit **Nicholas of Flüe** (canonized in 1947), whose conciliatory intervention left an indelible mark on the Swiss patriotic temperament. Born in 1417 into a family of prosperous peasants, Brother Nicholas (Bruder Klaus), as his fellow-citizens called him, showed a keen taste for prayer and the contemplative life. He first assumed all the family and civic duties that a man of his merit could claim. And yet at the age of fifty, this father of ten children, obeying an irresistible vocation, separated from his family and lived the life of an ascetic in the solitude of Ranft *(qv)*, at the mouth of the Melchtal.

Meanwhile the confederates of the VIII Cantons of that time *(see the Historical Notes)* were faced with serious internal difficulties. Two policies were in opposition: that of the Towns, governed by cautious bourgeois oligarchies, and that of the Districts (Länder) in the mountains, which had remained faithful to the practice of direct democracy and were more open to outside views.

In 1477 the dwellers on the shores of Lake Lucerne became agitated when they learned that Lucerne, in agreement with Zürich and Berne, had made a separate alliance with Fribourg and Solothurn. When Lucerne maintained the pact, in spite of the entreaties of its neighbours Uri, Schwyz and Unterwalden, the conflict became acute. In despair the parish priest of Stans went to Ranft to consult Brother Nicholas. He returned with an admirable appeal for peace. A compromise (1481) was made.

BOAT TRIPS ⊘

For seasonal visitors a boat trip around the lake, followed by a climb to one of the surrounding summits, should not be missed. Some of the lakeside sights, namely the historic Field of Rütli, can only be reached by boat.

★★★① NORTH SHORES

From Lucerne to Altdorf
54 km – 34 miles – about 2 1/2 hours – Local map below

★★★**Lucerne** – *Time: 3 hours. See Lucerne.*

Between Lucerne, Küssnacht and Weggis, the road runs through rich country planted with walnut and fruit trees, and skirts the ramifications of Lake Lucerne and Lake Küssnacht as it approaches the slopes of the Rigi with their reddish outcrops. Far away, to the south, the mountainous foothills of the Nidwalden (Stans-Engelberg District) succeed one another in confusion, although Pilatus is still easy to distinguish by its rugged crests.

Merlischachen – Here wooden houses with pointed roofs offer some fine examples of the type of building found in Central Switzerland *(illustration p 30)*.

Chapel of Queen Astrid (Astridkapelle) – The road follows the walls of this small sanctuary, erected after the tragic accident of 29 August 1935, in which Queen Astrid of Belgium was killed, when the royal car crashed into an orchard. A plain cross marks the spot where the queen was found, now surrounded by a protecting fence.

Hohle Gasse – Facilities. *From Küssnacht, 3km – 2 miles Rtn by the road to Arth (no 2), plus 1/4 hour on foot Rtn.*

Leaving your car at the Hohle Gasse Hotel, take the sunken road (in German, Hohle Gasse) steeply uphill and roughly paved, where according to tradition William Tell lay in wait to do justice to Gessler. The road through the woods ends at the commemorative chapel which is a place of pilgrimage for the Swiss.

★★**Weggis** – Facilities. Weggis is the queen of the resorts situated on the shores of Lake Lucerne. It lies within view of Pilatus and the Unterwalden Mountains along a promenade quay which leads to the Hertenstein Promontory. Pleasure boating and walks on the last slopes of the Rigi, planted with vines and even some almost tropical species – the warmth of the Föhn *(qv)*, coinciding here with a site facing due south – plus the resort's social amenities, will satisfy every visitor.

From Weggis the lakeside road reveals a constantly changing landscape.

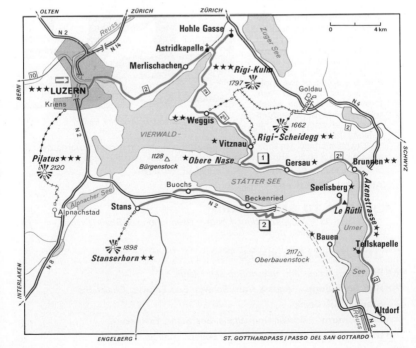

★**Vitznau** – Passing tourists may leave their cars for a few hours in this elegant resort, enclosed between the Rigi and the lake, to climb Rigi-Kulm by rack-railway. This was the first mountain railway built in Europe (1871).

★★★**Rigi-Kulm** – *From Vitznau, about 3 hours Rtn, including 1 1/4 hours by rack-railway. See Rigi.*

★**Obere Nase** – The very pronounced bend in the road as it passes this cape is arranged as a **belvedere**★. This "Nose", thrown out by a spur of the Rigi, and the Untere Nase, an extreme outcrop of the Bürgenstock facing it, enclose a channel only 825m – 2707ft wide connecting two very different basins. Within a short distance you pass from Lake Vitznau, bounded on the south by the wooded spur of Bürgenstock, to Lake Gersau-Beckenried, in a more open setting. Pilatus remains a familiar landmark.

★**Gersau** – Facilities. Lying in one of the most open **sites**★★ on the Alpine shores of the lake, the tiny "Republic of Gersau" – such was the status of the village between 1390-1817 – is now attached to the Schwyz Canton.

Near Brunnen the wooded Schwyz Basin, dominated by the twin Mythen Peaks, unfolds. On the right, under the arched Cliffs of the Fronalpstock, the terrace of Morschach appears. You will now begin to skirt the Bay of Brunnen, followed by the Seelisberg.

★★**Brunnen** – *See Brunnen.*

From Brunnen to Flüelen the Axenstrasse *corniche* overhangs the romantic **Lake Uri** (Urnersee), with its deep blue waters. Its shores are marked by places of patriotic pilgrimage recalling the birth of the Confederation (Rütli, Tell's Chapel).

★★**Axenstrasse** – This section of road, which is one of the best-known on the St. Gotthard route, is also one of the busiest in all Switzerland (about 10000 cars in mid-summer). It was cut last century through the cliffs which dip into Lake Uri. The section has two parts differing in character.
– Between Brunnen and Sisikon the road follows a *corniche* facing the Seelisberg Promontory – whose wooded slopes are interrupted by the green patch of the Rütli Field *(qv)* – within view of the twin Uri- Rotstock Peaks. The best sited belvedere is on the outside of a bend above the railway; here you are exactly opposite the Rütli.
– Between Sisikon and Flüelen the road has changed since a single tunnel was bored to take the place of the famous open gallery *(disused and closed to cars)* of which millions of photographs must have been taken.

William Tell Chapel (Tell-skapelle) – *From the Hotel Tellsplatte, 1/2 hour on foot Rtn by a steep path.* Built on a lonely **site**★ on the shore of **Lake Uri**, this chapel commemorates one of the most dramatic episodes in the story of William Tell: when he was Gessler's prisoner after the ordeal of the apple the valiant bowman was thrown into a boat which was assailed by a sudden storm; the bailiff and his minions had to appeal for

William Tell by F Hodler

Musée des Beaux-Arts, Soleure

their captive's help. He took advantage of this to steer the boat towards the shore, leaped onto a rocky shelf and kicked the boat back into the raging waves.

The first houses of Altdorf mark the end of the drive.

Altdorf – *See Altdorf.*

★② **ROAD TO SEELISBERG**
22km – 13 1/2 miles – about 1 hour – Description see Stans: Excursions – Local map on previous page

ADDITIONAL SIGHTS

★★★**Pilatus** – *Access and description see Pilatus.*

★★**Rigi Scheidegg** – *Access from Schwyz. See Schwyz: Excursions.*

Stans – *See Stans.*

★★**Stanserhorn** – *Access from Stans. See Stans: Excursions.*

★**Bauen** – *Access from Altdorf. See Bauen: Excursion.*

Michelin map ᴍ19 fold 8 or ᴍ27 fold 24 – Local map below – Alt 273m – 896ft – Facilities

The "Queen of the Ceresio" lies at the end of a beautiful bay framed between the wooded Mount Brè and Mount San Salvatore. It faces south and is an ideal tourist and health resort, particularly appreciated in the spring and autumn. The organization of the innumerable fêtes and amusements for visitors (beaches, tennis courts, 18-hole golf-course, riding, boating and casino) is a credit to Switzerland. Lugano is a convenient excursion centre for visiting the three lakes – Maggiore, Lugano and Como.

It is pleasant to stroll under the arcades of the Via Nassa and down the magnificent shady promenade along the lake shore from the Municipal Park *(see next page)* to Paradiso (views). A most enjoyable time can be had sitting in one of the pavement cafés on the Piazza della Riforma.

★★**Lake Lugano** – Most of the lake is in Swiss territory. The Italians, who call it Ceresio, have only the northeast branch (Porlezza), part of the southwest shore (Porto Ceresio) as well as a small enclave located on the east shore (Campione d'Italia).

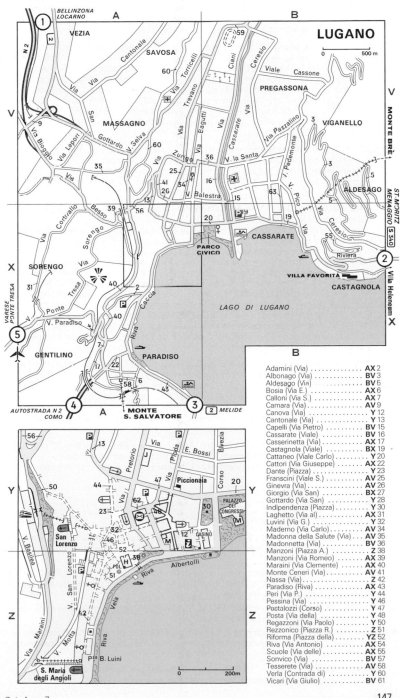

Adamini (Via)	**AX** 2
Albonago (Via)	**BV** 3
Aldesago (Via)	**BV** 5
Bosia (Via E.)	**AX** 6
Calloni (Via S.)	**AX** 7
Camara (Via)	**AV** 9
Canova (Via)	**Y** 12
Cantonale (Via)	**Y** 13
Capelli (Via Pietro)	**BV** 15
Cassarate (Viale)	**BV** 16
Casserinetta (Via)	**AX** 17
Castagnola (Viale)	**BX** 19
Cattaneo (Viale Carlo)	**Y** 20
Cattori (Via Giuseppe)	**AX** 22
Dante (Piazza)	**Y** 23
Franscini (Viale S.)	**AV** 25
Ginevra (Via)	**AV** 26
Giorgio (Via San)	**BX** 27
Gottardo (Via San)	**Y** 28
Indipendenza (Piazza)	**Y** 30
Laghetto (Via al)	**AX** 31
Luvini (Via G.)	**Y** 32
Maderno (Via Carlo)	**AV** 34
Madonna della Salute (Via)	**AV** 35
Madonnetta (Via)	**BV** 36
Manzoni (Piazza A.)	**Z** 38
Manzoni (Via Romeo)	**AX** 39
Maraini (Via Clemente)	**AX** 40
Monte Ceneri (Via)	**AV** 41
Nassa (Via)	**Z** 42
Paradiso (Riva)	**AX** 43
Peri (Via P.)	**Y** 44
Pessina (Via)	**Y** 46
Poctalozzi (Corso)	**Y** 47
Posta (Via della)	**Y** 48
Regazzoni (Via Paolo)	**Y** 50
Rezzonico (Piazza R.)	**Z** 51
Riforma (Piazza della)	**YZ** 52
Riva (Via Antonio)	**AX** 54
Scuole (Via delle)	**AX** 55
Sonvico (Via)	**BV** 57
Tesserete (Via)	**AV** 58
Verla (Contrada di)	**Y** 60
Vicari (Via Giulio)	**BV** 61

Lake Lugano looks wilder than Lakes Maggiore and Como. It is set among the steep but beautiful slopes of the Alps, on which the silvery leaves of olive trees make pale patches. It is irregular in shape, with a total length of 33km – 21 miles and a maximum depth of 288m (947ft – 150 fathoms). Unfortunately, a causeway carrying the St. Gotthard road and railway cuts it into two basins.

SIGHTS

★★**Municipal Park (Parco Civico) (BX)** – A delightful garden where fine trees spread their shade. The pleasant setting is further enhanced by a number of fountains and statues (a sculpture of Socrates executed by the Russian artist Autokolsky).
During the summer season, and providing the weather is fine, one can attend open-air concerts in the park.

"Piccionaia" (Y) – At the junction between the Corso Pestalozzi and Via Pioda, and in the northeast corner (set back from the street) this lovely house, known under its Italian name meaning dovecote, is said to be the oldest in the city. It has a façade embellished with painted friezes.

Cathedral of St Lawrence (Cattedrale di San Lorenzo) (Y) – This has an elegant façade with three delicately decorated Renaissance doorways. At the end of the south aisle is the early 16C tabernacle by the Rodari brothers of Maroggia. There is a view from the esplanade of Lugano and the lake.

Church of St Mary of the Angels (Santa Maria degli Angioli) (Z) – This former conventual church, begun in 1499, contains three of the finest **frescoes★★** of Bernardo Luini (c1480-1532). The most impressive one, adorning the partition that cuts off the nun's choir from the nave, represents a *Passion,* striking on account of its huge size and great expressivity. Below it are pictured St Sebastian and St Roch. In the first chapel you come to on the right, on the left-hand wall, note the fresco *Virgin with Child and St John,* which was taken from the cloisters: its beauty is believed to be "worthy of the great Leonardo". The nave bears a representation of the Last Supper.

★★★**Monte San Salvatore** ⊘ – Alt 912m – 2 996ft. *About 3/4 hour Rtn, including 20 minutes by funicular, starting from the Paradiso quarter* (**AX**).
An admirable view of Lugano, the lake and the Bernese and Valais Alps (belvedere with viewing balconies). You can return to Lugano from the summit by marked paths.

★**Villa Favorita (BX)** ⊘ – At Castagnola. *Take bus no 2 leaving from Piazza Manzoni and get off at Villa Favorita.*
Access to this late 17C building, consisting of three staggered storeys, is through a long, narrow garden park overlooking the lake, planted with boxwood, cypress, palm and monkey puzzle trees and dotted with statues.
The greater part of the remarkable collection of paintings gathered from 1920 to the present day by the Thyssen-Bornemisza, the famous German steel industrialists, has been transferred to the Thyssen-Bornemisza Museum in Madrid *(see Michelin Green Guide Spain)*. However, the Villa Favorita regularly holds exhibitions of works taken from this collection, concentrating on a given theme or a given artistic movement. One of these, titled *Europe and America: 19 and 20C Paintings and Watercolours* was a wonderful opportunity to appreciate the Luminist and Hudson River Schools, as well as the great American Impressionists and the West European painters.

Villa Heleneum (BX) – *Take bus no 2 leaving from Piazza Manzoni. Get off at San Domenico, then continue on foot for 5 min along Via Cortivo.*
On the edge of the lake, a Neo-Classical mansion houses the **Museum of Non-European Culture** (Museo delle Culture Extraeuropee). The collections displayed here feature around 600 exhibits, mainly wooden sculptures from Oceania, Asia and Africa. Each of the three floors presents the culture of a particular ethnic group, focusing on a given theme (social life, environment).

★★**Monte Brè** ⊘ – Alt 925m – 3 051ft. *About 1 hour Rtn, including 30 minutes by funicular, starting from Cassarate* (**BX**). *You can also go up by car.*
A very sunny summit. From the terraces there is a fine view of the lake and the Alps.

EXCURSIONS

by car or mountain railway

★★★**Monte Generoso** – Alt 1 701m – 5 581ft. *The excursion takes a full half-day. 15km – 9 miles by* ③ *and the road to Como as far as Capolago, where you turn right to reach Riva San Vitale.*

Riva San Vitale – A 5C baptistry containing 14 and 15C frescoes (restored); also the graceful 16C Church of the Holy Cross (Santa Croce), surmounted by an octagonal dome and adorned with frescoes.

Return to Capolago where you will leave the car and take the rack-railway. Time for the journey: 2 hours Rtn.

★★★**Monte Generoso** ⊘ – From the summit the splendid **panorama★★★** extends over the Alps, Lugano, the lakes and the Lombardy Plain to the distant Apennines on a clear day.

★**Monte Lema** – *17km – 10 1/2 miles northwest via Bioggio. Leave Lugano by* ④.
From Bioggio the road winds through woods before entering Cademario.

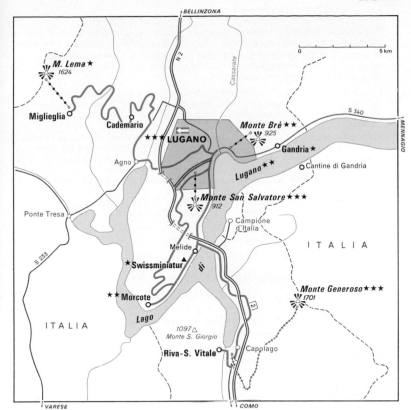

Cademario − From this terraced village there is a nice **view** (especially near the parish church) of the plain below, part of the west side of Lake Lugano and the surrounding mountains. As you leave the village following directions to Lugano, the old **Church of San Ambrogio** ⊙ stands alone with its campanile in the Lombardy style and its façade with its partly-erased 15C frescoes. Inside are interesting 13C polychrome frescoes: in the nave, on the pillar, there is a Crucifixion, on the south wall another Crucifixion and the martyrdom of St Ambrose and in the apse there is a Christ Blessing (in the Byzantine style) surrounded by angels and Apostles.

Miglieglia − At the foot of the wooded Monte Lema lies the village and its church, St Stefano (15C). The interior houses 16-17C frescoes: note in the chapel across from the side entrance God the Father above Mary in prayer then visited by the Holy Ghost; in the chancel are Evangelists and their symbols, the Nativity and Crucifixion, under a Christ Blessing (in the vaulting).

★**Monte Lema** ⊙ − Alt 1 624m − 5 328ft. *Access by chairlift from Miglieglia.*
The climb, above a landscape of fern and rocks, presents a bird's-eye view of Miglieglia and the Church of St Stefano. From the restaurant of the upper station climb to the top *(20 minutes Rtn along a steep path)* between a television relay station and a large metal cross for a **panorama**★ which extends westwards to Lake Maggiorre and Monte Rosa and eastwards to Lake Lugano and Monte Generoso.

★★**Morcote** ⊙ − Facilities. Round tour of 26km − *16 miles − about 2 hours − starts along a fairly hilly road. Access by boat.*

Leave Lugano through Paradiso (by ③*) and then take the high road to Morcote.*

This route via Pazzallo and Carona offers magnificent **bird's-eye views**★★ of the lake and distant glimpses as far as the Monte Rosa massif.

★★**The village** − The Lombardic arcaded houses of Morcote are reflected in the calm waters of Lake Lugano ot the foot of the last slopes of Mount Arbostora carpeted with Mediterranean flora. By a staircase and alleys offering many vistas you will reach the Church of Santa Maria del Sasso containing remarkable 16C frescoes. The lake, the church, the baptistry, the cypresses and a cemetery form a remarkable **picture**★★.

Return to Lugano taking in the road along the lake shore, which is most attractive. Switzerland in Miniature is located before **Melide.**

★**Switzerland in Miniature (Swissminiatur)** ⊙ − This replica of the main sights of each Swiss canton reproduced in miniature is a joy to children and grown-ups alike.
Spread over 1ha − 2 1/2 acres of verdant and flowery land on the edge of the lake, the exhibit displays the country's main tourist attractions; monuments (reproduced in stone), bridges etc... and evokes the country's main economic activities as well. Trains (3km − 2 miles of network), boats and cable-cars all function.

Boat Trips

The steamer services on Lake Lugano, by which you can make an hour's trip at short notice or a complete half-day tour, are among the attractions of the resort.
In addition to the localities sited below the steamship company on Lake Lugano stops regularily at Porlezza Ponte Tresa, Campione, etc. A tour of the lake Grande Giro del Lago starts from Lugano.

★ **Gandria** – *1 hour Rtn if you do not go ashore.* Amid a maze of stepped streets this village, with terraces planted with geraniums, trellises, leafy bowers, arcaded houses and a small baroque church form a charming picture much appreciated by artists.

Customs Museum ⊘ – *At Cantine di Gandria on the south shore of the lake (access by boat 1 3/4 hours Rtn including visit to the museum).* Located on the lake shore in a Swiss customs house, the museum explains the role, past and present, of the customs officer (maps, photos, models dressed in uniform).
On the second floor the devices (traps, weapons...) used by the smugglers are exhibited.
Perhaps the museum's most interesting object is the inflatable boat which was captured in 1946 – its inflation compartments held salami!
On the third floor are temporary exhibitions.

★★ **Morcote** – *See Lugano: Excursions.*

MALOJA Graubünden (Grisons)

Michelin map **218** fold 15 or **427** fold 17 – Local map see GRISONS – Alt 1 815m – 5 955ft – Facilities.

The Maloja crossing, used by a great international route establishes communications between the Valleys of the Inn and the Mera.

Pass Belvedere – Opposite the Maloja Kulm Hotel a smooth rocky outcrop, edged with a balustrade, gives a bird's-eye **view** of the Bergell shelf and the hairpin bends in the road going down to it.

Castle Belvedere – *From Maloja village, 1/2 hour on foot Rtn along an uphill road beginning level with the Schweizerhaus Hotel.*
From the top of the tower – a relic of a great unfinished project of the last century – the **panorama**★ embraces the Bergell Mountains (Gletscherhorn, Piz Cacciabella) and, on the Engadine side, extends beyond Lake Sils to the Rosatsch-Corvatsch chain. The former castle park contains a few eroded potholes (below the tower near the fences surrounding these cavities).

MARBACH Lucerne   Pop 1 220

Michelin map **217** folds 7 and 8 or **427** fold 14 – Local map see EMMENTAL

In a valley adjacent to the Entlebuch Valley, Marbach is a good departure point for excursions.
Note its large Catholic church with its richly-adorned baroque interior.

EXCURSIONS

★ **Marbachegg** ⊘ – The cable-car leaves Marbach, rides over a countryside made up of spruce forests and meadows, and arrives *(12 minutes)* on Marbachegg Mountain where the village of Lochsitenberg (alt 1 483m – 4 865ft) is perched. The restaurant's terrace commands a lovely **view**★ of the area. From east to south the following can be seen: the Schrattenflue Cliffs which are flanked on the right by the Schibengütsch, on the horizon gleam the shiny white Fiescherhorn and Eiger Peaks and in the foreground the snowy torrents of the Hohgant Summit. Just below is a fine wooded valley.

★ **Schallenberg Pass Road** – *33km – 20 1/2 miles from Marbach to Thun.*
This picturesque road, winding along the foot of the Hohgant and between the peaks delimiting the Emmental to the south, offers good glimpses of the Schrattenflue, the Hohgant and, after the narrow Schallenberg Pass (alt 1 167m – 3 829ft) and a lovely spruce forest, the peaks of the Jungfrau Massif. Starting at Süderen Oberei, villages succeed one another alternating with meadows and fir trees; the road then skirts the deep, wooded Zulg Valley (left) with a view of Rüti Peak. After Kreuzweg continue down to Steffisburg, the industrial centre of Thun – on the left note Thun Castle. Continue to Thun.

★★ **Thun** – *See Thun.*

Michelin Maps (scale 1:200 000), which are revised regularly, provide much useful information:
covers the whole of Switzerland, showing
- latest motorway developments and changes
- vital data (width, alignment, camber and surface) of motorways and tracks
- the location of emergency telephones.

Keep current Michelin Maps in the car at all times.

MARTIGNY Valais

Michelin map **74** fold 9 or **427** fold 21 – Local map see VALAIS – Alt 476m – 1 562ft
– Facilities – Town plan in the current Michelin Red Guide Switzerland

The town of Martigny, dominated by La Bâtiaz Tower, is an international road junction and a choice halting-place for tourists.

In this elbow of the Valais Rhône, where the Drance joins it, the flow of traffic from the Simplon and the Great St. Bernard routes, and that from the Forclaz Pass all converge.

Martigny boasts a number of stone ruins dating back to Roman times. Forum Claudii Augusti was a small town situated in the Forclaz Pass, linking Italy directly to France. Originally founded between 41 and 47 AD, under the reign of the Emperor Claudius, it was subsequently renamed Forum Claudii Vallensium.

SIGHTS

Cross the Drance to reach Rue de la Bâtiaz.

La Bâtiaz Tower – *20 minutes on foot Rtn by the Chemin du Château.* Set in a strategic site, high on a rocky promontory, the circular keep and its defensive wall are all that remain of a 13C fortress. From the tower there is a lovely **view★** of the Martigny Basin and the vineyards around.

Just before the bridge, turn right along the west bank of the river.

Our Lady of Compassion Chapel – This 17C sanctuary contains an elegant baroque gilt altarpiece and an unusual collection of ex-votos in the form of small paintings.

Cross the 19C wooden covered bridge (pont couvert) *and go down Avenue Marc-Morand.*

At no 7 the 16C **Grand'Maison**, recognizable by its elegant spire-like shingled roof, was a hostel where a number of notable 18 and 19C Europeans stayed.

On the right, at the beginning of Avenue du Grand-St-Bernard, is a powerful bronze bust by Courbet of a woman symbolising Liberty.

Return to Place Centrale and enter the 19C town hall (**H**) to see the brilliant **stained-glass window★** (55m² – 592sq ft) which illustrates the Rhône contemplating the Drance. There are also other stained-glass windows worth nothing which depict the Four Seasons, the Zodiac..., all the work of Edmond Bille, the painter from the Valais.

Continue as far as the parish church (Our Lady of the Fields) behind the town hall on place du Midi.

Our Lady in the Fields (Notre-Dame-des-Champs) – Rebuilt in the 17C in the Tuscan style and flanked in the 18C by a Neo-Gothic bell tower (50m 164ft high), this church is elegant with its monumental doorway with finely carved panels. There are handsome **furnishings**, carved by local artisans of the 17 (baptismal font, pulpit) and 18C (reredos of the high altar, statues or the Apostles, chancel stalls) as well as a large Crucifix (1495).

Go as far as the Rue des Alpes to see the **Supersaxo House** (restored) an interesting example of a 15C building. Take Rue de la Délèze, Rue Octodure, and Rue du Forum. The latter passes in front of the Forum Claudii Vallensium, a Gallo-Roman site *(entrance Rue d'Oche).*

Continue along Rue du Forum as far as the modern building which houses the museum.

★★ **Pierre Gianadda Foundation** ⊙ – Léonard Gianadda opened this cultural centre to honour the memory of his brother, who died in 1976 after sustaining serious injuries in a plane crash. In addition to its permanent collections, the foundation also hosts temporary exhibitions of a very high standard, exhibiting works by such renowned artists as Goya, Renoir, Picasso, Klee, Braque, Botero, Degas and Modigliani.

The **Gallo-Roman Museum**, arranged in galleries overlooking the Roman ruins, displays statuettes, coins, jewellery, domestic utensils and fragments of sculpted stones dating back to the 1-4C. Especially worth noting are the bronzes of Octodurum, small fragments of statues including the tricorne head of a bull, and a leg and arm belonging to a titanic god or legendary hero.

The **Automobile Museum** presents a splendid collection of early vehicles, still in perfect working order, dating from 1897-1939, some of which are unique models. The oldest is a 1897 Benz with a maximum speed of 25km/h – 25 mph... All the great

Martini 1903

names of the car industry are present: Rolls-Royce (1923 model in polished aluminium which travelled to Mandelieu, on the French Riviera, in 1988), Bugatti, De Dion-Bouton, Delaunay-Belleville (1914-1917 torpedo commissioned by the Czar Nicholas II for his hunting parties; delivery was cancelled on account of the Russian Revolution). The museum also displays cars made in Switzerland: Pic-Pic (1906 double-phaeton), Sigma (1910-1911), Martini (1912 torpedo), and Fischer (1913 six-seater torpedo).

The **Garden**, dotted with archaeological ruins, may be seen as an open-air museum of sculpture. The permanent collections feature works by Henry Moore, Joan Miró, Alicia Penalba, Jean Arp, Brancusi, Dubuffet, Segal and Rodin.

Turn left into Chemin de Surfrête, then left again into Route du Levant.

Roman Amphitheatre – It has taken many years of excavation and restoration work to reinstate this arena, one of the smallest of the Roman empire, able to seat an audience of 6000. The podium wall which ran along the sides of the amphitheatre (47m – 155ft x 35m – 115ft; Nîmes: 133m – 436ft x 101 – 330ft, seating capacity 24 000) was flanked by an outer rampart reaching a height of 1 to 2m – 3 to 7ft. The podium itself was surmonted by a parapet so as to protect the spectators from the wild beasts. Six ramps led to the cavea, where numbers of the public sat on wooden steps. A number of carceres opened into the arena: these small cells were used for storing equipment and locking up the animals. The *pulvinar*, or official tribune, is located above one of these cells. It is approached by a long vaulted corridor.

Turn around; Route du Levant leads back to Place du Bourg.

Place and Rue du Bourg – Pleasant small square with its turretted house (1609 – heavily restored) and picturesque street. On the left note the old town hall (Maison de Commune du Quartier du Bourg – 1645) with arcades supported by seven marble columns.

EXCURSION

From Martigny to Salvan – *7km – 4 miles – about 1/2 hour. Leave Martigny to the northwest.* This region surrounding the **Trient Valley** is perfect for long mountain walks because of its impressive setting and lush vegetation. Its slopes are particularly suitable for cross-country skiing and alpine skiing during the winter season. *After the covered bridge or the new bridge over the Drance, turn left into the Salvan by-road, which climbs, sometimes through the rock, above the Rhône Valley.*

★★**Gueuroz Bridge** – Leave the car at the exit from the bridge. This reinforced concrete bridge with its slender framework was thrown over the Trient Gorges, at a height of over 180m – 600ft in 1934. When crossing the bridge on foot you will enjoy a bird's-eye view of the gorge, very rocky downstream – this part of the floor has been arranged for visitors – and wider and wooded upstream.

From the road, which becomes very winding, there are glimpses of the bridge.

Salvan – Pop 932. Facilities. This pretty mountain resort is built around a small square.

Salvan is the starting-point for two excursions: Van Valley and Les Marécottes.

Van Valley (Vallon de Van) – The narrow road overhanging the Rhône Valley at a height of 800m – 2 600ft provides an exciting route to Van d'en Haut, where the road comes to an end in a wild, hostile setting.

The drive back to Salvan offers some impressive views of the Van Valley and Martigny.

Return to Salvan, then follow the Trient Valley until you come to Les Marécottes.

Les Marécottes – Pop 350. A pretty mountain village with wooden chalets. A cable-car takes you up to **La Creusaz** (alt 1 777m – 5 800ft), where you can enjoy a sweeping perspective of Mont Blanc and the Valais Alps.

On your way down, stop in at the **Marécottes Zoo** ⊙, located on the right, not far from the village. A wide variety of alpine species can be visited, set in their natural environment and separated by enclosures: chamois, beavers, reindeer, ibexes, Valais goats, moufflons, etc.

★ **MEIRINGEN** Berne   Pop 4 346

Michelin map **217** folds 8 and 9 or **427** fold 14 – Local map see BERNESE OBERLAND – Alt 595m – 1 952ft – Facilities

Meiringen is the chief town in the Hasli Valley (the Upper Aare Valley – above Lake Brienz). Since the coming of the motor-car it has become an important tourist centre. It is now not only the starting-point for well-known excursions to the Aare Gorges and the Reichenbach Falls but also a convenient halt on the Grimsel and Susten roads.

On the square named after the Scottish novelist **Arthur Conan Doyle** (1859-1930), the father of Sherlock Holmes, stands a bronze statue of the celebrated fictitious detective, executed by the English sculptor John Doubleday. Conan Doyle, who loved Switzerland, was made an honorary citizen of Meiringen.

The **Sherlock Holmes Museum** ⊙ is a reconstitution of the famous London drawing-room at no 221B Baker Street. It contains memorabilia belonging to the sleuth and his faithful assistant, Doctor Watson. In 1891 Holmes fell to his death in the Reichenbach Falls *(qv)* in a struggle with Professor Moriarty. But fortunately for his readers, who refused to accept the demise of their hero, Conan Doyle resuscitated his character a few years later.

Church – It stands in the upper part of the village, where a few wooden houses recall old Meiringen, ravaged by fire in 1879 and 1891. The present church (1684) is the fifth built on this spot, succeeding others ruined and swept away by the disastrous flooding of the Alpbach, a torrent which forms a waterfall behind the building. For this reason, its imposing detached Romanesque tower has foundations over 7m – 23ft deep. During restoration work the remains of the original 11C structure, now the crypt, and a series of Romanesque frescoes in the upper church, representing scenes from the Old Testament, were discovered.

EXCURSIONS

★★**Aare Gorges (Aareschlucht)** ⊘ – 2km – 1 mile – plus ¡/2 hour sightseeing. The road leaving to the gorges' car park branches off from the Grimsel road (no 6) on leaving Meiringen for Innertkirchen, 200m upstream from the bridge over the Aare. The gorges cut by the Aare through the Kirchet "bolt" between Meiringen and Innertkirchen are one of the most popular curiosities in the Bernese Oberland.
The viewing galleries lead into the narrowest part of the gorges, the walls of which, sometimes sheer, sometimes curiously polished and hollowed by erosion (traces of "pot-holes" and glaciated rocks), are very impressive. Stranger still, however, is the dim light in the depths of the cleft where the jade-green stream of the Aare flows.

> After about 1.5km – 1 mile within view of a tributary waterfall you arrive at the far end of the gorge (the last hairpin bend before Innertkirchen).

★★**Rosenlaui Valley** – 12km – 8 miles – about 1 hour – by a very narrow mountain road (passing impossible between halts). The road is stony, sometimes walled-in and very steep on leaving Willigen. Cars for six or more persons are not allowed through.

> Leave Meiringen by the Grimsel road.

At Willigen, turn right on the road to Rosenlaui, which after a series of sharp hairpin bends enters the lonely Reichenbach Valley, dominated on the left by the extraordinary rock formations of the Engelhörner. Soon you will see ahead, from left to right, the Rosenlaui Glacier, the Wellhorn and the Wetterhorn. A bridge over the canalized bed of the Reichenbach leads you to the fields of Gschwandtenmad, from where there is a striking view★★★: the rocky shoulder of the Welhorn rises beyond a foreground of fir woods to the right of the Rosenlaui Glacier. This flanks the icy cone of the Wetterhorn, which stands above the Grosse Scheidegg Depression, a broad shelf over which you can walk from Rosenlaui to Grindelwald.
Rosenlaui – This mountaineering resort has given its name to a climbing school which has trained several candidates for the conquest of the Himalayas.
Here tourists may visit the **glacier gorges★** (Gletscherschlucht) ⊘ hollowed out by the waters from the melting ice of the Rosenlaui Glacier (3/4 hour of rather difficult walking). The scenery now becomes quite rocky. On arriving at Schwarzwaldalp, at the end of the motor road, you will find a slope wholly planted with maples.

★**Reichenbach Falls (Reichenbachfälle)** ⊘ – 1km – 1/2 mile – plus about 1/2 hour Rtn, including 10 minutes by funicular.

> Leave Meiringen by the road to Grimsel. After the bridge over the Aare, at a crossroads, turn to the right and leave your car at the lower station of the Reichenbach funicular.

Crossing the lower falls on a viaduct, the funicular ends at a terrace from where you can admire the great Reichenbach Waterfall, the site of the fictional disappearance of Sherlock Holmes and Moriarty.

★ MISOX CASTLE Graubünden (Grisons)

Michelin map ▦ fold 13 or ▦ fold 16 (ruin south of Mesocco) – Local map see GRISONS

The feudal ruins of Misox Castle, the most impressive and evocative in the Grisons, command the Mesolcina Valley and the San Bernardino Defile, from a high rock peak. This massive fortified group, where the heavy shape is broken by the vertical lines of a graceful campanile, once belonged to the Counts of Sax-Mesocco. The castle was sold in 1483 to the Trivulce of Milan and was dismantled by the Grisons "Leagues" in 1526 (read commentary on the Grisons coat of arms, p 26). It was saved from complete destruction by the intervention of Swiss students in 1924-25.

TOUR about 1/2 hour

Santa Maria del Castello Chapel ⊘ – This church with a much pierced Romanesque campanile standing at the foot of the castle, contains an interesting series of 15C **frescoes★**. St George slaying the dragon is depicted with the features of a very young knight. St Bernardino of Siena, patron saint of the valley – the San Bernardino Pass was called after him – is the thin-faced monk holding in his hand the monogram of Christ which is surrounded by rays of light. The symbolism for the months of the year, spaced out on the lower panel, mingles scenes of courtly love with those of rural life as known on the Italian slopes of the Alps.

Castle – Access by the grass track climbing from behind the chapel to the entrance drawbridge. The most remarkable feature of this fortress is the Romanesque campanile of its chapel, with five storeys of arches. To enjoy a superb bird's-eye **view★** of the Mesolcina Valley and the village of Soazza turn to the left as soon as you find a gap between the ruined buildings and make for an uncrowned wall on the edge of the escarpment, the top of which can be reached by a staircase without a balustrade.

Michelin map **217** fold 14 or **427** fold 12 – Local maps see Lake GENEVA and VAUD ALPS – Alt 398 m – 1 305ft – Facilities – Plan of the conurbation in the current Michelin Red Guide Switzerland

Thanks to its beautiful **site**★★ and pleasant surroundings – which have won literary fame since Rousseau chose the village of Clarens, now a suburb, as the setting for *La Nouvelle Héloïse* – Montreux, extensively modernised, is the most frequented resort on Lake Geneva and has acquired an international reputation. The town stretches along the shores of a large bay facing south and rises in tiers to heights covered with woods and vineyards which shelter it from the north and east winds. Its sumptuous palaces, all fronted by yellow blinds, and Edwardian hotels are reminiscent of the French Riviera. Montreux is also an important cultural city: it hosts a great many festivals and major world events such as the International Choral Festival (week after Easter), the Golden Rose Television Festival (spring), a jazz festival (July) and the September Musical Concert *(see the Calendar of Events)*.

A number of local trains, leaving from Montreux station, will take you to the nearby summits, offering panoramic views of Geneva, the Mont Blanc, the Matterhorn, etc.

Steamboat cruises are available for those wishing to tour the Upper Lake.

Montreux

★★**General View** – It is pleasant to go up through old Montreux to the terrace of the church and see the district of Clarens-Montreux-Territet, the lake with Chillon Castle on its rocky islet, the mountains of the Savoy Chablais and the sparkling Dents du Midi.

Vaud Riviera – The mildness of its climate (average annual temperature 10 °C – 50 °F) makes Montreux a climatic resort all the year round and earns the name of Vaud Riviera for its lake shore. This exceptional climate, the mildest on the north side of the Alps, produces varied and luxuriant vegetation: vines grow at an altitude of nearly 600m – 2 000ft, walnut trees up to 700m – 2 300ft and fruit trees up to 1 000m – 3 250ft.

On the shores of the lake you will find fig, bay, almond and mulberry trees and even cypresses, magnolias and palm trees flourishing in a truly Mediterranean temperature. In the spring the fields overlooking the town are covered with narcissi, which lend a special charm to the hillsides.

History Museum of Old Montreux (Musée du Vieux Montreux) ⊘ – *40 Rue de la Gare*. A former 14C citadel, heavily restored during the 18C, houses the collections of this small local history museum or historical museum of the Swiss Riviera. An exhibition of photographs explains how the city gradually developed over the centuries. The day-to-day life of the Montreux population is illustrated by the reconstitution of interiors (kitchen, bedroom) and crafts (carpenter's workshop). Farming, the mainstay of the local economy, is presented to visitors through an exhibition on viticulture and the reconstruction of a mountain chalet. The last room is devoted to arms, pewterware, weights and measures.

EXCURSIONS

★★★**Naye Rocks** (Rochers de Naye) ⊘ – 2 042m – 6 699ft. *About 3 hours Rtn, including 2 hours by rack-railway.*
During this trip you will enjoy seeing the hill sites of **Glion** (alt 689m – 2 260ft), a pleasant country holiday resort at medium altitude, and of **Caux** (alt 1 050m – 3 448ft), another balcony-resort with a tourist reputation of long standing.
From the summit you will enjoy a bird's-eye view of Lake Geneva and a splendid panorama of the Bernese, Valais and Savoy Alps and the Jura.

★★**Chillon Castle** – *3km – 2 miles to the south. It can also be reached of foot, by following the shores of the lake. See Chillon Castle.*

★★**Avants-Sonloup Tour** – *25km – 14 miles – about 1 hour. Follow the route marked with arrows on the plan above.*

    Leave Montreux by the route marked Les Avants-Fribourg.

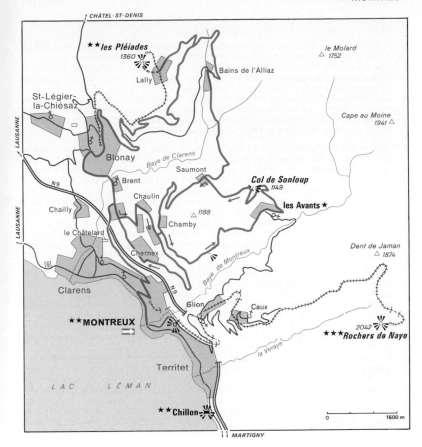

On the left the road overlooks the town and the lake, while the Castle of Le Châtelard, with its big rectangular 15C battlemented tower, stands out on the crest of a vine-clad slope.

Climbing steeply, the road affords fine views of the lake and the Alps.

4km – 2 miles from Montreux turn right towards Chernex-Les-Avants. Turn left 200m farther on before Chamby (two bends) and cross the railway line, then turn right for Les Avants.

★ **Les Avants** – Alt 968m – 3 175ft. Facilities. This small resort overlooked on the southeast by the Dent de Jaman and the Naye Rocks is beautifully sited.

Sonloup Pass (Col de Sonloup) – Alt 1 149m – 3 770ft. A fine **view**★ of the Naye Rocks, the Dents du Midi and the Savoy Alps.

The return to Montreux is made by way of the Saumont-Chamby-Chernex road.

Narrow at first this road reveals new glimpses of the lake and of the Vevey-Blonay Region.

★★ **Les Pléiades** – *36km – 22 miles – plus 1/2 hour on foot Rtn.*

To get to Saumont follow the directions explained above. Turn right at Saumont towards Bains de l'Alliaz and then take the road which climbs steadily among fields and fir woods to the hamlet of Lally, where you will leave the car. You can also reach Lally by rack-railway from Blonay.

★★ **Panorama** – *From Lally 1/2 hour on foot Rtn.* From the Les Pléiades Summit (alt 1 360m – 4 462ft) you will see a fine panorama of Lake Geneva, the Molard, the Dent de Jaman, the Naye Rocks, the Savoy Alps and the Mont Blanc Range.

Return by the Blonay road which gives frequent glimpses of the lake and reveals, to the right, **Blonay Castle**, dating back to the 11C.

Shortly after Brent, turn right to return to Montreux.

★ MORGES Vaud

Michelin map **217** northwest of fold 13 or **427** fold 11 − Local map see Lake GENEVA − Alt 378m − 1 240ft − Facilities

The little town of Morges is an important wine-growing centre on the Vaud hillside. It has a pleasant site on the shore of Lake Geneva, facing the Savoy Alps.
The port, built from 1691-96 is now used as a **pleasure boat harbour**. Before the expansion of the railway network, it enjoyed great commercial activity sustained by trade between the Vaud District and Geneva.
From the quay, near which stands the castle − a former residence of the Bernese bailiffs − there is an excellent **view★** of the lake at its widest point and beyond it of the Alps, from Mount Salève to the Fribourg Alps, including the Savoy Alps among which the Dent d'Oche and Mont Blanc are prominent.

★★**Alexis Forel Museum** ⊙ − *54 Grand'Rue*. Founded by Alexis Forel, the engraver, and his wife, the museum is housed in part of the Blanchenay mansion. This handsome residence of the 15, 17 and 18C was built into two blocks joined at each storey by a Tuscan gallery; note inside the panelled ceilings (15 and 16C), the 17C carved Burgundian doors and the two monumental chimneys.
Each exhibition room pays tribute to a particular period in history, thanks to its lavish decoration: 15-19C French and Swiss furniture, most of which Forel collected himself; mementoes (17 and 18C salons), porcelain from Nyon and the East India Company; 16-19C glasswork, 18 and 19C silverware. An exhibition of dolls occupies two floors, displaying numerous 18-20C dolls together with their accessories.

Castle − Built on a strategic location west of the town, this massive 13C fortress, flanked by four circular corner towers defining four bulwarks arranged around a central courtyard, houses the collections belonging to three museums.
The **Swiss Figurine Museum** (ground floor) presents a series of dioramas involving lead or tin soldiers which illustrate the major historical events from Antiquity to the 19C (Babylonia, the Aztec rebellion against the Spanish settlers, the Field of the Cloth of Gold, Berezina Crossing...). Each figurine has been painstakingly reconstructed with minute attention to detail.
The **Vaud Military Museum** ⊙ (ground floor and first floor) presents an exhaustive review of the different weapons, uniforms and types of headdress associated with the Swiss Army from Napoleonic times up to the present day (this includes the celebrated pontifical guard). A succession of rooms re-create various periods of history, for instance, the Tower of Justice or the Tower of Torture, the Davel Room, devoted to Major Jean-Daniel Abraham Davel, a Vaud patriot executed in 1723 for having fought against the Bernese authorities, or the room paying tribute to General Guisan, Commander-in-Chief of the Swiss Army between 1939 and 1945 (military record, personal belongings).
The **Artillery Museum**, set up in a series of fine cellars enhanced by barrel vaulting, displays around forty real exhibits along with miniature models which explain the development of this particular weapon: early artillery pieces from the 16C, mountain artillery carried by beasts of burden, 75 mm field canon and carriage; an unusual boule-shaped 12mm mortar able to revolve around its axis, adjustable on slopes, with a range of 3km − 2 miles.

Protection of Alpine flora

In Switzerland the picking of the following Alpine flowers (Cyclamen, Alpine Aster, Primrose and Edelweiss) which are particularly threatened is strictly controlled.

★ MORGINS VALLEY

Michelin map **217** fold 14 or **427** fold 12

The Morgins Pass is the only international route in the pre-Alpine Chablais Massif joining the pastoral Valleys of Dranse d'Abondance and Morgins, with their many large chalets. On the Valais side it is a modern road offering views of the Dents du Midi.

FROM MONTHEY TO CHÂTEL

34km − 21 miles − about 2 hours − Itinerary **8** *of the Valais local map*

Swiss customs control near the pass, French customs at Vonne.

On leaving Monthey the road climbs quickly in hairpin bends above the Rhône Valley, overlooked (going upstream) by the summits of Les Diablerets, the Grand Muveran and the Dent de Morcles. Ahead, in line with the Illiez Valley, are the snowy Dents Blanches and the Dents du Midi. Fields planted with walnut trees succeed vineyards.

★**Champéry** − Facilities. Champéry lies on the mountainside at the beginning of the **Illiez Valley★★**, in the shadow of the Dents du Midi Range. The resort clusters around its single narrow street and has a family atmosphere in spite of its international situation. It is a favourite place for rock-climbers.
A local feature is the church **belfry** roofed with a curious pierced stone crown. In winter the Panachaux Basin, served by several ski lifts, offers fine, sunny slopes to skiers.

★★ **Culet Cross (Croix de Culet)** ⊘ – *From Champéry, about 3/4 hour, including 1/4 hour by cable-car and 1 hour on foot.*
From the upper station of the Planachaux cable-car, climb on foot, along the crest, to the cross (alt 1 963m – 6 539ft). There is an open view of the various peaks of the Dents du Midi, Mount Ruan, the Dents Blanches and the Vaud Alps.
The road continues to make hairpin bends, offering a widening **view**★ of the Rhône Valley, to the south of the Illiez Valley, the Dents du Midi cliffs and, to the right of these, Mount Ruan.
The road then becomes a *corniche* above the wooded ravine of the Vièze; it then reaches the floor of the softly-shaped Alpine coomb of the Morgins Valley.
Here the chalets nestle under wide-eaved roofs covered with shingles. In a vertical line from the gable, their two-storey balconies have a double overhang, forming a gallery.

Morgins – Facilities. This peaceful mountain resort is restful both in summer and in winter.

★ **Morgins Pass** – Alt 1 369m – 4 491ft. The road, falling slightly, slips into this forest dell containing a small lake in which the fir trees are reflected. Southeastwards, in the middle distance, the Dents du Midi summits can be seen.
The steeper descent into the Drance d'Abondance Valley reveals the majestic **site**★ of Châtel *(description in Michelin Green Guide Alpes du Nord – in French only)*. Ahead, the horizon is now barred by the slopes of Mount Chauffé (left) and Cornettes de Bise (right).

MOUDON Vaud   Pop 4 336

Michelin map **217** fold 4 or **427** fold 12 – Alt 522m – 1 713ft

Moudon was for a long time the capital of the Savoy Vaud District. It is situated in the Broye Valley, in the centre of a rich agricultural area. Moudon was an important halt on the road between Rome and Vindonissa (Windisch, near Brugg) in Gallo-Roman times. It enjoyed a period of great prosperity in the 14C under the Counts of Savoy – most of the buildings which give the present town its medieval air date from that time. From the bridge over which the N1 secondary road crosses the Broye there is, in the foreground, a pleasing view of the Church of St Stephen and, behind it, of the old quarter with its 15-17C houses. These with great roofs overhanging in front, stand huddled at the foot of the hill crowned by the old Rochefort and Carrouge Castles and the ancient Broye Tower.

SIGHTS

St Stephen's (Église St-Etienne) – This was built in the second half of the 13 and the beginning of the 14C. It is flanked by an imposing fortified belfry, once part of the town walls. The Gothic nave, roofed with vaulting, bearing coats of arms, has lovely stained-glass windows and an organ (1764). The chancel contains fine stalls dating from the early 16C; early 17C stalls can be seen on the left as you enter the church. Original 16C frescoes, which have undergone extensive restoration, are noteworthy.

Rue du Château – *Start at Place de la Grenette.* This is the main street of the old quarter. At the beginning of the street is an amusing fountain depicting Justice (polychrome statue sheltering under its robe four dwarf-sized magistrates); as you walk up the street you will find standing, on the right, the 12C Broye Tower (in ruins); and on either side of the street are several 15, 16 and 17C houses; mid-way to the left the view overlooks the river spanned by a covered bridge; at the end of the street are the museums (on the right) and a second fountain (1557) called Moses.

Old Moudon Museum ⊘ – The Castle of Rochefort contains the Old Moudon Museum, which includes collections of ancient arms and uniforms, wrought-iron signs and Roman statuettes and pottery. A trade section housed in two galleries, recalls the former economic activities of the district.

Eugène Burnand Museum ⊘ – The Bâtiment du Grand'Air houses works by the native-born artist E. Burnand (1830-1921), a painter of peasant life and illustrator to the Provençal poet Frédéric Mistral (1830-1914).

MICHELIN GUIDES

The Red Guides (hotels and restaurants)
Benelux - Deutschland - Espana Portugal - Main Cities Europe - France - Great Britain and Ireland - Italia - Switzerland

The Green Guides (fine art, historical monuments, scenic routes)
Austria - Belgium - California - Canada - England: the West Country - France - Germany - Great Britain - Greece - Ireland - Italy - London - Mexico - Netherlands - New England - New York - Paris - Portugal - Quebec - Rome - Scotland - Spain - Switzerland - Washington
... and the collection of regional guides for France.

★★ MUOTTAS MURAGL Graubünden (Grisons)

Michelin map **218** fold 15 or **427** fold 17 – north of Pontresina – Local map see GRISONS

The grassy ridges of Muottas Muragl, easily reached by funicular from the Samedan Basin, form the classic belvedere of the Upper Engadine.

★★ Climb to Muottas Muragl ⊙ – *From the lower station at Punt Muragl, about 1 hour Rtn, including 1/2 hour by funicular.*
From the upper station (hotel), at an altitude of 2 453m – 8 048ft there is a **view★★** of the Upper Engadine Gap, framed by the small Piz Rosatsch and Piz Julier Ranges, with its chain of lakes between St. Moritz and the Maloja. Farther to the left are the Roseg corrie and the shining peaks of the Bernina Massif: Piz Morteratsch, Piz Bernina and Piz Palü.
Many tourists will enjoy walking on this high ground, famous for its flora and fauna, along broad, gently-sloping paths superbly sited on the mountainside. Such is the Hochweg which leads down, in three and a half hours, to Pontresina.

★★ MÜRREN Berne

Michelin map **217** northeast of fold 17 or **427** fold 14 – Local map see INTERLAKEN: Excursions – Alt 1 638m – 5 374ft – Facilities

Perched on a shelf of Alpine pasture forming a balcony over the steep cleft of the Lauterbrunnen Valley, Mürren faces the Jungfrau Massif. The view extends from the Eiger on the left to the Breithorn on the right and the Gspaltenhorn group on the extreme right.
The **site★★** of this village, completely cut off from motorized civilization, and the sporting character of its ski slopes, which bristle with every imaginable obstacle, account for the popularity of the resort with the British, who have created a resort very British in atmosphere.
It is at Mürren that the Kandahar Ski Club was formed in 1924 and started the famous Arlberg-Kandahar competition, which is now regarded as the unofficial world championship of the Alpine countries.

Approach ⊙ – Motorists are advised to drive to Stechelberg, at the end of the Lauterbrunnen Valley road. There, take the Schilthorn cable-car to Mürren.
You can also drive to Lauterbrunnen, then leave the car in the car park before taking the funicular to Grütschalp. From there a train will take you to Mürren.

EXCURSION

★★★ Schilthorn ⊙ – Alt 2 970m – 9 744ft. *About 1 1/4 hours including 35 minutes by cable-car.*
From the top, in a desolate landscape of torrents and scree a **panoramic view★★★** of the Jungfrau Massif with only the Lauterbrunnen cleft between that and the observer. Part of Thun Lake is visible.

★★ MURTEN (MORAT) Fribourg   4 601

Michelin map **217** fold 5 or **427** fold 12 – Alt 458m – 1 503ft – Facilities

Overlooking the east shore of the lake that bears its name, Murten has a yachting marina which attracts visitors. It is famous in history for the defeat there of Charles the Bold by the Swiss. This former fortified city, which has kept most of its ramparts and towers, has a picturesque charm.

Battle of Murten – Anxious to erase the check he had suffered at the hands of the Swiss Confederates at Grandson *(qv)* on 2 March 1476, the Duke of Burgundy, **Charles the Bold,** hastily gathered a new army. Leaving Lausanne on 27 May, he marched on the Broye Valley and on 9 June arrived before Murten, to which he laid siege. The arrival of the Confederate Army on 22 June reversed the situation. Hemmed in by the lake, the troops of Charles the Bold were massacred. Many drowned in the lake; the Duke himself was able to flee. Nearly 8 000 Burgundians perished. A rich booty of fabrics, furs and arms fell into the hands of the victors.

Lake Murten (Murtensee) – This tranquil rectangular-shaped body of water is parallel to the northern part of Lake Neuchâtel and is linked to it by the Broye Canal.
Lake Murten, abounding in fish, with a migratory bird sanctuary on its north shore, and a beach (facilities) on its south shore, is bordered on its eastern side by the town of Murten.

SIGHTS

★ **Main Street (Hauptgasse)** – This runs through the heart of the Old Town and displays a fine degree of unity with arcaded houses, overhanging roofs covered with brown tiles, fountains and a gate, the Berntor (**B**), surmounted by a graceful pinnacle.

Take the street which begins on the right just before the Berntor and go around the German Protestant church, behind which a stairway leads to the walls.

★ **Town Walls (Stadtmauer)** – Take the wall-walk to the right. It affords pretty views over the clustering roofs of the old town, the castle and the lake, while Mount Vully and the Jura foothills rise on the horizon.

Take the first downward stairway you come to.

This ends at a door in the ramparts giving access to a small square from which there is a good view of the outside of the walls.

Come back through the door and turn left towards the castle.

You will cross the end of the main street in front of the Rübenloch (**D**), a fine old house.

Castle (Schloss) – Built in the 13C by Duke Peter of Savoy, this is a grim, impressive structure. From the inner court there is a fine view of Lake Murten and the Jura.

Historical Museum (M) ⊙ – The museum is located in the town's former watermill, restored as it looked in the 18C. On five levels (start on the top floor) are exhibited: prehistoric and Gallo-Roman relics (pottery, arms, jewellery); exhibits evoking local history from the Middle Ages to the 18C (coins, pewter, glassware, stained-glass windows, utensils), Burgundian treasures (swords, armour, cannon...) and slides and a diorama on the Battle of Murten. *The lift takes you back to the top floor and the exit.*

★ **MÜSTAIR** Graubünden (Grisons)   Pop 752

Michelin map 218 fold 17 or 427 fold 18 – Local map see GRISONS

Chief town of the Müstair Valley, Müstair is the only part of Swiss territory in the Adige Basin. The church which, according to tradition, was founded by Charlemagne, stands at the end of the village on the Italian side still enclosed in the boundaries of the Abbey of St John the Baptist (a Benedictine monastery). It is one of the most ancient buildings in Switzerland.

★ **Church** – Its triple apse has oven vaulting. The nave, which was originally in the style of basilica, was transformed in the 15C into an ogive-vaulted Gothic structure with two aisles. The **frescoes**★★ on the walls offer the art-lover the most imposing cycle of wall paintings in the Confederation: some of the series have been transferred to the National Museum in Zürich. This painted decoration goes back to Carolingian times (first half of the 9C), and is partially covered by Romanesque frescoes (1150-70) which are in good condition.

Among the other works of art are a 12C statue of Charlemagne and an 11C low relief of the Baptism of Christ.

NÄFELS Glarus   Pop 3882

Michelin map 216 fold 20 or 427 fold 16 – Alt 437m – 1 434ft

Näfels lies in the alluvial plain between Lakes Zürich and Walen, the site of an important battle in Swiss history.

★ **Freuler Palace (Freulerpalast)** ⊙ – This building's architecture and the memories it enshrines take us back to the times when the most natural calling for the sons of certain important Swiss families was to serve in the armies of foreign rulers. Erected between 1642-47, its ornamentation places it in the late Renaissance period (the gate, great staircase and woodwork).

On the ground floor note the hall paved with marble, its arches decorated with stucco, in the Italian manner. On the first floor do not miss the **state rooms**★★ where masterpieces of inlaying are lavished from floor to coffered ceiling. The upper floors contain the collections of the original museum of the Glarus District. Many visitors will be impressed by the section devoted to the development of fabric-printing.

A SELECTION OF PICTURESQUE VILLAGES

Village	Canton	Village	Canton
Gandria	Ticino	Morcote	Ticino
Giornico	Ticino	St-Ursanne	Jura
Gruyères	Fribourg	Soglio	Grisons
Guarda	Grisons	Stain am Rhein	Schaffhausen
Kippel	Valais	Zuoz	Grisons

★★ NEUCHÂTEL Ⓒ

Michelin map 216 fold 13 or 427 fold 12 – Local map see Swiss JURA – Alt 440m –
1 444ft – Facilities

Neuchâtel enjoys a charming site between its lake, with 4km – 3 miles of quays,
and Chaumont Hill. The pleasant, smiling town stands in the midst of vineyards; its
pale ochre houses made Alexandre Dumas say it was carved out of a block of
butter. The silhouettes of the collegiate chuch and the castle dominate the scene.

Lake Neuchâtel – This is the largest wholly Swiss lake, being nearly 38km –
24 miles long and 8km – 5 miles wide. It is teeming with fish. Canals used by
pleasure boats join it with Lakes Biel and Murten. Its many-coloured waters, its
hilly, vine-clad shores, are favourite subjects for painters and writers (André Gide).

HISTORICAL NOTES

The name of Neuchâtel is derived from a structure built as a stronghold in the
second period of Burgundian rule (1011). The town then became, by inheritance,
the property of the French Orléans-Longueville family.

It is said that in order to celebrate his entry into the town during the visit he made
in 1657, Henri II of Orléans had 6 000 litres – 1 300 gallons of the local red wine
poured into the Griffin Fountain, which can still be seen in the Rue du Château.

Again by inheritance, Neuchâtel became the personal property of the King of
Prussia after 1707. Its intellectual and cultural life was highly developed and the
ideas of the Encyclopaedists flourished there.

Struggle for independence – After being placed from 1806-14 under the rule of
Marshal Berthier (the Chief of Staff of Napoleon I) as a principality, Neuchâtel
joined the Swiss Confederation in 1815 and was then in a peculiar political position.
It became a Swiss canton while remaining bound to the King of Prussia. A Liberal
party was then formed and tried to take power in 1831 but failed. The attempt was
repeated in 1848, and this time the Republic was proclaimed. In 1857 the King of
Prussia at last recognized the canton's independence but kept the courtesy title of
Prince of Neuchâtel. Today Neuchâtel is an important watch and clock research
centre, the observatory of which gives the official time to all Switzerland. It is also
a wine market, and a great wine harvest procession takes place there in September
(see the Calendar of Events). As the seat of a university it keeps up its reputation
as a centre of French learning. The French spoken at Neuchâtel is considered by
many to be the purest heard in Switzerland.

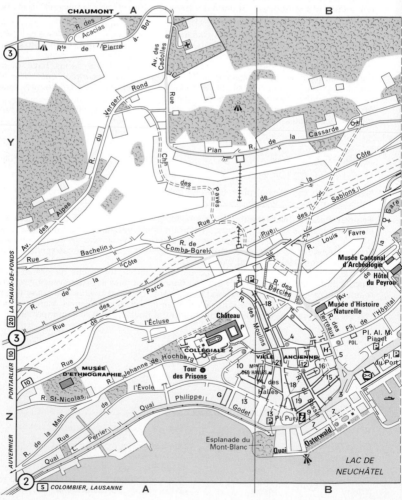

SIGHTS

★ **Old Town** (Ville Ancienne) (ABZ) – A picturesque quarter (Rue du Château, Rue du Trésor, Rue du Pommier, Rue des Moulins) with old houses, 16 and 17C fountains and defensive towers, extends between the Town Hall (1788), a classical building by the architect and painter Paris (1747-1819) from Besançon, and the group formed by the collegiate church and the castle.

On the oblong Place des Halles (Market Square) are 17C houses, and, at the far end, a Renaissance house called les Halles (Maison des Halles), flanked by turrets and bearing the shield with the fleur-de-lis of the Orléans-Longueville family.

★ **Collegiate Church and Castle** ⊘ – These two curious buildings form a single monumental ensemble.

The **Collegiate Church**, a fine 12 and 13C construction with multi-coloured glazed tiles, was converted in 1530, because of the Reformation, and heavily restored during the 19C. The east end is Romanesque, as is demonstratred by the three apses and their overhead arcatures ornamented with human and animal heads. Skirting the east end to the right, you reach the 15C cloisters, of which there remains a row of Romanesque arcades propped up against the wall.

Facing the main entrance of the church stands a statue of the reformer Guillaume Farel (1489-1565), whose sermons led the population of Neuchâtel to adopt the reformed cult. The nave, with its ribbed vaulting, is typical of the Gothic style. At the transept crossing is a lantern-tower. Under an arcade in the chancel (historiated Romanesque capitals), the cenotaph of the Counts of Neuchâtel (14C) is a striking example of medieval sculpture: this superb stone composition comprises fourteen stiff and impressive polychrome statues depicting knights and noblewomen at prayer.

The south portal, Romanesque, decorated with archivolts and carved capitals, is flanked by the statues of St Peter and St Paul.

The **Castle** (15 and 16C, restored), formerly the residence of the Neuchâtel lords, is today the seat of the cantonal government; it still retains some vestiges of the 12C, like the Romanesque gallery pierced by seven blind bays int the southwest façade. The main entrance gate, evidently defensive, is sided by two towers crowned with machicolations and embellished with broken arches. Under the passageway, the arms of Philippe de Hochberg, Lord of Neuchâtel, can be seen at the point of intersection of the ribs. In the northern wing, the first one to be built, you may visit the former kitchen area (fireplace with a wooden hood), the antechamber (clock by Jacquet-Droz, *The Blessing of the Plough in Franche-Comté*, painted by Robert Ferrier), the semicircular Great Council Hall, the seat of the cantonal government, 115 members elected for four years (note the stained-glass windows by Georges Froidevaux, representing municipal coats of arms), the grotto, a small room with barrel vaulting which once housed regional archives, and the Knights' Hall, the largest room in the castle, used for receptions (fine ceiling, arms on either side of the fireplace, portraits of all the State Councillors). In the south wing visitors are shown round the room named after Mary of Savoy, niece to Louis XI and wife to Count Philippe de Hochberg in 1478 (the count's arms hang above the stone fireplace), the Philippe de Hochberg Gallery, where the State Councillors meet, and the States' Room or Tribunal Room, whose walls recount the history of the Neuchâtel district (emblazoned coins). The wall-walk offers lovely views of the town.

Prison Tower ⊘ At the foot of the hill on which the castle stands, in the Rue Jehanne-de-Hochberg, there is a high crenellated tower known as the Prison Tower. Its base is the oldest piece of architecture in the town.

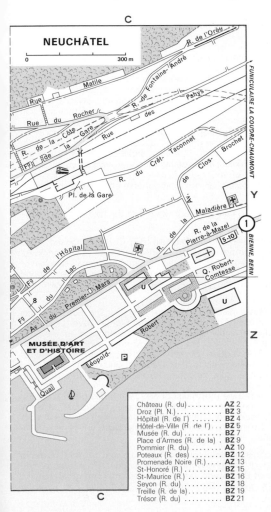

Château (R. du)	**AZ** 2
Droz (Pl. N.)	**BZ** 3
Hôpital (R. de l')	**BZ** 4
Hôtel-de-Ville (R. de l')	**BZ** 7
Musée (R. du)	**BZ** 9
Place d'Armes (R. de la)	**BZ** 9
Pommier (R. du)	**AZ** 10
Poteaux (R. des)	**BZ** 12
Promenade Noire (R.)	**AZ** 13
St-Honoré (R.)	**BZ** 15
St-Maurice (R.)	**BZ** 16
Seyon (R. du)	**BZ** 18
Treille (R. de la)	**BZ** 19
Trésor (R. du)	**BZ** 21

The interior contains two wooden dungeons used until 1848 and two maquettes of Neuchâtel from the late 15 and late 18C. The belvedere affords a nice **panorama** of the collegiate church, the town and the lake.

★★**Art and History Museum** (Musée d'Art et d'Histoire) (CZ) ⊙ – *Start on main floor.*

Fine Arts – *Main floor.* A sweeping staircase decorated with allegorical frescoes by Paul Robert and stained glass by Clement Heaton leads to this part of the museum. Eight out of the nine galleries are devoted to temporary exhibitions, or 19 and 20C works, executed by Swiss painters, in particular local artists. These are displayed in rotation, except for the rooms reserved for Léopold Robert *(Weeping Woman at the Water's Edge),* Ferdinand Hodler *(Autumn Evening)* and Albert Anker *(Bernese Peasant Reading his Newspaper).*

Automaton: The Musician

History and Decorative Arts – *Ground floor and mezzanine, on the right.* The largest gallery contains a multitude of objects, remarkably well displayed, evoking local crafts and the local way of life in the past. Other rooms retrace the history of the canton and display collections of gold and silver plate (cups of the various guilds), coins, porcelain and ceramics (made by rural craftsmen). Gallery 4 includes clocks from Neuchâtel and three **automata★★**, marvels of ingenuity made in the 18C by Jaquet-Droz and Sons as well as by Jean-Frédéric Leschot: they are the Musician, the Writer and the Draughtsman.

On the mezzanine (note the signs of Neuchâtel inns in the staircase) are old glassware, arms, 16 and 17C stained glass ornamented with municipal coats of arms, and the admirable **Strübin Collection★**, presenting weapons, armour, helmets and uniforms from the French Revolution, the First Napoleonic Empire, the Restoration and the Second Empire.

★**Ethnography Museum** (AZ) ⊙ – It is housed in an early 20C villa surrounded by a park. The modern annexe, called the "Dynamic Museum", is used exclusively for temporary exhibits focusing on a specific theme: the northern façade is embellished with a huge fresco executed by the Swiss painter **Hans Erni,** *The Conquests of Man.*

Many of the sumptuous collections on the ground floor, permanently on display, illustrate African ethnography: the Egypt of the Pharaohs (statuettes, funerary boats), Negro art (masks, symbolic figures of tutelary spirits, jewellery, royal dishes, tribal chief's throne) and Oceanian traditions (New Guinea, Polynesia). On the first floor lies the private study of the great traveller and collector Charles-Daniel de Meuron (1738-1806), containing the exotic objects encountered on his many voyages: Madagascan fan, Chinese porcelain, quiver with arrows, etc. There is also an interesting exhibition devoted to Bhutan, a small central Asian country wedged in between India and China. The artefacts on show were bequeathed by the late King and by members of the royal family: rugs, traditional costumes, musical instruments, domestic objects, an amazing portable altar in the shape of a three-tiered pagoda, etc.

Osterwald Quay (BZ) – *Viewing table.* Superb **view★★** of the lake and the Alpine range.

Natural History Museum (Musée d'Histoire Naturelle) (BZ) ⊙ – It is housed in the former School of Commerce, an imposing 19C residence built with yellow brick. As well as the exhibitions of mammals, the museum features several species of aquatic and sylvan birds, displayed in dioramas which reproduce their natural setting; note the recordings of the different songs, twitters, squawks and screeches.

Archaeological Museum (Musée cantonal d'archéologie) (BY) ⊙ – The oldest artifacts on display originate from Cotencher Cave (Rochefort) and Bichon Cave (La Chaux-de-Fonds); among these objects is the skull of an adult belonging to the Cro-Magnon race from the Upper Palaeolithic Era. The excavations, which have taken place along the lake shore (Auvernier, Bevaix), have uncovered a variety of different articles: a wooden sickle with a flint blade (c 3000 BC), wood and wickerwork combs, a cup with a ladle belonging to the late Neolithic Age and pottery from the late Bronze Age.

Discovered in 1857, the site of **La Tène** (northeast of Neuchâtel) has given its name to the second stage of the Iron Age – La Tène Culture – a number of arms (decorated sword sheaths), tools and Celtic jewellery have been salvaged from the area. From the Gallo-Roman era admire the marble bust portraying Julia, daughter of Drusus and Livilla.

DuPeyrou House (BZ) – This graceful building was erected in the 18C for a financier, DuPeyrou, a friend of the philosopher Jean-Jacques Rousseau. A fine entrance gate affords a view of the façade, which has pure lines and great unity of style, and gives access to a garden. The statue in the pool, *The Bather,* is by A. Ramseyer.

EXCURSIONS

★★ **Chaumont** – *8km – 5 miles. Take the road to Chaumont on the right (northwest of the plan –* **AY***)*. Leave your car at the upper Neuchâtel-Chaumont funicular station (alt 1 087m – 3 576ft) . To the left of and behind the station is an observation tower ☉. An immense panorama *(viewing table)* of the Bernese Alps and Mont Blanc Massif unfolds . *It can also be reached by the funicular* ☉ *from La Coudre, 3km – 2 miles from the centre of Neuchâtel. Time of trip: 12 minutes.*

Auvernier – *4.5km – 3 miles by the Rue de l'Évole* (**AZ**)*, prolonged by a by-road typical of those that go through the Neuchâtel vineyards.* A charming wine-growing village which is residential as well. In the vicinity of Grand-Rue stand fountains, a 15-18C church and a pretty 16-17C château.

Colombier – *7km – 4 miles by the Yverdon road (leave by* ②*). See Colombier.*

Boudry – *10km – 6 miles by* ② *along the Yverdon road.*
This small medieval-looking town was the birthplace of the French revolutionary leader **Jean-Paul Marat**, the editor of *L'Ami du Peuple*, murdered in his bath tub by Charlotte Corday in 1793. A sculpture called *Marat-L'Œil* has been erected in his honour near his native house. This 14m – 46ft high structure in painted steel slowly revolves, creating dazzling effects of light. The renowned chocolate manufacturer **Philippe Suchard** was born at no 7 of the Rue Louis Favre in 1797. He spent many childhood years in the house at no 37 of the same street; now the Town Hall.
The 13-16C castle, which served alternately as a counts' residence and a prison, houses the **Wine Museum** ☉, founded by the "Compagnie des Vignolants". The wines of Neûchatel, produced according to long-standing traditions, are made with grapes grown on a vineyard extending between Neûchatel Lake and the Jura. The visit, which begins with a "study of the wine bottle", ranging from the amphora to the wine box, provides a comprehensive review of the history of regional wine making from the 18C up to today. The exhibition, relying on photographs, paintings, tools, machines, explains the work of the wine grower, defined by the four seasons, the equipment used, diseases of the vine, grape harvesting and the vinification process right up to bottling.

Cailler, Suchard, Kohler, Nestlé, Lindt, Tobler...
Attractive presentations, mouth-watering contents characterise the high-quality confectionery of the Swiss chocolate-makers.
During the 19C and early 20C Swiss chocolate-makers acquired an international reputation for their delectable products.
Like a good wine, one should savour the aroma and taste. Dark, white or milk, chocolate comes in many forms — cake, mini-slabs, sweets and a variety of shapes — and is often combined with various other ingredients (nuts, raisins, ginger).

LA NEUVEVILLE Berne   Pop 3 324

Michelin map **216** fold 13 or **427** fold 12 – Local map see Swiss JURA – Facilities

La Neuveville, a pleasant town, is situated on the shores of Lake Biel across from **St Peter's Island** (St Petersinsel – *qv*); its economic activity includes wine-producing, precision engineering and tourism. An old-world feeling lingers about the town with its paved streets, lanterns and five towers (remains of the fortifications).

Rue du Marché – This street, which serves as the main square, is charming with its catch drain, lovely Renaissance fountains (with bannerets – *p 29*), flower-decked houses (two of which date from 1647 and 1697) and its old gates (Tour Rouge and Tour du Rive) which close the street at each end.

Blanche Église ☉ – *East of town towards Biel, on the left.* This Carolingian building remodelled in the Gothic period and restored in 1915 is surrounded by 17 and 18C tombstones. There are more tombstones inside as well as a painted wood pulpit (1536) and remains of 14C frescoes on the right of the chancel: Temptation of Christ, Christ Reviled, Entrance to Jerusalem, Adam and Eve.

★★ NUFENEN PASS ROAD

Michelin map **217** folds 19 and 20 or **427** folds 14 and 15

This spectacular road which links the Ticino and Valais regions is the most recently constructed of the St Gotthard Massif roads.

FROM AIROLO TO ULRICHEN

40km – 25 miles – about 1 1/2 hours – Itinerary **3** *on the St.Gotthard Massif map*

Nufenen Pass is usually closed November to May.
From **Airolo** (alt 1 142m – 3 747ft – facilities) to 8km – 5 miles from Nufenen, the climb up the Bedretto Valley (and from the Ticino River to its source) takes place between slopes covered with fir trees. From Airolo to Fontana there are audacious examples (above and to the right) of the engineers' ingenuity when constructing the road. Then after Ossasco you can see a series of villages half-way up the slope, Bedretto being one of them. Beginning at the hamlet of All'Acqua *(cable-car on the left)* the foliage becomes scarcer and the climb steeper, the hairpin curves offer a succession of views behind onto the valley's slopes. You then ascend the barren right side of the Bedretto Valley. The climb stops abruptly at the Nufenen Pass.

★★**Nufenen Pass** (Passo della Novena) – Alt 2 478m – 8 130ft. You have just climbed more than 1 300m – 4 265ft since Airolo. This pass offers an amazing landscape of incredible desolation. Higher up *(to the left of the restaurant)* the view encompasses the glacier and the Gries Reservoir. The view★★ also extends (northwest to southwest) onto the Upper Valais Range, Bernese Oberland (Finsteraarhorn Summit) and in the foreground the black, vertically-grooved face of the Faulhorn. The downhill road on the Valais side, after a close-up view of the greyish-coloured Gries glacier and its meltwater lake, plunges dizzily into a mineral landscape, brightened only by patches of very short grass and thistles. The glacier and Faulhorn can still be seen followed soon by a hanging valley and its waterfall.

Some 5km – 3 miles after the pass the view takes in the Upper Rhône Valley. The road then follows the diminished course of the Agene River, which has become the overflow of the Gries Dam and is hardly visible in its rocky bed, at the foot of the precipitous rock-face of the Blashorn, on the right.

The valley becomes more welcoming and is blanketed with larch as you approach the "Walser" village of **Ulrichen**, huddled around its church.

★ NYON Vaud

Pop 14 747

Michelin map **217** fold 12 or **427** fold 11 – Local maps see Lake GENEVA and Swiss JURA – Alt 410m – 1 345ft – Facilities

A pleasant town above lake Geneva, Nyon was founded by Caesar under the name Colonia Julia Equestris (succeeding the Helvetian burg of Noviodunum). In the 16C Nyon was occupied by the Bernese. Examples of their style of architecture can be seen in the castle and the arcaded houses on Place du Marché.

SIGHTS

★**Walk around the town walls** (Promenade des Vieilles Murailles) – Arranged in the 19C so as to be sheltered from the north wind and to overlook the lakeside quarter, the walk skirts the walls covered with creeper and widens onto the Esplanade des Marronniers from where there is a pretty view of the town, the Little Lake as far as Geneva, the Salève and Mont Blanc. The Roman columns add a romantic touch to the scene.

Castle – Considerably altered in the 16C, the feudal castle has five different towers all crowned with pepper-pot roofs. From the terrace there is a nice **view** of the Rive quarter and the Little Lake *(viewing table).*

History and Porcelain Museum ⊘ (Musée historique et des porcelaines) – It was in 1781 that the porcelain factory of Nyon officially opened its doors. This museum presents numerous collections of porcelain and earthenware pieces pre-20C. In 1813, owing to economic factors, earthenware was to replace porcelain. The most precious exhibits include coffee services (monochrome with cornflowers and gilt ornamentation), tea services, soup bowls and a set of crockery

NYON

Bel-Air (Pl.) 2
Château (Pl. du) 3

Colombière (R. de la) 4
Gare (R. de la) 5
Jura (Promenade du) 6
Morâche (R. de la) 7
Porcelaine (R. de la) 9

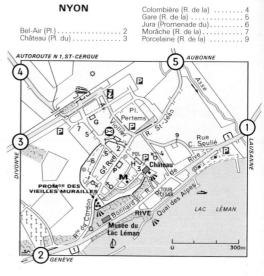

which belonged to Joachim Murat, Maréchal de France and the King of Naples in 1808. One room contains furniture made by local craftsmen: a walnut wardrobe, a dresser with a top in black marble. The Burkhard Reber Collection, named after a chemist attached to Geneva Hospital, consists of apothecary's pots made of majolica and earthenware (16-18C), displayed together with various measuring devices.

Roman Museum (M) ⊘ – This underground museum is indicated "above ground" by a statue of Caesar. Also indicated on the ground is the location of the Forum's old basilica. On the façade of the neighbouring house there is a drawing of how the Forum must have looked during the Roman era.

This vast public building (1C) forms by its excavated part (more than a third of its foundations) the main interest of the museum. Around it are artefacts excavated from digs at Nyon and its environs: fragments of mosaics with simple geometric patterns or foliage motifs (including the famous Artemis mural), stone debris (capitals, military milestones), domestic objects (lamps, ceramics, crockery, coins) and a host of amphorae of different origins...

Lakeside – A park and quays with attractive flower beds border the small sheltered yachting harbour and provide views of Lake Geneva and France on the far side. Further along in Quai des Alpes stands the 11C Caesar's Tower. Note high up the Roman masque of the god Attis, consort of the Great Mother of the Gods (Cybele).

Lake Geneva Museum (Musée du Lac Léman) ⊙ – The museum is housed in an 18C hospital overlooking the harbour and it makes a good introduction to any visit to the region. The origins of Switzerland's largest lake, its flora and fauna (aquariums are home to various species of fish) are the themes of the first exhibitions. The next section illustrates the various activities associated with the lake: fishing (boats, nets and tools), forestry and timber working (the barges used to transport the logs prior to the advent of the railway) as well as the history of shipping (from the early lateen-sailed fishing boats so typical of the lake to machinery from the steamer *Helvétie I*).

EXCURSIONS

Crans – *6km – 4 miles southwest of Nyon by* ②. The château, which boasts good lines and proportions, is a fine example of the Louis XV period. The small church nearby offers a nice view of the vineyards, the lake and, in the far distance, the French mountain range.

OLTEN Solothurn   Pop 17 805

Michelin map **216** fold 16 or **427** fold 5 – Local map see Swiss JURA – Alt 399m – 1 309ft – Facilities – Town plan in the current. Michelin Red Guide Switzerland

Olten is pleasantly situated at the boundary of the Jura, on the banks of the Aare. A wooden covered bridge (Alte Brücke), reserved for pedestrians, leads to the old town.
Since the beginning of the century the appearance of the town, which continues to spread on both sides of the Aare, has been changed by its great industrial activity – soap and cement works, foodstuffs and the workshops of the Federal Railways.

SIGHTS

Fine Arts Museum (Kunstmuseum) ⊙ – The museum has a good collection of paintings and sculpture of the 19 and 20C. The most interesting works on display are on the second floor and include excellent caricatures, studies and drawings by **Martin Disteli** (1802-44). This talented painter and caricaturist has interpreted scenes from Swiss military history and political life, as well as fables.

Historical Museum (Historisches Museum) ⊙ – This museum contains various collections relating to local art and customs, furniture and regional costumes, and also a well-known prehistory section.

EXCURSIONS

★**Säli–Schlössli Panorama** – *5km – 3 miles southeast. Leave by Aarburger-strasse and take Sälistrasse on the left.*
The street soon starts climbing, in hairpin bends, the wooded hillside to reach the ruins of the feudal stronghold of Wartburg. From the top of the crenellated tower ⊙ of the small Neo-Gothic Castle, standing amidst the ruins, there is a **panorama★** of Olten and Aarburg below, and the Aare Valley away to a horizon of green hills.

Zofingen – *9km – 5 1/2 miles. Leave Olten by Aarburgestrasse.*
The old part of the town is contained within the quadrilateral formed by the alleys which have taken the place of its ramparts. The Pulvertum, a square 12C tower, is all that remains of the old ramparts. Zofingen's large square, the Thut-Platz, has a fountain with a banneret and numerous 17 and 18C houses. The Church of St Maurice (altered), has preserved its 17C bell tower (Renaissance aspect). Dating from the Roman period there are two large mosaics (under shelter) which can be seen as you leave the town from the south *(behind Römerbad Hotel).*

ORBE Vaud   Pop 5 084

Michelin map **217** fold 3 or **427** fold 11 – Local map see Swiss JURA – Alt 483m – 1 585ft

Orbe, terraced on a hill surrounded by the meander of the river of the same name (derived from the Latin name *Urba*), is a small attractive town with an old-world atmosphere.
From the Place du Marché, with its fountain with banneret (1753), take the alleyway which leads to the 15 and 16C Reformed Church (interior: side aisles with unusual keystones) and then to the terrace of the old castle from where there is a good view of Orbe and its valley. From the end of the flower-decked Rue des Moulinets – a picturesque scene can be appreciated of the Roman bridge and the covered bridge.

Urba Mosaics ⊙ – *2km – 1 mile north of Orbe on the road, to Yverdon.* Alongside the road, four isolated pavilions house Roman mosaics (early 3C). The subjects are (in order of their proximity to the farm nearby): Calendar of the Divinities, the loveliest, made of polychrome medallions; pastoral scene with chariots, the most evocative; the maze with lion and birds; and a geometric mosaic in black and white.

ORON-LE-CHÂTEL Vaud   Pop 169

Michelin map 🔲 south of fold 4 (north of Oron-la-Ville) or 🔲 fold 12 – Alt 720m
– 2362ft

This little village situated in the Haute-Braye on the left bank of the Flon, a
tributary of the Broye, is dominated by the imposing mass of its fortified castle.

Castle ⊙ – This solid construction, firmly established on its rocky promontory, was
built in the late 12 and early 13C. Despite the many alterations it has undergone, it
still conveys the image of a stern, forbidding citadel. Several families have occupied
the premises in succession, as can be inferred from the impressive coat-of-arms
display in the main hall. For 241 years the castle was the official residence of the
Bernese bailiffs. The rooms on the first floor give one a good idea of how French
middle-class families lived in those days. The dining-hall houses some superb
collections of Sèvres and Limoges porcelain, as well as pieces of Wedgwood. The
library (beautiful 15C coffered ceiling) is believed to contain around 18 000 books
dating from the 16 to the 19C. The visit ends with a series of tastefully-decorated
rooms: music room (the piano is thought to have belonged to Mozart), smoking
room with wallpaper decorated with hunting scenes, playroom and study for the
children, tea parlour (Louis XV commode in rosewood), prior's bedroom, etc.

★ PASSWANG PASS ROAD

Michelin map 🔲 folds 4 and 15 or 🔲 fold 4

The harsh Lüssel Valley with the welcoming Birse Valley make up the major part of
this itinerary which winds between the Aare and Rhine Rivers.

FROM OENSINGEN TO BASLE

73km – 45 miles – about 2 1/4 hours – Itinerary ⑥ *on the Swiss Jura local map*

Between Oensingen and Balsthal, the road follows the bottom of the Klus or
transverse valley, cutting at right angles across the small Weissenstein Range. The Von
Roll foundries pour their smoke into the corridor, keeping up the metalworking tradition
of the Jura. In the valley lies **Alt-Falkenstein Castle**, unfortunately overly-restored.
Between Balsthal and the Passwang Pass, the road makes an angle at the foot of
the proud ruins of the *Burg* (fortress) of **Neu Falkenstein,** dominated by a round tower,
and enters the agricultural **Guldental** through a new – but very short – rock tunnel.
The last bends in the road before the Passwang Tunnel give bird's-eye views of
this secluded valley, as the Bernese Alps appear in the distance. The excursion
from the Passwang Pass to the Passwang Summit is recommended.

★★**Passwang Summit** – Alt 1 204m – 3 950ft. *From the north exit of the Passwang
Tunnel, 2km – 1 mile along a narrow road with sharp gradients (close the gates
behind you), plus 3/4 hour on foot Rtn. Leaving the car at the "Wirtschaft Ober-
Passwang" café-restaurant, continue the climb on foot. On coming out of a wood,
after passing through a gate, leave the road and climb, to the right, to the summit.*
From this point a varied **panorama**★★ extends, to the north, over the last undulations
of the Basle Jura, the Plain of Alsace (note the double ribbon of the Rhine and the
Kembs Canal, part of the great Alsace Canal) framed between the Vosges and the
Black Forest, and to the south, to the Solothurn Jura and part of the Bernese Alps.
Between the pass and Laufen, the lonely Lüssel Valley shrinks to a narrow wooded
cleft. Between Erschwill and Büsserach, the ruins of Thierstein, a massive tower
flanked by a turret, stand like a sentinel. You come out in the Laufen Basin where
the tilled, undulating floor lies spread before the forest ridges of the "Blauen".
Between Laufen, a little town with fortified gates, and Aesch, the **Birse Valley** continues
green and smiling in spite of increasing industrialisation. The **Angenstein Castle's** keep,
a former residence of the bishops of Basle, seems to block the last defile.
At Grellingen take the road to the east.

Seewen – On the outskirts of this charming village, huddled in a wooded basin at
the foot of its white church, stands the **Museum of Musical Automata** (Musikautomaten-
Museum) ⊙. Its galleries house a total of 800 objects dating from the 18 to the early
20C and all in good working order: mechanical pianos, barrel organs, street organs,
music boxes, orchestrions (imitating orchestra instruments) and especially amusing
automata designed to resemble a bird, a painter, a magician...

Goetheanum ⊙ – *The way is marked on leaving Dornachbrugg or Arlesheim.*
The design of the Goetheanum, standing on the slopes overlooking Dornach and
Arlesheim, surprises the visitor. This is the international centre of the "Universal
Anthroposophical Society" and also of a "Free University of Spiritual Science" in
which, among other activities, public performances are given; namely the entire
Faust by Goethe and the four mystery-dramas by Rudolf Steiner. The building and
its annexes, even the most utilitarian among them, are designed down to the last
details in accordance with the principles of anthroposophy, whose founder Rudolf
Steiner (1861-1925) was strongly influenced by Goethe, using the metamorphosis
as a basis for his own work.

Arlesheim – The **collegiate church**★ (Domkirche) ⊙ of Arlesheim is one of the most
charming successes of baroque art in Switzerland. Built in 1680 for the chapter of the
episcopal principality of Basle, it was later transformed to the rococo style (1769-71).
It stands in a quiet, shady little square bordered by the former canons' houses. The
inside of the church, of which the harmony is unblemished by any detail, is adorned
with stucco discreetly picked out in pink or pale yellow, while the low vaulting bears
large, misty compositions in pale colours by Joseph Appiani (1760).
You now enter the outer suburbs of Basle.

★★★**Basle** – *Time: 3 hours. See Basle.*

★ PAYERNE Vaud   Pop 7 393

Michelin map **217** fold 4 or **427** fold 12 – Local map see Swiss JURA – Alt 450m – 1 476ft

Payerne is situated in the rich Broye Valley and has a remarkable abbey church, once attached to a Benedictine abbey. This abbey is believed to have been founded in the 10C by the Empress Adelaide, wife of Otto the Great, first of the Holy Roman Emperors and daughter of the legendary Queen Bertha, nicknamed Bertha the Spinner, the widow of Rudolf II, King of Trans-Jura Burgundy.

★ **Abbey Church** – The 11C church is almost all that remains of this once large abbey. The church fell into disuse in the mid 16C when the Bernese introduced the Reformation to the Vaud District. It was then transformed into a storehouse and barracks and subsequently suffered considerable damage. Large-scale restoration work has restored this Romanesque church to its former glory.

★★ **Interior** ⊘ – *Photograph in the Introduction (p. 31).* The very plain nave is lit by tall windows and roofed with barrel vaulting, while the aisles have groined vaulting and the apse has oven vaulting. Purity of line and harmony of proportion give the visitor an impression of grandeur but also of severity, accentuated by the absence of decoration (except for the attractive combination of golden limestone and grey sandstone).

Remarkable capitals adorn the tall windows of the chancel and the transept pillars. Their crude but expressive design dates them back to the abbey's founding. Frescoes adorn the arms of the transept. The room above the narthex or St Michael's Chapel (13C frescoes) houses the abbey museum.

Contiguous to the church, the elegant **chapterhouse** with groined vaulting houses temporary exhibitions. Opposite the abbey church, the Protestant church contains frescoes and old tombstones.

PICHOUX GORGES

Michelin map **216** folds 2 and 14 or **427** folds 3 and 4

From Lake Biel to the Ajoie Region (area around Porrentruy), deep gorges, pastures, fir or deciduous forests follow the road, which in the Sorne Valley, runs between the Franches Montagnes and the Delémont Regio.

FROM BIEL TO PORRENTRUY

61km – 38 miles – about 2 1/2 hours – Itinerary 5 *on the Swiss Jura local map*

★ **Biel** – *Time: 1 hour. See Biel.*

From Biel to Sonceboz the road climbs quickly above the suburbs of Biel and half-way up the slope threads its way through the Taubenloch Gorges (Taubenlochschlucht – *lovers of deep defiles should visit these gorges preferably on foot, walking along the floor by the route described under Lake Biel*). The road goes up the industrialized Suze Valley *(big cement works at Reuchenette)*, narrowed by rock tunnels marking the successive ridges of the Jura.

Pierre-Pertuis – Between Sonceboz and Tavannes, the Pierre-Pertuis section resembles the crossing of a small Alpine pass. This corridor, already used since the beginning of the 3C by the Roman road from Aventicum (Avenches – *qv*) to Augusta Raurica (Augst – *qv*), gets its name from the artificial arch which was then built and under which the former road passed on the Tavannes slope. The **site** is well-known throughout the region. A clearing at the pass with benches may be used for a halt.

Tavannes – The name of this prosperous, hard-working little town, situated in the Upper Birse Valley, at the foot of the rock of Pierre-Pertuis, is known for its clock-making. The modern Roman Catholic church was decorated by artists of the Société St-Luc, a school of sacred art well-known in Romansh Switzerland. The mosaic on the façade, representing the Ascension, is by Gino Severini.

The countryside becomes High Jurassian and in some places the road forms an avenue bordered by fir trees.

Bellelay Abbey ⊘ – The 18C buildings of the former abbey, occupied by the Premonstratensians from 1136-97, has kept the distinctive appearance of a monastery.

The **abbey church**, built between 1710-14, has an imposing array of baroque architecture in the interior, which art lovers may compare to that of St-Urban and Rheinau. The **interior**★ is remarkably impressive, although it lacks furnishings. The Fathers of Bellelay are believed to hold the secret of making **Monk's Head**, a semi-hard cheese which cuts into appetizing flakes.

After winding through wooded pastureland where the bay horses of the Franches Montagnes roam free, the road glides into the depths of the gorges cut by the Sorne.

★ **Pichoux Gorges** – This cutting, in which the road shares the bed of the stream, is the deepest of the *cluses* hollowed out by the Sorne between Le Pichoux and Berlincourt. The gorges have limestone cliffs to which cling forests of fir.

The **climb**★ from Boécourt to Les Rangiers Pass at first crosses the flank of an open slope planted with birch and gnarled oaks. Here you can appreciate the spaciousness of the Delémont "Valley" which is gracefully curved and dotted with prosperous small industrial towns. The Doubs slope is reached when the road joins the itinerary called the Jura Corniche, but you can only guess at the course of the great Jurassian river.

The rest of the itinerary is described under Weissenstein Road, in the opposite direction, starting at Porrentruy.

Pilatus (highest point: 2 129m – 6 985ft at the Tomlishorn) dominates the western basins of Lake Lucerne with its sharply defined ridges. It is both a useful landmark for the visitor to central Switzerland and a barometer popular in all the Lucerne area, if the following proverb is to be believed:

> "When Pilate hides his head,
> Sunshine below will spread;
> When Pilate's head is bare,
> Of rain beware".

For a long time the massif inspired superstitious dread, for legend declared that the spirit of Pontius Pilate haunted a small lake near the summit and that any bold man who approached this accursed spot would cause fearful storms. The mountain has become one of the attractions of the Swiss Alps.

Pilatus

CLIMB TO PILATUS

From Alpnachstad, about 2 hours Rtn, including 1 hour by rack-railway ☉

The line, with a maximum gradient of 48% (1 in 2, it is the steepest in the world for this form of traction), is particularly impressive where it crosses the slopes of the Esel.

★★★ **Pilatus-Kulm** – From the upper station, which has two mountain hotels, you will climb in a few minutes to the Esel Summit (alt 2 121m – 6 959ft), a belvedere from which the eye, dazzled by the Alpine range, follows the winding waters of Lake Lucerne, narrowed in the centre by the promontories of the Rigi and the Bürgenstock. A walk through the gallery with openings cut out of the rock of the Oberhaupt is also recommended.

You can also reach the Pilatus-Kulm by cable-car starting from Kriens, in the suburbs of Lucerne, and make a circular tour (see details under Lucerne: Excursions.

Every year
*the **Michelin Red Guide Switzerland***
revises its selection of establishments which

- *serve carefully prepared meals at a reasonable price*
- *include service on the bill or in the price of each dish*
- *offer a menu of simple but good food at a modest cost*
- *provide free parking.*

It is well worth buying the curent edition.

★★ PONTRESINA Graubünden (Grisons)   Pop 1 604

Michelin map **218** fold 15 or **427** fold 17 – Local map see GRISONS – Alt 1 777m – 5 863ft – Facilities

Pontresina is the leading mountaineering resort of the Engadine. It lies at the mouth of the Bernina Valley within view of the Roseg corrie and the snowy ridges of the Piz Palü. Pushing up the Roseg or the Morteratsch Valleys, lovers of the high mountains start out from here for magnificent glacier climbs in the Bernina Massif, especially the famous Diavolezza tour. Walkers can continue along the woodland paths of the forest of Tais (Taiswald) or climb, via a *corniche* path from Muottas Muragl *(7km – 4 miles)*, the last foothills of the Piz Languard. The winter season at Pontresina lasts far into spring. It offers long-distance excursions for skiers and the sunny ski-runs served by the ski tows of the Languard Alp and the funicular of Muottas Muragl.

Chapel of St Mary (Santa Maria) ☉ – This little Romanesque church near the 12C Spaniola Tower contains a series of mural paintings (restored) done mostly by an artist of the Quattrocento (15C). The series devoted to the story of Mary Magdalene will interest tourists familiar with the Golden Legend and the great Provençal traditions.

★★**Muottas Muragl** – *3km – 2 miles by the road to Samedan as far as Punt Muragl, plus about 1 hour Rtn, including 1/2 hour by funicular. Access from Punt Muragl and description under Muottas Muragl.*

PORRENTRUY Jura   Pop 6 857

Michelin map **216** south of fold 2 or **427** fold 3 – Local map see Swiss JURA – Alt 445m – 1 460ft –Facilities

Porrentruy, once fortified, lies in the middle of the Ajoie region. On annexing this little district with its Comtois character to French territory, the Revolution made Porrentruy the capital of the Mont-Terrible Department, which included the present Jura Canton and Bernese Jura as far as Biel. This was a great honour for a modest, wooded height whose real name was Mount Terri (alt 804m – 2 638ft – south of the village of Cornol).

The **old town** stands on a spur overlooking the Allaine Valley and has a good number of interesting buildings. The castle of the Prince-Bishops of Basle, whose proud Refousse Tower is 45m – 147ft high (fine view), included several structures built since the 11C. Below the castle, the Porte de France is one of the few vestiges of the former walls.

In the Rue Pierre-Péquignat and the steep Grand'Rue you can see the market and the town hall, both 18C, the Samaritan Fountain, the 17C Swiss Fountain and the former hospital (1765), which has fine wrought-iron gates. This hospital houses a **museum** ☉ displaying old documents and manuscripts. The former hospital pharmacy next to the library may also be visited.

★ Bad RAGAZ St Gallen   Pop 4 325

Michelin map **218** fold 4 or **427** fold 16 – Alt 502m – 1 647ft – Facilities

Bad Ragaz, located in one of the Alpine Rhine Valley's fine settings and facing the rugged crests of the Falknis is a leading Swiss spa. Since the 11C the resort has utilized slightly mineral waters rising at a temperature of 37° C (98°F) in the Tamina Gorges below the village of Pfäfers. It is particularly recommended for circulatory troubles, rheumatism, paralysis and the after-effects of accidents.

Bad Ragaz has been a mid-winter skiing centre since a cable-car and ski-tows linked the town with the great snowfields in the Pizol District.

EXCURSION

★★**Tamina Gorges (Taminaschlucht)** ☉ – *2 hours Rtn on foot by the road branching off the road to Valens on the left, southwest of Bad Ragaz.*

To take the waters, before these were piped, patients were lowered on ropes to the bottom of this tremendous fissure.

★ RAPPERSWIL St Gallen   Pop 7 463

Michelin map **216** fold 19 or **427** fold 6 – Local map see ZURICH: Excursions – Alt 409m – 1 342ft – Facilities

The little town of Rapperswil occupies a pretty site on a short peninsula on the north shore of Lake Zürich. The upper town has kept its medieval appearance, emphasized by the imposing mass of its castle. Rapperswil is a pleasant place to stay in summer, with plenty of walks and drives around the lake and in the neighbourhood.

SIGHTS

Castle – This is a massive structure flanked by three grim-looking towers, built by the counts of the district in the 13C. From the outer terrace there is a fine **view** of the town below, of Lake Zürich and, beyond it, of the Glarus Alps and St Gallen. On the opposite side, above the former ramparts and overlooking the lake, a deer park has been laid out.

Polish Museum ⊘ – *First floor.* Founded by Polish immigrants, this museum contains six galleries *(plus one for temporary exhibitions)*. One gallery is devoted to Chopin and Adam Mickiewicz, one to the 2nd Polish Division, which fought in France in 1940, one to provincial costumes and the last three to Polish history (documents, arms, paintings, memorabilia, etc.).

Local Museum (Heimatmuseum) ⊘ – This museum, installed in a 15C house, contains many relics of the Roman era and collections of weapons and works of art displayed in rooms with painted ceilings and fine old furniture.

Children's Zoo (Kinderzoo) ⊘ – *Behind the railway station. Access by Schönbo-denstrasse then right on Obersee Strasse.*
Belonging to the Knie National Circus, the zoo presents different attractions (Noah's Ark, whale aquarium and a train) as well as a limited selection of animals (zebras, camels, rhinoceroses, monkeys, parakeets...). Dolphins perform.

EXCURSION

From Rapperswil to Pfäffikon – *22km – 13 1/2 miles north. Leave Rapperswil on the road to Zürich, then bear right on the road to Winterthur; at Rüti bear left towards the motorway, after going underneath it, bear right; 300m before Bubikon take the signposted path (marked Ritterhaus).*

Commandery of Bubikon (Ritterhaus) ⊘ – Founded in 1192 and rebuilt in the 15 and 16C, the Commandery of the Order of the Hospital of St John of Jerusalem, whose outbuildings have been converted into a farm, is a museum. It recounts the history of the Hospitaller Order, from its origins with the aid of documents, arms, paintings...
Also to be visited are the ossuary, chapel (frescoes), 16C kitchen, library and large common rooms with their trompe l'œil ceilings and panelling, fireplaces, and Gothic-Renaissance furnishings.

Return to the Winterthur road.

After having skirted the Pfäffikersee, you arrive at the entrance to Pfäffikon. On the left is the tumulus of the ancient Roman camp of Irgenhausen.

Fortress of Irgenhausen (Römisches Kastell) – *Leave the car in the factory's car park, level with the fortress, then 1/4 hour on foot Rtn (pass underneath the railway line).*
This small citadel (held a maximum of 200 legionaries), built 285-305 AD, was part of a line of forts placed strategically to defend against an attack by the Alemans. The fort was strategically set on a mound overlooking both the lake and the town. Although the walls of the fort still stand, only foundations remain of the four defensive towers on the lake side.

★ RHEINAU Zürich   Pop 1 769

Michelin map **216** folds 7 and 8 (on the Rhine) or **427** fold 6 – Alt 372m – 1 220ft

This little town is prettily placed in a bend of the Rhine south of the famous Rhine Falls *(for access see Schaffhausen).* It was the seat of a Benedictine abbey (now converted into a mental hospital) on an island in the river. Its abbey church is an outstanding example of baroque art. In 1956 a large hydro-electric power station and dam were completed across the Rhine downstream of Rheinau.
Its reservoir stretches for 6.5km – 4 miles up to the Rhine Falls.

Abbey Church (Klosterkirche) ⊘ – The church, with a rather severe façade, was rebuilt, except for its 16C south tower, at the beginning of the 18C.
The **interior★** is striking for its rich decoration in the purest baroque tradition. The nave, the vaulting of which is covered with frescoes, is flanked on either side by four chapels adorned, like the high altar, with a profusion of marble and gilding. A balustrade runs under the clerestory. The chancel, enclosed by an elaborate grille, has beautiful stalls. The organ dates back to 1715. In a small room containing the treasure, to the left of the chancel, is some fine inlaid furniture.

Knie the Swiss National Circus

In 1803 Friedrich Knie, son of Empress Maria-Theresa's personal physician, was studying medecine at Innsbruck. A chance encounter with a horsewoman from a troupe of travelling artistes soon put an end to his studies. Friedrich joined the troupe and became an acrobat. Later he was to found his own troupe and marry in 1807 Antonia Stauffer, a barber's daughter. Their travels took them through Germany, Austria, Switzerland and France and Friedrich rapidly became famous as a tightrope walker. His children and grandchildren carried on the tradition and continued to entertain enthralled audiences in the open. In 1900 the Knie family acquired Swiss nationality. In 1919 Friedrich's most cherished dream came true when the Knie Circus was founded. Today the Knies are one of the great circus families and their "one-ring circus" is still a family affair with the 6th generation now active in the business. The troupe is Switzerland's national circus, although it remains financially independent. The circus and its travelling zoo are on the road and rail from the end of March to the end of November and they give 375 shows under the big top to capacity audiences of 3 000 in some 60 towns. The winter quarters are in Rapperswil. In 1994 the circus celebrated its 75th anniversary.

RHINE (RHEIN)

Michelin maps 216 and 218 or 427

The Rhine is Swiss for barely 1/4 of its course, for it reaches Basle after 388km – 242 miles. In this relatively short distance it falls from 2 200m to 250m – 7 218ft to 820ft and has the appearance of a wild and fast-flowing river.

GEOGRAPHICAL NOTES

An Alpine river – The Rhine Basin is by far the largest river basin in Swiss territory. It extends to all the Swiss cantons except those of Geneva, Valais and Ticino.

With its low water in winter and its spate in summer at the melting of the snows, the Rhine is a typical Alpine river. It rises in the Grisons (Graubünden); its two main arms, the Vorderrhein – principal headstream of the Rhine – and the Hinterrhein – lesser headstream of the Rhine – meet at Reichenau, above Chur, and provide the power for the large-scale hydro-electric works. The courses are followed respectively by the San Bernardino *(qv)* and the Oberalp roads *(qv)*.

The river is swollen at Chur by the Plessur and soon afterwards by the Landquart and the Tamina. It follows the **Rheinthal** cleft, which resembles Alsace by its north-south orientation, its size and its varying vegetation (maize, vines, etc.). It then flows into **Lake Constance** which acts as a regulator for it, as Lake Geneva does for the Rhône.

An inland sea, the Bodensee – Lake Constance, the Bodensee, is 12km – 8 miles wide and at the most 64km – 40 miles long. Though a little smaller (54 000ha – 33 400 acres) than Lake Geneva, it gives an impression of immensity which sometimes recalls the sea. At Constance, the Rhine, now limpid, leaves the main basin for the Lower Lake (Untersee), from which it escapes at Stein am Rhein.

Crossing the Jura – Between Schaffhausen and Basle the character of the river changes. Hemmed in between the slopes of the Black Forest and the Jura foothills, it has to force its way among slabs of hard rock. This is the case below Schaffhausen, where the valley narrows, the flow becomes faster and the river plunges between the rocks, forming impressive falls *(description see Schaffhausen)*. Farther on, other rocky slabs produce rapids *(Laufen)*, whose presence accounts for place names like Laufen and Laufenburg.

All these breaks in the level make navigation impossible but they have enabled hydro-electric power to be fully developed from power stations on the river banks, the most recent of which may be seen in the power-dam at Rheinau *(see opposite)*.

Confluence with the Aare – The Aare makes an important contribution to the Rhine. This is the largest all-Swiss river and its basin covers 2/5 of the area of Switzerland. It flows in succession through Lakes Brienz and Thun (Brienzersee and Thunersee), waters Berne and Solothurn and receives many tributaries, the most important being the Reuss and the Limmat.

The rivers meet near Koblenz, upstream from Waldshut, where the Aare has covered a greater distance than the Rhine (280km – 175 miles against 274km – 170 miles). The scene is spectacular, for the Aare brings more water than the Rhine into which it flows. From now on the Rhine is a great river and carries international traffic below Basle. *A visit, which is extremely interesting, to the port of Basle is described on p 52.*

THE PICTURESQUE RHINE

Between Lake Constance and Basle, driving along the Rhine Valley is complicated by the meandering border of the Canton of Schaffhausen. Therefore do not try to follow the course of the Rhine very closely in Swiss territory.

It is better to choose a few of the most characteristic observation points and make excursions to them:
the **Höhenklingen Castle,** near Stein am Rhein *(qv)*;
the **Munot terrace,** at Schaffhausen *(qv)*;
the **Laufen Castle,** at the Rhine Falls *(see Schaffhausen)*;
at **Laufenburg** (Swiss shore), the terrace laid out below an old tower.

Steamer services – Steamers based at Constance, Romanshorn, Arbon and Rorschach ply the main part of Lake Constance and on Lake Überlingen (in German territory). Excursion steamers also sail between Schaffhausen and Kreuslingen on the Rhine and the Lower Lake (Untersee), offering incomparable glimpses of the romantic river banks, overlooked by some ruined castles, and of the charming little towns of Diessenhofen, Stein am Rhein, etc.

Rhine-Main-Danube Canal

Ever since Roman times emperors, kings, engineers and visionaries have dreamed of linking the Rhine and Danube waterways. Charlemagne began the great enterprise, hence the name Charlemagne's Ditch (Fossa Carolina), Bavaria's Ludwig I made another attempt when he built the Ludwig Canal. However it was bargeloads of 20C dignitaries who were the first to cross the watershed between the Rhine and the Danube on the 25th September 1992.
The 177km – 110 mile-canal with its hundreds of locks takes the barges up and down the 245m – 800 ft climb and 12 centuries after it was orignally started, the idea of a waterway linking Europe from the North Sea to the Black Sea has become a reality.

Michelin map **217** fold 6 or **427** fold 13

As you enter the town from the north (Berne road) bear right onto the road to the Abegg Foundation, the modern buildings of which are located on the mountainside in a verdant and tranquil setting.

★★**Abegg Foundation** (Abegg-Stiftung) ⊘ – The institute founded in 1961 by Werner Abegg contains some rare collections of applied art of varied origin and different periods. The exhibits dating back to early civilisations feature Neolithic ceramic pieces from Anatolia and Persia, small-size sculptures from the Cyclades, silverware from Marlik (Persia), two buckets, one in bronze and one in silver, shaped as ram's heads, ivory plaquettes from the pre-Achaemenid era (the Achaemenid dynasty ruled Persia from 556 to 330 BC), an elegant lapis-lazuli tumbler in the shape of an ibex, bronzes from Luristan (this part of Persia flourished artistically between the 14 and 7C BC, producing a great many bronzes decorated with animals). The museum also pays tribute to ancient Egypt.

Fondation ABEGG, Berne

Silk hanging with partridge motif
(Lyon, c1770)

The tapestry gallery houses two huge hangings portraying Meleager and Atalanta, as well as Dionysos, Ariache, Pan and other mythological figures, a textile mural depicting the goddess Artemis and another illustrated by scenes taken from Genesis and Exodus. The exhibitions devoted to the Near East include Sasanian silverware (Persan dynasty which ruled from the 3 to the 7C), liturgical vases from Byzance and 10 and 11C Persian textiles. Contributions to Romanesque art come from Sicily, southern Italy (ivory sculptures), France (capitals, Limoges enamels, mural paintings) and Spain (carved pieces, silk fabric). One of the most treasured exhibits is the chasuble of St Vital, once the property of Salzburg Abbey. Gothic art is represented by an embroidered cope from England (opus anglicanum), tapestries from Touraine and Bruxelles, sculptures (a *Virgin with Child* by Hans Multscher), caskets, silverware and a collection of paintings executed by Botticelli, Lorenzetti, Fra Angelico, Van der Weyden, displayed in a separate room. The Renaissance period is also represented by jewellery, silk and velvet fabric, amber candelabra and fine Italian vases made of gold and rock crystal. The 18C silk hangings displayed alternately in the last gallery were, for the moste part, manufactured in Lyon.

Michelin Maps (1:200 000) which are revised regularly, indicate
- golf courses, sports stadiums, racecourses, swimming pools, beaches, airfields
- scenic routes, long-distance footpaths, panoramas
- forest parks, interesting sights...

The perfect complement to the Michelin Green Guides for planning holidays and leisure time.

★★★ RIGI

Michelin map **216** south of fold 18 or **427** fold 15 – Local map see Lake LUCERNE

Isolated on all sides by a depression largely covered by the waters of Lakes Lucerne, Zug and Lauerz, this "island mountain", to use the graphic description of German geographers for this type of feature, rears its heavy wooded shoulders, scarred by reddish escarpments, to an altitude of 1 797m – 5 896ft. It has been famous for a century for its highest point, the Rigi-Kulm, on the summit of which, according to tradition, one should spend the night to see the sun rise over the Alps.

On the other hand, those who like easy walks among woods and Alpine pastures, or on mountain roads, which always offer interesting views, should stay in one of the high-altitude hotels scattered on the mountainside. One of the best-situated resorts of this kind is **Rigi-Kaltbad** (facilities).

A great spectacle – For generations of "sensitive souls" the sunrise seen from the **Rigi-Kulm** was the climax of a visit to Switzerland. The splendour of the spectacle drove away memories of the harsh preliminaries, and the shivering, sleepy-eyed crowd reached a state of collective exaltation when the first rays of the sun lit up, according to Victor Hugo , that "incredible horizon", that "chaos of absurd exaggerations and frightening diminutions".

CLIMB TO RIGI-KULM

From Arth-Goldau or from Vitznau the climb by rack-railway ⊙ to the Rigi-Kulm takes 35 minutes. Another way is to take the cable-car from Weggis to Rigi-Kaltbad and change there to the rack-railway for Rigi-Kulm.

★★★ **Panorama** – Alt 1 797m – 5 896ft. *From the terminus station, near which there is a large hotel, 1/4 hour on foot Rtn to the signpost and the cross standing on the summit.* Your eye may wander from end to end of the Alps' tremendous back-cloth rising between Säntis and the Bernese Alps (Jungfrau) and including the Glarus and Uri Alps and the Titlis Massif. The opposite half of the horizon is less dazzling but more attractive. On this side the rounded hills of the Zürich countryside stretch into the distance, beyond Lakes Lauerz, Zug and Lucerne, to merge with the line of the Jura, the Vosges and the Black Forest.

★ ROMAINMÔTIER Vaud   Pop 428

Michelin map **217** folds 2 and 3 or **427** fold 11 – Local map see Swiss JURA – Alt 676m – 2 163ft

This old village nestles around a plain but graceful Romanesque church belonging to the abbey founded in the 5C by St Romanus and handed over to the monks of Cluny in the 10C.
The abbey controlled 7 priories, 20 parish churches, 30 villages and 50 fiefs.

★ **Church** – You will reach it by passing under the fortified gateway of the former monastery.
Replacing two chapels of the 5 and 7C (the plan is shown on the floor in the nave), the church was built of fine, pale Jura stone in the 11C and was later modified. Its design was directly inspired by that of the former abbey church of Cluny, St-Pierre-le-Vieux, which preceded the great building erected in the 12C; the plan, elevation and decoration based on Lombard bands and arcading are, therefore, typically Burgundian. The transept, dominated by a central tower, and the nave date from the 11C. A large, early 12C narthex is preceded by a 13C Gothic porch. Inside, the groin-vaulted two-storey narthex contains 13C murals. In the nave 13C pointed arches have replaced the original timboring, but the aisles still have their semicircular vaulting. The transept crossing is roofed with a dome supported on squinches. The chancel and apsidal chapels were modified in the 14 and 15C. The chancel contains priors' tombs and an ambo (a sort of pulpit) of the 7C. The church has been Protestant since 1536. A magnificent lime tree grows behind the east end of the church.
50m to the right of the façade stands the former prior's house (now a tea room) dated 1605 – but going back to the 13C – with a pepperpot-roofed turret and an embossed doorway.

ROMONT Fribourg   Pop 4 098

Michelin map **217** fold 4 or **427** fold 12 – Alt 760m – 2 736ft

The little town of Romont was built by Peter II of Savoy in the 13C. It is still encircled by some of its ramparts and it occupies a picturesque **site**★ on a crest overlooking the Valleys of the Glâne and the Glâney.

Our Lady of the Assumption (Collégiale Notre-Dame-de-l'Assomption) – This is one of the finest Gothic churches in Romansh country. The original building dated from the 13C, but it was largely destroyed in 1434. It was immediately rebuilt and displays two aspects of the Gothic style (13 and 15C). The 15C **chancel**★ is closed by a grille and adorned with carved stalls and panelling of the same period.
The church is lit by fine 14 and 15C stained-glass windows, one of which is an Annunciation and an Assumption of Burgundian origin.
A bronze group of the Assumption, dating from 1955, dominates the modern high altar. A series of modern windows by the painter Cingria depicts the Twelve Apostles, another by the French master of stained-glass windows, Sergio de Castro, depicts characters from the Old Testament.
Before leaving, note the Romanesque Virgin and Child which adorns the altar in one of the chapels on the left.

Castle – The castle dates from the 13C as can be seen from the keep of Peter II of Savoy, but has been remodelled several times. The main gateway (16C) is surmounted by several coats of arms of Fribourg and Romont.
Since 1981, the castle houses the **Swiss Museum of Stained Glass** ⊙. This collection includes medieval stained glass and Swiss heraldic glass as well as works by non-Swiss glassmakers. The works date from the early 20C, signifying the renaissance of stained glass. An audio-visual presentation recounts the making of stained glass and its history through the centuries. Temporary exhibits consist of works of art from all over the world.

The highway code states that on difficult mountain roads the ascending vehicle has priority.
On "postal" roads drivers must comply with the directions of the drivers of the post bus service.

RORSCHACH St. Gallen   Pop 9535

Michelin map 216 folds 10 and 11 or 427 fold 7 – Alt 398m – 1312ft – Facilities

Rorschach stands on the Swiss shore of Lake Constance. It is an important transit and business centre which was kept busy as the "maritime" outlet of the St Gallen area. Today the port is also a good centre for pleasure boating and trips on the lake. In the main street (Hauptstrasse) are several houses with carved and painted oriel windows.

Local Museum (Heimatmuseum) ⊙ – The museum is housed in an old granary (Kornhaus) near the lake. It contains prehistory, natural history and popular art collections. There are also reconstructed lake dwellings, dioramas of animals, and models (one of which is of Rorschach – 1797). The lace room with its loom illustrates the main occupation of the district.

RUTLI Uri Lake

Michelin map 218 fold 1 – Local map see Lake LUCERNE
Access by boat leaving from Brunnen.

The Rütli or Grütli prairie dominating Uri Lake symbolises the foundation of the Swiss Confederation and proudly carries the Swiss banner. It was indeed on this land that, on 1 August 1291, Walter Fürst, Werner Stauffacher and Arnold von Melchtal, representing respectively the Valleys of Uri, Schwyz and Unterwalden, met to conclude a permanent alliance; they were accompanied by William Tell, as required local tradition *(p 144)*. Before becoming an important place of pilgrimage for patriots, this historic location was used as a meeting-point for military leaders in the event of a serious crisis. In July 1940, under the threat of the German troops, General Guisan, Commander-in-Chief of the Swiss Army, summoned several hundred officers to the prairie.
To celebrate the 700th anniversary of the Swiss Confederation, a pedestrian footpath of around 35km – 22 miles has been laid out, leaving from Rütli and circling Lake Uri. Known as the **Swiss Way**, this route is divided into as many sections as there are cantons and half-cantons (26 altogether), separated by milestones. The length of these sections was established on the basis of each canton's population. The Swiss Way ends on the Place des Suisses de l'Etranger in Brunnen, on the edge of the lake. All along the circuit, you may admire a succession of commemorative spots and natural sites of great beauty.

★ SAANEN Berne   Pop 6090

Michelin map 217 fold 15 or 427 fold 13 – Local map see VAUD ALPS – Alt 1010m – 3312ft – Facilities

Lying at the point where the road from Lausanne to Interlaken (via Bulle or the Mosses Pass) leaves the Sarine Valley (Saane in German) to reach the Saanenmöser shelf and from there the Simme Valley, Saanen enjoys very favourable conditions in which to display its old-fashioned character. There is indeed an intriguing contrast between this quiet, picturesque township and its brilliant but impersonal neighbour, Gstaad. It retains a certain independence in winter through its all-embracing winter sports facilities (chairlift: Kalberhöni-Vorder Eggli).

★**Wooden houses** – The houses along the road through the town have weather-browned gables covered in the Bernese Oberland style *(illustration p 30)* by huge overhanging roofs. The oldest buildings date from the 16C *(read the inscriptions)*.

Church – Its sturdy tower is visible afar. Inside, the chancel is decorated with a series of 15C **mural paintings★** representing scenes from the Bible and episodes from the life of the Virgin and the martyrdom of St Maurice *(light switch below the pulpit)*.

★★ SAAS-FEE Valais   Pop 1242

Michelin map 219 fold 4 and 5 or 427 fold 23 – Local map see VALAIS – Alt 1790m – 5873ft – Facilities

Nicknamed the "Pearl of the Alps", Saas-Fee, which in the past was a Valais village, is now an attractive resort perched up in the mountains. It enjoys a magnificent **setting★★★** offering to the newcomer sudden and dazzling contact with mountains over 4000m – 13123ft high.
Combustion engines are forbidden *(peripheral car parks – fee)*; electric vehicles are used. The resort was officially opened in the 19C. One of its founders was the abbot Johann Joseph (1806-1869), whose statue proudly adorns the church square.
The view you embrace ranges from the icy dome of the Allalinhorn to the rocky group of the Mischabel (highest point: the Dom – alt 4545m – 14941ft – recognizable by its forked peak), it is caught by the flattened snow-capped Alphubel Summit, and then traces the course of the huge Fee Glacier (Feegletscher), which eventually divides into two tongues around the rocky promontory of the Längfluh.
Saas-Fee is a well-known mountaineering centre. For the sports enthusiast who likes ski-touring it has become the terminal of the famous **High route** (Haute Route) (Chamonix – Saas-Fee or more often Verbier – Saas-Fee).

View of Saas-Fee

Degonda/O.VS.T

In winter for downhill skiing, the cable-cars of Plattjen and Längfluh serve the area; the Feldskinn cable-car works in summer and since 1984 an underground funicular to Mittelallalin (alt 3 500m − 11 483ft).

Saas Museum (Saaser Museum) ⊘ − This former thermal establishment (1732) houses a museum devoted to regional folklore. Domestic and Alpine activities are brought to life by reconstructed interiors, farming implements, local costume and headgear, and a collection of liturgical objects. Special attention is paid to the development of the spa: the growing expansion of tourism, accommodation, climbing, winter sports and the introduction of new, sophisticated equipment (compare a 1906 ski with one belonging to the Swiss champion Pirmin Zurbriggen). One of the rooms presents personal mementoes of the writer Carl Zuckmayer, a one-time resident of the city of Saas.

SACHSELN Obwalden   Pop 3 819

Michelin map **217** fold 9 or **427** fold 14 − 3km − 2 miles south of Sarnen − Alt 472m − 1 549ft

The town of Sachseln is prettily situated on the shore of Lake Sarnen − and with the sacred soil of the Ranft forms a moving place of pilgrimage. Swiss Catholics affirm their attachment to their faith and their patriotic fervour by coming here to pray to St Nicholas of Flüe.

Church − The great baroque building, supported by columns of black Melchtal marble, enshrines the relics of **St Nicholas of Flüe** on a special altar at the entrance to the chancel. The remains are enclosed in a large, embossed recumbent figure (1934).

Go around the building to reach, at the foot of the detached Romanesque bell tower, the funeral chapel, where the faithful come to meditate before the tombstone, which was carved in 1518 with the effigy of the saint. Below is the worn step of the original sepulchre.

EXCURSION

From Sachseln to Ranft − *3km − 2 miles − plus 1 1/2 hours walk and visit. Leave Sachseln eastwards on the Flüeli road (uphill behind the church). Leave the car at the car park on the central esplanade of Flüeli.*

Flüeli − The rustic character of this hamlet, where Brother Nicholas led the life of a mountain patriarch surrounded by his numerous family, has been preserved. The chapel (1618) can be seen on its mound from far off; it is reached by stairs and an esplanade.

From the terrace there is a pleasant, open view of the Valley of Sarsen, Lake Sarnen and Pilatus on one side and the deep cleft leading into the Melchtal on the other. Besides this sanctuary, pilgrims still visit the birthplace (the oldest wooden house − 14C − in Switzerland) and the family home of Nicholas.

★ **Ranft** – *Approaches are marked on leaving Flüeli.* By a steep descent (ramp or stairs) towards the floor of the Melchaa Valley you will first reach the hermitage-chapel. The church dating from the 17C is decorated with painted panels *(follow the order of numbering)* recalling the life of the recluse; outstanding is a fine Gothic **Christ**★ taken from former Sachseln church.
The cell nearby – where the hermit could not stand upright – was built in 1468 by his fellow-citizens (of Obwalden).
Below, another chapel was built in the 16C on the spot where the Virgin appeared to Nicholas.

On returning from Flüeli, motorists who are bound for Lucerne will take the fork to the right towards Kerns; they will then cross the Melchaa on the **Hohe Brücke**★. This covered bridge was thrown across the torrent at a height of 100m – 329ft in 1943 by Swiss Army Engineers.

SACHSELN ROAD

Michelin map ▨▨ fold 17 and ▨▨ folds 8 and 9 or ▨▨ fold 14

This pleasant route, lined with lovely lakes, offers a hilly road (to **Brünig Pass**) and an excursion to the famous Pilatus Mountain.

FROM LUCERNE TO BRIENZ

98km – 60 miles – 2 1/2 hours

★★★ **Lucerne** – *Time: 3 hours. See Lucerne.*

> *To get out of Lucerne quickly you should take the Stans motorway, the first of its kind to be built in Switzerland. Turn off at the exit "Hergiswil". The next section, as far as Alpnachstad, runs along the lake shore.*

The bends in this road offer views from many different angles of the Rigi Massif, the wooded spurs of the Bürgenstock and the isolated Stanserhorn Summit.

> *The trip by rack-railway from Alpnachstad to Pilatus is recommended.*

★★★ **Pilatus** – *From Alpnachstad, about 2 hours Rtn, including 1 1/4 hours by rack-railway. Access and description see Pilatus.*
The road crosses Sarsen (facilities) and skirts the lake of the same name.

Sachseln – *See Sachseln.*

> *Turn right when you reach Giswil.*

Sörenberg – The road, while climbing up in hairpin bends to the **Glaubenbüelen Pass,** offers lovely views of Sarnen Lake and the surrounding countryside.
At the pass you discover the snowy basin of **Brienzer Rothorn***(qv).* The road then descends amidst fir trees, passes the base of the Brienze Rothorn (on the left is the cable-car station to the mountaintop) and continues on to Sörenberg, a ski resort located in a mountainous cirque.

> *Return to Giswil.*

Between Giswil and Kaiserstuhl, you will get a good distant view of the Pilatus ridges rising above the shallow depression, dotted with farms and clumps of trees, partly submerged by Lake Sarnen. Upstream and in the far distance, the three snowy peaks of the Wetterhorn group appear through the Brünig Gap.
From **Lungern** (facilities) to the Brünig Pass, there are pretty glimpses between the fir trees and maples of Lake Lungern (Lungernsee), with its curving shores. On the Bernese side of the pass the gradient becomes very steep but the excellent layout of the road and its easy bends will enable you to enjoy a wide **panorama**★ of the cleft of the Aare, hollowed out by former glaciers between the terraces of the **Hasliberg** (facilities) and the Schwarzhorn foothills, from which the Wandelbach and Oltschibach cascades pour down.
You may halt at the point where the road is cut through the rock before tackling the last stage to Brienz.

★ **Brienz** – *See Brienz.*

SAILLON Valais   Pop 1 169

Michelin map ▨▨ south of fold 15 or ▨▨ fold 21 – Local map see VALAIS – Alt 522m – 1 713ft

Saillon was formerly a bridgehead and a strategic position of great importance before the Rhône changed its course in this part of central Valais.
The old fortified city within its rampart ruins stands on a rocky outcrop in a picturesque **site.**
An attractive group is formed by impressive ruins of the castle, the grey roofs of the old town nestling under the ramparts and the church which is built on a terrace and has a Romanesque belfry surmounted by a stone pyramid.

★ **View** – From the village, a steep path leads, in a few minutes, to the foot of the great tower of the castle – a former keep – from which you can overlook the village and the church, the terraced vineyards on the slopes and the alluvial plain with its orchards. The Pennine Alps can be seen like a massive wall in the distance.

★ ST-CERGUE Vaud

Pop 1332

Michelin map **217** northeast of fold 11 or **427** fold 11 – Local map see Swiss JURA – Alt 1044m – 3480ft – Facilities

A high-altitude resort in the Jura long known both to the Genevese and to the French for its bracing mountain climate, St-Cergue stands at the point where the corridor of the Girvine Pass debouches within sight of the Mont Blanc Massif and Lake Geneva. There are many belvederes near the resort from which there are good views of the forest-clad foreground and the "giant of the Alps" and its retinue.
Those interested in botanical phenomena should go to the Borsattaz meadow, where giant pine trees, known locally as *gogants,* grow; they are only to be found in the Jura.
You reach the meadow from the Lausanne road; after 1.5km – 1 mile turn left into a tarred road ("Route de la Prangine et du Plumet"); 1.5km – 1 mile farther bear right at the "Carrefour des Fruitières".
St-Cergue offers more than 50km – 31 miles of trails for cross-country skiing and a variety of training grounds and fairly difficult ski-runs for downhill skiing.

★★**Old Castle Belvedere (Belvédère du Vieux Château)** – *1/2 hour on foot Rtn by a path signposted "Le Vieux Château".* Splendid view of Lake Geneva and Mont Blanc.

EXCURSION

★★★**Dôle** – Alt 1677 – 550ft. *21km – 15 miles – about 2 1/2 hours. Leave St-Cergue by the road to Nyon, turn right and drive on until you reach Gingins. Then take the road to Dôle and La Barillette.*
Leave the car at the foot of Dôle and continue on foot. Follow the path on the left, marked out in yellow. It leads to the summit, where a navigation beacon and radar station have been constructed.
A vast **panorama**★★★ extends over the Alps right up to the peaks of the Valais (Matterhorm) and the Oisans (Meije). Between towers Mont Blanc with Lake Geneva in the foreground. Looking right round, you can see the Jura including Mount Tendre and the Chasseron on one side and the Valserine as far as the Reculet, on the other.

★★ ST. GALLEN Ⓒ

Pop 75327

Michelin map **216** fold 21 or **427** fold 7 – Local map see APPENZELL DISTRICT – Alt 668m – 2201ft – Town plan in the current Michelin Red Guide Switzerland.

An abbey, founded in 720 on the spot where **Gallus** (companion of the Irish monk Columban) died, established the fortunes of St Gallen. The town spreads over the nearby hills, which are scattered with huge blocks of buildings such as the St. Gallen Graduate School of Economics, Business and Public Administration (Hochschule für Wirtschafts und Sozialwissenschaften), decorated by many artists of the sixties.

The abbey's golden age – By the 8C the abbey had become an important Benedictine monastery thanks to St Otmar.
In the 10C it enjoyed extraordinary intellectual influence and its fame spread throughout western Europe. The monastery buildings proving too small with the passing years, from the 9C onwards a larger edifice was planned as shown by the Carolingian plan of the monastery (now in the abbey library).

The cathedral chancel

Vadian and the Reformation – Joachim von Watt – known under the scholastic name of **Vadian** – a doctor, a humanist and mayor of the town, introduced the Reformation to St. Gallen en 1524, thus striking a deadly blow to the abbey.

From that time, following the split brought about by the Reformation, the abbey experienced many upheavals. It was only in the middle of the 18C that is resumed its expansion with the building of the abbey church and the library. The abbey was secularized in 1805 and in 1846 it became the seat of a bishopric.

Cradle of the Swiss textile industry – As long ago as the Middle Ages, workrooms in the monastery and in the town wove linen; the fabric acquired a great reputation. Later, fine cotton fabrics and embroideries gained the upper hand and supplied an important industry all over the canton.

St. Gallen, through its creative skill, is today the centre of the Swiss cotton and embroidery industry. The best items are exported to the industrialized countries.

SIGHTS

Former Abbey – From the Klosterhof (monastery courtyard) there is a fine general view of the former Benedictine abbey. The abbey buildings are attached to the cathedral; they now house the bishop's residence, the famous abbey library, the Cantonal Government and several schools. With Einsiedeln *(qv)* it is the most important baroque structure in Switzerland

★★ **Cathedral** (Kathedrale) – This was built from 1755-68 on the site of a 14C Gothic edifice. Two elegant towers crowned with domed belfries flank the east face which has on its pediment a low relief depicting the Coronation of the Virgin, a 1933 replica of the original work by Joseph Anton Feuchtmayer.

The exterior is plain, forming a surprising contrast with the interior, which is a triumph of the last period of expression of the baroque style. The harmony of the building, a masterpiece of the **Vorarlberg** school, depends on the main dome over a rotunda in the exact centre of the great structure. From the rotunda the chancel and the nave extend east and west.

The decoration is rich but not vulgar. The casein paintings on a blue ground adorning the central dome *(The Eight Beatitudes)* are by the painter Joseph Wannenmacher. Other mural paintings decorate the nave and the chancel. The very fine stucco mouldings were done by Christian Wenzinger.

The **chancel** ★★★ is altogether remarkable. It is enclosed by admirable grilles and adorned with a high altar executed in the Empire style in 1810. The great stalls, of rare delicacy, and the confessionals form a remarkable whole.

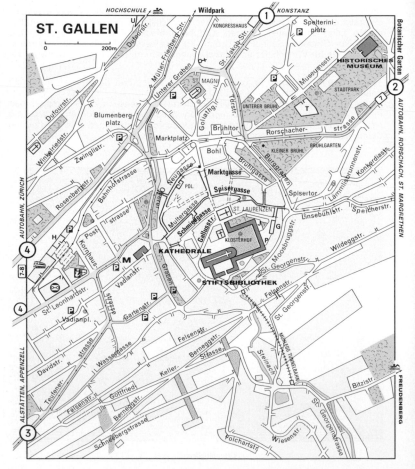

★★★**Abbey Library** (Stiftsbibliothek) ⊙ – When the abbey was secularized in 1805 the library fortunately remained in use as such. Its valuable collections, displayed in admirable surroundings, include about 100 000 volumes, some of the rarest of which are 2 000 St. Gallen manuscripts mostly dating from the early and later Middle Ages (8-12C). There are also 1 650 early printed books (pre-1500). Apart from these works there are a number of illuminated manuscripts of the 15 and 16C, bearing witness to the colourful art of the Renaissance.

The main hall of the library, considered to be the finest rococo room, was built during the same period as the cathedral (1758-67) and by the same architects. Its lines are wonderfully graceful and harmonious.

Dazzled by such magnificence, the visitor hardly knows what to admire most: the parquet floor, inlaid with stars in alternating light and dark wood, the rich woodwork adorned with columns with gilded capitals, the painted ceilings with their many human figures or the monochrome (grisaille) paintings above the eight-storey gallery.

★**Old Town** – Not far from the cathedral is a picturesque quarter which used to lie within the ramparts. Here are many 16 and 18C houses, sometimes with painted façades, often adorned with wrought-iron signs and carved and painted wood oriel windows.

The tourist will find it pleasant to stroll along the streets. Among the most typical are the **Spisergasse★**, the **Gallusstrasse** ("Zum Greif" house★), the **Schmiedgasse** ("Zum Pelikan" house★) and the **Marktgasse**.

Textile Museum (Textilmuseum) ⊙ – The museum contains the most complete collection of needlework throughout the ages, the **Iklé and Jacoby Collection★★** from countries all over the world. Admire the many specimens of lace and embroidery as well as the various kinds of fabrics.

★**Historical Museum** (Historisches Museum) ⊙ This museum contains important exhibits on the history and monuments of St. Gallen. Special attention should be paid to the reconstruction of the abbey as it was in the 9C and that of the town in 1642, as well as to tapestries, local costumes, coins and porcelain. There are also ethnological collections (Asia, Africa and South America).

Botanical Gardens (Botanischer Garten) ⊙ – In the suburb of Neudorf; via ② and then bear left on the Stephanshornstrasse.

These gardens (1.5ha – 3 1/2 acres) which serve as a scientific observation centre, are also of interest to the tourist because of the variety and unusual aspect of the species exhibited. Stroll along the paths lined with tropical or Alpine flora, originating from each of the continents (rhubarb from Chile – note its incredibly large leaves) or rest beside the pergola set near the pool where rushes and reeds grow or visit the two tropical greenhouses with cacti, palm trees, orchids...

EXCURSIONS

★**Freudenberg** – Alt 884m – 2 900ft. 2.5km – 2 miles. Leave St Gallen by the Bitzistrasse (southeast of the plan). A pleasant road among the pines will then take you to the Freudenberg Summit.

The belvedere affords an almost circular panorama of St Gallen, the surrounding hills towards Lake Constance (Bodensee) and the Alpstein Massif (Säntis).

"Peter and Paul" Wildlife Park (Wildpark) – 3.5km – 3 miles. Leave St Gallen by the Müller-Friedbergstrasse (north on the plan). A pleasant zoological park (deer, chamois, ibex) in an open setting. At the entrance to the park, by following a little path to the right along the boundary fence for a few steps, you will get a fine **view★** of the site of St Gallen and the Alpstein Range beyond it.

★ ST. GOTTHARD MASSIF

Michelin map **217** folds 9, 10, 19 and 20 and **218** folds 1, 2, 11 and 12 or **427** fold 15

This is the kernel of the Swiss Alps and the watershed which supplies the two longest rivers in western Europe. In the St. Gotthard Massif the two greatest longitudinal valleys, the Rhône and Rhine, and the two greatest transverse valleys, the Reuss and Ticino, of the Swiss Confederation converge at Andermatt. For the traveller, the name of St. Gotthard calls to mind a road and a series of walled-in sites rather than a grand mountain landscape. Here the summits are massive, and surprisingly, rise to a uniform height – they vary around 3 000m – 9 843ft.

St. Gotthard road – In spite of its reputation, this is far from being the oldest route in the Alps, for traffic along it could be developed only after the 13C when the terrible Schöllenen Gorges had been forced. It was, however, a vital artery for Switzerland. Without the St. Gotthard road the Forest Cantons (p 144), and especially the canton of Uri, which held the keys to this coveted highway, would have had more difficulty in winning their emancipation from the emperor and from the Habsburgs.

Today, by road or rail, the St. Gotthard is a first-class route for communications between German-speaking central Switzerland and Italian Switzerland, as well as an international highway.

Other roads in the massif – The Oberalp, Lukmanier and Furka roads (pp 81, 205 and 94) complete the network for circular tours, starting from Andermatt.

TOUR

Recommended itineraries – Organized according to time (longest to shortest) needed.

★ 1 **Lukmanier Pass Road** – From Biasca to Disentis/Mustér – about 2 1/2 hours. *See Ticino Alps.*

★ 2 **St. Gotthard Pass Road** – From Andermatt to Biasca – 2 hours. *See Ticino Alps.*

★★ 3 **Nufenen Pass Road** – From Airolo to Ulrichen – 1 1/2 hours. *See Nufenen Pass Road.*

4 **Schöllenen Road** – From Altdorf to Andermatt – 1 1/2 hours. *See Schöllenen Road.*

★ 5 **Oberalp Pass Road** – From Disentis/Mustér to Andermatt – about 1 hour. *See Disentis/Mustér.*

★ **ST-MAURICE** Valais   Pop 3 731

Michelin map **217** fold 14 or **427** folds 12 and 21 – Alt 422m – 1 384ft

The little town of St-Maurice, dominated to the west by the Dents du Midi and to the east by the Dent de Morcles, occupies a picturesque site★.

Agaune (from the celtic name acauno, meaning a rock) was the chief village of the Nantuates tribe. After the Roman conquest it became the capital of the present Valais under the Emperor Augustus.

The field of martyrs – At the end of the 3C a legion recruited in Africa – the Theban Legion, commanded by the Primicerius **Maurice** – was massacred near the town for having refused to worship the gods of Rome. In the following century a community took charge of the martyrs' tombs.

The foundation of the Abbey of St-Maurice by King Sigismund of Burgundy in 515 was due to the desire to perpetuate the memory of Maurice and his comrades. The abbey was richly endowed from the start and it attracted many of the faithful throughout the Middle Ages. In the 9C the town took the name of its illustrious patron saint. In 1125 it welcomed the regular Canons of the Order of St Augustine and on 22 September every year it still celebrates the memory of its martyrs with fervour. In the course of centuries the abbey changed and grew; gradually a rich treasure, formed from the gifts of pilgrims and Christian princes, was amassed. St-Maurice became one of the holy places of Christianity.

SIGHTS

Abbey Church (Église Abbatiale) – The fine **belfry**★ is 11C, the stone spire 13C, although the church itself dates only from the beginning of the 17C and has been restored (since 1949). The nave is plain. A Carolingian pulpit has been reinstalled in the outer chancel, recently restored. The chancel itself is large and adorned with fine stalls. On the altar there is a fine mosaic by Maurice Denis.

★★**Treasury** ⊘ – This is one of the richest ecclesiastical treasuries in the Christian world. Its excellent arrangement displays exceptional pieces of goldsmiths' work. Among the oldest pieces, pay special attention to a sardonyx vase decorated with scenes from Greek mythology, the Merovingian casket of Theodoric made of gold encrusted with pearls and cameos, the golden 9C ewer, said to be Charlemagne's, whose enamelwork seems to derive from the purest Oriental technique, and the reliquary of St Maurice, whose decoratives features – Christ the King, the Virgin, Angels and Apostles – probably came from an embossed and gilded altarpiece of the 12C (the medallions on the roof of the reliquary depict the story of original sin in six scenes). Two other reliquaries of the 12 and 13C, the reliquary-bust of St Candid depicted with a noble look (on the plinth, his martyrdom by beheading) and the reliquary-monstrance given by St Louis complete the priceless collection.

Martolet Excavations ⊘ – Near the belfry, at the foot of the rock overlooking the abbey, excavations have recently uncovered the foundations of the buildings that preceded the present church from the 4C onward; their plan stands out clearly. You may also see traces of a baptistery and graceful modern cloisters in the Romanesque style. It is possible to visit the catacombs, narrow underground galleries leading to the crypt and tomb of St Maurice.

Castle ⊘ – Overlooking the Rhône and niched against the forested eastern slopes of the Dents du Midi, this small castle dates from the early 16C. The square keep and bastions were added in the 18C and now house the **Cantonal Military History Museum.** On display are banners, medals, arms and uniforms. The section on the second floor includes models of the fortifications built along the Swiss borders during both World Wars. The dungeons house heavy artillery from the Second World War while anti-aircraft guns occupy the courtyards of the bastions. On the ground floor the elegantly furnished reception room is typical of the 18C.

Fairies' Grotto (Grotte aux fées) ⊘ – *Reached by a steep uphill path starting from the level of the castle and the bridge over the Rhône at the north entrance to the town.*
This grotto is formed by a natural gallery about 900m – 2/3 mile long leading to an underground lake and waterfall.
From the terrace of the nearby restaurant there is a fine **view**★ of the site of St-Maurice and the Dent de Morcles.

★★★ **ST. MORITZ** Graubünden (Grisons)   Pop 5 426

Michelin map ⑱ fold 15 or ㊷ fold 17 – Local map see GRISONS – Alt 1 856m – 6 089ft – Facilities – Town plan in the current Michelin Red Guide Switzerland

Living under the sign of the sun, St. Moritz (in Romansh, San Murezzan) with its twin resorts, is the most famous Swiss ski resort.
St. Moritz-Dorf, which has the world's oldest ski school (1927), is grouped half-way up the slope at the foot of a leaning campanile (Schiefer Turm), the only vestige of the original village.
St. Moritz-Bad is the spa quarter, whose extensive installations spread over the flat floor of the Inn Valley. The curative qualities of the waters rich in iron (for rheumatological, neurological, gynaecological, cardiological, etc... disorders) of St. Moritz have been used since the Bronze Age.

View of St. Moritz

SIGHTS

★**Engadine Museum** (Engadiner Museum) ⊙ – This visit is a useful preliminary to an excursion through the villages of the Engadine. With its arcaded gallery, its windows with outer embrasures, its oriel windows and its sgraffito *(qv)* the building itself is a reconstitution of local styles. A Sulèr *(qv)* leads to the rooms with their collections of furniture, mostly brought from lordly or peasant homes and decorated with carved pine woodwork. The stoves will interest experts in porcelain.

The **Engadine Room No II** (Zuoz house) has an elegant ceiling with beams. **State Room No IX** (the Visconti-Venosta house at Grosio) is the most luxurious. **State Room No VII** (a nobleman's house at Marca de Mesocco) is simple and comfortable but has more character.

Segantini Museum ⊙ – This rotunda contains several works by the painter Giovanni-Segantini (1858-99), who is very popular in Switzerland, especially the symbolic **trilogy**★ *To Be – To Pass – To Become,* where details of the upper mountain landscape are illustrated.

★★**Piz Nair** ⊙ – Alt 3057m – 10029ft. *About 3/4 hour, including 1/2 hour by funicular to Corviglia and then by cable-car, and 1/4 hour on foot Rtn.*
From the terrace of the upper cable-car station you can look down on the Upper Engadine and its lakes. Then go on foot to the highest point to enjoy the circular **panorama**★★ embracing the Bernina Summits.

★JULIER AND ALBULA PASS ROADS

Round tour starting from St Moritz

96km – 59 1/2 miles about 5 hours – Itinerary ③ *of the Grisons local map*

> *Leave St Moritz to the south.*

In the bends of the uphill road after Silvaplana lie, surprisingly near the Lakes of Silvaplana and Champfèr. As the road climbs to the pass and, on entering a bend on the right, a **panorama**★★ opens out over the Upper Engadine.
It extends from the mountains overlooking Zernez on the left to the Piz de la Margna on the right, taking in (from left to right), the Piz Vadret – Piz Muragl group, dominating Pontresina, the Piz Rosatsch and the Piz Corvatsch, between which the marked depression of the Fuorcla Surlej reveals the snowy Piz Bernina Summit (alt 4049m – 13284ft) in the middle distance.

Julier Pass – Alt 2284m – 7493ft. The Latin and imperial ring of this name is enough to attract an archaeologist's attention. Two pylons, set up like milestones on either side of the road, are parts of a single column from a "shrine to the pass" built by the Romans. It may have served as the plinth of a statue (as the Joux column at the Little St. Bernard).
The road down from the pass loses 500m – 1640ft altitude in 9km – 5 1/2 miles. The valley grows more and more desolate but near the chalets of Mot a flourishing Arolla pine with a very straight trunk stands all alone.
Etymologically, the name **Bivio** means fork. Here the Septimer road, quite disused today, branches off from the Julier road at the entrance to the village, turning into a path running southwards, reaching the Septimerpass (alt 2310m – 7788ft) before joining Bregaglia Valley at the village of Casaccia.

Marmorera Dam ⊙ – This work, which has drowned the hamlets of Cresta and Marmorera, is unusual for having been built of earth. Over 2.7 million m³ – 95 million cu ft – of material has been used to make a dam 400m long, 90m high and 400m thick at the base – 1312ft x 230ft x 1312ft.
The essential purpose of the water storage of 60 million m³ – 13200 million gallons is to feed all the hydro-electric power stations on the Julia and the Albula during the winter period of low water. The town of Zürich financed the works.
The new reservoir blends well with the austere landscape.
During the winding descent, after the dam, three torrents, impressively full at the melting of the snows – especially the Ava de Faller – are crossed within 1km – 1/2 mile.

Savognin – Facilities. Lovers of religious art may drive to the Church of St Martin, at the forest edge on the last slopes of the Piz Arlos (leave the Julier road near the post office to go down into the valley, and after crossing the Julia on a hump-backed bridge take the second road to the right).
This small, isolated church, the tallest of the three in the village, is distinguished by its classical pediment and the dazzling whiteness of its walls. The crowning dome was decorated inside by the Milanese painter, Carlo Nuvolone (1681). The various celestial hosts are arranged in concentric circles, as though in galleries, around the Holy Trinity and the Virgin, with a surprising effect of perspective.
Below the village of Riom, on the valley's other side the ruined walls of the old bishop's Castle of Raetia Ampla appear on a mound. The exit from Oberhalbstein takes you through the short defile of the Crap Ses.

Tiefencastel – This little town lies on the floor of the Albula Valley at the point where the main road, from Chur to the Engadine by the Julier Pass, goes through the gap. The profile of its church, southern in style, will be remembered by the traveller coming down from Lenzerheide as the first evidence of Romansh civilization *(see Gruyères)*. Between Tiefencastel and Bergün, the Albula Valley becomes more densely forested (fir trees, larches and Arolla pines) and unin-habited with Alvaneu and its sulphur spings on the left. It then becomes narrower and more steeply walled-in until the road is obliged to cut through rock in the **Bergüner Stein Defile**★.

Bergün – Facilities. This village, which is overshadowed by the triangular face of the Piz Rugnux, a spur of the Piz Ela, of which you get repeated glimpses, has several Engadine-style houses with oriel windows *(illustration p 29)* and window grilles, which are more rustic than those of the Inn Valley.

From Bergün to Preda, while the road climbs steeply through mossy woods and fields, you will see the extraordinary contortions (loops and spiral tunnels) imposed upon the railway to gain height.

Arrival at the level of Preda is marked by an opening-out of the mountainous horizon. The rocky Igls Dschimels Peaks and the Piz da las Blais are impressive. Between Preda and the pass, there are pleasant pastures as far as the little green Palpuogna Lake. Higher up, beyond the Crap Alv, the road rises among rocky ledges as it skirts a marshy plateau, where numerous small cascades indicate one of the sources of the Albula. You then reach the grassy coomb marking the pass.

Albula Pass – Alt 2 312m – 7 585ft. *The pass is usually blocked by snow from November to June. You can use the rail-car service leaving from Tiefencastel for Samedan.*

The pass divides the Albula Basin to the north, a tributary of the Rhine from the Val d'Alvra, to the south, a tributary of the Inn. Between this and La Punt, where clumps of larches reappear, you will get a quick glimpse, on the floor of the Inn Valley, of the nearby villages of La Punt and Chamues-ch., watched over by the ruins of Guardaval. From La Punt to Samedan follow the flat floor of the Inn Valley until the peaks of the Bernina Massif appear through the Pontresina Gap.

★**Samedan** – *See Samedan.*

★**Celerina** – *See Celerina.*

From Celerina the road returns to St Moritz.

★ ST-PIERRE-DE-CLAGES Valais

Michelin map **217** fold 15 or **427** fold 21 – between Ardon and Riddes – Alt 526m – 1 729ft

This village has a Romanesque **church**★ which one belonged to a Benedictine priory. The small 11-12C building shows fine unity of style. You must stand behind the east end to see the building at its best, with its apsidals decorated with a pilaster strip and its two-storey octagonal tower surmounting the transept crossing. The nave is very dark, with ribbed vaulting supported by massive pillars. The transept does not project and is marked only by a widening of the last bay before the chancel.

★ ST URBAN Lucerne

Michelin map **216** fold 16 or **427** fold 5 5km – 3 miles – northeast of Langenthal

The tourist will be surprised by the imposing mass of the former Cistercian Abbey of St Urban. The buildings are at present occupied by a psychiatric clinic.

★**Church (Klosterkirche)** ☉ – This is a fine specimen of the baroque style, built in the early 18C. The façade, plain and unusually broad, is flanked by two tall, symmetrical towers detached from the body of the church. The well-proportioned nave is lit by high windows underneath which runs a gallery with balustrades. The stucco decoration, with some gilding, is not overloaded – the capitals have carved acanthus leaves. The chancel, enclosed by a fine **grille**★, is adorned with magnificent carved 18C **stalls**★★.

★ ST-URSANNE Jura   Pop 918

Michelin map **216** fold 13 and 14 or **427** fold 3 – Local map p 117 – Alt 494m – 1 621t

Lying away from the main roads deep in the Doubs Valley, St-Ursanne, a little old town which has remained unchanged since the beginning of the 19C, makes a charming place to stop when crossing the Swiss Jura *(qv)*. It originated with the hermitage that Ursicinus, a disciple of Columban, set up in the 7C.

You enter the town through fortified gates surmounted by a bear carrying the symbolic crosier of the prince-bishops of Basle. An agreeable scene is presented of fountains and houses, flanked by turrets, with great brown, pointed roofs, adorned with wrought-iron signs.

★**View from the bridge** – From this picturesque structure, guarded by a statue of St John Nepomucene, the patron saint of bridges, there is a well-composed picture of the fortified gate, framed in the façades with overhanging wooden balconies of the riverside houses, the roofs of the town dominated by the church tower, the slopes of the valley and, on the crest, the scant ruins of a 14C castle.

Collegiate Church – The building has a sober look (restored). The east end and the apse are Romanesque and comprise a fine, single-arched **doorway**★ adorned with statues of the Virgin and St Ursicinus. It has a pretty tympanum and capitals. Inside, the Romanesque chancel contains a baroque canopied altar; the crypt is also Romanesque whereas the nave is early Gothic (13C). The church has large Gothic cloisters on its north side as well as a lapidary museum containing 7 to 9C sarcophagi.

★ **STE-CROIX-LES-RASSES** Vaud   Pop 4 321

Michelin map 🔲 fold 3 or 🔲 fold 11 – Local map see Swiss JURA – Alt 1 069m – 3 507ft – Facilities

The twin townships of Ste-Croix and Les Rasses lie on a sunny shoulder of the Chasseron, facing the Alps.
They deserve a special place among Swiss Jura resorts for their commanding situation and their excellent tourist organisation.
In winter Ste-Croix-les-Rasses is recommended for the novice or medium skier who wants to enjoy himself rather than to break records. Where cross-country skiing – the speciality of the Jura – is concerned, the resort offers more than 80km – 50 miles of marked trails.

The village of sound – The history of Ste-Croix since the mid-19C is a good example of the adaptability of Swiss industry to international economic changes. About 1850, like most of the small towns in the Jura, the village was making watches. The establishment in the United States of great watch and clock-making factories with perfected machine tools caused a grave crisis at Ste-Croix, which turned to the musical-box industry. But when Edison developed the phonograph, the public lost interest in little musical boxes with their tinkling notes, which were thought childish. Ste-Croix had to convert itself to the making of gramophones. Since then the popularity of radio has required another conversion of the workshops, but nowdays musical boxes again play an important part in local industry and Ste-Croix is still "the village of sound".

International Centre of Mechanical Musical Instruments (**Centre International de la mécanique d'art**) ⊘ – Step into this old music box factory (display of disused machinery) and you will be transported into a wonderful, magic world where you will discover the vibrant melodies coming from beautiful hand-made instruments, masterpieces of acoustics and cabinetmaking. Thanks to this museum, musical boxes operated by discs or cylinders (the first model dates from 1815), radio sets, phonographs, pianos, street organs, automata (clowns, acrobats, Pierrot writing to Colombine), barrel organs and bird-organs are given a new lease of life.

The resorts – **Sainte-Croix** lies in a pastoral basin well protected from the winds at the mouth of the wooded pass of the Covatannaz Gorges, through which a wide section of the Bernese Alps can be seen.

Les Rasses★, this tourist annexe of Ste-Croix consists of several hotels and a few scattered chalets enjoying a magnificent terraced **site★★** within view of the Alps. For those interested in rambling, there are more than 200km – 124 miles of paths.

EXCURSIONS

★★★ **Chasseron** – Alt 1 607m – 5 272ft. *From Les Rasses, 3km – 2 miles – 1 1/4 hours by a small, winding, tarred road (there is also a chairlift ending at Les Avattes, about an hour's walk from the summit).*
Follow the road from Ste-Croix to Les Rasses, 500m – about 1/3 mile beyond the Grand Hôtel des Rasses. Turn to the left on the Chasseron road. At the Avattes crossroads, bear right towards the Hôtel du Chasseron. On emerging from the woods, leave the car at the hotel car park.
Walk to the Hôtel du Chasseron and the summit *(sign-post)* where you will see a vast panorama of the Alps, the Jura and Lake Neuchâtel.

L'Auberson – Pop 699 – *4km – 3 miles west of Ste-Croix (Pontarlier road). Turn left at the Col des Étroits.*

Baud Museum ⊘ – This small museum displays and keeps in working order an exceptional **collection of ancient musical instruments★** (Utrecht organ, barrel organ, player organ...) and phonographs (note especially the ones dating from 1900, 1912 and 1920). Also exhibited and functioning are automata and animated scenes.
In display cases, music boxes, mechanisms, bonbonnières, etc. can be admired.

★★ **Mount Baulmes** – Alt 1 285m – 4 216ft. *From Ste-Croix 4.5km – 3 miles – about 1/2 hour by a narrow mountain road, steep towards the end but wholly tarred, plus 1/4 hour on foot Rtn.*
Leave Ste-Croix by the level-crossing at the railway station and continue through the hamlets of La Sagne and Culliairy. Leave the car at the Chalet-Restaurant of Mount Baulmes, and go along an avenue to the viewing table, on the edge of the precipice, for a bird's-eye view of the Swiss plateau, its lakes (in particular, Lake Neuchâtel) and the Alps.

★ **SAMEDAN** Graubünden (Grisons)   Pop 2 875

Michelin map 🔲 fold 15 or 🔲 fold 17 – Local map see GRISONS – Alt 1 709m – 5 607ft – Facilities

At the entrance to the little triangular plain where the great resorts of the Upper Engadine have found room for a golf course, an aerodrome and glider field, Samedan's horizons are bounded by the high summits of the Bernina to the south: Piz Morteratsch and Piz Palü.
The village is a simple resort attractive to tourists who seek local colour. Its **Engadine houses** *(qv)* are the most typical in the immediate neighbourhood of St Moritz. You will also notice, in the heart of the village, facing the Community House, the imposing double Planta House (Chesa Planta – from the name of one of the oldest families in the Grisons) containing the Romansh Library, an institution devoted to the preservation of the local language and traditions.

★★ SAN BERNARDINO PASS ROAD

Michelin map **218** folds 4, 12, 13 and 14 or **427** folds 15, 16 and 25

The San Bernardino Pass, on this great transalpine road, links Bellinzona (near Lake Maggiore) in the sunny Lower Ticino Valley to Chur, the historical capital of the Grisons, located downstream from the confluence of the Vorderrhein and Hinterrhein.

The San Bernardino Pass is usually blocked by snow from November to May. The itinerary outlined below follows the old road (blue signposts). The motorway which is parallel to this itinerary is not indicated on the map.

FROM BELLINZONA TO CHUR

194km – 120 miles – allow one day – Itinerary **2** *on the Grisons local map*

Bellinzona *– See Bellinzona.*

After Bellinzona the road climbs the Mesolcina Valley watered by the Moesa.
On leaving Roveredo, the valley becomes narrower and runs northwards. On the way to Soazza (alt 623m – 2044ft) look out for the last signs of typically Mediterranean farming and vegetation: plane trees, maize, vines and figs (as far as Cama).
After admiring the double **Buffalora Waterfall,** follow the old road which runs through Soazza and pass the great church. The road to the pass starts climbing.

★**Misox Castle** *– See Misox Castle.*

Beyond the village of **Mesocco,** which clusters on a ledge at the foot of its castle's ruins, the climb is resumed, still pleasantly among grassy mounds (note the outline of the motorway and its many structures), to the **San Bernardino** ledge. This is the highest and most frequented resort in the Mesolcina Valley and it has an unusual circular church. From the village of San Bernardino to the pass, the road, after skirting the pretty Moesola Lake, follows a wayward course which leads it from level to level among fir woods and Arolla pines. *(For details of these conifers read Alpine Vegetation in the Introduction).* Eastwards, in the foreground, the coloured escarpments of the Pizzo Uccello appear as a rugged spur parallel to the Pan di Zucchero (Sugar Loaf).

San Bernardino Pass *– Alt 2065 – 6775ft.* This pass is littered with rounded rocks left behind by Quaternary glaciers. Open between the Zapporthorn and the Pizzo Uccello, the pass marks the dividing line between the Moesa, southwards, a tributary of the Ticino and thus of the Po and the Hinterrhein, northwards. The old road is very hilly and difficult near the pass.
On the north side, the **Upper Inner Rhine Valley** (Hinterrhein) presents as far as Splügen a landscape which is open and pastoral but still severe.
From the approach to the Hinterrhein, the **view**★ opens out upstream towards the massif containing the sources of the Rhine. The range is also remarkable for the size of its glaciers: the great Zapportgletscher, overlooked by the flattened cone of the Rheinquellhorn, is particulary impressive.

Avers-Cresta

Between Splügen and Andeer the road runs through dense woods of Norway spruce, skirts the vast Sufers Reservoir and crosses the deepest section of the Rheinwald, the Roffla Defile, which corresponds with the northward bend of the valley.

★ **Roffla Gorge (Rofflaschlucht)** ⏱ – The galleries, 300m – 984ft long, arranged between 1907-14 in this gorge through which the Rhine flows, end under an impressive waterfall, which passes just above the spectator's head.

As you leave this gorge you will notice the Bärenburg Reservoir, another example of the engineering works on the Hinterrhein.

From Roffla, proceed to the southeast and follow directions for Innerferrera.

★★ **Averserrhein Valley** (Ferrera Valley, Avers Valley) – The Averserrhein, a tributary of the Hinterrhein, carves its route through a picturesque valley in the Piz Grisch and Piz Platta Massifs.

Following the torrent, the road climbs through the **Ferrera Valley** (facing south) within view of the rocky Piz Miez, which serves as a backdrop, and crosses the village of Ausserferrera, located in a lovely wooded site (waterfalls). After **Innerferrera**, which overlooks a large dam, the road deviates southeasterly. It follows a hilly landscape, interrupted by long tunnels (between the tunnels, a pretty waterfall is visible on the left and behind), and opens out onto the Avers Valley and its first village, **Campsut**, which is set in a basin whose sides are covered with fir trees, ravines and small waterfalls. Starting at Cröt, a sudden rise in the road gives you a good view: **Avers-Cresta** (charming white church) beyond the tree-line, a hanging valley, on the right is closed off by the Tscheischhorn snowfields. The road ends at **Juf** (alt 2126m – 6975ft) in a desolate site surrounded by high mountains (glaciers).

Continuing down the Hinterrhein, downstream from Andeer, the road enters the agricultural Schons Basin, whose west slope is open and dotted with villages.

Zillis – *To reach the church leave the through road and follow the road marked "Zur Kirche".* The **ceiling**★★ of the Zillis church is one of the most valuable pieces of painting left to Switzerland by the artists of the Romanesque period. It reveals the hand of an illuminator of manuscripts in its workmanship, and is believed to date from the 12C. The 153 square panels are arranged in two separate cycles. Those on the perimeter symbolize the Original Ocean and the Sea of the Apocalypse with waters teeming with fabulous monsters and, in the four corners, the Angels of the Last Judgment, shown with the attributes of the Four Winds. The inside panels (follow the scenes from left to right, walking backwards away from the chancel) refer to the Life of Christ and a few scenes from the life of St Martin.

Mathon – This rustic mountain village (alt 1521m – 4990ft) is situated in a privileged **site**★ on the verdant slopes of Piz Beverin, overlooking the Schons Basin and in view of the snowy peaks of the basin's east side. Below the church and hanging over the precipice are the ruins of a former church (1528, parts of which date from the 9C).

★★ **Via Mala** – *Time: 1/4 hour, not including the walk through the galleries.* This famous stretch of road, which for centuries has been the main obstacle to the development of traffic along the **Untere Strasse** (Low Road – *p 111*) is divided into two gorges separated by the small, verdant Rongellen Basin.

The **upstream defile**★★ – the Via Mala proper – plunges between formidable schist escarpments connected by four successive bridges. Leave the car by the pavilion at the entrance to the galleries and go towards the "Second Bridge" (upstream bridge) and take up a position preferably on the old bridge dating from 1739 and now restored. This spans the gorge at the bottom of which gushes the Rhine, 68m – 223ft below.

To enjoy the famous view of the site of these bridges and to get as close as possible to the bed of the Rhine you can go down to the **galleries**★ ⏱ *(341 steps – 1/2 hour Rtn)*. The road avoids the floor of the ravine downstream and the section called the Verlorenes Loch (Lost Hole). This was considered inaccessible until a carriage road through these depths was opened in 1822.

From the top of the opposite escarpment you can see the feudal ruins of Hohenrätien, a site worthy of an engraving by Gustave Doré.

Thusis – Thusis is a busy little town below the ruins of Hohenrätien (a "refuge castle" and a church destroyed in the 15C). The ruins are perched 200m – 650ft above the Via Mala at the point where this gorge opens into the Domleschg Basin. The section between Thusis and the Rothenbrunnen Bridge runs along the bottom of the Domleschg Depression, where the Hinterrhein flows between steep sides. The steeper and more thickly wooded slopes of the Heinzenberg face the east slope – the **Domleschg** proper – dotted with villages nestling amid orchards and the ruins of feudal fortresses.

Two sentinels watch over the entrance to the Domleschg Gap: upstream the Citadel of Ortenstein, and downstream Rhäzüns Castle, perched above the deeply-cut course of the Rhine.

Reichenau – *See Disentis/Mustér.*

On leaving the ravine, the road runs through the Rhine Valley opposite the rocky slopes of the Calenda, to the north. The hummocky ground in the vicinity of Domat is said to be the result of a landslide in prehistoric times.

★ **Chur** – *See Chur.*

With this guide use **Michelin Maps** *nos* 216, 217, 218 *and* 219 *or* 427.

186

★★★ SÄNTIS

Michelin map **216** middle of fold 21 or **427** fold 7 – Local map see APPENZELL DISTRICT

Säntis, with an altitude of 2 502m – 8 207ft, is the highest peak in the Alpstein Massif and, as an advanced bastion of the Pre-Alps between Toggenburg, the Rhine Valley and Lake Constance is the chief belvedere of eastern Switzerland.
The summit itself with its calcareous shoulders, sometimes gently folded (north face), sometimes sharply ridged (Wildhuser Schafberg), is one of the most easily-identified in all the range.

Climb to the summit ⊘ – *From Schwägalp, the terminus of the roads coming from Urnäsch or Neu-St-Johann: about 1 hour Rtn, including 20 minutes by cable-car.*
From the upper station you can easily reach the summit where an observatory is installed.
The **panorama**★★★ of the Vorarlberg Mountains, the Grisons, Glarus and Bernese Alps and the lakes of Zürich and Constance is incredibly grand. Its immensity is, however, often difficult to appreciate in full summer, especially in the middle of the day, when a heat haze obscures distant features.
To get nearer bird's-eye views you may go down steps to the Hôtel du Säntis, built above the wild valley of the Seealpsee *(qv)*.

LA SARRAZ CASTLE Vaud

Michelin map **217** fold 3 or **427** fold 11

Overlooking the village, this 11C castle, altered in the 15 and 16C, is surrounded by a small park. The main building, featuring rounded corner turrets, is preceded by two massive machicolated square towers.

Visit ⊘ – Step inside and discover a series of beautifully-furnished rooms with fine silverware, porcelain, 17 to 19C timepieces, paintings and various objets d'art.
A former chapel situated near the castle houses an astonishing 14C carved **cenotaph** of the Count of La Sarraz; the recumbent figure of the Count, covered with snakes and toads, is dutifully guarded by his wife, his daughter and his two sons.
A **Horse Museum** has been set up in one of the outbuildings: collection of horse-driven vehicles, remarkable exhibition on the different types of harness for warfare, circus performances, hunting parties, etc.

★ SCHAFFHAUSEN Ⓒ   Pop 34 225

Michelin **216** fold 8 or **427** fold 6 – Alt 403m – 1 322ft – Facilities

The old city of Schaffhausen, built on terraces on the north bank of the Rhine at the foot of the Munot Keep, is one of the most attractive towns in Switzerland because of its wonderful Renaissance and classical buildings. The most northerly of the Swiss cantons, Schaffhausen is also the capital.
This is the starting-point for a visit to the Rhine Falls (Rheinfall), a traditional attraction of romantic Switzerland.

An important depot – As the Rhine Falls compelled boatmen to unload their cargoes here, merchants settled in the town and set up a depot which soon became important. By the end of the 12C Schaffhausen had become a Free Imperial City. It entered the Swiss Confederation in 1501.
Nowadays, Schaffhausen depends largely on its situation as a communications junction and bridgehead. It has also become an industrial centre, drawing electric power from the river itself.
Machine and electrical goods factories, spinning mills and steel works have been set up outside the old city of Schaffhausen, which has thus been able to keep its medieval appearance.

SIGHTS

★**Old Town** – This is dominated by the remains of the ramparts crowned by the **Munot**, a massive 16C keep, which forms a choice **belvedere**★ ⊘ overlooking the town and the Rhine Valley *(to the platform of the keep: by stairs and a footbridge across the moat, now turned into a deer park)*.
The lower town contains fine houses with painted façades, often adorned with oriel windows.
The **Vordergasse**★ is one of the most typical streets, with its houses adorned with stucco and carvings and crowned with fine brown roofs, pierced by numerous dormer windows.
The "Haus zum Ritter" (**A**) – the Knight's House – deserves a special mention: the paintings adorning the façade were restored in 1938-1939 by Care Roesch, who respected the style and spirit of the original frescoes, signed by the famous Schaffhausen artist, Tobias Stimmer. Some of these murals, executed around 1570, can be seen in the All Saints' Museum. The themes chosen were inspired by Roman history and mythology.
You must also see the pretty fountains in Fronwagplatz and the Regierungsgebäude (Government House – **P**), a 17C building with a fine sculptured façade and a stepped gable.
★**All Saints' Museum** (Museum zu Allerheiligen) (**M¹**) ⊘ – The museum is in the buildings of the former Abbey of All Saints. It contains prehistorical collections from excavations carried out in the district, manuscripts and early printed books, mostly 15C, which belonged to the monastery library and works of Swiss artists from 15-20C. The most remarkable exhibit is an onyx (early 13C), mounted on gold and encrusted with precious stones. The exhibits also include fragments of the

paintings (*c*1570) which originally adorned the façade of the Knight's House. These were the work of the Schaffhausen master Tobias Stimmer and they portrayed subjects from mythology and the history of Rome.

A historical section traces the city's history, whilst another gallery concentrates on natural history. Several rooms are devoted to the industries of Schaffhausen. Models and excellent documentation make the exhibition most interesting.

All Saints' Church (Münster) **(B)** – This 11C Romanesque abbey church was built of yellow ochre-coloured stone on the old basilical plan. Its interior was recently restored; tall columns support a wooden ceiling; the chancel ends in a flat east end. The cloister, abutting against the south aisle of the church, has a gallery with Gothic bays and contains numerous tombstones.

A bell known as Schiller's Bell, which inspired the poet's *Ballad of the Bell,* is kept in a small courtyard close by. A medicinal garden nearby is planted with a wide variety of herbs and spices.

Contemporary Art Hall (Hallen für neue Kunst) **(M²)** ⊘ – Situated along the banks of the Rhine, this former textile factory dating from the turn of the century houses works representing the main European and American art trends of the 1960s and 1970s; they are laid out over a total area of $5\,000\text{m}^2$ – $53\,820\text{sq ft}$ and arranged on three levels. The interior has been carefully and tastefully arranged to accommodate largish compositions requiring a lot of light and space. Artists such as Joseph Beuys, Carl André, Richard Long (Land Art), Jannis Kounellis and Mario Merz (Arte Povera) are well represented in this attractive setting.

★★RHINE FALLS
(RHEINFALL)

The Rhine Falls are the most powerful in Europe. The river plunges from a height of 21m – 70ft. Its flow sometimes reaches $1\,070\text{m}^3$ – $37\,500\text{cu ft}$ per second (average flow, 700m^3 – $25\,000\text{cu ft}$ per second). The spectacle, which Goethe described as "the source of the Ocean", is best seen in summer, at the season of high water (July).

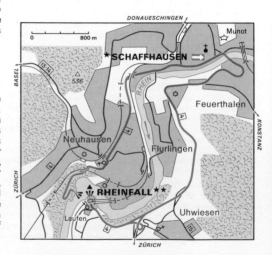

Scene from the north bank (Rheinfallquai) – 4km – 3 miles by ④ and Neuhausen, *where you will leave the Basle road and follow the Rheinfallstrasse.*

Close views from the south bank – 5km – 3 miles – plus 1/2 hour on foot Rtn. *Leave Schaffhausen by ④ on the road to Zürich, which you will then leave to turn right towards Laufen. Park the car at the entrance to* **Laufen Castle***, which is now a restaurant.*

Belvederes ⊙ – Enter the courtyard of the castle. You will go down a staircase to the level of the falls. From the top of the staircase you will see, from a little kiosk with coloured windows, the huge mass of water below. Lower down, various platforms and gangways go very near the falls and make it possible to see them from the most varied viewpoints.

Boat trips ⊙ – These can be made to the rock in the middle of the falls and also from one bank to the other.

★★ SCHÖLLENEN Uri

Michelin map **217** fold 10 or **427** fold 15 – 3km – 2 miles north of Andermatt – Local maps see BERNESE OBERLAND and ST-GOTTHARD MASSIF

Between Göschenen and Andermatt the granite walls of the Reus Valley, remarkably smooth and polished, form a bottle-neck. This is the legendary Schöllenen Defile which was the chief obstacle to the development of traffic on the St Gotthard route until about the 13C when a road was boldly driven through it. Modern road works may arouse a feeling of anti-climax in the visitor to the defile – in which case a walk along the old road is recommended.

Devil's Bridge (Teufelsbrücke) – This bridge took the place, in 1830, of the bridge built, according to legend, at the instigation of the Devil and paid for with the soul of the first to cross it – a billy-goat driven across by the crafty people of Uri. Since motor traffic has ceased to use it, the bridge has made an ideal belvedere from which to admire the foaming **Reuss Falls** *(best seen in sunlight around noon).*

Slightly downstream a cross hewn in the rocky wall of the east bank and accompanied by an inscription in Cyrillic characters, commemorates the hazardous venture of the Russian corps of General Suvorov, who, having forced the passage on 24 September 1799 in pursuit of the French army, debouched on the plain too late to prevent Masséna from defeating the Allies at Zürich.

SCHÖLLENEN ROAD

Michelin map **217** fold 10 or **427** fold 15

The itinerary, starting in the Lake Lucerne District and following the Reus Valley, penetrates into the heart of the St Gotthard Massif. Its most unusual site, the Schöllenen Defile, is at the end of the itinerary.

FROM ALTDORF TO ANDERMATT

56km – 35 miles – about 1 1/2 hours – Itinerary ④ *on the St. Gotthard Massif local map*

Between Altdorf and Göschenen, a motorway runs along the road we recommend.

Altdorf – See Altdorf.

From Altdorf to Amsteg, as the valley narrows, the majestic conical Bristen Peak, rising sheer to 3 072 – 10 079ft, catches the eye. The populous centre of Erstfeld marks the point where the line begins to climb the ramp to the north entrance of the St Gotthard Tunnel, 600m – 1 968ft higher.

Between Amsteg and Wassen, the floor of the Reuss Valley, where the mountain section of the road begins, contains pretty shaded nooks. Bends in the road – especially before arriving at Wassen, whose church can be seen directly after leaving Gurtnellen – give glimpses, below, of the shapely pyramid of the Kleine Windgällen.

Pfaffensprung – From the car park, downstream from the bridge over the Reuss, cross the road to reach a belvedere overlooking the Parson's Leap. The overflow of the dam built in this reach sometimes forms a spectacular cascade, with beautiful iridescent effects.

Wassen – Wassen became well-known when the builders of the St Gotthard railway made two successive loops in the track, partly underground, on either side of the village. The amazement of the uninitiated traveller, when he sees three successive views, from different angles, of a church which his imperturbable neighbour in the train assures him is still that of Wassen, has never ceased to be a subject of amusement. The building of the Susten road on the slope of the Reuss, has stimulated local tourist traffic.

From Wassen to Göschenen the bottom of the corridor is partly obstructed by landslides among which can be seen an enormous single rock called the Devil's Stone (Teufelsstein). Impressive road construction has been realized on this section.

Göschenen – Göschenen is best known for its railway station at the north end of the St Gotthard Tunnel (15km – 9 miles long, opened in 1882). It is a useful halt for tourists, who will find it pleasant to stand near the small central bridge and admire the icefield of the Upper Dammastock, which can be seen through the Göschenertal Gap.

★★Göscheneralp Lake – The road that leads to this lake-reservoir offers close-up views of the Dammastock Glaciers (on the east side of the Rhône Glacier), which feed it.

The road climbs the wild, narrow Göschenen Valley, with, at the end of the ride, *corniche* sections along the side of superb rock faces.

Leave the car at the car park near the restaurant (alt 1 783m – 5 850ft) and go to the centre of the dam's grassy crest (quite close). This dead weight dam (capacity 9.3 million m³ – 204 600 million gallons; 700m – 2 297ft thick at base; 155m – 508ft high; 540m; 1 772ft length of crest) retains a reservoir-lake.

Ahead is a magnificent **landscape★★** with the dam, the cascades falling right and left and, separated by a rocky cone, the gleaming glaciers below the Winterberg crests. Look behind you and admire the rocky cirque, opposite, sprinkled with fir.

★★Schöllenen – *See Schöllenen.*

★Andermatt – *See Andermatt.*

For a pleasant and quiet hotel in a convenient location.
*Consult the current edition of the annual **Michelin Red Guide Switzerland.***

★★ SCHULS (SCUOL) Graubünden (Grisons)   Pop 1 889

Michelin map **218** fold 7 or **427** fold 18 – Local map see GRISONS – Alt 1 244m – 4 081ft – Facilities

This mineral water and climatic spa, whose centres are scattered over the slopes of the widest basin in the Lower Engadine, is much appreciated for its setting of forests and rocky heights, among which the Lower Engadine Dolomites stand up against the sky. It also has a dry, sheltered climate and bright sunshine.

Different springs at Schuls and Tarasp are used to treat gastro-intestinal troubles and disorders of metabolism, circulation, the kidneys and the bladder.

THE RESORTS

Walkers can avoid the main roads by using the paths linking the three resorts of Schuls, Tarasp and Vulpera.

Alte Durchgangsstrasse	2	Gurlaina	8
Ragnera	3	Punt	9
Bahnhofstrasse	4	S.-charl (Via da)	10
Bogns (Via da)	6	Stradun	12

★Schuls – This village on the tilled slope of the valley has become a tourist and business centre maintained by traffic using the international Engadine-Austria route (St Moritz-Landeck). At the same time, below the through road, Lower Schuls, the former nucleus of the community, still stands around two paved squares built in a purely Engadine style.

The most imposing building is the **"Chagronda"** (Chasa Gronda) (**M**), which can be recognized thanks to its two superimposed galleries. It houses a Lower Engadine Museum ⊙.

Tarasp – The watering-place of Tarasp lies in an enclosed site on the floor of the Inn Valley.

★★Vulpera – Facilities. Four hotels built on a terrace of the wooded valley side, among burgeoning flower beds, form the nucleus of the resort.

EXCURSIONS

★Road to Ardez – *12km – 7 1/2 miles west by a narrow winding road.*

The climb to **Ftan** will enable you to appreciate the site of Tarasp Castle. Coming down to Ardez *(p 87)*, the bend at the exit from the Tasna Valley and the return to the main valley provide an excellent **belvedere★★** overlooking the mountain setting of the Schuls Basin and Tarasp Castle.

From Tarasp to Kreuzberg – *From Kurhaus Tarasp, 4km – 3 miles – about 1/2 hour – by a narrow, steeply winding road – plus 1/2 hour on foot Rtn to the Kreuzberg.*

Cross the Inn and start the climb to Vulpera; directly after the Hotel Schweizerhof (**F**) turn right (hairpin bend).

Leave the car at the entrance to Tarasp Fontana and take the road climbing to Tarasp-Sparsels, at the foot of the castle. At the end of Sparsels turn right along a road running into the fields within view of the cross on the grassy mound of the Kreuzberg.

Tarasp Castle

★**Kreuzberg** – Alt 1 477m – 4 845ft. From this belvedere you can admire the **site**★★ of the castle as well as a **panorama**★ embracing the whole of the Lower Engadine with its "Dolomites" (Piz Lischana and Piz Pisoc) and its perched villages (Ftan and Sent).

★**Tarasp Castle** (School Tarasp) ⊘ – This remained an Austrian enclave in the Grisons until 1803. After many vicissitudes damaging to its interior arrangements, which are now of uneven quality, the fortress was restored (1907-16) and is now used at certain seasons by the Prince of Hesse-Darmstadt.

Sent – *4km – 2 1/2 miles northeast*. To reach Sent drive along a little road shaded by maples, traced along the flank of the ridge, within view of the Lower Engadine Dolomites and Tarasp Castle.
Sent is a fine village with houses perfectly kept by emigrants from the Grisons who spend their holidays here. The baroque gables, known as "Sent gables" are curiously decorated.

★ **SCHWYZ** Ⓒ   Pop 12 872

Michelin map 216 south of folds 18 and 19 or 427 fold 15 – Alt 517m – 1696ft

This quiet little town, which has the honour of having given to the Swiss Confederation both its name and its flag, occupies a majestic **site**★ at the foot of the twin Mythen Peaks, between Lakes Lucerne and Lauerz. *For the history of the original cantons, see "The Swiss national sanctuary" under Lake Lucerne.*

The resort of Stoos (alt 1 295m – 4 249ft; facilities), built on a sunny terrace, forms its mountain annexe.

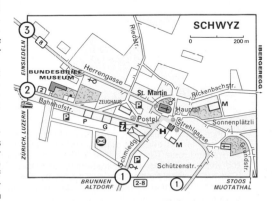

Soldiers of fortune – When foreign princes recruited mercenaries for their service from the 16C onwards, the men of Schwyz enlisted in their armies, especially in French regiments.
Their bravery and military qualities enabled many to return, to their country, having made their fortunes and covered with honours and glory. They settled in their native land and then built the sumptuous homes that their descendants still own.

SIGHTS

★**Federal Charters Museum (Bundesbriefmuseum)** ⊘ – A modern building, with a fresco by H. Danioth on its façade, has been erected to house the most precious original documents of the Confederation.
In the great hall adorned with a fresco, *The Oath* by W. Clénin, and with banners of the Schwyz Canton, are displayed the Pact of 1291 (Bundesbrief – *p 144),* the Pact of Brunnen of 1315 (Morgartenbrief), charters of freedom and pacts of alliance concerning the "XIII Cantons" *(p 21).*

St Martin's – The church has sumptuous 18C baroque decorations. The nave is adorned with stucco and frescoes; the high altar, the altars in the side chapels, the marble **pulpit★** (supported by atlantes and adorned with a frieze carved in high relief) and the baptistry are all elaborately decorated. In the transept are the reliquaries of St Polycarb (left) and St Lazarus (right).

Town Hall (H) ⊙ – Burnt down and rebuilt in the 17C, the town hall is ornamented on the outside with mural paintings (1891) recalling episodes in Swiss history. Inside are rooms with decorative woodwork and stained-glass windows.

EXCURSIONS

From Schwyz to Rigi-Scheidegg – *12km – 7 1/2 miles. Leave Schwyz by ② and at Seewen take road no 2 towards Lucerne.*

Lauerz Lake (Lauerzer See) – The scene of this lovely stretch of water, bordered by reeds and waterlilies, and embellished by two wooded islets, is, unfortunately, marred by the quarry at its east end.

★★**Rigi-Scheidegg** ⊙ – Leave Goldau from the south and take a narrow, winding road for 3km – 2.5 miles to the "Station Kräbel" *(also the mid-station for the rack-railway to Rigi-Kulm)* and take the cable-car to Scheidegg.

At the top of the Rigi-Scheidegg (alt 1 665m – 5 268ft) there niches the small resort of the same name. Climb atop the hillock behind the chapel and admire the immense **panorama★★**, similar to that of the Rigi-Kulm *(qv)*, but blocked to the northwest by the Rigi-Kulm's promontory.

★**Ibergeregg Road** – Michelin map **218** fold 1 – *11km   7 miles. Leave Schwyz east via the Rickenbachstrasse.*

Beginning at the hill's slope, right after crossing Rickenbach, views open out on the left to the Mythen and on the right on part of the Lakes Lucerne and Lauerz, separated by the Hochflue. After a magnificent stretch of corniche through woods above the deep Muotatal Valley and, in a bend in the road, there is a beautiful **view★** behind of this valley and the Lake Lucerne District. During the steep climb that follows, the snowy summits of the Glarus Alps can be seen. At the **Ibergeregg Pass** (alt 1 406m – 4 613ft) admire the remarkable **views★** of the neighbouring valley.

★**Hölloch Cave** (Höllochgrotte) – Michelin map **218** fold 1 – *15km – 9 miles by the Muotatal road (southeast of the plan) plus 1 hour tour. See Hölloch Cave.*

When doing this trip you can also go to **Stoos** in a funicular and then to the magnificent belvedere of the **Fronalpstock** (alt 1 922m – 6 306ft).

★ SEELISBERG Uri   Pop 569

Michelin **218** fold 1 or **427** fold 15 – southwest of Brunnen – Local map see Lake LUCERNE – Alt 845m – 2 772ft – Facilities

Seelisberg stands on a wooded spur dipping into Lake Lucerne within view of the Bay of Brunnen and the Schwyz Basin. It is overlooked by the twin peaks of the Mythen. As one of the exclusive summer resorts in central Switzerland, this luxurious retreat is characterized by its isolation, the majesty of its panorama and the quality of its tourist amenities.

Access – You can go up to Seelisberg:
– by car, from Stans *(22km – 13 1/2 miles – by a road described under Stans Excursions)*
– by funicular ⊙, from the Treib landing-stage *(services connecting with the steamers on Lake Lucerne – time for the climb: 8 minutes).*

★★**View from Seelisberg** – From the public belvedere-promenade there is a view of the Fronalpstock and Lake Uri.

SEMPACH Lucerne   Pop 3 096

Michelin map **216** fold 17 or **427** fold 14 – on the shore of Lake Sempach – Alt 518m – 1 699ft

Founded by the Habsburgs, Sempach is built near the lake to which it gave its name; for a long time it owed its activity and prosperity to the considerable traffic on the St Gotthard route (Basle-Lucerne-Milan), which now follows the opposite shore.

The main street has an old-fashioned air with its Witches' Tower, its town hall (Rathaus) with a façade made cheerful by a red and white pattern, its flower-decked fountain and its houses with brown tile roofs.

A national hero – On 9 July 1386 a decisive battle took place near Sempach between the Swiss Confederates and the Austrians commanded by Duke Leopold. **Arnold von Winkelried** spurred forward, and grasped as many spears as he could hold in order to make a breach in the Austrian square, bristling with pikes, and by his heroic sacrifice secured the victory of the Confederates when Duke Leopold lost his life.

A monument perpetuates the memory of that day which heralded the decline of the Habsburg rule in Switzerland.

Swiss Ornithological Centre (Schweizerische Vogelwarte) ⊙ – The centre is devoted to local birds, the survival of species and bird migration.

Kirchbühl – *2km – 1 mile north-east.*

The object of this trip is the old church of Kirchbühl, from beside which (stand in the former cemetery) you will get a fine **view★** of Lake Sempach and the Alps. A low porch roofed with tiles leads into the 13C nave. Among the damaged paintings, you will distinguish the *Last Judgment,* the *Passion* and the *Resurrection of Christ.* A 16C altarpiece adorns the chancel.

SIERRE Valais   Pop 14 143

Michelin map ZIZ fold 16 or ₄₂₇ fold 13 – Local map see VALAIS – Alt 534m – 1 752ft – Facilities

Sierre is one of the sunniest cities in Switzerland *(details of the climate under Valais)*. It lies in the valley of the Valais Rhône below the vineyards of the Noble Country (Noble Contrée) and at the mouth of the Anniviers Valley. A huge landslide in prehistoric times explains the strange **site**★ of the town, in a landscape like "a gravel pit dug and turned over with a spade". Sierre (Siders) marks the language boundary between French and German *(map p 22)*.
Several strongholds such as the Castle of the Vidomnes and the Goubin Tower, perched on its rock, recall the part played by Sierre at the time of episcopal and feudal Valais.

SIGHTS

Town Hall – Formerly a manor house and an hotel, this building dates from the 17 and 19C. The **interior**★ is sumptuous in its decoration (elegant painted ceilings, frescoes, paintings and stained-glass windows) and yet it retains a certain intimacy. It houses two small museums: the **pewter museum** ⊙ (in the cellar) displays in show-cases approximately 180 objects (tableware, utensils) of the 17-19C.

Rue du Bourg – A small picturesque street with old houses. Note the unusual building with bartizans, the said "Château des Vidomnes" and the Catholic Church of St Catherine (17-19C). Inside the church are a baroque chancel, a carved pulpit and a lovely organ loft.
At no 30, on the ground floor, the Maison Pancrace de Courten houses the **Rilke Museum** ⊙, a tribute to the Austrian author Rainer Maria Rilke who before he died in 1926, had taken up residence in the former Château de la Cour, presently serving as the Town Hall.

Château Mercier – This attractive manor house (19C) is privately owned, and not open to the public but you can stroll in the **Pradec Park,** surrounding the manor house and overlooking the town (views of the town through the trees).

Villa Château – The **Valais Museum of Wine** ⊙ has been set up in one of the château outbuildings. The visit begins with a video film about traditional techniques for pressing grapes. The two following rooms are devoted to wine presses. The second one explains the work of a cellarman. The visits ends with a display of the different types of containers (bottles and labels, pewter pots, barrels) associated with the commerce of wine and the role it plays in society.

EXCURSIONS

Salgesch – A 6km – 3.8 mile **Wine Route** linking Sierre to Salgesch (**Salquenen** in French) enables you to discover part of the vineyard. The route is dotted with signposts which describe the different grape varieties (Chasselas, Pinot, Sylvaner, Malvoisie), the quality of the soil, the various pruning methods and the long-standing tradition of *"vignolage"* (a day's work in the vineyard in springtime, accompanied by fife and drum music). In this quiet, little village, the 16C **Zumofen House**, easily recognisable by its double-gabled wooden roof, presents an exhibition which complements those of the Villa Château Museum. Several rooms enlighten visitors on the art of winemaking: soil, grape varieties, techniques and tools used in winemaking, and finally grape harvesting, conducted with the blessing of Saint Théodule, the patron of this noble profession.

Gourmets...
The chapter on Food and Drink in the Introduction to this guide
describes Switzerland's gastronomic specialities and best national wines.
The annual **Michelin Red Guide Switzerland**
offers an up-to-date selection of good restaurants.

★★ SIMPLON PASS ROAD

Michelin maps ZIZ folds 18 and 19 and ZI₉ fold 6 or ₄₂₇ folds 14 and 23

The Simplon road is not the boldest in the Alps – the Splügen and even the St Gotthard have more daring structures – but it is the noblest and most majestic. It is impossible not to feel the beauty of such a **siting**★★★ as that which unfolds between the Simplon Pass (alt 2 005m – 6 578ft) and Brig, on the Rhône Valley slope. This gentle winding along the mountain flank, without sharp hairpin bends, is a model of adaptation to topography.
The picturesque interest of the run lies in the succession of enclosed sites in the Valleys of the Diveria or Divedro (south slope) and the panoramic ledges of the north slope.

To get the guns through – As early as the 17C the Great Stockalper *(see Brig)*, making the most of his monopolies and the position of Brig, adapted the Simplon road, used until then mainly by smugglers and mercenaries, to commercial traffic. He organised a mail service and built two hostels, which still stand at Gondo. But all this was for mule trains, not for wheeled traffic. The modern Simplon is a product of Napoleon's genius.

Seeing that an expedition like that to the Great St Bernard was doomed to remain an exceptional feat – a detachment sent at the same time to Italy via the Simplon had forced the passage only by dint of perilous manoeuvres – the First Consul decided in September 1800, three months after Marengo, that "the road from Brig to Domodóssola must be made passable for artillery". The low altitude of the pass and its relatively scanty snowfall determined his choice. It received absolute priority after being a mere alternative to one for Mount Cenis. The undertaking was confided to a man from Champagne Nicolas Céard, chief engineer of public works in the Léman Department, who drew up plans for a road 7 to 8m – 22 to 25ft wide with a maximum gradient of 10% (1 in 10).

The road was officially opened to traffic on 9 October 1805, but Napoleon never had occasion to use it.

FROM DOMODÓSSOLA TO BRIG

65km – 40 miles – about 3 hours – Itinerary ② *on the Valais local map*

The Simplon Pass is sometimes blocked by snow from December to May in spite of the galleries built to keep it clear at all times of the year.

The really Alpine section begins at Crévoladossola, where you leave the warm inner plain of the Ossola, somewhat Mediterranean in character with its bushy, stony floor exposed to the meanderings of the Toce River

From Crévoladossola to the border, the narrow Diveria Valley offers little interesting scenery. A few campaniles and the greenery of thickets of hazel, walnut and ash are not enough to make it attractive. A short distance from Crévoladossola, on the left, can be seen, the ruins of the little village of San Giovanni, which was razed by a landslide in 1958. The ruins increase still further the bleakness of the valley.

Italian and Swiss Customs control are at Paglino and Gondo respectively.

★**Gondo Gorges (Gondoschlucht)** – The wildest section of this long defile, hemmed in by granite walls, is the confluence of the Alpienbach and the Diveria, whose falls join at the foot of a spur pierced by a road tunnel.

Between Gstein (Gabi) and the pass the road, leaving the Laggintal in the southwest where it penetrates towards the higher levels of the Weissmies (4023m – 13199ft), climbs gradually among the Alpine pastures of the lower Simplon coomb.

Above the village of Simplon the rugged appearance of the terrain still shows the devastating effects of the terrible avalanche of 1901 started by the collapse of a whole section of the Rossboden Glacier (Rossbodengletscher). The pile of debris can still be seen. Dominating this glacier, the Fletschhorn is the most attractive and dominant feature of the landscape. The larches thin out as you enter the upper hollow of the pass.

★★**Simplon Pass** – Alt 2005m – 6578ft. The road runs halfway up the side of this long, winding defile, with its uneven floor. It is overlooked from the south by the Böshorn, in the middle distance, by the snowy Fletschhorn and from the east by the greenish slabs of the Hübschhorn and the Chaltwassergletscher, coming from Mount Leone.

Of the three main features of this scene none is more remarkable than the Alter Spittel (a former hostel built by Stockalper), which is high and flanked by a 17C tower and bell turret. The present hostel (Hospiz) was built (incomplete) at the same time as the road and is kept by the monks of the Great St Bernard. A stone eagle commemorates the watch kept on the frontier during the Second World War.

The **belvedere**★★ of the pass is at the highest point, that is, just before the hollow on the Valais side. Beside the Hotel Simplon-Kulm, it is possible to pick out the summits of the Bernese Alps which can seen between the Schinhorn and the Finsteraarhorn (highest point of the Bernese Alps – alt 4274m – 14022ft) A small section of the giant Aletsch Glacier can also be seen.

On the Rhône side the course of the road, between the pass and a tunnel called the Kapfloch, exceeds all the other sections for bold siting. The road clings to the upper precipices of a rocky cirque laced by the icy waters of the Chaltwassergletscher which can be seen above, protected by a series of concrete galleries and roofs.

Approaching the Kapfloch Pass through a gap you will see the Fletschhorn, flanked on its right by the Böshorn.

From the Kapfloch to Rothwald a long stretch of *corniche* road under larch woods finally reveals, 1000m – 3281ft below, the town of Brig framed in the opening of the Saltine Gorges. The mountains separating the Rhône Valley from the Lötschental now unfold on the horizon: from left to right, the Bietschhorn, the Briethorn, the Nesthorn and the Schinhorn.

Between Rothwald and Schallberg, the road makes a detour into the **Gantertal**. On the north slope of this beautiful valley are many crooked Arolla pines *(see Alpine Vegetation in the Introduction)*.

After having crossed the modern Ganter Bridge, and as you leave the Gantertal you will see, very high now, the road near the pass.

Between Schallberg and Brig the road at first overlooks the Saltine Gorges (Saltinaschlucht), the floor of which cannot be seen. It then leaves the forest and drops to the well-tilled slopes of the Brigerberg.

The towers of the Stockalper Castle and of the churches of Brig become clear, while, below, the shining ribbon of the Rhône is shrouded by the factory smoke of Visp.

Brig – *See Brig.*

Michelin map **217** folds 15 and 16 or **427** folds 13 and 22 – Local maps see SION: Excursions and VALAIS – Alt 512m – 1 680ft – Facilities

The town of Sion is 2 000 years old. It lies in the inner Valais plain on a **site**★★ which can be fully apreciated when coming from Martigny or again when climbing to Savièze. The appearance of the two rocky Valère (Rhône side) and Tourbillon (mountainside) Peaks, each crowned with episcopal fortresses, gives an immediate sense of history.

The Bishopric of Sion – The Bishopric of Sion was founded in the 4C, and in spite of rivalry with the House of Savoy, played a considerable part in religion and politics of the Middle Ages. The bestowal of the County of Valais on the church of Sion at the beginning of the 11C by the last King of Trans-Juran Burgundy, Rudolf III, made the bishop a temporal lord and a real sovereign prince, who enjoyed full royal prerogatives: the dispensing of justice, the levying of many fines, the striking of coinage and the presidency of the Diets or General Assemblies. When the Communes were emancipated these privileges disappeared one by one. However, until 1848, the Bishop of Sion, was elected jointly by the canons and the Valais Diet and subsequently by the Grand Council until 1918. From then on, the appointment has been the sole responsibility of the Vatican.

Sion and the Valère peak

★**VALÈRE**   *2 1/2 hours*

The hill of Valère, which overlooks the valley from a height of 120m – 394ft, has on its summit a fortified-church, former residence of the Chapter of Sion.
Leave the car on a small square, at the car park between Valère and Tourbillon, at the end of the Rue des Châteaux, which goes up through the old town. You will reach the precincts and a grassy esplanade from which you may enjoy the **view**★ of the Rhône Valley, looking far upstream.
Now enter the fortified area. At the end of a ramp there is a terrace *(viewing table)* which affords a fine **view**★ of Sion and of the Lower Valais, looking downstream.

★**Our Lady of Valère** (**Église Notre-Dame-de-Valère**) ⊘ – The church is built on the top of the hill and has all the appearance of a fortress, with its curtain wall, battlemented tower and north wall and internal wall-walk. Building began in the early 12C and continued until the mid-13C.
The nave displays ogive vaulting and is shut off from the chancel by a rood-screen which breaks the harmony of the building. It meets the exigency of the site by two steps to the chancel. Magnificent 17C **stalls**★★, with panels depicting various scenes taken from the Passion adorn the chancel, which has historiated capitals dating from the Romanesque period and 16C frescoes. The organ-loft and organ are both early 15C.

★**The Canton's Historical and Ethnographical Museum** (**M³**) ⊘ – Originally the canon's residence, this 12C castle, the interior of which was recently renovated, houses alternate exhibitions presenting the history of the Valais area. Displays of sacred art, popular religious art (sculptures, gold and silver plate, pictures), military tradition (armour, weapons) and daily life (furniture) are organised in rotation. In the large hall, enhanced by its fine sculpted fireplace and wooden beams, you can admire several painted murals (facing the firplace) depicting the Nine Valiant Knights, three pagan heroes (Hector, Alexander and Julius Caesar), three Jewish heroes (Joshua, David and Maccabees) and three Christian heroes (Arthur, Charlemagne and Godefroy de Bouillon), seen as paragons of chivalry.

TOURBILLON *1 hour*

From the car park, a path leads up to the imposing ruins of a former stronghold whose crenellated walls circle the hill. During the ascent (rather steep), the **view★** of Valère and its church-fortress, and of the surrounding hillsides planted with vines, is breathtaking.

The building and the chapel were erected in the late 13C by the bishop Boniface de Challant. Although originally conceived as a defensive structure, the castle was

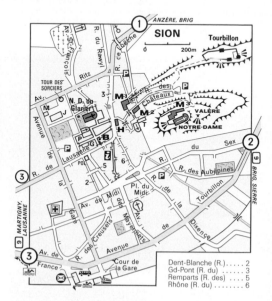

Dent-Blanche (R.) 2
Gd-Pont (R. du) 3
Remparts (R. des) 5
Rhône (R. du) 6

used as a summer residence for bishops in times of peace. Repeatedly besieged and rebuilt in the 15C, it was razed by a terrible fire in 1788.

After walking through a first doorway, pierced in a ring of ramparts, one enters the enclosure of the castle, dominated by its keep. Inside the chapel, supported by ribbed vaulting ending in columns ornamented with carved capitals, one can admire a few fragments of mural paintings.

ADDITIONAL SIGHTS

Our Lady of Glarier Cathedral – The 11 and 13C Romanesque **belfry★** is adorned with Lombard arcades and ends in a graceful octagonal steeple. The ogive-vaulted nave was completed at the beginning of the 16C. The chancel contains 17C stalls and is decorated behind the high altar with a gilded wood **triptych★** of the Tree of Jesse.

Town Hall (H) ⊙ – This is a 17C building. Just at the entrance is an elaborately carved wooden **door★**. In the entrance hall are exhibited Roman inscriptions, one of which is Christian (377).

The **Burgesses' Council Chamber★** (on the first floor) has splendid woodwork and gorgeous furnishings.

Supersaxo Mansion (B) ⊙ – This sumptuous dwelling was built in 1505 by Georges Supersaxo, who wished to dazzle his rival, Cardinal Matthew Schiner, with his luxury. The house has a very large, high **room★** with a radially patterned woodwork ceiling with a huge rose-shaped pendant in the centre showing the Nativity of Christ. Around the room are twelve niches containing busts of the Magi and the prophets.

The Canton's Museum of Fine Arts (M¹) ⊙ – The Majorie and the Vidomat were formerly the residences of episcopal officers. They now house the Valais Fine Arts Museum (old prints, paintings by Valais artists – past or present). From the various floors of the Majorie, especially the third floor, there is a fine general **view★** the fortified church of Valère and the ruins of Tourbillon Castle.

The Canton's Archaeological Museum (M²) ⊙ – On the ground floor of this small museum are exhibited carved prehistoric steles, copies of the bronzes of Octodurum (the originals are in the Gallo-Roman Museum at Martigny) as well as Roman and Islamic glassware.

In the basement are amphorae and Gallo-Roman statuettes together with remarkable Greek and Etruscan ceramics and Neolithic vestiges: arms, jewellery, pottery and fibulae.

EXCURSIONS *local map opposite*

Underground Lake of St Léonard (Lac Souterrain) ⊙ – *6km – 3 1/2 miles by ② on the road to Brig and then left; from the car park 10 minutes on foot Rtn.*

The lake and cave were formed by water infiltrating the gypsum bed and dissolving it little by little. The lake and cave were explored as of 1943 and arranged to receive tourists – the level of the lake is maintained by pumping (its dimensions are: 300m long, 20m wide, and 15m deep – 984ft x 65 1/2ft x 49ft). The electric lighting enhances the site: the tormented relief and contrasting shades of colour (whitish gypsum, coaly schist and grey marble) of the vaulting and rocky surfaces reflect onto the lake surface.

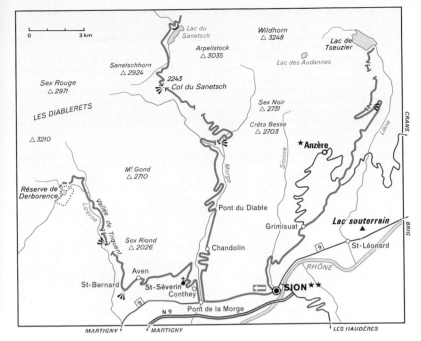

★Anzère – Facilities. *16km – 10 miles by* ①.
This pleasant modern sports resort is very well equipped for winter and summer sports.
Located at 1 549m – 5 082ft, its **site★** was beautifully chosen – on the side of the Wildhorn Massif and overlooking the Liène Valley with, on the horizon, the Valais Alps beyond Crans-Montana.

★Derborence Road – *24km – 15 miles. Leave Sion by* ③ *and follow road no 9 as far as Pont de la Morge.*
The road climbs through vineyards and crosses the villages of Conthey, Sensine and **St Séverin** (church with stone bell tower) where you go left. After Erde, vineyards are replaced by shrubbery; in the bend before Aven's chalets, there is a good view of the Rhône Valley. After St Bernard's Church (last nice view of the valley), the road goes northwards and along the wild Triquent Valley, where the Lizerne runs. After the first tunnel, there is a view of Les Diablerets blocking the coomb to the north, yet the landscape is picturesque: scree topped by snowfields here and there, pine trees, a torrent (the Lizerne, which the road crosses three times) surrounded by erratics, cascades...
The valley then opens out into a grandiose **cirque★★** of rocks, pine and larch. Bear left onto the rocky path, which ends in the Derborence Nature Reserve *(strictly protected)* in a rock **corrie★** created in the 18C, after an avalanche of Les Diablerets.

★★Sanetsch Road – *33km – 20 1/2 miles. Leave Sion by* ③ *and follow road no 9 until you reach Pont de la Morge.*
After having crossed the Morge, the narrow road through the vineyards climbs to Chandolin, offering pleasant views of the neighbouring slopes covered with vineyards and the Rhône Plain. At Pont du Diable the *corniche* road descends, cut by a tunnel, and meets up with the torrent. The road then climbs into a more welcoming landscape with fir trees, while on the opposite slope is a lovely cascade.
At the junction of the road to Conthey (on the left), the rocky Crêta Besse Summit stands straight ahead. A steep climb (15% – 1 in 6 1/2) through woods ends at the chalets of Plan-Cernay.
2km – 1 mile farther, in front of the Zenfleuron Inn, the road crosses the Morge and in a *corniche* stretch passes the east slope, offering, after a tunnel, a **view★** of the valley and at the opposite end onto the mountaintops (where tumble three torrents from melting glaciers) followed by a climb along the slope which opens, before the second tunnel, at the foot of the rocky face of Sex Noir facing the snowy barrier of Les Diablerets.
After the last tunnel, the route continues its spectacular climb to the **Sanetsch Pass** (2 243m – 7 359ft; lovely **view★★** of Les Diablerets preceded by the Tsanfleuron Glacier) and then descends to the dam's reservoir (Sanetsch Lake) where the road eventually ends.

★Tseuzier Road – *23km – 14 miles. Leave Sion on the road to Crans-Montana to the north.* 3km – 2 miles after Grimisuat bear left onto the road to Ayent and at St-Romain follow the narrow but easy road signposted "Barrage de Zeuzier", which climbs amidst fir trees above the Liène Valley and soon offers some lovely glimpses of the valley and the terraced resort of Crans – Montana beyond (a wide **view★**, especially at the entrance to the first tunnel).
At the end of the road *(restaurant)* these is the small lake of Tseuzier Dam in its rocky basin.

Michelin map 216 fold 15 or 427 fold 4 – Local map see Swiss JURA – Alt 436m – 1 430ft – Facilities

Solothurn lies at the foot of the last ridge of the Jura (Weissenstein) and today extends to both banks of the Aare.

On the north bank of the river the old nucleus of the town, still encircled by its 17C walls, has some fine Renaissance and baroque buildings. The Krummturm (Twisted Tower) is the most striking feature of this fortified group.

From 1530 to 1792 Solothurn remained Catholic and was chosen as a residence by the French ambassadors to the Swiss Diet. Intellectual and artistic exchanges flourished between the two countries; Bourbon court fashions were adopted and the town's fortifications were built from 1667 according to the principles of the famous French military engineer Vauban.

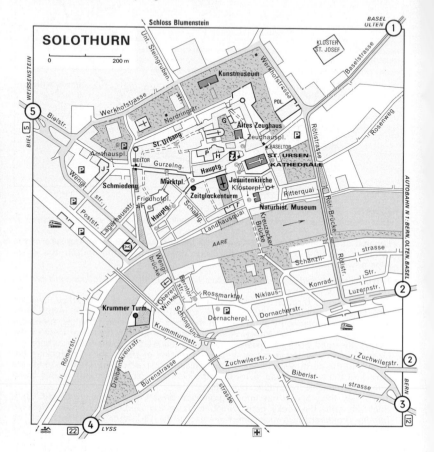

SOLOTHURN

SIGHTS

★ **Old Town** – The Basle Gate (Baseltor) and the Biel Gate (Bieltor) give access to the old quarter. Many of the streets are charming and picturesque with brightly-painted shutters, wrought-iron signs and widely overhanging roofs. The Hauptgasse, St-Urbangasse and Schmiedengasse are noteworthy. The Marktplatz, which is the centre of the old town, is adorned with a fountain with painted figures of the 16C (St-Ursen-Brunnen). It is dominated by the 12C clock tower (Zeitglockenturm) whose astronomical clock-face is surmounted by three figures (the King between Death and Saint Ursus, patron saint of the town).

★ **Cathedral of St Ursus (St. Ursenkathedrale)** – This imposing baroque building was designed in the Italian style in the 18C by two Ticino architects, and took the place of the cathedral dedicated to Saints Ursus and Victor, martyrs from the Theban Legion who, having escaped the massacre of Aguane *(see St-Maurice)*, were beheaded at Solothurn.

The vast nave is supported by piers with engaged pilasters and floriated capitals. This decoration continues along the false gallery under the clerestory. A dome surmounts the transept crossing. The carved pink marble pulpit and the paintings in the chancel and at the transept crossing are the main decorative features of this building, which has a fine unified appearance. Pleasant gardens are laid out behind the east end of the cathedral.

Jesuits' Church (Jesuitenkirche) – This was built at the end of the 17C; it has a nave★ of three bays decorated with frescoes and stucco. A gallery runs along the first two bays, so that the third seems to form a transept.

The gigantic high altar is adorned with a great painting representing the Assumption, framed between two large green marble pillars. The double organ-loft is delicately decorated.

Former Arsenal (Altes Zeughaus) ⊙ – Presently converted into a museum, this old arsenal contains a large collection of weapons and uniforms dating from the Middle Ages up to the 17C. The second floor boasts 400 breast-plates and suits of armour, whilst the ground floor displays a German tank used in the Second World War and a collection of cannon, both old-fashioned and modern.

Museum of Fine Arts of Solothurn (Kunstmuseum Solothurn) ⊙ – Most of the exhibitions are devoted to Swiss art from 1850 onwards. The most interesting collections are on the first floor. Alongside works by Ferdinand Hodler, Maurice Barraud and Cuno Amiet, all contemporary painters, note two stunning portraits executed by bygone masters. **Virgin with Strawberries** ★ is a painting on wood of the Rhenish School (*c* 1425), remarkable on account of its strong, vivid colours (blue, green, gold, crimson, ruby) and the graceful attitude of the two characters. As for **The Madonna of Solothurn** ★ – the work of Holbein the Younger – it is full of majesty and shows strict composition in which gold, red and blue predominate.

Natural History Museum (Naturhistorischesmuseum) ⊙ – The museum instructs the visitor on European fauna (alive and fossilized): mammals (ground floor – dioramas of animals and human beings), birds, fish, reptiles (first floor). The second floor contains displays on Swiss geology and mineralogy.
The basement houses temporary exhibitions.

Blumenstein Museum ⊙ – *Access northwest of the town centre (follow directions for Schloss Blumenstein) via the Untere Steingrubenstrasse, the Herrenweg on the right and the Blumensteinweg on the left.*
This large 18C building, surrounded by a small park, exhibits various collections of different periods: furniture, tapestries, sculpture (religious and cult objects), costumes, ceramics, musical instruments... On the ground floor's verandah are lovely 16C stained-glass windows, together with a model of the town.

★ **SPIEZ** Berne   Pop 11 182

Michelin map **217** fold 7 or **427** fold 13 – Local map see BERNESE OBERLAND – Alt 628m – 2 060 – Facilities

This charming little town on the south shore of Lake Thun and at the foot of the Niesen has a beautiful **site** ★ best seen from a terrace at the exit from the town beside the road to Interlaken.
Spiez is a pleasant summer resort and a good excursion centre.

Spiez

SIGHTS

Castle – The medieval castle, crowned with several massive towers, stands on a spur of the Spiezberg overlooking the lake and the bay. It was built in the 12 and 13C and has been enlarged and restored several times. From the public garden on the esplanade in front of the castle entrance, you overlook the harbour containing sailing and pleasure boats. Many chalets nestle among the greenery on the far shore.

Museum ⊙ – The various rooms contain mementoes of the former owners of the castle, the Erlachs and Bubenbergs, and some fine Gothic, Renaissance and baroque inlaid furniture. The rooms are adorned with rich woodwork and stained-glass windows. From the top of the great tower there is a fine **panoramic view** ★ ★ of the site of Spiez, Lake Thun, the Niesen in the south and the Beatenberg in the east.

Old Church (Alte Kirche) – This Romanesque church (late 10C, now disused), near the castle, is on the basilical plan, with three aisles and semicircular apses (fine frescoes). To the left of the chancel are the tombs of Sigismond of Erlach and Jeanne of Budenberg.

STANS ⓒ Nidwalden   Pop 6 217

Michelin map **217** fold 9 or **427** fold 14 – Local map see Lake LUCERNE – Alt 451m
– 1 480ft – Facilities

Stans has remained an agreeable town of purely local interest, making a good
excursion centre – especially for going by funicular and cable-car up to the
magnificent Stanserhorn belvedere *(see below)* – or a convenient halt when the
hotels in the Lucerne district are full.
It was in the Diet at Stans in 1481 that Nicholas of Flüe *(qv)* saved the still fragile
structure of the young Confederation by his conciliatory intervention.

SIGHTS

Church – Its large Romanesque **belfry★**, with four tiers of arcades, towers above
the main square. The spire was added in the 16C. The spacious interior, in the early
baroque style, is impressive. The statues which adorn it stand out in dazzling white
on altarpieces carved from the local black marble.
Nearby the Chapel of the Ossuary, in Late Gothic style, contains frescoes on the
north wall of the nave and a charnel-house in its crypt.
Below the church note the well-known monument commemorating the sacrifice of
Arnold von Winkelried at the Battle of Sempach *(qv)*.

EXCURSIONS

★★**Stanserhorn** ⊘ – Alt 1 898m – 6 227ft. A pleasant ride in a funicular and cable-car
takes you to the upper station (the huge serrated wheels of the winch, which
hoisted the old funicular, can be seen) from where a portion of the view *(viewing
table)* seen from the top is offered. Walk to the summit *(20 minutes Rtn)* from
where there is a splendid **panorama★★** of: Lake Lucerne to the north, the peaks of
the Swiss Alps to the south (Titlis Glacier) and to the southwest, the peaks of the
Bernese Alps, including the Jungfrau Massif.

★**Road to Seelisberg** – 22km – 13 1/2 miles – about 1 hour – itinerary ② of the
Lake Lucerne local map.
Start at Stans, go under the motorway to the large town of **Buochs,** located on the
south bank of Lake Lucerne; continue along the lake shore via Niederdorf to the
charming village of **Beckenried.** (There are beaches.) After St Anna and a steep climb
look back and admire the silhouette of Mount Pilatus. After a stretch of road under
wood, at Emmetten, there is a lovely view to the left of the lake. The road then
drives through an undulating landscape. Before arriving at **Seelisberg★** *(qv)* there is
a view, below and to the right, onto the small Seeli Lake set at the foot of the
Niederbauen Chulm Cliffs.

The length of time given in this guide
- for touring allows time to enjoy the views and the scenery.
- for sightseeing is the average time required for a visit.

★★ STEIN AM RHEIN Schaffhausen   Pop 2 793

Michelin map **216** fold 8 or **427** fold 6 – Alt 413m – 1 355ft – Facilities

The picturesque medieval town of Stein am Rhein is built on the north bank of
the Rhine, close by the outflow of the Untersee – the western basin of Lake
Constance.

Painted houses

★★OLD TOWN *3/4 hour*

Its character is apparent as soon as you approach the bridge over the Rhine. On the right are half-timbered houses, whose foundations dip into the river. But the Town Hall Square (Rathausplatz) and the main street (Hauptstrasse) form an exceptional picture with their flower-decked fountains and their oriel-windowed houses, whose fully-painted façades develop the theme of each house sign: House of the Pelican, Inn of the Sun, House of the Red Ox, House of the White Eagle, etc.

Historical Museum (Historische Sammlung) ⊘ – *Housed on the second floor of the town hall (Rathaus).* Here weapons, Delft porcelain and historiated stained-glass windows of the 16 and 17C recall the town's past.

St George's Monastery (Kloster St Georgen) ⊘ – This former Benedictine monastery, set up at Stein in the 11C by the German Emperor Heinrich II, has kept its medieval character but has been converted into a **museum★** (history, local art). The various rooms are adorned with carved ceilings, panelling and inlaid furniture and are sometimes decorated with 16C monochrome paintings *(grisailles).*
You will notice the monks' cells, with their fine stone paving, the bailiff's room, the cloisters and the chapterhouse. The Romanesque church, a 12C basilica with a flat ceiling and no transept, has been restored.

EXCURSION

★**Hohenklingen Castle** – *2.5km – 2 miles north.* A steeply uphill road running partly among vineyards, partly through woods, leads to the Hohenklingen Castle. From the tower you will see a **panorama★** of Stein am Rhein and its site, the Rhine, the surrounding hills and beyond them the Alps, from which the Säntis emerges.

SURSEE Lucerne   Pop 8143

Michelin map **216** fold 17 or **427** folds 5 and 14 – Alt 504m – 1654ft

The small old town of Sursee stands near the northwest corner of Lake Sempach. It has kept some of its atmosphere in spite of the fires that ravaged it between the 14 and the 17C.

SIGHTS

★**Town Hall (Rathaus)** – This fine building of the Late Gothic period was built in the middle of the 16C and is flanked by two towers. One ends in a curious little belfry. The other is hexagonal and is crowned with a dome.
The façade with a stepped gable is pierced by many mullioned windows.

Beck House – This house, built in 1631 for the mayor, Schnyder von Wartensee, has a three-storey façade in the Renaissance style. The frames of the mullioned windows are richly decorated.

Basle Gate (Baseltor or Untertor) – This town gate, a vestige of the former ramparts, is flanked by a half-timbered house whose white façade is intersected by red beams.

D'après photo Friebel

Town Hall

Mariazell Chapel – *On the outskirts of town near the Beromünster road.* Built in the 17C, this pilgrim's chapel is adorned with a ceiling decorated with naïve paintings representing Noah's Ark, the Tower of Babel and other scenes from the Old Testament.
From the open space near the gateway there is a **view★** of the lake, the Alps and the Jura.

EXCURSION

Beromünster – *7.5km – 5 miles northeast of Sursee.*

This little town, near which stand the transmitters of the Swiss National German-language Broadcasting Station, gets its name from the monastery (Münster) founded in 980 by Count Bero of Lenzburg and transformed in the 13C into a priory for lay canons.

Collegiate Church (Stiftskirche) – The church was built in the 11 and 12C but was almost entirely remodelled in the baroque period. The porch is adorned with many shields bearing the arms of former canons. The raised chancel is enclosed by a wrought-iron screen and furnished with remarkable **stalls★** (1609). Their carved panels represent episodes of the life of Christ. The treasury holds the reliquary of Warnebert (7C).

Castle-Museum (Schloss-Museum) ⊘ – The museum, housed in the castle's medieval tower, displays a collection of furniture, paintings, local costumes, tools and objects from Beromünster and its environs as well as a reconstruction of the Helyas Heyle print room where in 1470, the first book was printed in Switzerland.

SUSTEN PASS ROAD

Michelin map **217** folds 8, 9 and 10 or **427** folds 14 and 15

The Susten Pass road (Wassen to Innertkirchen) was built between 1938-45. It was the first great mountain road in the Confederation designed for motoring. It is an engineering masterpiece. It is better to cancel this trip or postpone it if the weather is not set fair. You should arrange your schedule so as not to find the Sustenhorner Glaciers in shadow.

FROM ANDERMATT TO MEIRINGEN

62km – 38 miles – about 2 1/2 hours – Itinerary ⓵ *of the Bernese Oberland local map*

★**Andermatt** – *See Andermatt.*

The principal feature of the Andermatt-Wassen run, which uses the St Gotthard road along the bottom of the Reuss Valley, is the steep sided Schöllenen Defile.

★★**Schöllenen** – *See Schöllenen.*

Göschenen – *See Schöllenen Road.*

Wassen – *See Schöllenen Road.*

From Wassen to Meiendörfli, the Susten Pass road (the word Susten means public goods depot), which cuts through the rock, is at first curiously interlaced with the railway track. The latter makes a great loop, largely underground, to cross the ridge between the main Reuss Valley and the hanging valley of the Meienreuss River (Meiental). Notice, straight ahead downstream in the Reuss Valley, the isolated pyramid of the Bristen.

The road from Meiendörfli to the pass, uphill all the way, climbs from ledge to ledge, higher and higher above the Meiental, which for a long time seems to be closed by the jagged peaks of the Fünffingerstöck (Five Fingers). As you approach the upper hairpin bends and the tunnel through the crest, the final cirque of the valley appears in its turn, with the symmetrical, triangular rocky faces of the Sustenspitz and the Klein Sustenhorn dominating the pass from the south.

A viewing table 700m – about 1/2 mile from the east end of the tunnel makes it possible to pick out the chief rocky summits of the Spannörter and Bristen groups.

★★**Susten Pass** – *Large car park at the west end of the tunnel (Bernese slope).* The road reaches its highest point (2 224m – 7 296ft) in the 325m – 1 067ft long tunnel driven under the pass (alt 2 259m – 7 411ft – *which can easily be reached on foot*).

The finest **scenery**★★★ in this section is henceforth on the Bernese slope. The 4km – 3 miles between the western entrance and the Himmelrank are a continual marvel and should be taken as slowly as possible. In the foreground the huge flow of the **Steingletscher** dies away under a mass of reddish morainic deposits; the foot of the glacier reappears on the shores of a small lake, where miniature icebergs float. To pick out the summits of the Sustenhörner group stop at the Swiss Touring Club viewing table 2km – 1 mile below the pass.

★★**Himmelrank** – *Park inside the bend.* The road-builders named this Paradise Bend; it winds across a rocky slope which used to be called Hell Upstairs by the people of Gadmental. They were more aware of the grim appearance of this section than of the **view**★★ downstream of the verdant coomb of Gadmen and upstream of the icy Sustenhörner Summits (Sustenhorn, Gwächtenhorn).

It is in the section between the Steingletscher Hotel and Gadmen that the engineers have shown the greatest audacity.

★**Gschletter hairpin bend** – *Park inside the bend; fountain.* This loop in steep country forms a **belvedere**★ overlooking the lower Gadmental and the majestic, ruin-like escarpments of the Gadmerflue and the Wendenstöcke.

Very high up, the massive crenellated walls of the Gadmerflue and the Wendenstöcke, detached from the Titlis, stand out against the sky. Near Gadmen the floor of the valley begins to show more smiling Alpine features with maple-planted fields.

Between Gadmen and Innertkirchen you will make two more descents: the Nessental shelf is pleasant with its many walnut and fruit trees but the valley is still narrow and lonely. As you pass the last rise before arriving in the Innertkirchen Basin, the view opens out to the snowy summits which enclose the Urbachtal, on the left of the dark and rugged crests of the Engelhörner.

Between Innertkirchen and Meiringen *(qv)* you follow the road to the Grimsel *(qv).*

★★**Aare Gorges** (**Aareschlucht**) – *From the road to Meiringen, 1km – 1/2 mile. See Meiringen: Excursions.*

★**Meiringen** – *See Meiringen.*

A SELECTION OF SKI RESORTS

Resort	Altitude
Arosa	1 742m-5 715ft
Crans-Montana	1 500m-4 921ft
Davos	1 563m-5 128ft
Gstaad	1 080m-3 543ft
St. Moritz	1 856m-6 089ft
Wengen	1 275m-4 183ft
Zermatt	1 620m-5 315ft

Michelin map **217** folds 6 and 7 or **427** fold 13 – Local maps see BERNESE OBERLAND and EMMENTAL – Alt 560m – 1837ft – Facilities – Plan of conurbation in the current Michelin Red Guide Switzerland

Thun is one of the most original towns in Switzerland. It occupies an admirable **site**★★ within view of the Bernese Alps. The city was first established on an islet in the Aare at the point where the river flows out of Thun Lake (Thunersee), and it gradually spread over the neighbouring shores at the foot of the Schlossberg, while passing from the hands of the Zähringens *(p 54)* to those of the Kyburgs. The second dynasty having become extinct in its turn, Thun passed under the control of the Gentlemen of Berne. The old quarters lie on the right bank of the Aare but the modern town with its iron works has spread westward over the left bank.

OLD TOWN

The bustling **Hauptgasse**★ has an amusing feature: the flower-decked terraces of the houses serve as footpaths, so that one walks on the roofs of the shops installed in the arcades at ground level. From the upper part of this street with its broad overhanging roofs a curious covered staircase (Kirchtreppe) leads to the church and Castle of Kyburg.

The **Rathausplatz**★ is surrounded by arcaded houses and adorned with a flower-decked fountain. With the castle which dominates it, the Rathausplatz makes a fine picture.

A covered bridge (Obere Schleuse), crosses the Aare.

THUN

Bahnhofbrücke 2
Berntorpl. 3
Gen. Guisanplatz 5
Grabenstr. 6
Kirchentreppe 9
Marktgasse 10
Maulbeerpl. 12
Obere Hauptgasse 13
Rathauspl. 14
Unter-Bälliz 15

★ **Castle** (Schloss) – Reached by the covered staircase (Kirchtreppe) mentioned above. It rears its massive keep, flanked by four towers, which now contains the Historical Museum, at the north end of the Schlossberg.

★ **Historical Museum** (Historisches Museum) ⊙ – The magnificent Knights' Hall contains beautiful tapestries – one from the tent of Charles the Bold, seized by the Confederates after the Battle of Grandson – and standards, chests and carved coffers.
The popular arts of Thun and the Bernese Oberland are represented by furniture, pottery and rustic utensils, while pictures recall the history of the town. Above the Knights' Hall is a retrospective exhibit of the Swiss Army in the 19C (firearms, uniforms).
From the top floor of the tower you can reach the four corner turrets which afford a wide **panorama**★★ of the town and the Aare, Thun Lake and the Bernese Alps from the Stockhorn in the west to the Niesen in the south, embracing the Jungfrau, the Eiger and the Mönch.

Church (Stadtkirche) (B) – The parish church stands at the other end of the Schlossberg. Its large octagonal tower with a belfry covered with small round tiles dominates a fresco-decorated porch.
From the church terrace there is a fine **view**★★ of the town, the lake and the Alps.

THE LAKE SHORE

★★ **Jakobshübeli** – From this hill equipped as a belvedere (viewing table), there is a semicircular **panorama**★★ towards the Stockhorn and the Jungfrau.

Schadau Park (Park Schadau) – Set on the lake shore, this pleasant garden surrounding a castle offers a fine **view**★★ *(viewing table)* of the summits of the Bernese Alps, particularly the Finsteraarhorn (alt 4 274m – 14 022ft), which is the highest point of this mountain group.

Wocher Panorama ⊙ – The park is the setting for the rotunda housing Marquard Wocher's panorama portraying Thun and its environs around 1810. These "pictures without boundaries" were popular at the end of the 19C.

EXCURSION

Einigen – 11km – 6 1/2 miles south via ③.
Halfway between Thun and Spiez, the charming village of Einigen is located on the south bank of Lake Thun, across from a lovely mountain landscape.
The small Romanesque church, with a brilliant roughcast, is topped by a pinnacle turret. With the tiny cemetery surrounding it, and sloping down in terraces to the lake, the church forms a picturesque **scene**★.
The church's interior is decorated with 15 and 16C stained-glass windows.

★★ THUN LAKE

Michelin map **217** fold 7 or **427** fold 13

18km – 11 miles long, almost 4km – 2 1/2 miles wide and 217m – 7 1/2ft deep, Thun Lake (Thuner See) is one of the loveliest and largest sheets of water in Switzerland and very much appreciated by the tourist who admires its location amidst green mountains with snowy summits (among them the Jungfrau).
Motor-boat service links the different localities on the lake shore.

FROM THUN TO INTERLAKEN

23km – 14 miles – about 1 hour – Itinerary **5** *on the Bernese Oberland local map*

★★**Thun** – *Time: 1 1/2 hour. See Thun.*

From Thun to Oberhofen the road, after emerging from the pretty residential suburbs of Thun, remains within view of the summits of the Bernese Alps (Eiger-Mönch-Jungfrau and, more to the right, the three characteristic snowy ridges of the Blümlisalp). In the foreground, on the opposite shore, the Niesen pyramid and the rocky Stockhorn are prominent.

Hünegg Château ⊘ – Located in a wooded park which slopes down to the lake, this large edifice (1863), in spite of its size, cannot be seen from the road.
Inside, the apartments (1900) have been arranged into a museum of the *Jugendstil (Art Nouveau)*. There is also a room evoking the life of the Swiss student at the time (uniforms, duelling weapons etc.) and on the second floor there is an exhibition of works by the Bernese painter Martin Lauterburg (d 1960).

Oberhofen – A **castle** ⊘, jutting into the waters of the lake, forms an enchanting **picture★** *(illuminated at night)*, opposite the summits of the Bernese Alps, making Oberhofen a place of artistic interest for visitors to the Oberland.
Originally, in the 12C, the castle was a dwelling-tower. It owes its present appearance to enlargement and restoration carried out from the 17 to the 19C. It is now a branch of the Bernese Historical Museum *(p 58)*, specially used for the display of period furniture (Louis XIV, Louis XV, Empire) and collections of popular art illustrating life in the Bernese Oberland.
The landscaped park laid out on the shore of the lake is one of the most pleasant features of the visit.
Between Oberhofen and Merligen, there is a superb **run along the quays★★**, facing Spiez and the mouth of the Kander Valley, the best side of the lake for sun and flowers. The Blümlisalp Massif, clearly visible through this gap, now draws near.
Merligen marks a definite change of surroundings. The road now becomes a *corniche* along the steep slopes of the Nase (Nose) promontory over the eastern basin of the lake, whose lonely shores form a contrast with the little Riviera you have just come through.
During the descent through several tunnels, beginning 1km – 1/2 mile after Beatenbucht (the starting-point of the Beatenberg funicular), the view will open out over the Bödeli Plain, enclosed between the wooded chains of the Harder (on the left) and the Rugen (on the right) and dominated in the background by the rocky points of the Schynige Platte. This is the site of Interlaken.
Before Unterseen, the road passes at the foot of the Beatushöhlen Grottoes, hidden in a impressive cliff, with a cascade tumbling down.

★★★**Interlaken** – *Time: 1 hour. See Interlaken.*

Protection of Alpine flora

In Switzerland the picking of the following Alpine flowers (Cyclamen, Alpine Aster, Primrose and Edelweiss) which are particularly threatened is strictly controlled.

★ TICINO ALPS

Michelin map **218** folds 1, 2, 11 and 12 or **427** fold 15

The Ticino, the southernmost canton of the Confederation, is Italian-speaking and Roman Catholic and yet, since the Middle Ages, attached politically to Switzerland. Mainly a mountainous region with the Lepontine Alps in the north, the canton is divided by three river systems with the Ticino River as the main system. It cuts into the southern face of the St. Gotthard from the Lombard Plain to the highest peaks of the St. Gotthard Massif.
The barrier, formed by the massif, shelters the shores of Lakes Maggiore and Lugano, offering these resort areas a pleasant Mediterranean climate.
The mountainous aspect of the country at this southernmost part of the Alps can be fully appreciated when taking the St. Gotthard and Lukmanier Pass roads *(see below and overleaf)* as well as the Nufenen Pass road *(qv)*.

★THE ST GOTTHARD PASS ROAD

See the St.Gotthard Massif for the history of this road.
Most of the present siting dates from 1830 but extensive resurfacing and widening of the roadway – especially necessary in the Tremola Valley – has improved it considerably. On the Ticino side the road is much faster than along the Reuss.
The St. Gotthard road carries heavy traffic.
The St. Gotthard Pass is usually blocked by snow from November to June.
The St. Gotthard road tunnel between Göschenen and Airolo, which was opened at the end of 1980, holds the new world record in length: 16km – 10 miles.

FROM ANDERMATT TO BIASCA

65km – 40 miles – about 2 hours – Itinerary ② on the St. Gotthard Massif local map

★ **Andermatt** – *See Andermatt.*

The last climb to the St. Gotthard begins on the Andermatt slope at the foot of the ancient Hospental Watch-tower. The road climbs above the Urseren Valley, barred, to the right of the Furka Pass, by the snowy Galenstock Peaks. After this, the road slips into the inhospitable Gams Valley.

St. Gotthard Pass (Passo del San Gottardo) – Alt 2 108m – 6 919ft. In a mournful setting of rounded rocks and scattered lakes, the pass owes its name to a chapel erected about 1300 in honour of St Gotthard, Bishop of Hildesheim (near Hanover).

Tremola Valley – *Access in August only. 13km – 8 miles from St. Gotthard Pass.* The road coils loop over loop in this steep corridor with the alarming name of Trembling Valley. Seen from below (stand on the disused bridge at the bottom of the ravine) the road, with its multiplicity of apparently interlaced sustaining walls, gives a good idea of the road-builders' enterprise.

The modern road, an exceptionally bold piece of work, avoids the difficult crossing of the Tremola Valley by a change of route. It follows the mountainside with only three hairpin bends – one of which is built partly on a curved viaduct, another is a **belvedere★** – and a tunnel 700m – about 1/2 mile long.

The descent is very steep within sight of the Upper Leventina, which lies wide open between slopes dotted with villages nestled at the foot of a campanile, with their Ticino stone houses and Alpine chalets with wooden upper storeys.

The Ambri-Piotta Basin, enclosed between woods of firs and larches, among which you will see the conduits of the Ritóm power station, opens out between Airolo (facilities) and the Piottino Defile.

Below the Piottino Defile the valley is gradually shut in by steep spurs with wild ravines the torrents of which end in waterfalls.

Faido – Facilities. Thanks to its hotel accommodation and a neighbourhood rich in woodlands and running water (La Piumogna Cascades) this township, although the administrative centre of the Leventina, is considered a summer holiday resort.

The semicircular main square with shady lime trees, a statue dedicated to local glories, houses covered by curious conical stone roofs and cafés timidly setting up a few chairs in the open air, makes a lovely Italian scene.

As you are leaving Faido, look out for the attractive, high-perched Church of Calonico.

★ **Giornico** – *See Giornico.*

The lower level of the Leventina shows espalier vines. Although marred by the smoke from the chemical factory at Bodio, this section has an attractive wild aspect among the steep shoulders of the Cima Bianca, the Pizzo di Mezzodì and the Madone Grosso.

Biasca – *See the Ticino Alps.*

★ THE LUKMANIER PASS ROAD

From Biasca to Disentis/Mustér

66km – 40 miles – about 3/4 hours – Itinerary ① on the St.Gotthard Massif local map

The Lukmanier Pass is usually blocked by snow from November to May.

Biasca – This small town, at the intersection of the Ticino and Brenno Valleys, is dominated by the 12C Church of Saints Peter and Paul, which is built into the rock and accessible by a long stairway. This Romanesque church made of local granite has a tall bell tower with arches. Its façade, decorated with a fresco of Christ Blessing (partly worn away), has a peristyle and double flight of steps.

Inside, the nave is vast with a flat, decorated ceiling; the chapel (south side) is in the baroque style; remains of interesting polychrome **frescoes** ⊘ may be seen in the aisles (14-15C) and apse (17C).

Malvaglia – The Romanesque **campanile★** of the church, the arches of which approach the summit in the Lombard fashion, is the most graceful in the Blenio Valley. The barrenness of the lower **Blenio Valley**, accentuated by the destructive work of the tributaries of the Brenno, decreases beyond Dongio.

A more verdant basin now opens out, while the bold pyramid of the Sosto rises ahead.

Lottigna – This village stretches along the valley in terraces. Located in the former bailiffs' house (15C), which is decorated with the coat of arms of the first Swiss cantons, is the **Blenio Museum** ⊘. It houses an ethnographic collection (tools, utensils and traditional regional costumes), religious art (sculpture, ecclesiastical ornaments) and a large arms collection (14C to the present).

At Aquarossa bear left onto the small road which runs along the western side of Blenio Valley.

Prugiasco – The baroque interior of St Ambrose is delightful: altar table in carved gilt wood, in the chapel (south) above a statue of Madonna and Child are stucco and painted medallions.

Left of the church take the street which climbs, then narrows and follow it for 2km – 1 mile to the foot of a grassy knoll, on top of which stands the lone sanctuary of Negrentino.

★**Negrentino San Carlo Church** ☉ – *1/2 hour on foot Rtn.* This small Romanesque church (11C) turns its east end – double apse flanked by a campanile decorated with twin windows – towards the valley. The interior is painted with an admirable series of polychrome **frescoes**★★ (11-16C): Nativity, Crucifixion, etc...

Via Castro (small 1730 church), Ponto-Valentino, you arrive at Aquila and the direct road to Lukmanier. From Olivone to Acquacalda the road avoids the Olivone dead-end in two series of hairpin bends separated by the Camperio shelf. Soon the **view**★ opens eastward to the snowy peaks of the Adula Massif.

Lukmanier Pass (Passo del Lucomagno) – Alt 1 916m – 6 286ft. The pass marks the parting of the waters, the change from one language to another – Romansh to Italian – and a cleavage between two types of local architecture: to the south, the villages are groups of stone buildings around slender campaniles; to the north they have wooden chalets and domed churches. The Lukmanier is the lowest of the Swiss transalpine routes, but owing to its roundabout approaches on the north slope of the Alps it has long yielded its place to the St Gotthard for international traffic. On the Rhine side part of the high Alpine hollow is flooded by the waters of the Santa Maria Dam.

Between the Santa Maria Dam and Disentis/Mustér, beyond a valley choked with debris and thickets formed of a few clumps of dwarf alders and rhododendrons, the road crosses the clear Cristallina Rhine and, as conifers begin to reappear, debouches into the central basin of the Medel Valley. With its sloping pastures cut by zigzag ravines, dark chalets and the domed belfry of Curaglia, this little mountain retreat makes a most attractive **picture**★. Notice the vertical silos in which grain is left to finish ripening, after being harvested early because of the severity of the climate.

Medel Gorges (Medelserschlucht) – The Rhine Falls at Medel roar in this rocky cleft, where the road passes through many tunnels. The old road, which can now be followed only on foot after the lower mouth of the second tunnel (over 500m – 1/3 mile long), is more spectacular. Below, the white Abbey of Disentis and the Tödi Massif soon appear through the gap of the Medel Gorges.

Disentis/Mustér – *See Disentis/Mustér.*

TRAVERS VALLEY

Michelin map **216** fold 12 and **217** fold 3 or **427** folds 11 and 12

The Areuse River wends its way through this wide lush valley where fields of crops are interspersed with attractive towns, and slopes are blanketed with firs. This valley, one of the main crossover points between France and Switzerland – the road from Pontarlier to Neuchâtel passes through – presents to the tourist, at its furthest eastern point, two pleasant walks: Areuse Gorges and the Creux du Van Nature Reserve.

FROM FLEURIER TO NOIRAIGUE

28km – 18 miles – about 3 hours – Local map see Swiss Jura

Môtiers – This pleasant village has preserved several 17 and 18C houses and a church, a former Gothic abbey church rebuilt in 1679. Its two small **museums** ☉ are worthy of attention: the Jean-Jacques Rousseau Museum (memorabilia) located in the house Rousseau lived in from 1762-65 and the local museum, and 18C home with a carved façade, known locally as the "maison des Mascarons".

Travers Asphalt Mines – The very first deposit was discovered in 1711 by Eirini d'Eyrinys, a Greek physician who subsequently published a book by the title of *Essay on Asphalt or Natural Cement*. This precious mineral, a water-resistant combination of limestone and bitumen, was exported to all corners of the world from 1830 to 1986, after which its exploitation ceased. During this period, a total of two million tonnes of rock were extracted, covering a distance of 100km – 62 miles of galleries excavated by man. Visitors are first shown the Mining Museum (geological cross-sections, diagrams explaining the extraction and exploitation of asphalt, photographs of miners at work, display of early mining equipment, lumps of asphalt, etc.), from where they continue on foot through several galleries (helmets and electric torches are provided). There are a number of stops at which the various operations are commented (destruction by explosives, ventilation, supporting structures, loading, transportation), bringing to life an important chapter in the industrial and social history of the Travers Valley.

La Brévine – This small area of plateau has received the nickname "Swiss Siberia" because of its very cold winters – it registers the lowest temperatures in Switzerland! The ride up offers views of Travers Valley. The plateau, surrounded by dark green fir trees squared off by walls enclosing crops and pastures (cattle, horses) and sprinkled with chalets, has as its centre La Brévine (alt 1 043m – 3 422ft) at the edge of an immense coomb of high mountain pastures.

★★**Creux du Van** – *From the Ferme Robert allow 2 1/2 hours Rtn to walk up to Le Soliat by a path to Dos d'Ane, 1km – 1/2 mile east of Le Soliat.* This nature reserve (flora and fauna – chamois, ibex – are protected) covering 11km² – 4sq miles, includes this typical example of a Jura blind valley crowned by a superb cirque of cliffs which open in a U-shape towards the Areuse Gorges and look down on rubble blanketed by fir trees.

From its highest point, Le Soliat (alt 1 463m – 4 800ft), there is a magnificent **view**★★ to the south onto Neuchâtel Lake and the peaks of the Alps beyond. From the paths running along the top of the cliffs, there are pleasant views onto the verdant hills of the nature reserve and to the north onto the Jura heights.

Return to Noiraigue.

★**Areuse Gorges** – *Time: 1 1/2 hours. See Areuse Gorges.*

TROGEN Appenzell (Ausser-Rhoden)   Pop 2 042

Michelin map **216** northeast of fold 21 or **427** fold 7 – 10km – 6 miles southeast of St Gallen – Local map see APPENZELL DISTRICT – Alt 903m – 2 963ft

Trogen is built on a hill in the picturesque district of Appenzell within view of Lake Constance. It has many middle-class houses, some of which are real palaces built by rich merchants of former days.

Landsgemeindeplatz – The traditional meeting *(see the Introduction: Democracy in Action)* of the half-canton of Appenzell – Ausser-Rhoden – takes place every even year in the Landsgemeindeplatz, while, in uneven years, the ceremony is held at Hundwil. Among the fine houses around it you will notice the Zur Krone, an inn with its overhanging roof and two superimposed gables. The many-windowed façade is ornamented with repeated patterns in which grey-blue, brown and green tones predominate.

Town Hall (Rathaus) – This severe-looking building was the former Zellweger mansion.

Children's Village of Pestalozzi – *1km – 1/2 mile south by the Bühler road.* The houses are reserved for war orphans of various nations. Pestalozzi, a citizen of Zürich (1746-1827), is honoured all over Switzerland for his educational work and his teaching methods.

UTZENSTORF Berne   Pop 3 356

Michelin map **216** fold 15 or **427** fold 13 – Local map see EMMENTAL

This lovely shaded and flowered village has a small church with 16C stained-glass windows.

Landshut Château – North of Utzenstorf, in a lovely park, stands this 17 and 18C white turretted edifice, surrounded by water (trout, ducks, swans) and nicely shaded by rare species of trees. The château was the residence of the bailiffs of Berne until 1798. To be seen inside are heavy period furnishings and huge porcelain stoves. Some of the rooms house the **Swiss Hunting Museum** ⊙ with dioramas of animals, trophies, decoys (second floor) and a remarkable collection of seignorial hunting arms from the 16 to 20C (knives, cross-bows, pistols, guns and their accessories). Located in the attic is the Museum of the History of Swiss Agriculture (tools, utensils, machines).

★★ VALAIS (Wallis)

Michelin map **217** folds 14 to 19 and **219** folds 1 to 5 or **427** folds 12 to 14 and 21 to 23

In the mosaic of Swiss cantons, the Valais includes one of the most isolated districts of the Alps: the Upper Rhône Valley from the Furka to Lake Geneva. This wide fissure, almost complety cut off from the economic centres of German Switzerland, has been kept busy for 2 000 years by intense international traffic through the Great St Bernard and Simplon Passes. It owes its well-marked regional character to the Mediterranean clarity of its sky, the deeply Catholic beliefs of its people and its impressive indus-

Raccard or mazot
The stone discs keep out rats

trial development, which does not prevent the survival in the high valleys of the most ancient ways of life.

Here you must not expect pastoral scenes, but heroic memories evoked by such places as St Maurice and Sion and unforgettable high mountain landscapes like those of the **lateral valleys★★★**, dotted with chalets and *raccards* or *mazots* (small barns perched on piles and used as granaries or store-houses).

In these wild, uninviting regions, it is common to come across wayside calvaries (wooden crosses bearing the Instruments of the Passion), set up to protect travellers and local residents from the dark dangers of the mountain.

THE VALAIS RHONE

From the glacier to the vines – Issuing from the famous terminal cataract of the Rhône Glacier, the great river is born at an altitude of 2 200m – 7 217ft, crosses the desolate Gletschboden Basin and enters the broad Valley of Conches or Goms.

Its volume is doubled at Brig when it receives the waters of the Massa flowing down from the Aletsch Glacier. It then ceases to be a mountain torrent and flows on the floor of the alluvial plain between steep rocky banks dimmed by the smoke of the factories at Visp (Viège) and Gampel.

The double obstacle created by the cone of debris of the Illgraben, cloaked in the Finges Forest (Pfynwald), and by the Sierre landslide, results in a wide break in the longitudinal profile of the valley. This is where the traditional boundary between the German-speaking Upper Valais and the French-speaking Valais has developed *(map p 22)*.

A first taste of Provence – The Central Valais between Sierre and Martigny is sheltered from the ocean winds by gigantic mountain barriers and is the driest area in Switzerland. Favoured by this Mediterranean climate, the local vines *(details of Valais wines in the Introduction)* flourish on the rugged, sun-baked ridges of the slope facing south, opposite the wooded and pastoral slopes of the **mayens** (pastures where the herds wait in May for the snow to melt on the higher Alps). The Valaisan peasants had to carry earth, washed down by the rain, laboriously up to the narrow terraces *(tablards)* on which their vines grew. *A route through the vineyards has been signposted between Martigny and Sierre.* As soon as river flooding could be prevented, the alluvial Rhône Plain was covered with orchards and plantations of asparagus and maize. Even strawberries are cultivated in the valleys of Bagnes and Entremont within sight of eternal snows.

From the orchard to the lake – At Martigny, the Rhône receives the Drance and turns sharply north, adopting the direction of its powerful tributary. Deflected towards the last foothills of the Bernese Alps by the cone of debris from the St Barthélemy Torrent, the river passes through the rocky gateway of St Maurice and debouches into the Lower Valais. This marshy plain, which spreads as it extends towards the shores of Lake Geneva, belongs politically to the Valais on the left shore of the lake.

The tumultuous natural phenomenon of the waters' meeting *(details p 105)* is the last sign of this 170km – 106 mile long mountainous Rhône.

Cow Fights
These highly popular cow fights take place in spring and autumn in Valais. At each gathering there are at least 100 contestants and they are grouped into categories according to their age and weight. The cows are usually of the Herens breed, a sturdy, muscular race of cattle with curving horns and a lively even belligerent character and are good for both meat and milking. The cows fight before being put out to grass, or being taken up to the summer pastures or when they meet another herd. The springtime fights decide the Queen Cow who leads the herd up to the summer pastures. Heads are lowered for the clash and the locking of the horns and then the struggle begins. The weaker one will retreat often chased by the winner. Organised fights are arranged to determine regional and cantonal queens where a jury awards prizes to the first six in each category. The queens then fight for the overall championship and title of Queen of Queens.

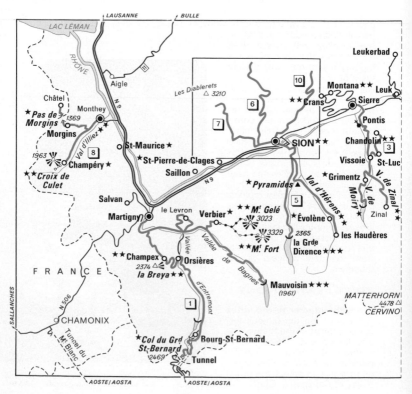

LIFE IN THE VALAIS

Valaisans and Walser – All along the Rhône Valley the traveller, seeing the signs of religious unity throughout the country – the first trace, dating from 377, of the Christian conversion of Switzerland was found at Sion – might think he is in contact with a purely Latin civilization. But beyond Sierre and especially in the vicinity of Brig the guttural sounds of a Germanic dialect begin to strike the ear and the name Valais yields to Wallis. This is because the Upper Valais was invaded from the 6C onwards by Germanic peoples who probably came down from the Grimsel and pushed on as far as Sierre. Later, these restless "Walser" often infiltrated into other southern Alpine valleys, forming permanent centres of Germanization in French-speaking districts, as at Davos for instance. In the political evolution of the country these hardy mountaineers – especially the inhabitants of the Conches Valley, represented the most fiercely democratic element. The great castle-wreckers (Raron, Saillon), ceaselessly reducing the temporal rights of the prince-bishops of Sion and the claims of local feudal lords by force, if necessary *(for the episcopal Valais see p 195),* found no difficulty in reconciling their ideal of independence with persecution of the French-speaking peoples of the Lower Valais.

The "Cardinal of Sion" – The character of **Matthew Schiner,** a Valaisan, in whom the customary tenacity of a race of mountaineers was allied with the fertile mind, fired by the universalist ideas of a man of the Renaissance, is that of all Swiss. Though his great designs led the Swiss into the camp of the vanquished at Marignano, the fact remains that this prelate was one of the great pioneers of the present Confederal system. To this period of cordial relations with the Holy See (1506) may be traced the system of recruiting still in force, by which Julius II reserved for the Swiss alone, and especially for the Valaisans of the Conches (Goms) Valley, the right to wear the picturesque uniform of the Papal Guard, designed by Michelangelo.

The union of the Valais with the Confederation dates from 1815 *(see the Historical Notes).* Before that the country was merely allied with the XIII Cantons; then, it had the status of a protected Republic and then a French Department under the name of Simplon.

The bisses – In the middle section of the Valais (from Martigny to Brig) the cultivation of the tablelands overlooking the Rhône Valley raised difficult problems of irrigation. The paucity of rain and the enclosure of torrents in the depths of inaccessible gorges gave the Valaisans here a chance to display a tenacity and inventive spirit which found expression in the *bisses.*

These narrow canals, which numbered 207 at the beginning of this century and with a total length of 2 000km – 1 250 miles, drew the glacier waters of the Rhône tributaries almost from their sources and carried them, with an imperceptible drop in level, along the mountainsides. When a rocky wall blocked their path they ran through dizzily suspended wooden troughs, the upkeep of which demanded dangerous acrobatics. The maintenance of the irrigating *bisse* and the careful distribution of its water among those who are entitled to it, hold an important place in the lives of the small mountain communities. The filling of the canals at the beginning of spring is still accompanied in some places by a religious ceremony, including a blessing. Technical progress in water supply has led to the abandonment of many of these rustic aqueducts, but some sections of them – in the woods, for instance – still offer tourists charming scenes for walks on level ground. In the Valais – above Verbier, for instance – they also have an ingenious way of transporting milk by pipe-lines. These "milk ducts" which run between the Alpine pastures and the dairies have a total length of about 220km – 138 miles.

TOUR OF THE RHONE VALLEY (UPSTREAM)

From Martigny to Glestsch

129km – 80 miles – about 2 1/2 hours – Local map see VALAIS

Between Martigny and Sion the long, straight stretches of a road edged with poplars by Napoleon's engineers do not encourage idling. Do, however, pause to visit the historic city of Sion which also makes an ideal excursion centre.
Between Sion and Brig, we recommend to tourists who have an hour to spare, the excursion from Sierre to the high terrace of Montana *(qv)*.
From Brig to Gletsch we describe *(see Conches Valley)* the Valley of Conches (Goms), a high section of the Rhône Valley through which motorists rushing to cross the Furka often pass too quickly.

TOUR

Recommended itineraries – Organized according to time (longest to shortest).

★⚀ **Great St Bernard Pass Road** – From Martigny to the Great St Bernard Pass – about 3 1/2 hours. *See Great St Bernard Pass.*

★★⚁ **Simplon Pass Road** – From Domodóssola to Brig – about 3 hours. *See Simplon Pass Road.*

★⚂ **Anniviers Valley** – From Sierre to Zinal – about 2 1/2 hours. *See Anniviers Valley.*

★★⚃ **Conches Valley** – From Brig to Gletsch – about 2 hours. *See Conches Valley.*

★★⚄ **Hérens Valley** – From Sion to Les Haudères – about 2 hours. *See Hérens Valley.*

★★⚅ **Sanetsch Road** – Starting from Sion – about 1 1/2 hours. *See Sion: Excursions.*

★⑦ **Derborence Road** – Starting from Sion – about 1 hour. *See Sion: Excursions.*

★⑧ **Morgins Valley** – From Monthey to Châtel – about 1 hour. *See Morgins Valley.*

★⑨ **Lötschental** – From the road fork Gampel to Kippel – about 3/4 hour. *See Kippel.*

★⑩ **Tseuzier Road** – Starting from Sion – about 1/2 hour. *See Sion: Excursions.*

VALLORBE Vaud   Pop 3 271

Michelin map **217** fold 2 or **427** fold 11 – Local map see Swiss JURA – Alt 769m – 2 530ft

Lying on the south side of the small Jurassian chain of Mount Or, the town of Vallorbe owes its activity to its varied industries (light engineering, plastic products) and especially to its frontier station, well-known to users of the Simplon line.
For the motorist coming from France, Vallorbe is a good excursion centre for charming one day tours in the Vaud Jura (Romainmôtier, Joux Valley, Dent de Vaulion, etc).

Iron and Railway Museum (Musée du Fer et Chemin de Fer) ⊙ – *Enter through the Tourist Information Centre.*
Iron Museum – Nestling on the banks of the Orbe, on the former site of the Grandes Forges, this museum evokes the metallurgical vocation of the region and presents the history of the iron industry. Two early forges are exhibited: one has remained untouched since it was last used while the other is operated by a smith according to old-time techniques. The museum displays objects from the Iron Age (anvils, grinding-stones and other tools manufactured by the *Grandes Forges*), as well as modern products made through precision engineering. The energy is supplied by three paddle wheels set up outside.
Railway Museum – Vallorbe's golden age as one of the stops on the Simplon line is vividly evoked by slides and a diorama and a maquette of the station in 1908: railway tools and equipment, tickets, old posters and an inspector's uniform illustrate the history of rail transport in the area. On the second floor, visitors can follow the adventures of their favourite train on a miniature toy circuit.

Fort de Pré-Giroud ⊙ – This stronghold, carved out of the rock and facing the French border, was built shortly before the Second World War. It consists of three small forts and six heavily-guarded blockhouses and watch turrets, connected by a maze of underground galleries. To your astonishment, you will discover, 30m – 100ft below ground level, a machine room (air filters, production of electric current), ammunition dump, telephone exchange, barracks, dormitory, kitchen, mess, canteen, infirmary, dental surgery and operating theatre. Figurines, weapons, documents and sound effects complete this evocation of military life in the Fort de Pré-Giroud, which could house around one hundred men.

EXCURSION

Source of the Orbe – *3km – 2 miles – plus 1/2 hour on foot Rtn.* Leave Vallorbe by the road to the Joux Valley, and then take the road to the left marked "Source-Grottes", sloping gently downhill. Leave your car near the power station. Going on foot along a shady path you will reach the end of the little rocky hollow where the Orbe rises. This is really a reappearance of the waters of Lakes Joux and Brenet.

Caves ⊙ – As you come out of the tunnel 80m – some 85ft, there is a gallery which has been built taking in the series of pillars, draperies and delicately shaped stalactites and stalagmites. You end at the dark cave affording a view of the surging waters of the Orbe hemmed in by the curious rock walls.

The **Fairies Treasure** (Trésor des Fées) ⊙ is a large collection of local minerals.

★★ VAUD ALPS

Michelin map **217** folds 14 and 15 or **427** folds 12 and 13

The Vaud Alps are divided between the Rhône and Aare Basins (Upper Sarine Valley). They owe their strong individuality to their landscape of wide green valleys and limestone escarpments, forming majestically snowy summits.

Their mountain peoples speak French, are Protestants, and build houses like those of the Bernese Oberland *(illustration p 30)*.

The Ormonts and Enhaut district valleys, served by roads described below, are excellent as means of communication between the district of Lake Geneva and the Bernese Oberland. Tourists wishing to relax a while will find peace and quiet in such holiday resorts as Château-d'Oex or Les Diablerets, while higher up, on their terraced sites 1 000m – 3 280ft above the Rhône Valley and facing the Dents du Midi, Leysin and Villars-Chesières draw the world of sport and fashion.

A striking feature of the local landscape is the extraordinary scattering of chalets over the slopes above the Grande Eau and the Sarine.

★★ ① ORMONTS VALLEY

From Aigle to Saanen

45km – 28 miles – about 1 1/2 hours – Local map above

The Pillon Pass (Col du Pillon) is usually blocked by snow from November to April.

Aigle – See Aigle.

Then the road enters, at high altitude, the wooded **gorges**★ cut by the Grande Eau.

Leysin – Facilities. *From the touring route, 4km – 2 1/2 miles by a road on the left before reaching Le Sépey.* The splendid terraced **site**★★ of Leysin, overlooking the Rhône Valley and facing the Dents du Midi, enjoys a mild climate and strong sun. It has now been equipped to receive summer holidaymakers and winter skiers.

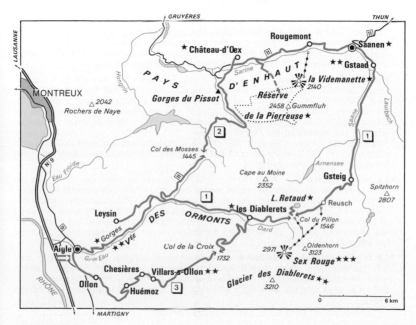

The next delightful sight is the village of Les Diablerets, at the foot of the escarpment of the same name, especially when seen during the slight descent immediately before reaching the centre of the resort.

★**Les Diablerets** – Facilities. Chief town of the Ormonts Valley. The resort is spread over a widening basin of meadows dotted with ash trees and maples. The **site**★★ is both smiling and impressive. The visitor will see very fine chalets, built and decorated in the traditional style of the Bernese Oberland.

Here the Les Diablerets Mountain wall curves deeply in a cirque (Creux de Champ) between the Sex Rouge spur and the Culan.

Between Les Diablerets and the Pillon Pass, a bend in the ravine crossed by the Bourquin Bridge gives glimpses, between the trees, of curious whitish monoliths, formed by the dissolution of gypsum. On the opposite slope the Dard Torrent escapes in thin cascades from two overlapping rock **cirques**★.

★★★**Sex Rouge** ⊙ – *Access: 35 minutes by cable-car leaving from Pillon Pass or by cable-car leaving from Reusch.* During the ascent you will see marmots and chamois and yet your attention will be caught by the view of Les Diablerets Basin and the splendid escarpment seen immediately before reaching the upper station. From the upper station, a staircase *(open only in summer)* leads to the Sex Rouge Peak (alt 2 971m – 9 747ft) from where there is a magnificent **panorama**★★★: southwards, in the distance, of the Swiss Alps (Matterhorn) and French Alps (Mont Blanc) to the nearby peaks of Les Diablerets (Oldenhorn on the left) and the superb **Les Diablerets Glacier**★★ (an extension to the north of the Tsafleuron Glacier), northwards the view extends to the Tornette and Palette Peaks which rise up behind the Ormonts Valley.

★**Lake Retaud** – *1.5km – 1 mile by a narrow mountain road from the Pillon Pass.* This pretty sheet of green water fills an Alpine hollow opposite the double cirque of the Dard, dominated on the left by the Oldenhorn and on the right by the Sex Rouge.

A third cirque will be found between the northeast spurs of the Oldenhorn (in the Valley of Oldenbach) on the way down from the Pillon Pass to Gsteig. This ends within sight of the solidly-buttressed Spitzhorn pyramid.

Gsteig – A church with a sharply-pointed timber steeple is an essential feature of this pretty village **site**★, the highest in the Sarine Valley.

The rocky hanging valley *(see "The Heritage of the Quaternary glaciers" in the Introduction)*, which appears farther upstream between the escarpments of the Spitzhorn and the Mittaghorn and from which a powerful cascade flows, leads to the Sanetsch Pass, a pass which used to be much frequented as a link between the Oberland and the Valais.

The Hotel Bären is a huge **building**★ in the Oberland style, its gable richly decorated with geometrical friezes and inscriptions.

The crane on the coat of arms alongside the Bernese bear recalls the time when the whole of the Sarine valley was part of the domain of the Counts of Gruyères *(see Gruyères)*.

★★**Gstaad** – *See Gstaad.*

The road runs northwesterly to Saanen.

★**Saanen** – *See Saanen.*

② ENHAUT DISTRICT

From Saanen to Aigle

45km – 28 miles – about 1 hour (not including visits) – Local map see Vaud Alps

Between Saanen and Château-d'Oex, the short **Allamans Defile** marks both the boundary between the cantons of Berne and Vaud and the change of language from French to German, as the name of the hamlet suggests. The slim, rocky point aptly named Rubli (the Carrot) continually catches the eye.

Rougemont – Facilities. This charming village, which was the site of a Cluniac priory between the 11C and the Reformation, has inherited from its monastic past a church, which nestles picturesquely under a huge sloping roof. Inside, the severe, three-aisled building is typical of early Romanesque structures on Swiss territory. In the stained-glass windows of the chancel note the crane, which is the symbol of the Gruyère region.

The buildings of the adjoining 16C château (entirely reconstructed and restored after a fire in 1973), which succeeded the priory, harmonize pleasantly with the hooded outline of the church.

★**La Videmanette** ⊙ – Alt 2 140m – 7 021ft. *Access by cable-car in 18 minutes leaving from Rougemont.* The upper station is on top of the Videmanette Mountain, which is situated between the Rubli and Rocher Plat Summits. From the restaurant's roof terrace, the **vista**★ encompasses (right to left): the three Summits of La Tornette, Les Diablerets, Lakes Arnensee and Retaud, behind the Gummfluh, the Oldenhorn Range, the Jungfrau Mountain range in the distance and, to the far left, rises the Eiger.

★**La Pierreuse Nature Reserve** – *On foot: allow 1/2 day.* At Les Granges bear left *(careful: very sharp bend)* into the downhill road from Gérignoz, which goes through a tunnel (single lane) and crosses a bridge over the Sarine.

Before a large sawmill bear right and take the road up the opposite side of the valley.

Leave the car before the Les Leyssalets Bridge.

The nature reserve covers approximately 1 000ha – 2 471 acres at the foot of the rocky north face of the Gummfluh.
It is in a **site**★ hilly with debris and covered by wood or pastures. The flora and fauna (spruce trees, ibex, marmots) are protected.
The twin Gummfluh Peaks appear through a gap formed by the tributary Valley of Gérignoz.

★ **Château-d'Oex** – *See Château-d'Oex.*

Pissot Gorges – A belvedere placed on a curve allows you to appreciate the depth and wooded nature of this rocky cleft, through which the Torneresse flows.
After passing through the Pissot Gorges, the road winds around the curve of the beautiful, pastoral Etivaz Valley, at the end of which there is a momentary glimpse of a small peak, the Cape au Moine. You will then come to the extensive lowland of Mosses with its woods and fields.
At La Lécherette you reach the upper valley of the Hongrin where there is a reservoir.
On the Ormonts slope the view extends downstream along the Comballaz to the icy domes of Les Diablerets ; on the left, observe the Sex Rouge and the Oldenhorn. Looking down the Grande Eau Valley you can pick out the spa and large hotels of Leysin and, on the horizon, the Dents du Midi.
Between Le Sépey and Aigle the road runs for a distance along a ledge above the wooded **Grande Eau Gorges**, and then, in a few hairpin bends, goes down to the floor of the Rhône Valley. The town of Aigle, marked by its castle, appears in a vineyard setting.

Aigle – *See Aigle.*

★★③ CROIX PASS ROAD

From Aigle to Les Diablerets via Villars

29km – 18 miles – about 1 hour – Local map see Vaud Alps

Aigle – *See Aigle.*

From Aigle, the road runs through vineyards, orchards and meadows dotted with beehives and within sight of the snowy peaks of the Grand Muveran and Les Diablerets.

Ollon – Charming wine growers' village clustered about its church.
The road now climbs, tortuous but excellent, along a *corniche* and under wood.
3km – 2 miles after Ollon a superb **view**★★ opens onto the Grand Muveran and Les Diablerets, separated by the Pas de Cheville Valley behind which is the silhouette of Gond Mountain.

Huémoz – A typical mountain village with old chalets.

★★ **Villars** – *See Villars.*

After Villars, the climb is extremely steep (13% – 1 in 7 1/2) and Les Diablerets Mountains fill the horizon with their snowy summits. Once at **La Croix Pass** (alt 1 727m – 5 666ft), the road offers excellent views of the imposing mountain range of Les Diablerets before descending to the wide basin and the resort of Les Diablerets spread out below.

★ **Les Diablerets** – *See Vaud Alps: Ormonts Valley.*

★ VERBIER Valais   Pop 1 800

Michelin map **219** north of fold 2 or **427** fold 21 – Local map see VALAIS – Alt 1 500m – 4 920ft (Verbier Resort) – Facilities – Town plan in the current Michelin Red Guide Switzerland

Preceded by **Verbier-Village** (with its two churches) the new Valais resort of Verbier, scattered over the sunny slope of the Bagnes Valley within view of the Grand Combin and Mont Blanc Massifs, continues its expansion with luxurious hotels and chalets in this privileged **site**★★.
The cirque of regular slopes converging on the new settlement offers ideal topographical and climatic conditions for the great majority of present-day skiers, who find here spacious and restful surroundings and considerable mechanical equipment suitable for downhill skiing.
Verbier is also known to long-distance skiers as the starting-point of the High Road run, of which Zermatt or Sass-Fee is the terminus.

★★ **Mont Fort** ☉ – Alt 3 329m – 1 994ft. *Access (allow 45 min): by cable-car from Verbier to Les Ruinettes; by shuttle (5 min) or on foot (30 min) up to La Chaux; by jumbo cable-car to Les Gentianes, then take another cable-car up to the top.*
A great favourite with skiers and snowboard fans on account of its lasting snow and ice, including in summer, Mont Fort on a clear day offers a **sweeping panorama**★★ *(viewing tables)* of the Alps, covering a wide geographical spectrum indeed: Italy (Matterhorn), France (Mont Blanc), the Valais (Mont Fort, Grand Combin) and the Bernese Oberland (Eiger).

★★ **Gelé Mountain** ☉ – Alt 3 023m – 9 918ft. *Access (about 3/4 hour) via cable-car from Verbier to Les Ruinettes, then change and take another cable-car to Attelas I and change again for Attelas II (near the top).*
From the cross, which indicates that you are at the rocky summit of Gelé Mountain, admire the **circular view**★★: to the south Grand Combin Massif and its glaciers; to the east Mont Fort and its glaciers; to the north the Peaks of Les Diablerets; to the west Pierre d'Avoi Mountain, Verbier below and the Entremont Valley.

Michelin map **217** fold 14 or **427** fold 12 – Local maps see Lake GENEVA – Alt 400m – 1 312ft – Facilities – Town plan in the current Michelin Red Guide Switzerland

Vevey occupies a beautiful **site★** facing the Savoy Alps at the mouth of the Veveyse Valley and the foot of Mount Pèlerin, with the blue sheet of Lake Geneva and the Alps making a splendid background.

Already capital of the Lavaux vineyards *(see under Lake Geneva)* Vevey, in the 19C, became the cradle of the Swiss industry of milk and dietetic products, and chocolate. The powerful Nestlé group has its headquarters here, together with its central laboratory and an experimental factory.

Vevey is today one of the most agreeable holiday resorts on the Vaud Riviera.

About every 25 years – the last occasion was from 30 July to 14 August 1977 – the town celebrates its "feast of the wine-growers" on a lavish scale. This is the greatest folk festival in Europe and it ends in a display in honour of Bacchus, the god of wine.

Regional lore also includes picturesque traditional markets (Saturday mornings in July and August) and the International Festival of Comic Films, held annually during the month of August.

SIGHTS

St Martin's Church (Eglise St Martin) – The present building which dates back to 1530, stands on a terrace overlooking the town. The site was originally occupied by an 11C sanctuary whose walls were discovered during excavation works. The church is dominated by a large, square tower and four corner turrets. The terrace *(viewing table)* affords a sweeping **view★** of the town, the Alps and Lake Geneva.

Jenisch Museum (Musée Jenisch) ⊘ – Installed in a large 19C building, the museum is divided into two sections.

The ground floor houses the **Prints Gallery,** presenting numerous engravings by the great masters of the past (Dürer, Rembrandt, Lorrain, Belletto, Corot) as well as by modern Swiss artists.

As for the **Fine Arts Museum** on the first floor, it displays paintings and watercolours by Swiss contemporaries (Steinlen, Hodler, Poncet, Robert, Bocion), although one can also admire works by Courbet (*Sunset on Lake Geneva,* bronze sculpture of a seagull), Tal-Coat, Bissier, Music, Valenti and Kokoschka.

History Museum of Old Vevey (Musée historique du Vieux-Vevey) ⊘ – This museum is housed in the castle which was once the residence of the Bernese bailiffs. It tells the history of the area and contains a fine collection of furniture from the Gothic period to the 18C, small wrought-iron objects and caskets, costumes and local mementoes. On the first floor, you may also visit the **Museum of the Wine-growers Fraternity** (Confrérie des Vignerons), where models of the costumes worn at earlier wine-growers' festivals (since 1819) are kept, together with prints, records and banners used during these festivities.

Swiss Museum of Cameras (Musée suisse d'appareils photographiques) ⊘ – The five floors of this museum display cameras and photographic equipment, both Swiss and foreign, dating from the late 19C to the present day, along with the reconstruction of a post Second World War dark room. Note the rare exhibits, such as a *camera obscura,* which led to the invention of the modern camera, the Chevalier lens used by Niepce and Daguerre, a series of 1885-1890 "foldings", a 1888 "photosphere" and a 1895 "physiograph". Visitors can also handle early models and test their knowledge of photography on two electronic computer games.

Alimentarium ⊘ – *Rue du Léman.* Since 1985 a neo-classical edifice has housed the Museum of Nutrition, founded by Nestlé. The three sections, currently open to the public, explain the different aspects of nutrition (production, processing, preservation, preparation and, ultimately, consumption).

This didactic and modern display also shows that the problems linked to food vary according to epoch, geographical location and ethnic and social types. The visit ends with a series of audio-visual presentations and electronic games.

EXCURSIONS

★★Mont-Pèlerin Resort – Alt 810m – 2 657ft. *Round tour of 25km – 16 miles – about 1/2 hour. Consult the local maps under Lake Geneva.* Leave Vevey by the Châtel-St-Denis-Fribourg road 2.5km – 2 miles after having passed the road to Chardonne on your left, turn left towards Attalens, then sharp left again towards the Pèlerin or Pilgrim Mountain. Several of these roads run *corniche* fashion among the vines.

From a point near the arrival station of the funicular there is a wide open **view★★** of Lake Geneva and the crest of the Vaud Alps (Dent de Jaman, Naye Rocks, Aï Tower). The drive back through Chardonne and Chexbres takes you along roads magnificently sited within view of the Dents du Midi and the summits of the Haut-Chablais in Savoy.

La Tour-de-Peilz – *2km – 1 mile by road no 9 heading toward Montreux.* The castle commissioned in the 13C by the Comtes de Savoie was subsequently altered in the 18C. Of its defensive vocation, there remain the ramparts, the moats and two corner turrets. The inside of this former keep houses the **Swiss Museum of Games** ⊘ (Musée suisse du jeu), which assembles miscellaneous games from all countries and all eras.

These are split into five groups: educational games, strategic games, simulation games, games of skill and games of chance. Each section stresses the qualities required for playing and is illustrated by a series of examples. Visitors may test their own natural ability by playing, learning and even creating new games. Several exhibitions have genuine artistic appeal, as is the case with the chess figurines carved in ivory or bone.

If you skirt the castle on the left, you will come to the yachting harbour; from there you can take a pleasant walk along the shores of the lake. Opposite stands the Grammont, dominating the Swiss landscape from a height of 2172m − 6 800ft.

Blonay − *4km − 2.5 miles east.* The Blonay-Chamby **Railway-Museum** ⊘ has given a new lease of life to a railway section which opened in 1902 and closed down in 1966. Electric trams and early steam-driven trains take travellers along a steep, winding route covering a distance of 2.95km − 2 miles. Half-way up the hill stands the former shed. It has been converted into a museum displaying old machinery, a 1914 postal van, a 1904 tram from the Fribourg area, a steam engine once linking Le Locle to Les Brenets, etc.

★★ VILLARS-SUR-OLLON Vaud

Michelin map **217** east of fold 14 or **427** fold 12 − Local map see VAUD ALPS − Alt 1 253m − 4 111ft − Facilities

Together Villars, Chesières and Arveyes form a resort perched 800m − 2 625ft above the lower Valais. It is the most highly developed mountain resort in French Switzerland and one of the most accessible for the inhabitants of the lowlands, affording a semicircular panorama of the French Alps, the Dents du Midi and the Muverans Range with the Mont Blanc, the Trient Glacier and the peaks of Les Diablerets in the distance.

THE RESORTS

Villars − The main part of the town lies along an esplanade of parkland enjoying intense sunshine within view of the Dents du Midi, which stand opposite. From the range of hotels to the golf course and the swimming pool, the local equipment makes every provision for a pleasant stay, for both sports enthusiasts or tourists seeking a restful stay.

In winter, after preliminary training on the slopes near the hotels, skiers take the rack-railway or two cable-cars to the Roo d'Orsay, Les Chaux or Bretaye, from which a fan-shaped network of ski-lifts enables them to reach the crests of the Chaux Ronde and Chamossaire (highest point: 2 113m − 6 942ft).

The artificial skating rink draws skaters at all times of the year, and also attracts spectators to watch the first class performances and entertainment held there.

Chesières and Arveyes − These resorts are recommended to residents who desire rest rather than fashionable society.

The panorama from Chesières includes the Mont Blanc Massif, between the Trient Glacier and the Aiguille Verte.

EXCURSION

From Villars to Pont de Nant − *22km − 13 1/2 miles.* Leave Villars to the south on the road to Bex. As it dips, the road presents a plunging view of the wooded Gryonne Valley crossed by a concrete bridge. La Croix de Javerne and the Dent de Morcles stand straight ahead.

La Barboleusaz − Alt 1 211m − 3 973ft. This winter sports resort is located in a lovely site overlooked by Les Diablerets. From here you can get to the ski fields of **Les Chaux★** *(5km − 3 miles by a narrow, winding road; in winter access by cable-car)* or to the **Solalex Refuge★** (alt 1 466m − 4 809ft) − via a small picturesque road (6km − 3 1/2 miles) following the Avançon torrent − in a cirque of Alpine pastures at the foot of Les Diablerets.

Gryon − Alt 1 114m − 3 655ft. Pop 827. Facilities. Old terraced village overlooking the Avançon Valley.

The road descends rapidly, winding its way between fir and larch. 2km − 1 mile before Bex bear left towards Les Plans.

At Frenières note on the left the perched village of Gryon. After Les Plans the road climbs through woodland, running parallel to a torrent.

★Pont de Nant − Lovely cirque at the base of the Grand Muveran Glaciers.

An Alpine rock garden can be visited (waterlily pond; more than 2 000 kinds of Alpine or medicinal plants from the world over).

★★ WALENSEE

Michelin map **216** folds 20 and 21 or **427** fold 16

Lake Walenstadt or the **Walensee** spreads its tarnished mirror beneath the gigantic rock bastions of the Churfisten, a sight remembered by travellers coming from Zürich, who pass through the Wessen-Sargans Gap on their way to the Rhine Valley, Austria and the Grisons.

Between Näfels and Murg, the new course of the road, which runs beside the lake, parallel with the railway, has called for large-scale civil engineering undertakings, including the construction of six tunnels and nine stretches of road cut into the mountainside above sheer drops.

It is still possible to go by the old, steep road which, as it climbs to the wooded terrace of the Kerenzerberg, affords many **bird's-eye views★★** both westwards to the Glarus Valley of the Linth and the low alluvial plain into which the torrent flows, and eastwards to the lake and Churfirsten.

★★★ WEISSENSTEIN Solothurn

Michelin map 216 fold 15 or 427 fold 4 – 10km – 6 miles north of Solothurn – Local map see Swiss JURA

The crests of Weissenstein, standing like a rampart above the Solothurn lowland, offer the excursionist one of the most impressive panoramas in the Jura.

Access ⊙ – *From Solothurn (qv), 10km – 6 miles – about 2 hours – by ⑤, Oberdorf and then a section of mountain road of which the most difficult part can be avoided by taking the chairlift from Oberdorf station to Kurhaus Weissenstein (time: 16 min). From Delémont (qv), 24km – 15 miles by road no 6 to Moutier, then by road no 30 to Gansbrunnen from where a small mountain road (for the most part not tarred) leads to the summit.*

★★★ **Panorama** – When coming from Solothurn or Gänsbrunnen by car, the summit of the climb is marked by a pastoral coomb. Turn into the road to the Kurhaus, which stands on the crest at an altitude of 1 287m – 4 222ft. *Walk down the "planetary" path more than 7km – 4 miles long on the road to Gänsbrunnen.* Leave the car in front of this establishment and make for the terrace (by the passage to the left of the building if you do not intend taking refreshments there), from where the great barrier of the Alps can be seen from the Säntis, on the left, to Mont Blanc on the right. The **bird's-eye view**★★★ of the Mittelland *(qv)* is unequalled in the northern Jura. Berne and Lakes Neuchâtel, Murten and Biel can be distinguished in clear weather.

★★ WEISSENSTEIN ROAD

Michelin map 216 folds 2, 14 and 15 or 427 folds 3 and 4

This itinerary through the Jura, with many woodland and gorge sections reserves, for its final phase, the opportunity to discover a superb panorama at Weissenstein.

FROM PORRENTRUY TO SOLOTHURN

102km – 64 miles – about 4 1/2 hours – Itinerary ① on the Swiss Jura local map

Between Gänsbrunnen and Oberdorf, the small Weissenstein road, usually blocked by snow from December to May, takes the form of a narrow roadway in bad repair on the north slope of the mountain and is very steep on the Solothurn side (gradients up to 22% – 1 in 5 – approach the hairpin bends very carefully).

Porrentruy – See Porrentruy.

After Porrentruy the road has to make a big hump to cross the Mount Terri Chain at Les Rangiers Pass.
Below Les Malettes, just before this threshold, a steep descent through the woods leads to the **Ajoie Plateau,** which is in fact part of the Franche-Comté joined to Switzerland, where belfries crowned in the style of the Franche-Comté can be seen here and there.

★ **St-Ursanne** – See St-Ursanne.

This hilly, nearly always wooded section is none the less pleasant and not too slow, but open views are rare. The popular Rangiers Sentinel, a monument commemorating the mobilization of the Swiss Army during the First World War, marks the beginning of the pass.

   Start driving towards St-Brais.

★ **Jura Corniche** – See Franches Montagnes.

Road no 6 from the pass to Delémont affords similar conditions.

Delémont – See Delémont.

From Delémont to **Moutier,** the Birse, whose rapid course you now follow, has hollowed out two cross valleys separated by the village of Roches. The lower cross valley is definitely industrial (the ironworks at Choindez). The upper cross valley much narrower, cuts through the Raimeux Chain, whose name it bears, and runs between great rocky walls pierced by a succession of short railway tunnels. *For more on cross valleys see the Introduction: Swiss Jura.*

Chalières Chapel – In Moutier's cemetery. Leave the town westwards on the road towards Perrefitte. This Romanesque chapel (very restored), has inside its apse early 11C frescoes – on the vault is a Christ in Glory surrounded by angels, a unicorn and a griffon.

★★★ **Weissenstein** – Access and description see Weissenstein Road.

The very hard section over the wooded Weissenstein Chain – the forest is densest on the Solothurn side – ends at last in the lush orchards of the Mittelland which mark the arrival at Solothurn.

★ **Solothurn** – Time: 1 hour. See Solothurn.

★★★ WENGEN Berne

Michelin map **217** fold 8 or **427** fold 14 – Local maps see BERNESE OBERLAND and INTERLAKEN: Excursions – Alt 1 275m – 4 183ft – Facilities

Wengen is one of the most fashionable and the best-equipped mountain resorts in the Bernese Oberland. The **site★★★** of this shoulder of Alpine pastures and forests from which, after being dazzled by the Jungfrau, you can look along the Lauterbrunnen rift from a unique point of view, is a delight constantly renewed by walks along perfectly kept paths – regularly cleared of snow even in winter. In the skiing season your time can be divided between sport and rest, using the railway service to Kleine Scheidegg (or to the Eigergletscher resort in the spring) and the cable-car to Männlichen. The best-known international skiing competition is the **Lauberhorn race,** which takes place at the beginning of January.

★ WERDENBERG (BUCHS) St Gallen

Michelin map **216** fold 21 or **427** fold 16 – Local map see APPENZELL DISTRICT – Alt 451m – 1 480ft

At the north end of the populous settlement of Buchs, the old village of Werdenberg, framed in deep greenery and sleepy waters, forms a particularly welcome little **scene★** in the broad Rheinthal corridor *(qv)*, which is usually more striking for its agricultural prosperity than for its picturesqueness.
Leave the car on the promenade beside the road, alongside a pool. Opposite are the houses of Werdenberg, closely grouped at the foot of the castle of the Counts of Werdenberg.
Entering the tiny village and following the castle ramp or, better still, after taking a fork to the left, an alley bordered by a series of well-restored arcaded wooden houses, the stroller may conjure up the atmosphere of the little towns in the Rhine Valley in the 17 and 18C. He will be further helped in this by inscriptions, dates and multicoloured decorative patterns to be found on many of the house fronts.

WIL St Gallen   Pop 16 108

Michelin map **216** folds 9 and 20 or **427** fold 7 – Alt 571m – 1 873ft

Wil was formerly the residence of the abbot-princes of St Gallen. It is built on a mound at the entrance to the Toggenburg depression. The old town, with its Hofplatz and its Marktgasse, whose arcaded houses are adorned with corbels and covered by overhanging roofs, is picturesque.
From the terrace of the Church of St Nicholas (Stadtkirche) there is a fine **view★** of the Alpstein Massif (Säntis) and the Churfisten Range.

Municipal Museum (Stadtmuseum im Hof zu Wil) ⊙ – The "Hof", a massive 15C building on the summit of the hill, was once the residence of the abbots of St Gallen. The museum housed on the third floor contains a model of the city and documents recording the history of Wil.

★ WILDEGG CASTLE Aargau

Michelin map **216** north of fold 17 or **427** fold 5 – 5km – 3 miles north of Lenzburg

The impressive mass of **Wildegg Castle** ⊙, rising above the Aare Valley, was built in the 12C by a Count of Habsburg and has been enlarged and altered several times since (particularly by the Effinger family who were the owners for four centuries). It is now an outstation of the Swiss National Museum at Zürich.
The castle contains fine furniture dating from the 17 to the 19C. The Blue Room, the armoury and the library deserve special attention for the beauty of their ceilings and furnishings. From the upper storeys there is a wide view of a gently undulating landscape of fields and forests.

WILLISAU STADT Lucerne   Pop 2 866

Michelin map **216** fold 16 or **427** fold 14 – Alt 555m – 1 821ft

Founded in the 13C, Willisau still has a large section of its fortified wall. The main street of this little town leading to the Obertor, its former gateway, is a picturesque scene with its three fountains (with modern religious statues in cast-iron by Meyer-Kistler) and houses with painted façades, adorned with wrought-iron signs and covered by wide roofs, often with decorated gables.

Chapel of the Precious Blood (Heiligblutkapelle) – *In front of the Obertor, on the side opposite the parish church.* The chapel has a curious ceiling with painted panels. It is believed to have replaced, at the end of the 17C, a much older chapel which had been built on the site of a gaming-house. When one of the gamblers brandished his sword in the air, it is said, drops of blood fell on the card table. To make amends the Willisau community vowed to build a chapel here.

EXCURSION

Wolhusen – *10km – 6 miles southeast.* In the cemetary overlooking the church and Wolhusen, stands the **Chapel of the Dead** (Totenkapelle). The most interesting feature of this tiny sanctuary is the 1661 fresco which adorns its interior. It depicts a **Dance of Death** in brownish tones, subtitled by quatrains in German, attributed to each of the characters. Note the skeletons whose skulls protrude from the wall.

217

WINTERTHUR Zürich

Michelin map 216 fold 8 or 427 fold 6 – Alt 439m – 1 440ft – Town plan in the current Michelin Red Guide Switzerland

A town, under the name of Vitudurum, was established here during the Roman era. At the end of Middle Ages, Winterthur used to make the large porcelain stoves which can still be admired in some Swiss houses. The industrial development of the town, nowadays connected with the textile industry and mechanical engineering (railway equipment, diesel engines), has in no way interfered with its artistic fame, which has been kept up by patrons.
The public collections of Winterthur show a complete record of 19C European painting. The concerts given by the Collegium Musicum, founded in 1629, always draw a large audience.

SIGHTS

Oskar Reinhart Collection – Oskar Reinhart, a patron of the arts, who died in 1965, bequeathed his famous collection to the Swiss Confederation on the condition that it remain in his native town.

Oskar Reinhart Foundation ⊘ – *Stadthausstrasse 6.* Works by Swiss, German and Austrian painters from the 18, 19 and 20C are shown in this museum. Excellent drawings by Rudolf Wasmann, child portraits by Anker, works by Böcklin and Koller, paintings by the German Romantics and by artists of the Munich school as well as animal studies by Jacques Laurent Agasse may be seen. The many canvases by Ferdinand Hodler (1853-1918) show the importance attached to this leader of pre-1914 Swiss painting.

The Day Nursery by A Anker

★★**Oskar Reinhart Collection "Am Romerholz"** ⊘ – *Haldenstrasse 95.* The collector's house, set in large grounds overlooking the town, contains a very fine collection of paintings covering five centuries.
They include the German school with Cranach the Elder, the Flemish school with Bruegel, a painting by El Greco, drawings by Rembrandt, French works from the late 17 to the 19C with Poussin, Claude Lorraine, Watteau, Chardin and Fragonard, and several drawings by Daumier. The 19C is represented by artists whose works reflect the main contemporary trends in pictorial art, such as Corot, Delacroix, Courbet, Manet, Renoir and Cezanne as well as Van Gogh and closer to the present time, Picasso with drawings from the Blue period.

★**Fine Arts Museum (Kunstmuseum)** ⊘ – The town's collections include works of the 16C (Cranach), of the local schools of the 17 and 18C (Graff, Mayer, Füssli) and of Swiss and German painters of the 19 and 20C (Hodler, Vallotton, G. Giacometti, Auberjonois, Corinth and Hofer). The French schools are represented by Renoir, Bonnard, Vuillard and Van Gogh.
A part of the building is devoted to sculpture by Rodin, Maillol, Haller, Marini and Alberto Giacometti.
The museum also houses the town's library and a natural history section.

Technorama ⊘ – *Oberwinterthur, Technoramastrasse 1* – The museum presents recent scientific and technological achievements in an attractive and amusing way. This standing exhibition features several "experimental nooks" where visitors are encouraged to participate by operating various devices themselves. It is divided into eight areas: Physics (electricity, magnetism); Energy (solar rays, uranium); Water, Nature and Chaos; Mechanical Music; Materials; Textiles; Automatic Technology; Toy Trains (Bommer Collection of miniature trains).
To meet the ever-increasing demand for greater understanding, a number of demonstrations and audio-visual shows are staged at set intervals in one or several of these areas. The laboratory "Youth and Science" offers young people the opportunity to learn and have fun at the same time, under the supervision of trained instructors.

EXCURSION

Kyburg Castle (Schloss Kyburg) ⊘ – *6km – 4 miles south. Leave Winterthur by the Seen road. At Sennhof take the small road to the right and follow it along the Töss; after 1 km – 1/2 mile turn left to go to Kyburg village.*
This feudal castle was built in the 10 and 11C and passed successively from the line of the Counts of Kyburg to the Habsburgs. In 1424 it came within the bailiwick of the town of Zürich and remained so until 1798; since 1917 the castle has belonged to the canton.
Inside are remarkable collections of furniture and arms which will interest visitors with a knowledge of history and antiques. There is a good view of the surrounding countryside.

YVERDON-LES-BAINS Vaud   Pop 22 758

Michelin map 217 fold 3 or 427 fold 12 – Local map see Swiss JURA – Alt 439m – 1 440ft – Facilities – Town plan in the current Michelin Red Guide Switzerland

Yverdon-les-Bains is built at the south end of Lake Neuchâtel. It is a mineral-water spa, well known for the properties of its sulphur and magnesium springs. A group of menhirs situated outside the town, on the road to Estavayer-le-Lac, testify to the presence of human settlement in former times. This town was originally a Celtic settlement which later became Gallo-Roman. Of its Roman history it has kept only the remains of a *castrum* (fortified citadel), located near the local graveyard. The town hall, with its Louis XV façade, and especially the castle, are worthy of attention.

Castle – This castle dates from the 13C. In fact it was on the site of a former edifice, built some years earlier but not completed, that Peter II of Savoy, who had captured the town in 1259, erected this imposing fortress with its four round towers. It has lost its feudal character as the result of various changes, made mostly last century. The moats that surrounded it have been largely filled up.

Museum ⊘ – These collections, which take up several rooms of the castle, recall the history of the area since prehistoric times. Regional fauna is also represented. One of the rooms in the northeast tower presents an exhibition on the famous teacher **Pestalozzi** *(qv)*.

★★★ ZERMATT Valais   Pop 4 225

Michelin map 219 fold 4 or 427 fold 22 – Local map see VALAIS – Alt 1 616m – 5 302ft – Facilities – Town plan in the current Michelin Red Guide Switzerland

Zermatt can be reached only by rail either from Brig or Visp (Viège) where most tourists leave their cars, or from Täsch, which has a large car park. The resort is thus traffic-free and offers exceptional relaxation.
The town has two distinct aspects: from the railway station to the parish church it is a **street** of hotels and shops built in a style reminiscent of the Seilers, a family of hotel-keepers who launched the resort in 1855 (the year of opening of the Monte Rosa Hotel, on the façade of which is a medaillon dedicated to Whymper – *see below*). Beyond the church, **Old Zermatt** gathers its Valais chalets and its toast-coloured *mazots* (small barns – *qv*).
Zermatt was "discovered" a century ago by the English and it remains a mountaineer's sanctuary.
The **Matterhorn** (Mont Cervin – alt 4 478m – 14 692ft), whose hooked and inclined pyramid appears most boldly from the middle of the resort, is awe-inspiring.

CONQUEST OF THE MATTERHORN

In the 1860s, **Edward Whymper,** a young British illustrator thrilled by the mountain shapes that his publisher had asked him to draw, had been wandering for his pleasure over the Alps of the Valais, Savoy and Dauphiné, looking for unconquered peaks. He had already made the first ascents of the Barre des Écrins, the Aiguille Verte and the Grandes Jorasses, but he always came back to Zermatt or the Valtournanche, fascinated by the Matterhorn, which he had already vainly attempted eight times, starting from Breuil with the help of a well-known local guide, Jean-Antoine Carrel. In 1865, changing his plan of action, Whymper decided to attack the peak along its northeast ridge – that which faces Zermatt. On 13 July of that year the local people saw three British climbers and a guide from Chamonix – Douglas, Hudson and Michel Croz – join Whymper and his two guides from Zermatt, the Taugwalders, father and son, and set off for the mountain. Helped by ideal weather, with no falling stones, the climbers set foot on the summit of the Matterhorn on 14 July, early in the afternoon. They scored a victory over a party of climbers led by Carrel who unbeknown to them had set off from Breuil to make an attempt to reach the summit from the Italian side.
On the return journey, young Hadow, less experienced, slipped, dragging Croz, Hudson and Douglas, with him in his fall. The life-line snapped between Douglas and the elder Taugwalder. Whymper and his guides watched the frightful fall of their four companions, 1 200m – 4 000ft below. An impressive celestial phenomenon, the appearance of two crosses shining in a great arc of clouds, tested the survivors' nerves once more before they regained the valley. Carrel, approaching from the far side, reached the summit on 17 July.
This first great tragedy of the "Killer Alp" plays no small part in fostering the awesome atmosphere connected with the Matterhorn.

THE RESORT

Zermatt must be regarded essentially as a sporting resort at all seasons.

The attraction of the dozen "4 000s" (i.e. peaks over 4 000m high – about 13 000ft) to which Zermatt commands the approaches, is shown in summer by the crowd of mountaineers of all nationalities.

In winter, when the swish and jingle of sleighs take the place of the rumbling of omnibuses, tourists enjoy the sunny slopes of the Riffelberg, where skiers brought by the Gornergrat railway are in full view of the Matterhorn.

The cable-cars of the Stockhorn, the Klein Matterhorn, the Trockener Steg and the Unter Rothorn, and helicopter services up to the highest snowfields such as at Plan Rosa or the Theodule Pass make summer skiing easy at Zermatt.

Alpine Museum (Alpines Museum) ⊙ – Here relics of the first conquests of the Matterhorn (relief model) are kept and the memory of the first guides of Zermatt and of famous guests to the resort is perpetuated. An important section is devoted to Old Zermatt (reconstructions of mountain-dwellers' homes).

EXCURSIONS

★★★ **Gornergrat** ⊙ – Alt 3 135 – 10 272ft. *2 hours Rtn.*

This tour by rack-railway – the highest open-air railway in Europe – brings you not only to Riffelberg where there is a very good view of the Matterhorn but it also provides an unforgettable first sight of Mount Rosa (highest point: Pointe Dufour, alt 4 634m – 15 203ft) and its glaciers.

Spend half a day on this excursion, which you can prolong by taking the cable-car to the Stockhorn ⊙ (alt 3 407m – 11 135ft); *3/4 hour Rtn.*

★★★ **Ascent to the Klein Matterhorn** ⊙ – Alt 3 886m – 12 684ft. *Access by four successive cable-cars (time the entire trip up: 50 minutes including 1/4 hour on foot from Zermatt to the departure station).*

The first section rides above a steep corridor of rubble of which there is a view straight ahead from the mid-station of **Furi** (alt 1 865m – 6 119ft) to Zermatt.

From Furi to **Furgg** (alt 2 434m – 7 985ft) you first ride above rocky debris, then above grassy slopes where sheep graze; the Matterhorn is on the right; splendid views straight ahead onto the Théodule Glacier and behind, of the Pennine Alps.

★ **Schwarzsee** ⊙ – From Furgg a cable-car goes up *(3 minutes)* to the foot of the Matterhorn which reflects iself in this small lake nestled in a rocky verdant basin. A path goes around it. On its shore stands a chapel (restored; restored mural paintings inside).

Return to Furgg and continue the climb to the Klein Matterhorn.

The third section rides through a mineral-like landscape before ending at **Trockener Steg** (alt 2 929m – 9 610ft) where the **Théodule Glacier**★★ can be seen, its irregular-shaped pinnacles of ice in a cirque of reddish slopes streaked with cascades and topped by snowy peaks.

The fourth cable-car climbs over the glacier and stops at the highest altitude station in Europe (alt 3 820m – 12 533ft), perched on a small shelf on the side of Klein Matterhorn, 66m – 217ft from the top *(not accessible to walkers).* From this station, after going through a long tunnel, you come out over the snowfields, a paradise for summer skiers. The horizon is blocked by the Breithorn and Klein Matterhorn.

★★ **Rothorn** ⊙ – Alt 3 103m – 10 180ft. *Go up, from Zermatt by funicular (access by a long corridor) to Sunnegga, then by cable-car to Blauherd and then again by cable-car (time needed for the entire trip up: about 20 minutes including 5 minutes by funicular).*

The first part of the journey is underground; at **Sunnegga** (alt 2 285m – 7 497ft), on the edge of a plateau of Alpine pastures enhanced by a small lake, you get your first glimpse of the Matterhorn (southwest). From **Blauherd** (alt 2 577m – 8 459ft) the second mid-station in view of a lovely fir forest (on the right), the cable-car arrives on the flat, rocky summit of the Rothorn. From here the **panorama**★★ barred to the east by the Ober Rothorn stretches southwest to the Matterhorn (profile view), south onto Findelen Glacier, west onto Zermatt and north onto Nikolaital Valley.

Gorner Gorges ⊙ – *2 hours on foot Rtn. At the south exit from Zermatt, turn left (bridge) and follow the signposts.*

These impressive gorges are overlooked from a path cut in the sheer rock walls; far below the torrent surges on the floor of the ravine. Arolla pines and larch woods precede the picturesque hamlet of Blatten with its chapel, its *mazots (qv)* and its erratic boulders.

After Zumsee take the road leading back to Zermatt.

To plan a special itinerary
- consult the Map of Touring Programmes which indicates the tourist regions, the recommended routes, the principal towns and main sights.
- read the descriptions in the Sights section which include Excursions from the main tourist centres.
- Michelin Maps nos 216, 217, 218 *and* 219
(at a scale of 1:200 000) or 427 *(at a scale of 1:400 000) indicate scenic routes, places of interest, viewpoints, rivers, forests...*

ZERNEZ Graubünden (Grisons)

Michelin map **218** fold 6 or **427** fold 17 – Local map see GRISONS – Alt 1 474m – 4 836ft – Facilities

This large, picturesque village overlooks the confluence of the Spöl and Inn Rivers. The village is interesting chiefly due to its position near the Swiss National Park.

★OFEN PASS ROAD

From Zernez to Umbrail Pass

57km – 35 miles – about 2 1/2 hours – Itinerary ⑥ *on the Grisons local map*

The road links the Engadine with Val Venosta in Italy.

Swiss National Park ⊘ – The motorist is forbidden to leave the Ofen Pass road and the pedestrian must keep to the authorized paths.
The Val dal Spöl crosses the national park: small, wild valleys with their cloak of woodland left to grow quite freely – notice the dead trees left on the spot, a most unusual sight in Switzerland – are interrupted only by the torrents running through them, leaving an impression of solitude which is sometimes oppressive.
This was founded in 1909 at the suggestion of the Nature Protection League and forms a nature reserve of 16 000ha – 40 000 acres which is protected from all human interference. It is forbidden to camp, to light fires, to leave the authorized roads and paths, etc., so that the wild animals (deer, ibex, chamois, marmots) and the flora are completely protected.
From the tourist's point of view the most striking thing about the park, of which the motorist gets glimpses as he follows the Ofen road, is its lonely woodland. The lover of wildlife will also be deeply impressed by the things to be seen during the guided walks regularly organized during the season.

Ofen Pass – Alt 2 149m – 7 051ft. The pass separates the Val dal Spöl, to the north from the Val Müstair, to the south, whose torrent, the Rom, is a tributary of the Adige. From the pass to Tschierv several sections of *corniche* road afford pretty glimpses downstream and especially of the snow-capped Ortles. After Tschierv the road runs pleasantly between stretches of turf and larch woods. It owes some of its character to the Tyrolean note introduced by the domed belfries of Valchava and Fuldera.

Santa Maria – Lovely village whose roughcast houses recall the Engadine.

★Müstair – *See Müstair.*
Return to Santa Maria.
From Santa Maria to the Umbrail Pass the road climbs up Muraunza Valley, whose barren appearance and limited skyline contrast with the refreshing and harmonious **scene★** that greets you at the Alpenrösli Restaurant. From the restaurant's terrace you can look down into the Müstair Valley, a series of fields more and more narrowly bounded in the uphill direction by wooded slopes which culminate in the Ofen Pass.

★ ZUG (Zoug) © Pop 21 705

Michelin map **216** fold 18 or **427** north of fold 15 – Alt 425m – 1 394ft – Facilities

This charming little town is built at the northeast end of **Lake Zug★★** (Zuger See) among gardens and orchards on the shore of the lake, at the foot of the first wooded foothills of the Zugerberg. Excavations reveal that the site of Zug has been inhabited by man without interruption from the Neolithic era. In the Middle Ages it belonged successively to the Lenzburg, Kyburg and Habsburg families before it joined the Confederation in 1352. Its 13C castle has now been entirely restored.

SIGHTS

★The Quays – From the Seestrasse to the Alpenquai, a promenade beside the lake offers **views★** of the summits of central Switzerland (Rigi, Pilatus, Bürgenstock, Stanserhorn) and, in the background, of the Bernese Alps (Finsteraarhorn, Jungfrau, Blümlisalp).

★Old Town – Ruined fortifications – Powder Tower (Pulverturm), the Capuchin's Tower (Kapuzinerturm) – still mark the original nucleus of the town.
The quarter crossed by the Unter-Altstadt and the Ober-Altstadt, with its old step-gabled houses, strikes a delightfully medieval note. The Fischmarkt (Fish Market) has houses with painted weather-boards and overhanging balconies.
The **clock tower** (Zytturm) as a roof of tiles painted in the Zug colours (blue and white) and crowned with a slim belfry. Under the clock-face are the coats of arms of the first eight cantons of the Confederation – Zug having been the seventh canton to join alliance.
The **Kolinplatz** is surrounded by old houses, among them the Town House (Stadthaus – POL on the plan), a 16C building adorned with a fine flower-decked fountain.
This fountain bears the statue of the standard bearer Wolfgang Kolin, a local hero who performed brave feats to save his banner at the Battle of Arbedo (1422), when the Confederate forces, who were defending the Leventina, were defeated by the Duke of Milan's army. Kolin's son, to whom the banner had been passed, was also killed.

St Oswald's Church – This Late Gothic church was built in the 15 and 16C.
The interior, with ogive vaulting, is made dark by its massive pillars. The nave is separated from the chancel by a partition adorned with frescoes.
The interior decoration includes many statues of saints in the chancel and on either side of the nave, painted and gilded wooden triptychs in each of the side chapels, and frescoes on the vaulting of the nave and aisles.

EXCURSIONS

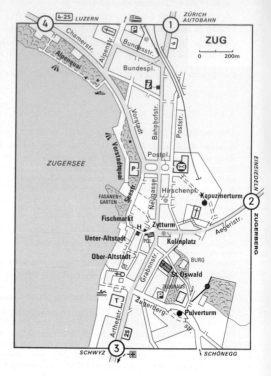

★Zugerberg – Alt 988m – 3 241ft. *7.5km – 5 miles – about 1/2 hour – by a very narrow, steeply uphill road, plus 1/4 hour on foot Rtn. Leave Zug by ②, the road to Schwyz via Ägeri.*

After 1km the narrow approach road to the Zugerberg, lying right of the town, affords fine views of the town and the lake.

Leave your car near the crossroads just before you come to the village of Schönfels. Then make for the Zugerberg Summit across the fields.

From the terrace you will get an almost circular **view★** to the northwest, of Zug and the lake, to the southwest of Pilatus, to the south of the Uri-Rotstock and the Uri Alps, and to the east – through a gap in the fir trees – of the village of Unter-Ägeri and its lake. To the north the hills of the Mittelland can be seen rising one behind the other towards Zürich.

★Former Abbey of Kappel – *8km – 5 miles by ①.*

The imposing abbey church's silhouette – buttresses, pointed roofs, slim bell tower – can be seen in the distance with its village huddled against it. It is located not far from where Zwingli *(qv)* was killed.

Built in the 13C (chancel) and 14C (nave), the abbey illustrates the Early Gothic style with its pure lines and the simplicity, entirely Cistercian, of its façades decorated with elegant lancet windows.

The interior is especially interesting: the construction of the vast nave and its aisles with ogive vaulting and wonderfully carved, painted keystones, a flat east end (modern stained-glass window), the chancel and 14C **stalls** – decorated with human or animal heads (note bitch with puppies) – are separated by a partition made of panels depicting amusing subjects; old tombstones, remains of 14C frescoes decorating the chancel walls (St Martin, Christ and Saints in medallions), **stained-glass windows★** (14C) up at the clerestory located on the south wall of the nave and retracing the scenes of the life of Jesus (the Crucifixion is near the entrance). Two of the former conventual buildings stand behind the abbey church.

★ ZUOZ Graubünden (Grisons)   Pop 1 199

Michelin map **218** northwest of fold 16 or **427** fold 17 – Local map see GRISONS – Alt 1 716m – 5 561ft – Facilities

Zuoz is a high-altitude resort, well-equipped for a stay in summer. It reserves for lovers of local colour a group of **Engadine houses★★**, mostly built by members of the Planta family, who played an important part in the history of the Grisons.

SIGHTS *1/4 hour*

★★Main Square – Its fountain is surmounted by the heraldic bear of the Plantas (the family arms include a severed bear's paw with the sole – *planta* – turned upwards). The square is bounded on the north by the Planta House, which consists of two distinct dwellings under one roof.

This building is designed according to the rules of the Engadine style *(see under Engadine)* but its unusual size and its outdoor staircase with a rococo balustrade give it a lordly air.

On the main street the Crusch Alva Inn (1570) has a gable decorated with a series of coats of arms. To the right of St Luzius, the church of the saint who converted upper Rhaetia, you will recognize the arms of the three Leagues *(see the Introduction: Swiss Cantons)*, those of the XIII Cantons of the period and finally those of the Salis (willow – *salix* in Latin), Planta and Juvalta families.

Go around the Planta House to pass under the arcades connecting this building with the 13C Planta Tower and walk down to the church.

Church – This is dominated by a slender tower and has a nave roofed with star-vaulting. The bear's paw motif often recurs in the interior decoration. Three windows contain modern stained glass: those in the apse, Hope and Charity, were designed by the contemporary artist, Augusto Giacometti; the Three Kings, by Gian Casty.

Michelin map **216** fold 18 or **427** fold 6 – Local map p 228 – Alt 408m – 1 339ft –
Town plans in the current Michelin Red Guide Switzerland

Zürich is built between the wooded slopes of the Uetliberg and the Zürichberg at
the point where the Limmat, emerging from Lake Zürich, receives the Sihl. It is
presently considered to be the most important financial, industrial and commercial
centre in Switzerland. It is also known to be particularly receptive to contemporary
trends associated with the younger generation.

HISTORICAL NOTES

Zwingli and the Reformation – When **Zwingli** was made parish priest of Glarus
in 1506 he did not hesitate to denounce from his pulpit the mercenary service
abroad which was draining the nation's manhood, as well as the venality of
magistrates. After two years at Einsiedeln he was given the pastorate of the
Grossmünster (cathedral) of Zürich. It was then that he sought to realize his
religious projects.

In January 1523, after a public debate at the Zürich Town Hall between supporters
and opponents of Zwingli, the priest was victorious, for the Council declared itself
in favour of the new ideas. Within three years the Reformation was firmly
established at Zürich. Zwingli obtained the abolition of pilgrimages, processions
and certain sacraments, advocated the marriage of priests and had the monasteries closed in the Zürich Canton, the home of the Reformation in German
Switzerland.

Zwingli's authority alarmed the Catholic cantons. Lucerne, Uri, Schwyz, Unterwalden and Zug allied themselves against Zürich and excluded it gradually from
the direction of federal affairs. Another great religious debate took place at Berne
in 1528. Again Zwingli had the advantage, but war, barely avoided in 1529, broke
out in 1531. On 11 October, Zwingli met his death at Kappel. But his removal did
not mean the failure of his religious theories, which gradually spread throughout
German Switzerland.

Tremendous growth   Zürich, which still had only 17 000 inhabitants in 1800,
expanded tremendously from the early 19C onwards. Though it had to cede the
title of federal capital to Berne in 1848, it became, six years later, the official seat of
the Federal Polytechnic School – the famous Polytechnicum. The democratic
constitution it gave itself in 1869 became the model for those of other cantons and
even, in part, for the Federal Constitution of 1874. At the beginning of the 19C the
town already extended beyond its fortifications and new buildings were springing
up in the surrounding country. Industrial suburbs subsequently developed along the
lines of communication. Today Zürich is, in fact, the economic capital of the
Confederation.

The Advent of the Dada Movement – On 5 February 1916, the **Cabaret Voltaire**
(1 Spiegelgasse) was inaugurated by the poet and director Hugo Ball and his wife
Emmy Jennings, in the company of many friends and artists from a variety of
backgrounds: Tristan Tzara, Marcel Janco, Jean Arp, Richard Huelsenbeck,
Sophie Taeuber, etc.

All were prompted by the desire to create a new and original art form, an avant-
garde movement seen as a reaction to existing art. They therefore decided to
disrupt conventional rules by staging dance performances, reciting poems and
exhibiting their paintings.

This unprecedented approach to cultural life proved a resounding success. The
term Dada was coined quite by accident when Hugo Ball and Richard Huelsenbeck
were trying to find a name for the cabaret singer. It was soon chosen to
designate the new group.

In 1916 the word appeared in the first issue of *Cabaret Voltaire*, a magazine
published in three languages, German, English and French: it expressed the first
quiverings of a moral and intellectual rebellion against the complacency of
contemporary society. Although the *Cabaret Voltaire* had to close down after only
six months of existence, the Dadaist magazine managed to survive.

View of the Quays

SIGHTS

Bahnhofstrasse (BYZ) – Built along the former site of the Fröschengraben (Frogs' Moat), the Bahnhofstrasse, which leads from the central station (Hauptbahnhof) to the shore of the lake, is the busiest street in the town and the most important business centre in all Switzerland.

All along this fine avenue planted with lime trees are luxury shops, great banks and the most modern buildings.

★★Quays (BCZ) – Along the banks of the Limmat and Lake Zürich (Zürichsee), the quays spread their magnificently-kept gardens – clumps of trees of various species, lawns and flower beds for the enjoyment of strollers – while the many sailing and motor-boats plying from the landing-stages offer pleasant excursions. By going as far as the **Mythenquai** (a prolongation of the General-Guisan-Quai, ④) you will find more and more open **views★** of the lake and the Alps (in the far distance the Oberland Massif).

Zürichhorn Gardens – By ③. There is an excellent **view★** of the town from the Zürichhorn Gardens (beyond the Utoquai) where a Le Corbusier Centre (the world-famous contemporary architect Le Corbusier was born in La Chaux de Fonds) has been built.

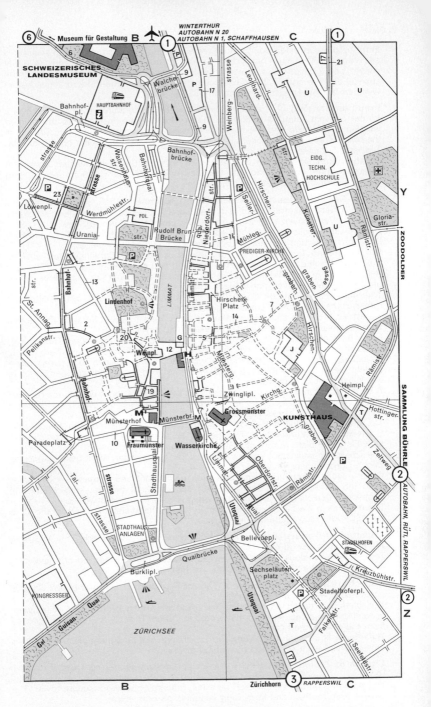

Weinplatz (BY) – South of the square, which is adorned with a pretty fountain surmounted by a wine-grower carrying his basket, you will find, on the opposite shore, some fine old houses with "Flemish" roofs, the Rathaus (**BY H**) – a graceful building in the Italian Renaissance style – and the Wasserkirche (**BZ**), a 15C chapel recently restored. The cathedral dominates the whole with its two tall towers.

Lindenhof (BY) – This tree-shaded esplanade, with its fountain, marks the summit of a hill, and because it was well placed to guard the crossing of the Limmat, it was the site of the Celtic and Roman settlements from which Zürich sprang. From the edge of the terrace overlooking the Limmat you will see the old quarters of the town rising in tiers on the east bank. The Predigerkirche stands opposite, to the right is the Grossmünster.

Cathedral (Grossmünster) (BCZ) ⊘ – This impressive building, erected between the 11 and the 13C, took the place of a collegiate church said to have been founded by Charlemagne. This cathedral is a symbol of the Reformation for the German speaking Swiss.

It was here that Zwingli *(qv)* began preaching the Reformation in 1519.

Its façade is flanked by two three-storey towers surmounted by wooden dom faced with metal plates. The south tower is crowned by a colossal sta (the original is in the crypt) of Charlemagne seated with a sword across knees.

Enter by the north side door, whose restored uprights are adorned with sculptures and capitals. The nave has pointed vaulting; the raised chancel ends in a flat chevet, and a gallery runs above the aisles. Traces of frescoes may be seen in the chancel and the crypt with its characteristic triple nave. The modern stained-glass windows are by Augusto Giacometti (1932).

Fraumünster (BZ) ⊘ – Built in the 12 and 15C, this church took the place of a former convent founded in 853 by Ludwig the German. Inside, note the pointed vaulting in the nave and the remarkable **stained-glass windows**★ by Marc Chagall in the chancel and south transept and by Augusto Giacometti in the north transept. Two arcaded galleries face one another.

On the south side of the church the remains of the Romanesque **cloisters**★★ (Kreuzgang) are ornamented with frescoes by Paul Bodmer (1920-31) representing the legend of the foundation of the abbey.

★★★ **Swiss National Museum** (**Schweizerisches Landesmuseum**) (BY) ⊘ – The collections of the national institution are rich and carefully selected. They illustrate every aspect of Swiss civilization from prehistoric times to the present day.

The prehistory collection (ground and first floors) is one of the most outstanding; those of the Roman era include both domestic and military pieces.

On the ground floor the most valuable specimens of Carolingian art are the frescoes from the church at Müstair *(qv)* and two small ivory plaques (9C).

Religious art in the Middle Ages is represented by numerous altarpieces, some painted, some of carved and gilded wood.

You will notice a curious *Christ with Palms* carved in the 12C, which, although rather clumsily executed, shows a great sense of movement.

Tapestries, frescoes and fine furniture (tables, chests and coffers) of the Gothic and Renaissance periods are also on view (mezzanine).

Many halls and rooms of the 16 and 17C have been reconstructed (first floor); panelled wooden partitions, carved and painted coffered ceilings, coffers, seats, tapestries, stained glass (the "study window", a form native to German Switzerland, which was all the rage throughout the 16C) and chinaware, contribute to the richness of the decoration.

A large Gobelin tapestry woven to cartoons by Charles Lebrun depicts the renewal of the alliance between Louis XIV and the Swiss in Paris in 1663. There is also a collection of Swiss clocks (16-19C).

The great ogive-vaulted Hall of Arms and Armour, decorated with frescoes by F. Hodler *(qv)* representing *The Defeat at Marignano (see Historical Notes)*, includes a complete review of military life from the 13 to the 18C.

The Treasure contains goldsmith's work, sacred and secular, some belonging to the Zürich Corporations.

On the second floor is a large collection of peasant and burgesses's costumes from the various cantons (18 and 19C) accompanied by interesting prints and engravings depicting the evolution of dress in every part of Switzerland.

The galleries in the basement are devoted to local handicrafts (bells from the 13 to the 18C) with reconstituted workshops.

Museum of Applied Arts of Zurich (**Museum für Gestaltung Zürich**) ⊘ – *Access by the Museumstrasse* (BY).

Temporary exhibitions, based on themes derived from the applied arts, architecture, graphic art and industrial design, are held in the galleries.

★ **Church of Sts Felix and Regula** (**Felix-und-Regulakirche**) – *Access by the Stauffacherstrasse, west of the plan* (AY).

This church is dedicated to Saints Felix and Regula, a brother and sister who, according to tradition, suffered martyrdom at Zürich. The tall bell tower is detached from the rest of the building.

The interior is unusual: the oblong church, shaped like an almond, is roofed with a barely curved vault supported by sloping pillars.

Church of Zürich-Altstetten – *Access by the Badenerstrasse, west of the plan* (AY).

This modern church is dominated by a tall, graceful, openwork square tower. The nave is asymmetrical and lit by high windows on one side.

Museum of Domestic Life (**Wohnmuseum**) (AZ) ⊘ – This museum is located in two adjoining houses (late 17C – very restored).

It presents on three floors *(lift)* many examples of furniture, stoves and utensils, etc... from mid-17 to mid-19C.

In the basement are a collection of dolls created in the 1920s by a local artist.

★★ **Rietberg Museum** ⊘ – *Gablerstrasse 15. Access by the Seestrasse* (AZ).

This museum is installed in the former Wesendonck Villa in the middle of a park and in view of the lake. It contains the valuable collections formed by Baron von der Heydt: statues from India, Cambodia, Java, China, Africa and the South Sea Islands. The collections of Japanese prints made by Willy Boller and Julius Mueller, works of art from the Near East, Tibet and pre-Columbian America, paintings from the Far East, a collection of Swiss masks and some Flemish and Armenian carpets complete the exhibition.

"Zur Meisen" House (BZ M[1]) – *Between Münsterhof and the Limmat.*

This corporation building (Zunfthaus) contains the collections of 18C ceramics (faience and porcelain) of the Swiss National Museum *(see above)*.

Fine Arts Museum (**Kunsthaus**) (CZ) ⊘ – The museum, in which temporary exhibitions are arranged, gives a prominent place to modern painting. There are also displays of sculpture of the early French and German Middle Ages and Swiss and German primitives of the 15C.

On the first floor are the most representative canvases of Ferdinand Hodler, who is considered as the leader of the Swiss school of the early 20C, and pictures by Valloton, Böcklin, Anker, Auberjonois and Barraud. The French school is represented by works by Toulouse-Lautrec, Renoir, Degas, Matisse, Léger, Picasso, etc. One room contains 14 works by Marc Chagall.

There is also the largest collection outside Scandinavia of the work of Edvard Munch. Finally the Alberto Giacometti Foundation has on view a considerable collection of that artist's works (1901-66).

★**Zoological Gardens (Zoo Dolder)** ⊘ – *Access by the Gloriastrasse* (**CY**).

Nicely laid out at Zürichberg, in a very pretty, leafy setting, this zoo houses more than 2 000 animals. Giant tortoises, an otter and a beaver can be seen playing in the water and on land. Fascinating are the monkeys and the elephants' bath *(around 0010)*, as well. A board at the main entrance announces the zoo's recent births.

★★**Foundation E.G. Bührle Collection (Sammlung Bührle)** ⊘ – *Zollikerstrasse 172. Access by the Zeltweg, east of town plan.*

A villa set in the lovely southeast suburb houses works of art (paintings and sculpture) collected by the industrialist Emil Bührle between 1934 and 1956.

Impressionism makes up the major part of the collection which includes works by such major artists as Manet *(The Swallows,* 1873; *A Garden Nook at Bellevue,* 1880), Renoir (the lovely portrait of *Little Irène,* a work painted just before the painter broke loose from Impressionism), three works by Sisley *(The Luminous Summer at Bougival)* – note his portrait painted by Renoir in 1868, Monet *(Garden*

at Giverny, 1895 and especially the *Poppies Near Vertheuil, c*1880, the figures represented with rapid brushstrokes blend into the poppy field), Eugène Boudin, Monet's teacher and a master of seascapes and beach scenes *(Sailboats,* 1890), Pissaro *(The Route de Versailles at Louveciennes)* and Degas *(Count Lepic and His Daughters).* The Post-Impressionist period is represented by Gauguin *(The Offering),* seven works by Van Gogh *(Blossoming of a Chestnut Tree* shows the influence of Japanese art) and Cézanne (with his famous, brightly-coloured *The Boy in the Red Waistcoat).*

Bührle aslo collected works of art created before and after the Impressionist movement had made its impact. Paintings by Delacroix *(Self-Portrait),* Corot and Ingres *(Portrait of Monsieur Devillers)* as well as works by the 16 and 17C Dutch School artists E. de Witte, Saenredam (church interiors), Salomon van Ruysdael *(View of Rhenen),* Van Goyen and Frans Hals are displayed. A gallery is devoted entirely to 16-18C Spanish and

Fondation Collector E. G. Bührle

Italian Girl by Picasso

Italian painters. Admire Canaletto's two representations of the Grand Canal belonging to a series of six views (1738-42), two works by Gaudi, Tiepolo *(Diana Bathing)* and Goya *(Procession in Valencia).*

Among the 20C works of arts are a still-life by Matisse, with its bright, luminous colours which contrast with *The Seine at Paris,* painted five years earlier. Also to be seen are works by Picasso, Braque, Gris, Modigliani and the Expressionists, Rouault and Soutine.

In the religious sculpture section (12-16C) Switzerland (15C *Pietà)* is one of the countries represented.

BOAT TRIPS ⊘

There exist a great many boat trips leaving from Zürich, ranging from the Short Tour of 11/2 hours stopping at Erlenbach and Thalwil, to the Great Tour taking half a day and including a visit to Rapperswil *(qv).* Main landing stage at the Bürkliplatz (**BZ**).

The chapter on art and architecture in this guide gives an outline of artistic achievement in the country providing the context of the buildings and works of art describrd in the Sights section.

This chapter may also provide ideas for touring. It is advisable to read it at leisure.

EXCURSIONS

★★**Uetliberg** ⊙ – Alt 874m – 2 867ft. *About 2 hours Rtn, including 50 minutes by rail.*
The railway journey is mainly through woods. From the arrival station, where you will already get a fine view of the snowy summits of the Alps, you walk up a steep path to the nearby terrace of the hotel-restaurant *(viewing table)*.
You can go on to the top of the belvedere tower *(167 steps)* from where you will have a sweeping **panorama**★★ of the whole Zürich district, the Limmat Valley, Lake Zürich and the Alpine range – from Säntis in the east to the Jungfrau and Les Diablerets in the southwest – while the ridges of the Jura and the Vosges are faintly visible to the west and northwest on the horizon.

★**Albis Pass Road** 53km – 33 miles. *Leave Zürich southwest via the Bederstrasse* **(AZ)** *and then road no 4.*
The road follows the Sihl Valley between the slopes of Uetliberg (right) and Lake Zürich (left), in front of which stretches the motorway and a string of towns. At Adliswil leave road no 4 and bear right on the road to Albis which crosses the Sihl Forest.

Langenberg Wildlife Park – This wildlife park (European species) extends on either side of the road (mostly left side of the road) north of Langnau am Albis on a couple of acres of forest and rocky hillocks. Deer, doe, chamois, marmot, wild boar... can be seen. The road climbs to Albis Pass (alt 793m – 2 602ft) from where magnificent views extend over the undulating countryside; then it descends between Lake Turler and Albis Mountain before turning left in the direction of Hausen at the foot of the Albishorn.

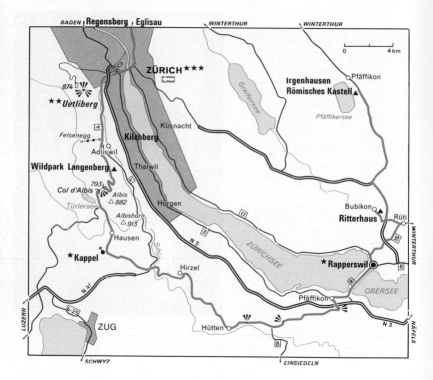

★**Former Abbey of Kappel** – *See Zug: Excursions.*
> *From Kappel descend to the left and bear left again to pick up road no 4 to Hirzel, then bear right towards Schönenberg.*

Some time after Hütten, there is a stretch of *corniche* road (2km – 1 mile) which overlooks the widest part of Lake Zürich.
The road then rises as far as Feusisberg in a charming countryside enhanced by glimpses of the lake; during the downhill stretch the two wooded islets of the lake can be seen.
After a winding section of road through woods, there is a plunging **view**★ which reveals both sections of the lake (Obersee on the right) which the Rapperswil causeway divides.

★**Rapperswil** – *See Rapperswil.*

Regensberg – Alt 617m – 2 024ft. 17km – 10 miles. *Leave Zürich by* ⑥ *and then turn left immediately into the road towards Dielsdorf. Turn left in the village to take a little road to Regensberg.*
Regensberg which is a small vine-growing village with a perfectly preserved atmosphere and old, half-timbered houses standing one beside the other all around its single square, is a charming and picturesque stopping-place.
There is an extensive **view** of the vineyards and the local countryside from the Romanesque watch-tower.

From Zürich to Eglisau – *23km – 14 miles. Leave Zürich by ① and road no 4. 5km – 3 miles after Kloten at the north exit of Seeb-Winkel, bear left on a small road which leads (500m – 1/3 mile) to the Roman ruins.*

Roman Farm of Seeb (Römischer Gutshof Seeb) – In a pleasant site, with wide views *(viewing tables)* of the plain and neighbouring heights, are scattered the remains of a large farm dating back to the 1C which was enlarged until the 3C and then destroyed and abandoned. The foundations of the west wing of the villa (living quarters) are under shelter. The pile of bricks of the hypocaust and part of the baths, an attractive black and white mosaic, a model of the farm, and a display case of pottery (found here) are on display.

Outside, the remains of the water-tower can be seen as well as a kiln and a piscina with a central well (6m – 19 1/2ft deep), etc.

Eglisau – Facilities. This picturesque old town, near the German border, is located in a charming **site★**, terraced amidst trees and vines on the north bank of the Rhine.

Above the domed church (transformed 18C) a shaded belvedere-terrace, with a bronze statue of a young woman, offers a lovely view of the river.

Kilchberg – *7km – 4 miles. Leave Zürich by ④.* Road no 3 runs along the west shore of the lake to Kilchberg, the residential suburb of Zürich. The Swiss poet Conrad Ferdinand Meyer (1825-98) and the German writer Thomas Mann (1875-1955) spent their last days in this area and are buried in the small cemetery.

ZURZACH Aargau   Pop 3 594

Michelin map **216** fold 6 or **427** fold 5 – Alt 339m – 1 129ft – Facilities

Near the Rhine on the site of the Roman town, Tenedo, Zurzach is now a spa centre (cures for rheumatic disorders). On its main street are some 17 and 18C monuments and houses and beside the river stands a 19C château.

August Deusser Museum ⊙ – The château houses this museum, which contains the personal collection belonging to the Germain painter August Deusser (1070-1942) as well as his own works of art. On the first floor are furnishings (some of which are in Louis XVI style), works of art, an 18C Chinese low relief and a carved gilt bed made for Ludwig II of Bavaria. The second floor presents works bequeathed by Deusser. A number of them evoke the war of 1870 and seem Impressionistic in style. In the park are modern sculptures by Johann Ulrich Steiger.

Basle Carnival

Practical
Information

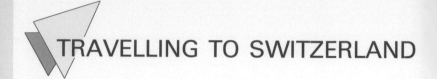
As administrative and customs formalities are subject to variation, readers are advised to apply to the Automobile Association, Royal Automobile Club, the Swiss Touring Club or one of the Swiss National Tourist Offices *(see under Tourist Information)* for the latest information.

Passport – Each member of a party must have a valid passport or British Visitor's Passport to enter Switzerland.

Visa – Generally speaking, visas are not required for a stay of less than three months. The nearest Swiss consulate or embassy will help if there is any doubt.

Customs – Tax free allowances for various commodities are decided by the EU. Under-17s are not allowed to import or export alcohol or tobacco.
There are no restrictions concerning the import, export and exchange of Swiss francs. Domestic animals brought into Switzerland require a veterinary certificate stating that the animal has been vaccinated against rabies and will be placed in quarantine.

By air – Set in the heart of Europe, Switzerland is a focal point of international air traffic. Numerous airlines - Swissair, American Airlines, TWA, Pan Am, Air Canada, British Airways operate scheduled flights to one of the country's three international airports (Basle, Geneva and Zurich). Further information on timetables, air fares and charter flights is available from travel agencies and airlines.
There are many flight options from Swiss airports to other European cities.
A Fly-Rail Baggage service is available for a charge of £9 per piece of baggage, so your luggage can be sent from your home airport direct to your destination in Switzerland, without your having to carry it yourself.

By rail – Over thirty high-speed Eurocity trains link Switzerland to many European countries. The extensive Swiss railway system operates a frequent and efficient service.

By road – Those driving from one of the Channel ports have two main routes to choose from: via **Calais** and French motorways through **France** (the A26 to Troyes, A5 to Langres, A31 to Beaune, A6 to Mâcon and A40 to Geneva - about 800km - 500 miles); or via **Oostende** and through **Belgium, Luxembourg, France** and **Germany** (along the E40 to Liège, the E25 to Luxembourg, the A31 to just north of Metz, the A4 to Strasbourg, where you cross the Rhine and the German border to pick up the E35 (A5) to Basle - about 700km - 450 miles).

The Channel Tunnel – In May 1994, the Channel Tunnel was inaugurated, the realisation of dreams of linking Britain to mainland Europe which date back over two hundred years. The Channel link consists of two single-track rail tunnels, (7.60m - 24ft in diameter) for passenger and freight transport, and one service tunnel (4.80m - 15ft in diameter), for safety and ventilation. The tunnels are 50.5km - 31 miles long, 37km - 23 miles of which are under the Channel. Most of the tunnel is 40m - 131ft beneath the seabed, in a layer of blue chalk. The trains (800m - 2 624ft long) have two levels for passenger cars (capacity 118 cars per shuttle) and one level for coaches and caravans. Special services will operate for heavy goods vehicles. British, French and Belgian trains, including French TGVs, will also use the tunnel. Journey time will eventually be 35 minutes, 28 minutes of which are in the tunnel at a maximum speed of 130km - 80 miles per hour.

36 15 MICHELIN Minitel Service – Michelin Travel Assistance (AMI) is a computerised route-finding system offering integrated information on roads, tourist sights, hotels and restaurants. 36 15 MICHELIN is one of the French Telecom videotex services. Foreign subscribers can access the service. For route planning give your point of departure and destination, stipulate your preference for motorways or local roads, indicate the sights to see along the way and it will do the rest. The same applies for that special restaurant, secluded country hotel or pleasant camp site along the chosen route.

TRAVELLING IN SWITZERLAND

By car

Documents – A valid driving licence, international driving permit, car registration papers (log-book) and a nationality plate of the approved size are required.

Insurance – An International Insurance Certificate (Green Card) is the most effective proof of insurance cover and is internationally recognised by the police and other authorities. Certain motoring organisations run accident insurance and breakdown service schemes for members.

Annual road tax (Vignette) – Instead of tolls on Swiss motorways, an annual road tax – **vignette** – is levied on all cars and motorbikes using Swiss motorways. The vignette is valid from 1 December of the year preceding until 31 January of the year following the year printed on it, and it must be affixed to all motor vehicles and trailers with a maximum total weight of 3.5 tonnes each. The vignette costs 30Frs (an additional 30Frs applies to trailers and caravans) and can be obtained at the border crossings, post offices, petrol stations, garages and cantonal motor registries. To avoid any delay at the border it is recommended that the vignette be purchased in advance from the Swiss National Tourist Office.

Rules of the road – The Swiss rules of the road are not difficult for foreigners, but the spirit in which they are observed may vary.
The minimum driving age is 18 years old. The laws listed below are strictly enforced and the police are authorised to collect fines on the spot.
Drive on the right and pass on the left *(see below)*.

Seat belts are obligatory and children under the age of 12 are required to sit in the back. Driving with side-lights is no longer permitted under any circumstances and **dipped headlights** are compulsory in road tunnels.
A red **warning triangle** or **hazard warning lights** are obligatory in case of a breakdown.
The use of the **horn** is to be avoided everywhere except on mountain roads with many blind corners, where it is recommended.
The use of **studded tyres** is forbidden on motorways and is subject to a speed limit of 80kmph – 50mph. The use of studded tyres is only permitted between 1 November and 31 March.
Remember to **cede priority** to vehicles coming from the right. Nevertheless, those who have the right of way should approach crossroads with care. The "STOP" signs at crossings should be strictly obeyed, and care should be taken to observe white lines painted on road surfaces.
It is strictly prohibited to pass on the right, even on motorways. When driving on **mountain roads**, if you want to pass another vehicle, remember that, if you meet an on-coming vehicle, it is for the car coming down to draw aside first and if necessary reverse back to a suitable stopping-place. However, if you meet a **post bus** – they can be recognised by their yellow colour, a black disc bearing a post horn or by their three-note horn (the first notes of the overture to *William Tell*) – you must obey the orders which the driver of the post bus or van is authorised to give you.

There are special regulations for cars towing caravans on mountain roads, enquire at the Swiss National Tourist Office before leaving. The Klausen Pass Road is closed to cars with trailers.

The **tram and light railway systems** are modern and run at high speed. The greatest care is advised at unguarded crossings, where warning is generally given by three red blinking lights, arranged in a triangle and connected with a bell.

Speed limits – The maximum permitted speed on motorways is 120km/h – 74mph, on other roads 80km/h – 50mph and in towns and villages 50km/h – 31mph. Cars fitted with studded tyres are subject to a speed limit of 80km/h – 50mph. Police Radar Speedtrap Detectors are not allowed to be taken into the country.

Road signs – Motorways are indicated by signs in white on a green background. There are priority roads which are numbered and marked by arrows in white on a blue ground, whereas the secondary roads are marked and numbered in black on white.

Petrol – The average price per litre in 1994 was: 1.21Frs for unleaded petrol; 1.29Frs for four-star (super); 1.24Frs for diesel (NB 4.54l = 1 gallon). Self-service petrol stations accept 10Frs or 20Frs notes only; larger petrol stations generally accept credit cards.

Emergency road service – The Touring Club of Switzerland (TCS), 9 Rue Pierre-Fatio, CH-1211 Geneva 3, ☏ (022) 737 12 12, the Swiss Automobile Club (ACS) Wasserwerkgasse 39, CH-3000 Berne 13, ☏ (031) 311 77 22, and "Touring Secours" breakdown service (☏ 140) have developed a complete emergency service covering the main Alpine roads and motorways

Route planning – The Michelin map **427** at a scale of 1:400 000 and the series **216**, **217**, **218** and **219** at a scale of 1:200 000 cover the whole of Switzerland *(see layout diagram on the back cover)*. In addition to a wealth of tourist information they indicate very narrow roads (single track where overtaking is difficult or impossible), gradients, difficult or dangerous stretches of road, tunnels and the altitudes of mountain passes.

The itineraries described in this guide often follow local roads which may intimidate the driver not familiar with mountain driving. All of these roads are accessible, at least in summer. The Michelin maps mentioned above indicate **snowbound roads** (with their opening and closing dates) as well as the location of emergency telephones.

The main road tunnels:

St Gotthard	16.9km - 10.5 miles (1980)
Seelisberg	9.9km - 6 miles (1981)
San Bernardino	6.6km - 4 miles (1967)
Gt St Bernard	5.8km - 3.5 miles (1964)

By rail

The Swiss rail network covers about 4989km - 3100 miles, offering a practical and comfortable alternative to driving. One of the things most commonly associated with Switzerland is the fact that trains run on time there! All the major cities and large towns have excellent connections and regular service. There is quite a variety of trains: fast Intercity trains (IC); regular direct trains; regional trains, which serve destinations normally considered quite off the beaten track; rack-railways in the mountains; scenic railways and steam railways, not forgetting funicular railways, cablecars, chair-lifts and underground trains. Car-carrying trains operate between Kandersteg and Goppenstein (Lötschberg), Brig and Iselle di Trasquera in Italy (Simplon), Thusis and Samedan (Albula), Oberwald and Realp (Furka) and Andermatt and Sedrun (Oberalp).

The main railway tunnels:

Simplon	19.8km - 12 miles (1906)
Furka	15.4km - 9.5 miles (1982)
St Gotthard	15.0km - 9.3 miles (1882)
Lötschberg	14.6km - 9 miles (1913)

Rail Passes – The Swiss Travel System offers a number of different passes. The passes should be purchased before leaving from a Swiss National Tourist Office or local travel agent.

The **Swiss Pass** enables you to travel freely all over the country – a network of 16 000km – 12 000 miles – using trains, boats, post buses, tramways and buses belonging to 25 Swiss towns. Moreover a 25% discount is made on excursions to the main summits. The Swiss pass is valid for 4, 8, 15 days or one month.

The Swiss **Flexipass** enables you to travel freely all over the country for three days. This pass is valid for fifteen days.

The **Swiss Card** entitles you to a return ticket to your holiday spot, leaving from either an airport or a station on the border. It also grants you a 50% discount on train, post bus and mountain train journeys. The Swiss Card is valid for one month.

The **Regional Pass**, available between 1 May and 31 October, enables you to travel freely for several days within a given region. It is issued on Swiss territory. Tourists can choose between several formulas.

Valid 7 days, entitling you to travel freely for three days in the region. On the other days, a 50% discount on train, boat and post bus trips.

Valid 7 days, entitling you to travel freely for two days in the region. On the other days, a 50% discount on train, boat and post bus trips.

Valid fifteen days, entitling you to travel freely for five days in the region. On the other days, a 50% discount on train, boat and post bus trips.

Valid for 7 days of unlimited travel in the region.

For more information on the famous Alpine Trains see under Discovering Switzerland.

Post buses – These famous post buses *(postauto)*, easily identifiable on account of their bright yellow colour and disk bearing the Swiss horn, are a common feature on the country roads. They usually leave from the train station or the Post Office and for many visitors are the ideal way of visiting some of the more remote villages.

By boat – It is possible to explore all the big Swiss lakes and parts of some of Switzerland's main rivers on one of the large white boats that can be seen cruising up and down. A few of the boats still have their original paddle-wheels. For further information see under Discovering Switzerland.

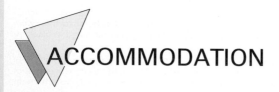

ACCOMMODATION

Places to stay – Consult the current **Michelin Red Guide Switzerland** for a selection of hotels and restaurants. The *Swiss Hotel Guide,* published annually, is available from the Swiss National Tourist Offices. In Switzerland rooms are charged per person.

The Swiss National Tourist Offices can usually provide information folders or leaflets on small guest houses located in the countryside *(E+G Hotels)*, on chalet, house and apartment rentals and on farm holidays *(Swiss Farm Holidays)*. Lists of people offering overnight accommodation are available from local tourist information offices, but also be on the lookout for the appropriate roadside signs (*B&B; Zimmer frei; Chambre à louer; Affitasi camere*). It is also possible to rent chalets and appartments through Interhome Ltd, 383 Richmond Road, Twickenham, TW1 2EF, ☎ 081 891 1294.

Youth Hostels – Switzerland's youth hostels (almost 100) are open to travellers with an international or national youth hostel card. There is no maximum age limit but priority is given to members under 25. Individuals are advised to reserve, and it is compulsory for groups to do likewise. A list of Swiss youth hostels is available from the Swiss National Tourist Office. The Swiss Youth Hostel Association (Schweizer Jugendherbergen) has its headquarters at Engestrasse 9, CH-3012 Berne, ☎ (031) 302 55 03.

Camping and caravanning – Camping is only permitted on authorised sites. A map and list of sites are available from the Swiss National Tourist Office. The two national associations are the Swiss Camping and Caravanning Federation (Schweizer Camping und Caravanning Verband), Habsburgerstrasse 35, CH-6004 Lucerne, ☎ (041) 23 48 22 and the Swiss Camping Association (Verband Schweizer Campings), Seestrasse 119, CH-3800 Interlaken, ☎ (036) 23 35 23.

Mountain Huts – The Swiss Alpine Club operates numerous mountain huts. For a list of these huts apply either to the Swiss National Tourist Office or the Swiss Alpine Club (Schweizer Alpenclub - SAC), Helvetiaplatz 4, CH-3005 Berne, ☎ (031) 351 36 11.

Tourism for the Disabled – The **Michelin Red Guide Switzerland** indicates hotels with rooms accessible to the disabled; as suitable rooms may be limited it is advisable to book in advance. A fact sheet and special hotel guide are available from the Swiss National Tourist Office or Mobility International Schweiz, Postfach, CH-8034 Zurich, ☎ (01) 383 04 97.

The following car rental company provides for wheelchair-bound drivers: Schweizerische Paraplegiker Vereinigung, Langsägestrasse 2, CH-6021 Kriens/LU ☎ (041) 42 1107.

EATING OUT

The **Michelin Red Guide Switzerland** offers a wide choice of restaurants which will enable you to discover and appreciate the best Swiss specialities. The establishments noted for their high gastronomical standards have been awarded stars (one to three). The localities possessing such establishments are mentioned in the introductory part of the guide.
In restaurants, it is not uncommon to pay for the bread served with the meal.
Station cafés offer decent meals at reasonable prices.
See the section on Food in the Introduction of this guide as well as the chapter on Wines and Local Specialities in the Michelin Red Guide Switzerland.

A few specialities

Take the time to enjoy a perch fillet caught in Lake Geneva, eaten on the terrace of a charming lakeside restaurant and accompanied by a glass of Fendant or Perlan, a cheese fondue with Gruyère or vacherin or even a combination of two cheeses, served with a dry white wine, a tasty raclette or tripe prepared in the Neuchâtel tradition with an Œil de Perdrix rosé.
For those who prefer game or meat why not try game from the Valais with a strong bodied Cornalin, dried and smoked beef from the Grisons enhanced by a velvety Pinot Noir, veal slices (geschnetzeltes kalbfleisch) cooked in the Zurich way with a Pinot Noir, the Bernese dish of assorted cold meats, spicy meat balls (polpettone) from the Ticino region with a full-bodied Merlot, rosti (delicious diced potatoes, fried then baked) and the traditional veal sausage, a nationwide speciality.
To round off a meal there are the imposing cream pastries, the sweetmeats made in German-speaking Switzerland, and of course the world-famous and mouth-watering chocolates.

Beverages

Wine – There are many famous wines made in Switzerland. The following are among the better-known grape varieties:
White wines: Fendant (Valais), Perlan (Geneva), Chasselas (Neufchâtel, Vaud) and Johannisberg (Valais).
Red wines: Gamay (Geneva), Pinot Noir (Grisons, Neuchâtel), Dôle (assemblage of Pinot Noir and Gamay, Valais), Merlot (Ticino).
Rosé wines: Œil de Perdrix (Neuchâtel), Merlot Rosato (Ticino).
The best recent vintages are 1989, 1990 and 1992.
The best "open" wines – ie those presented in a carafe – are served by the decilitre (2 to 5). For instance you may order 3 decilitres of Fendant.
In German-speaking Switzerland, the **Weinstub** provides a pleasant setting where you can sample the best wines by the glass in a cosy, friendly atmosphere.

Beer – In each canton, beer drinkers can appreciate a wide range of both draught beer and bottled beer (Adler, Cardinal, Egger, Eichhof, Feldschlösschen, etc).
In German-speaking localities, the **Bierstub** is to beer what the Weinstub is to wine.

Mineral water – It is not in the habits of the Swiss to drink ordinary tap water. In restaurants, it is recommended to order a bottle of mineral water, either fizzy or flat. The most common labels are Henniez, San Pellegrino and Passuger.

Coffee – This is often served with a small pot of cream (Kaffesahne). In the afternoon, treat yourself to a nice break in a café (tea room) offering an impressive choice of delicious cakes and pastries.

GENERAL INFORMATION

Language – Switzerland is a multilingual country. German is spoken in the centre and east, French in the west, Italian in the south and Romansh in the southeast. For further details see the map and tables in the introduction.

Medical treatment – It is strongly recommended that visitors take out insurance cover against personal accident and sickness as there is no state health service and you will be required to pay for all medical treatment. Special winter sports policies are also offered.

Currency – The following denominations are in circulation:
Coins (5, 10, 20, 50 centimes or rappen in the German-speaking areas); (1, 2, 5 Francs); Notes: 10, 20, 50, 100, 500, 1000 Swiss Francs.
Travellers cheques and bank notes are exchanged by banks and official exchange offices. Your passport is necessary as identification when cashing cheques in a bank. Commission charges vary with hotels charging more highly than banks. For current exchange rates enquire at your bank. Banks are open from 0830 to 1630 (Monday to Friday).

Post – All letters to Switzerland should have the international abbreviation CH and the postal code number before the name of the place eg CH-3000 Berne. The postal codes of all places mentioned in the guide are given in the index.
Airmail postcards and letters to the USA and Canada: 1.60Frs.
Airmail postcards and letters to UK (up to 20g): 1.00Frs.
Domestic: postcards and letters: 0.80Frs.

Opening times – Post offices are generally open from Mondays to Fridays 0830 (0730 in large towns) to 1200 and 1345 to 1830 and from 0700 to 1100 on Saturdays.

Telephone – The Swiss telephone network is entirely automatic and it is therefore possible to call any subscriber, at any hour of the day or night, from any public or private call-point. There are public telephone boxes in the most remote hamlets. The number is formed by a three-figure code, given in brackets, followed by another group of five, six or seven figures. When calling someone in the same telephone district do not dial the code. The minimum call is two 20 centime coins.
Telephone cards, called **Taxcards**, are available (10Frs or 20Frs) from post offices, newsagents, railway stations etc.

Useful telephone numbers:

111 addresses of chemists on duty; addresses of the nearest hospital and or doctor.

114 to place calls abroad when it is not possible to dial direct.

117 police in case of an emergency.

118 fire brigade.

120 in winter snow report and avalanche bulletin; in summer tourist information provided by the Swiss National Tourist Office.

140 the Touring-Secours motor breakdown service (open 24 hours).

162 weather forecasts.

163 information about snow-bound roads and whether you need chains etc.

191 international numbers and information about telephoning abroad.

There is a 24-hour **English-speaking** information and help line called Anglo-Phone: ☎ 157-5014, which costs 1.40Frs per minute.
The operators usually speak French, German and Italian depending on the region and English in the main cities and major resorts.

Working hours – In summer, offices and shops are open at 0800, sometimes even 0700, to 1200 and 1400 to 1700 or 1800; banks are open Mondays to Fridays 0830 to 1630. The five day working week is becoming more and more widespread except for shops, which stay open on Saturday afternoons, closing generally at about 1600. In large towns department stores are closed on Monday mornings but have late-night shopping until 2100 once a week.

Tipping – Tips are included on all restaurant and hotel bills, and in most taxi fares, so it is not usually expected to leave an extra tip.

Standard Time – In summer Switzerland operates a daylight saving scheme when clocks are advanced by an hour. The actual dates are announced annually but always occur over weekends in March and October.

Electricity – 220 volts (AC) is the usual voltage and most power sockets are designed for three pin round plugs.

National holidays – These general holidays are observed all over the country:

New Year's Day (1 January)
Good Friday
Easter Monday
Ascension Day
Whit Monday
Swiss National Holiday (1 August)
Christmas Day (25 December)
Boxing Day (26 December)

Other holidays tend to vary from canton to canton. Thanksgiving (*Jeûne féderal* in French; *Bettag* in German), not to be confused with the American holiday, is observed in all the cantons, but Geneva, the 3rd Sunday in September; the following Monday is a holiday observance in some of the cantons. The Geneva Canton observes Thanksgiving the 2nd Thursday in September.

Useful addresses

Swiss Embassies and Consulates

United Kingdom: Swiss Embassy, 16-18 Montagu Place, London W1H 2BQ, ☎ (071) 723 0701; **Consulate General of Switzerland**, Sunley Tower, 24th floor, Piccadilly Plaza, Manchester M1 4BT, ☎ (061) 236 2933.

Eire: Swiss Embassy, 6 Aylesbury Road, Ballsbridge, Dublin 4, ☎ (1) 692 515.

United States: Swiss Embassy, 2900 Cathedral Avenue NW, Washington DC 20008, ☎ (202) 745 7900 with consulates in Atlanta, Chicago, Houston, Los Angeles, New York and San Francisco.

Canada: Swiss Embassy, 5 Avenue Marlborough, Ottawa, Ont K1N 8E6, ☎ (613) 235 1837.

Foreign Embassies and Consulates in Switzerland

Great Britain: Embassy, Thunstrasse 50, CH-3005 Borne, ☎ (031) 352 50 21; **Consulate General of Great Britain**, Dufourstrasse 56, CH-8008 Zurich, ☎ (01) 47 15 20 and another consulate in Geneva.

Eire: Embassy, Kirchenfeldstrasse 68, CH-3005 Berne, ☎ (031) 352 14 42

United States: Embassy, Jubiläumstrasse 93, 3005 Berne, ☎ (031) 43 7011 with consulates in Geneva and Zurich..

Canada: Embassy, Kirchenfeldstrasse 88, 3005 Berne, ☎ (031) 44 6381 with a consulate in Geneva.

TOURIST INFORMATION

Swiss National Tourist Offices (SNTO) – For information (NB the SNTO publishes a comprehensive information brochure: *Switzerland – Travel Tips*), brochures, special listings, maps and assistance in planning your trip to Switzerland apply to the official tourist office in your country.

Swiss National Tourist Office Headquarters (Schweizerische Verkehrszentrale – SVZ) – Bellariastrasse 38, CH-8027 Zurich, ☎ (01) 288 1111.

Australia: 203-233 New South Head Road, PO Box 193, Edgecliff, Sydney NSW 2027, ☎ (02) 326 17 99.

Canada: 154 University Avenue, Suite 610, Toronto, Ontario M5H 3Y9, ☎ (416) 971 9734.

United Kingdom: Swiss Federal Railways, Swiss Centre, Swiss Court, London W1V 8EE, ☎ (071) 734 1921

United States: Swiss Center, 608 Fifth Avenue, New York City, NY 10020, ☎ (212) 757 5944.
150 North Michigan Avenue, Chicago, IL 60601, ☎ (312) 630 5840.
260 Stockton Street, San Francisco, CA 94108, ☎ (415) 362 2260.

There are also Swiss National Tourist Offices in the following cities: Amsterdam, Brussels, Chicago, Frankfurt, Los Angeles, Madrid, Milan, New York, Paris, Rome, Stockholm, Tokyo, Toronto and Vienna.

Tourist Information Centres 🛈 – Tourist Information Centres (verkehrsbüro; office de tourisme; ente turistico) are to be found in most large towns and tourist resorts and their phone numbers are given, along with other information, under the entry headings in the Admission Times and Charges section. The symbol 🛈 indicates their location on the town plans.

Swiss Hotel Association (Schweizer Hotelier – Verein – SHV) – Monbijoustrasse 130, CH-3001 Berne, ☎ (031) 370 41 11.

Automobilclub der Schweiz (ACS) – Wasserwerkgasse 39, CH-3000 Berne 13, ☎ (031) 311 77 22.

Touring Club der Schweiz (TCS) – Rue Pierre Fatio 9, CH-1211 Geneva, ☎ (022) 737 12 12.

Consult the map of Places to Stay at the beginning of the guide to choose a suitable location.

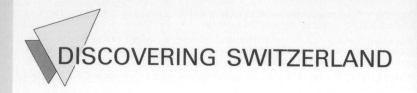

DISCOVERING SWITZERLAND

By rail on the famous Alpine trains

The **William Tell-Express** links central Switzerland to the Ticino area. By paddle-boat from Lucerne to Flüelen-Lugano/Locarno. After that, the journey continues by train.

The **Glacier Express** links Zermatt to St-Moritz or Davos (in summer only). An unforgettable journey through the majestic Alps.

The **Bernina Express** links Chur to Tirano (Italy), passing through the Bernina Pass. An impressive route.

The **Golden Pass Panoramic Express** offers panoramic views between Montreux and Zweisimmen.

The **Palm-Express** links St-Moritz to Lugano-Locarno/Ascona by post bus and Domo-dossola to Brig and Zermatt by train.

The **MOB (Montreux-Bernese Oberland)** with its Panoramic Express or its Super Panoramic Express travels through enchanting landscapes.

Small steam trains – With their nostalgic plume of smoke, they are now a charac-teristic feature of the Swiss countryside. They have been lovingly restored by volunteers and can be seen in service during the tourist season, especially at weekends.

Vaud Canton: **Blonay-Chamby** ☎ (021) 943 21 21, **Le Pont-Le Brassus** ☎ (021) 845 56 15, **Lausanne-Echallens-Berger**, nicknamed "La Brouette" (The Wheelbarrow) ☎ (021) 881 11 15, **Montreux-Claux-Naye Rocks** ☎ (021) 963 65 46.

Valais Canton: **Rive-Bleue Express** linking Le Bouveret to Evian (France) ☎ (025) 71 41 64.

Neuchâtel Canton: **St Sulplice-Travers** ☎ (038) 61 36 78.

Bernese Oberland: **Interlaken-Brienz or Grindenwald** ☎ (036) 51 32 77.

Bernese Mittelland: **Berne Weissenbühl-Interlaken Ost-Brienz** ☎ (031) 45 20 33, **Flamatt-Laupen-Gümmenen** ☎ (031) 747 74 16, **Huttwil-Ramsei-Huttwil** ☎ (034) 22 31 51, **Worblaufenworb Dorf/Solothurn** ☎ (031) 925 55 55.

Solothurn Canton: **Solothurn-Burgdorf-Thun-Solothurn** ☎ (034) 22 31 51.

Ticino Canton: **Capolago-Generoso Velta** ☎ (091) 48 11 05.

Steam boats on the lakes – Yet another familiar feature of the Swiss countryside. Proudly sporting the red flag and its white cross on their stern, these paddle-boats provide a wonderful opportunity to visit the Swiss lakes during summer. Enjoy the delicious meals served in luxurious dining rooms on many of these boats!

Greifensee	Lake Lucerne
Lake Brienz	Lake Maggiore
Lake Constance	Lake Thun
Lake Geneva	Lake Zurich

Tours of the lakes on traditional steam boats are also organised regularly.
The Swiss Boat pass (subscription 50% discount) entitles you to unlimited travel for one or two weeks. It is sold at Swiss National Tourist Offices, on board boats and at ticket offices in harbours.

THE SWISS NATIONAL PARK also see under Zernez

The purpose of this park is the preservation of Swiss flora and fauna and visits are subject to strict regulations. Drivers must leave their car in one of the car parks. Visitors are requested not to stray from the authorised paths, which are waymarked by a white sign on a red background. Nature lovers can explore 80km – 50 miles of paths, dotted with strategic observation points from where they can admire the lovely countryside and the different types of alpine flowers, and perhaps be lucky enough to espy a deer, marmot, ibex or an eagle. The various paths feature a great many explanatory boards.

For further information apply to a Swiss National Tourist Office or the **Visitor Centre (Maison du Parc)** in Zernez. In the latter you will find many books and maps to add interest to your visit.

Local tourist information centres propose guided tours as well as special routes. A brochure published by the Federal Commission of the National Park provides comprehensive information about the park and recommends certain excursions, complete with details of the routes.

Heritage trails – This initiative of the Swiss National Tourist Office is to offer tourists four specific itineraries noted not only for the beauty of their landscape but also for their historical importance. They are:

The Roman Way

Following in the Footsteps of the Pilgrims on the Way of St James

The Great Walser Route

The Swiss Way

The Swiss National Tourist Offices will provide a free brochure. Guides for specific routes and excursions can be purchased on their premises.

RECREATION

Fishing – Switzerland's many rivers and lakes are a paradise for the angler. For further information on regulations and licences apply to the Swiss National Tourist Office, local tourist information centres or the Swiss Fishing Federation, Klösterliallmend 3, 6045 Meggen.

Cycling – Certain railway stations offer a bicycle-hire service. It is often possible to start from one station and return it to another. The following towns, with their cantons in brackets, offer signposted itineraries for bicycles: Contone (Ticino), Grosswangen (Lucerne), Kallnach (Berne), Mendrisio (Ticino), Mettmenstetten (Zurich), Oberägeri (Zoug), Rebstein (St Gall), Saignelégier (Jura), Sion (Valais) and Yens (Vaud). The tourist information centres have brochures on local cycling paths.

Hill walking – There are many signposted paths for hill walking and hiking. The signposts with black on yellow backgrounds indicate the nearest village or town and distance. The trails and footpaths are indicated by yellow losenges. The Swiss National Tourist Office has a brochure on the various organised walks available and may provide information on geological and nature trails. There is also a choice of walks in the Swiss National Park and further information is available from the tourist information centres in Zernez, Zug, Schuls and Müstair.

Mountaineering and rock-climbing – The mountains of Switzerland are renowned for the variety of climbs they offer. The Swiss Alpine Club operates numerous mountain huts *(see under Accommodation)*. There are schools at all main resorts. Never venture onto the mountains unless you are properly clad and equipped. It is essential to have a guide when attempting any climb and there is a wide choice of organised expeditions under the supervision of highly-trained and qualified mountain guides or instructors.

Golf – Ask the Swiss National Tourist Office for a fact sheet on the 18 and 9-hole golf courses in the country. This will also indicate courses where visitors are welcome.

Sailing and surfing – There are sailing schools on most of the big lakes.

Water-skiing – Schools are available on most of the big lakes.

Canoeing, rafting and canyoning – Switzerland's wild Alpine rivers provide some of the best stretches of water for these adventure sports. Professional instructors with a thorough knowledge of the rivers put the eager sportsmen of all levels through their paces. The Saane, Simme, Upper Rhine known as the Swiss Grand Canyon, Lütschine and the Inn offer challenges and adventure galore for beginners and the more experienced with unforgettable scenery as an added extra. Official organisations provide certified rafts and hire out tested equipment: paddles, helmets, life-vests, wet suits and boots. The rafting season is from April/May to September.

Horse-drawn caravans – Discover the beauty of the Swiss countryside in a leisurely fashion, comfortably seated in a quaint, old-style caravan.

Hang-gliding and paragliding – For those who like Icarus yearn to lift, swoop and turn over treetops and mountain ridges Switzerland provides some ideal territory for the hang- and paragliders.

WINTER SPORTS

The season begins around mid-December and usually ends in mid-April The Swiss snowfields have long been known as the ski-playground of Europe. There are opportunities for all kinds of skiing from downhill to the more recent ski-touring and many schools to choose from for the beginner.

Alpine or downhill skiing, the oldest sport, reserved for those who thrive on speed and big thrills, is practised at all the resorts. Skis, sticks and boots can be hired locally.

Cross-country skiing became popular several years ago and a great many resorts have designed special routes for this sport, considered rightfully or wrongfully to be a less energetic activity. It is certainly a wonderful opportunity to discover the calm and beauty of the Swiss mountain landscapes. Engadine is a favoured spot for cross--country skiers. The skis are longer than for alpine skiing; the boots are lighter and they are not fastened to the heel.

Ski touring is a combination of cross-country skiing and downhill skiing. The boots are fastened to the heel for downward skiing, but left free for upward walking.

Ski-joring, in which the skier is pulled along by a galloping horse, requires an excellent physical condition.

Monoski, snowsurfing and free-styling are taught at several resorts.

Ice sports such as skating, curling and hockey can be played on many natural or artificial rinks, indoors or outdoors.

Sledge fans can indulge in their favourite sport on simple paths or officially marked out routes. Bobsleigh slopes too are available for those wishing to experience vertiginous sensations (descent with a pilot at St-Moritz and a few other resorts).

In the vicinity of all large resorts, visitors can also enjoy **sleigh rides** and **snowshoe walks** – decidedly more restful activities.

Sledges drawn by dogs can reach a speed of up to 40kmh - 24 mph.

As well as practising all these sports visitors may also watch as a spectator by attending the many competitions and championships held during the winter season.

Winter sports resorts – Many of the important winter sports resorts are located on the Places to Stay Map in the Introduction and a selection of resorts have been included in the list below. The Michelin Red Guide to Switzerland also has a map of the winter sports resorts.

The Swiss National Tourist Offices also have leaflets on the resorts and their skiing facilities.

	Altitude of the resort	Highest summit	Ski-lifts	Ski school	Cross country skiing	Ice rink	Indoor swimming pool
Adelboden BE	1 356	2 350	21	●	●	●	●
Alt. St. Johann SG	894	1 620	5	●	●		
Andermatt UR	1 436	2 963	9	●	●	●	
Anzère VS	1 500	2 462	12	●	●	●	●
Appenzell AI	785	922	1	●	●		●
Arosa GR	1 742	2 653	16	●	●	●	●
Bettmeralp VS	1 950	2 709	14	●	●		●
Bever GR	1 710				●	●	
Blatten/Belalp VS	1 322	3 100	9	●	●		●
Breil/Brigels GR	1 289	2 400	7	●	●	●	●
Bruson VS	820	2 200	6	●	●	●	●
Celerina/Schlarigna GR	1 720	3 030	9	●	●	●	
Cernier and Val-de-Ruz NE	822	1 435	18	●	●		●
Champéry VS	1 049	2 300	6	●	●	●	●
Charmey FR	981	1 630	8	●	●	●	●
Château-d'Oex VD	968	1 700	11	●	●	●	●
La Chaux-de-Fonds NE	994	1 234	2	●	●	●	●
Churwalden GR	1 230	2 865	11	●	●	●	
Crans-Montana VS	1 484	2 927	39	●	●	●	●
Davos GR	1 560	2 844	35	●	●	●	●
Les Diablerets VD	1 155	3 000	18	●	●	●	●
Diemtigtal BE	820	1 850	17	●	●		
Disentis/Muster GR	1 150	3 000	7	●	●	●	●
Einsiedeln SZ	900	1 113	3	●	●	●	
Engelberg OW	1 002	3 020	22	●	●	●	●
Falera GR	1 218	3 018	32	●	●	●	
Fiesch VS	1 062	2 869	10	●	●		●
Fleurier and Val-de-Travers NE	742	1 450	8	●	●	●	
Flims-Waldhaus GR	1 103	3 018	13	●	●	●	●
Flond-Surcuolm GR	1 081	2 280	18	●	●	●	
Flumserberg SG	1 390	2 222	16	●	●		
Grächen VS	1 617	2 920	12	●	●	●	●
Grindelwald BE	1 034	2 468	17	●	●	●	●
Gstaad BE	1 080	3 000	17	●	●	●	●
Hasliberg BE	1 230	2 433	4	●	●		
Haute-Nendaz VS	1 255	3 330	19	●	●	●	●
Hoch-Ybrig SZ	1 048	1 850	9	●	●		
Kandersteg BE	1 176	2 000	6	●	●	●	
Kloster GR	1 191	2 844	16	●	●	●	●
Laax GR	1 023	2 976	18	●	●	●	●
Lenk BE	1 068	2 098	14	●	●	●	●
Lenzerheide/Lai GR	1 476	2 865	22	●	●	●	●
Leukerbad/Loèche-les-Bains VS	1 411	2 700	17	●	●	●	●
Leyzin VD	1 268	2 300	17	●	●	●	●
Maloja GR	1 815	2 159	1	●	●	●	
Marbach LU	874	1 500	5	●	●	●	
Meiringen BE	595	2 245	9	●	●	●	●
Les Marécottes/Salvan VL	1 100	2 300	5	●	●	●	●
Les Mosses VD	1 448	1 900	12	●	●	●	
Morgins VS	1 320	2 277	16	●	●	●	
Münster MS	1 359	2 180	1	●	●		
Mürren BE	1 650	2 970	9	●	●	●	●
Oberiberg SZ	1 126	1 856	2	●	●		
Obersaxen GR	1 281	2 310	8	●	●	●	
Parpan GR	1 511	2 865	38	●	●	●	●
Pontresina GR	1 800	2 978	9	●	●	●	●
Riederalp VS	1 930	2 335	8	●	●		
Rougemont VD	992	2 156	4	●	●		
Saas-Fee VS	1 809	3 600	25	●	●	●	●
Saas-Grund VS	1 560	3 100	6	●	●	●	●
Saignelegier/Franches-Montagnes JU	978	1 260			●	●	●
St-Cergue VD	1 047	1 680	12	●	●		
St-Imier-et-Vallon BE	793	1 460	8	●	●	●	●

	Altitude of the resort	Highest summit	Ski-lifts	Ski school	Cross country skiing	Ice rink	Indoor swimming pool
St-Luc VS	1 650	2 580	9	✓	✓	✓	
Samedan GR	1 720	2 276	4	✓	✓	✓	
Samnaun GR	1 846	2 872	11	✓	✓	✓	✓
St-Moritz GR	1 850	3 030	12	✓	✓	✓	✓
St-Stephan BE	993	1 989	3	✓	✓		
Savognin GR	1 210	2 700	17	✓	✓		✓
Schwarzenburg BE	792				✓		
Schwarzsee FR	1 050	1 750	9	✓	✓	✓	✓
Scuol/Schuls GR	1 244	2 800	10	✓	✓	✓	✓
Sedrun GR	1 441	3 000	13	✓	✓	✓	✓
Le Sentier VD	1 024	1 476		✓	✓	✓	✓
Sils-Maria GR	1 815	3 303	6	✓	✓	✓	✓
Silvaplana GR	1 816	3 303	8	✓	✓	✓	✓
Sörenberg LU	1 166	2 350	12	✓	✓	✓	✓
Splügen GR	1 450	2 215	6	✓	✓	✓	
Tarasp-Vulpera GR	1 268	2 800	16	✓	✓	✓	✓
Ulrichen/Oberwald VS	1 347	2 080	5	✓	✓	✓	✓
Unteriberg SZ	931	1 856			✓		✓
Unterwasser SG	910	2 262	5	✓	✓		✓
Val D'Illiez VS	946	2 300	16	✓			✓
Val Müstair GR	1 248	2 519		✓	✓	✓	✓
Verbier VS	1 406	3 330	55	✓	✓	✓	✓
Veysonnax VS	1 235	3 300	10	✓	✓		✓
Villars-sur-Ollon VD	1 253	2 217	12	✓	✓	✓	✓
Wengen BE	1 275	2 440	18	✓	✓	✓	
Wildhaus SG	1 098	2 076	11	✓	✓	✓	✓
Zermatt VS	1 620	3 820	31	✓	✓	✓	✓
Zernez GR	1 471				✓	✓	✓
Zuor GR	1 750	2 500	4	✓	✓	✓	
Zweisimmen BE	1 000	2 000	7	✓	✓	✓	

Firework display, Geneva

J. P. Maeder — I.O.C.

BOOKS TO READ

Switzerland for Beginners by George Mikes (André Deutsch)
The Swiss Army by John McPhee
Switzerland's Amazing Railways by C J Allen
Turner in the Alps by David Hill (George Philip)
The Swiss and the British by John Wraight
The Man in the Ice by Konrad Spindler, translated by Ewald Osers (Weidenfeld and Nicolson)

Written in Switzerland or with Swiss connections

The Garden Party and Other Stories Katherine Mansfield (Penguin)
The Doll's House Katherine Mansfield
Sherlock Holmes detective series by Conan Doyle

Children's favourites

Swiss Family Robinson by Johann David Wyss, edited by his son Johann Rudolf Wyss
Heidi by Johanna Spyri

Swiss authors

Max Frisch playwright and novelist: *The Fire Raisers* (play) *Andorra* (play); *I'm Not Stiller* (novel); *When the War was Over* (novel); *Edge of Reason; A Wilderness of Mirrors* (novel); *Man in the Halocene* (novel).

Classics – well worth looking for a copy

Murray's Hand-Book for Travellers in Switzerland
Switzerland, her Topographical, Historical and Literary Landmarks by Arnold Lunn
Scrambles among the Alps in the Years 1860-69 by Edward Whymper
The Early Mountaineers by Francis Gribble

Famous Swiss

My Autobiography C Chaplin (Penguin)
François de Bonivard and his Captivity - The Prisoner of Chillon by Byron
The Le Corbusier Guide by Deborah Gans (Butterworth Architecture)

Works by the artist-travellers of the 19C

William Pars: watercolours of the Grindelwald and Rhône Graciers
William Turner: his many paintings and drawings give a colourful account of his six visits to the country. His sketch books are in the Tate Gallery, London. Well known canvases are *Chillon Castle looking towards the Dents du Midi*
Ford Madox Brown: characteristic Swiss landscapes

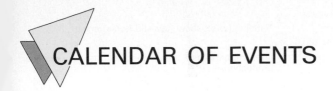

CALENDAR OF EVENTS

January
Solothurn . . . . Swiss Film Festival

1st Monday in Lent
Basle . . . . Carnival (3 days)

Early March
Geneva . . . . International Motor Show

February or early March
Ticino . . . . Travelling carnival with risotto served outdoors

3rd Monday in April
Zürich . . . . Sechseläuten: a spring festival to mark the end of
winter; corporations' procession; burning of "Böögg"
(old man winter)

One week in April
Basle . . . . European Watch, Clock and Jewellery Fair

Last Friday and Saturday in April
Aarberg . . . . Secondhand Market

Last Sunday in April
Appenzell . . . . Landsgemeinde: open-air assembly
Hundwill . . . . **216** fold 21 (1) Landsgemeinde (see above) (uneven
years)
Trogen . . . . Landsgemeinde (see above) (even years)

Mid-April to mid May
Morges . . . . Tulip Festival

Late April or late April early May
Montreux . . . . International "Golden Rose" Television Festival

1st Sunday in May
Glarus . . . . Landsgemeinde

One week in May
Berne . . . . International Jazz Festival in the Kursaal

Ascension Day
Beromünster . . . . Ascension Day Ride Out: over a hundred banner-
carrying horsemen accompany the cross and the mons-
trance with music and psalm singing on a morning ride
out. The cavalcade returns to the church in the afternoon for the traditional blessing.

Corpus Christi Thursday
**Appenzell, Fribourg, Saas-
Fee** . . . . Procession with local costumes

Corpus Christi and the previous Thursday
Kippel . . . . Procession and march-past of the "Grenadiers of God"

Late June-early September
Interlaken . . . . Open-air performances of Schiller's *William Tell*

July
Fribourg . . . . International Jazz Festival
(even years) . . . . Festival of Sacred Music
Lausanne . . . . Athletissima: International Athletics Meeting
Lugano . . . . Jazz Festival
Montreux . . . . International Jazz Festival
Nyon . . . . Paléo: International Open-Air Rock and Folk Music
Festival

Late July to early September
Gstaad/Saanen . . . . Classical Music Festival under the auspices of Yehudi
Menuhin
Altdorf . . . . Open-air performances of Schiller's *William Tell*

1 August: Swiss National Day
Throughout Switzerland . *See next page*

1st two weeks in August
Geneva . . . . Genevan festivities; floral floats and fireworks
Locarno . . . . International Film Festival

2nd weekend in August
Saignelégier . . . . National horse show, fair and horse racing

Mid-August to early September
Lucerne . . . . International Music Week: concerts, recitals, theatrical productions

Last week in August
Fribourg . . . . International Folk Festival

Last weekend in August
Aarberg . . . . Secondhand Market

Late August
Willisau . . . . International Jazz Festival

Late August to early October
Ascona . . . . International Classical Music Weeks
Montreux, Vevey . . . . Classical Music Festival

8 September
Saas-Fee . . . . Pilgrimage to the Hohen Stiege Chapel (local costumes)

2nd Sunday in September
Zürich (at the Albisgütli) . Knabenschiessen (Boys Shooting Contest): a competition for Zürich schoolboys, ending in the election of a "Shooting King", a procession and a prize giving

14 September
Einsiedeln . . . . Great Festival of the Miraculous Dedication; torchlight procession

2nd Fortnight in September
Lausanne . . . . Swiss Trade Fair

Fridays and Saturdays
Morges . . . . Autumn Festival

Last Friday and weekend in September
Neuchâtel . . . . Grape harvest festival: great procession and Battle of the Flowers

October
St-Gallen . . . . OLMA, National Show for the Dairy and Farming Industry

1st Friday and weekend in October
Lugano . . . . Grape harvest festival

First Sunday in October
Martigny . . . . Cow fights for the title of Queen of Queens in Valais

2nd weekend in October
Charmey . . . . Race of special mountain-type hay carts

3rd Sunday in October
Châtel-St-Denis . . . . 217 fold 14 *(1)* Bénichon (Benediction or harvest thanksgiving) festival to mark the end of heavy summer work; folklore procession, traditional *Bénichon* meals

4th Monday in November
Berne . . . . Zibelemärit: traditional onion market to mark the beginning of winter; battle of confetti December (date changes)

Geneva . . . . Feast of the Escalade: commemoration of the defeat of the Savoyard attack in 1602; historical procession; dancing

1st Saturday in December
Fribourg . . . . St Nicholas parade and fair

Fortnight before Christmas
Berne . . . . Christmas Market

---

(1) For places not described in the guide the number and fold of the Michelin map (at a scale of 1:200 000) are given.

A map of places to stay in the Introduction
shows the resorts, spas and ski areas
selected to make your holiday more pleasant.

The national festival – Every year all Switzerland fervently commemorates the anniversary of the perpetual alliance sworn on 1 August 1291, by the representatives of the three communities of Uri, Schwyz and Unterwalden *(qv)*. The evening of 1 August is given over to patriotic demonstrations. The historic sites of Lake Uri *(qv)*, especially the Rütli Field and the Axenstrasse, are floodlit, and in villages all over the country young people light bonfires on the heights, making a fascinating spectacle for anyone who can enjoy it from a summit in the Jura or Alps.

Music and art festivals – The great event of the summer season in Switzerland is the Lucerne Festival. International Music Weeks are organised in August under the most distinguished auspices. The programme includes daily public concerts, recitals and a series of theatrical productions.

In the early and late season other big resorts on the shores of the lake offer equally attractive programmes to their guests. This is the case with Zürich, Lausanne and Lugano in May and June and Montreux and Ascona in September.

In a different sphere, Basle hosts an International Art Exhibition in mid-June.

Fairs – In April Basle holds a Swiss Samples Fair *(Schweizer-Mustermesse)* at which Swiss and international industrial production are fully represented. In September the Lausanne Fair *(Comptoir Suisse)* attracts nearly a million visitors. Here the atmosphere is more relaxed, for amusements and gastronomy play their part as well as business. Another type of exhibition, OLMA, the Swiss agricultural and dairy farming show held at St Gallen every October, is more and more successful with every show held.

The Swiss penknife
The genuine Swiss penknife, an essential part of the good boyscout's kit, is recognisable by its red colour and white cross, circumscribed by a square with rounded corners. There exist over two hundred models, ranging from the most basic to the most sophisticated. The designers have even brought out a model specially intended for users who are left-handed!
This gem of the miniature cutlery industry was originally created to equip the Swiss Army more than one hundred years ago. But within a short time, the "Schweizer Militärmesser", later known as the Swiss penknife, became world famous and was adopted by all adventure lovers and do-it-yourself fiends.
It has many functions and can be used for cutting, slicing, filing, carving, sharpening, opening (tins for instance), removing caps and bottle tops, tightening, loosening, measuring, chipping, dismantling, piercing, finding one's bearings, etc. There is no doubt that it truly deserves its traditional nickname - the smallest toolbox in the world.

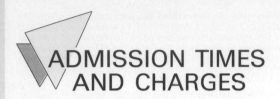

ADMISSION TIMES AND CHARGES

As admission times and charges are subject to modification due to increase in the cost of living, the information printed below is for guidance only.

The following list details the opening times and charges (if any) and other relevant information concerning all sights in the descriptive part of this guide accompanied by the symbol ⊙.

The prices quoted apply to individual adults but many places offer reduced rates for children, OAPs and some a family discount. Prices are given in Swiss Francs (abbreviated to Frs).

The times are those of opening and closure but remember that some places do not admit visitors during the last hour or half hour.

For most towns the address and/or telephone number of the local Tourist Information Centre, indicated by the symbol ☱ , is given below. Generally most efficient, these organisations are able to help passing tourists find accommodation (hotel, guest house, camp site, youth hostel, etc) and provide information on exhibitions, performances, guided tours, market days and other items of local interest.

City tours are organised regularly during the tourist season in many Swiss towns. See under each heading or apply to the Tourist Information Centre.

Sights which have facilities for disabled tourists are indicated by the symbol ⅙ below.

A

AARE
☱ Bahnhofstrasse 20 ☏ (064) 24 76 24

Gorges – Open early April (weather permitting) to late October daily 0900 to 1700; July and August 0800 to 1800; illuminations Wednesdays and Fridays in July and August between 2100 and 2300; 5Frs; ☏ (036) 71 32 14 .

AIGLE
☱ Rue de la Gare 4 ☏ (025) 26 12 12

Castle: Wine Museum – Open July and August daily 1000 to 1800; April to June, September and October, daily (except Mondays) 0900 to 1230 (last admission at 1130) and 1400 to 1800 (last admission at 1700); closed 1 November to 31 March; 6Frs; ☏ (025) 26 21 30.

ALP GRÜM

Train leaving from Ospizio Bernina – 4.40Frs.

ARENENBERG CASTLE

Napoleonic Museum – Open April to September 0900 to 1200 and 1330 to 1800; October to March 1000 to 1200 and 1330 to 1600; 5Frs; ☏ (072) 64 18 66.

ARLESHEIM

Collegiate Church – Closed between 1400 and 1600.

AROSA
☱ ☏ (081) 31 16 21

Weisshorn Cable-Car – Every 10 minutes or 20 minutes depending on the demand; in winter 0820 to 1620, in summer 0820 to 1220 and 1340 to 1700; 28Frs; ☏ (081) 31 18 28.

L'AUBERSON

Baud Museum – ⅙ Guided tours (1 hour) July to mid-September, Mondays to Fridays 1400 to 1700; the rest of the year Sundays and public holidays 1000 to 1200 and 1400 to 1800; 6Frs; ☏ (024) 61 24 84.

AUGST (AUGUSTA RAURICA)

Roman House – Open March to October, daily (except Monday mornings) 1000 to 1200 and 1330 to 1800 (1700 November to February); closed 1 January, Good Friday, 24, 25 and 31 December; 5Frs; ☏ (061) 811 11 87.
Museum – ⅙ Same opening times as above.
Ruins/Excavated site – Open 0800 to 1630.

AVENCHES
☱ 3 Place de l'Eglise ☏ (037) 75 11 57

Roman Museum – Open daily (except Tuesdays) 0900 to 1200 and 1300 to 1700; closed 1 November to 1 March, on 1, 2 January and 25 December; 2Frs; ☏ (037) 75 17 30.

B

BADEN

Bailiff's Castle – Open Tuesdays to Fridays 1200 to 1700; Saturdays, Sundays and public holidays 1000 to 1700; closed for Easter, Whitsun and Christmas; 5Frs; ☎ (056) 22 75 74.

BALLENBERG

Ballenberg Open-Air Museum – ♿ Open 15 April to 31 October daily 1000 to 1700; 10Frs; ☎ (036) 51 11 23.

BASLE

City tour – Apply to the Tourist Information Centre.

Cathedral – Open Easter to 15 October, Mondays to Fridays, 1000 to 1800, Saturdays 1000 to 1200 and 1400 to 1700, Sundays 1300 to 1700; 16 October to Easter Sunday, Mondays to Saturdays 1000 to 1200 and 1400 to 1600, Sundays 1400 to 1600.

Cathedral Tower – 2Frs.

Ethnographic Museum – Open May to November Tuesdays to Sundays as well as Easter Monday and Whit Monday 1000 to 1700; the rest of the year 1000 to 1200 and 1400 to 1700; closed Mondays, 1 January, Good Friday, 1 May, 24, 25 and 31 December as well as the afternoons of Ash Wednesday and 1 August; 3Frs; ☎ (061) 29 55 00.

Town Hall – Guided tours; apply to the Tourist Information Centre ☎ (061) 261 50 50.

Fine Arts Museum – ♿ Open daily (except Mondays) 1000 to 1700; closed 1 January, Wednesday afternoon during Carnival, Good Friday, 1 May, 1 August, 24, 25 and 31 December; 6Frs (free Sundays and public holidays); ☎ (061) 271 08 28.

Paper Museum – Open Tuesdays to Sundays 1400 to 1700; closed Mondays (except Easter and Whit Mondays), 1 January, the Wednesday prior to Easter, Wednesday during Carnival, Ascension Day, 1 May, 1 August, 24, 25 and 31 December; 7Frs; ☎ (061) 272 09 93.

Museum of Contemporary Art – ♿ Open daily (except Mondays) 1100 to 1700; closed on the same public holidays as the Fine Arts Museum; 5Frs; ☎ (061) 272 81 83.

Zoological Garden – ♿ Open May to August 0800 to 1830; March, April, September and October 0800 to 1800; November to February 0800 to 1730; 9Frs (children 3.50Frs); ☎ (061) 281 00 00.

Kirschgarten Museum – Open daily (except Mondays) 1000 to 1700; 5Frs (free the first Sunday of each month).

Historical Museum – Open daily (except Tuesdays) 1000 to 1700; 5Frs (free the first Sunday of each month); ☎ (061) 271 05 05.

Museum of Antiquities – ♿ Open daily (except Mondays) 1000 to 1700; closed 1 January, Good Friday, 1 May, 1 August, 24, 25 and 31 December as well as Monday during Carnival and Ash Wednesday; 5Frs; ☎ (061) 271 22 02.

Museum of Casts – Open daily (except Mondays) 1000 to 1200 and 1400 to 1700; closed on the same public holidays as the Museum of Antiquities, as well as on Easter and Whit Mondays; 3Frs (free Sundays); ☎ (061) 271 22 02.

Museum of the City and Cathedral – Open Tuesdays to Fridays 1400 to 1715; Sundays and public holidays 1000 to 1715; 5Frs (free Sundays and public holidays); ☎ (061) 267 66 25.

Historical Museum of Pharmacy – Open Mondays to Fridays 0900 to 1200 and 1400 to 1700; ☎ (061) 25 79 40.

Collection of Old Musical Instruments – Open Wednesdays and Fridays 1400 to 1700; also open Sundays 1000 to 1200.

Museum of Architecture – Open Tuesdays to Fridays 1300 to 1800, Saturdays 1000 to 1600, Sundays and public holidays 1000 to 1300; closed Easter Monday, Good Friday, 1 May, Whit Sunday, 1 August, 25 and 26 December and during Carnival; 5Frs; ☎ (061) 261 14 13.

General View – From the silo terrace of the Swiss Navigation Co; open March to October daily 1000 to 1200 and 1400 to 1700; the rest of the year Wednesdays, Saturdays and Sundays 1000 to 1200 and 1400 to 1700; closed 1 January, Ash Wednesday, Maundy Thursday, 24, 25 and 31 December; 4Frs; ☎ (061) 66 33 49.

"From Basle to the High Seas" Exhibition – Open March to November daily (except Mondays) 1000 to 1700; the rest of the year Tuesdays, Saturdays and Sundays 1000 to 1700; closed 1 January, 1 August, 24, 25 and 31 December; 6Frs; ☎ (061) 631 42 65.

Tour by boat – From early May to early October; apply to the Basler Personenschiffahrts-Gesellschaft AG, Blumenrain 2; 12Frs; ☎ (061) 261 24 00.

BEATENBERG

Niederhorn chairlift – Closed mid-April to late May and late October to mid-December; the rest of the year operates 0830 to 1730 in summer and 0830 to 1630 in winter; 22Frs Rtn; ☎ (036) 41 11 96.

BELLA LUI See Crans-Montana

BELLELAY

Abbey Church – Open 0800 to 1800 (1600 in winter); exhibitions mid-June to mid-September 1000 to 1200 and 1400 to 1800; 5Frs; ☎ (032) 91 91 22.

BELLWALD

Richinen Chairlift – Operates mid-June to late October and mid December to late April; 8Frs; ☎ (028) 71 19 26.

BERNE
🚉 Bahnhof ☎ (031) 311 66 11

Guided tours – Apply to the Tourist Information Centre.

Clock Tower – Guided tours (3/4 hour) May to October daily until 1630; the rest of the year on request; tickets available from the Tourist Information Centre; 5Frs; ☎ (031) 22 76 76.

Albert Einstein's House – Open February to November Tuesdays to Fridays 1000 to 1700, Saturdays 1000 to 1600; closed Mondays, Sundays and public holidays; 2Frs; ☎ (031) 31 20 01.

Bear Pit – Open early April to October 0700 to 1800; the rest of the year 0900 to 1600.

Cathedral of St Vincent – Open from Easter to 31 October Mondays to Saturdays 1000 (Sundays 1100) to 1200 and 1400 to 1700; the rest of the year Tuesdays to Fridays 1000 to 1200 (Saturdays 1700); closed Sunday afternoons.
Cathedral Tower – Closed 1/2 hour before the cathedral.

Federal Palace – Guided tours (3/4 hour) daily (except Saturdays) at 0900, 1000, 1100, 1400, 1500 and 1600 (except Sundays); visitors may attend some of the sessions from the benches; ☎ (031) 61 85 22.

Fine Arts Museum – Open Wednesdays to Sundays 1000 to 1700, Tuesdays 1000 to 2100; closed Mondays; 4Frs; ☎ (031) 311 09 44.

Natural History Museum – Open Tuesdays to Saturdays 0900 to 1700, Sundays 1000 to 1700, Mondays 1400 to 1700; closed 1 January, Good Friday, Easter Sunday, Ascension Day, Whitsun, 3rd Sunday in September and at Christmas; 3Frs; ☎ (031) 350 71 11.

Bernese Historical Museum – Open daily (except Mondays) 1000 to 1700; closed 1 January, Good Friday, Easter, Whitsun and Christmas; 5Frs; ☎ (031) 351 18 11.

Swiss Alpine Museum – Open all year Mondays 1400 to 1700; open the other days of the week mid-May to mid-October 1000 to 1700 and mid-October to mid-May 1000 to 1200 and 1400 to 1700; 4Frs; ☎ (031) 351 04 34.

Swiss Postal Museum – ♿ Open daily (except Mondays) 1000 to 1700; closed public holidays; 2Frs; ☎ (031) 62 77 77.

Dählhölzli Zoo: **Vivarium** – ♿ Open daily 0800 to 1830 in summer, 0900 to 1700 in winter; 5Frs (children 1.50Frs); ☎ (031) 351 06 16.

BEROMÜNSTER

Castle-Museum – Guided tours (1 hour) May to October Sundays and public holidays 1500 to 1700; 3Frs; ☎ (045) 51 29 34.

Collegiate Church – Open daily 1000 to 1600; ☎ (045) 51 38 68.

BERTHOUD see Burgdorf

BEX
🚉 ☎ (025) 63 30 80

Salt Mine – Guided tours (2 1/4 hours) 1 April to 15 November; 13Frs. It is essential to book in advance. ☎ (025) 63 24 62. Take a warm jumper or cardigan as the average temperature is usually around 17°C-63°F.

BIASCA
🚉 ☎ (092) 72 33 27

Church of St Peter and St Paul – Apply to the presbytery or the address mentioned on the door.

BIEL
🚉 Verkehrsbüro, Zentralstrasse 60 ☎ (032) 22 75 75

Schwab Museum – Open Tuesdays to Saturdays 1000 to 1200 and 1400 to 1700, Sundays 1100 to 1700; 3Frs; ☎ (032) 22 76 03.

BLONAY
🚉 ☎ (021) 943 10 15

Blonay-Chamby Railway Museum – Operates 10 May to 17 October Saturdays 1400 to 1800, Sundays 0940 to 1800; 10Frs Rtn including the museum; ☎ (021) 943 21 21.

BLUE LAKE

The site is open from May to October; 4Frs including the boat trip.

BOUDRY

Wine Museum – Open Thursdays to Sundays 1400 to 1700; closed 24 December to 10 January; 5Frs; ☎ (038) 42 38 32.

LE BOUVERET
🚏 Route cantonale 42 ☎ (025) 81 11 01

Swiss Steam Park – Open 16 May to 25 September 1330 to 1800 (weekends 1000 to 1800); 28 September to 30 October weekends 1000 to 1800 and Wednesday afternoons 1330 to 1800; 1 April to 15 May weekends and public holidays 1000 to 1800 and Wednesday afternoons 1330 to 1800; 8Frs; ☎ (025) 81 44 10 and (025) 26 23 92 (after opening hours).

BRENETS LAKE

Boat Excursion to the Doubs Falls – Summer service from 23 May to 26 September; boats leave daily every 45mins after 1000; 10Frs Rtn; ☎ (039) 32 17 17.

LA BREYA

Chairlift – Operates mid-June to mid-September 0830 to 1215 and 1330 to 1700; ☎ (026) 83 13 44.

BRIENZER ROTHORN
🚏 Brienz ☎ (036) 51 32 42

Rack-railway from Brienz – Operates from June to October; departures every hour; 58Frs Rtn; ☎ (036) 51 32 42.

BRIG
🚏 Bahnofplatz ☎ (028) 23 19 01

Stockalper's Castle – Guided tours (50mins) May to October daily (except Mondays) at 0900, 1000, 1100, 1400, 1500, 1600 and 1700; 4Frs; ☎ (028) 23 19 01.

BRISSAGO ISLANDS

Access to the Main Island – A boat service operates from April to October; for all enquiries apply to the Tourist Information Centres in Ascona or Losone or to the offices of the Navigazione Lago Maggiore in the port of Ascona. There are tropical gardens and an art exhibition on the island.

BRUDERHOLZ

Water Tower – Open from 25 March to 25 September 0700 to 2000; the rest of the year 0800 to 1700; 0.50Frs; ☎ (061) 20 52 67.

BRUGG

Vindonissa Museum – Open 2 January to 24 December daily (except Mondays) 1000 to 1200 and 1400 to 1700; closed from Good Friday to Easter, at Whitsun and Christmas; 4Frs; ☎ (056) 41 21 84

BUBIKON

Commandery – Open early April to late October Thursdays to Sundays 0900 to 1100 and 1400 to 1800; closed Easter and Whitsun; 4Frs; ☎ (055) 38 12 60.

BULLE
🚏 ☎ (029) 280 22

Museum of the Gruyère Region – ♿ Open Tuesdays to Saturdays 1000 to 1200 and 1400 to 1700; Sundays and public holidays 1400 to 1700; closed 1 January and 25 December; 4Frs; ☎ (029) 272 60.

BURGDORF
🚏 ☎ (034) 22 24 45

Castle-Museum – Open early April to late October Mondays to Saturdays 1400 to 1700, Sundays and public holidays 1000 to 1700; 4Frs; ☎ (034) 23 02 14.

BÜRGLEN

Tell Museum – Open July and August 0930 to 1730; May, June, September and October 1000 to 1130 and 1330 to 1700; 3Frs; ☎ (044) 241 55.

C

CADEMARIO

San Ambrogio Church – Apply to the presbytery ☎ (091) 59 47 35, the Post Office ☎ (091) 59 24 02 or the Town Hall ☎ (091) 59 24 18.

CANTINE DI GANDRIA

Customs Museum – Open Sunday prior to Easter to the second last Sunday in October 1430 to 1730; ☎ (091) 28 48 11.

CELERINA
🚏 ☎ (082) 339 66

St John's – Open Tuesdays 1400 to 1600, Wednesdays 1600 to 1700, Fridays 1030 to 1200.

CHASSERAL

Toll road – Cars and motorcycles: 3Frs.

CHÂTEAU-D'OEX

☎ ☎ (029) 477 88

Enhaut Traditional Museum – Open Tuesdays, Thursdays and Fridays 1000 to 1200 and 1400 to 1630; Saturdays, Sundays and public holidays 1400 to 1630; closed 1 January and 25 December, as well as Easter and Whitsun; 4Frs; ☎ (029) 465 20.

CHAUMONT

Observation tower – 1Fr.

Funicular from La Coudre – Departures every hour; 5.40Frs (8.60Frs Rtn).

LA CHAUX-DE-FONDS

☎ Rue Neuve 11 ☎ (039) 28 13 13

International Museum of Horology – ♿ Open June to September 1000 to 1700; the rest of the year 1000 to 1200 and 1400 to 1700; closed Mondays (except public holidays), 1 January, 24, 25 and 31 December; 8Frs; ☎ (039) 23 62 63.

Fine Arts Museum – ♿ Open 1000 to 1200 and 1400 to 1700 (2000 Wednesdays); closed Mondays, 1 January, Good Friday and 25 December; 8Frs; ☎ (039) 23 04 44.

Museum of Natural History – Open 1400 to 1700 as well as 1000 to 1200 on Sundays and public holidays; closed Mondays, 1 January and 25 December; ☎ (039) 23 39 76.

History and Medal Museum – Open Tuesdays to Fridays 1400 to 1700 (1800 Saturdays); Sundays and public holidays 1000 to 1200 and 1400 to 1800; closed 1 January and 25 December; 3Frs; ☎ (039) 23 50 10.

Zoological Garden – ♿ Indoor vivarium open 1000 to 1200 (except Tuesdays) and 1400 to 1700; ☎ (039) 276 430.

Peasant Museum – Open May to October daily (except Fridays) 1400 to 1700; the rest of the year Wednesdays, Saturdays and Sundays 1400 to 1700; closed 1 January and 25 December; 3Frs; ☎ (039) 26 71 89.

CHILLON

Castle – Open July and August 0900 to 1900 (last admission at 1815); April, May, June and September 0900 to 1830 (last admission at 1745); October 1000 to 1730 (last admission at 1645); November to February 1000 to 1200 and 1330 to 1645 (last admission at 1600); March 1000 to 1200 and 1330 to 1730 (last admission at 1645); 5.50Frs; ☎ (021) 963 39 12.

CHUR

☎ Ottostrasse 6 ☎ (081) 22 18 18

Cathedral of Our Lady: Treasury – Open Mondays to Fridays 1000 to 1200 and 1400 to 1600; closed Sunday mornings and Holy Week to Corpus Christi; 1.50Frs; ☎ (081) 22 92 50.

Rhaetic Museum – Open 1000 to 1200 and 1400 to 1700; closed Mondays, Good Friday, Ascension Day, Whitsun, 3rd Sunday in September and at Easter and Christmas; 5Frs; ☎ (081) 22 29 88.

Fine Arts Museum – ♿ Open daily (except Mondays) 1000 to 1200 and 1400 to 1700 (2000 Thursdays); admission price varies according to the exhibition; ☎ (081) 21 28 68.

CIMETTA see Locarno

COLOMBIER

Museum – Guided tours (1 hour) from March to October Wednesdays, Thursdays, Fridays and Sundays at 1500; ☎ (038) 43 96 25.

COPPET

Château – Guided tours (35mins) April to October 1000 to 1200 and 1400 to 1800 (last admission 30 mins before closing time); closed on Mondays except in July and August; 6Frs; ☎ (022) 776 10 28.

CRANS-MONTANA

☎ ☎ (027) 41 21 32 and (027) 41 30 41

Bella Lui – Cable-car from Crans and Montana towards Cry d'Err 0830 to 1230 and 1345 to 1700, operating continuously July to September. Every 20 minutes in summer leaving from Cry d'Err, operating continuously in winter; 15Frs (22Frs Rtn).

CULET CROSS

Cable-car from Champéry – In July and August departures every 1/2 hour 0900 to 1800; 18 June to 1 July and 20 August to 25 September irregular departures 0900 to 1700; 4 to 17 June and 26 September to 30 October departures 0900 to 1700 (in fair weather only); during the winter season departures 0800 to 1700; 15Frs Rtn; ☎ (025) 79 12 28.

The chapter on art and architecture in this guide gives an outline of artistic achievement in the country providing the context of the buildings and works of art describrd in the Sights section.

This chapter may also provide ideas for touring. It is advisable to read it at leisure.

D - E

DAVOS
☎ (081) 45 21 21

Funicular and cable-car from Weissfluhgipfel – The service operates from 30 June to 21 October; 27Frs Rtn.

Funicular from Schatzalp – Service operates all year round; 8Frs Rtn.

DELÉMONT
☎ (066) 22 97 78

Art and History Museum of the Jura Region – Open 15 May to 15 October daily (except Mondays) 1400 to 1700; the rest of the year Sundays 1400 to 1700; closed 24 December to 3 January, Easter and Carnival Day; 4Frs; ☎ (066) 22 80 77.

DIABLERETS GLACIER see Sex Rouge

DIAVOLEZZA

Cable-car – Operates mid-June to mid-October and early December to late April; departures every 1/2 hour; 24Frs; ☎ (082) 664 19.

EBENALP

Cable-car – Departures every 1/2 hour 27 May to 29 September 0740 to 1800; 30 September to 1 November 0830 to 1730; the rest of the year 0830 to 1700; the cable-car service does not operate 4 April to 11 May and 2 November to 17 December; 19Frs Rtn; ☎ (071) 88 12 12.

ÉCHALLENS

Bread and Grain Museum – Open 15 January to 20 December 0900 to 1800 (last admission at 1715); closed Mondays, 7Frs; ☎ (021) 881 50 71.

EGGISHORN

Cable-car from Fiesch – & Departures every 20 or 30mins; closed in May and November; 36.40Frs; ☎ (028) 71 27 00.

EINSIEDELN
☎ (055) 53 44 88

Abbey Great Hall – Open 1330 to 1800 (1645 Sundays and public holidays when there is a concert); 2Frs, ☎ (055) 53 24 32

EMOSSON

Cable-car from Barborine, Little Train and Miniature Funicular of the Dam – Service operates late June to mid-October Tuesdays, Thursdays, Saturdays and Sundays; 30Frs Rtn; ☎ (026) 68 12 36 (during the tourist season) or (026) 22 47 40.

ENGELBERG
Dorfstrasse 34 ☎ (041) 94 11 61

Abbey – Open 1000 (1030 Sundays and public holidays) to 1600; 2Frs; ☎ (041) 94 13 49.

ERLENBACH
☎ (033) 81 14 58

Cable-car from Stockhorn – Service operates June to October 0810 to 1740; 15 December to March 0940 (0840 Saturdays and Sundays) to 1710; 33Frs Rtn; ☎ (033) 81 21 81.

ESTAVAYER-LE-LAC
Grand-Rue 108 ☎ (037) 63 12 37

Museum – Open July and August 0900 to 1100 and 1400 to 1700; March to June, September and October Tuesdays to Sundays 0900 to 1100 and 1400 to 1700; November to February weekends only 1400 to 1700; 3Frs; ☎ (037) 63 24 48.

F

FIRST

Chairlift from Grindelwald – Chairlift operates 12 May to 23 October and 23 December to early April; 40Frs; ☎ (036) 53 36 38.

FLIMS
☎ (081) 39 10 22

Cassons Grat Chairlift and Cable-Car – Service operates mid-December to late May or early June to late October; 30Frs Rtn; ☎ (081) 39 28 22.

Crap Sogn Gion and Crap Masegn Cable-Cars – Departures every 1/2 hour; from Laax-Murschteg to Crap Sogn Gion 20Frs Rtn; from Laax-Murschteg to Crap Masegn 30Frs Rtn; from Laax-Murschteg to Vorab 32Frs Rtn; closed late April to mid-October.

FORCLAZ PASS

Footpath – For further information on possible routes apply to the Tourist Information Centre at Les Marécottes; ☎ (026) 61 15 89.

🛈 Square des Places 1 ☎ (037) 81 31 75

City Tour – Apply to the Tourist Information Centre.

Cathedral of St Nicholas – Open Mondays to Fridays 0930 to 1730; Sundays 1400 to 1730.

Art and History Museum – Open Tuesdays to Sundays 1000 to 1700 (late opening Thursday evenings 2000 to 2200); closed 1 January, Good Friday and 25 December; 5Frs; ☎ (037) 22 85 71.

Franciscan Church – Open Mondays to Fridays 0900 to 1800, Saturdays 1000 to 1200 and 1600 to 1800, Sundays 1400 to 1800.

Natural History Museum – ♿ Open 1400 to 1800; closed 1 January, Good Friday and 25 December; ☎ (037) 82 63 91.

FURKA PASS

The pass is usually snow-bound between November and May. A motorail service operates between the stations at Oberwald and Realp. Trains leave every hour between 0600 and 2100; the price of the ticket (28Frs) covers the car and passenger(s).

G

LA GARENNE

Zoo – Open 0900 to 1800; 6Frs (children aged 6-15 3Frs); ☎ (022) 366 32 57 or (022) 366 11 14.

GENEVA **🛈** Gare Cornavin ☎ (022) 738 52 00

City Tour – Apply to the Tourist Information Centre. Bus tours: Keytours SA. Pedestrian tours: several "thematic" routes are available (Association des Guides de Genève).
During the summer season, the Léman-Mont-Blanc train leaving from Genève-Eaux-Vives offers visitors sumptuous views of the surrounding mountains and the shores of Lake Geneva.

History of Science Museum – Open daily (except Mondays) 1300 to 1700; closed from Good Friday to Easter Monday, from Saturday to Monday during Whitsun, and on 1 and 3 January, 1 May, Ascension Day and 25 December.

Botanical Garden – ♿ Open 1 April to 30 September 0800 to 1930; 1 October to 31 March 0900 to 1700. The greenhouses are open daily (except Fridays) 0930 to 1100 and 1400 to 1630.

Rath Museum – Open 1000 to 1700 (Wednesdays 1200 to 2100); closed Mondays; 5Frs.

University Library – Open 0900 to 1200 and 1400 to 1700; closed Saturday afternoons, Sundays and public holidays as well as from 24 December to 2 January and from Thursday prior to Easter to the following Wednesday; ☎ (022) 320 82 66.

St Peter's Cathedral – Open June to September 0900 to 1200; November to February 0900 to 1200 and 1400 to 1700; March to May and October 0900 to 1200 and 1400 to 1800; ☎ (022) 738 56 50.
Access to the tower – Same opening times as the cathedral; 2.50Frs.

Archaeological Site – Open 1000 to 1300 and 1400 to 1800 (earphones with recorded commentary); closed Mondays; 5Frs; ☎ (022) 738 56 50.

Maison Tavel – ♿ Open daily (except Mondays) 1000 to 1700; ☎ (022) 311 43 88.

Town Hall: Alabama Room – Guided tours (1/4 hour) 15 June to 30 September Mondays to Fridays (included in the visit of the Old Town); ☎ (022) 738 52 00.

Zoubov Collection – Guided tours (50mins) 15 June to 30 September Mondays to Fridays at 1545 (the visit is included in the walking tour of the old town); the rest of the year open Thursdays at 1800, Saturdays at 1430 and 1530; ☎ (022) 311 92 55.

St Germanus' Church – Open daily (except Sundays) April to October 1400 to 1700.

Ariana Museum – ♿ Open daily (except Tuesdays) 1000 to 1700; free for standing exhibitions, 5Frs for temporary exhibitions; ☎ (022) 740 25 25.

Palais des Nations – ♿ Guided tours (1 hour) July and August 0900 to 1200 and 1400 to 1800; the rest of the year 1000 to 1200 and 1400 to 1600; closed Saturdays and Sundays in November and December; 8Frs; ☎ (022) 907 45 60.

UN Philatelic Museum – Open 2 January to 15 December 0900 to 1200 and 1400 to 1630; closed Saturdays and Sundays and certain public holidays: Easter Monday, Whit Monday, second Thursday in September and the following Friday; ☎ (022) 907 48 82.

International Red Cross Museum – ♿ Open 1000 to 1700 (last admission at 1545); closed Tuesdays and on 1 January, 24, 25 and 31 December; 8Frs; ☎ (022) 734 52 48.

Art and History Museum – Open 1000 to 1700; closed Mondays and on 1 January and 25 December; an admission fee is charged for certain temporary exhibitions; ☎ (022) 311 43 88.

Musical Instruments Museum – The museum is scheduled to reopen in 1994; ☎ (022) 346 95 65.

Baur Collection – Open 1400 to 1800; closed Mondays, 1 January, Good Friday, 24, 25 and 31 December; 5Frs; ☎ (022) 746 17 29.

Petit Palais: Museum of Modern Art – Open 1000 to 1200 and 1400 to 1800; closed Monday mornings; 10Frs; ☎ (022) 46 14 33.

Natural History Museum – ৬ Open 0900 to 1700; closed Mondays and public holidays; ☎ (022) 735 91 30.

Horology and Enamels Museum – Open 1000 to 1700; closed Tuesdays; ☎ (022) 736 74 12.

Barbier-Mueller Museum – Open daily 1100 to 1700; 5Frs; ☎ (022) 312 02 70.

Russian Orthodox Church – Open June to September 0900 to 1200 and 1430 to 1630; the rest of the year 0900 to 1200; closed Mondays; ☎ (022) 346 47 09.

Ethnographic Museum – Open 1000 to 1200 and 1400 to 1700; closed Mondays and on 1 January and 25 December; ☎ (022) 328 12 18.

Voltaire Institute and Museum – Open 1400 to 1700 Mondays to Fridays as well as on Easter Monday, Ascension Day, Whit Monday and the second Thursday in September; closed 2 January, Good Friday, 24, 25 and 31 December; ☎ (022) 344 71 33.

Historical Museum of the Swiss Abroad – Open 1000 to 1200 and 1400 to 0800; closed Mondays, 1 January and 25 December; 5Frs including admission to Geneva's Military Museum; ☎ (022) 734 90 21.

Geneva's Military Museum – Open 1000 to 1200 and 1400 to 1800; closed Mondays and 24 December to 10 January; 1.50Frs (5Frs for a combined ticket giving access to the above museum); ☎ (022) 734 90 21.

GENEVA LAKE

Boat service – See p 104.

GIESSBACH

Falls – In summer there are 7 trips daily; starting from Brienz 12.40Frs Rtn; starting from Interlaken 22.40Frs Rtn (includes funicular).

GLETSCH

Ice Grotto – Open June to October; 4Frs; ☎ (028) 73 11 29.

GOETHEANUM

Tour – From 0830 to 1230 and 1400 to 1800; ☎ (061) 701 42 42.

GORNER

Gorges – 3Frs.

GORNERGRAT

Rack-railway from Zermatt – 53Frs Rtn.

Stockhorn cable-car – Operates late May to late September with departures every 20mins; 20Frs Rtn.

GRANDSON

Castle – Open March to October daily 0900 to 1800; the rest of the year Saturdays 1400 to 1700, Sundays 0900 to 1700; 7Frs; ☎ (024) 24 29 26.

GREAT ST. BERNARD PASS

Museum – Open July and August 0800 to 1900; June and September 0900 to 1800; 6Frs; ☎ (026) 87 12 36.

GREAT ST. BERNARD PASS ROAD

Tunnel – Access at Bourg-St-Bernard. Toll: cars 27Frs (38Frs Rtn), motorcycles 27Frs (30Frs Rtn).

GRINDELWALD 🅱 ☎ (036) 53 12 12

Glacier Gorge – Access from 20 May to end October; 5Frs; ☎ (036) 53 12 12.

GRUYÈRES 🅱 ☎ (029) 610 30

Castle – Open June to September 0900 to 1800; March to May and October 0900 to 1200 and 1300 to 1700; January, February, November and December 0900 to 1200 and 1300 to 1630 (last admission half-hour before closing time); closed Christmas; 4Frs; ☎ (029) 621 02.

Cheese Dairy – Open daily 0730 to 1900. Cheese-making demonstration 1000 to 1100 and 1400 to 1500 (1200 to 1300 Sundays); ☎ (029) 614 10.

GURTEN

Funicular – 7Frs Rtn; ☎ (031) 54 23 23.

GUTTANNEN

Crystal Museum – Open June to September Mondays to Fridays 0800 to 1100 and 1400 to 1700; 3Frs; ☎ (036) 73 12 47.

H

HALLWIL

Castle – Open early April to late October daily (except Mondays) 0930 to 1130 and 1330 to 1730 (0930 to 1730 Sundays); closed 2 November to 31 March; 5Frs; ☎ (064) 54 11 21.

HARDERKULM

Funicular – Operates May to October with departures every 1/2 hour; 18.40Frs; ☎ (036) 22 45 85.

HAUTERIVE

Abbey – Guided tours (45mins) late March to late September weekdays 1400 to 1700 (1045 to 1130 and 1445 to 1645 Sundays and public holidays); the rest of the year weekdays 1400 to 1630 (1045 to 1130 and 1400 to 1600 Sundays and public holidays); ☎ (037) 42 10 83.

HEIMWEHFLUH

Funicular – Operates late March to late October 0930 to 1730 with departures every 1/4 hour or 1/2 hour; 6.40Frs; ☎ (036) 22 34 53.

HOHER KASTEN

Cable-car from Brülisau – Operates every 1/2 hour from early April to mid-January; 15 November to 23 December weekends only when the weather is good; 24 December to 2 January, operates daily when weather is good; 20Frs Rtn; ☎ (071) 88 13 22.

HÖLLOCH

Cave – Guided tours (1 hour) Wednesdays to Fridays at 1030, 1330 and 1600; Saturdays and Sundays at 1000, 1300, 1500 and 1700; 8.80Frs; ☎ (062) 71 27 71. It is advisable to wear stout walking shoes.

HÜNEGG

Château – Open mid-May to mid-October Mondays to Fridays 1400 to 1700; Sundays 1000 to 1200 and 1400 to 1700; 4Frs; ☎ (033) 43 19 82.

I

INTERLAKEN
🛈 Höheweg 37 ☎ (036) 22 21 21

Tourist Museum – Open early May to mid-October 1400 to 1700; 3Frs; ☎ (036) 22 63 41.

J

JEGENSTORF

Château – Open mid-May to mid-October daily (except Mondays) 1000 to 1200 and 1400 to 1700; closed third Sunday in September; 3Frs; ☎ (031) 96 01 59.

JUNGFRAUJOCH

By train – Round trip ticket Interlaken to Jungfraujoch: 140Frs; by one of the two early morning trains and their connections; 97Frs.

Round trip ticket Interlaken-Petite Scheidegg-Interlaken (does not include ascent of the Jungfraujoch) 54Frs.

Return ticket from Lauterbrunnen: 124Frs; by one of the two early morning trains: 81Frs.

Return ticket from Grindelwald Grund: 120Frs; by one of the two early morning trains: 77Frs.

K

KANDERSTEG
🛈 ☎ (033) 75 22 33

Lake Oeschinen – Chairlift operates mid-May to late October and late December to mid-April; 10Frs Rtn; ☎ (033) 75 11 18.

KLEIN MATTERHORN

Cable-cars – Departures from Zermatt every 20mins; 49Frs Rtn.
Cable-car from Schwarzsee - 26Frs Rtn.

KÖNIGSFELDEN ABBEY

Church – Open April to October 0900 to 1200 and 1400 to 1700; the rest of the year 1000 to 1200 and 1400 to 1600; closed Mondays, 1 and 2 January, 1 May, Good Friday to Easter, 1 August, 25 and 26 December; 2Frs; ☎ (056) 41 88 33.

KYBURG

Castle – Open March to October 0900 to 1200 and 1300 to 1700; November to February 1000 to 1200 and 1300 to 1600; closed Mondays and public holidays; 4Frs; ☎ (052) 232 46 64.

L

LANGNAU IM EMMENTAL
🛈 ☎ (035) 234 34

Local Museum – Open February to November daily (except Mondays) 0900 to 1130 and 1330 to 1800; closed on all public holidays; 3Frs; ☎ (035) 242 52.

LAUSANNE
🛈 Avenue de Rhodainie 2 ☎ (021) 617 73 21

City Tour – Apply to the Tourist Information Centre.

Olympic Museum – ♿ Open May to September 1000 to 1900 (2000 Thursdays); the rest of the year 1000 to 1800 (2000 Thursdays); closed Mondays (except Whit Monday), Easter and third Sunday in September; 12Frs; ☎ (021) 621 65 11.

Elysée Museum – Open 1000 to 1800 (2100 Thursdays); closed Mondays, 1 and 2 January, 25 December; 5Frs; ☎ (021) 617 48 21.

History Museum of Lausanne – Open 1100 to 1800 (2000 Thursdays); closed Mondays, 1 January, Easter and Christmas; admission charge for temporary exhibitions; ☎ (021) 312 13 68.

Cathedral – Closed in the afternoon 1 January and 25 December and all day 2 January (except on a Sunday).

Tower – Ascent March to September 0830 to 1130 and 1330 to 1730 (1400 to 1730 Sundays); the rest of the year 0830 to 1130 and 1330 to 1630 (1400 to 1630 Sundays); 2Frs.

Pipe and Tobacco Museum – For information call the Gallery ☎ (021) 323 43 23.

Fine Arts Museum – Open 1100 to 1800 (2000 Thursdays); 12Frs; ☎ (021) 312 83 32.

Museum of Geology, Palaeontoly and Zoology, Archaeological and Historical Museum – Open 1000 to 1200 and 1400 to 1700; closed 1 January, Easter and 25 December; ☎ (021) 692 48 18 and (021) 312 83 34.

Collection of Spontaneous Art – Open 1000 to 1200 and 1400 to 1800; weekends and public holidays 1400 to 1800; closed Mondays, 1 January and 25 December; 5Frs; ☎ (021) 647 54 35.

Hermitage Foundation – Open 1000 to 1300 and 1400 to 1800 (2200 Thursdays); closed Mondays; 13Frs; ☎ (021) 320 50 01.

Museum of Decorative Arts – Open daily (except Mons) 1100 to 1800 (2100 Tuesdays except in summer); closed 1 January and 25 December; 2.50Frs; ☎ (021) 323 07 56.

Botanical Garden – ♿ Open in March, April and October 1000 to 1200 and 1330 to 1730 (1830 May to September); ☎ (021) 26 24 09.

Museum of Contemporary Art – ♿ Open 1000 to 1800 (2000 Fridays); closed 1 January, Easter Sunday and 25 December; 12Frs; ☎ (021) 29 91 46.

Museum at Pully – ♿ Open 1400 to 1800; closed Mondays and from 24 December to 3 January; 3Frs; ☎ (021) 729 55 81.

Roman Villa at Pully – Open early April to late September daily (except Mondays) 1400 to 1700; the rest of the year weekends only 1400 to 1700; ☎ (021) 728 33 11.

LOCARNO
🛈 Via F. Balli 2 ☎ (093) 31 03 33

Excursions

Cimetta – Chairlift from Cardada operates all year round (except in November) 0800 to 1200 and 1330 to 1700; 6Frs; ☎ (093) 31 26 79.

LE LOCLE
🛈 Hôtel de Ville ☎ (039) 31 13 12

Museum of Horology – Open May to October 1000 to 1200 and 1400 to 1700; the rest of the year 1400 to 1700 only; closed Mondays (except on public holidays), 1 January and 25 December; 6Frs; ☎ (039) 31 16 80.

Fine Arts Museum – Open daily (except Mondays) 1400 to 1700; closed 1, 2 January, 24, 25 and 26 December; 6Frs; ☎ (039) 31 13 13.

Underground Mills at Col-des-Roches – Guided tours (1 hour) May to October 1000 to 1200 and 1400 to 1730 (last admission at 1700); 7Frs; ☎ (039) 31 62 62; temperature 7°C-45°F take a warm cardigan.

LOTTIGNA

Blenio Museum – Open weekdays 1400 to 1700; Saturdays, Sundays and public holidays 1000 to 1200 and 1400 to 1700; closed Maundy Thursday and 1 November; 4Frs; ☏ (092) 78 17 65.

LUCERNE

🏢 Frankenstrasse 1 ☏ (041) 51 71 71

Guided tours – Apply to the Tourist Information Centre.

Picasso Collection – Open in summer daily 1000 to 1800; in winter 1100 to 1300 and 1400 to 1600; 5Frs; ☏ (041) 51 35 33.

Historical Museum – & Open Tuesdays to Fridays 1000 to 1200 and 1400 to 1700; Saturdays, Sundays and public holidays 1000 to 1700; 4Frs; ☏ (041) 24 54 24.

Swiss Transport Museum – & Open March to October daily 0900 to 1800; the rest of the year Mondays to Saturdays 1000 to 1600 (1700 Sundays and public holidays); closed 24 and 25 December; 15Frs; ☏ (041) 31 44 44.

Fine Arts Museum – Open July to September daily 1000 to 1700 (2100 Wednesdays); the rest of the year daily (except Mondays) 1000 to 1200 and 1400 to 1700 (2100 Wednesdays), no lunchtime break on Sundays; 6Frs; ☏ (041) 23 10 24.

Richard Wagner Museum – Open 1 February to 31 October 1000 to 1200 and 1400 to 1700 (daily except Mondays in summer); the rest of the year Tuesdays, Thursdays, Saturdays and Sundays 1000 to 1200 and 1400 to 1700; 5Frs, ☏ (041) 44 23 70.

Great Panorama of Lucerne – Open March to November 0900 to 1700; 3Frs; ☏ (041) 52 99 42.

Glacier Garden – Open May to mid-October 0800 to 1800; mid-October to mid-November 0900 to 1700; mid-November to February 1030 to 1630 (except Mondays); March and April 0900 to 1700; 6.50Frs; ☏ (041) 51 43 40.

Musegg Ramparts – Open Easter to All Saints Day 0900 to 1830; ☏ (041) 51 71 71.

Museum of Natural History and Archaeology – & Open Tuesdays to Sundays 1000 to 1200 and 1400 to 1700 (no lunchtime break on Sundays); closed Thursday following Carnival Day, 24 and 25 December; 4Frs; ☏ (041) 24 54 11.

Gütsch – The funicular operates from 0700 to 2400 with departures every 10 minutes; 2Frs; ☏ (041) 22 02 72.

Boat trips – The Compagnie de Navigation operates a series of steam and other boats on Lake Lucerne linking Lucerne to the many lakeside villages and historic sites. Choose between the commented trips, the evening ones with music and dancing, excursions scheduled to link up with the cable-cars or funiculars of the lakeside summits or the William Tell Express to discover the St. Gotthard line.
During the tourist season there are hourly departures from Lucerne for boats heading for Flüelen and Alpnachstad.

LUGANO

🏢 Riva Albertolli 5 ☏ (091) 21 46 64

Guided tours – Apply to the Tourist Information Centre or the travel agency Danzas, Via Balestra 18.

Villa Favorita – Open early April to late October 1000 to 1700; closed Mondays; 8Frs (12Frs during temporary exhibitions); ☏ (091) 51 61 52.

Monte San Salvatore – Access by funicular operating mid-March to mid-November, July and August with departures every 1/2 hour until 2300; 14Frs Rtn.

Monte Bré – Access by funicular (closed January); departures every 1/2 hour; 15Frs Rtn.

M

MARMORERA

Dam – Guided tours (1 hour) all year round; ☏ (081) 81 12 10

MARBACHEGG

Cable car from Marbach – Operates 0800 to 1200 and 1300 to 1730 (no lunchtime break Saturdays and public holidays); closed 10 April to late May and in November; 8Frs Rtn; ☏ (035) 637 95.

LES MARÉCOTTES

Zoo – Open in summer 0900 to sunset; in winter 1100 to sunset (except Mondays and Tuesdays); 7Frs (children aged 6 to 15 4Frs); ☏ (026) 61 15 62.

MARTIGNY

🏢 Place Centrale 9 ☏ (026) 21 22 20

Pierre Gianadda Foundation – Open June to October 0900 to 1900; November to January 1000 to 1200 and 1330 to 1800; February to May 1000 to 1800; closed the morning of 25 December; 12Frs; ☏ (026) 22 39 78.

MEIRINGEN

🏢 ☏ (036) 71 43 22

Sherlock Holmes Museum – Open May to September daily 1000 to 1800; October to April 1500 to 1900 (except Mondays and Tuesdays); 3.50Frs; ☏ (036) 71 42 21.

MELIDE
🅱 Via Pocobelli 14 ☏ (091) 68 83 83

Switzerland in Miniature – ಈ Open mid-March to October 0900 to 1800 (2200 mid-July to mid-August); 9Frs (children 5Frs); ☏ (091) 68 79 51.

MISOX

Santa Maria di Castello Chapel – Apply to the Town Hall in Mesocco; ☏ (092) 92 17 17.

MOLÉSON-SUR-GRUYÈRES

Cheese Dairy – Open 15 May to second Sunday in October 0930 to 1830; cheese making demonstration at 1000 and 1500; 3Frs; ☏ (029) 624 34 or (029) 610 44.

Moléson Observatory – Cable-car leaves from the village of Moléson-sur-Gruyères; the service operates daily with no lunchtime break; closed mid-April to mid-June and mid-October to mid-December; 18Frs Rtn (children 9Frs).

Wax Museum – Open 0900 to 2200; closed Tuesdays and in November; 3Frs; ☏ (029) 624 34.

MONTE GENEROSO

Rack-railway from Capolago – Operates early April to late October departures every hour; 39Frs Rtn; ☏ (091) 48 11 05.

MONTE LEMA

Cable-car from Miglieglia – Operates April to October daily 0830 to 1730; 1 December to 31 March weekends only; 18Frs Rtn; ☏ (091) 71 29 86.

MONTREUX
🅱 ☏ (021) 963 12 12

History Museum of Old Montreux – Open April to October daily 1000 to 1200 and 1400 to 1700; 6Frs; ☏ (021) 963 13 53.

MOOSFLUH

Cable-cars – See under Riederalp.

MORCOTE

Access by boat from Lugano – Time: about 1 hour. For further information apply to the Società Navigazione del Lago di Lugano ☏ (091) 51 52 23.

MORGES
🅱 Grand-Rue 80 ☏ (021) 801 32 33

Alexis Forel Museum – Open Easter to October 1400 to 1800 (1700 the rest of the year); closed Mondays, 1 and 2 January, 25 and 31 December; 5Frs; ☏ (021) 801 26 47.

Vaud Military Museum – Open 1000 to 1200 and 1330 to 1700; Saturdays, Sundays and public holidays 1330 to 1700; closed 15 December to 1 January; 5Frs; ☏ (021) 801 26 16.

MÔTIERS

Museums – Guided tours 15 April to 30 September 1400 to 1700; closed Mondays and Fridays; 5Frs; ☏ (038) 61 35 51.

MOUDON

Old Moudon Museum – Closed for restoration work.

Eugène-Burnand Museum – Open 15 March to 15 December Wednesdays, Saturdays and Sundays 1330 to 1730; 6Frs; ☏ (021) 905 33 18.

MUOTTAS MURAGL

Funicular – Departures every 1/2 hour; closed 10 April to 7 May; 24Frs Rtn; ☏ (082) 682 32.

MÜRREN

Cable-car from Stechelberg – Operates May to April with departures every 1/2 hour; 58Frs Rtn; ☏ (036) 23 14 44.

MURTEN
🅱 Franz Kirchgasse 6 ☏ (037) 71 51 12

Historical Museum – Open May to September 1000 to 1200 and 1400 to 1700; the rest of the year open daily 1400 to 1700; closed Mondays all year and Saturdays and Sundays in January and February; 3Frs; ☏ (037) 71 31 00.

Michelin Maps (scale 1:200 000), which are revised regularly, show at a glance:
main roads linking the main towns and sights
regional roads
side roads for a leisurely drive.
Keep current Michelin Maps in the car at all times.

N

NÄFELS
☎ (058) 34 21 88

Freuler Palace – Open early April to late November daily (except Mondays) 1000 to 1200 and 1400 to 1730; closed Easter, Good Friday and Whitsun; 3Frs; ☎ (058) 34 13 78.

NAYE ROCKS

Rack-railway – 8 trains daily in summer with departures on the hour except at noon; in summer steam train Saturdays and Sundays; in winter last train 1500; 45Frs Rtn.

NEGRENTINO

San Carlo Church – If closed, apply to Prugiasco Restaurant or Leontica Restaurant. A deposit is required in exchange for the key.

NEUCHÂTEL
🛈 Rue de la Place d'Armes 7 ☎ (038) 25 42 42

Guided tours – Apply to the Tourist Information Centre.

Castle – Guided tours (1 hour, includes Collegiate Church) early April to late September Mondays to Fridays at 1000, 1100, 1200, 1400, 1500 and 1600; Saturdays at 1000, 1100, 1400, 1500 and 1600; Sundays and public holidays at 1400, 1500 and 1600; ☎ (038) 25 42 42.

Prison Tower – Open Easter to late September 0800 to 1800; 0.50F.

Art and History Museum – Open June to September 1000 to 1700 (2100 Thursdays); closed Mondays, 1, 2 January, 25, 26 December and in the afternoon 24 and 31 December; 7Frs (free Thursdays); ☎ (038) 207 920 or 925. The automata can be seen in action the first Sunday of each month at 1400, 1500 and 1600.

Ethnography Museum – Open daily (except Mondays) 1000 to 1700; ☎ (038) 25 03 36.

Natural History Museum – Open daily (except Mondays) 1000 to 1700; closed 1 January, last weekend in September, 24, 25 and 31 December; 5Frs; ☎ (038) 20 79 60.

Archaeological Museum – Open daily (except Mondays) 1400 to 1700; ☎ (038) 25 03 36.

LA NEUVEVILLE

Blanche Église – Open 0800 to 1200 and 1400 to 1830 (Saturdays 1400 to 1600); ☎ (038) 49 49.

NIESEN

Cable-car from Mülenen – Operates late May to late October; 26Frs Rtn; ☎ (033) 76 11 12.

NYON
🛈 Viollier 7 ☎ (022) 61 62 61

History and Porcelain Museum – Open April to October daily 0900 to 1200 and 1400 to 1800; 5Frs (ticket valid for all Nyon museums); ☎ (022) 363 82 82.

Roman Museum – ♿ Open April to October daily 0900 to 1200 and 1400 to 1800; November to March Tuesdays to Sundays 1400 to 1700; closed 1 January, 24, 25 and 31 December; 5Frs (ticket valid for all Nyon museums); ☎ (022) 363 82 82.

Lake Geneva Museum – ♿ Same opening times as the Roman Museum; 5Frs (ticket valid for all Nyon museums); ☎ (022) 363 82 82.

O

OBERALP PASS

Train – Between Andermatt and Sedrun in winter; for the timetable and reservations ☎ (044) 672 20 or ☎ (081) 949 11 37.

OBERHOFEN

Castle – Open May to mid-October 1000 to 1200 and 1400 to 1700; closed Monday mornings; 4Frs; ☎ (033) 43 14 19.

OLTEN
🛈 ☎ (062) 3230 84

Fine Arts Museum – Open Tuesdays to Fridays 1400 to 1700; weekends 1000 to 1200 and 1400 to 1700; closed New Year, Easter, Whitsun, Ascension and Christmas; 2Frs; ☎ (062) 32 86 76.

Historical Museum – Open Tuesdays to Saturdays 1400 to 1700; Sundays 1000 to 1200 and 1400 to 1700; closed public holidays; ☎ (062) 32 89 89.

ORBE

Urba Mosaics – Open 25 May to 31 October 0900 to 1200 and 1330 to 1730; Saturdays, Sundays and public holidays 1330 to 1730; 3Frs; ☎ (024) 41 31 15.

ORBE, SOURCE OF THE

Caves – Guided tours (1 hour) July and August 0900 to 1800; September to November and June 0900 to 1700; April and May (except Mondays) 0900 to 1700; 12Frs; ☎ (021) 843 25 83.

Fairies' Treasure – & Same times and charges as the Caves.

ORON-LE-CHÂTEL

Castle – Guided tours (1/2 hour) March to November daily (except Mondays) 1000 to 1200 and 1400 to 1800; 5Frs; ☎ (021) 907 90 51.

P

PARPANER ROTHORN

Cable-car – Operates in summer 0800 to 1200 and 1300 to 1700, in winter 0800 to 1715; 23.20Frs Rtn; ☎ (081) 34 16 61 or 34 10 50.

PAYERNE
🛈 Hôtel de Ville ☎ (037) 61 61 61

Abbey Church – Open April to October weekdays 0900 to 1200 and 1400 to 1800 (Sundays and public holidays 1000 to 1200 and 1400 to 1800); the rest of the year 1030 to 1200 and 1400 to 1700 (Sundays and public holidays 1000 to 1200 and 1400 to 1700); closed 1, 2, 3 January and 25 December; 3Frs; ☎ (037) 61 61 61.

PILATUS

Rack-railway from Alpnachstad – Closed late November to mid-May; 53Frs Rtn.

PIZ CORVATSCH

Cable-car – Operates July to mid-October and December to April; 27Frs Rtn; ☎ (082) 482 42.

PIZ LAGALB

Cable-car from Curtinatsch – Operates early July to late September and early December to late April; 19Frs; ☎ (082) 005 91.

PONTRESINA
🛈 ☎ (082) 664 88

Chapel of St Mary – Open July to mid-October

PORRENTRUY
🛈 5 Grand-Rue ☎ (066) 66 18 53

Hospital Museum – & Open Wednesdays, Fridays and last Sunday of each month 1500 to 1700; closed Easter, Christmas and 23 June; ☎ (066) 66 72 72.

R

RAPPERSWIL
🛈 Seestrasse 6 ☎ (055) 27 70 00

Polish Museum – Open 1300 to 1700 (in March weekends only 1300 to 1700); closed January, February, November and December; 4Frs; ☎ (055) 27 44 95.

Local Museum – Open April to October Saturdays 1400 to 1700, Sundays 1000 to 1200 and 1400 to 1700; July and August also open 1600 to 2000; 3Frs; ☎ (055) 27 71 64.

Children's Zoo – Open 15 March to late October daily 0900 to 1800 (1900 Sundays and public holidays); 5Frs (children 3Frs); ☎ (055) 27 52 22.

REICHENBACH FALLS

Funicular – Operates from Whitsun to third Sunday in September daily 0800 to 1150 and 1315 to 1800; 4Frs (6Frs Rtn); ☎ (036) 71 43 22.

RHEINAU

Abbey Church – Open Tuesdays to Saturdays 1400 to 1600, Sundays and public holidays 1330 to 1730; closed November to April; ☎ (053) 43 31 00.

RHEINFELDEN
🛈 Marktgasse 61 ☎ (061) 831 55 20

Feldschlösschen Brewery – Guided tours (1 hour) by appointment Mondays to Fridays at 1000 and 1400; closed 1 January, Easter Monday, 1 May and 25 December; ☎ (061) 86 01 11.

RHINE FALLS

Belvedere of Laufen Castle – 0.50Frs.

Boat trips – 4Frs Rtn to the rock.

RIEDERALP
🛈 ☎ (028) 27 29 32

Cable-car from Mörel – Departures every 1/2 hour; 3.60Frs Rtn; ☎ (028) 27 22 27.

Cable-car from Riederalp to Moosfluh – Operates mid-June to late October and mid-December to late April; 10Frs Rtn; ☎ (028) 27 22 67.

RIGGISBERG

Abegg Foundation – & Open May to October 1400 to 1745; 5Frs; ☎ (031) 809 12 01.

RIGI

Rack-railway to Rigi-Kulm – Trains leave from Arth-Goldau, Vitznau and Weggis; 48Frs Rtn; ☎ (041) 83 18 18.

RIGI-SCHEIDEGG

Cable-car from Kräbel – Operates late April to July with departures every 1/2 hour; 20Frs; ☎ (041) 84 18 38.

ROFFLA

Gorge – Open 0800 to 1900; 2Frs; ☎ (081) 61 11 97.

ROMONT   🗓 84 rue de l'Eglise ☎ (037) 52 31 52

Swiss Museum of Stained Glass – Open early April to late October daily (except Mondays) 1000 to 1200 and 1400 to 1800; the rest of the year weekends and public holidays only 1000 to 1200 and 1400 to 1800; closed 1 January and 25 December; 5Frs; ☎ (037) 52 31 52.

RORSCHACH   🗓 Neugasse 2 ☎ (071) 41 70 34

Local Museum – Open Tuesdays to Saturdays 0930 to 1130 and 1400 to 1700; Sundays 1000 to 1200 and 1400 to 1700; usually closed mid-November to mid-April; 2.50Frs; ☎ (071) 41 40 62.

ROSENLAUI

Glacier Gorges – Open late May to late October 0900 to 1700 (late June to late September 0800 to 1800); 5Frs; ☎ (036) 71 43 22.

ROTHORN

Funicular and cable-cars – 13Frs.

S

SAAS-FEE   🗓 ☎ (028) 57 14 57

Saas Museum – Open June to 20 October daily (except Mondays) 1000 to 1200 and 1400 to 1800; December to April Mondays to Fridays 1400 to 1800; 3Frs; ☎ (028) 57 14 75.

ST. GALLEN   🗓 Bahnofplatz 1a ☎ (071) 22 62 62

Abbey Library – Open May to October weekdays 0900 to 1200 and 1330 to 1700; Sundays and public holidays 1030 to 1200 (also 1400 to 1600 June to August); November to March Tuesdays to Saturdays 0900 to 1200 and 1400 to 1600; April 0900 to 1200 and 1400 to 1700 (except Sundays); closed 1 January, Whit Sunday, 24 December (afternoon), 25 and 31 December as well as the last three weeks in November; 3Frs; ☎ (071) 22 57 19.

Textile Museum – Open 1 April to 31 October Mondays to Saturdays 1000 to 1200 and 1400 to 1700; 2 November to 31 March Mondays to Fridays 1000 to 1200 and 1400 to 1700; closed 1 January, Good Friday, Easter, Ascension Day, All Saints' Day and Christmas; 4Frs; ☎ (071) 22 17 44.

Historical Museum – & Open daily (except Mondays) 1000 to 1200 and 1400 to 1700 (no lunchtime break on Sundays); closed 1 January, Good Friday, Easter, Whitsun, Ascension Day, National Day, All Saints Day, 24, 25 and 31 December; 4Frs; ☎ (071) 24 78 32.

Botanical Gardens – & Open 0800 to 1200 and 1330 to 1700; the greenhouses are open to the public 0930 to 1200 and 1400 to 1700; ☎ (071) 35 15 30.

ST-IMIER

Church – Open May to October 0800 to 1800.

ST-LÉONARD

Underground Lake – Boat trips (1/2 hour) July and August 0900 to 1830; June and September 0900 to 1800; 15 March to 1 November 0900 to 1700 (1730 weekends and public holidays); 5.50Frs; ☎ (027) 31 22 66.

ST-MAURICE   🗓 ☎ (025) 65 29 70

Abbey Treasury – Guided tours (1/2 hour) July and August at 0930, 1030, 1430, 1530 and 1630; May, June, September and October at 1030, 1500 and 1630; November to April at 1500 and 1630; closed on Sunday mornings and religious holidays and during church services. Donations welcome. ☎ (025) 65 16 72.

Martolet Excavations – Temporarily closed for restoration work.

Castle (Valais Military History Musem) – Open 1000 to 1200 and 1400 to 1800; closed Mondays, 1 January and 25 December; 4Frs; ☎ (025) 65 24 58.

Fairies Grotto – Open July and August daily 0900 to 1900; 15 March to 15 November 1000 to 1800; closed the rest of the year; 5Frs; ☎ (025) 65 10 45.

ST. MORITZ

Engadine Museum – Open June to October Mondays to Fridays 0930 to 1200 and 1400 to 1700 (Sundays 1000 to 1200); December to April Mondays to Fridays 1000 to 1200 and 1400 to 1700 (Sundays 1000 to 1200); 4Frs; ☎ (082) 343 33.

Segantini Museum – Open early June to 20 October Tuesdays to Saturdays 0900 to 1230 and 1430 to 1700 (Sundays 1030 to 1230 and 1430 to 1630); December to April Tuesdays to Saturdays 1000 to 1230 and 1500 to 1700 (Sundays 1500 to 1700); closed public holidays; 7Frs; ☎ (082) 3 44 54.

Piz Nair – Cable-cars leave every 20mins 19 June to 17 October; 30Frs Rtn; ☎ (082) 388 88.

ST. PETER'S ISLAND

Access from Biel – Departures April to mid-October; 15.60Frs Rtn.

Access from La Neuveville – Departures April to mid-October; 8.60Frs Rtn.

ST.URBAN

Church – Open 1000 (Sundays 1100) to 1700 (1900 in summer); ☎ (063) 48 50 01.

STE-CROIX-LES-RASSES

International Centre of Mechanical Musical Instruments – & Guided tours (1 hour) 1330 to 1800 (last admission at 1700); closed Mondays and 25 December; 8Frs; ☎ (024) 61 44 77.

SÄLI-SCHLÖSSLI

Panorama – Access through the Château-Restaurant; closed Mondays, Good Friday, 24, 25 December and January to mid-February.

SÄNTIS

Cable-car from Schwägalp – Departures every 1/2 hour; 19Frs Rtn.

LA SARRAZ

Castle – Guided tours (3/4 hour) May to September 1000 to 1200 and 1400 to 1730; April and October weekends and public holidays only 1000 to 1200 and 1400 to 1730; 5Frs; Horse Museum 5Frs; combined ticket for Castle and Horse Museum: 8Frs; ☎ (021) 866 64 23; apply at the castle to see the cenotaph.

SCHAFFHAUSEN

Munot Belvedere – May to September 0800 to 2000; the rest of the year 0900 to 1700.

All Saints'Museum – Open Tuesdays to Saturdays 1000 to 1200 and 1400 to 1700; closed 1 January, Easter, 1 May, 1 June, 1 August, third Saturday in September and 25 December; 3Frs; ☎ (053) 25 43 77.

Contemporary Art Hall – Open 2 May to 31 October Tuesdays to Saturdays 1500 to 1700 (Sundays 1100 to 1500); ☎ (053) 25 25 15.

SCHILTHORN

Cable-car from Stechelberg – & Operates in summer 0725 to 1625, in winter 0755 to 1555; 78.40Frs Rtn; ☎ (036) 23 14 44.

SCHÖNENWERD

Boot and Shoe Museum – Guided tours (1 1/2 hours). It is advisable to book two weeks in advance to be incorporated into a group ☎ (064) 40 26 82 or (064) 40 26 40.

SCHULS

Chagronda: Lower Engadine Museum – Open June, September and October Tuesdays and Thursdays 1500 to 1700, July and August Tuesdays to Fridays 1000 to 1130 and 1500 to 1700; 3Frs; ☎ (084) 864 10 36.

SCHWYZ

Federal Charters Museum – Open 0930 to 1130 and 1400 to 1700; closed Good Friday, 24 and 25 December; 30Frs; ☎ (043) 24 20 64.

Town Hall – Guided tours (1/2 hour) Mondays to Fridays at 1000 and 1500; closed public holidays; ☎ (043) 21 42 66.

SCHYNIGE PLATTE

Rack-railway from Wilderswil – Operates May to October with departures every 40mins; 42Frs Rtn; ☎ (036) 22 45 85.

SEELISBERG

Funicular from the landing stage in Treib – Operates all the year round; 7.60Frs; ☎ (043) 31 15 63.

SEEWEN

Museum of Musical Automata – Guided tours (1 hour) Tuesdays to Saturdays 1400 to 1700; 8Frs; ☎ (061) 911 02 08.

SEMPACH

Swiss Ornithological Centre – Guided tours (1 1/2 hours) early April to late September Mondays to Fridays 0800 (1000 Sundays) to 1200 and 1400 to 1700; also Saturdays 1400 to 1700; 2Frs; ☎ (041) 99 00 22.

SERVION

Zoo – ᴖ Open 0900 to 1900 (1700 November to March); last admission 1 hour before closing time; 8Frs (children 4Frs); ☎ (021) 903 16 71.

SEX ROUGE

Cable-cars from Pillon Pass or Reusch – Access to Les Diablerets glacier is assured alternately from either of these two departure points daily July to May and at weekends only in June. For further details phone Pillon Pass ☎ (025) 53 13 77 or at Reusch ☎ (030) 5 10 70; 37Frs Rtn.

SIERRE
🄑 Place de la gare ☎ (027) 55 85 35

Pewter Musem – Open Mondays to Fridays 0800 to 1200 and 1400 to 1700; ☎ (027) 57 01 11.

Rilke Museum – Open daily (except Mondays) 1500 to 1900; closed Christmas; 3Frs; ☎ (027) 56 26 46.

SION
🄑 Place de la Plante ☎ (027) 22 85 86

City Tour – Apply to the Tourist Information Centre.

Our Lady of Valère – Open 1000 to 1200 and 1400 to 1800; closed Mondays, 1 January and 25 December; ☎ (027) 21 69 22.

The Canton's Historical and Ethnographical Museum – Open 1000 to 1200 and 1400 to 1800; closed Mondays, 1 January and 25 December; 5Frs; ☎ (027) 21 69 22.

Town Hall – Open Mondays to Fridays 0800 to 1800. In July and August this visit is included in the guided tour of the town.

Supersaxo Mansion – Open Mondays to Fridays 0800 to 1200 and 1400 to 1800.

The Canton's Museum of Fine Arts – Open May to October 1000 to 1200 and 1400 to 1800; closed Mondays, 1 January and 25 December; 5Frs; (027) 21 69 02.

The Canton's Archaeological Museum – Open 1000 to 1200 and 1400 to 1800; closed Mondays, 1 January and 25 December; 4Frs; ☎ (027) 21 69 16.

SOLOTHURN
🄑 Kronenplatz ☎ (065) 22 19 24

Former Arsenal – Open May to October daily (except Mondays) 1000 to 1200 and 1400 to 1700; the rest of the year Tuesdays to Fridays 1400 to 1700; also weekends 1000 to 1200; closed 1 January, Easter, Whitsun and Christmas; ☎ (065) 23 25 28.

Fine Arts Museum – Open Tuesdays to Sundays 1000 to 1200 and 1400 to 1700 (2100 Thursdays); ☎ (065) 22 23 07.

Natural History Museum – ᴖ Open weekdays 1400 to 1700 (2100 Thursdays); Sundays 1000 to 1200 and 1400 to 1700; closed Mondays, 1 January, Good Friday, Easter, Whitsun and 25 December; ☎ (065) 22 70 21.

Blumenstein Museum – Open weekdays 1400 to 1700; Sundays 1000 to 1200 and 1400 to 1700; closed Mondays, Tuesdays, 1 January, Easter, Whitsun and Christmas; ☎ (065) 22 54 70.

SPIEZ
🄑 ☎ (033) 54 21 38

Museum – Open 1000 to 1700; closed Monday mornings and 15 October to 31 March; 4Frs; ☎ (033) 54 15 06.

STANSERHORN

Funicular then cable-car from Stans – Operates May to October with departures every 1/2 hour without interruption when busy; 36Frs Rtn; ☎ (041) 61 14 41.

STEIN

Cheese-making demonstration – ᴖ Open 0800 to 1900; closed 24 December and afternoon of 25 December; ☎ (071) 59 15 21.

STEIN AM RHEIN
🄑 Dorf 29 ☎ (071) 59 11 99

Historical Museum – Apply in advance to Stadtpolizei; ☎ (054) 41 54 25.

St George's Monastery – Open March to October 1000 to 1200 and 1330 to 1700; closed Good Friday, Easter, 1 May, Whitsun, 1 August, 3rd Sunday in September; 3Frs; ☎ (054) 41 21 42.

SURSEE

Guided tours – Apply to M Röllin; ☎ (045) 23 25 25.

Gourmets...

The annual **Michelin Red Guide Switzerland**
offers a selection of good restaurants.

T

TAMINA

Gorges – ♿ Open first Saturday in May to last Sunday in October 1000 to 1700; 4Frs; ☏ (081) 302 71 61.

TARASP

Castle – Guided tours (1 hour) in June and 21 August to mid-October Mondays to Saturdays at 1430; 1 to 10 July daily at 1430 and 1530; 11 July to 19 August daily at 1100, 1430, 1530 and 1630; in winter Tuesdays and Wednesdays at 1700; 6Frs; ☏ (081) 864 93 68.

THUN
🚉 Bahnhofplatz ☏ (033) 22 23 40

Historical Museum – Open June to September 0900 to 1800; early April to late May and early October to 7 November 1000 to 1700; 4Frs; ☏ (033) 23 20 01.

Wocher Panorama – Open July and August daily (except Mondays) 1000 to 1800; September, October, May and June 1000 to 1700; 4Frs; ☏ (033) 22 23 40.

TITLIS

Cable-cars – Operate early December to late October; 66Frs; ☏ (041) 94 15 24. A revolving cable-car - the "Rotair" - operates on the upper section between Strand and Titlis: the trip lasts 5mins. Thanks to this exceptional cabin, revolving around its axis, visitors can enjoy breathtaking views of the surrounding landscape.

LA TOUR-DE-PEILZ

Swiss Museum of Games – ♿ Open daily (except Mondays) 1400 to 1800; closed 1 January and 25 December; 6Frs; ☏ (021) 944 40 50.

TRACHSELWARD

Castle – Open first and third Sundays of the month 1300 to 1800 or by appointment; it is advisable to book in advance ☏ (034) 71 23 97.

TRÜMMELBACH

Falls – Open June to August 0830 to 1800; April, May and October 0900 to 1700; 8Frs; waterproof clothing necessary.

TRUN

Cuort Ligia Grischa – Open Mondays, Wednesdays, Saturdays and Sundays 1400 to 1700; closed 15 November to 15 April, Easter and Whitsun..

U

UETLIBERG

By Train – Departures every 1/2 hour from the main station in the centre of Zurich; 6.30Frs (12.60 Rtn); ☏ (01) 202 88 84

URNÄSH

Folklore Museum – Open April Wednesdays, Sundays and public holidays 1330 to 1700; May to October 1330 to 1700; 4Frs; ☏ (071) 58 23 22.

UTZENSTORF

Swiss Hunting Museum – Open 2nd Sunday in May to mid-October 1000 to 1200 and 1400 to 1700; closed Mondays, 1 August and third Sunday in September; 4Frs; ☏ (065) 45 40 27.

V

VADUZ
🚉 ☏ (075) 232 14 43

Liechenstein State Art Collection – Open daily 1000 to 1200 and 1330 to 1730 (1700 1 November to 31 March), closed 24, 25 and 31 December; 3Frs; ☏ (075) 232 23 41.

National Museum – Temporarily closed for restoration work. ☏ (075) 232 23 10.

Postage Stamp Museum – Open daily 1000 to 1200 and 1330 to 1730; closed Christmas; ☏ (075) 236 61 01.

VALLORBE

The Tourist Information Centre sells a combined ticket (Carte Trèfle: 18Frs) valid for a season for the sights given below.

Iron and Railway Museum – Open April to November 0930 to 1200 and 1330 to 1800; closed Mondays except when it is a public holiday and in April and May; 9Frs; ☎ (021) 843 25 83.

Fort de Pré-Giroud – Guided tours (1 1/2 hours) in July and August 1200 to 1730; April to June and September to November Saturdays, Sundays and public holidays 1200 to 1730; 8Frs; ☎ (021) 843 25 83.

Orbe Caves – See under Orbe.

VERBIER

Cable-cars to Mont Gelé and Mont Fort – Mount Gelé: operates December to April only. Mont Fort: operates December to April and late June to late August; ☎ (026) 31 61 01.

VEVEY

Jenisch Museum – ᕯ Open March to October daily (except Mondays) 1030 to 1200 and 1400 to 1700; the rest of the year 1400 to 1730; closed third Sunday in September; 6-10Frs for temporary exhibitions; ☎ (021) 921 29 50.

History Museum of Old Vevey – Open March to October 1030 to 1200 and 1400 to 1730; November to February 1400 to 1730; closed Mondays, 1 January, 25 and 26 December; 4Frs; ☎ (021) 921 07 22.

Swiss Museum of Cameras – ᕯ Open March to October daily (except Mondays) 1030 to 1200 and 1400 to 1730; the rest of the year 1400 to 1730 only; 4Frs; ☎ (021) 921 94 60.

Alimentarium – Open daily (except Mondays) 1000 to 1200 and 1400 to 1700; closed 1 January and 25 December; 4Frs; ☎ (021) 924 41 11.

VIA MALA

Galleries – Open April to October daily 0900 to 1700; 2.50Frs; ☎ (081) 81 11 84.

LA VIDEMANETTE

Cable-car – Operates June to September and mid-December to mid-April 0900 to 1700; 17Frs (22Frs Rtn).

VUFFLENS-LE-CHÂTEAU

Castle – Not open to the public.

W

WEISSENSTEIN

Chairlift from Oberdorf – Operates from mid-April to late October Mondays to Fridays 0830 to 1210 and 1325 to 1800 (Saturdays and Sundays 0800 to 1800); the rest of the year 0900 to 1200 and 1320 to 1700 (Saturdays and Sundays 0800 to 1700); 15.80Frs Rtn; ☎ (065) 22 02 64.

WETTINGEN

Abbey – Restoration work scheduled until 1996.

WIL

Municipal Museum – Open Wednesdays 1400 to 1700 and the first and third Sundays of the month 1400 to 1700; closed Easter and Christmas; 2Frs; ☎ (073) 22 04 57.

WILDEGG

Castle – Open mid-March to October Tuesdays to Sundays 1000 to 1200 and 1400 to 1700; 2Frs; ☎ (064) 53 12 01.

WINTERTHUR

Oskar Reinhart Foundation – Reopening scheduled for mid-1995. Open daily (except Mondays) 1000 to 1700; closed 1 January, Easter, Whitsun, 1 May and Christmas; 6Frs; ☎ (052) 267 51 72.

Oskar Reinhart Collection – Open Tuesdays to Sundays 1000 to 1700; closed on certain public holidays; ☎ (052) 213 41 21.

Fine Arts Museum – Open Tuesdays to Sundays 1000 to 1700 (2000 Thursdays); closed 1 January, Good Friday, Easter, Ascension Day, 1 May, Whitsun and Christmas; 7-10Frs; ☎ (052) 267 51 62.

Technorama – Open Tuesdays to Saturdays 1000 to 1700; closed 25 December; 12Frs, children 6 to 16 6Frs; ☎ (052) 243 05 05.

Y

YVERDON-LES-BAINS

Museum – Open June to September 1000 to 1200 and 1400 to 1700; the rest of the year afternoons only; closed Mondays, 1 January, Good Friday, Easter, Whitsun and third Sunday in September; 4Frs; ☎ (024) 21 93 10.

Z

ZERMATT

Alpine Museum – Open daily in summer (except Saturdays) 1000 to 1200 and 1600 to 1800; 3Frs; ☎ (028) 67 41 00.

ZERNEZ

Swiss National Park – Guided tours (6 hours) on request, apply to the visitor centre; ☎ (082) 813 78.

ZOUG

Guided tours – Apply to the Tourist Information Centre.

ZÜRICH

Cathedral – Open April to September 0900 (1200 Sundays) to 1800; the rest of the year 1000 (1200 Sundays) to 1600; ☎ (01) 252 61 44.

Fraumünster – Open May to September 0900 to 1200 and 1400 to 1800; October, March and April 1000 to 1200 and 1400 to 1700; November to February 1000 to 1200 and 1400 to 1600; ☎ (01) 211 41 00.

Swiss National Museum – Many of the rooms are closed for refurbishment. Open Tuesdays to Sundays 1000 to 1700 (Tuesdays and Thursdays guided tours at 1800), ☎ (01) 218 65 65 or 218 65 11.

Museum of Applied Arts – Open Tuesdays, Thursdays and Fridays 1000 to 1800; Wednesdays 1000 to 2100; weekends 1000 to 1700; 4 and 6Frs; ☎ (01) 271 67 00.

Museum of Domestic Life – Open mid-June to mid-September (except Mondays) 1000 to 1700 (1600 Saturdays); the rest of the year 1000 to 1200 and 1400 to 1700 (1600 Saturdays); 5Frs; ☎ (01) 218 65 11.

Rietberg Museum – ও Open Tuesdays to Sundays 1000 to 1700 (2100 Wednesdays); closed public holidays; 8Frs; ☎ (01) 202 45 28.

Fine Arts Museum – Open Tuesdays to Thursdays 1000 to 2100; Fridays to Sundays 1000 to 1700; closed public holidays; ☎ (01) 251 67 55.

Zoological Gardens – Open in summer 0800 to 1800 (1700 in winter); 7.70Frs (children 6-16 3.30Frs); ☎ (01) 251 54 11.

Foundation E. G. Bührle Collection – Open Tuesdays and Fridays 1400 to 1700 (Wednesdays 1700 to 2000); 7Frs; ☎ (01) 422 00 86.

Boat Trips – Special lunch trips are organised at noon; evening trips with music and dancing on Saturdays in June and September; Wednesdays, Fridays and Saturdays in July and August.

ZURZACH

August Deusser Museum – ও Open 1300 to 1800; closed first three weeks in February, second, third and fourth weeks in July, Good Friday, Maundy Thursday, Easter and Christmas; 6Frs; ☎ (056) 49 20 50.

INDEX

Aare Gorges

5000

Bonivard, François de

Isolated sights (castles, abbeys, dams, passes, waterfalls...) are listed under their proper name.

Towns, sights and tourist regions followed by the name of the canton.

Postal code.

People, historical events, artistic styles and local terms explained in the text.

MANUFACTURE FRANÇAISE DES PNEUMATIQUES MICHELIN

Société en commandite par actions au capital de 2 000 000 000 de francs

Place des Carmes-Déchaux - 63 Clermont-Ferrand (France)

R.C.S. Clermont-Fd B 855 200 507

© Michelin et Cie, Propriétaires-Éditeurs 1991

Dépôt légal 4ᵉ trim. 91 — ISBN 2-06-701563-X — ISSN 0763-1383

Printed in the EC 12-94-30/2

Photocomposition : M. C. P., Fleury-les-Aubrais — Impression et brochage : AUBIN, Poitiers

**FRANCE • BENELUX
DEUTSCHLAND • ESPAÑA PORTUGAL
GREAT BRITAIN AND IRELAND
ITALIA • EUROPE
SUISSE SCHWEIZ SVIZZERA**

216

Suisse
Schweiz
Svizzera

Neuchâtel-
Basel-St-Gallen

1/200 000 – 1 cm : 2 km

217

Suisse
Schweiz
Svizzera

Genève-
Bern-Andermatt

1/200 000 – 1 cm : 2 km

427

Suisse
Schweiz

Répertoire des localités
Ortsverzeichnis

1/400 000 – 1 cm : 4 km

218

Suisse
Schweiz
Svizzera

Andermatt-St-Moritz-
Bolzano/Bozen

1/200 000 – 1 cm : 2 km

CARTE ROUTIÈRE ET TOURISTIQUE
MICHELIN

219

Suisse
Schweiz
Svizzera

Aosta/Aoste-
Zermatt-Milano

1/200 000 – 1 cm : 2 km

CARTE ROUTIÈRE ET TOURISTIQUE
MICHELIN